ALSO BY EVAN THOMAS

The Wise Men
(co-author with Walter Isaacson)

The
Man
to See

Edward Bennett Williams Ultimate Insider; Legendary Trial Lawyer

EVAN THOMAS

SIMON AND SCHUSTER
NEW YORK   LONDON   TOKYO   SYDNEY   TORONTO   SINGAPORE

SIMON & SCHUSTER
Simon & Schuster Building
Rockefeller Center
1230 Avenue of the Americas
New York, New York 10020

Designed by Irving Perkins Associates
Manufactured in the United States of America

10   9   8   7   6   5   4   3   2   1

Library of Congress Cataloging-in-Publication Data

Thomas, Evan.
    The man to see : Edward Bennett Williams : ultimate insider ;
legendary trial lawyer / Evan Thomas.
        p.   cm.
    Includes bibliographical references and index.
    1. Williams, Edward Bennett.   2. Lawyers—Washington (D.C.)—
Biography.   I. Title.
KF373.W466T46   1991
370'.092—dc20
    [B]   91-25131
                                                               CIP
ISBN: 0-671-68934-7

To my father
Evan W. Thomas II

Contents

I

The Man to See

Chapter One

EDWARD BENNETT WILLIAMS wanted to be in control to the end, and a little beyond. Before he died, his family suggested that the funeral be held at Holy Trinity, a lovely neo-Georgian church in Georgetown. Too small, said Williams. He wanted the service to be held in St. Matthew's Cathedral, a Romanesque monstrosity downtown. His children teased him for his vanity. They assumed that the church would be half empty, since most of official Washington had fled the city's late-summer torpor for the mountains or the seashore.

But when the Williams family arrived at the cathedral on that muggy Tuesday morning in August 1988, they found it overflowing. Over two thousand mourners had gathered, filling the immense nave and spilling out onto the street which was lined with black limousines. Senators and Supreme Court justices, felons and bookmakers, waiters and doormen, billionaires, professional ball players, and Georgetown society jammed under the domed ceiling to sit before the plain mahogany casket.

Katharine Graham, the owner of the *Washington Post,* had flown back from the Republican National Convention in New Orleans. (The night before, as he headed to New Orleans to accept his party's nomination for president, George Bush had stopped at Gawler's Funeral Home to pay his last respects.) In one row in the crowded church, a former Miss America, Yolande Fox, sat beside boxing champion Sugar Ray Leonard, soothsayer Jeane Dixon, and a janitor from Williams's office building. Baseball commissioner Peter Ueberroth chatted quietly with football commissioner Pete Rozelle (Williams was the only professional team

13

owner to win both the Super Bowl and the World Series in one year, 1983). The Kennedy clan had turned out—Ethel and four children, Eunice and Sargent Shriver—and so had Joe DiMaggio. Outside the cathedral door, Justice Thurgood Marshall stopped to tell reporters that Ed Williams was "a great lawyer, a great American, a great man."

Sitting along one aisle, Michael Milken, the junk bond king, looked stricken. The Justice Department was closing in on the empire he had built out of vision, guile, and larceny. Frightened, Milken had done what many powerful men had done when they had a serious problem. He had done what Senator Joseph McCarthy, Teamster boss Jimmy Hoffa, Mafia don Frank Costello, LBJ aide Bobby Baker, singer Frank Sinatra, Soviet spy Igor Melekh, industrialist Armand Hammer, New York Yankees owner George Steinbrenner, Democratic party chairman Robert Strauss, *Playboy* owner Hugh Hefner, Texas governor John Connally, financier Robert Vesco, Senator Thomas Dodd, CIA director Richard Helms, Chrysler chairman Lee Iacocca, Reverend Sun Myung Moon, and President Gerald Ford had all done before him: He had gone to Edward Bennett Williams.

People in deep trouble turned to Williams because of his reputation as a miracle worker who could make the guilty go free. They also found him a source of comfort and even forgiveness. Williams had an Irish Catholic's deep pessimism about the essential sinfulness of man, and an equally great faith in the power of redemption. He would sometimes mock clients behind their backs, but he would not pass moral judgment on them. Clients felt that Williams understood them, that he felt their grief and fear. When Milken, anxious and uncertain, came to him in November 1986, Williams had comforted and reassured him. He was the only man, the junk bond trader believed, who could get him through his ordeal. The only question had been whether Williams would live long enough to do it.

Because of his empathy and shrewdness, Williams became an adviser to the rich and powerful not just on legal matters, but on career choices, business decisions, personnel problems, or almost any personal vexation. Williams's *X*-factor, the quality that set him apart from thousands of others peddling advice and access in Washington, was his intuition. "I have a gypsy's instinct," he told his second wife, Agnes. He meant that he could see what others would do before they knew it themselves. Men became addicted to Williams. Marvin Davis, the billionaire tycoon whom Williams had rescued from a grand jury and then had helped buy 20th

Century–Fox, called Williams every day. When Williams died, Davis was unable to remove Williams's speed dial number from his telephone. "I ask myself," he said a year later. "What would Ed tell me to do?"

As he helped hoist Williams's coffin onto its pedestal in St. Matthew's, *Washington Post* executive editor Ben Bradlee wondered as well what he would do without his old friend. During his two decades running the paper, Bradlee had always turned to Williams for help in resolving problems large and small. In June 1971, when Bradlee was desperate to catch up to the *New York Times,* the *Post*'s regular lawyers had counseled against publishing the Pentagon Papers, the secret study of America's roots of involvement in Vietnam. They were afraid the Nixon administration would prosecute the *Post*. Bradlee called Williams in Chicago, where he was trying a fraud case. "What's Nixon going to do?" Williams scoffed. "Put every major publisher and editor in jail? Nixon doesn't have the balls to go after you, Bradlee." Relieved, emboldened, Bradlee pressed ahead and the *Post* published the Pentagon Papers. For the *Washington Post,* the decision was a coming of age (and Williams shortly thereafter became the Washington Post Company's regular lawyer).

Humor columnist Art Buchwald and Ed Williams had an unusual Washington friendship: neither wanted anything from the other. "That's why it was such a good friendship," said Buchwald. What Buchwald missed about his lost friend was his company. Williams was very funny and quick, a raconteur with a rich store of lore—his own career—to draw upon. To be sure, Williams's humor was calculated; like Churchill, he spent his spare time rehearsing his extemporaneous remarks. Williams prepared for humor the way he prepared for trial. He kept a file of jokes in his office (most of them ethnic or off-color), and for days he would try them out on the lawyers in the firm before he would incorporate them into an "informal" talk. He knew all the rhetorical tricks of story-telling: how to stretch out the windup to the punch line, how to modulate his voice to draw the listener forward, and then jolt him upright with a burst of laughter. But Williams's sense of humor was too great to be contrived. So much of his humor came from his physical magnetism, the raw and undiluted energy and zest that seemed to flow from him. Sitting next to him, especially when liquor had loosened his tongue and eased his mood, was "roughly akin to having your breath sucked out of you by a tornado," recalled Pierce O'Donnell, a young associate of Williams's in the seventies. Williams had the power to make men shake and weep with laughter. He seemed to have direct access to his emotions. His face and body were a register of all the pleasure and pain, anger and exultation he had ever felt. When he was sullen or angry he looked like one of his mobster clients making a hit; when he was happy he looked like a little boy about to eat a Good Humor after school. When he was tired and drunk, the tears would suddenly come welling up, and his tension and fear would spill out.

"He never crossed his arms," recalled Barbara Howar, a Washington socialite in the 1960s. "His body language was totally open." He was physical, constantly touching and holding and sometimes hitting, whacking a seatmate at a football game to celebrate a bruising tackle. David Brinkley, the longtime television anchorman and commentator, recalled his slight shock when, at a cocktail party, Williams playfully reached down and squeezed Brinkley's buttocks. "It was a gesture of informality and friendship," said Brinkley. "He'd grab you by the ass."

When Williams died, his old friends Bradlee and Buchwald wondered if there would be a memorial service where they could stand up and say a few words of farewell. But from his deathbed, Williams had ruled out eulogies from his old buddies. In the way of the Old Church, he wanted only priests. In life, Williams had not advertised his piety. "He didn't want anyone to think he was nutty," said Bob Flanagan, his financial adviser. "On a business trip, when he said, 'meet you for breakfast,' he meant mass." Williams went to morning mass 365 days a year, yet he could be irreverent about the church. "They think if they sprinkle a little Holy Water on you, you're going to give an endowment," he told friends, without telling them that he gave Catholic charities well over $100,000 a year. Williams was, in effect, a favor bank for the archdiocese. When he was President of the Washington Redskins, the first row of the owner's box at Robert F. Kennedy Stadium was usually lined with priests in Roman collars. Once, while playing a word game in his office, a lawyer had prompted Williams by saying "Priests." "Tickets," he immediately shot back.

James Cardinal Hickey had broken off a papal mission to Australia to preside over Williams's funeral, flying all night to arrive three hours before the service. Over two dozen priests, resplendent in white robes, swinging vessels of incense, followed the Cardinal into the nave. The presidents of Georgetown University and the College of the Holy Cross each rose to exalt the dead. Father Tim Healy of Georgetown compared Williams to Sir Thomas More, torn between service to God and country. Father John Brooks of Holy Cross went further. He said, "I can honestly say this morning that in all my life I have never known a man or woman who more fully reflected the person of Jesus Christ than did Ed Williams.'' In the congregation, Williams's friends and law partners smiled and rolled their eyes. The sadness of his seven children was mixed with exuberance and joy. ''God, Dad would have loved this,'' said one of the boys.

HE WAS CALLED ''the magic mouthpiece, the man who can get you out of bad trouble'' by *Life*, the ''nation's hottest lawyer'' by the *New York Times*, the ''country's top criminal lawyer'' by *Time*. The myth of Williams, which he carefully nurtured all during his life, persists after his death in 1988 at the age of sixty-eight. Lawyers still argue whether he was the greatest lawyer of his time or just the greatest trial lawyer. In an age of specialization, the fact that he could handle jury trials, Supreme Court arguments, and corporate takeovers with equal facility is a source of lawyerly awe. A whole generation of trial lawyers mimics his courtroom moves and lifts the best lines of his jury summations.

After a few late night drinks, Williams would sometimes tell the eager young acolytes who came to his firm, hoping to follow his example, that they could not. There would never be another lawyer like him. The practice of law had changed too much, in no small measure because he had changed it. Williams was sui generis. There were other lawyers who were just as smart or hard-working, but somehow Williams was bigger, literally and figuratively. His appetite, his ego, his emotions, his memory, and even his body—particularly his enormous, leonine head—were all outsize.

Williams was not content just to be a great lawyer. He wanted power, and he wanted to be seen as a force for larger ends than the narrow representation of his clients. He was, at least in the beginning, an effective crusader for individual freedom. In the name of civil liberties and protecting the rights of the criminally accused, he helped spark a judicial revolution against unchecked police power in the 1950s and 1960s. Before anyone else, Williams exposed the illegal acts of the Federal Bureau of Investigation (FBI)—the wiretapping and break-ins, the bugging and ''black-bag jobs''—that were rotting J. Edgar Hoover's empire from within. Behind the scenes, he played a little-known but critical role in revealing and ultimately dethroning the abusive power of Richard Nixon's White House. Williams not only urged Ben Bradlee to print the

Pentagon Papers, he helped give the *Post* editor the courage—and quite possibly, the inside information—to press forward with the newspaper's probe into Watergate when the rest of the establishment press was turning the other way.

Yet, having exposed the abuse of power, Williams went on to protect it. Apparently without a second thought, Williams defended the very people exposed by the scandals that he had helped unearth. He defended a half dozen private and public powerbrokers from charges brought by the Watergate special prosecutor. He defended Central Intelligence Agency (CIA) director Richard Helms against accusations that he had authorized an illegal break-in and lied to Congress. He defended the FBI's top specialist against charges of having performed "black-bag jobs." And in the secret councils of the White House, he argued *against* restricting CIA eavesdropping on U.S. citizens.

Williams saw no irony in playing both sides. He was an advocate, and he was intent on winning. If he could expose a scandal and then turn around and get off the people embroiled in it, so much the better. He won both ways. He always had. In the 1950s, he had represented Communists and fellow travelers before the House Un-American Activities Committee (HUAC) while at the same time he represented the greatest red-baiter of them all, Senator Joe McCarthy. Throughout his career, Williams appeared to be involved in a variety of conflicts of interest. But to Williams, representing clients on different sides of an issue was not a conflict at all. He believed he could represent everyone's interests at once, and often he succeeded in finding a middle way. Certainly he served his own interests. His individual clients were almost always happy as well. But viewed from a distance of years, Williams's ceaseless maneuvering sometimes seemed to add up to one vast zero-sum game.

Williams loved games, and the games he played were exhilarating. He could be found squarely in the middle of most of the crises or scandals that gripped the nation's capital over three decades, dispensing advice and counsel to one side or the other, and sometimes both at once. And in the process, he seemed to become more powerful, more important, than the people he advised. That he could be perceived as such a force in Washington is a testimonial to Williams, but it also says something less inspiring about Washington.

Williams came to Washington, D.C., in 1941, just as it was beginning its transformation from sleepy Southern town to center of the Western world. He had $12 and endless ambition. He saw Washington as a place free of anti-Catholic prejudice, where power belonged to those clever and driven enough to grasp and hold it. Over $100 million richer yet in some ways still unfulfilled, he died just as the city, and the country it governed, seemed in decline, militarily still strong but strangely paralyzed by its problems at home. Williams himself was one of a kind, but his career stands as a metaphor for the city of his dreams.

Far more vital than many of the drones who shuffle in and out of Washington's so-called revolving door, Williams could be witheringly funny about the climbers of Washington, and even make fun of his own grasping. Always teasing, armed with a healthy sense of the absurd, he poked fun at Washington's hothouse atmosphere that hyped ordinary foibles into scandals. In the post-Watergate Washington of the press's fevered imagination, there were "no errors, only conspiracies," he said. For his own part, he saw himself as a moral man, and in most ways he was. "Fast Eddie" was the nickname he hated most, but it was one that he earned.

With Eugene McCarthy, the Democrats' poet-peace candidate of 1968, Williams liked to talk about what C. S. Lewis called "the temptation of the inner ring," the ambition to be on the inside. "Ed knew that it made good men do bad things," said McCarthy. Yet Williams was unable to resist the temptation himself. He relished being a one-man Legal Services Corporation for the establishment, a kind of Washington monument that important people visited just to say they had. "He loved the power of it, that when the shit hit the fan, they all came to him, and he'd tell them what to do," said Bill Graham, son of *Washington Post* owner Katharine Graham and a former lawyer in Williams's firm. Though Williams liked mavericks and hated snobs, he wanted to be on Kay Graham's A-list for dinner. He wanted membership in the inner sanctum. He was pleased to be rumored as Deep Throat, the secret source who blew open Watergate for the *Washington Post,* and never denied that he was. "Whaddya know?" he would ask Sally Quinn, the well-wired *Post* "Style" section writer and wife of Ben Bradlee. "He wanted to know everyone's secrets, and he knew the worst there was to know about anyone," she recalled. "Nothing shocked him."

Williams's cynicism did not bother the powerful, who needed him too much. Their wives, however, would occasionally question his defense of crooks and wrongdoers. In Washington, a man's town, wives were, for the most part, spectators, and thus freed to see what their all-consumed husbands could not. Sitting in church one day in the early 1980s, Eunice

Shriver turned to Williams and asked, "How can you defend evil?" He patiently replied that "everyone is entitled to a lawyer. In the law," he explained in the precise, deliberate way he used when he was making a subtle point to laymen, "there is a presumption of innocence. It is a legal concept, not a moral one. I defend my clients from legal guilt. Moral judgments," he concluded, "I leave to the majestic vengeance of God."

It was a good little speech, and he had given it many times before: to TV talk shows, graduation audiences, law school seminars, his friends, and particularly to his friends' wives, who would corner him at dinner parties. But he was getting tired of it. "The wives!" he would roar. Thinking them moralistic and naive, he would mock their exasperating questions. "How *can* you defend such *terrible* people?" he would screech in a whiny voice. When he began to give his everyone's-entitled-to-a-lawyer speech to Ann Jones, the wife of his family doctor, she had riposted, "Yes, but they're not entitled to *you*." Williams did not bother to respond with his standard parry: "You mean they're entitled to a defense, but not the *best* defense?" He just poured himself another drink. "He'd put up with it from the wives," said David Povich, a partner in Williams's firm. "But if a young lawyer in the firm tried it, he'd unload on him. 'Why is this guy in the law?' he'd ask."

Williams would defend anyone, he liked to say, as long as they gave him total control of the case and paid up front. He would represent Mafia dons and pornographers for enormous fees. He would also represent priests, judges, and attractive women in distress for little or nothing. Yet he did not like to represent clients who stood for causes. He thought it was a mistake to mix ideology with law, and he worried that political activists would not give him the total control he demanded. He refused to represent Dr. Benjamin Spock and several other antiwar activists indicted for inciting students to burn their draft cards in 1970. "They don't need a lawyer," he scoffed. "They need a toastmaster."

WILLIAMS WAS DETERMINED to control and shape his public image. He hated and feared the press—he called reporters "pygmies with dart guns"—but he carefully cultivated those who could help or hurt him. Over the years, he gave the same interview over and over again, word for word. He concocted an anecdotal story of his life that was romanticized and selective. He first dissembled about his war record and then never spoke of it. He kept almost every word ever written about himself in forty-eight bound volumes of press clippings, but he left out articles that cast him in a bad light.

Williams was a man of enormous, seemingly bewildering contradictions. "He loved liberty and hated raw power, unless he was exercising it," said Peter Fleming, a New York trial lawyer who worked with Williams. "He was a devout Catholic, yet he was totally able to separate the world of Peter from the world of Caesar," said Arthur Liman, another well-known trial lawyer who was close to Williams. "He had unshakable faith, yet in worldly affairs he was a complete skeptic." Williams hated yes-men, but he was sometimes surrounded by sycophants. He saw sin in everyone, yet hero-worshiped like an eleven-year-old subscriber to *Boy's Life*. He was pious and profane, shy and sociable, cruel and kind, warm and cold. He could be all or any of these on command. He showed only the side he wanted to show; he compartmentalized his feelings and was a master of manipulation. Yet if he used people, they were for the most part happy to be used by him.

He was not insincere; his friendships were not feigned. Like an actor, he had the capacity to become whatever role he was playing, to genuinely feel the emotions he was projecting. While self-absorbed, he was also extremely loyal, generous, and considerate. He had dozens of "best friends." At one time or another, he managed to convince most of his seven children that they were closer to him than any of the others.

Williams needed to be loved even more than most people. "He needed constant public reaffirmation of self," said Mike Tigar, a trial lawyer who was a protégé of Williams's. Late at night, after he had a few drinks, Williams would sometimes announce that he was running for office, for the Senate perhaps, or even for president. "We're going to New Hampshire!" he'd exclaim, envisioning a shocking groundswell for EBW in the first primary. With beautiful women, he would sometimes posture as a statesman manqué. Lauren Bacall remembers Williams, in his cups after midnight, lamenting that he had not been chosen for the Supreme Court. But his closest friends and his wife, Agnes, doubted that he really wanted to take a government job, much less run for office. Two presidents had offered to make him director of the CIA, a job that fascinated him, but he had turned them down. "He believed public life was so intrusive," said his law partner Brendan Sullivan. "I don't think he wanted to expose himself in that way." A confirmation hearing, said Mike Tigar, was "his idea of living hell."

Williams never wanted to lose control. He was angry when Ben Bradlee was quoted calling him a "primitive." Bradlee had meant to be complimentary, that in bland and colorless Washington here was a man of elemental emotions, a man who could cry and laugh and bay at the moon. But Williams preferred to project an image of certainty and control, of being completely in charge of his destiny.

Williams's philosophy of life, he was fond of telling reporters, was "contest living." In life, he said, "every effort is marked down at the end as a win or a loss." Some found his obsession with winning unattractive, even pathological. He could rant and cry like a small child when he lost something as inconsequential as a firm softball game. One of his law partners saw his public espousal of "contest living" as a "convenient marketing device," since "what you want from lawyers is Fighters! Warriors!" But really, Williams's "contest living" was about losing, or learning to live with defeat. When he had been drinking, Williams showed flickers of self-awareness about the unrelenting pressure he had imposed on himself, and he sought to ease the burden with barroom philosophizing. On the night he hired Vince Lombardi to be coach and general manager of the Washington Redskins, Williams had said to the legendary coach, "You and I must always win, Vince. But nobody *always* wins. I don't care how great you are, you've got to lose. You've got to learn to deal with that."

Williams never did. His drive was too great. After a long day in court and a long night of drinking, Tigar recalls watching Williams rocking slowly back and forth, his great body sagging with exhaustion, as he urinated against the wall in a deserted alley at Third Avenue and 55th Street in New York. "Ed was drained, all done in," recalled Tigar. "He could never say, 'this is enough.' " Williams preached to his children: "Life is not a plateau. You either move up or you fall back." He was determined that he would never fall back to Hartford, Connecticut, and to the dark little house on Adelaide Street.

II

Dreams

Chapter Two

JOE WILLIAMS WAS a dapper, meticulous little man who wore a carnation and worked as a floorwalker in a department store in downtown Hartford. The son of a Welsh immigrant who had been converted to Catholicism by his Irish wife, he read the Bible cover to cover and brewed foul-tasting beer in his basement. He also had a touch of gentle blarney; "when better kisses are made, a Williams will make them," he trilled. But mostly he was quiet. At dinner he was speechless. He had a hiatal hernia that made him gag and cough when he swallowed food. His wife, May, however, was gabby. She liked to play bridge and gossip, and she didn't like to cook. Because of Joe's hernia, the food had to be bland. Her dinners were tasteless and heavy and served in large portions. The pie crust was so thick, her cousin Geraldine Ray recalled, that the dough was raw inside.

May never criticized Joe for being a poor provider, but she was not happy with him. He never took her out to a show or a movie or a restaurant; mostly, he would sit in the front room and read the paper. May told her nieces, "Once you get married, the fun stops and the boredom starts." She said she was envious of her sister, who went out all the time, and wished she had married her sister's husband.

May and Joe married late. May was forty-four when she had her first child, a son. The next child was stillborn, and she never had another. The double-decker house at 36 Adelaide Street was gloomy inside. The furniture, dominated by a burgundy upholstered couch and an imitation mahogany breakfront stuffed with knickknacks, was heavy and dark. The shades were always drawn to keep the fabric from fading. At dinner the

25

young Edward Bennett Williams silently ate his mother's doughy pie and listened to his father's quiet gag.

"I knew I was going to break out," Williams said years later. "I knew I wasn't long for there." In describing his Hartford childhood, Williams portrayed himself as an urban Tom Sawyer who was constantly slipping out the back window at night to go to baseball games and boxing matches. He vividly remembered running three miles in the dark to East Hartford when he was nine years old to watch the city's own Bat Battalino outbox Andre Routis of France for the Featherweight Championship of the World. At Bulkeley Stadium, a rickety minor league park occupied by the Hartford Senators of the Eastern League, he sold "ice colds and red hots" in the summer and watched Hank Greenberg, "the $9,000 Flash," hone his skills for the majors. At night, Edward dreamed of pitching the seventh game of the World Series at Yankee Stadium.

Williams decided to become a lawyer, he once said, the day he saw an enormous crowd outside the Hartford courthouse craning to catch a glimpse of Gerald Chapman, a playboy thief on trial for murder. Williams claimed that he walked the two miles down to the courthouse every day to watch the trial. Since he was not quite five years old at the time, it is not clear how much of the legal maneuvering he appreciated, or whether he actually made it to the courtroom. Nonetheless, he carried a memory of his mother leaning over him as she pointed to the prosecutor, Hugh Alcorn, and saying, "He's a great man—someone you should look up to!"

In Williams's recounting of his childhood, there is a certain amount of Hardy Boys self-mythologizing. Williams's neighborhood playmate and best friend David Rosen has a somewhat less theatrical memory of Williams's boyhood. Rosen remembers "Eddie" as a dutiful child who always came when his mother called—by blowing on a police whistle. On the first day at Burr Elementary School, when the other boys jumped him and pushed him down, Eddie ran home in tears to his mother. He was quiet, Rosen recalled, and very studious. He loved sandlot baseball but he was not much of a player. He was usually picked last or nearly last and then put out in right field or, because he was tall, at first base. Rosen recalled climbing over the Bulkeley Stadium wall with Williams, but he added that a sympathetic policeman gave them a leg up. They did not sneak out at night, he said, because there were no night games. Bulkeley Stadium had no lights.

Williams's cousins remember him as soft-spoken and bashful in an engaging sort of way. Sometimes, in describing something that had happened to him, he would get excited and start to act out the scene. Then he would suddenly catch himself and sit down, looking about shyly. As he grew older, he became more interested in acting, and more assertive about it. In the evening, he would stand on a chair in the kitchen and imitate Franklin D. Roosevelt giving radio speeches. By the time he was twelve, he liked to play Broadway director, organizing his friends to put on plays that he had seen performed at a public park in Hartford. He also showed an early interest in gambling. When he was eight, his cousin Jack Williams showed him how to play a simple numbers game by betting on the U.S. Treasury balance in the evening paper. Williams and Rosen set up their "own little numbers racket," selling chances at three for a nickel. The pot, they advertised, was $100. They panicked when they realized that one of their customers might actually guess the winning number. For the rest of the afternoon they hid out, until Mrs. Williams blew her police whistle for dinner.

OTHER FRIENDS BEGAN to notice a deliberate, purposeful quality to Williams. "He was the most premeditated kid I've ever seen," said Charles Buck, a classmate. "He thought everything out, what he was going to do, how he was going to do it." His early political skills were rewarded. By the seventh grade he was the recognized teacher's pet. "At high school I practically ran the place," Williams later boasted. ("He ruled with an iron hand," agreed the 1937 Bulkeley High yearbook.) As the editor of his high school paper, *The Torch,* he wanted to know all the gossip; he named his column "Inside Stuff" and earned the nickname "Walter Winchell." Tall and skinny, with intense eyes and an impish smile, he was genuinely popular, often amusing his classmates with a mild streak of mischief. Reporting in the *Torch* on a school dance he printed a sophomoric double entendre headline—"Herbie Hind Says Great Dance Friday Night"—that took the faculty a week or two to comprehend (Her Behind . . .).

He wore a suit and tie to school every day—the same suit, a shiny brown pinstripe. On cold days he wore a beige sweater underneath. His family couldn't afford to buy him a new suit or a coat. In later years, Williams liked to say he had grown up "dirt poor." His relatives back in Hartford are slightly bothered and puzzled by his poor-mouthing; after all, they said, there was always food on the table, and Adelaide Street, while a little shabby, was hardly a slum. But when Williams was about fourteen, his father was laid off. The Depression had settled over Hartford, and the Brown Thomson Department Store where Joe Williams worked was losing business. Young Edward saw his sacked father come home in tears. For Williams, the experience was terrifying. He knew his parents had meager savings, and he had seen the hobos living in rags in squalid shacks down in the weeds by the Connecticut River. Joe Williams got his job back, with his salary cut from $42 to $37 a week, but Williams never forgot the fear in his father's face.

Williams himself went to work pumping gas to help support his family. In the summers, he later claimed, he worked eighty-four hours a week, 8:00 A.M. until 1:00 A.M., and was paid eleven cents an hour. Years later, when he had become a famous trial lawyer, the oil company that owned the gas station where Williams had worked tried to hire him to defend it in a criminal matter. Williams refused. "We couldn't agree on the fee," he dryly explained to a magazine reporter. "Ed was cheap," recalled Jerry Waterhouse, Williams's high school girlfriend. "He never spent more than thirty-five cents on a date—twenty-five cents for the movie, ten cents for the Coke. We walked miles because his family didn't have a car." Williams was bitter, she remembered, when he had to bum a ride for the two of them to the prom.

Waterhouse found Williams shy and upright. He urged her to be a better Catholic and never did more than kiss her on a date. "His only security was his intelligence," she said. "He didn't know much about girls." He never talked about his mother or father, but he talked a great deal about himself. He told her, "I want to make money." "That's what he talked about," she recalled. "He wanted to buy things. In later years he told me he was driven by power, but I always thought it was money."

For an Irish Catholic in Hartford in the 1930s, the opportunity to make money was limited. The city of 150,000 was then, as now, dominated by insurance companies. Back then, their WASP owners did not like to hire the Irish, at least for white-collar jobs. The Irish and Italians lived in tenements and double-deckers in South and East Hartford. The WASPs lived on tree-lined streets in West Hartford; they referred to the neighboring ridge occupied by the well-to-do Jews as "Kike's Peak." At the beach on Long Island Sound favored by Hartforders in the summer, the Irish sat at one end and the Yankees at the other. The Irish side was called the House of Commons and the WASP side was called the House of Lords.

Williams was not exposed firsthand to discrimination, but only because the city was so segregated. He later joked that he didn't meet his first Protestant until the age of twelve, yet he found Hartford, with its stratified social structure and small-town ways, oppressive and confining. He knew the best way to get out of Hartford was to go to college. He was not interested in a scholarship to the local college, Trinity, an Episcopalian school of modest reputation. He wanted Yale. But there was only one Yale scholarship at Bulkeley High, and it went to the top student. Too busy with the school paper and pumping gas, Williams did not have the best grades in his class. After an all-nighter at the *Torch,* he would corner Jerry Waterhouse in the hallway and demand that she read him her Latin translation before class; she remembers being stunned by his photographic memory. Fortunately, Williams was a special pet of Miss Jane Dargan, the vice principal, who had close ties to a number of Jesuit colleges. She was able to arrange a full scholarship to Holy Cross in Worcester, Massachusetts.

Williams's father was against his going to college. He wanted his son to stay home and produce a paycheck for the family. After a bitter quarrel, Williams packed his bags for Holy Cross. "I left Hartford," he told a young lawyer at his law firm in Washington, "and never looked back." Years later, after his parents died, his relatives in Hartford asked him if he wanted the mementos and photos and knickknacks from his mother's home. "Forget it," he replied.

WHEN GRADUATES OF the old Holy Cross try to describe their school to an outsider, they sometimes use martial analogies: The College of the Holy Cross was as strict as West Point, as tough as the Marine Corps. It was boot camp for the mind and spirit, with Jesuits as drill sergeants. Like a military academy, Holy Cross had a clearly defined mission: to produce humanistic gentlemen devoted "To the Greater Glory of God." To the weak and slow, the training was an ordeal; to the survivors, it could be a glorious crucible.

The rule book Ed Williams was handed when he entered Holy Cross in September 1937 was, by modern standards, laughably strict. Students could not play cards. They could not listen to the radio before 3:00 P.M. or after 7:00 P.M., or have a woman in their room, ever. "To have in one's possession any books or writing of immoral tendency, obscene pictures or illustrations, or to circulate the same, may entail dismissal from the college,'' the rule book warned. Anyone caught drinking alcohol or staying out of his dormitory without permission after 10:00 P.M. faced expulsion. "The plea of first offense," the rule book cautioned, "will not be considered."

Life at Holy Cross, however, was not as repressive as the rule book implied; the Jesuits would wink at a certain amount of youthful exuberance. Still, there was, on the bleak hilltop occupied by the college, an air of cultivated innocence. When the Holy Cross football team hosted the University of Georgia, in Williams's sophomore year, the governor of Georgia, Eurith Rivers, was asked to address a pregame rally in the basement of the Holy Cross chapel. To lighten up the occasion, the governor made a mildly off-color joke—none of the Holy Cross students laughed. Naturally, there were a few hell-raisers who would sneak out at night to drink beer in downtown Worcester, ignoring the rumors that barbed wire had been put on the drain pipes to keep them from shinnying down. There was even a fast crowd, centered around George Curley, the son of the mayor of Boston, who had a car and could drive his pals into the big city. But Williams was never among them.

Williams was not about to risk his scholarship by breaking rules. He was cautious and subdued in his first year at Holy Cross, according to Robert Maheu, who was a class ahead. They were both poor boys who had to wait on tables and eat after the other students, and they had taken a solemn vow not to smoke or drink in college. Williams was a relentless grind. As a freshman, he occasionally woke at 1:00 A.M. to study, using a flashlight under the bedclothes so as not to disturb the twenty other boys snoring in the iron cots crowded into the fourth-floor dormitory of O'Kane Hall. During his first two years, he could not find the time to attend football games. Because he spent his Saturday nights in the library, his classmates inevitably dubbed him "Leatherpants." There was no dishonor in studying hard at Holy Cross, but even so, Williams's work habits seemed excessive. "You have to have a *little* fun," classmate Brutus Clay reproached him. "The fun will come later," Williams replied.

FIRST CAME "SECTION A." Williams had been placed in the fast-track class with about twenty of the brightest boys. Many had prepared at Jesuit high schools, and Williams felt at a disadvantage. Section A was taught— driven is perhaps a more accurate description—by Father John Dwyer, a

Jesuit priest with a bulldog face, hunched shoulders, and piercing eyes. The atmosphere, said Bill Richardson, Williams's classmate in Section A, was one of "tense merriment." Dwyer meant to elevate his mostly lower-middle-class charges: He ordered them to read twenty classic English novels "that every educated man should know," and demanded three different translations of Juvenal's *Satire X*: one for the schoolteacher, one for the editor of *The New Yorker,* and one for the streets. "Faster, faster," Father Dwyer would exclaim, twirling his finger, as students stumbled over their Cicero. Picking imaginary pieces of lint off his black cassock, he would stalk between the students' desks, pausing to flick his cincture, the sash around his robe, in the face of a recalcitrant pupil. On the very rare occasion when a student talked back, "Tiger," as his students called him, would thrust out his finger and command, "Change your manner!"

The *ratio studiorem,* the Jesuit curriculum, stressed reason and logic, but it did not particularly encourage original thought. The Jesuits at Holy Cross believed that medieval scholasticism had pretty well exhausted the possibility of human thought several centuries before. Logic was to be used to defend truths already discovered against the attacks of skeptical philosophers like Immanuel Kant and René Descartes. Holy Cross students were given courses in "apologetics," in how to prove or justify the existence of God. "We swallowed dogma whole," recalled Father John Brooks, who graduated from Holy Cross in 1949 and became the college's president in 1970. "Faith was structured on the argument that one believes because the Church teaches it."

To make this argument, Holy Cross gave its students powerful tools. Williams spent hours in Tiger Dwyer's rhetoric class outlining and studying the speeches and debates of the great orators—Edmund Burke and William Pitt, Henry Clay and Daniel Webster. Dwyer's students labored to learn deductive reasoning, syllogisms and enthymemes. Although Dwyer's emphasis was more on logic than flourishes, Williams was exposed to a variety of rhetorical styles, from the orotund circumlocutions of Cicero and Burke to the sharp declarative jabs of Demosthenes and Pitt the Elder. In later years, they would all echo in the cadence of Williams's closing arguments to juries.

Though Williams was not particularly outspoken in class, his classmates began to notice that he had what Jesuits call a *continuatsio verborem,* literally a continuity of words, an ability to speak naturally and fluently. Translating Juvenal's satires for Tiger Dwyer, Williams was able to find the right phrases, the right metaphors—what Horace called the *callida junctura,* a happy combination of words. Tiger encouraged vividness as well as felicity, and told those who did not know that Juvenal's "punishment of the mullet" meant a scaly fish jammed up the victim's rear end.

The one extracurricular activity that Williams allowed himself was debating. In that pretelevision era, Williams later said, "debating was big league," particularly among Catholic schools. On a Saturday night in Worcester, a Holy Cross debate might attract a crowd of several hundred and a radio audience of thousands more. The school's debating coach, a precise, fastidious priest named Father James Dolan, was extremely concerned about the public image of his team when it traveled to debate other schools. He instructed his debaters to address each other as "Mister," to wear neckties, to use the right fork, to chew with their mouths closed, and to dry out the sinks in the lavatory after they washed. Williams carefully followed Dolan's instructions on how to make others feel important: Listen before speaking and be solicitous of the "little people," the waiters and conductors and trainmen.

Williams came to regard Dolan as a tinhorn martinet, but he always heeded the debating coach's advice on thorough preparation. "When I tried to fly by the seat of my pants, Ed would get mad at me," said Robert Maheu, his debating partner junior year. "He told me we'd lose if we were unprepared." Williams's senior year debating partner, Bill Richardson, said that Williams was particularly adept at using facts and statistics. Richardson was perhaps more skilled at enunciating overarching principles, but Williams was quicker at taking apart a debating point. "He had a corkscrew mind," Richardson said. "He would bore in on a sinuous or tortuous argument." Williams's style was low key; the theatrical ability he showed in court would come later. "He was all head," Richardson remembered. "He'd drape himself over the podium and speak in a low voice."

But he was very effective. His win-loss record was not preserved by Holy Cross, but his classmates said that he seldom lost. After Holy Cross defeated Harvard in Williams's senior year—a sweet victory for a small Jesuit school—most of Williams's classmates went off to town to celebrate. Williams went back to his room to study. In the corridor late that night he encountered several members of the Harvard team who were staying overnight in the Holy Cross dorm, and with great glee he explained to them how they could and should have won.

Like all good debaters, Williams could take either side of an argument with equal facility. To confound their opponents, he and Richardson would think up gimmicks. One time, in the midst of attacking FDR's Keynesian economic policies, Williams suddenly stopped, as if he had forgotten what to say. As his rebuttal time ran down, and the audience and even Richardson began to squirm, Williams suddenly announced, "In the last minute, the U.S. government has spent $12,000. . . ." Williams would try to make the opposition waste time by arguing points he would then concede. He would selectively use facts and statistics to make his case, while ignoring the statistics that made the opposite point. "We were cute and cozy," recalls Richardson. "We were not interested in resolving the issues. We were interested in winning."

In some ways, Williams's debating experience mirrored his education at Holy Cross. To be sure, the Jesuits taught absolute truths, certain "natural laws," and the commandments of the Bible. But they also recognized that mere mortals were bound to fall short of the high moral standards set by the Scripture. The students at Holy Cross, like Catholics everywhere, were taught that man was a victim of Original Sin, and thus essentially weak. Forgiveness was divine, but it could be helped along by baptism and confession. In their traditional role as confessors, Jesuit priests acted as advocates, not judges. They sought, through reason and logic, to ease the heavy burden of guilt on a penitent and to make the harsh laws of God and nature more humane. So severe was the penalty for committing a mortal sin—eternal damnation—that the forgiving priests in the Society of Jesus strained to find some mitigating circumstance that could excuse a mortal sin, or at least reduce the charge to mere veniality. In theology and philosophy classes, Holy Cross students explored, on a case-by-case basis, the boundaries of sinfulness. Stealing was a mortal sin, but what about stealing to feed your family? What was a white lie? How late could you arrive at mass without having to go again in the afternoon?

The question of how far you could go without going to Hell had particular application to sex. In teaching the sacrament of marriage and the Sixth Commandment in junior-year theology, Father Luke O'Connor was at once explicit and broadminded. Sex outside marriage and masturbation were mortal sins, but Father O'Connor recognized that the young men in his class had hormones. They were bound to want sex. How much was permissible? Kissing but not soul kissing? Petting but not heavy petting? After long debate, accompanied by a certain amount of winking and tittering, Father O'Connor would draw the bottom line: Orgasm, he lectured, was out.

Williams took thirty-six hours of philosophy in his last two years at Holy Cross. The course names today sound obscure and esoteric—epistemology, metaphysics, cosmology—but the training was immensely useful for applying facts to law in a way that excused actions that might be immoral or wrong but were not, strictly speaking, unlawful. There is an academic word—casuistry—to describe what the Jesuits were teaching their charges. In essence, it is the study of how ethical principles can change, depending on the circumstances. What was wrong in one case, the Jesuits taught, was not in another. "What it boiled down to was how to get off the hook," said Father Tim Healy, who was trained at Holy Cross's sister institution, Fordham. The Jesuits' charges learned to grasp legalistic distinctions. "We understood that a plea of not guilty doesn't mean 'I didn't do it.' It just means, 'You've got to prove it,' " said Healy.

The training helped make students sympathetic to human foibles, but inevitably, casuistry could be twisted. Clever students learned to argue by specious analogy, to sweep bad conduct along with good, to excuse conduct that adhered to the letter of the law while violating the spirit. The Jesuit priests mocked by Enlightenment writers were adept at this sort of legalistic reasoning in the royal courts of the sixteenth and seventeenth centuries. So, too, was Ed Williams in the American courtrooms of the twentieth century.

Still, there is some evidence that he struggled with the question of moral absolutes while he was in college. In March 1941, his senior year, he wrote a prize-winning essay entitled "Towards the True Norm of Morality." In it he called for "absolute standards for evaluating human acts." According to the student newspaper, the *Tomahawk,* Williams's essay "decried the variable, subjective norms existing today as manifested, for example, in the condemnation of Hitler for having broken trusts, while at the same time they condone and tolerate the practice of divorce."

He had tried to apply the same rigid standards to his sex life a few months earlier. His old high school girlfriend, Jerry Waterhouse, was now a senior at nearby Smith College. Because Williams lacked the funds or the time, they had not seen much of each other in college, but Williams had loosened up a little in his last year, and he invited Jerry to a football weekend. On Saturday night, Williams snuck out of his dorm and made his way to the boardinghouse where Waterhouse was staying. For an hour or two, they "kissed," Waterhouse recalled, but then Williams suddenly got up and left. ("He was sexually shy," she said.) But instead of going back to the dorm, she recalled, Williams spent the night wandering the streets of Worcester so his friends would think he spent the night with a girl.

ALONG WITH MORALITY, Holy Cross sought to imbue its students with what Ignatius of Loyola, the founder of the Society of Jesus, called "political insight." From Ignatius onward, Jesuits have believed that political power was necessary to spread the Word of God. In Europe, that meant penetrating the aristocracy, a task the Society accomplished so effectively that the wily Jesuit courtier became a stock villain to Voltaire and other writers of the Enlightenment. In New England, however, the aristocracy, or what passed for one, was largely closed to Catholics. Threatened by the waves of immigrants from Ireland and Italy, the Anglophile Boston Brahmins looked down from Beacon Hill on the "papists" swarming into the North End. No matter how successful, Catholics were constantly reminded of their lower status. Joseph Kennedy, a big man in Harvard's Class of 1912, never forgot the bitterness he felt standing in the cold street outside the Porcellian Club, wondering why his WASP roommate, Robert Sturgis Potter, got in and he didn't. In the early part of the twentieth century, about the only elite a Holy Cross graduate could aspire to was the Society of Jesus.

By the late 1930s, banking and finance in Boston were still WASP preserves. But the "No Irish Need Apply" signs were coming down elsewhere. With the large influx of Irish and Italian immigrants, political power was shifting to the more numerous Catholics, embodied by the colorful mayor of Boston, James Michael Curley. The year Ed Williams entered Holy Cross, Joe Kennedy was appointed ambassador to the Court of St. James's by Franklin Roosevelt.

Like other Jesuit colleges, Holy Cross played an essential role in breaking down the class and ethnic barriers. For the children of immigrants, the best way to respectability was through the professions, and law schools and medical schools were open to anyone with a good education.

"Holy Cross was full of the sons of firemen aspiring to become doctors," Richardson recalled. "We were told that Harvard Medical School was eager to have us." The fathers of most of Williams's classmates had never been to college, but their sons were determined to become lawyers, doctors, teachers, and priests. Like most of his classmates, Williams did not brood about the oppression of his ancestors, at least in dormitory bull sessions. His outlook was more optimistic. He had long since set his sights on becoming a lawyer, and Holy Cross offered the way.

Making money, Richardson thought, was only a peripheral goal to Williams. Rather, like his models Webster and Clay, "he wanted to be involved in the great debates of the time"—and it did not particularly matter on which side. Williams was not a crusader for social reform. Though he was nominally a New Deal liberal, he did not have a burning social conscience. What he wanted, said Richardson, "was power and influence."

The night of the prom in the spring of 1941, Richardson found taped to his door a note from Williams, excitedly telling him that they had both received full scholarships to Catholic University Law School in Washington. The next morning, a Sunday, the two debating partners slipped downtown and began drinking beer in a cafeteria. Williams was full of dreams and plans: They would room together in law school, then apprentice apart for five years, then rejoin to form a firm that would put Webster and Clay to shame. Giddy with beer and promise, Richardson was swept along.

There was, however, one problem: Richardson had decided to join the priesthood. A few weeks later, he told his friend of his vocation. Williams was disappointed but not altogether surprised. The best scholars and leaders at Holy Cross were encouraged to listen for God's call. Williams told Richardson that he, too, had considered the priesthood, but he wasn't sure that priests were, as he put it, "for real." He was suspicious of Fulton Sheen, the urbane Catholic apologist who was perhaps a little too polished. Williams would stick with the law.

He wanted to go to law school in Washington, says Richardson, "because the action was there. The New Deal was still on, and the nation was on the eve of war." A few weeks after he heard from Catholic U., Williams got a full scholarship to Georgetown Law School, a better-known institution in the nation's capital. By the end of his senior year, Williams was a good catch for any law school. Though he had struggled in his first two years, he graduated summa cum laude, first in his class of 346. On his final oral examinations he received a grade of 97 only because, awed classmates joked, his Jesuit inquisitors did not believe in human perfectability.

Williams also received a partial scholarship to Yale Law School. He was tempted by the Yale name, but to go there, he would have had to borrow $1,500 for the three years. His father told him he would never be able to repay such a sum. In fact, Joe Williams did not want his son to go to law school at all. When Edward came home from Holy Cross in June and announced that he intended to go to law school, his father burst into tears. Joe Williams was having increasing trouble with his health, and he wanted his son to come home and help support the family. Angry and upset, Ed turned and ran from the house on Adelaide Street, making his way to St. Augustine's Church, three blocks away. His mother found him there, kneeling at the altar, bowed in prayer.

Chapter Three

WILLIAMS ARRIVED IN Washington in September 1941 with $12 in his pocket. He was assigned a fourth-floor garret in Old North on the Georgetown campus and was required to "proctor" the undergraduates, mostly by making sure they were in their rooms at night. Law school bored Williams at first. He particularly disliked property class, learning arcane and hoary rules about fees simple and contingent remaindermen. The old common law, imported from Britain, had been written to favor property rights over human rights—English landlords over Irish peasants—and Williams found studying it not only dull but depressing. Tied down with his law books and handing out demerits to undergraduates, Williams did not have much time to explore the arenas that had drawn him to Washington—the Capitol and the courts. His financial situation did improve somewhat in November: He won "beer money for the year" by betting on Holy Cross against Boston College at ten to one odds. The Crusaders won 55–21.

The Japanese freed Williams from Real Property I by bombing Pearl Harbor on December 7. At first, Williams does not appear to have been eager to jump into combat. On December 19, he applied for a job as a clerk at the Federal Bureau of Investigation. Although the FBI examiner rated him "undoubtedly above average intelligence," Williams was rejected as "too smart aleckie." FBI files show that he became impatient waiting in line with the other applicants and tried to "pull a fast one" by presenting himself for an interview in the Chief Clerk's office. Having failed to become a clerk, Williams next went to the opposite extreme and enlisted to become an aviator in the Army Air Corps. The glamour of being an officer in an elite unit appealed to him, he told a fellow enlistee, Fen Seton. He didn't give much thought to the flying part, which turned out to be a mistake. Williams was sworn in as an Air Corps cadet on January 15 in Hartford. He was given a train ticket on the overnight sleeper to Montgomery, Alabama, and told to bring some underwear. At Maxwell Air Force Base, he shared a crude barracks with eleven other cadets. The February rains quickly turned the tent city into a mud hole, but the young cadets were treated as officers and gentlemen, with servants to make their beds and shine their shoes. Basic training, called "pre-flight," lasted ninety days, during which they were drilled in math, algebra, meteorology, calculus, and, quaintly, skeet shooting (to learn how to lead an airborne target).

Williams was very quiet and unassertive, recalled Seton, his tentmate. But he could "destroy you with a couple of words if he had to." Most of his verbal deftness was used on Southern rednecks who taunted Williams for being a Yankee and a "mackerel snapper." Williams did well at the academic and physical training; he was by now an imposing presence, a strapping 180-pound six-footer with close-cropped curly hair and eyes that could turn hard. On weekends, the cadets would cut loose in the honky-tonks of Montgomery, drinking and picking up girls. Williams did not join the carousing, recalled Seton. Rather, he spent hours and hours listening to the jukebox, particularly a song called "Tangerine" sung by Helen O'Connell, a beautiful young singer with the Tommy Dorsey band.

In mid-April, Williams graduated from preflight school. Before heading to "primary" flight school in Bennettsville, South Carolina, he and Seton went back to Hartford for the weekend. Seton remembered Williams's exultation as he collected salutes and smartly returned them while strolling around his hometown in his new uniform.

By June, however, after less than five months in uniform, Williams was back at his desk at Georgetown Law School, dressed again in ordinary civilian clothes, drearily poring over his property case book. What happened? His own account changed over time. Some Georgetown classmates said Williams told them he had crashed in a bomber, en route to North Africa via Brazil, on takeoff from Maxwell Field. Williams had been the co-pilot but not at the controls. Everyone aboard the plane but Williams had died. Badly injured in the head and back, he had been given a medical discharge. He told Peter Maxson, a Holy Cross friend, that the accident happened the day after he got his wings. "He took it hard that all his friends in the bomber had died," Maxson said.

Williams told his family doctor, Steve Jones, that he had fractured his head in the crash and needed a metal plate attached to his skull. But Jones never saw any scar from a surgical incision.

In later years, Williams amended his story. He said that he had crashed a biplane, a training plane, while attempting a landing. The plane had "ground-looped," flipped over nose first. The cause was a "mechanical defect" or "engine failure"—not pilot error. Williams told his first bi-ographer, Robert Pack, that he had been discharged for medical reasons as a lieutenant. In his *Who's Who* listing, Williams put down "USAAF 1941–43." In fact, Williams washed out of the Army Air Corps as a cadet "for reason of flying deficiency" on June 10, 1942. The report on Williams's discharge, released to the author under the Freedom of Infor-mation Act in 1991, states:

> Williams has had a total of 17 hours and 20 minutes flying instruction, of which 16 hours have been dual. This student has made very slow progress and since soloing he has been unable to progress. His coordination is extremely weak and erratic. His decisions in the air are slow and unde-pendable. He fails to profit from repeated correction. As a result, the Board found the appointee to have conclusively demonstrated that his military flight training should be immediately discontinued due to the fact that he has exhibited traits while operating an aircraft which are a source of danger to his own life as well as the lives of others. The board recommended that he be relieved from flight training and be discharged from military service.

Williams never admitted the true story to his friends or even his family. He never liked to talk about his time in uniform. On the typed draft of a résumé prepared in the late 1950s, he wrote in pencil "military service:" but never filled out the rest. The résumé just shows erasure marks. The closest Williams came to acknowledging the truth was a note he penned on a letter he wrote to his old tent mate Seton nearly forty years later. "I still can't fly!" Williams wrote. "What a mistake the A.A.F. made."

Jerry Waterhouse, his old girlfriend, remembers seeing Williams back in Hartford in the summer of 1942, after his discharge. His jaw was twitching, he complained of a head injury, and he seemed depressed.

Williams had fulfilled his military obligation and he was free to resume law school. But it is not surprising that he felt low about going back to school. Most young men were off at war in the summer of 1942, or preparing to enter the military. To be out of uniform, grinding away at Trusts and Civil Procedure, must have been very disheartening. "Georgetown was a very quiet and lonely place at the time," said his classmate Tom Rover. Indeed, Williams was so discouraged and so bored that twice that first year he considered dropping out of law school, coming back each time after a couple of miserable weeks with nowhere to go but Hartford.

By the summer of 1944, however, Williams had begun to cheer up. He was poor, but he could afford an occasional beer at Mrs. Morris's Silver Dollar Cafe in Georgetown. At the "Silver Buck" he would jaw and drink with fellow students with names like Murphy, O'Brien, and O'Rourke. Some nights he got a little carried away. Walking down M Street after a particularly liquid evening, he stopped with his buddies to buy hamburgers at the Little Tavern. Suddenly, recalled Bill Ragan, who was along on the bender, Williams vaulted across the counter. Wild-eyed, he seized a machete used for slicing rolls and chased the terrified short-order cook out of the joint. When Williams returned to campus, instead of heading for his dorm, he climbed up onto the statue of the college's founder, Bishop John Carroll, and proceeded to relieve himself. Then he passed out. The next morning, when a priest found him asleep in Bishop Carroll's lap, Williams had to use every bit of Tiger Dwyer's rhetorical training to avoid losing his scholarship.

To mitigate the boredom of wills and trusts, Williams began slipping away from the Georgetown Law School, then located across the street from the federal courthouse on 6th Street, to watch real lawyers argue cases in court. Most of them, he concluded, were dreadful, but he learned from watching their mistakes. At night he pored over Irving Stone's biography of Clarence Darrow, the great trial lawyer, marveling at Darrow's ability to make jurors weep with the passion of his arguments.

SOME AFTERNOONS, HIS classes over, Williams would wander about the city of Washington. He relished the grandeur of the capital. He looked with wonder at the vast Greco-Roman temples of government that lined the broad avenues; he mounted the wide staircases and gazed down the vistas; he stood in the Capitol, where Daniel Webster and John Calhoun had debated; he read with awe the frieze above the marble columns of the Supreme Court promising "Equal Justice Under Law."

Many Northerners who came to Washington had a less romantic view of the place. Built on a swamp, the city was unlivable in the summer during the years before air-conditioning. Even after the population doubled with war-related personnel, the city remained drowsy and slow-moving. "People from real cities—Boston, New York, Chicago, cities with factories and immigrants and subways—thought it astonishing," wrote David Brinkley in *Washington Goes to War*. "They found few restaurants offering anything not fried in deep fat. . . . There was one legitimate theater, dark half the time. A baseball team, the Senators, usually in last place in the American League, played in ancient Griffith Stadium, widely regarded as a firetrap."

Coming from Hartford, which had only a minor league team, Williams was not much bothered by the lack of culture or high cuisine. He didn't have any money to spend anyway. To Williams, Washington had advantages that no other city could offer. According to Bill Richardson, Williams had been drawn to Washington because it was becoming "the center of the world." And the city's preeminence was even more apparent as the war wound down, leaving the empires of the Old World in ruins. For any ambitious young man eager to make a public name for himself, Washington was a good place to be in 1945. But for Williams, it had a special appeal: It was a place where a young Irish Catholic male found no barriers to his advancement.

In cities like Boston and New York, the waves of Irish immigrants had seemed threatening to the upper classes. In Boston, the Brahmins built a large stone armory to protect themselves in case the teeming hordes rioted or revolted. While Washington was not an immigrant town, it was a racist one, and the locals felt threatened by the influx of poor Southern blacks who built shanties and squalid hovels in the alleyways. Senator Theodore Bilbo of Mississippi, called the mayor of Washington because he was chairman of the Senate District Committee that actually ran the city, hated the fact that nearly half the residents of the city were black. "If you go through the government departments," said Bilbo, "there are so many niggers it's like a black cloud all around you." But Washington was fairly free of prejudice against the Irish, whose small community was well integrated into the city.

The Irish were particularly well represented in the law. At Gonzaga, the local Jesuit high school, the students "were beaten with rods and switches to create lawyers and doctors," said Thomas Kelly, a Gonzaga graduate and lifelong Washingtonian. Those who graduated were automatically given half-scholarships to Georgetown. The two big law schools in Washington—Georgetown and Catholic University—fed the local bar with Irish Catholic lawyers, so the bench in Washington was dotted with Irish names like Curran, McClough, and Maguire. The New Deal had drawn in a smattering of Harvard and Yale Law grads to work in the agencies and clerk for the Supreme Court, but the Justice Department and the U.S. Attorney's Office were well-stocked with Georgetown grads.

If Williams had gone to Boston, he would have had to overcome Yankee prejudice and the lack of a Harvard degree. Even on Wall Street, still the center of the legal universe, he would have had to queue up behind Ivy Leaguers and WASPs. Washington had a snobby upper class, the Cave Dwellers, who drew back from the pushy New Dealers into their sedate houses in Kalorama and their exclusive clubs—Chevy Chase, the Metropolitan, and the Sulgrave. But Williams never saw the Cave Dwellers, and as a law student, he might not even have been aware of their existence. All Williams knew was that Washington was a city on the way up, and that a bright young man, even an Irish Catholic, could rise with it.

THE WAR HAD left Washington with something it would never experience again: a lawyer shortage. The growth of government brought on by the New Deal and the war effort had provided plenty of legal business, but many of the lawyers had disappeared into uniform. At Hogan & Hartson, one of Washington's leading firms, the chief trial lawyer, Howard Boyd, went prospecting for new talent at Georgetown Law School. Standing on a street corner outside Boyd's office, Georgetown law professor Al Philip Kane told Boyd about the "brightest student" he had ever had, a "flier who bumped his head and is draft proof." Boyd asked to meet him. Finding Ed Williams "young, handsome, and virile," he later recounted, "I hired him on the spot."

Williams went to work for Hogan & Hartson in the summer of 1944, before he had even graduated or passed the bar. While a leading firm, Hogan & Hartson was not the most prestigious in Washington. Covington & Burling, with a large federal appellate and regulatory practice, drew the Harvard and Yale Law School grads and the Supreme Court clerks.

Hogan & Hartson was more of a local firm, but of these it was the biggest and best, representing the department stores, the banks, the transit company, and the utilities. Half of Hogan's eighteen lawyers had graduated from Georgetown, and Williams's Jesuit pedigree made him an easy fit. Ironically, much of what Williams did was insurance work, defending the same insurance companies that refused to hire Irish Catholics in Hartford.

When Williams graduated (again first in his class) and passed the bar in the fall of 1944, he began going to court nearly every day. His guide and tutor was Howard Boyd, a genial redhead and extremely able trial lawyer. Like Father Dolan at Holy Cross, Boyd stressed preparation. Never go to court, he instructed Williams, without knowing more about the facts than your opponent, your client, or anyone else. Williams quickly showed Boyd his capacity for work and his attention to detail. Years later, Boyd still liked to recall how Williams had defended the Capital Transit Company in a lawsuit filed by a woman named Ella Thomas, a somewhat neurotic spinster who claimed she had been injured when the bus in which she was riding collided with another bus. The collision had been minor, and Miss Thomas was the only passenger to claim an injury. The doctors could find nothing wrong with her, but her complaints kept worsening; she often ran a high fever, and she kept coming back to the hospital for further examination. Meanwhile, the medical bills mounted. Before the trial, Williams stayed up all night reading her hospital records. He began noticing a certain pattern: Every time she recorded a high temperature, the nurses' notes showed that she had asked for a hot water bottle a half hour earlier. During his cross-examination, Williams asked Miss Thomas about her fevers. She vividly described feeling flushed and pained. Then Williams began asking about the hot water bottle. She squirmed uncomfortably, bit her lip, and nervously eyed the jury. Finally, she broke into tears. "You think I put the thermometer in the hot water bottle don't you? . . . Well, how else could I make them know how sick I was?"

Williams also learned by his mistakes. In another Transit Company case, he wanted to show that a pedestrian run down and killed by a streetcar was not an innocent victim but a drunken bum. The man's son had been seen at the scene of the accident, bending over the body of his father. Williams felt confident that the boy had been removing a bottle from his father's back pocket. On cross-examination, he closed in on the boy. "You leaned over him, didn't you?" asked Williams. "Yes," the boy replied. "You were sniffing his breath for alcohol, weren't you?"

"No, sir," replied the boy. "You were reaching into his pocket for a bottle, weren't you?" he pressed. "No, sir," insisted the boy. "Other witnesses have testified that they saw you bending over your father. Now why *were* you bending over him?" Williams demanded. "Because he was my father," said the boy, "and I wanted to kiss him good-bye." Williams immediately asked the judge for a recess, went to a pay phone in the hall, and recommended to the insurance company that they settle the case. He also learned never to ask a question on cross-examination unless he knew the answer.

Boyd liked to use gimmicks in his trials, and Williams, already a master of debating tricks, was an eager accomplice. One of Boyd's clients had been injured when his chair collapsed at a Washington hotel, and the man was suing the hotel. "Ed got hold of the chair and during the course of the argument to the jury he would pick it up in a certain way and the thing would fall apart with a great clamor and then crash down on the floor in front of the jury. With pretended embarrassment, Ed would pick it up and put it back together," recalled Boyd, still richly amused forty years later. Boyd and Williams sometimes tested the limit of the judge's patience. In another case, their best witness had been killed in the war before the case came to trial. So instead, they put the private investigator who had interviewed him on the stand. Boyd asked him, "Can you tell us where the witness is?" Williams and Boyd had prompted the detective to lower his head and say in a dramatic voice, "He died for his country." The judge immediately interrupted this little theatrical production to call Williams and Boyd to the bench to admonish them, even threatening a new trial if they won.

Though he was a gamesman, Boyd was also a gentlemanly sort who taught Williams to be polite to his opponents and never to play the bully in court. Boyd recognized that Williams was extremely aggressive. In his very first case at Hogan & Hartson, Williams defended a bicyclist who had been sued for knocking down a pedestrian; Williams's strategy was to countersue the pedestrian for not getting out of the way (the client won $500). Williams simply would not accept defeat. In an early case, he defended a department store sued by a woman who had hurt herself sitting down at a counter. The stool had no seat, and the woman wasn't looking when she sat down. Williams lost at trial, and insisted on appealing. Boyd told him that it would cost the insurance company more to appeal the case than pay the judgment. Williams managed to persuade the insurance company to go along. Williams lost—and insisted on appealing again. This time, he had to do it free of charge. He won, and the woman recovered nothing.

Williams was always in the office when Boyd arrived, and he was always there when he left. He worked Saturdays, and often on Sundays and holidays. He was living at Mrs. Murphy's boardinghouse, and he was sick of the food. He relaxed only late at night, often in bars where, Boyd said, "he drank a little too much." He was lonely, and he wanted to find a wife.

Chapter Four

VERA HARTSON, THE wife of one of the name partners in the firm, liked to play matchmaker. On Friday nights, she would invite some of the young men of Hogan & Hartson over to dinner to meet eligible young ladies. One Friday in the winter of 1946, she invited Ed Williams and a young woman named Dorothy Guider. Williams disliked going to Mrs. Hartson's get-togethers; he complained to friends that she was always trying to set him up with "dogs." But he couldn't very well refuse the boss's wife, especially since the female guest that evening was the favorite granddaughter of the firm's founder, Frank Hogan.

Meat rationing was still in effect in postwar Washington, and Mrs. Hartson wanted to treat the hungry young lawyer by broiling a steak. But when the Filipino waiter placed a thick cut of red sirloin in front of Williams, he created a moral dilemma for the young Catholic, who was prohibited from eating meat on Fridays. Williams solved the problem by dipping his finger in the water glass, sprinkling a few drops on the steak, and declaring that his definition of a fish was anything that swims. As Williams dug in to his dinner, Dorothy Guider laughed and winked. By 10:00 P.M. that evening, Williams and the boss's pretty granddaughter were dancing at the Shoreham Hotel and arguing flirtatiously over drinks.

As Williams later told the story, he and Dorothy danced under the stars on the hotel terrace. As they stared dreamily at one another, a man who had been watching them sent over a bottle of champagne with a note that read: "Name the first baby for me." Like many of Williams's stories, this one is slightly embellished. They could not possibly have danced on

47

the hotel terrace; it was the middle of winter. (In a tempered version of the story, the note accompanying the champagne bottle read: "To celebrate your engagement.")

In any case, Williams did ask Dorothy to marry him that very night. When she got home, Dorothy called her sister Betty to tell her the news. There was no mention of dancing on the terrace or strange admirers with champagne. Rather, Dorothy said, Williams had been unromantically complaining about the inferior cuisine at Mrs. Murphy's boardinghouse. It didn't matter. Dorothy told her sister, "I'm in love and I'm getting married." Betty asked, "What does he look like?" "Sort of average," Dorothy replied, but he's "bright and funny."

Dorothy Guider came from a world far removed from Adelaide Street. She had grown up in wealth and comfort. Though Irish Catholic, she had attended Madeira in the Virginia hunt country, a horsey school favored by WASPy rich girls, and Smith College, one of the proper Seven Sisters. Summers were spent aboard a yacht owned by a client of her doting grandfather. She had been schooled in the social graces and given a sense of privilege. For a poor boy from Hartford, she was a prize—pretty, witty, and rich. She did, however, have a startling physical defect. She had been born with a stunted arm that ended just below the elbow. As Williams danced with her that night, he must have been conscious of the stub of her left arm resting lightly on his shoulder.

Inevitably, Williams was a suspect on all the usual counts: gold digging, social climbing, and marrying the boss's daughter in order to take over the boss's job. Certainly he was fascinated by Dorothy's grandfather. The son of poor Irish immigrants, Frank Hogan had in one generation become a fixture in the Washington legal establishment. He was a friend and confidant of Broadway stars, professional athletes, and politicians, whom he entertained lavishly in a large mansion in Kalorama, where the Cave Dwellers lived. Frank Hogan was, in fact, exactly what Williams wanted to be, and a logical first step, then, was to marry into his family.

Nonetheless, Dorothy's family did not regard Williams as an opportunist. Indeed, they embraced him as a bright young man on the way up. "We're brain snobs, not social snobs," said Betty Guider Killay. Williams immediately struck up a fast friendship with Dorothy's father, Duke Guider, whom he called "Captain" after his wartime rank in the navy. Shanty Irish himself ("descended from horse thieves," he claimed), Duke Guider was quick and charming and a clever lawyer. But he was also an alcoholic and a philanderer whose rough edges made enemies in Washington. After his father-in-law Hogan died in 1944, Guider had left Hogan & Hartson and moved to New Hampshire, where he invested in radio and TV. According to his daughter Betty, Guider became so fond of Williams that he began slighting his own son, Frank, who over time came to resent Williams for shoving him aside in his father's affections.

Though vivacious, Dorothy was not well. In addition to her stunted arm, she had weak lungs. Two months after her engagement to Williams, the doctors diagnosed her—incorrectly, as it turned out—as having tuberculosis. She was ordered to bed for six months. In haste, the wedding was arranged at her parents' eleven-bedroom house in New Hampshire. Dorothy told her fiancé to wear a blue suit, assuming he would know to wear dark blue. Instead, Williams waited at the altar in a *light* blue suit. He just didn't know any better; he had never been able to afford any decent clothes before. No one said anything to him about his faux pas, but he never wore the suit again.

Dorothy—D.A. to her friends, after her full name, Dorothy Adair Guider—had a brief and necessarily subdued honeymoon before taking to her bed. When she got up six months later, her lungs stronger but still troublingly weak, she set up housekeeping for Williams in Washington. The apartment, on 16th Street, up Washington's "Gold Coast," was spacious and sunny but not lavish. Although Dorothy had the expectation of a sizable inheritance, she did not have a large income. Besides, Williams wanted them to live on his salary, then about $5,000 a year (roughly $40,000 in 1990 dollars), a perfectly comfortable sum for a young couple without children in Washington after the war.

To help her overcome her deformed arm, Dorothy's parents had taught her at an early age small acts of self-sufficiency, like tying shoes with one hand. Over time, she learned how to play the piano and to hand-beat egg whites without holding the bowl with the other hand. She even crocheted argyle socks for her new husband (it took him eight years to work up the courage to tell her that he hated argyles, which he regarded as dandyish). Although Williams had to cut her meat for her and she couldn't curl her hair, "D.A. could do just about everything else," her sister Betty said, "and she hated to be helped." As a child, schoolyard teasing had made her sensitive and easily hurt. "She was not easygoing," said Betty Killay. "Life was a fight." Eventually, adversity toughened her. She had a temper and strong opinions, which she did not hesitate to voice, and she tended to view the world in terms of black or white. Politicians were either good or evil. According to her sister, she was deeply angry at her father, whom she regarded as a skirt-chaser and a drunk. Williams, who saw more shades of gray, would try to moderate her views, particularly toward her father. When Dorothy started in on his drinking, Williams would protest, "The Captain sloshed is smarter than most men sober."

Despite her anger, Dorothy had a quick wit and an infectious laugh. Smiling and teasing, she could put down her husband, usually without impinging on his pride. "Oh, come on Ed," she would laugh when he told a tall tale, "you don't know what the hell you're talking about." He knew she loved him, and would tease her back, but he needed to dominate, and over time the teasing between them became edgier and more hostile.

JUST BEFORE THE wedding, Ed Williams had had lunch with his old debating partner Bill Richardson, who was studying at a Jesuit seminary. Williams told Richardson that he had been phenomenally successful in his first year of private practice. He had won thirteen of his first fifteen cases, and one had ended in a mistrial. And he had begun to teach evidence and criminal law at Georgetown Law School at night. But he was, he confessed, already a little restless at the law firm. The real fun, he said, was not defending insurance companies in streetcar cases. The true challenge was defending human beings accused of a crime.

In his first year at Hogan & Hartson, Williams had volunteered to take court-appointed criminal cases. At school, criminal law had interested him far more than commercial law, and he was curious to see how it was actually practiced in the courts. What he found was a neglected and disreputable backwater. There was a real streak of Babbitry in the American bar of that era. A 1947 survey of the nation's lawyers conducted by the American Bar Association found that the average lawyer was "squarely in the great American middle class." He (only 2.5 percent were she) was "also a good joiner and a good neighbor." This definitive survey of American legal practice devoted exactly two out of 340 pages to criminal law. Criminal lawyers in the 1940s tended to come from ethnic backgrounds, have inferior educations, and much lower incomes. They were widely thought to be dishonest and unprincipled—like the clients they served. The public's idea of a criminal lawyer had been shaped by a 1941 best-seller called *The Great Mouthpiece,* a biography of

Broadway lawyer William J. Fallon, who destroyed evidence, drank too much, and so cleverly bamboozled juries that he was dubbed "the jail robber" by the newspapers. Fallon got rich defending hoodlums, but in general, the courtroom was regarded by much of the bar as a poor place to make a living. Indeed, many large law firm lawyers of that era wanted to stay out of court altogether. The big fees were to be made advising corporations how to avoid litigation, not trying cases. At Hogan & Hartson, the litigation department was the least profitable in the firm.

Williams was the only member of his firm, he said, to volunteer for court-appointed criminal cases. At the time, there was no such thing as a public defender or legal-aid program in Washington, D.C. Indigent defendants were assigned lawyers by the court. The lawyer received no fee, unless he could gouge one out of the poor defendant's family. Most court-assigned cases went to so-called Fifth Street lawyers who kept offices down near the courthouse on Fifth Street and hung around hoping to pick up any case they could. A Fifth Streeter's hope was that if he took enough criminal cases for free, the judge would appoint him guardian or trustee in a civil case that provided a fee. Naturally, lawyers spent as little time as possible preparing criminal cases. "Are you ready for trial, Mr. Miller?" a judge asked Bob Miller, a well-known Fifth Streeter of that era. "Yes, Your Honor, you may proceed," Miller responded. Then he turned to his client and asked, "What's your name?"

Williams's first criminal defendant was a sixteen-year-old black girl named Mary Elizabeth Lofton. She was accused of stabbing her boyfriend in the heart with a nail file. The murder had occurred in a sleazy bar in a rundown neighborhood on U Street, and Williams went out to find some patrons who had witnessed the crime. When he came to court with two witnesses, the U.S. attorney was amazed. Normally, criminal defense lawyers didn't bother to do any legwork in a case like this. Williams argued that Lofton had killed in self-defense. The witnesses supported the defendant's claim that the murder victim was about to throw a beer stein at her head. After deliberating for two hours, the jury acquitted the girl. Williams's client was overwhelmed with gratitude. Sobbing with relief, she told Williams that she wanted to become his maid. Forever, she said. For nothing. Touched, amused, Williams respectfully declined, but he felt an enormous sense of satisfaction, much greater than any he felt protecting Yankee insurance companies from the claims of injured bus passengers.

In this era before the sweeping liberal reforms of the Warren Court, criminal defendants did not have many rights. In state courts, they did not even have the right to counsel. In federal courts, like the District of Columbia's, they theoretically had the protections guaranteed by the Bill of Rights—the right against self-incrimination, the right to due process, and the right to a fair and speedy trial. But, in practice, those safeguards were widely ignored. Upon arrest, the accused were not read their rights by police. Two decades would pass before the Supreme Court established the Miranda warning, requiring police to tell suspects they have a right to a lawyer and the right to remain silent. In serious cases, criminal suspects were more commonly subjected to intense questioning, often under threat of a beating. And in not-so-serious cases as well: In 1947, Williams represented a Georgetown student arrested for public drunkenness who had been beaten bloody by a rubber truncheon because the police thought he was an insolent college boy. Poor black defendants had even fewer rights; young black men would often be swept up by the dozen in "drag-nets" and left to sit in jail until one confessed.

Williams did not have a hard time figuring out why there were more procedural safeguards in civil cases than in criminal cases. The monetary rewards were greater in civil cases, so lawyers devoted more attention to making sure they were fair. In civil cases, the bar had eliminated "trial by surprise" by pushing for extensive pretrial "discovery." But the criminal courts stayed mired in the nineteenth century.

There was not much money to be made trying criminal cases, Williams knew, but there was another reward: publicity. Williams collected his first headline in August 1946 representing a serviceman named Robert Chisholm, who had been accused of collaborating with the Japanese in World War II. Dubbed "Lord Haw Haw of the Orient," Chisholm had made radio propaganda broadcasts while imprisoned by the Japanese, who, he claimed, had put a gun to his head. After the war, he languished in a U.S. Army jail in Shanghai. Williams was able to get "Lord Haw Haw" released on a writ of habeas corpus because he had never been formally charged.

Williams began to keep a scrapbook of newspaper clippings, the first of the forty-eight he would fill over the next four decades. Now when he argued in court, he often had his own claque of Georgetown students to cheer him on. Williams savored the attention and adulation. The little boy who had acted out plays for his friends and cousins in Hartford, shyly seeking their approval, now had a built-in audience for his theatrics. The years of lonely grinding, of sublimating his ego in the hopes of some

distant reward, were finally at an end. Now he could find instant grati-
fication for his public performance.

But he also felt a deep private reward in defending the criminally
accused. In streetcar cases, Williams was defending a corporation. In
criminal cases, he later reflected, "you have a person sitting right there
who is dependent upon you—a flesh and blood breathing person instead
of a corporate entity." He often found that he came to personally like the
defendant, who was generally scared and humbled. "When they are in
deep trouble they are usually less arrogant, less obnoxious," Williams
told a newspaper reporter who, some years later, was helping him write
about his experiences. Williams enjoyed the satisfaction, he went on, of
"bringing out the best of the worst" as he consoled and prepared his
clients for trial. Williams never put it this way himself, at least publicly,
but at moments he must have felt like a Catholic priest, offering forgiveness and redemption to the sinners who sought his help.

The challenge of keeping his clients out of jail imposed an emotional
and physical cost on Williams. Every morning before he argued a criminal case, he would vomit. He may have appeared perfectly at ease in
court, but his emotions were in a constant state of riot. It is hard to
imagine that a child actor/college debater/daily courtroom litigator would
not have conquered stage fright along the way, but Williams could never
escape his obsession with winning and losing.

At first, he lost his breakfast before arguing civil cases, too, but gradually he got over his nerves in those. After his occasional setbacks in
streetcar cases, he said, "I felt bad about losing Capital Transit's money
but I never felt *very* bad about it." But when he lost a client to jail, he was
desolate. His response, typically, was to vow not to lose again. The very
difficulty of that challenge—the prosecution wins most cases that go to
trial—made Williams embrace it all the more.

He could not stand still. He had argued every kind of streetcar case
imaginable, and he was bored at Hogan & Hartson. In the summer of
1949, he decided to leave the firm and go into practice on his own.

Throwing away the security and reward of working for one of the city's
top law firms to enter the uncertain world of solo practitioners seemed
like a bold move. But Williams was bold, as well as impatient. Like most
big law firms, Hogan & Hartson expected each "class" of associates to
move in lockstep and wait six or seven years to make partner. With some
justification, Williams thought he was already a better lawyer than most
of the partners in the firm, much less the other associates. He did not want

to wait another couple of years to become a partner, and a junior one at that. He thought he could have a more interesting practice on his own, and he correctly predicted that he could have a more lucrative one in short order.

Dorothy did not oppose the decision, despite the prospect that her husband would lose his stable income by leaving her grandfather's firm. She was financially secure herself, and knew that her family would come to the rescue in a pinch. She also understood that her own grandfather was the model for her husband's ambitions. Though the firm had become staid and genteel, Frank Hogan's own practice had been flamboyant. In a sensational trial during the Teapot Dome Scandal in 1930, he had managed to get millionaire oilman Edward Doheny—owner of the yacht that Dorothy had summered aboard as a girl—acquitted of charges that he had bribed Interior secretary Albert B. Fall. He succeeded even though Fall, in a separate trial, had been convicted of taking the $100,000 bribe from Doheny. Doheny paid Hogan a fee of $1 million. "The ideal client," Hogan liked to say, "is a rich man who is scared." It was a line Ed Williams would quote for years to come.

Chapter Five

As he argued a criminal case in district court in the winter of 1949, Nicholas Chase had the sense that he was being closely watched. Chase asked the judge, Matthew McGuire, if he knew the tall man with reddish hair who had been sitting in the back of the courtroom. Ed Williams, a hot-shot young lawyer, replied the judge. After the trial, Williams approached Chase and introduced himself as a fellow graduate of Bulkeley High in Hartford and as a trial lawyer with Hogan & Hartson. Williams said he was only making $7,000 a year at the Hogan firm, and he felt he could do better on his own. Would Chase care to join him as a partner? Finding an office wouldn't be a problem, he explained. His wife's family owned a handsome ten-floor office building at the corner of 17th and I streets, the Hill Building. They could move into a suite on the tenth floor, overlooking Farragut Square. Chase accepted.

Nick Chase was thirty-five, seven years older than Williams. He had worked with William Leahy, who, after Frank Hogan's death in 1944, was regarded as the top trial lawyer in Washington. Chase had trial experience in well-publicized cases, defending price-fixers and corrupt politicians. A few years earlier, he had helped represent Mayor Curley of Boston, who had been convicted in a scheme to bilk investors in government contracts (Curley continued to serve as mayor from his jail cell). A small, intense man with an ornate speaking style, Chase was not universally admired by his peers. Howard Boyd, Williams's mentor at Hogan & Hartson, counseled Williams against going into practice with

Chase. "He's mean," Boyd told him. "He enjoys destroying witnesses on cross-examination." Asked to join Williams and Chase in their new office, a couple of young Georgetown Law School grads, Bill Ragan and Paul McArdle, declined. They predicted a clash of egos.

The first clash came over the name of the firm. Names were not a trifling issue to either man. Williams now referred to himself by his full name, Edward Bennett Williams. His stated reason for using his middle name on his stationery and court documents was prosaic enough—to avoid being confused with another lawyer in town named Edward B.Williams. But the full name, marching off the tongue in stately fashion, Ed-ward Ben-nett Wil-liams, had a certain resonance, even grandeur, that he felt enhanced his presence in a courtroom. Chase, for his part, had been born Ciccone. He had anglicized his name as a young lawyer in Washington during the war to avoid any ethnic aspersions. Williams originally wanted to call the firm simply the Law Offices of Edward Bennett Williams—or at the very least Williams and Chase. But Chase had more experience and a bigger name in the Washington bar. So the firm name, announced on white engraved cards mailed out in March of 1949 to members of the bar, the press, and certain potential clients, was Chase and Williams.

Williams wanted a criminal practice, but he had no intention of becoming a social worker. He wanted to find clients who could pay high fees. At the time, however, criminal law enforcement was aimed mostly at poor people. Aside from the occasional politician caught with his hand in the till, there were not many so-called white-collar cases. Although the term *white-collar crime* had been coined by Edwin Sutherland, a sociologist writing about corporate crime in 1940, it would be another two decades before the government looked hard at crime in the executive suite and in the political arena. Rich gangsters were only sporadically targeted. In New York, the District Attorney's Office had a reputation for racket-busting. But in Washington, FBI director J. Edgar Hoover was still insisting that organized crime did not exist. "They're just a bunch of hoodlums," he would say, as if that somehow diminished the problem.

The criminal defendants who could pay big fees in Washington were for the most part gamblers. The numbers rackets were so well organized in the nation's capital after the war that the top gambling bosses divided up the city into districts. Illegal off-track betting was equally pervasive; brazen bookmakers would routinely make the rounds of respectable business offices. The biggest gamblers in the District were represented by a colorful lawyer named Charlie Ford, the self-proclaimed president of the Fifth Street Bar Association. Ford became a figure of fascination for Williams. A slab of a man, the hulking, red-faced Ford was masterful with juries: "corny, scornful, humble, tricky, laughing, tear-stained—you name it," wrote a young *Washington Post* reporter named Benjamin Bradlee, who had been assigned to cover the municipal courts. Ford, who liked to joke that he was "aiming only for purgatory, not Heaven," could make juries laugh at the priggishness of law enforcement. William Beckler, a former D.C. prosecutor, recalls watching Ford get a police officer to describe in detail the bump-and-grind of a dancer he had just arrested for indecent behavior. "Like this?" Ford would ask, doing a ridiculous fat man's hoochie-goochie while the jury convulsed with laughter. But for all his theatrics, Ford was no clown. Unlike other Fifth Street lawyers, he knew how to use the law books, and he was constantly filing motions attacking the prosecution's case on one technicality or another. Ford also knew how to make valuable friends, among them the District's police superintendent Robert J. Barrett, whom Ford took to ball games at Griffith Stadium. Ford got on with beat cops just as well, and represented the Policeman's Benevolent Society free of charge. Irked by his pipeline into the police station, prosecutors scoffed that Ford knew more about their cases than they did. Williams, however, closely studied all of Ford's moves, including his Robin Hood fee schedule—a pittance for poor people charged with serious crimes, ten times as much for the rich no matter how minor the offense.

Williams made it his business to get to know Ford, and within a few months of leaving Hogan & Hartson, he was sharing a counsel's table with him. A congressional subcommittee was holding hearings into the existence of after-hours clubs, so-called bottle clubs, that were violating the city's blue laws and drawing gamblers and prostitutes. Ford was representing several establishments with names like the Turf and Grid Club and the Stardust Whist Club. Williams was representing the Atlas Club, a popular gaming joint up above a delicatessen at 13th and E Streets, in the heart of Washington's old downtown. The Atlas Club was owned by a gambler named Gary Quinn, a burly former University of Georgia football player. Williams had begun representing Quinn after he was caught in a police sting of a back-room bookie joint in Bladensburg, Maryland. (Williams got Quinn off; when the not-guilty verdict was announced, the judge admonished the jury for ignoring the evidence.) At the congressional hearing, indignant lawmakers asserted that the bottle clubs were "detriments to the community" and "breeding places of crime." A newspaper account noted insinuatingly that the Atlas Club was "long patronized by some of the city's prominent professionals and businessmen."

Among the Atlas Club regulars was Edward Bennett Williams. He liked the raffish crowd, the gamblers and hookers mixing with the cops and politicians after the legal establishments closed at midnight. The teacher's pet and mama's boy who had been such a dutiful grind back in school was also the boy who slipped out the back window after dark and sneaked into prizefights. The more victories Williams racked up in court by day, the more he gave vent to his free spirit at night. As the ice tinkled, the dice rattled, and the slot machines rang in the back room of the Atlas Club, Williams would listen raptly to Charlie Ford spinning tales from the underworld.

Some evenings, Williams would be joined by the aristocratic young reporter from the *Post*, Ben Bradlee, who had left his Harvard crowd, the Supreme Court clerks and Foreign Service officers, to slum it for an evening. Bradlee and Williams had struck up an immediate friendship. In some ways, their class backgrounds worked against the match: The only Irish Catholics admitted to Bradlee's club at Harvard were waiters who served drinks on trays. But Williams was actually much better educated than Bradlee, who had forgotten most of his boarding school Latin and nearly flunked out of college. In the navy, Bradlee had learned how to swear and affect a rough-and-ready manner. Newspaper reporters were considered déclassé at the time; Bradlee thought he was being rakish, and wore a loud checked suit to blend in with the bookies.

Just as Bradlee wanted to fit in with the Fifth Streeters, Williams wanted to be accepted by the WASPs. Williams was disdainful of fops with inherited wealth, but he was drawn to power, and he was shrewd enough to recognize that even in Washington, with its relative social mobility, Old Money had a leg up. Throughout his career, Williams would make fun of WASPy types and "preppies," but at the same time he craved social respectability.

In personality, Williams and Bradlee were well matched: both were charming; both knew how to temper their swagger with self-deprecation; and both had a keen sense of life's absurdities and possibilities. In a peculiar way, they were bonded as well by the Depression. Like Williams, Bradlee had seen his father laid off after the Crash. Frederick "Be" Bradlee had lost his job as a stockbroker—as well as much of his fortune—in 1932. He was forced thereafter to depend on his wife's trust fund and the charity of friends. Be Bradlee's penury was far more genteel than Joe Williams's, but no less crushing to his ego. Seeing their fathers humiliated had given both Williams and Bradlee a powerful incentive to achieve—and to keep on achieving—in their own lives. As they poured down the booze at the Atlas Club, they loudly teased each other and silently plotted the careers that would cross many times in the years ahead.

EVEN AFTER THE influx of servicemen during the war, Washington remained a buttoned-up town. Most government bureaucrats hurried through a blue-plate special at lunch, served in compartmentalized platters, forty cents and no substitutions. In the evening they went home. Determined to protect the capital against rowdy saloons, President Roosevelt had personally written the District's liquor laws in 1933. Customers could not be served standing up. Perched on bar stools, they could only drink beer or wine. For hard liquor, they had to sit at tables and be served by waiters. In deference to the churches, bars had to close at midnight on Saturday and stay closed all day Sunday.

Precisely because the city was so determinedly dull, Washington was bound to have places like the Atlas Club. Williams was drawn by the ambience of illicit pleasure. His fascination with sin was well repressed during the workday, but after a few drinks, his inhibitions would drop, and he would entertain the after-hours crowd by listing the Seven Deadly Sins. Williams delighted in the words themselves, and he would draw them out in an almost sensuous way, as if they tasted like forbidden fruit: " . . . *Glut*-to-nnyyy, AV-a-rice, gr-e-e-e-ed, *LUST!*" If Williams wanted to conjure up a truly terrible fate, he would imagine his victim stripped naked, placed in a department store window, and left there until a class of parochial schoolchildren, led by nuns, walked by. He could easily summon up the terror he had felt at the hands of the nuns at St. Augustine's. When Williams wanted to sound threatening, he would glower with mock seriousness, "The nuns! The *nuns* will get you!"

Williams particularly enjoyed making fun of the chief of the Vice Squad, Sergeant Roy Blick, who led his men into the men's room of theaters and bus depots in clownish pursuit of homosexuals, whom Blick invariably called "queers." Late at night at the Atlas Club, Williams would imitate Blick standing at a urinal for hours, hoping, *praying* that a "queer" would come along and grab his penis—so he could make a morals arrest, of course.

Over time, Williams's boyhood shyness had fled. But he was not yet the dominating presence he would become. Ben Bradlee noticed that "he wouldn't show you all his cards. He wouldn't react until you reacted." Still, his sense of fun and mischief had become more readily accessible. Friends who had known him as withdrawn and cautious at Holy Cross and Georgetown were struck by his growing ebullience. He was a gifted story-teller who knew how to drag out the punch line. He could mimic his subjects, and when he got going, he would jump up and act out the story, swinging his large body about and drawing pictures with his meaty hands. With his dancing eyes and puckish smile, he put other men at ease and made them laugh. His bemusement was contagious; Williams could make an old joke seem funny again just because he thought it was funny and would laugh and chortle as he told it (and retold it).

Liquor made Williams jolly, at least on the way up. "Ed was not what we called an MID—a Mean Irish Drunk," said his sister-in-law, Betty Killay. He was not sullen or nasty, but he had a temper, and from time to time he got into bar fights. Beneath the charm, some sensed a lurking anger in Williams. "I don't think he had worked through certain feelings," said Frank Waldrop, the executive editor of the *Washington Times-Herald,* then the city's biggest paper. Williams had befriended Waldrop while trying to keep the name of one of his clients out of the paper. The client was a State Department employee who had been caught in an "indecent act" by one of Sergeant Blick's men in the men's room at Lafayette Park. The man was married with a family, and Williams begged Waldrop to spare him public humiliation. Waldrop was moved by Williams's plea and went along. He felt Williams had genuine empathy for his client. But as he got to know Williams, Waldrop began to speculate about the source of that empathy. Williams was emphatically heterosexual, yet Waldrop wondered if Williams felt for his clients because he shared, at some level, their darker urges. In his cups, Williams could become maudlin. "He'd start crying and say, 'I can't stand seeing anyone put behind bars.' It was trashy and sentimental," said Waldrop. But it reflected a crack in Williams's emotional defenses. Other friends in later years would glimpse Williams's repressed drives when liquor lowered his inhibitions. Watching Williams drunkenly weep, "you could feel the straight shots from his id," said Ben Heineman, a lawyer in Williams's firm in the 1970s.

Turning thirty in 1950, Williams was a man's man who was also attractive to women. Though he looked well fed and prosperous, he had not yet turned to fat. The skin was still smooth on his face, and his large body carried weight gracefully. His hair was a wavy reddish-brown, and his eyes twinkled. Columnist Mary McGrory once described his voice as a "plush tenor." Actually, Williams's voice varied, depending on his purpose and his mood. When he was telling macho stories to barflies, he could be growly and gruff. When he was one of the boys, he affected a street accent that was part Hartford, part Hollywood tough guy. In court, he spoke with precision and lucidity and no trace of accent. With women, he purred and flirted. His body language was open and welcoming, he freely touched and stroked women with an eagerness just shy of pawing. To a woman who wanted to be touched, Williams could come across as a walking invitation to sin.

Williams did not always resist temptation. "He whored and then he felt guilty about it," said Waldrop. Roughly speaking, Williams divided women into two groups: There were proper wives, who bore your children and raised your family and served as moral anchors, and there were loose women, party girls, fun girls you flirted with and, if you were drunk or foolish, slept with. Williams believed that "the woman you marry is the Madonna, and everyone else is a prostitute," said Betty Killay. She saw genuine sexual attraction between Dorothy and Williams, but she saw his confusion and wandering eye as well. "Ed had all the hang-ups of the Irish Catholic male," she said. "He was hung up about sex."

LATE ON THE night of Sunday, January 28, 1951, Williams arrived at the Atlas Club after a dull black-tie dinner with an earnest group of young lawyers called the Barristers. He was in a buoyant mood, looking for a good time. He had been representing a top official of the U.S. Postal Service named Harold Ambrose, who had been charged with running a get-rich-quick stamp deal that fleeced investors of $600,000. The case had gotten almost daily headlines in the Washington papers. Ambrose himself had been conned into the scheme by Joe Adonis, the boss of the Brooklyn rackets and a very big-time hood by Washington's fairly small-time standards. Ambrose was unquestionably guilty, but Williams had once managed to get the indictment thrown out for various technical violations of grand jury procedure (a tactic he turned into an art form in later years). Ambrose had been reindicted, but Williams believed that he had worked out a deal with the prosecutor. Ambrose had pleaded guilty to a couple of counts, but in return, the U.S. attorney would recommend no jail sentence to the judge. It was practically a sure thing, Williams told Ambrose: He would walk free.

On this Sunday night, the eve of his sentencing, Ambrose had also come to the Atlas Club. He morosely nursed a drink at his table. Williams, meanwhile, danced with Mrs. Ambrose. A lawyer named Eugene Gott, who had come to the Atlas Club with Williams from the stuffy black-tie dinner, thought his fellow Barrister had developed a large crush on his client's wife. Dance after dance, Gott watched Williams and Mrs. Ambrose move together, cheek-to-cheek, gliding around the cramped dance floor through the smoky haze.

By 3:00 A.M., Williams moved on from Mrs. Ambrose to banter with another of his clients, Gary Quinn, the club's owner. When the Atlas closed down at four, the whole group, thoroughly inebriated by now, pushed on to a low-rent dive frequented by all-night cabdrivers and doormen called Pete Haley's, down in Foggy Bottom. Williams began dancing with Mrs. Ambrose again. The sun was rising when Williams tossed off his last drink.

Williams's hangover did not improve in court the next morning. Contrary to his expectations, the judge did not buy the defendant's plea for clemency. He sentenced the hapless postal official to two to seven years in prison. Ambrose burst into tears; Mrs. Ambrose had to be carried out of court by the marshals.

Williams's own judgment awaited him at home on 16th Street that evening. Dorothy was deeply worried about her husband's night prowling. Her own father was a philanderer, and she suspected her husband was repeating the same pattern. "There were big fights," recalled Betty Killay. Williams would be contrite and remorseful after these unhappy domestic scenes, but he wouldn't promise to stay out of the Atlas Club.

The other person who was not happy about the company Williams kept was his law partner, Nick Chase. He accused Williams of hustling cases. The bar ethics of the time prohibited lawyers from soliciting clients. These stodgy rules were widely ignored, but Chase told Williams he didn't want him offering the firm's services to gamblers and gangsters and the sort of lowlife found in the Atlas Club. Chase said that he did not want to get tagged as a Fifth Streeter, that he wanted nothing to do with the bottle-club crowd. He quoted Emerson: "If you put a fish in a can of milk, it's never the same can of milk." According to Chase, Williams would promise to reform, his head hanging, his shoulders drooping, but then he would come back in with another gambling case. He defended his pursuit of high-profile cases by quoting dramatic passages from Irving Stone's biography of Clarence Darrow. "He wanted to get involved in causes célèbres," said Chase. "This meant handling big-name publicity cases. . . . He came to know the gambling and related underworld figures in Washington. Don't kid yourself. These people didn't come to him at first. He had no string of wins. . . ." It wasn't that Williams didn't care about social acceptability. As an associate at Hogan & Hartson, Williams had joined the Metropolitan Club, the exclusive all-male bastion of the Washington Establishment, for which his father-in-law had put him up. It was important, Williams joked to Chase, to get into the Metropolitan Club as a young man, before you had a chance to make enemies. But to Chase, Williams cared more about glory than respectability.

One afternoon in early 1950, Williams arrived back in the office from a trip to New York holding the legal file of a legendary gangster, Charles "Lucky" Luciano. Deported to Naples by the U.S. government in the late 1940s, Luciano was looking for a good lawyer to get him back into the United States. Williams wanted to take the case. Chase shook his head. "The only way we'll get him back into the United States is as a vice consul," he lamely joked. Williams pressed; this was a big case, with novel legal issues. Moreover, the publicity would be tremendous. Publicity-conscious Williams understood that the newspapers would build his practice faster than his legal skills would. "I don't want to get tied up in this crap!" Chase exclaimed. "When you fool around with skunks you get pissed on! I don't want to come home one night for dinner and have one of my kids say, 'Hey, Dad, what about this guy and this case?' " Chase says that he told Williams that representing Luciano in this matter was "doubtfully moral, and it can be unethical."

Chase's recollections of his partnership with Williams are colored by bitterness. But a secretary/clerk who worked for the two men, Robert McChesney, recalls overhearing Williams and Chase arguing over Luciano, and he confirms Chase's account. McChesney, who was at the time a Georgetown law student and remained on friendly terms with Williams in later years, recalls Chase seething with anger over Williams's choice of clients. "We shouldn't have taken that case," he would mutter, hinting broadly to McChesney that Williams's legal ethics left something to be desired. McChesney attributes some of Chase's ire to jealousy; though Chase was the senior member of the partnership, Williams was getting all the press attention. It was a partnership that could not last, and by the summer of 1950, the law firm of Chase and Williams was dissolved. Chase never got over his anger at Williams; when his onetime partner applied for membership to the Congressional Country Club twenty years later, Chase tried unsuccessfully to get Williams blackballed.

WILLIAMS'S FASCINATION WITH the underworld was matched by his interest in political power. Handling the legal problems of congressmen and administration officials gave him entree into their world, not to mention a steady source of newspaper headlines. Big-time political corruption cases were hard to come by, in part because the government was not trying very hard to catch crooked politicians the way it would in the post-Watergate era. But Williams was willing to help the powerful with almost any problem. Before he left Hogan & Hartson, he defended Senator Milton Young of North Dakota after a taxi driver accused the senator of punching him in a fare dispute (the suit was dropped). In addition to the State Department official accused of committing an "indecent act" in the men's room of Lafayette Park, Williams represented another State Department aide who was a party in an "alienation of affections" case. Williams's defense of his client's infidelity, quaint in retrospect, was that his wife had forced him to cook his own breakfast (the case ended in a mistrial).

Williams's own political allegiances had shifted since his arrival in Washington as a New Deal Democrat. In the summer of 1948, as President Truman languished in the polls, it appeared that the long Democratic reign was ending in the capital. The Republicans, who had already recaptured Congress, felt certain they would win the White House as well. Williams's father-in-law, Duke Guider, was urging Williams to join the GOP. So when Senator Young, grateful to Williams for protecting him from the irate cabbie, asked his young lawyer to accompany him to the Republican National Convention in Philadelphia, Williams eagerly accepted. At the convention, Williams backed the wrong horse, Harold Stassen, against Thomas E. Dewey, and, along with most of the rest of the country, he underestimated Harry Truman, who defeated Dewey in November. But Williams did have the occasion to meet an obscure senator from Wisconsin, Joseph R. McCarthy.

III

Fame

Chapter Six

WHEN ED WILLIAMS met Joe McCarthy, the senator had not yet discovered the Communist threat. In fact, he was just a hack, about to be voted the worst U.S. senator in a poll of the reporters covering Congress. But in the winter of 1950, McCarthy made his famous Lincoln's Day speech in Wheeling, West Virginia. No one ever knew if the list McCarthy waved in the air that night named 205 or 57 Communists in the State Department—the number kept changing over the next few weeks: 205, 57, 87—but the details really weren't important. The timing was perfect. That winter, Americans were bewildered: How did the technically backward Russians build their own atomic bomb? Who in Washington had "lost China" to the Communists? What secrets did State Department official Alger Hiss hand over to the Kremlin? The country was looking for scapegoats, and the junior senator had found some. Each time McCarthy announced that he had discovered another Communist hiding in the government, he got an explosion of headlines. It didn't seem to matter that he was never able to prove that the unfortunate souls he fingered actually *were* Communists, or even Communist sympathizers. He just kept charging, and the feckless press of the time kept on printing lurid stories that ruined careers and fed McCarthy's insatiable appetite for publicity.

A few reporters stood up to McCarthy. One was the muckraking columnist Drew Pearson, who in fifty-eight syndicated columns during 1950 attacked McCarthy for various financial improprieties. At a dinner party at the Sulgrave Club that December, a drunk McCarthy told Pearson's wife, Luvie, that he was planning to deliver a speech on the Senate floor so devastating to her husband that it would "cause a divorce in the family." Luvie said nothing, but Pearson quipped, "Joe, how is your income tax case coming along?" Later in the cloakroom, McCarthy kneed Pearson in the groin and slapped him to the floor. Subsequently, he issued a thirty-seven-page speech calling Pearson "an unprincipled, greedy, degenerate liar" as well as "a Moscow-directed character assassin." Pearson sued McCarthy for $5 million.

McCarthy needed a lawyer. According to William F. Buckley, who was close to McCarthy, he got Edward Bennett Williams without even asking. Williams had simply walked into McCarthy's office and offered to represent him, free of charge. Williams later disputed Buckley's account, and said that he had been referred to McCarthy by another lawyer, John Sirica. Sirica's recollection is that McCarthy had telephoned him and asked, "Did you ever hear of a kid lawyer around town by the name of Ed Williams?" Sirica, who replaced Williams in the litigation department of Hogan & Hartson (and would two decades later win fame as the federal judge who helped break open the Watergate scandal), told McCarthy that Williams was an ambitious, hard-working, talented lawyer. McCarthy said that he had met with Williams and was going to give him a try. If Williams did volunteer his services to McCarthy, it was neither the first nor the last time that he solicited a famous client.

Williams soon became a trusted adviser to McCarthy. As the Pearson case rattled inconclusively around the courts, Williams helped McCarthy with a variety of legal problems. He took over McCarthy's representation in a libel suit against Senator William Benton of Connecticut after the Wisconsin senator, trying to represent himself, botched his deposition of Benton. He defended McCarthy in a long and complicated tax dispute with the IRS, finally proving that McCarthy had actually overpaid his taxes. And he represented one of McCarthy's operatives who had staged a clumsy but effective campaign of dirty tricks against Senator Millard Tydings of Maryland. After McCarthy's Wheeling speech, Tydings had called McCarthy's charges of Communists in the State Department a "fraud and a hoax." McCarthy got even by orchestrating what a Senate subcommittee later characterized as a "despicable back street campaign" against Tydings that cost the Marylander his Senate seat in November 1950. The campaign manager for Tydings's opponent was a hired gun named Jon Jonkel, a public relations man with close ties to the McCormick family, owners of the archconservative *Chicago Tribune*. When a grand jury and a congressional subcommittee began questioning Jonkel's handling of campaign funds, McCarthy brought in Williams to represent him.

Even given Williams's devotion to the right to counsel, it is difficult, in retrospect, to understand why he was so eager to represent Joe McCarthy. Williams felt bound to represent *criminal* defendants who faced jail; he did not have the same sense of obligation in civil cases. McCarthy did not stand accused of any crime. In later years, Williams said that he found McCarthy more ridiculous than menacing. He told friends that McCarthy was an engaging rogue. He wasn't really dangerous, said Williams; the senator was driven more by a desire for personal glory than power over others. Nonetheless, Williams was in a position to know what harm McCarthy could cause. He saw firsthand the dirty tricks McCarthy used to defeat Senator Tydings. Throughout his career, Williams held himself out as a defender of civil liberties. It is hard to imagine anyone more contemptuous of civil liberties than Joseph McCarthy. Williams knew it was fundamentally unfair for a headline-hungry congressman to drag someone who had never been accused of a crime into a public hearing room and force him to take the Fifth Amendment. After McCarthy died, Williams publicly expressed his disapproval of these tactics. But at the time, when McCarthyism was at its peak, he said nothing.

On a personal level, Williams felt a genuine kinship with McCarthy. The two Irish boyos shared a taste for gin and palaver, although Williams had great self-control, and McCarthy absolutely none. Williams could understand McCarthy's terrible black moods, having experienced some himself. Williams was also deeply anti-Communist. Unlike McCarthy, Williams did not see Communists under every bed, but then he thought McCarthy was only pretending, that for the senator from Wisconsin, witch-hunting was more of a sport than a crusade. It was important to Williams that McCarthy observed meatless Friday and went to confession. Although McCarthy was regarded as an ogre in liberal circles, he was a hero to many of his fellow churchmen. Francis Cardinal Spellman, the archbishop of New York, repeatedly praised McCarthy for trying to exorcise godless communism. Williams wanted to be accepted by WASP society and valued his membership in such groups as the Metropolitan Club, but he also shared McCarthy's Irish distrust of aristocracy. Williams and McCarthy were both "anti-Harvard, anti-sissy, anti-genteel," said columnist Murray Kempton. They shared resentment against those fancy-pants prigs at the State Department, those effete Ivy League WASPs who treated Irish Catholics like servants.

On a more cynical level, Williams understood that McCarthyism was good for business. America in the fifties had plunged into an Age of Accusation. In 1950, Senator Estes Kefauver of Tennessee had discovered the immense power of television by holding a series of hearings into organized crime, with cameras whirring and klieg lights shining. Williams watched with envy as Charlie Ford sat at the counsel table alongside his gambler clients who had been summoned to testify. Suddenly, Ford was not just a Fifth Streeter, he was a national figure. "Television! This is the way to get clients!" Ed exclaimed to another lawyer, Paul McArdle, over drinks one night in the men's grill at the Shoreham. Cameras were not allowed into the hearing room of the House Un-American Activities Committee, where a parade of frightened ex-Communists, fellow travelers, and liberals who had belonged to organizations retroactively branded Communist (and some innocent bystanders as well), were taking the Fifth or naming names. But there were plenty of reporters and photographers in the room.

And the witnesses appearing before the committee needed counsel to defend themselves. In that paranoid time, people accused of Communist ties—no matter how tenuous or remote—sometimes had difficulty finding a lawyer to sit alongside them. Red baiting was so poisonous that charges, baseless or not, stuck to family members, colleagues, business associates, even legal counsel. People went to extraordinary lengths to avoid being tarred. Walt Disney testified that he had resisted Communist efforts to make Mickey Mouse follow the Party line. The Cincinnati Reds felt compelled to change their name, briefly, to the Redlegs. For a lawyer to defend someone caught up in the hysteria took real courage. Williams's belief in the right to counsel was sincere, but he also appreciated that he was fairly well insulated from guilt by association. After all, he was Joe McCarthy's lawyer. How could he be a pinko? Williams felt free to work the other side of the street. Representing "comsymps" and "security risks" who had been dragged before a congressional committee, fired from their jobs, or blacklisted became a major—and lucrative—part of his law practice in the early fifties.*

---

*One of Williams's tenants in the Hill Building, a young Harvard Law School grad named Murdaugh Madden, represented a number of government employees who had been fired from their jobs by the Loyalty Review Boards established by the Truman administration to appease the Right. Williams's representation of McCarthy and Madden's representation of alleged security risks led to some interesting run-ins. One Saturday morning, Madden recalled, he was talking to a client "with a Russian last name whose crime had been playing chess and attending a labor summer music camp." Suddenly, his office door swung open. It was Senator McCarthy himself, asking if Madden had seen Williams. The Russian security risk looked as if he had been visited by the Devil Incarnate. As Williams liked to tell the story, the man bolted from the office and was never seen by Madden again.

Williams's most prominent clients during the Red Scare were Hollywood writers and producers who were being summoned before the House committee. HUAC was already terrorizing the show business world, imprisoning the Hollywood Ten, a group of leftist screenwriters and directors, and destroying careers with mere subpoenas. Witnesses facing the committee were presented with a terrible dilemma. They could take the Fifth Amendment—and be presumed guilty, blacklisted, and ruined—or they could name names and bring into the glare of hot lights their friends and colleagues. The latter course was "less courageous," Williams noted dryly, "but it had the virtue of also being less dangerous."

The first client Williams represented before HUAC, a screenwriter name Martin Berkeley, set a record for naming names: 154 of them, everyone he knew in the movie business associated in any way with the Communist party between 1936 and 1943. In Hollywood, the grim joke was that Berkeley had copied his list from the menu of a celebrity hangout in Hollywood. Even HUAC's chief investigator, William Wheeler, felt that Berkeley had gone overboard. Wheeler told Victor Navasky (the author of *Naming Names*) that "when Berkeley came down with his list of 154 names, I told him, I said, 'Don't name that many. You're just going to get yourself in big, deep trouble.' I said, 'We don't need all this.' "

So why did the screenwriter squeal so indiscriminately? Richard Collins, the Hollywood screenwriter who had named Berkeley to the committee, believes Berkeley "panicked." Wheeler opined that Berkeley gave so many names because "his asshole lawyer Edward Bennett Williams insisted." Williams later told biographer Robert Pack that he had *not* urged Berkeley to name names. He blandly stated that he "didn't have a feeling" about whether his client should or not.

If Williams did press Berkeley to name names, is there anything wrong with that? It is perfectly common for lawyers to suggest that their clients finger someone else in order to save their own skins. In cases of white-collar crime, low-level employees routinely seek immunity from prosecution by offering to testify before a grand jury against their corporate higher-ups. From a legal point of view, there was nothing unethical about Williams's role in the security cases. Still, it created an apparent conflict. Because of his close ties to McCarthy, Williams seemed to be serving two masters, the congressional witch-hunters as well as his clients, in a way that was financially very rewarding to him.

Williams was an inside player in a shabby business called "clearance." Getting off the blacklist became a small industry in the McCarthy era. In 1950, three former FBI agents began publishing *Red Channels,* a compendium of entertainers and their Communist-front links. In 1953, Aware Inc. joined the vigil. Show business executives used these handy aids to witch-hunting by paying to have the names of their employees checked against "the files." Aware Inc. charged $5 to vet a name for the first time, $2 for a recheck. These lists were not immutable, but to get off them you needed really good connections.

Most lawyers who represented security risks were leftists themselves and had no friends among the McCarthyites. Williams did. Sidney Cohn, a leftist lawyer who represented dozens of blacklisted movie producers and writers, used Williams as a go-between in dealing with Red hunters in Washington. "Williams was a good friend of Scott McLeod's at State and had the reputation of being a violent anti-Communist," Cohn recalled. (McLeod ran the State Department's loyalty/security program; he had been placed there by the McCarthyites in Congress.)

In 1953, Cohn sent producer Robert Rossen to Williams to get cleared by HUAC. Rossen, ironically, had won an Oscar for a movie about political demagoguery—*All the King's Men*—in 1949. Rossen liked Williams. His widow, Sue, later contrasted her impressions of two lawyers that she and her husband had consulted for advice: "One had plush offices and he was charging seventy-five dollars a minute and he was very proper and distant. Then we went to see Ed Williams, who was in a cubbyhole, very informal, sitting there in his shirtsleeves. He was very impressive. I said, to use one of Bob's favorite expressions, 'It's the difference between chicken shit and chicken salad.' " At first, Williams told the Rossens that he could take care of their problems without Rossen having to name names, at least publicly. Williams had the contacts to arrange "private" audiences with the committee. But in the end, Rossen named fifty-seven others, including Ring Lardner, Jr., and Budd Schulberg. He was shunned by some members of the film community for cooperating with the committee, but he was taken off the blacklist.

Through Senator McCarthy, Williams was close to George Sokolsky, a right-wing Hearst columnist who was known as the Great Clearer for his power to remove names from the blacklist. Sokolsky enjoyed playing confessor, like a monk at the Inquisition. The day after Robert Rossen admitted the error of his ways to HUAC and named others who had erred with him, Williams pasted Sokolsky's column into his scrapbook: "Sought New Gods—Found Clay Monkeys," read the headline.

Williams was not all coziness with the Red hunters. He could threaten if need be. When Howard Koch, co-author of *Casablanca,* was blacklisted, he went to Williams for help. Williams found Koch's accuser in the Red-baiting network and told him, "My client, Howard Koch, is off your list or we sue you for a million dollars." According to Koch, he was off the list "the next day." Yet Williams never tried to expose the system itself. From his work with McCarthy, Williams knew full well the shoddy procedures and shaky information that frequently characterized "Redbaiting" investigations. These tactics were ripe targets for the sort of "scorched earth" attacks that Williams would later popularize. Still, no such attacks were ever pursued.

Williams was eager to profit from handling security cases. When Cohn asked Williams to help him defend Carl Foreman, scriptwriter of *High Noon,* Williams said his fee would be $50,000 plus 10 percent of Foreman's next picture. Williams asserted that he could arrange for a "private hearing" with HUAC. Cohn balked at this. It was not unusual for Williams to take a piece of his client's next film as partial payment, though the gamble rarely paid off. Robert Rossen gave him 10 percent of a bomb called *Alexander the Great.* Williams had made the mistake of turning down a 10 percent interest in Harold Hecht's production company, which a year later made *Vera Cruz* and *Marty.* Still, Hecht is a good example of how naming names was good for Williams's business. Hecht had been named to the committee by Williams's talkative client, Martin Berkeley. The week after Williams represented Berkeley before HUAC, he represented Hecht.

BY THE SUMMER of 1953, as the Eisenhower era began, McCarthy was beginning to flail. He predicted wildly that Beria, Stalin's chief of police, would defect and come testify before his committee. He falsely accused several State Department officials of "shaking down" a Central American country for $150,000. He announced that he would investigate "lax security" at the Central Intelligence Agency. Then, in the winter of 1954, he accused the U.S. Army of harboring subversives. At a public hearing he charged that Gen. Ralph Zwicker, a decorated combat veteran, was not "fit to wear the uniform" of an army officer because he had failed to discharge a pink dentist from the base he commanded. Zwicker, McCarthy bellowed, "did not have the brains of a five-year-old child."

McCarthy was starting to eat his own, the patriotic Americans he claimed as his constituency. He was no longer just beating up on Harvard professors and "pansy" diplomats. He had taken on a hero of the Battle of the Bulge. The army counterattacked—in true Washington fashion—by leaking an internal investigation critical of McCarthy. The most titillating revelation was that Roy Cohn, McCarthy's chief aide, had improperly pressured the Pentagon for special favors for his friend David Schine, who was then a private in the army. Meanwhile, McCarthy's colleagues in the Senate were losing patience. He had abused several of them as well, calling Senator Guy Gillette of Iowa "dishonest," Senator Robert Hendrickson of New Jersey "the only human who ever lived without brains or guts," Senator Ralph Flanders of Vermont "senile," and Senator William Fulbright of Arkansas "half bright." In April 1954, a special Senate committee was appointed to look into McCarthy's charges against the army, and the army's against McCarthy.

McCarthy asked Williams to advise him at the hearings. Williams refused. He told McCarthy that he didn't want to be a "bag carrier" for him. "You don't need me," Williams said. "You want to run the case yourself." Maintaining control was very important to Williams, but McCarthy's unwillingness to let him cross-examine witnesses was not the only reason he refused to sit alongside McCarthy in the hearing room. Williams was not quite as eager to be identified with the junior senator from Wisconsin as he had been when McCarthy first burst upon the scene in 1950. McCarthy had outlived his usefulness to Williams. The lawyer sensed that the Eisenhower administration was finally turning on McCarthy, and that the public was about to. The Cold War hysteria was beginning to ebb in 1954. Stalin had died, and new Kremlin leaders were openly seeking better relations with the West. Edward R. Murrow, the leading broadcaster of the day, had been mute about McCarthyism up until now, but in March his prime-time program "See It Now" on CBS mocked the demagogue with film clips of him patronizing the president, giggling uncontrollably, belching, and picking his nose.

Williams himself was beginning to pay a price for representing McCarthy, particularly when he traveled to New York City on business. Manhattan held a special fascination for Williams; it was the big time, and Williams badly wanted to be known and recognized there. Largely by representing show business figures targeted as security risks, he had

gained entree into the world of actors and television and sports personalities who gathered in watering holes like Toots Shor's and Sardi's. But
one night in the summer of 1953, he was having dinner at Toots Shor's
with actor Eddie Dowling when Shor himself came over to the table and
blasted Williams, whom he barely knew. Shor always humorously
taunted his patrons as "crum-bums and creeps," but he was serious as he
tore into Williams. The restaurateur later apologized—and the two men
began a long and memorable friendship that lasted until Shor finally drank
himself to death in 1977—but Williams was taken aback. Not long afterward, his representation of McCarthy almost provoked a fistfight in the
dining room at Sardi's. Williams was having dinner with actor Eddie
Albert and his wife when director Leonard Spigelgass came over to their
table and sat down. "Aren't you the lawyer who represents McCarthy?"
Spigelgass demanded. "How could you defend that rotten bastard? How
could you prostitute yourself like that?" Williams thought Spigelgass was
angry enough to take a swing, but instead he walked away, saying that
he wouldn't sit at the same table with someone who had a relationship
with McCarthy.

When necessary, Williams could sound like a true believer. Imploring
William F. Buckley to aid in McCarthy's defense in 1954, Williams
declared, "We've got to save Joe! It's important to save the country from
the Communist threat." Buckley recalls that he thought Williams was a
"good 100 percent witch hunter." (With arched eyebrows, he adds,
"and two years later I discovered he was Mr. ACLU.") By 1954,
Williams had put some distance between himself and the senator. In
private, he had always chided McCarthy for his methods, and as the
senator became more outrageous, Williams's criticism became more
pointed. Jean McCarthy, the senator's wife, grew suspicious of
Williams's convictions. When the senator told her that he might retain
Williams to defend him at the Army-McCarthy hearings, Mrs. McCarthy
expressed reservations; she felt that Williams would not be sufficiently
zealous. Dorothy Williams, for her part, wanted nothing to do with
Senator McCarthy. She forbade Williams from bringing him into her
house.

Williams did not refuse to help McCarthy altogether with the
hearings—he just refused to do it publicly. A half dozen times, Williams
met with McCarthy and his underlings in the evening after the hearings to
review the day and plot strategy. It may have pained Williams to pass up
the chance to appear daily at the nationally televised hearings, but in

terms of his own reputation, Williams was shrewd to lay low: The hearings were blustery and chaotic. Witnesses squabbled and senators postured. McCarthy kept whining "Point of order! Point of order!" to bring even more disorder to the proceedings, dragging in new smears and recycling old ones. A few weeks into the hearings, at one of the nightly postmortems, McCarthy suggested that he had a new weapon to use against the army. Through his numerous spies, McCarthy had learned that Fred Fisher, a young lawyer on the army's defense team, had once been a member of the National Lawyers Guild, an organization that had been branded "subversive" by HUAC. McCarthy told Williams that he planned to drop this grenade at the appropriate moment. Williams urged him not to. He knew that McCarthy ran the risk of slashing too hard, and he was wary of the army's able counsel, Joseph Welch of Boston. Williams warned McCarthy that bringing up Fred Fisher's past could backfire. Roy Cohn, who was also at the meeting that night, seconded Williams. Cohn had an especially urgent reason to keep Fisher out of it: He had made a deal with the army's counsel that if McCarthy did not mention Fisher's affiliation, Welch would not bring up the fact that Cohn had been a draft-dodger in World War II.

McCarthy, however, could not resist "touching wet paint," as Williams later put it. He promptly dragged Fisher into the hearings. Acting shocked and wounded, Joe Welch rose theatrically to the occasion. "Until this moment, Senator, I think I never really gauged your cruelty or your recklessness," said the bespectacled Boston lawyer, blinking shyly, for effect, into the klieg lights. When McCarthy blundered ahead, Welch finished him off. "Have you no decency, sir, at long last? Have you no sense of decency left?"

Millions were watching. Two out of three Americans who owned television sets were tuned to the hearings, and while the hearings aired, department stores were reporting a fall-off in sales—but a run on TVs. When the hearings ended after thirty-six days and 2 million words, little had been proved but everyone involved looked bad. The judges—the senators on the committee—had appeared just as foolish as the combatants. McCarthy's contempt for the orderly processes of the Senate grated on lawmakers. It was all very fine for him to attack pinkos and fellow travelers, even if his evidence was flimsy (when McCarthy had first started looking for subversives in 1950, Senator William Taft, the distinguished majority leader, had whispered to him, "If one case doesn't work, try another"), but now McCarthy was fouling his nest. He was, in the words of his fellow Red hunter, Senator William Jenner, "the kid who came to the party and peed in the lemonade."

In June, Senator Ralph Flanders, whom McCarthy had recommended "catching in a net and taking someplace safe," introduced a motion to censure the senator from Wisconsin. In August, the measure was referred to a special committee of six senators, all of them members of the Senate's "Inner Club," under the chairmanship of Senator Arthur Watkins of Utah, a former judge. Similar committees had been appointed only four other times in the Senate's history, and three of them recommended censure. This time McCarthy really did need a lawyer. Once again, he called on Ed Williams.

Williams had not spoken to McCarthy since the Fred Fisher incident. He had refused to come to any more evening postmortems during the hearings and departed for Germany in July to lecture at the University of Frankfurt. When he stepped off the plane from Germany at Idlewild Airport in New York on August 15, carrying a double chin from six weeks of lager and knockwurst, he read in the newspaper that McCarthy intended to use him as his lawyer. Irritated at McCarthy's presumption, he refused even to take a telephone call from the senator. "The Army-McCarthy fiasco was fresh in my mind, and I was determined not to participate in a carnival of that character," he later said. But he finally relented on one condition: that McCarthy give his lawyer complete control of his defense.

The Watkins Committee was only too glad to have Williams, not McCarthy, in charge. They were even willing to put Williams on staff and pay him a salary. Williams declined; it was unseemly for him to be on the payroll of a committee that was judging his client, and "less altruistically," as he put it, he did not want to be disqualified from other cases during the hearings because of a conflict of interest. He agreed to handle McCarthy's case free of charge, knowing that the publicity would be more valuable than any fee. In this goal, he was at cross-purposes with Chairman Watkins, whose intention it was to "get off the front page and back among the obituaries."

When the censure hearings began on August 31, 1954, the atmosphere contrasted starkly with the Army-McCarthy spectacle, which had been performed under klieg lights in a smoky, jam-packed room. Cameras were now banned; Watkins, a strict Mormon, even prohibited smoking. Either Williams or McCarthy was allowed to question witnesses, but they couldn't question the same witness—and there would be no more "points of order.'' The tidiness of the proceeding was too much for McCarthy. After squirming in his seat through one long and dull exchange between Williams and the senators, McCarthy tried to interrupt, politely at first. Watkins immediately cut him off by reminding him of the rules: "when your counsel speaks on one matter, that precludes you from addressing the Chair of the committee on the same matter.'' Angrily, McCarthy seized the microphone from Williams and began his familiar nasal whine. "I should be entitled to know whether or not . . .'' Bang! went Watkins's gavel. "The Senator is out of order!'' Two more times McCarthy tried to interrupt; Williams could be heard whispering to him, "Now don't get excited . . .'' Again Chairman Watkins brought down the gavel. "The Senator is out of order. We will not be interrupted by these diversions. The committee will be in recess.'' Spluttering, McCarthy pushed Williams aside and headed for the lobby, where the TV cameras and lights were waiting. "This,'' he muttered to reporters, "is the most unheard of thing I've ever heard of.''

Spoiled by the Army-McCarthy theatrics, the newspapers were quickly bored by the staid proceedings. "McCarthy Drama Is a Turkey; Even Principal Players Yawn'' read the headline over a Mary McGrory story in the *Washington Star* on September 2. McGrory noted that Watkins had used his gavel six times in fifteen minutes, and that empty seats had started appearing in the gallery. As the committee tediously rehashed McCarthy's familiar transgressions, about the only new angle to write about was McCarthy's impressive young lawyer. "McCarthy's Counsel Jousts with a Pointed Legal Lance'' read the *Star*'s headline on September 8. "No one has contributed more to the judicial atmosphere of the censure hearings than young Mr. Williams, a lynx-eyed, wavy-haired, smooth-tongued young man who wears shirts with button-down collars and has an air of fierce attention,'' wrote McGrory. Williams's "voice was quiet, his manner humble,'' reported the *Washington Post*; he began most sentences with "If I may, sir . . .'' But Williams was not suppliant. When he wanted to argue a point, his "ankles would hook onto the outside of the chair legs, his grip tighten on the tops of the armrests.'' He looked, the *Post* reported, "as if he was about to take off.''

Williams's defense strategy was essentially pot-calling-the-kettle-black, a tactic known by Holy Cross debaters as *Tu Quoque* ("You're another''). He did not try to deny that McCarthy had done all the things he'd been accused of. He argued, instead, that other senators had done the same in the past and not been punished for it. True, McCarthy had called Senator Flanders "senile," but in an earlier speech, Senator Flanders had likened McCarthy to Hitler and hinted that he was a homosexual. Chairman Watkins was not moved. He ruled that evidence about the actions of other senators was irrelevant. Williams declared himself "shocked" and complained that Watkins had cut "the heart and soul" out of his defense.

Gaveled into silence by Watkins, muzzled by Williams, McCarthy behaved himself inside the hearing room. *Outside* the room was another matter. Whenever he got bored, he would tell Williams that he had to go to the bathroom; then he would go into the lobby and make a few intemperate remarks to reporters, sometimes stopping in the men's room on the way for a little nip. "No one blames Mr. Williams for these outbursts," wrote the *Washington Star*. But Williams blamed himself. He had made McCarthy agree to give him complete control only inside the hearing room. Whether he could have kept McCarthy leashed the rest of the time is doubtful, but Williams regretted not having tried. He was especially sorry when McCarthy—without telling him—slipped a speech into the Congressional Record attacking the Watkins Committee. "The Communist party," McCarthy declared, "has now extended its tentacles to the United States Senate." The Watkins Committee members, he charged, had become "the unwitting handmaidens" of the Kremlin. Senators on both sides of the aisle were indignant. "Does the Senate of the United States have enough manhood to stand up to Senator McCarthy?" demanded Senator Sam Ervin of North Carolina. As Williams trudged out of the Senate that evening, a reporter stopped him. "Ed, your boy sure isn't trying to win friends and influence people is he?" Williams wearily replied, "That's the book Joe didn't write."

Still, there was one last chance to save McCarthy from censure. Working with Vice President Richard Nixon, a group of Republican senators that included Majority Leader William Knowland of California, Barry Goldwater of Arizona, and Everett Dirksen of Illinois cooked up a compromise: The Senate would pass a resolution to the effect that it would not "condone" McCarthy's actions, but it would not censure him either. The Senate would then pass rules to prohibit such conduct *in the future*. Dirksen had rounded up enough votes. It just remained for Williams to sell the deal to his client. McCarthy at the moment was holed up in Bethesda Naval Hospital, nursing an infected elbow and playing for time.

He wasn't interested in working out a compromise; he was waiting for his legions to rise up and demand exoneration, or perhaps launch him on a third-party ticket for the presidency in 1956. A group modestly called Ten Million Americans Mobilizing for Justice had delivered to the Capitol a petition with 1,000,816 signatures via an armored truck. McCarthy envisioned thousands of rallies and vigils all around the country, where people would sing his theme song, "Nobody Loves Joe But the People" ("the *pee*-pul").

On a cold evening in late November, Williams and Goldwater slipped through a back entrance at the naval hospital to avoid reporters camped in the lobby. They found the senator drinking bourbon, which he kept in a bottle under his mattress, out of a water glass. Williams tried to persuade him to sign letters of apology to Senators Watkins and Hendrickson. McCarthy just "threw the pen across the room, started swearing at both of us, and pounded the table," Goldwater recalled. He sneered at the idea of asking other senators to "condone" him. "You're going to lose, you're going to lose, you're going to go down to defeat," Williams pleaded. The commotion was so loud that the floor nurse called for a doctor, who called for the admiral in charge of the hospital, who threatened to call the Shore Police. After Williams and Goldwater glumly departed, Senator Dirksen arrived with another letter of apology (and a new bottle of whiskey). McCarthy calmed down a little. "I don't crawl," he told Dirksen. "I learned to fight in an alley. That's all I know."

On December 2, 1954, the Senate voted to censure McCarthy, 67–22. "From here on out," said Senator Mike Monroney of Oklahoma, "McCarthy will bear a scarlet *C* on his chest." Now when McCarthy stood up to speak on the Senate floor, the chamber would empty. When he sat down with his colleagues in the Senate dining room, they would make excuses and leave. The press that had helped create McCarthy now ignored him. At the White House, President Eisenhower greeted his cabinet with a little joke. "Have you heard the latest?" he asked. "McCarthyism is McCarthywasm."

Williams was depressed by the defeat. If anything, he took it harder than McCarthy, who had resigned himself to being "lynched." Still, Williams was cheered by his press notices. "McCarthy Counsel, 34, Rated Tops," extolled his old hometown paper, the *Hartford Courant*. Williams was "recognized by White House observers as probably the most talented young trial lawyer in town." "McCarthy's Censure Counsel Is a Young and Tough Battler," headlined the *Washington Star*. "He has a relaxed, casual manner and he talks easily and fluently, with a disarming and boyish air,'' read the Associated Press story. In *The New Yorker,* Richard Rovere wrote, ''Edward Bennett Williams is one of the most capable trial lawyers in Washington and an extremely personable young man.''

Chapter Seven

WITH FRIENDS, WILLIAMS was gleeful about his notices. His friend Frank Waldrop, the executive editor of the *Washington Times Herald,* remembers Williams lying, half drunk, on the floor of his house one night. "There are three things in life," Williams said. "Money, power, and public relations. My wife is rich, and I wouldn't know what to do with power, but give me those press clippings!"

Williams's pursuit of press clippings was enhanced in the early 1950s by his association with a fast-talker named Eddie Cheyfitz. Red-haired, dapper, and effusive, Cheyfitz was an unusual character. A poor boy from Toledo, Ohio, he had become a Communist in the 1930s and even moved to the Soviet Union for two years. Shocked by Stalin and Hitler in 1939, he had climbed aboard what leftists called the "Moscow-Rome Express" and became a Catholic. Cheyfitz had renounced the Party with the zeal of a convert and had become a public relations man and lobbyist in Washington. Like other influence peddlers, Cheyfitz decided a law degree would make him more respectable, so he started taking night courses at Georgetown. Among his teachers was Edward Bennett Williams. Williams sensed immediately that Cheyfitz could be useful to him, and when Cheyfitz graduated from Georgetown in 1952, Williams rented him an office in the Hill Building.

Williams wanted to promote himself with the press, but he didn't want to be too obvious about it. He preferred understatement. After he had worn the wrong shade of blue to his wedding, he had discovered Brooks Brothers and gray flannel. Cheyfitz, by contrast, had a taste for tailored suits and baroque furnishings, and he had no inhibitions about flaunting himself or his friends. He was happy to call reporters and talk up Williams's latest triumph. "Ed would use Cheyfitz to do what he didn't want to do," said Waldrop. "Cheyfitz would B.S. me a lot about Ed, [who] was smart enough not to do it himself. Cheyfitz was a natural born watercarrier."

According to Tom Kelly of the old *Washington Daily News,* Williams was not particularly warm to the ordinary beat reporters who covered the courts. "I found him cold and calculating," said Kelly, who covered several of Williams's trials. In speaking to courthouse reporters and on the record, Williams was careful, formal, and precise. He used the same lines and told the same stories, with exactly the same language, over and over again. Williams was friendlier, more informal with editors and the big-name journalists in town, men like Waldrop and Arthur Krock, the senior columnist of the *New York Times.* Speaking off-the-record with them, he was open, funny, and engaging.

When he had to defend himself, Williams could be very persuasive. Krock took a liking to Williams and invited him to dinner one night during the McCarthy censure hearings. Some other prominent reporters were there, and they started in on Williams for defending McCarthy. How could he defend such a terrible man? Williams was tired that night, and a little dour and defensive, recalls columnist Rowland Evans, another guest. After moodily listening to the badgering, he began, "Well, it's a funny thing. A doctor is driving along the road at night and there's a terrible accident. He rushes over. The driver is bloody. The doctor immediately tries to save his life. Or a priest is on a boat and he sees a passenger crushed by a boom. The priest runs over to administer last rites. Neither one of them has asked the character of the victim. But when a lawyer rushes in," Williams looked at his accusers, "this is what happens!" The dinner table quieted. The questioning stopped.

Williams's logic was clever, but a little specious and self-serving. His speech, which became his stock reply to critics, smacks of Holy Cross debating tricks. Williams was arguing by inapposite analogy. Unlike lawyers who hold themselves out to criminal defendants, the doctor and the priest are not deliberately seeking money by helping the victims they chance upon, nor are they seeking to excuse the criminal acts of their patients/penitents. A priest has a duty to God; he cannot refuse a penitent. A lawyer, however, is not compelled to defend Joe McCarthy. The fact is that lawyers are not required to represent everyone who asks them to, and Williams himself often said no. Williams had a genuine sense of duty about the right to counsel, but it is fair to say that he was more interested in marketing himself and getting headlines than playing the Good Samaritan. He had little interest in cases that were unexceptional or uninteresting. He wanted cases that were notorious or lucrative—and preferably both.

By 1953, THE fees were beginning to roll in. Williams was making at least five times as much as the $7,000 he earned in his last year at Hogan & Hartson. Still in his early thirties, he was beginning to deserve the reputation as a miracle worker with juries. When Williams had first gone to work at Hogan & Hartson, a partner at the firm told him why he had been hired. "You have an affidavit face," he said, meaning that Williams radiated a sincerity and credibility that, for jurors, carried the force of a sworn statement. Defending a lawyer named Robert Dudley in the summer of 1953 in a fairly routine bribery case, Williams was able to make the jury weep out of sympathy for the defendant. Dudley was acquitted so fast that one observer joked that the first juror was coming out to announce the verdict as the last one was going in to deliberate. (That night Williams and Dudley got happily drunk at his house, staying up most of the night and singing songs. The piano player was Dudley's neighbor, Vice President Richard Nixon.)

Only a month before, Williams had won a $50,000 libel judgment against columnist Drew Pearson. Pearson had written that Williams's client Norman Littell was under investigation by the Justice Department for failing to register as a foreign agent. Although he had been sued dozens of times, Pearson had never lost before, and he wasn't very worried about this case, particularly since the story he had written was true. But after watching Williams totally dominate the courtroom on the first day of trial, Pearson's wife, Luvie, came home and said to her husband, "You know, Drew, we've lost."

Williams was also a shrewd operator behind-the-scenes. After his acquittal by a weeping jury, Robert Dudley proceeded to get in legal trouble again, this time by acting as a front so that shipping magnate Aristotle Onassis could illegally gain control of surplus U.S. vessels from World War II. Once again Williams got Dudley off—as well as a number of other businessmen implicated in the scam—by a series of esoteric legal maneuvers combined with straight horsetrading. During litigation, the government had tied up much of Onassis's fleet in U.S. harbors along the eastern seaboard. Williams went with Onassis to discuss the case with U.S. Attorney General Herbert Brownell. As the lawyers argued back and forth, Williams could see that Onassis, who had come to the meeting wearing sunglasses and blue suede shoes, was getting impatient. Finally Onassis broke in: "General," he said to Brownell, "let's cut the bullshit! What's the ransom for my ships?" It took about a year, but the answer finally came back: $7 million in fines. Williams loved to tell this story in later years, imitating Onassis's heavy Greek accent ("'Ge-ne-ral, let's cut the bo-o-olsheet . . .'").

Other Washington lawyers watched these feats—and listened to Williams tell stories about them—with a certain amount of envy. Williams was popular enough to get himself elected vice president of the D.C. Bar Association in 1952, but the establishment bar did not quite know what to make of him. He was not a Fifth Streeter, but he was a little slick for downtown. Inevitably, his rapid rise provoked backbiting. Some lawyers grumbled that he was too much of a hustler, that he had married the boss's granddaughter and wormed his way into conservative political circles to feed his ambition.* William Hitz, a prosecutor whom Williams faced on a number of occasions, was irritated by the claque of Georgetown law students who would come to court every day and stare adoringly at Williams. "Do you require your students to come watch you?" Hitz would sarcastically ask. And for the first time, Williams began to suffer what he called "guilt by client."

VIEWED FROM AFAR, it's easy to picture Williams as a hustler. To those who knew him, however, he seemed genuinely modest and affable. He never seemed to take himself too seriously, even when he was openly grasping. The night he exclaimed "give me those press clippings!" he had had an impish smile on his lips. Williams also had the capacity for great personal loyalty. He would do anything for a friend, and often did, since his friends would come to him with their problems. Though he was eager to make money, he would often swallow the fee as a favor. By his

---

*When the Republicans won the White House in 1952, Williams decided to make use of his political connections. In January 1953, he quietly asked to be named U.S. Attorney for Washington, D.C. President Eisenhower's chief of staff Sherman Adams vetoed the appointment. It fell to Vice President Nixon to tell Williams why: He had represented Joe McCarthy, and Eisenhower did not want anyone who was in any way associated with McCarthy in that job.

basic decency and solicitude, he could turn foes into allies. The case of Drew Pearson is an example. Not only had Williams won a $50,000 libel judgment against Pearson, he had gone on to defend Pearson's archfoe, Joe McCarthy, in a libel suit brought by Pearson. Yet by the mid-fifties, Williams and Pearson were pals. Luvie Pearson recalls Williams arguing and flirting with her at the Republican convention in 1956; Williams, she says, became one of her husband's best sources, feeding the columnist tidbits of Washington gossip. When Pearson died, Williams helped Luvie settle his estate, free of charge.

Williams understood that even saints could be sinners, and he was there to help them when they fell from grace. The Washington cognoscenti was surprised to learn that Williams had become a friend of Joseph Welch, the great lawyer who shamed Joe McCarthy on national television. No one knew that Williams was more than a friend. After the Army-McCarthy hearings, Welch, the very model of probity and moral rectitude on television, shacked up with a woman at the Carlton Hotel one night. The woman was married, and her husband suspected her of infidelity. He had her shadowed and even bugged her conversations with Welch. The husband was about to file for divorce, naming Welch as the co-respondent; Welch called Williams in desperation. Williams went to the U.S. attorney in Baltimore, Bernard Flynn, and asked him to indict the husband for wiretapping, a federal offense. The husband quickly dropped his case. A month later, in the sort of irony that Williams relished, Welch called to say that he had just been named Father of the Year by the Boston newspapers.

WILLIAMS HATED VACATIONS. His family joked that he was always looking for excuses to quit relaxing and go back to work. He was sitting, bored and restless, at his in-laws' house in Littleton, New Hampshire, on a Friday evening in August 1955 when a man named Aldo Icardi reached him on the telephone. Icardi was in terrible trouble; could Williams come to Washington? Williams told him he'd be there Monday morning. He had never met Icardi, but he knew all about his case; he'd been reading about it in the newspapers. Williams couldn't wait to get back to work. The case that awaited him, he later said, had everything: espionage, murder, and treachery.

Aldo Icardi had been a spy. In 1944, on a secret mission for the Office of Strategic Services (OSS), the wartime precursor of the CIA, he had parachuted into Nazi-occupied Italy to aid the partisans. During the mission, his commanding officer, Maj. William V. Holohan, mysteriously disappeared. Six years later, Holohan's body was found—he had been shot twice in the head, zipped into his sleeping bag, and dumped into Lake Orta. In a lurid story in the September 1951 issue of *True* magazine, Icardi was identified as the murderer. Despite an internal investigation that had earlier cleared Icardi, the Pentagon issued a press release confirming the *True* story.

Because of a quirk in the law at the time, Icardi could not be prosecuted for murder. He could not be tried in civilian courts because he was abroad in uniform at the time of the crime, and he couldn't be tried in the military courts because he had since returned to civilian life. He had, however, been tried and convicted in absentia in Italy. And in 1953, he had been set up for a fall by the House Armed Services Committee. After testifying under oath before the committee that he had not murdered Holohan, he was indicted on eight counts of perjury. By the time he came to Williams's office in August 1955, he already "stood convicted in the court of public opinion and sentenced to infamy," Williams wrote. The small, bespectacled, bald-headed man was desperate and despondent. Icardi had two children and his wife was pregnant again, but because of his notoriety he could not get a license to practice law, his profession. His neighbors were calling him a "dago murderer" and, worse in that era, hinting that he was a Communist. If convicted, he faced up to forty years in prison.

Williams was touched by Icardi's plight and wanted to help. He could also see the potential for a headline-grabbing trial. He asked Icardi for $1,000 so he could go to Italy and investigate the case. Then he called his old Holy Cross debating partner Robert Maheu and asked him if he wanted "to go on a *really* exciting trip." A former FBI agent, Maheu had formed his own private detective agency. (Although Williams did not know it at the time, Maheu was also on the payroll of the CIA.) Maheu eagerly accepted Williams's offer, and the two set about plotting the necessary skulduggery. The first step was to sneak into the country so that they would not be followed by U.S. intelligence and Italian authorities. They made false reservations to fly into Rome, and then slipped over the border by train from Geneva. Maheu remembers Williams, too wound up to sleep, staring out at the moonlight from their train compartment, talking in excited and agitated tones as they passed through the Alps.

It took two and half days for the authorities to catch up, and by then Williams and Maheu had found what they were looking for. At first the partisans who had fought with Icardi were not friendly. One flicked his switchblade throughout the interview before finally throwing them out with a burst of obscenities. But the two Americans picked up their first hint of what had really happened to Major Holohan when they obtained photos of his corpse. The photographs showed that Holohan's hand had been chopped off—the gruesome signature of the Communist underground in northern Italy. Then they found the man who had ordered the murder: Vincenzo Moscatelli, a leader of the Communist partisans in the Po Valley where Holohan was killed.

Before interviewing Moscatelli, who had become a respectable member of the Italian House of Deputies, Maheu prepared a new gadget he had brought along: a tape recorder hidden in a briefcase. The two Americans plied Moscatelli with wine over lunch at a little café in Rome, the Ristorante Pancrazia, while trying hard to stay sober themselves. As the tape recorder silently spun in Maheu's briefcase, Moscatelli freely told them that he had decided to remove Major Holohan—a Wall Street lawyer who spoke no Italian and insisted on wearing his uniform so he would not be shot as a spy if captured by the Germans—because he was a liability to the partisans. Icardi, he said, had nothing to do with the murder. That night, before Moscatelli could have second thoughts, Williams and Maheu packed their bags and flew home.

Williams was convinced that his client was innocent. But he knew that his evidence—a secretly taped conversation—was not admissible in a U.S. court. He would do his best to exonerate Icardi publicly by laying out all the facts in his opening statement to the jury. Williams knew he needed a legal argument to get Icardi acquitted. Congress had trapped Icardi by getting him to testify and then sending his testimony to the grand jury for the perjury indictments. Now Williams would set a trap for Congress.

Williams played possum with the reporters who flocked around him in the days before the trial. He simply insisted Icardi was innocent. He made a point of taking Icardi to lunch at the National Press Club (where Williams was a member)—not to hold a press conference, but to allow reporters to chat with Icardi and judge for themselves whether this shy would-be lawyer from Pittsburgh, Pennsylvania, was a cold-blooded assassin. Just in case his legal strategy failed, Williams wanted to make sure that he had warmed up the jury. Anthony Lewis, then covering the courts for the *New York Times,* recalls sitting in the courtroom of Federal District Judge Richmond Keech as the case went to trial in April 1956.

During jury selection, the prosecutors called the jurors by number. Williams called them by name; he had memorized the names of every prospective juror in the pool of several dozen.

After a dramatic and exhaustive two-hour opening statement, in which he promised to identify the true murderer, Williams sat back as the government presented its first witness, Congressman Sterling Cole of New York. On cross-examination, Williams asked Cole why he had summoned Icardi to testify before his committee. Was it to aid the committee in drafting new legislation? Williams pointed out that Congress had already plugged the loophole in the law that prevented the trial of discharged soldiers for crimes committed during their service. Since a congressional hearing on that subject was not really necessary, why had Icardi been asked to testify? Williams then took a chance. He broke the basic rule Howard Boyd had taught him when he had cross-examined the son of the drunk run down by a streetcar: Never ask a witness a question unless you know the answer. Williams asked Congressman Cole if he had talked to anyone about setting up a perjury case against Icardi. If the answer had been no, Williams's legal attack would have been finished before he had a chance to launch it. But Williams had a hunch about Cole, whom he regarded as dim-witted, and sure enough, the congressman began hemming and hawing. Williams pressed: The congressman *had* discussed bringing a perjury case with his colleagues, hadn't he? "I cannot deny that happened," Cole said, squirming. "On the other hand, I cannot swear that it did happen." Slowly, Williams wrenched the truth out of Cole.

WILLIAMS: And your best recollection here today is that it did happen?
COLE: It could very well have happened.
WILLIAMS: And that is your best recollection here today?
COLE: I would not swear that it did, but it is my recollection.
WILLIAMS: It is your recollection that it did, is that your answer, sir?
COLE: Yes, sir.
WILLIAMS: I have no further questions.

This investigation, Williams told Judge Keech, had been exposure for the sake of exposure, a hearing for the sake of headlines. The government had not shown that the Holohan inquiry had any valid legislative purpose. It was just for show. Yet it was worse than that. It was a carefully laid perjury trap. Congressman Cole had just admitted it. Williams, who had brought a dozen law books with him to court, proceeded to cite a long string of precedents on the separation of powers that barred the legislative branch from usurping the power of the executive and judiciary. Then he moved for an acquittal.

The next morning, Judge Keech read a long opinion from the bench criticizing the "inquisition-type" tactics of the congressional committee. He ended by stating, "I shall ask the Marshal to call in the jury and I shall direct a verdict of acquittal for the defendant." Icardi collapsed, sobbing, into Williams's arms. The prosecutors, who had spent four years and a half million dollars on the investigation, looked stunned. One of the eighteen witnesses flown in from Italy at U.S. government expense turned to a Justice Department official and asked, "Who reached the judge?" Williams, with Icardi still draped around him, just picked up his briefcase and said to his client, "Let's go." He did not stop to answer reporters outside on the courthouse steps. When they arrived at the Hill Building, Williams gently told Icardi, "Go back to your family." Icardi asked, "What do I owe you?" Williams replied, "You don't owe me any-thing."

Williams's reward was the headlines the next morning. The story was on the front page of newspapers all over the country, and Williams himself was profiled as the *New York Times*'s "Man in the News." Under a headline that read "Sixth Amendment Lawyer," the *Times* story began by noting the irony that the same man who defended Joseph R. McCarthy had just "won a spectacular case today on the ground that his client had been abused by a congressional committee." Williams, however, saw no irony in this. He explained to the *Times,* "I just have a pretty solid conviction that the Sixth Amendment means what it says when it gives every accused a right to counsel." Then he added, "We don't refuse anyone who wants to hire us." Senator McCarthy, he said, "was just another client." The article went on to state, "the only problem in hiring Mr. Williams may be the limits of his time. He has made a phenomenal success as a trial lawyer in Washington in eleven years of practice, and he is not likely to become less busy after today's events." The article pictured Williams precisely the way he wanted to be seen. "Mr. Williams's courtroom manner is in contrast to the traditional flamboyance of the trial lawyer. He appears sincere, relaxed, and boyish-looking. He wears his suits with a Brooks Brothers air—including a gray flannel. . . . Mr. Williams voices his emotions with restraint." The next week, *Life* magazine devoted a two-page spread to an artist's rendering of "a brilliant attorney in action." The drawings of "the star of the trial" as he presented his opening argument to the jury, *Life* wrote, sought to "capture his massive sincerity."

Judge Keech's ruling was the first reported case in seventy-five years to hold that a congressional committee had exceeded its constitutional powers. The courts up until then had been passive about the abuses of the McCarthyites and the House Un-American Activities Committee. But Williams's cross-examination of Congressman Cole was the first blow in a series of rulings over the next few years that effectively restrained Congress from witch-hunting. The Icardi case "shook the curse" of defending McCarthy, Williams later recalled. His independence and integrity had been firmly established, certified by no less an authority than the *New York Times*. Now he was free to defend anyone he wanted.

Chapter Eight

FRANK COSTELLO, THE Prime Minister of the Underworld, Boss of Bosses, *Capo di Tutti Capi,* needed a good lawyer. In May 1956, he had been sentenced to five years in a federal penitentiary for income tax evasion, and now the U.S. government was trying to deport him back to Italy. His personal lawyer, George Wolf, told him he didn't have a case, since he had clearly lied on his immigration forms about his occupation (Costello had put down "real estate"). Costello ordered Wolf to find a lawyer who could make a case. But Wolf couldn't find any: In 1956, the best lawyers in New York wouldn't touch the Mafia don.

Wolf's partner, the noted civil liberties lawyer Morris Ernst, was lamenting the timidity of the bar as he stood with a group of lawyers that spring at a reception for the American Civil Liberties Union in Washington. One of the lawyers listening was Edward Bennett Williams. "Tell Wolf to call me," said Williams. Ernst reported back to Wolf that Williams was interested, and Wolf told Costello. The Mafia don was wary. "Isn't he the guy who defended Joe McCarthy?" Costello asked.

In later years, Williams loved telling the story about Costello's response. It was such a disarming anecdote, a clever way of deflating the blowhards who kept asking, "How could you *possibly* defend that awful . . ." Costello's lawyer, however, recalls a somewhat more prosaic exchange with Costello. Wolf says he recommended that Costello hire Williams, but warned, "He'll come high." Costello grunted, "Let's get him while I can still afford him."

Williams's one concern about taking on Costello was that he would offend Georgetown University. Williams was Georgetown's general counsel as well as a part-time professor in the Law School. He decided to feel out Father Francis Lucey, the Law School dean. With his best choirboy air, he told Father Lucey that he had qualms about defending a mobster like Costello, but added that, ethically, he could not deny him his right to counsel. Father Lucey thought for a moment and came up with a solution: Offer to represent him, but charge such a high fee that he'll turn you down. Lucey suggested $50,000 down and $1,000 a day.

But Williams also had to convince his colleagues in the Hill Building. He had loosely associated himself with a pair of lawyers, a former prosecutor named Tom Wadden and a tax lawyer named Colman Stein. Though the "firm" was later called Williams, Wadden & Stein on its letterhead, it was never in any real sense a partnership. Wadden and Stein were really more Williams's tenants in the building than his partners. On cases they shared, Williams called the shots and handed out the fees. Still, Wadden and Stein had to be consulted. Both had their doubts. Wadden worried that his children would be mocked at school. "Is this a good career move?" asked Stein. Williams said he wanted to take the case. "Okay," said Stein, "but when we set fees, the sky's the limit."

In June 1956, Williams flew to Manhattan to see Costello in his jail cell. In addition to demanding payment up front, Williams set forth his usual requirements: total control for Williams and total candor from the client. Costello hedged on the candor. "I can't promise that I will answer everything that you ask me," he said, "but I can promise you that everything I answer will be the truth." Williams said that would not be satisfactory. Costello offered a compromise: He would tell Williams everything "unless it involves some living person who has held a position of public trust." In other words, he did not want to tell Williams which judges and politicians he had paid off. Williams agreed and made one last request: "Don't wear an expensive suit to court. Just wear what you have on." Costello nodded, but he looked unhappy. As Williams was getting up to go, Costello stopped him. "Just one thing, counselor. It's about the suit." What about it? asked Williams. "It's just that I'd rather blow the case than wear *this*." He looked down at his prison garb.

Frank Costello was a vain and fastidious man. In prison, his shoes were professionally shined, his nails manicured, and his denim trousers creased. He had perfect manners; he knew which fork to use, and he always stood when ladies entered a room. Costello had an almost comic craving for respectability. Well read but painfully self-conscious about his street accent, he dropped large words into his conversation ("tangible," "recoup," "authentic"), stumbling only occasionally ("importancy"). Although he had amassed his fortune illegally—through gambling, bootlegging, and murder—many of his businesses—nightclubs, liquor companies, oil wells—were legitimate. Costello did not regard himself as a crook. A criminal, he believed, was someone who dealt heroin or held up banks. He thought the numbers rackets should be legal, and bribery was just a cost of doing business. He hated hard-core pornography and complained that Times Square had been ruined. He gave to charity, and he liked to read nursery rhymes to other people's children.

It was just this desire for respectability that had helped bring Costello down. Summoned before the Kefauver hearings on organized crime in 1951, Costello had refused to take the Fifth Amendment like most gangsters. He somehow hoped that he could convince the committee that he was an honest and reputable citizen. His testimony was a disaster. For two days he sweated and parried with his congressional interrogators. At the start of the third day, he had stalked out of the room. "When I testify, I want to testify truthfully, and my mind don't function," he muttered. The hearings were watched by 20 million Americans, twice the audience of the 1950 World Series. The federal government had to do something: The IRS set up a special rackets unit and Costello was convicted of cheating on his taxes. Meanwhile, the immigration service commenced deportation proceedings.

Williams formally entered Costello's tax and naturalization cases on June 27, 1956. It was his first big case in the Southern District of New York, which, to Williams, was the center of the legal universe. He appeared, solemn and humble, before Judge J. Sylvester Ryan, a hard-nosed Irishman. Columnist Murray Kempton was watching as Williams folded his hands before him and, like a Jesuit novice, cast his still-boyish face up to the bench. "Your Honor, I'm not very familiar with the rules of this circuit, and I hope you will bear with me and correct me if I err." He then proceeded to subpoena the district attorney, the New York police commissioner, the New York commissioner of investigations, and the heads of the Manhattan offices of the U.S. Treasury Department, U.S. Immigration Service, U.S. Internal Revenue Service, and the tax unit of the federal Alcohol and Tobacco Agency. "Mr. Williams, I'm not sure you were not being overmodest," Judge Ryan dryly observed a few days later.

Williams was looking for evidence of illegal wiretapping. The law on electronic eavesdropping was thoroughly confused in 1957. A federal statute banned wiretapping, but New York ignored it, permitting court-sanctioned wiretapping in the state. The New York law plainly conflicted with federal law, but it would be years before the courts would throw it out. Unquestionably, the New York police had eavesdropped on Costello. A court-approved tap in 1942 had picked up a conversation between Costello and Thomas Aurelio, a grateful nominee for the New York State supreme court. "I want to assure you of my loyalty for all you have done. It's undying," the new judge told the Godfather. Williams argued that Costello had been "continuously" tapped for eleven years, from 1943 until his income tax conviction. Six policemen, working in teams of two, had listened in on Costello around the clock, overhearing not only Costello's conversations but those of everyone in his household who used his phone. "The most confidential and intimate family secrets, the tender words of sweethearts" had been laid bare, Williams protested. "Wiretapping," he said, is "like an atom bomb. You can't pick your victims. As many people can be killed by the fallout as by the hit."

In those pre–Warren Court days, it was difficult to get a conviction thrown out by proving that the evidence had been illegally obtained through electronic eavesdropping. To get the tax conviction overturned and stop the deportation proceeding, it was not enough to show that Costello had been tapped. Williams also had to show that the federal authorities had used the evidence from the New York State taps in making their cases. This required an enormous amount of legwork. Tom Wadden interviewed scores of New York detectives and policemen, looking for the link. His records show him interviewing a former New York gumshoe while sitting in a Pontiac in a parking lot in Miami at 11:15 at night. Wadden's notes describe the detective as a "nervous wreck." Under Wadden's persistent cajoling and questioning, the detective finally admitted that he had, indeed, passed logs of Costello's phone conversations to the federal agents. In open court, however, Williams was never able to shake the insistence of U.S. attorney Arthur Christie that the feds had not used any evidence from the New York taps. Even so, Williams won a temporary stay in the deportation case when the judge ruled that the "wiretapping was so extensive and of such far-reaching nature" that it was "well-nigh impossible" for him to sort the evidence that was not "tainted" by wiretapping from the evidence that was.

Williams had also argued for a delay because Costello was a "very sick man" with an "active coronary disease." Costello testified that he was "a dying man in terrible pain." Leaving the court after winning his temporary stay, Costello gave reporters a hearty greeting and waved at the cameras. "This verdict makes me feel better already," he said. In March 1957, Williams managed to get Costello freed from prison on bond while the Supreme Court reviewed the question of whether his five-year sentence on tax evasion was too long for a sixty-five-year-old man. Costello was ecstatic. Forgetting his urge for respectability for a moment, he used the argot of the betting shop to praise his lawyer: "I've had forty lawyers," crowed the don, "but Ed's the champ. Ed's the champ. It's like playing dice. Man throws six, he can't pay off. Ed makes the point. Ed makes the point."

Williams liked Costello, too. He described the gangster as "a very pleasant fellow" who "had his own strong moral code," even though it may not have been "exactly your code or my code." Williams had demanded the truth from Costello, and he felt that the Mafia don had not lied to him (unlike so many of the congressmen and corrupt lawyers he represented). Williams liked Costello's company in part because he was fascinated by Costello's world—the New York demimonde of the 1950s, the nightclubs populated by gamblers, professional ball players, and show business celebrities. Costello would take Williams to the Copacabana, where they met Frank Erickson, the longtime bookmaker for the Vander-bilts and other swells. When Costello wanted to pay a check, float a loan, or place a bet, "Big Jim" O'Connell, a "flotilla commander" from Costello's bootlegging days, would suddenly appear and start peeling off hundred-dollar bills from a fat roll. When a starlet or a pretty showgirl sat beside Costello, there would be a C-note staring at her when the waiter removed her plate. Williams watched the high-rolling with laughter and wonder. This was a long way from dancing with Mrs. Ambrose at the Atlas Club.

One day while Costello was still in jail, Williams had complained to him that he couldn't get tickets to take his wife to the new Broadway sensation *My Fair Lady*. That afternoon at the hotel, Dorothy answered a knock on her door to find a sinister-looking man holding a box. "Open it," he growled. With some trepidation, Dorothy opened the box. Inside were a $100 bottle of Joy perfume and four orchestra seats for that evening's performance of *My Fair Lady*. In later years Williams would jokingly wonder whether the people who were supposed to sit in those seats "got cement shoes instead."

As a young man, Williams had enjoyed reading the stories of Damon Runyon, the legendary chronicler of Broadway's guys and dolls. Runyon's gangsters were all colorful rogues, while policemen—"coppers"—were hopeless flatfoots. Morals were relative. Crime was romanticized, portrayed with a mixture of ironic detachment and soft-focus bemusement. In New York City after the war, it was still possible to believe that Mafia dons were men with a code of honor and that cabdrivers had hearts of gold. After sitting through congressional hearings in Washington, defending mobsters by day and enjoying the bright lights at night was a romantic and mildly wicked life.

The clubhouse of the Runyonesque world that Williams sought out was Toots Shor's, a saloon on East 54th Street. Bernard Shor—known by everyone, including his mother, as Toots—had been a bouncer at Runyon's old hang-out, Billy LaHiff's, during Prohibition. Large, loud, and crude, he greeted patrons that he especially liked by insulting them. Frank Sinatra—"Sinat"—was "you skinny dago." "Whitey, Yogi," Shor would greet Whitey Ford and Yogi Berra, the Yankee pitcher and catcher, after a tough loss, "you bums play lousy but I feed you anyway." Shor was "particularly skillful at using the technique with some of his more serious celebrities," wrote David Halberstam in his book about the glory days of the Yankees, *Summer of '49*. "It allowed them to shed some of the burden of their fame and relax—while being treated as VIPs. Shor was surprisingly nimble, indeed almost delicate, in knowing how far to go, and when to stop." When Shor went too far, he would apologize—as he did after the night he tore into Williams for defending McCarthy.

Most diners said that the food at Shor's was terrible, but Shor's was not really about eating. It was about drinking. Standing by the huge circular bar at the front of his restaurant, Shor himself showed the way. The only night of the year he did not drink, Shor boasted, was New Year's Eve, because that was "amateur night." Drinking was a macho sport: One night, Williams and Jackie Gleason bet Shor $100 he couldn't drink a bottle of Scotch and remain standing. Shor obliged in an hour. Williams himself could keep pace: A couple of martinis before dinner and four or five Scotches afterward was a moderate evening.

Most evenings one would find Ed Williams at Shor's. "We used it as an office," says Tom Wadden, when he was working with Williams on the Costello case. "We got our messages there." Witty and masculine, a mesmerizing raconteur, Williams was quickly accepted into what sportswriter Red Smith called "the mother lodge." "The man's coming!" Shor would declare when Williams arrived, and usher him to one of the "celebrity banquettes" along the wall. There, Williams would hold court, chatting with the ball players and show biz personalities who would stop by for a few cocktails. Often the courtiers were columnists: This was the heyday of the gossip column, and a dozen of them wrote for the eight daily papers still being published in New York. Williams would joke with them: Leonard Lyons reported on September 30, 1956, that Williams had to fly down to Washington and defend an oil lobbyist accused of bribery. "Yes, that's me," Williams told Lyons. "Costello and the oil lobbyists. I'm always for the underprivileged." But Williams would also use the columnists to buff his reputation, telling Lyons that Costello and McCarthy had each objected to Williams serving as lawyer for the other. And Williams was not above trying his cases in the press: He told Earl Wilson that he was going to "blanket the town with subpoenas" to show that "high-level wiretapping" convicted Costello.

The celebrity that Williams most enjoyed seeing was also the shyest. In some ways, Joe DiMaggio was an unlikely match for Williams. The baseball star was quiet and reserved, neither clever nor articulate. But he had been the greatest Yankee since Babe Ruth, and Williams was overjoyed to call him a friend. His playing days behind him (he retired in 1951), DiMaggio carefully rented out his celebrity with occasional endorsements and spent the evenings roaming New York's night spots, often with a showgirl on his arm. He was a lonely insomniac who, Halberstam wrote, "wanted to touch the bright lights of the city, but not be burned by them." With Williams, he would talk, earnestly and for hours, about the burden of fame. The two men had in common a terrible fear of not living up to their reputation. DiMaggio would tell Williams about the pressure he felt to get a hit, even playing in a meaningless game before a crowd of a few hundred in St. Louis at the end of the season, because "there might be some fan who's never seen me hit one before." Williams would tell DiMaggio about the tremendous pressure he felt to win every case, even though he knew the best lawyers lose "40 percent of the time." DiMaggio's career in sports was finished, while Williams's star as a lawyer was just ascending, but each knew exactly what the other felt.

Another banquettemate of Williams's was a saucy girl by the appropriately Runyonesque name of Leonore Lemmon. Shor's was a man's place; if a man brought his wife, she was coolly welcomed by Shor as "the missus," and she would not be brought again soon. But Lemmon, or "Lem" as she was called by the barflies, was a mascot. Buxom, with jet-black hair, white skin, and slightly bucked teeth, Lem was boisterous and occasionally outrageous. Shirley Povich, a sportswriter for the *Washington Post,* recalls watching her dance one night in a tight tank top and stiff skirt. Suddenly, she just peeled off the skirt and danced in the leotard she was wearing underneath, shocking behavior in 1957. The daughter of a renowned ticket scalper, Lemmon knew all the night spots and everyone in them. Although she occasionally did some public relations work by day, she was a creature of the evening, a Holly Golightly who lived off Frank Costello's hundred-dollar bills. She took it upon herself to educate Ed Williams in the ways of New York nightlife.

"He was the least sophisticated guy you ever met," she recalled thirty years later. "I called him 'Freshman.' " He was completely "wide-eyed" about the glitter world, she recalled, and slightly afraid of the more high-tone café society haunts like El Morocco. Socialites made him uncomfortable; he was happier eating steak and drinking booze with ball players. "He loved to hear himself talk and nothing frustrated him. I'd ask him, 'What are you going to do when you grow up, Ed?' He'd say, 'I want to own a ball club and be president.' I didn't think he was kidding." Fueled by liquor and fantasy, refusing to recognize loneliness and fatigue, Williams developed an infatuation with Lemmon. He flirted with her, sending her presents and love notes, "but he had not a clue about women," she said.

He occasionally went to bed with her, but apparently he was not very aroused. According to Lemmon, Williams was impotent. "He was the world's worst lover. He was not really interested in sex. He thought it was something you had to do after you took a girl to dinner," Lemmon said. Actually, Williams was very interested in sex. He loved to ogle shapely women and make raunchy jokes and comments to his male buddies. When his law firm hired a pretty secretary, he was known to walk down the hall just to look at her. But Williams's strict Irish Catholic upbringing had taught him that sex was sinful. Sins could be forgiven, but some more easily than others. Extramarital sex was truly damnable. When Williams went to bed with Leonore Lemmon, he was drunk, and later full of guilt. In the morning, Williams would get up and go to St. Patrick's Cathedral for confession. "Got to hit the rail," he'd say to Lemmon, as he pushed off, hung over, to mass.

"I'M IN NEW York so much that even if I run down to the store and somebody asks Jobie where I am, he invariably answers, 'Daddy's in New York,' " Williams told *Life* magazine in October 1957. "Jobie" was Joseph Williams, Ed and Dorothy's four-year-old adopted son. Williams and his wife had been unable to have any children of their own. "D.A. wanted them desperately," recalled her sister Betty. "It was a big sadness in her life." However, she refused to take tests to find out why she was unable to have children. "She didn't want to find out if it was Ed. She didn't want to diminish him." Instead, the Williamses adopted a little boy, Joe, in 1954 and a little girl, Ellen, in 1955.

Williams, like many ambitious men in the 1950s, was an absentee father. Raising children, he believed, was for wives. "He was scared of babies and diapers," recalled his oldest daughter, Ellen. In later years, when he had a second family, he became a warm and affectionate father. But with his older children, he showed no real interest until they could talk and show some personality. His distance was especially unfortunate for Jobie, who was a hyper child. "I think Jobie's got problems," Dorothy told her sister when the child was four, and she had to cope with this difficult child largely without her husband's help.

In order to have space for children to play, Ed and Dorothy had moved to the suburbs. In 1952, Williams paid $135,000, a considerable sum then, to buy a glass-and-redwood split-level home in the Tulip Hill sub-division of Bethesda, Maryland, nine miles from Williams's downtown office. Dorothy's mother said the house looked "like a motel," but it was light and airy and decorated in a contemporary style. Dorothy wanted a modern feel because she had grown up with antiques (Williams called antiques "secondhand furniture"). She wanted to live on her husband's salary, but she was willing to use her own money to buy something if he refused to pay. In the mid-fifties, she sold a jewel she had inherited, a star sapphire, to redo her kitchen. When her husband balked at adding a new wing to the house, she promptly put the house on the market. The high bids persuaded Williams that it would be worthwhile to add the new wing.

Williams was not in any sense a homebody. He hated raking leaves or cleaning the gutters. Hopelessly unmechanical, he had to ask the neighbors to assemble toys. One of them, Thomas Taylor, recalls Williams's helplessness as a Santa Claus on Christmas Eve, fumbling ineptly with train sets and dollhouse kits. One cold winter's night at Tulip Hill, his furnace broke, and he called a repairman. "Where's the furnace, bud?" asked the man. Williams just stared at him blankly. "He had no idea," recalled Betty Killay, who was visiting at the time. His one skill was cooking steaks on the grill, and his one domestic pleasure was making a pitcher of martinis to quench his thirst as he toiled over the coals. His recreation was watching television, preferably boxing matches. He read books about political figures and power in Washington. He did not read novels or go to museums. Dorothy occasionally dragged him, protesting, to the theater. She liked modern art and collected some, but he was bored by it. Her friends tended to be WASPy country club women, former schoolmates at Potomac and Madeira, for whom Williams had no use.

Williams did make it a point to come home around six most evenings, at least when he wasn't traveling. But he brought his work home and he was often distracted by it. He could be very engaging with his friends at lunch, but in the evening he was often removed and preoccupied. "Ed and Dorothy barely chatted," said Betty Killay. "She served him dinner and he went to his study to work some more." He moved his study, originally on the first floor, to the basement in order to get away from the noise of children, and practiced his courtroom speeches in the quiet.

If Dorothy knew about Leonore Lemmon, she never told her sister. "But she was jealous, and she worried about him and other women," said Betty Killay. Williams rarely showed any romantic attentiveness toward Dorothy unless he had been drinking. Then he would place his hand lightly on her neck. From time to time, they would have bitter fights, shouting and slamming doors. Dorothy had a tendency to put on weight. She was taking cortisone for her lungs, and the medicine made her retain water. Williams usually joked about how he liked "zaftig women—I like them Rubenesque and soft." But sometimes he would ride Dorothy about her weight, publicly as well as privately. Robert Scott, who later became a D.C. judge, recalled an evening at his house in Shirlington, Virginia, when Williams became surly and drunk. He teased Dorothy so harshly about her extra pounds that she wept.

Despite the tension and the fighting, Dorothy remained devoted to Williams. She could still banter and tease with her husband, and she was proud of his achievements. She liked to go out in the evening and enjoyed watching the parade of ball players, reporters, and politicians who came by their table every Saturday night at Duke Ziebert's, Washington's answer to Toots Shor's. She had no use for Joe McCarthy, but she was not uncomfortable with Williams's other clients. Costello was very courtly with her; ever eager to learn respectable habits, he wanted Dorothy to educate him about food and wine. Dorothy often wore the diamond bracelet Costello had given her. She was, however, taken aback one day when a pair of hoodlums drove up to her house in a truck loaded with toys. They were a gift to Jobie and Ellen from Albert Anastasia, the chairman of the board of Murder Inc. and Costello's chief button man. Anastasia had taken a particular liking to Williams and always met him at the airport. The toys had been salvaged from a warehouse torched by the mob. Williams thanked Anastasia and sent them to an orphanage.

For all her spunk, Dorothy was not well, and she had trouble keeping up with her husband. Although she had been diagnosed as tubercular in 1946, she was in fact suffering from bronchiectasis, a degenerative lung condition that left her progressively weakened and short of breath. Steve Jones, their family doctor and Williams's friend from Georgetown days, recalled that on one trip to New York she tired visibly. Late one night at Toots Shor's apartment, as the others caroused, she asked Dr. Jones to take her back to her hotel room. Williams stayed on, said Jones, "pouring down the booze."

Williams could stay up all night drinking and appear energetic and sharp the next morning. He never seemed to have a problem mixing booze and working. Driving, however, was another matter. In the winter of 1954, Betty Killay noticed that Williams was going to mass every morning. She asked her sister about it. "We can't talk about it," Dorothy answered, seeming distraught. Killay asked Williams directly, and he replied, "If I get through this, I'll go to mass every day for the rest of my life." Whatever "this" was, it seemed so awful that Killay began to wonder if Williams had had an illegitimate child or killed someone. What had gone wrong?

At about 8:00 P.M. on the night of December 23, 1953, as he was driving home from a Christmas party at his office, Williams swerved into the oncoming lane on Rock Creek Parkway and struck another car head on. Williams was bruised, as was the other driver. The other driver's wife, Corinne Grant, was badly hurt—a concussion, broken teeth, lacerations on her face embedded with glass, and serious internal injuries. The Grants sued Williams for $100,000. Williams claimed that he had been struck from behind and knocked into the oncoming lane. He testified in a deposition that, during the course of the two-hour party, he had had one drink and "freshened it."

The policemen who interviewed Williams at the scene testified that Williams appeared sober. Deposed by their lawyer, a park policeman testified that he saw three vertical marks on Williams's left bumper, "just like if you would take a knife and cut chrome, I think." The implication, of course, was that Williams had cut the scratches himself to simulate the impact of a crash. There was also conflicting testimony about another car, a yellow roadster, that may have briefly stopped at the scene of the crash. The driver of such a car was arrested drunk later that night but absolved of any responsibility in the accident. Nothing was ever proved. The case never went to trial; Williams settled out of court for an undisclosed amount in 1956.

Williams may have been saved from serious trouble by Tom Wadden. According to Wadden, he was at his apartment off Wisconsin Avenue, trimming his Christmas tree, when he got a call from a Georgetown law student. The student had just driven by a wreck near the P Street bridge and had seen Williams standing, dazed and bleeding, by his car. Wadden rushed to the scene. He told the police, who had just arrived, to "forget about it." Wadden had just left his job as a prosecutor in the D.A.'s office. "I knew a lot of cops and they knew me," he said. Wadden was accompanied to the scene of the crash by his friend William Tayler. "We were so worried because Ed was drunk," Tayler recalled in 1991. "We were afraid he'd be charged. But Wadden was very smooth with the cops." There was never any mention of the car crash in the press, at the time or in any of the dozens of stories written about Williams in later years. Williams wanted to push his car crash, like his aborted military career, into a black hole. When Robert Pack wrote about the accident and sent Williams a draft, Williams threatened to sue him for libel, even though Pack's information was drawn from public documents filed in court. Pack said that he removed his account of the accident to avoid litigation.

Chapter Nine

ON THE NIGHT of March 14, 1957, Williams was exhausted. Three days before, he had managed to spring Frank Costello from prison. Now, worn out by his efforts in New York, Williams was thinking of taking his family to Florida for a vacation. He was just climbing into bed when the phone rang. It was Eddie Cheyfitz. "Jimmy Hoffa's been arrested!" the PR man exclaimed. Forgetting all about Florida, Williams got dressed and headed downtown to the courthouse.

He found the Teamster boss and Robert F. Kennedy, the young investigator for the Senate Labor Rackets Subcommittee, standing in the hallway, glaring at each other. They had been debating who could do more push-ups. Hoffa said he could do thirty-five; Kennedy claimed he could do more. Kennedy's wife, Ethel, was also present; she had "never been to an arraignment before," and this one was "very exciting," she told a *Washington Star* society reporter. She had not come along just to watch; her husband had asked her to alert reporters, and now, at one o'clock in the morning, fifty of them were waiting outside. "What is this all about?" Williams asked Kennedy. He refused to answer. Williams turned to Ethel, who was knitting like Madam Defarge at the guillotine. "What are you doing here?" he asked. "Why aren't you home with the kids?" Ethel smiled tightly. "Mr. Williams," she said. "You'll find out."

Williams, Kennedy, and Hoffa had been brought together that night by the interplay of scheming and chance that passes for destiny in Washington. Williams had met Bobby Kennedy in church in the early fifties. After morning mass at St. Matthew's Cathedral, the two young men began having breakfast together. They had much in common: They were both Catholic, ambitious, and tough. At the time, Kennedy worked for the Senate Permanent Subcommittee on Investigations, chaired by Williams's client Joe McCarthy. Kennedy was born rich and had gone to Harvard, and Williams was slightly envious of his princely past. Still, "we were very, very close friends," Williams recalled. In 1956, when Williams was vice president of the D.C. Bar Association, he asked Kennedy to sit with him at his table at the association's annual dinner. Between bites of roast beef, Williams invited Kennedy to become his law partner. Kennedy declined; he wanted to stay in government a few years longer. He had just become the general counsel of the Senate Select Committee on Improper Activities in the Labor and Management Field. Although his father was a former bootlegger and cringed at the idea, Bobby wanted to go racket busting.

Kennedy's other dinner partner that night, Eddie Cheyfitz, was eager to steer the would-be bloodhound down the right trail. Cheyfitz did public relations for the Teamsters Union. He wanted to tell Kennedy about a dynamic new labor leader by the name of Jimmy Hoffa, who was going to boot out the corrupt leadership of the Teamsters and transform the union. Cheyfitz had first attracted the notice of Teamster president Dave Beck back in 1949 by planting a damaging story about the Teamsters. When Beck complained, Cheyfitz got the same reporter to write a favorable story about Beck. The Teamster leader was so impressed that he put Cheyfitz on retainer. Cheyfitz had given more to the Teamsters than PR. He had found them a good lawyer—his friend Edward Bennett Williams. Indeed, the union leaders needed the best lawyer they could find. By the mid-1950s, the Teamsters' legal problems were erupting all over the country.

The union was thoroughly corrupt. It had been "mobbed up," infiltrated by gangsters lured by the union's $250 million pension and welfare fund. Teamster leaders rigged elections and stole union funds. Their goons threw acid and planted dynamite. Teamster president Beck postured as a statesman of trade unionism and tried to gain political influence in Washington, making some connections at the Eisenhower White House. Conceited and pompous, he shrilly denounced racketeering. But he was himself a crook who embezzled from a trust fund set up for a friend's widow.

Though he had been hired by Beck, Cheyfitz could see that the aging Teamster leader was vulnerable to both federal investigators and younger

Teamsters. Quietly, Cheyfitz switched his allegiance to a new force in the union, the president of Local 299 in Detroit, head of the Central Conference of Teamsters, and ninth vice president of the International, James Riddle Hoffa. Built like one of his trucks, Hoffa had a thick, compact body and abnormally short, muscular arms. His eyes would dart nervously as he twisted a ruby ring around and around on his stubby finger. Hoffa was ruthless, sardonic, and devious. He was a good family man, but otherwise completely amoral.

Cheyfitz tried to peddle Hoffa as a sincere young reformer; meanwhile, he undermined Beck. To camouflage his intentions, he took Bobby Kennedy to see the Teamsters' marble palace on Pennsylvania Avenue and asked him to give President Beck an autographed copy of his brother's new book, *Profiles in Courage*. Secretly, he fed Kennedy bits of damaging information about Beck. Cheyfitz succeeded in getting young Kennedy to pay attention to the Teamsters, but not quite in the way he had intended.

Working from a cluttered office in Room 101 of the Russell Building on Capitol Hill, Kennedy began looking into the corrupt union. By the time he finished thirty months later, his staff had grown to 100 lawyers, accountants, and investigators and more than 1,500 witnesses had testified in over 500 hearings and spoken 14 million words that filled 20,432 pages. What the testimony showed was a pattern of squandered and stolen union funds, sweetheart contracts, conflicts of interest among employers and union leaders, phony "paper locals," and a general disregard for the welfare of the rank and file. Increasingly, the man that Kennedy blamed for all this was not Dave Beck—but Cheyfitz's new champion, Jimmy Hoffa.

On February 15, 1957, Kennedy received a visit from a private investigator named John Cye Cheasty. "I have some information that will make your hair curl," Cheasty announced. The day before, he said, he had been offered $18,000 by Jimmy Hoffa to spy on Kennedy's committee. (Hoffa also told Cheasty to find out what Cheyfitz was doing to earn his $60,000-a-year retainer, and why Cheyfitz's buddy Ed Williams was eating lunch twice a week with Bobby Kennedy.) Saying that Hoffa had given him $1,000 in cash, Cheasty dumped out $700 on Kennedy's desk. A former naval officer, Cheasty (rhymes with "hasty") felt that it was his patriotic duty to tell the government. What he failed to tell the government was that he had spent $300 of the $1,000 for his personal use.

Kennedy decided to set a trap. He would hire Cheasty as a staffer on the committee and use him as a double agent. Periodically, Cheasty would feed Hoffa the information he wanted, and Cheasty would accept his $2,000-a-month retainer from Hoffa. Meanwhile, the FBI would watch—with cameras. It would be the perfect sting.

On February 20, Cheasty had his first assignation with Hoffa, passing him some committee documents at the corner of 17th and I streets while FBI men watched from the shadows. By coincidence, Hoffa was scheduled to have dinner that night with Bobby Kennedy. The two men had been invited to Eddie Cheyfitz's house; it was all part of Cheyfitz's campaign to persuade Kennedy that Hoffa was an honest and upright labor leader. Not wanting to arouse suspicion, Kennedy decided to go. As they shook hands, Kennedy awkwardly remarked that from what he'd heard about Hoffa, he "probably should have worn a bullet-proof vest." Hoffa snarled, "I do to others what they do to me, only worse." Cheyfitz offered Hoffa a drink. "I don't drink," said Hoffa. "I don't either," said Kennedy (who did). Over the roast beef, the conversation was stiff and strained. At 9:45, Kennedy got a call from Ethel. "Better hurry up, Bob," said Hoffa. "She probably called to see if you're still alive." At the telephone, as Hoffa listened, Kennedy said, "I'm still alive, dear. If you hear a big explosion, I probably won't be." The evening did not get any lighter. Hoffa thought Kennedy had treated him "like the butler" and complained to his aides that Kennedy was a "spoiled little jerk." Remembering how short (five feet four) Hoffa was, Kennedy told his aides that Hoffa needed to show that he was a "tough guy."

On March 13, Cheasty turned over some committee files to Hoffa, and, as the cameras whirred, Hoffa slipped his spy a wad of forty fifty-dollar bills. It was the next night, when Ed Williams was putting on his pajamas and thinking about his Florida vacation, that Hoffa and Cheasty met again in the lobby of the Dupont Plaza Hotel. This time the FBI moved in, and an hour later Williams found Hoffa and Kennedy glaring at each other in the courthouse hallway while Ethel tended to her knitting and public relations duties. After a storm of publicity about the arrest, Hoffa was released on $25,000 bond. A week later, the Teamster leader was indicted for bribing a government official. Cheasty, meanwhile, was given a gun and put under armed guard. *Newsweek* called Kennedy the Democrats' "bright new star," the man who "dug up the evidence and planned the strategy of the Teamsters' investigation." He was, the magazine added, "a man with political ambition himself." Kennedy was feeling cocky. When newsmen asked him what he'd do if Hoffa was acquitted, he replied, "I'll jump off the Capitol."

More shrewdly, Eddie Cheyfitz immediately set about downplaying public expectations for Williams. "If Hoffa is convicted, it's what everyone expects," he told reporters. "If Hoffa is acquitted, then Williams is a hero. It will put him in a class with Darrow." Williams was less philosophical. He was on a hot streak. He had not lost a case in two years, and he was determined to keep on defying the odds. Clients now flocked to him. "The byword in difficult federal cases," wrote the *New York Post* on March 24, "is, when in trouble, get Ed Williams."

Williams was tremendously overworked. On May 2, a *Washington Post* reporter found him in his office complaining that he was so busy that he had been forced to give up teaching law at Georgetown. His children had the mumps, and he was afraid he would get them, too, which would interrupt his work schedule. In addition to Costello and Hoffa, he was representing a Radcliffe girl accused of shooting her boyfriend. Then, while in a meeting with other lawyers on the Onassis shipping case, he got a call from Polly Adler, the famous New York madam, asking him to represent her in a deportation proceeding. That evening, another reporter called Williams to tell him that his old client, Joe McCarthy, had just died.* The phone rang again and it was Teamsters president Dave Beck, asking Williams to represent him before the Senate Rackets Committee the day after next. (On Williams's advice, Beck would take the Fifth 140 times, refusing to acknowledge that he knew the name of his own son.) The phone rang again and Williams learned that Frank Costello had just been shot in the head at point-blank range while leaving his apartment building. ("This is for you Frank," said the gunman, whose aim was poor: The bullet just creased Costello's skull. Although Costello knew perfectly well who shot him, he refused to testify and break the code of *omerta*. He later invited the gunman, Vincent "the Chin" Gigante, over for dinner to show he had no hard feelings.)

Early the next morning, as Williams tripped wearily through La Guardia terminal on his way to see Costello, he noticed the headlines on

---

*Williams felt bad about McCarthy, who had tried to dry out and clean up his life with the help of his wife, Jean (Williams was the godfather of their adopted daughter, Tierney). Williams blamed Roy Cohn, whom he loathed, for McCarthy's death. Cohn had conned McCarthy into investing his last savings in a penny stock and then "pulled the plug"—sold his own stake and left McCarthy stuck with useless shares when the stock plummeted. McCarthy had started drinking again and died a year later.

a New York tabloid: "McCarthy Dead; Frank Costello Shot; Dave Beck Recalled Before Senate Rackets Committee." All three, he realized with great satisfaction, were his clients. What other lawyer, he thought to himself, would have not one but three clients on the front page of the newspapers?

Dorothy, meanwhile, was beginning to get worried about her husband's obsession with winning. "Look, Ed, it's not the end of the world if you lose a case," she told him as they were having dinner with Robert Maheu, the private detective, at their house in Tulip Hill one evening that spring. "One day you *will* lose a case, and you have to be prepared for it." Actually, Williams was struggling with a way to ease the immense pressure he felt. His solution, Maheu recalled, was to predict certain defeat. "This is the worst case," he would moan as the Hoffa trial grew near. "The wo-o-o-rst case. We can't *possibly* win. It's hopeless."

In fact, the Hoffa case *was* pretty hopeless. The government, after all, had movies of Hoffa bribing a government official. Williams's initial strategy was to play for time. He threw up a blizzard of motions, accusing the government of illegal wiretapping and prejudicing the case with publicity. He argued that he couldn't defend Hoffa and Costello at the same time, and that the government would have to decide whom they wanted to prosecute first. He told the judge in the Hoffa case, Burnita Shelton Matthews, that he was "physically exhausted" and needed time to switch gears from Costello to Hoffa. "I really need this, Your Honor," he pleaded. He was hoping to at least delay the Hoffa case until the fall. The unstated motive was to allow Jimmy Hoffa to get elected president of the Teamsters at the union's annual convention in September before he was sentenced to jail. On June 14, while Williams was in New York representing Costello, Williams's associate, Agnes Neill, appeared on his behalf in court in Washington. In 1954, Williams had hired Miss Neill out of Georgetown Law School, where she had been on the Law Review. His first question to her reflected the era: "Can you type?" Together, Williams and Neill were friendly but correct; no one in Williams's office guessed that their professional relationship would one day mask other stirrings. Pretty and prim, Neill was a talented brief writer, but she felt uncomfortable in court. She asked for a delay until the end of July. Judge Matthews agreed. Then she let slip that Williams planned to go to London in July for a bar association conference. Judge Matthews was getting tired of the Hoffa defense team's delaying tactics. "If that's the case," the judge said, "then the trial will start Monday."

Williams was already prepared to go to court, but he could never be well enough prepared to suit his perfectionist standards. As always, he had gone into training for the ordeal of trial. He had quit drinking a month earlier, although he had gained fifteen pounds by eating peanut butter and crackers in his kitchen late at night when he rehearsed his arguments. He became so focused that he seemed almost catatonic to Vince Fuller, another young Georgetown lawyer whom he had hired. The joking and laughing had pretty well stopped. On the Sunday night before trial, Robert Scott, a friend, saw Williams at a children's birthday party for Jobie. Scott asked him how he planned to defend Hoffa. "At Georgetown, I always tell my students to plead 'em if the government has moving pictures," Williams replied. "And the government has moving pictures." So what are you going to do? Scott asked. "I'm going to the candles," said Williams.

Aside from praying, Williams's strategy was to destroy the government's chief witness, John Cye Cheasty. In the process, he nearly destroyed Cheasty as a person. Before trial, Williams had sent Bob Maheu out to research Cheasty's past, and Maheu had not come back empty-handed. Then, in early June, Williams got a break when the Supreme Court handed down a decision in *U.S.* v. *Jencks* ruling that the prosecution had to give the defense access to certain FBI reports, including the statements of government witnesses, before trial. Williams was overjoyed to discovery that Cheasty had not turned over all of Hoffa's bribe money to the government, but instead had spent some, buying shoes for his children and Valentine's Day candy for his wife. That revelation did not exactly blow a hole in Cheasty's credibility, but it at least gave Williams a wedge to chip at.

Cheasty looked pudgy and gray when he took the stand on June 27. He had a heart condition severe enough to force him out of the navy with an 80 percent disability. Indeed, the prosecution was afraid Cheasty would have a heart attack under cross-examination; the witness carried nitroglycerine pills in his left coat pocket. As he began his cross-examination, Williams insinuated that Cheasty was not just a heart patient, but a dope addict. "Have you taken any form of narcotics?" he demanded. The prosecutor, Edward Troxell, came angrily to his feet. "I object, Your Honor. This is an infraction which is disgraceful!" The judge sustained the objection. Williams began questioning Cheasty about a "sidekick" named Jones, the same Jones "who was convicted of bigamy in New

York by the name of Joseph Leo Monaghan?'' Up again shot Troxell, spluttering, ''Disgraceful!'' Objection sustained. Had Cheasty tried to bribe the police in Miami in order to set up a friend in a ''gambling joint or illegal still?'' Williams inquired. ''No!'' declared Cheasty, straining in his chair.

In later years, the Hoffa trial would be remembered for its tawdry racial politics. Williams believed that a black jury would be more sympathetic to Hoffa, picturing him as a champion of the underdog. So Williams had used all of his sixteen peremptory challenges to keep whites off the jury. As a result, eight of the twelve jurors were black. As he warmed to his cross-examination of Cheasty, Williams played his first race card. He asked Cheasty if he had used a ''fictitious identity'' when he was ''employed by the City of Tallahassee to investigate the National Association for the Advancement of Colored People?'' ''I object to that!'' Troxell fairly shouted. Cheasty, however, remained calm and replied that, yes, he had used a fictitious name, but that he had recommended that the city abandon the color line and allow blacks to sit anywhere on the bus. Williams, sensing that his question had backfired, tried to cut him off, but Cheasty went on to describe brutal beatings of blacks, including the pistol whipping of an eighteen-year-old pregnant woman.

Williams, who had begun this line of inquiry, had the gall to move for a mistrial because of Cheasty's ''inflammatory statements.'' Judge Matthews was shocked by Williams's nerve. ''*You* have introduced this now, and now you are moving'' for a mistrial? she demanded. ''You could have avoided the whole thing.''

Williams tried a different tack. He began asking Cheasty if he had worked for both Hoffa and the Senate committee. Cheasty said that he was working for the Senate committee, and that Hoffa believed he was working for him. So you were *pretending* to work for Hoffa, Williams asked. Yes, said Cheasty. But you were not really working for him, said Williams. Then you were deceiving him. Cheasty fenced with Williams, but grudgingly he admitted that he had deceived Hoffa. You told him falsehoods, didn't you? pressed Williams. Well, yes, said Cheasty. Indeed you told him *lies* did you not? asked Williams. ''There were a few lies in there, yes, sir,'' said Cheasty. Then Williams stuck in the hook: ''By your standard of morals, sir, is there ever a time when it is moral to lie?'' he asked, in his most churchly voice.

Unable to stand any more, Troxell objected. Williams withdrew the question. But he had planted the idea in the minds of at least some jurors that Cheasty was not altogether trustworthy. Nor was he finished. He went on to hint that Cheasty might have been fired from a job because he padded an expense account. He asked Cheasty why he wore sunglasses to hide his face at all times, even on snowy nights. Slowly, steadily, Cheasty began to deteriorate on the stand, to lose his defiance and take on a slightly beaten-down countenance.

Late in the second day of cross-examination, Williams questioned Cheasty about a call he had made to his wife from the airport when his plane was late one night returning from Detroit. "What did your wife ask?" Williams inquired. "She wanted to know if I had taken up drinking again," said the exhausted Cheasty. Williams just let his answer hang in the air.

Read from a transcript thirty years later, Williams's cross-examination of Cheasty seems like one cheap shot after another, even given the rough and tumble of the adversary system. But as Williams swung his powerful body around in the warm courtroom of Judge Burnita Matthews in late June 1957, it is doubtful that he was worrying about the seemliness of his actions or abstract ethical considerations. He was looking for just one juror to hold out against conviction, and he was using every technique he knew. His next victim was Robert Kennedy. Hoffa had baited Williams before the trial. "Kennedy's a friend of yours so you'll go easy on him," Hoffa had teased. But Williams made Kennedy squirm. By his questions, he showed that Kennedy routinely leaked to the press, handing out committee documents to reporters from United Press, the *New York Herald Tribune,* the *New York Times,* Scripps Howard, the *Detroit Times,* Cowles Publications, and the *Washington Post.* If Kennedy were willing to be so indiscreet about the committee's internal workings, what was so sacrosanct about the documents that Cheasty had allegedly stolen? Why, Kennedy was so open that he had had dinner with Hoffa himself only a few weeks before Cheasty was arrested!

Williams had scored some points against the prosecution's case. He had also begun to rattle the prosecutor, the thin-faced, ramrod-straight Troxell. In a stage whisper, Williams baited and teased the prosecutor until Troxell finally complained to the bench (three decades later, Troxell still seethed over Williams, muttering that his opponent was "no lawyer"). But now it was time for Williams to put on his own case. The question for Williams was the difficult one faced by every defense lawyer: Should he put the defendant on the stand? A defendant, presumed innocent, is not required to testify; the prosecution has the burden of proving guilt. Troxell felt sure Williams would not let Hoffa testify. Williams, however, had been doing some research. He found that in almost every case where the defendant refused to take the stand, he was convicted. In practice if not in law, juries held a presumption of guilt. "Nowadays," Williams told a reporter, "if a defendant doesn't take the stand, he might as well take his toothbrush to court on the last day and say good-bye."

Defense lawyers are not supposed to suborn perjury—to incite their clients to lie on the stand. Generally speaking, Williams followed this rule, for practical as well as ethical reasons. "A lie is the prosecutor's best weapon to destroy you," he told his young associates. But most lawyers believe they have considerable leeway to help a client fashion a plausible story. Over the years, Williams proved extraordinarily adept at coaxing a defensible "theory" of the case out of a defendant without actually putting words in his mouth or making up the facts. In the case of Jimmy Hoffa, Hoffa could hardly deny certain facts: He had been photographed handing money to Cheasty. Why was Hoffa paying Cheasty? What did Hoffa *believe* he was hiring Cheasty to do? Did Hoffa even know that Cheasty was on the payroll of the Senate Rackets Committee? As Williams explored these questions with Hoffa, the Teamsters leader began to see the light. He told Williams what he wanted to hear, and then Williams helped him say it better. Again and again, the two men rehearsed the story until Hoffa could deliver it with complete sincerity.

Dressed in a light brown suit, white socks, and a white tie, the same uniform he wore all through the trial, the Teamsters boss seemed self-assured when he took the stand on July 16. He confidently pushed away the microphone. Why had he hired Cheasty? Williams asked. As a legman to help him prepare for the Senate Racket Committee hearings, Hoffa replied. Under oath, he said he had no idea that Cheasty worked for the committee. Cheasty, he testified, had told him that he got the information from newspapermen—buttressing the idea that Kennedy leaked like a sieve. Hoffa, with Williams's deft coaching, had found a clever way out of an airtight trap.

Troxell was caught totally by surprise. His cross-examination of Hoffa, lasting only thirty-two minutes, was feeble. Troxell's own colleagues were stunned when he sat down after failing to ask Hoffa about his criminal past. Sitting in the audience, young Vince Fuller watched in disbelief. It was as if the government had capitulated.

*   *   *

HOFFA CAME TO court every day accompanied by an entourage. "Hoffa had an army of supporters. They descended on the town like locusts," Williams later said, and were "constantly criticizing and second-guessing" Williams's trial strategy. Williams refused to let any of them sit at the counsel's table during trial. He explained that he wanted to sit alone so that it would appear that the prosecution's team of five lawyers was "ganging up" on him. In fact, he wanted to keep as much distance as possible between Hoffa's henchmen and himself.

Two weeks into the trial, a new face appeared in the front row of spectator seats occupied by Hoffa supporters. A black woman lawyer named Martha Jefferson had been flown in from Los Angeles to join the Hoffa defense team. According to an article in the *Washington Afro-American*, a black newspaper, the "pert" and "widely known" Miss Jefferson had come to assist "that widely known pro-labor barrister, Edward Bennett Williams, sometimes referred to as the Sir Galahad of the legal arena." The July 6, 1957, edition of the *Afro-American* carried a full-page advertisement identifying Hoffa as a "hard-hitting champion" for the "167,000 colored truck drivers in America." Prominently displayed with the ad was a picture of Miss Jefferson shaking hands with Williams. The government prosecutors quickly responded by hiring a black lawyer, Harry Alexander, for their side. U.S. attorney Oliver Gasch later conceded that Alexander's presence in the courtroom "may have been tit for tat. They had Jefferson; we had Alexander."

Cheap stunts, perhaps, but not egregious, at least by the norms of the criminal courtroom. But then the Hoffa team went way over the line. Copies of the *Afro-American* were delivered to all eight blacks on the jury. Judge Matthews was furious. Ordering that the jury be isolated from the public for the rest of the trial, she demanded to know how this could have happened. Williams pleaded complete innocence. He insisted that he didn't even know Jefferson's name; she was just a lawyer from some-where "out west." It was, he wrote in 1962, "the darkest day of my professional life. I have never before nor since been so upset about any incident connected with a trial." Williams *was* in fact innocent; thirty years later, even members of Hoffa's own entourage admitted that Williams had nothing to do with Jefferson or the *Afro-American* incident. William Bufalino, a Detroit lawyer who represented a local of jukebox employees and had himself been tried and acquitted on extortion charges, told the author that he had paid Miss Jefferson $5,000 to come to Washington.

Williams did bring to Washington a far more prominent black to sit in the courtroom: Joe Louis, the heavyweight boxing champion. Louis was listed as a potential character witness for Hoffa. It is somewhat doubtful that Williams ever really intended to call Louis to testify, since any questions about Hoffa's character would open the door to a dangerous line of inquiry. Indeed, two weeks into the trial Williams told the court that he did not plan to call any character witnesses after all. Nonetheless, the next day Louis still appeared in the courtroom.

What happened next would haunt Williams for the rest of his career. Outside the courtroom on the afternoon of July 15, Clark Mollenhoff, a reporter for the *Minneapolis Star Tribune,* who would win a Pulitzer the following year, stopped Louis in the hall to ask him why he was in town. "I'm just here to see what they are doing to my old friend, Jimmy Hoffa," said the Brown Bomber. Williams, who was standing nearby, joked, "We've got Joe down here to punch you in the nose." Louis drifted into the courtroom, and Jimmy Hoffa began chatting with Mollenhoff. Then, as the afternoon session was beginning, Hoffa walked into the courtroom. As he came to where Louis was seated, on an aisle seat to the right, the Teamsters leader clapped a hand on the big fighter's shoulder. Louis put his hand on Hoffa's arm, and the two chatted. Mollenhoff noticed a juror elbow his neighbor and point to this touching scene.

Mollenhoff's account, printed in his best-selling book *The Tentacles of Power,* became a legend that spread like a stain on Williams's reputation. "The Joe Louis incident" was used by Williams's detractors to picture him as a hustler, a gamesman who would stoop to low tricks to win. The story infuriated Williams. "It never happened!" he shouted at Robert Pack in 1981. "He never greeted Hoffa in the courtroom. That was hokum! One hundred percent hokum! It's all mythology. It just didn't happen. It's just bullshit." The prosecutors insist that it did happen, and so does Dave Previent, who was Jimmy Hoffa's general counsel. Even Williams's associate Vince Fuller agrees that Hoffa and Louis greeted each other in court, though he asserts that the jury was not in the courtroom at the time.

It was certainly Williams's idea to bring Louis into the courtroom to begin with, under the dubious prospect that he would be a character witness. But it is impossible to know whether Williams staged the warm greeting between Hoffa and the boxer. In his newspaper column a month

after the trial, Drew Pearson laid the responsibility for the stunt on Eddie
Cheyfitz. The idea may have come from one of Hoffa's hangers-on, a
former hoodlum named Barney Baker, who tried a similar ploy with
Monsignor George Higgins, a prominent Catholic priest in Washington.
Baker told Higgins that it would give Hoffa "a lot of consolation if you
could come sit down in the front row of the courtroom tomorrow."
Higgins replied that this was not the sort of "spiritual consolation" that
he gave out. It was Baker who made all the travel and lodging arrangements to bring Louis to Washington; he could have easily arranged the
courtroom scene as well.*

Interestingly, two of Williams's best friends think it entirely possible
that Williams set up the handshake. "It seems totally plausible," commented Father Bill Richardson, Williams's Holy Cross debating partner.
"This is the kind of thing we did. I can see him planting the idea then
having deniability." Ben Bradlee was more certain. "Oh shit, there's no
doubt in my mind who brought Louis in," he said. "Does he really deny
bringing Louis in? Oh, bullshit." The best evidence that Williams was
not responsible for the incident comes from his then law partner Tom
Wadden. The day of the incident, Wadden recalls, Williams returned to
the office furious at Hoffa and his men for pulling the stunt. "He was
ranting. If you've ever seen Ed mad, it's a terrifying . . . he runs around
and rants like a small child. He was mad at Jimmy, he was mad at
everybody."

By the last day of the trial, Williams was fairly well fed up with
Hoffa's men. In the courtroom after Judge Matthews had instructed the
jury, Mollenhoff approached Williams and asked him if he would defend
Hoffa in any more criminal cases. "I've about had it," Williams replied.
"I didn't know what I was getting into with Hoffa and his friends. You
get into a case like this, and it is hard to get out before it is over. It isn't
worth it. I can get plenty of other clients, and there won't be that bunch
of Teamsters second guessing every move."

Williams was drained by his two-hour final argument to the jury.
Troxell was as dull and plodding as ever. Williams had been theatrical
and passionate. He was brutal to Cheasty: ". . . from this man's lips we
learn that he lies. From this man's lips we learn that he falsifies. From this
man's lips we learn that he deceives. What kind of man is it who, while

---

*Louis later became a greeter at a casino owned by the Teamster. He married Martha Jefferson.

carrying a symbol of the truth, honesty, beauty, a symbol of faith some of us hold dear, the Rosary, can lie and deceive and falsify at the same time. . . .'' Hoffa was sainted: ''Ladies and gentlemen,'' Williams concluded, in his most solemn manner, ''Jimmy Hoffa has fought many battles for labor. He has fought for the people that he loves. He has fought with his head held high. He has fought with a mind and heart without fear, and he has never betrayed a trust. . . . Now he is in a fight for his own life. I ask you to send him back to the good fight.''

In the pressroom an hour later, columnist Murray Kempton typed, ''They will, in our lifetime, run excursion trains to Washington so that young lawyers can watch Edward Bennett Williams postpone the frying of some damned soul. To watch Williams and then to watch a Department of Justice lawyer contending with him is to understand the essential superiority of free enterprise to government ownership.''

That night, Kempton got drunk with Williams at the Metropolitan Club. Kempton had observed that Hoffa was an arrogant little dictator who had failed to show much appreciation for Williams's miracles on his behalf. After Williams had made two jurors weep during his opening argument (compelling Troxell to ask the judge to instruct the jury that this was not a capital case, there was no risk that the defendant could be hanged), Hoffa had groused to his entourage, ''Is that all Williams is going to say about this fraud and deceit?'' Hoffa greeted his lawyer coldly when he finished. Hoffa, remarked Kempton, ''would treat St. Peter like a headwaiter.''

Williams just shook his head. He was so exhausted he could barely see. ''You know, Jimmy is just like Joe McCarthy. If he beats this case, he'll be like a guy who jumped out a sixth-floor window and survived. He'll take the elevator up to the eighth floor and jump again.'' Williams turned to Eddie Cheyfitz. ''There's no saving this guy, Eddie,'' said Williams. ''He's just like Joe. He's a jumper.''

At 3:45 the next afternoon, the jury acquitted Hoffa on all counts. The labor skates in the courtroom began to cheer wildly; Judge Matthews ineffectually banged her gavel for silence. Williams rested his forehead on the counsel table and said a prayer. Hoffa got up and walked toward the exit, waving at the jury. ''If one of you boys ever drives a truck, just give me a call,'' he yelled across the courtroom. Hoffa had not a word of thanks for his lawyer. (When Williams described Hoffa's ingratitude to Frank Costello, the Mafia don replied, ''I told you Hoffa was no gentleman.'' Still, Costello was pleased with the verdict: He had bet $1,000 at a hundred to one odds on an acquittal and he used the $100,000 to pay his own legal fee to Williams.)

Bobby Kennedy was sitting behind the rostrum at a Rackets Committee hearing over at the Capitol when the verdict came in. An aide slipped him a note with the bad news; the young gangbuster looked "deathly sick," wrote Mollenhoff. Bob Scott—the same friend who had heard Williams say he was "going to the candles" on the eve of trial—reached Williams by telephone shortly before midnight. He sounded "drunk as a skunk," Scott recalled. "Bobby Kennedy said he'd jump off the Capitol if Hoffa won," Williams exuberantly exclaimed to Scott, "and I'm going to send him a parachute!" (Williams actually did.)

Jimmy Hoffa was now free to take over the Teamsters—and their multimillion-dollar pension fund. John Cye Cheasty was ruined; he had trouble getting work and ended up eking out a living on his navy pension. Williams's performance was called "dazzling" by *Time* magazine. "He is Washington's cleverest and busiest criminal lawyer." But for the first time ever, he also began to get some bad publicity. Newspaper reporters in that era tended to be malleable and far too cozy with their sources. Williams was able to count on his many friends in the press to protect him. One of the more powerful, Arthur Krock of the *New York Times*, managed to persuade Bobby Kennedy to delete from his book about labor racketeering, *The Enemy Within*, an unflattering reference to Williams. Even so, the grumbling of other lawyers about Williams's zeal in the Hoffa case made its way into the newspapers. "Hoffa Lawyer's Halo Tarnished" read a headline in the *New York Mirror*. Drew Pearson chastised Williams for playing the race card, and Williams did not help his own case by bragging to Joe DiMaggio and Ed Wynn at a bar one night that "Joe Louis and I beat the Hoffa rap." The remark was picked up in a gossip column and spread around town.

Williams had difficulty coming down from the case. It was "as though I had the bends," he later told *Life* magazine. "I couldn't sleep. I went to movies and sat through double features and came out without knowing what I'd seen. I tried a drink—one was enough to make me dizzy." When he sobered up, the first thing he did was to set about repairing his reputation.

Chapter Ten

WILLIAMS WAS BEGINNING to feel a chill from his own church. *America,* the influential Jesuit weekly, assessed the roles of the three Catholics in the Hoffa case—Williams, Cheasty, and Kennedy—and concluded: "In view of the nature of the defense conducted by Edward Bennett Williams, Hoffa's lawyer, our sympathy goes out to Mr. Kennedy." Ethel Kennedy had been upset by Williams's tough cross-examination of her husband at the trial. "They have no right to ask him those questions!" she exclaimed to reporters after Williams grilled Kennedy about leaking to the press. (Even Williams later admitted that he may have "overcompensated" in the cross-examination because Hoffa had baited him about his friendship with Kennedy.)

Now, playing the sort of hardball more normally associated with her husband, Mrs. Kennedy put pressure on Georgetown to fire Williams as the university's counsel. After uneasy internal debate, Georgetown kept Williams on. But over at Catholic University, Father Maurice Sheehy, the university's head of religious studies, attacked Williams for representing Frank Costello, telling Williams, "You ruined your life the day you took on that man." In New York, Fordham University, a Jesuit institution, responded to Williams's successful defense of Jimmy Hoffa by canceling a lecture Williams was supposed to give.

To be sure, Williams's notoriety had given him some social cachet. He and Dorothy were invited to the big, somewhat impersonal parties give by professional Washington hostess Gwen Cafritz. In the same society-page column that described "Jackie [Kennedy] in a short, pale blue taille that simply shouted Paris" at a Cafritz party in June 1957, Williams was referred to as "effervescent young Edward Bennett Williams, nationally famous criminal lawyer." But Williams was still shunned by the upper reaches of society. At Dorothy's urging, Williams asked their neighbor, Tom Taylor, to put them up for the Chevy Chase Club, the city's most exclusive country club. Taylor bluntly advised, "Don't make the run. You will get slaughtered." Williams insisted, and Taylor gathered up the necessary letters of recommendation. Williams heard nothing from the club for several years. Finally, he withdrew the application. He professed not to care. "Country clubs!" he exclaimed to *Washington Post* reporter Jim Clayton in 1959. "What the hell is that?" But when a friend asked him why he had not joined Chevy Chase, he replied with some bitterness, "You could start a pretty good club with all the people that have been rejected by that place."

Williams was also blackballed by the Lawyers' Club, a stuffy dinner group for members of the Washington bar—none of them criminal lawyers. Just going out for dinner could be an inquisition for Williams after the Hoffa verdict. "There was a tremendous groundswell of anger, of ostracism. Somebody was always saying something," Williams told Clayton in an unpublished interview in 1959. Williams had a "hell of a fight" one night with Chalmers Roberts of the *Post* at a lawn party in Bethesda. Roberts's wife asked Williams how he could represent Hoffa, and Williams, who had already consumed several drinks, "got angry about it. I got muscular instead of just saying I was defending a client. I started to take the offensive." The next day, Williams felt bad enough to send a letter of apology.

LAWYERS ARE OFTEN asked how they can defend the guilty. To laymen, the question is valid and troubling, a genuine moral issue. To Williams, however, the question was mostly an annoyance—a nuisance, not a cause for soul-searching. He was no different from other criminal lawyers in this respect. "The fundamental mindset of most criminal defense lawyers toward defending the guilty is one of staggering indifference to the question," writes Stanford Law School professor Barbara Babcock, who worked for Williams in the sixties. Some years after Clarence Darrow won an acquittal in a famous case, an acquaintance asked him if the defendant had committed the crime. Williams understood perfectly his hero's response: "I don't know," replied Darrow. "I never asked him."

There are a number of reasons for this lawyerly indifference toward the question of guilt, and Williams invoked all of them at one time or another. Some lawyers embrace the high moral purpose of defending the Bill of Rights. The criminal defense attorney is not just defending a criminal, the argument goes, he is defending the Sixth Amendment right to counsel, the Fourth Amendment freedom from unreasonable search and seizure, and the Fifth Amendment right against incrimination. By defending the rights of the accused, he is defending all of our rights. Williams went to great lengths to wrap himself in this mantle.

Then there is what Babcock calls the "legalistic-positivist approach." This attitude holds that truth cannot really be known, that facts are evanescent, that guilt is not the truth but merely a legal conclusion. Williams liked to draw the distinction between *legal* guilt and *moral* guilt. The latter, he liked to say with appropriate reverence, "I leave to the majestic vengeance of God."

Some criminal defense lawyers, particularly politically active ones, claim they are defending the poor and the downtrodden by representing criminal defendants who are often poor themselves and, in some sense, the "victims" of society. By giving the poor all the legal protections enjoyed by the rich, a criminal defense lawyer works against alienation and class resentment and thus fosters respect for the "system." As a young man, Williams held himself out as the protector of the downtrodden. As he got older and politically more conservative, and as his clientele became increasingly wealthy, this justification became unavailable to him. But he always viewed himself as someone ready to help those in great need.

In his more candid moments, Williams would admit that the real reason he loved criminal law was that it was dramatic and exciting—much more fun than the dreary work lawyers usually do and Williams once did, such as trying insurance cases. Williams loved winning above all else, and winning at trial is particularly sweet for the criminal defense attorney. It is public and final: There is no appeal from a "not guilty" verdict. Although Williams made a great fetish out of "contest living" in his later years, he was careful not to advertise himself as an egotist early in his career. The image he sought to present was not that of a quick-draw gunslinger, but rather the thoughtful guardian of an individual's constitutionally guaranteed rights.

Before the Hoffa trial, Williams had begun giving speeches to bar groups and journalists about the right to counsel. It was his way of rebutting what he called "guilt by client." In a speech to the New York State Bar Association in January of 1957, he warned that this "insidious identification" would scare off lawyers from "standing by the unpopular or degraded." In a metaphor that he would use again and again, Williams said, "When a doctor takes out Earl Browder's appendix, nobody suggests that the doctor is a Communist. When a lawyer represents Browder [the head of the American Communist party], everybody decides that lawyer must be a Communist, too." Williams added, "I don't take clients on the basis of their politics or religion or their color or the social obnoxiousness of their activities. Those are matters of complete indifference to me."

In the month after the Hoffa trial, Williams decided to take his Sixth Amendment sermon on the road. He signed up to give a series of lectures at nine different law schools, including Harvard, Georgetown, and the University of Virginia. In Gaston Hall at Georgetown, a Jesuit priest asked him how he could defend the likes of Frank Costello and Jimmy Hoffa. Williams responded that "Nothing that I ever learned at Georgetown convinced me that I was unethical." At Harvard, a snide law student with a society drawl accosted him: "Tell me, Mr. Williams, did you feel proud of having Joe Louis make an appearance at the Hoffa trial?" Williams looked down at this young man in his tweed jacket and club tie. "Truthfully, no," Williams deadpanned. "I wanted Floyd Patterson." The audience roared. Williams had the flu that evening and his mood was sardonic. Another hostile young barrister inquired, "When you defend a man whom you feel is guilty and you get an acquittal, how do you feel?" "Wonderful," Williams replied sarcastically, "just wonderful."

To deflect the charge that he was a mouthpiece for criminals, Williams identified himself with liberal institutions that protected civil liberties and civil rights. The day after Frank Costello was released from jail, Williams joined the board of the American Civil Liberties Union (ACLU). After the Hoffa trial, Williams became the chairman of the D.C. Bar Association Committee on Civil Rights. He did not actually *do* much for either organization, however. "He was very anxious to be on the board. It was key to his rehabilitation campaign," said the former director of the ACLU's Washington office, Irving Ferman. "But he never came to any meetings. Peter Malen, the executive director of the ACLU, was suspicious. He thought Williams and Eddie Cheyfitz were trying to use the ACLU to serve their personal ends." In later years, Williams liked to say that he had played a leading role in integrating the D.C. bar. But several lawyers active in the fight dispute this. "Ed was just a front," says Superior Court Judge Paul McArdle, a former president of the D.C. bar. "He was a name. He did no lobbying." When a dissident group brought a legal challenge to the D.C. bar's decision to accept black lawyers, Williams was one of three lawyers chosen to defend the bar association in court. But Williams was a "no show," says Howard Westwood, one of the three. "I never had one lifted finger from Ed Williams. He was conspicuously absent."

Williams had some of the prejudices of a poor Irish boy from Hartford, and in private he would call blacks "shines" and "spades." But for his time he was liberal on the subject of race. He vocally opposed the legal inequality that still existed in the 1950s. He thought it was "disgraceful" that schools, jobs, and housing were segregated. He quietly consulted with senators like Estes Kefauver on civil rights reform legislation and publicly lobbied for a fair-housing law in nearby Baltimore. Through his criminal law practice, Williams saw firsthand how unfairly the system treated blacks. In the winter of 1958, he was visited by an agitated young black man who had been swept up in a dragnet after a local restaurant was robbed by three men. This young man had been one of ninety blacks between the ages of fifteen and twenty-three thrown in jail for the night (those who complained to the police that they would lose their jobs if they failed to show up on time were told "That's too bad"). Arrested as he left a movie theater, the young man had been released, after the morning line-up, to his worried parents, but he was still stricken with shame and fear. The reason went right to Williams's heart: The young man wanted to be a lawyer, and he was sure that having an arrest on his record would disqualify him.

Williams did not like to be called a "criminal lawyer." He called himself a "trial lawyer who practices criminal law." At a time when criminal lawyers were regarded with contempt, the distinction was important. But Williams was willing to stand up for the criminal bar. In 1958, a criminal lawyer named Sam Dash—who would later become a television hero as the chief counsel of the Senate Watergate Committee—formed a National Association of Criminal Lawyers. "We were the dregs, the loners, so we formed this group to bolster the morale of criminal lawyers and give them some respectability," Dash recalled. "We asked Williams to join us and he did." Williams did not do a whole lot for the new association, but he didn't have to. "He was the model," said Dash.

"He represented what we were looking for. He was not a shyster or a mouthpiece. He was dignified and prepared."

He was also extremely visible. "Defending the Unpopular" was the headline in *Life* magazine in October 1957. In the article, Williams tried to elevate criminal lawyers to make them look like saints among thieves. "The trouble is that the defense of liberty has lost its prestige," he said grandly. "The defense of property pays off better in dollars and cents, and so we lawyers have become a profession of business negotiators and hand-holders." Yet the article also reported that Williams's salary in the "defense of liberty" was $150,000 a year, and the photographs showed him living a life at once glamorous and purposeful. The three-page spread in the magazine, with its circulation of 5 million, showed pictures of Williams consulting with Jimmy Hoffa and Frank Costello, laughing it up with Toots Shor and Joe DiMaggio, taking a call in the elegant apartment of actress Faye Emerson, meeting late at night at the office of the ACLU, and advising a Catholic priest at Georgetown, as well as some more homey shots of him playing with his dog and his children.

Williams was laying it on for *Life*. The reality was he spent a lot more time at Toots Shor's than he did at the ACLU. But the image was convincing. Mario Cuomo was a law clerk that autumn, just out of St. John's Law School. "You've got to remember what he was to us young lawyers," Cuomo recalled thirty years later. "Lawyers had been stained by association with crime. But Edward Bennett Williams made representation what it was supposed to be. He elevated the whole system by the way he did it. He seemed like a family man, a good Catholic, upright, full of integrity." Yale Kamisar was a young law student at the University of Minnesota. "Most criminal lawyers were not scholars, but Williams was," he said. "He was thorough and most aren't. He was respectable and most aren't." Williams's example inspired Kamisar to devote himself to the rights of the criminally accused. Kamisar, Henry King Ransom Professor of Law at the University of Michigan, is now a nationally recognized authority on the Constitution.

Williams could turn around the most hardened skeptic. In 1965, Warren Burger, then a strict law-and-order judge on the U.S. Court of Appeals for the District of Columbia, was charged with writing a new set of ethical standards for the criminal courts. "Burger thought criminal lawyers had horns and tails," said Sam Dash, whom Burger had hired as a consultant. "He believed that criminal lawyers routinely counseled their clients and witnesses to commit perjury." Dash told Burger, "Ed

Williams doesn't." Burger did not believe him, so Dash arranged a meeting between the celebrated criminal lawyer and the future chief justice of the Supreme Court. "Ed put on a show," recalled Dash. "He told Burger, 'I never put on a client to lie. I tell them that I only present the facts and the law. If they don't like it, then here's the door.' " Burger was tremendously impressed by the presentation. His report proceeded to describe criminal lawyers as pillars of the system, held to the kind of high ethical standard exemplified by Ed Williams.

BOBBY KENNEDY HAD a less exalted view of Williams. After Hoffa's stunning acquittal, Kennedy became obsessed with getting the Teamsters leader, and Williams remained a significant obstacle in his path. Williams refused to represent Hoffa in any more criminal matters, but as a reward for getting Hoffa off on the bribery charge, he had been made general counsel of the Teamsters Union on a $50,000-a-year retainer.* Williams continued to appear with Hoffa as union counsel before the Senate Rackets Committee, where he often sparred with Kennedy. When Kennedy bore in on Hoffa in his flat, nasal Boston accent, Williams sniped back at the committee counsel for his "reckless charges." There was no doubt whom Kennedy was referring to when he publicly stated, "The two hundred lawyers who take their money from the Teamsters are legal prostitutes. . . . Most of them are criminal lawyers. They spend their time trying to keep Mr. Hoffa in office rather than representing the union membership."

Hoffa had been overwhelmingly elected president of the Teamsters two months after his acquittal, but the election was rigged: Hoffa's goons poured bagfuls of the opposition's ballots down a hotel laundry chute. Working closely with Kennedy, a group of dissidents challenged the election with a lawsuit. In two months of secret meetings with the dissidents, Williams hammered out a compromise: Hoffa would keep his title, but three monitors—one appointed by the dissidents, one by Hoffa, and one acceptable to both sides—would "supervise" the union. The swing vote, the "outside" monitor, was a Georgetown professor named Martin O'Donoghue. At first, Williams thought O'Donoghue would be

---

*Hoffa faced various criminal proceedings in New York, Tennessee, and Florida at the time, but Williams could not have ethically represented both Hoffa and the union, in part because Hoffa was accused of stealing from the union. "I had to choose the individual or the institution," Williams told newspaperman Frank Waldrop, "and I figured the institution would last longer."

easy to deal with, since he was a former general counsel of the Teamsters and an old friend. But O'Donoghue turned out to be a crusader for reform who wanted to clean up the union. Hoffa, not surprisingly, bitterly resisted.

Publicly, Williams posed as a union reformer. "What the labor movement needs now is a moral czar," he told a magazine reporter in January 1958. His model was Kenesaw Mountain Landis, who cleaned up professional baseball after the Black Sox scandal of the 1920s. "I'm not sure I'd take the job, but I might," Williams said modestly. "It would be an important thing." But within the councils of the Teamsters, Williams was hardly a crusader. "We were convinced that there was a lot of corruption in the locals, but Ed didn't push for reform," said Ray Bergan, a Georgetown law grad who had gone to work in Williams's firm. "Ed was a great compromiser. He was Henry Clay." He agreed with Hoffa that the monitors had no right to dictate morality to the union. But he urged Hoffa, whose machismo made him totally inflexible, to give a little. The monitors would go out of existence in a year, he told Hoffa. Anyone can get along for a year.

Williams himself was finding it increasingly difficult to get along with Hoffa. The Teamster boss continued to treat Williams like a doorman. "Jimmy liked to get the upper hand over people with education who were taller," said Joseph Konowe, Hoffa's administrative assistant. "Don't yell at your attorneys, Jimmy!" Williams would snap at Hoffa. "If it wasn't for your attorneys, you wouldn't be here." Williams got so riled up in one shouting match that he broke a blood vessel under his eye. His humor did not improve when it was widely rumored that Hoffa had given him a shiner in a fistfight.

The breaking point came one day when Williams handed Hoffa some papers, and the Teamster boss threw them across the table and onto the floor. "Pick them up," said Hoffa. "Not me," said Williams. He walked out and drafted a letter of resignation. The news that Williams was planning to quit leaked to the press, and he reconsidered. The $50,000-a-year retainer was hard to give up. Williams's solution was to do very little Teamsters work himself, instead letting his associate Ray Bergan deal with Hoffa and the union. Williams barely spoke to Hoffa after 1959, but his firm represented the Teamsters for another fifteen years.

*   *   *

THAT YEAR, THE Teamsters connection again caused grief for Williams. The episode occurred after Eddie Cheyfitz died of a sudden heart attack in May, 1959. The Washington PR man and fixer had become a close friend of Williams's, but he also left behind a tangled mess that would produce a charge, sworn under oath before the Senate Rackets Committee, that Edward Bennett Williams had offered a bribe.

In his effort to oust Hoffa as head of the union, Bobby Kennedy had made a strange alliance with a man named Godfrey Schmidt, a fierce anti-Communist who had founded Aware Inc. to catch "pinko" movie producers and organized Ten Million Americans Mobilizing for Justice to save Joe McCarthy from censure by the Senate. At Kennedy's urging, Schmidt had brought suit on behalf of Teamster dissidents challenging Hoffa's election as union president. As part of the settlement, Schmidt had been appointed one of the three monitors to oversee the union.

In the summer of 1959, what Schmidt wanted most from the Teamsters was to be paid. The father of six, he was so broke that his electricity had been turned off. He sued the Teamsters for $105,000 in legal fees for the dissidents' case and $45,000 in back pay for serving as a monitor. The Teamsters refused to pay him the legal fees, and claimed that his salary demands were excessive, since they had already paid him $35,000. To collect the rest of the money, Schmidt hired Bartley Crum, a well-known New York lawyer who had represented William Randolph Hearst and Rita Hayworth.

At a hearing before the Senate Rackets Committee on July 13, Crum made a sensational charge. He alleged that Eddie Cheyfitz had offered Schmidt a deal: If the pro-dissident lawyer would resign as a monitor, the Teamsters would pay his legal fees. He then charged that four days before the hearing, Williams had offered to pay Schmidt's fees the very next day if Crum would not appear before the Rackets Committee. This, said Crum, was "an immoral exercise of power." Committee chairman John McClellan of Arkansas cautioned Crum that he was making a "pretty serious charge," and reminded him that he was under oath. "Well," said Crum, "it is the truth."

Williams's large face turned beet red with anger. Grabbing the microphone, he demanded to testify immediately in response. His intensity seemed to border on "ferocity," wrote *Washington Star* reporter Mary McGrory, who noted that Williams was so agitated that he didn't even bother to put down the cigarette he was holding when he raised his right hand to be sworn. "I have a reputation," he began, barely able to contain his fury. "I am not going to allow it to go without being defended against [the] false, vicious, and contrived smear that I have heard here this afternoon." He flatly denied that he had offered Schmidt any inducement to resign or had in any way tried to stop Crum from testifying. Williams fenced with Bobby Kennedy, who saw a chance to wound his antagonist. When Kennedy appeared shocked at Williams's conduct, Williams took a dig at Kennedy's lack of legal experience: "I'm not surprised you don't understand it, Mr. Kennedy," he said sarcastically, "but I hope the lawyers of the committee will."

After the hearing, which was front-page news all over the country, Williams said he was in "agony." He met Crum again a few days later in the chambers of Supreme Court Justice Felix Frankfurter, who was holding a conference on the Teamsters case. Williams blurted out, "How could you have done this thing? How in the name of God could you have perjured yourself and slandered me in this way?" Meekly, Crum responded, "I didn't mean it to come out that way." Frankfurter, who was listening, said, "Then you go correct it." Crum did. He went to Williams's office and signed an affidavit withdrawing his charge that Williams had offered a bribe. Williams made the affidavit available to the *Washington Post*, which wrote an editorial entitled "About Face" chastising Crum for smearing Williams.

What really happened? Since the principals are now all dead, it is impossible to know for sure. Crum was not the most reliable witness: According to Williams, he was an alcoholic who was having mental problems. He died five months after his spectacular charge, leaving no will and an estate of only $16,000—a small sum for a well-known lawyer who had won a million-dollar divorce judgment for Rita Hayworth against the Aly Kahn. On the other hand, Cheyfitz and Williams may have seen the Teamsters' fee dispute with Godfrey Schmidt as a lever to get the pro-dissident lawyer to resign. Such a move would be ethically reprehensible, but Williams, in the spring and summer of 1959, was a man on the edge.

Chapter Eleven

IN OCTOBER 1958, as Williams was fencing with Hoffa and trying to decide whether to quit the Teamsters, a *Washington Post* reporter observed in the young lawyer's hazel eyes "a weary sense of strain." Williams began talking to the reporter about his philosophy of life. "If a man does a brilliant job and loses, people don't say he is brilliant. They say he lost. This is the price of reputation. My friend, Joe DiMaggio, and I have talked about it often." Williams, the *Post* reported, "shrugged in his Ivy League suit, drained his whiskey glass, and lit another cigarette." Success, he said, is like a "narcotic." He was an addict. "Now you're the champ, now you must never lose," said Williams. "The thought of any single failure becomes immense."

To every celebrated scoundrel in the country, Williams had become the man to see. After New England industrialist Bernard Goldfine gave Sherman Adams a vicuña coat, causing a scandal that brought down President Eisenhower's chief of staff, the government found that Goldfine had evaded about a million dollars in taxes. Goldfine hired Williams to defend him in November 1958. So did Adam Clayton Powell, the flamboyant congressman and pastor of Harlem's First Abyssinian Baptist Church, who was indicted for tax evasion. To handle these clients, as well as several others, Williams had to travel constantly. In February 1959, he flew to New York to see Powell, to Boston to confer with Goldfine, across the country to San Francisco and Los Angeles to meet with two other tax clients, to Florida for a Teamsters convention, and to Atlanta to see Frank Costello, who was back in jail. His schedule, Williams told a newspaper reporter, was "normal."

His resting place was as often Toots Shor's in New York as it was at home with Dorothy in Tulip Hill. The male camaraderie and boozy jollity allowed Williams to slough off, for an evening, the terrible burden of "contest living." He had become a center of attraction at Shor's. Leonore Lemmon would regale the regulars with a little ditty she composed about him: "Oh, there is scarcely a gangster now alive / Who has not dialed Metropolitan eight, six five, six five!" (ME 8-6565 was Williams's office phone number in Washington.) One night, Toots Shor was arrested for hitting a customer, a loud tourist who had mistaken Shor's restaurant for a public accommodation. The arresting officer was a beat cop who did not quite appreciate the rules of conduct in saloon high society, circa 1958. Shor was immediately released, and after the restaurant closed that night, a mock trial was held. Shor was the defendant. Williams was his lawyer. The presiding judge was the New York police commissioner, Stephen Patrick Kennedy, a crony of Shor's. With much hilarity, Shor was convicted, despite Williams's impassioned defense. Shor became a real client of Williams's as well, though not as lucrative as some. When one of Shor's waiters got arrested for beating up a patron, the saloon owner called Williams at 6:00 A.M. "For chrissakes, Toots, there are a million lawyers in New York. Why are you calling me at this hour?" Shor answered, "Because you don't charge me."

Williams liked performing small legal services for celebrities. When actress Faye Emerson wanted a divorce from bandleader Skitch Henderson in 1957, Williams represented her. He also openly flirted with her. A Broadway actress and television "personality" who made B-movies (*A Coffin for Demetrius* with Peter Lorre), Emerson was a poor girl from Texas who had shed her panhandle accent and acquired a veneer of sophistication. Wearing her blond hair in a trademark bun, she was elegantly dressed and cocktail-party literate. She could be tough; if a man was rude in the bar, she would pour her drink into his lap. Once married to FDR's son Elliot Roosevelt, she had entree into café society (a close friend was Marie Morgan, granddaughter of J.P.) and liked to entertain at her town house, where she served scrambled eggs and Bobby Short played the piano, after midnight. Emerson introduced Williams to Eleanor Roosevelt; Williams introduced her to professional boxing. As Emerson sat beside him at ringside at Uhline Arena before a fight in the late fifties, the usher informed her that women were not allowed to sit in the first row.

Emerson looked up from under her designer hat and remembered her Texas accent. "Go fuck yerself," she drawled.

Emerson also had a boyfriend, a handsome ex-marine named Jack Walker, who lived with the actress at her town house on 61st Street. In the summer of 1958, Emerson told Walker that she was driving that night up to Boston with Williams. Walker had drunk a few cocktails and he was the jealous type. "Why are you doing this?" he asked. Emerson said she felt sorry for Williams, that he was lonely and trapped in a bad marriage. "That sounded like a line of shit to me," Walker later said. When Williams arrived around 8:00 P.M., Walker grabbed a small paring knife and announced, "I'll kill the son of a bitch!"* After a tense moment at the doorway, Emerson calmed Walker down, and Williams drove her to Boston. He was on his way up to New Hampshire to join his family at Dorothy's parents' house.

In the winter of 1959, Williams developed an infatuation with a glamorous divorcée named Jean Barry Pochna. The daughter of a Cornell football star, Mrs. Pochna, née McCormick, was "real lace" Irish, raised in a home with marble fireplaces and a membership at Longwood Country Club in Massachusetts. Her first husband was a lawyer for J. Paul Getty and Aristotle Onassis; her sons' godfathers were Prince Rainier of Monaco and Gen. Walter Bedell Smith, Eisenhower's wartime aide-de-camp. In a gossip column announcing Pochna's separation from her husband in October 1958, "Suzy" described her as "one of Europe's foremost hostesses" who gave "celebrity-studded parties" at Villa de Iris, her home in the South of France. She had moved into a suite at the Pierre when she met Williams through their mutual friend Leonore Lemmon.

"Madcap" was the word gossip columnists of the day used to describe people such as Lemmon and Pochna. Williams was traveling to New York so much that he had rented an apartment at 55th Street and Lexington Avenue, and he gave both Lemmon and Pochna keys. The two party girls were appalled by the taste of the decorator Williams had hired. On the wall of the living room were the initials EBW in six-inch-high

---

*Four years later, as Walker entered P.J. Clarke's, another New York saloon, a very drunk Williams threw an arm around him. "This SOB tried to kill me one night!" he exclaimed to a group of drinking buddies seated nearby. Williams was laughing. He wrote down his phone number on a waiter's ordering pad and gave the slip to Walker, who carried it in his wallet for the next thirty years. "If you ever need help, just call me," Williams told him. "Ed loved it that he had made me jealous," Walker said.

brass letters. "It was too tacky," Pochna recalled, "so we took it down." But when they removed the initials from the wall, there were three large plaster holes. The solution: the girls went over to P.J. Clarke's, only a couple of blocks away, and stole a photograph of a fighter named Little Abe off the wall. Pochna carried it out under her coat and hung it where the initials used to be.

Pochna and Williams began having late night adventures together. Williams had become a close friend of Sugar Ray Robinson, the middle-weight boxing champion, and one night in the winter of 1959 they went up to a nightclub that Sugar Ray owned in Harlem. Pochna taught Williams the words to "Mack the Knife," and the lawyer became so inspired by the music and flowing alcohol that he climbed up onto the stage and began playing the drums, to the astonishment of the band. "When he was drinking," Pochna recalled, "he'd do anything." Including get into fights: At an after-hours bottle club in Washington, Williams got into a wrestling match with sportswriter and novelist (*Something of Value*) Robert Ruark, who was also courting Mrs. Pochna. Williams accused Ruark of living most of the year in Spain to avoid taxes. Ruark retorted that Williams was "into mob money." Williams jumped Ruark; Duke Ziebert, the owner of the restaurant across the street, pulled the two apart before they could do much damage.

Williams was increasingly manic in the winter of 1959, wooing Lemmon, Emerson, and Pochna on successive nights. Echoing Lemmon, Pochna recalled, "I don't think sex was that important to him. He didn't have a big drive." Williams was often too drunk to perform, she said, which she added was not altogether unusual for nightclubbing men in that heavy-drinking era. But while Williams would take her to bed and inef-fectually fumble when he was drunk late at night, he never made a pass while he was sober. "He could have made the scene before cocktails, like other men, but he didn't," she said. Several women who had romantic flirtations with Williams echoed the same theme about his sexual reti-cence. "He loved to touch, he loved to talk about sex, to say he wanted to go to bed," said one. "But he wasn't really interested."

With Lemmon, Williams would sometimes become maudlin. "Booze and nerves would give him crocodile tears," she recalled. He was frus-trated by the troubles of his son Jobie. "I can't get to him," he would say to Lemmon, throwing up his arms in despair, not acknowledging that one reason he couldn't reach the boy was because he rarely saw him. When Williams was especially drunk, Lemmon recalled, he would propose marriage—not only to her, but to Faye Emerson as well. "He'd ask us to marry him," Lemmon recalled. " 'Yes, dear,' we'd say. It got to be a joke. He was crazy." Lemmon said to Williams, "How can you do this to your wife?" Full of grief, guilt, and booze, Williams once responded, "She's going to die."

Dorothy Williams was, in fact, dying. She had been dying, very slowly, for years. Her asthma and recurrent bronchitis had progressively damaged her lungs. In the early fifties, Dorothy had been faced with a difficult choice: The doctors had told her that they could put her on steroids and cortisone to keep down the wheezing and help her breathe, but the medication would reduce her immunities and make her more susceptible to infection. With two little children, Dorothy wanted to be active; she had always fought her disabilities. She chose the medication. "But every time she got a cold, it went into her lungs," said her sister Betty. "She was terrified of pneumonia." Both Williams and his wife knew that Dorothy's life would not be a long one. In 1958, they adopted a third child, Bennett, "so Dorothy could have a baby," said Betty. "She loved babies and Ed thought it would make her happy."

In the early spring of 1959, while Williams was away on business, Dorothy had to rush a sick child to the doctor. Driving a convertible with the top down, she got caught in a downpour and came down with a bad cold. A chest surgeon cleared her lungs, but he couldn't combat her infection with the antibiotics available at the time. Her lungs filled with fluid again. She was sent to the hospital and put in an oxygen tent, where she begged the doctors to suck out her lungs with a bronchioscope, a very risky and painful treatment.

Williams escaped from the horror of his wife's slow drowning by plunging into work. He spent much of the spring of 1959 trying to get Bernard Goldfine out of jail. Few clients were less deserving. A textile manufacturer who handed out bribes like tips, Goldfine had two senators and a governor on his payroll, as well as President Eisenhower's chief of staff, Sherman Adams. After refusing to answer questions about his influence-buying schemes at a circuslike congressional hearing in the fall of 1958, Goldfine had gone to jail for contempt. Williams went to court in April 1959 to get him out. His defense was that Goldfine had been illegally bugged by a congressional committee staffer and investigative reporter Jack Anderson, who had eavesdropped on Goldfine with an electronic recording device from an adjacent hotel room.

Williams's actions that spring show a man under terrible strain. First of

all, he tried to cut an ethically questionable deal with columnist friend
Drew Pearson, who was Jack Anderson's boss. He offered to leak to
Pearson any inside news he picked up about the Sherman Adams situation
if, in return, Anderson would testify that his eavesdropping had produced
the evidence that Congress used to question Goldfine. Although Pearson
rarely turned down a cozy deal with a source, he balked at this one.

When Anderson took the stand, Williams again made the amateur's
blunder: He asked Anderson a question without first knowing the answer.
Williams demanded to know just what Anderson had heard when he
eavesdropped on Goldfine's hotel room. Anderson told him: Goldfine
arguing with his wife about his adultery with a showgirl. The courtroom
tittered with laughter. Williams risked contempt of court by exposing a
confidential file that one of his many sources in the police department had
given to him. And then, in the most bizarre scene, he tried to interrogate
a witness in the hospital. Tom LaVenia, a congressional investigator, was
lying sick in his bed when Williams came in the door and began quizzing
him. "I will say this, he was pretty strong on that visit, pecking away [at
LaVenia] at the hospital . . ." LaVenia testified. A nurse had to ask
Williams to leave.

Down the hospital hall from LaVenia's room, Dorothy Williams lay
near death. Robert Maheu recalls Williams in a panic, telling him that his
wife had decided not to fight anymore. He had to rush to the hospital to
change her mind, he said. In her hospital room, Dorothy had asked that
the oxygen tent be unzipped so she could reach out her hand to her
daughter, Ellen, who was four years old. "I can't say good-bye," she
wept.

"The last two weeks were sheer terror," said Betty Killay. "But at the
end, she calmed," and tried to make light of the fact that she had become
a morphine addict. Death came early Sunday morning on May 10, 1959.
Dorothy's mother answered the phone call from the hospital. Williams
heard the phone ring and came into the kitchen in his pajamas. His head
dropped "like he'd been given a karate chop," said Betty, who was
standing nearby. He went back and sat on his bed for an hour. On the way
to the funeral home, Betty asked him how he felt. "Numb," he said.
Back home, sitting in the kitchen with Paul McArdle, he finally broke
down and wept. By the time of the funeral mass, he was full of anger,
lashing out at the priest for speaking too long. "I'd like to get my hands
on him," he seethed. At the wake, he got drunk. Joe DiMaggio tried to
console him. A new friend, Phil Graham, the owner of the *Washington*

Post, handed him a note: ''Any time you want to walk or talk—if it's 2:00 A.M.—I'm here.''

Williams was stricken with ''grief and guilt,'' said Betty. ''I'm never going back to work again,'' he told her, adding wildly in his despair, ''I only did it for Dorothy.'' He refused to see the neighbors. His law partners, Tom Wadden and Colman Stein, took turns coming out to sit with him in the evening. They dreamed up imaginary crises at the firm to lure him back. Finally, after a couple of weeks of moping about, he was reassured by his loyal housekeeper Rosa that she would never leave the children, and Williams went back to work.

No MATTER HOW guilty his clients, Williams was usually able to find some way to attack the prosecution for violating the defendant's rights or to find some exculpatory way to explain his client's conduct. But the case against Bernard Goldfine severely tested his ingenuity. Goldfine was accused of failing to pay about $800,000 in taxes between the years 1953 and 1957. At the time, it was the biggest tax evasion case ever brought by the IRS. When Williams looked into the case, he discovered that Goldfine had not even filed tax returns for those years. For that matter, the millionaire New England textile manufacturer refused to respond to subpoenas from the Federal Trade Commission (FTC) or make filings with the Securities and Exchange Commission (SEC). A disciple of the old school of corruption, Goldfine believed that cash payments to key politicians would suffice. In 1958, for instance, he sent ''Christmas presents'' to thirty-two members of Congress and the administration.

Goldfine hired so many lawyers that prosecutors joked that he didn't have an attorney, he had a bar association. His counsel ranged from Sam Sears, a well-known Boston trial lawyer, to Ralph Slobodkin, who collected unpaid bills, procured girls for Goldfine, and ran out for cigarettes. In the winter of 1960, Williams went to see Goldfine as he sat in jail for contempt of Congress for refusing to answer questions in the Sherman Adams affair. Williams found an old, gray-haired man with a heavy Yiddish accent. After making small talk for a few minutes, Williams raised the fact that Goldfine had not filed any returns for the years in question. ''I'm sorry,'' Williams said, ''but you don't have a defense.'' Goldfine greeted this news stonily. A few minutes later, when Williams excused himself to go to the men's room, Goldfine turned to Sam Sears and said, ''Who does that young *momzer* from Washington think he is, telling me I have no defense? Defense? If I had a defense, I'd still have Slobodkin!''

Over the years, Williams would tell that story over and over again. It became part of the monologue he used to warm up audiences, especially clients. The story was funny, especially as Williams told it, eyes twinkling as he mimicked Goldfine's accent and his scorn. But the story also had an important subliminal meaning that Williams wanted to convey without putting it into words: When you're in deep, deep trouble, when you have no defense, the man to see is Edward Bennett Williams.*

Williams and his partner Tom Wadden carefully reviewed Goldfine's records and learned that the industrialist had pretended not to exist as an individual, at least for tax purposes. He paid for everything with corporate checks—his daughter Gwendolyn's divorce lawyer, his maid, his cemetery plot. His wife, Charlotte, had to scrounge kickbacks from the cook and gardener to get cash for herself. When he had finished his investigation, Wadden said to Williams, "The only way this guy is going to get off is if he pleads insanity."

In essence, that *was* Williams's defense. Williams demanded psychiatric examinations to show that his client was mentally incompetent to stand trial. Goldfine was sent to St. Elizabeth's in Washington, where he was diagnosed with a chronic brain syndrome associated with arteriosclerosis. His narrowed blood vessels were starving his brain cells, leading to mental deterioration. A very serious condition, the psychiatrists all agreed.

The U.S. attorney who was prosecuting Goldfine was a young Boston Brahmin named Elliot Richardson. Although Richardson had graduated from Harvard the same year Williams had graduated from Holy Cross, he had never tried a case. He was thoroughly intimidated, he recalled, by Williams's "air of authority and self-confidence." Williams "gave me the feeling he was pressing every minute for every advantage. I didn't see the humor or the exuberance or the joy that I later knew. I was insecure, and I resented his aggressiveness, particularly when I found that any

---

*Williams told the Slobodkin story so often, and with such relish, that the younger lawyers in his firm began to assume it was apocryphal. Williams was always using mock-Yiddish expressions, and the name Slobodkin sounded suspiciously like a Williams invention. But after some digging, a lawyer in the firm was able to find a copy of the real Ralph Slobodkin's admission to the Massachusetts Bar. The firm presented it to Williams on his sixtieth birthday, along with a portrait of EBW by Karsh of Ottawa.

remark I made would be turned to some use before a judge. So I clammed up.''

Richardson, however, was blessed with a useful family connection. His brother was a professor at Harvard Medical School. He was able to show Richardson that there was no sound medical evidence to support Williams's claim that arteriosclerosis led to brain deterioration. It was a theory without proof. At the hearing on Goldfine's fitness to stand trial in February 1961, Richardson was able to effectively cross-examine the battery of psychiatrists Williams had brought along. Richardson put on a Harvard doctor who declared that the defense's psychiatric theory was nonsense. He further showed that Goldfine had continued to conduct business from the psychiatric ward at St. Elizabeth's. Richardson won; Judge George C. Sweeney ordered Goldfine to stand trial.

Williams immediately began to plea bargain, but he couldn't keep his client out of jail. Goldfine was astonished. He couldn't believe that he couldn't fix the case, and even tried to donate $10,000 to Judge Sweeney's favorite charity. Williams went out to Sweeney's house in Newton to try to persuade him not to jail Goldfine, but got nowhere. As he was leaving, he waved good-bye to Sweeney and called out, ''Have a nice long sleep, judge.'' Williams turned to Richardson and whispered, ''That's Mafia talk for drop dead.'' The judge sentenced Goldfine to jail for a year and a day and fined him $110,000, a not terribly harsh penalty by the standards of modern white-collar crime, but unusual in an era when rich businessmen generally did not go to jail.

Chapter Twelve

THEY CALLED HIM "Mr. Jesus." The congregation would weep and shout "Amen" through the sermons of Adam Clayton Powell, Jr., the charismatic pastor of Harlem's Abyssinian Baptist Church. Powell had inherited Abyssinian's pulpit from his father, who had suffered a nervous breakdown in 1936. The elder Reverend Powell dealt in real estate as well as religion, and Adam's mother had been an illegitimate heiress of the Schaefer Brewing Company. The Powells vacationed in Bar Harbor, Maine, a summer oasis of the rich. When Adam heard his call to the ministry, his mother sent him on a chauffeur-driven tour of the Holy Land. Powell grew up "with a taste for expensive clothes, fancy cars, European trips, and Upmann cigars," reported *Time* magazine.

Powell was so light-skinned that he could pass for a white man, and did when he joined a rich boys' fraternity at Colgate in the 1930s. Then the fraternity learned that Powell was black and threw him out. Powell nursed his wounds with a mixture of vengeance, bemusement, and pride. On train trips through the segregated South, he would ride in the Whites Only dining car, and when his tablemates started making racial asides, he would stand and announce, "Gentlemen, I *am* a Negro." Elected to Congress from Harlem in 1944, he was a persistent advocate for civil rights. "I am an irritant," he said. "I see myself that way. Just to keep turning the screw, turning the screw. Drip, drip, drip makes a hole in the marble." On every housing, school, or labor bill, Powell would try to attach a desegregation rider. He almost always failed, but he was admired by many for his persistence.

He was, however, not admired for his absentee rate, usually the highest in Congress. And his swanky life-style—he liked to drive a silver Jaguar with the top down—was a source of envy and suspicion. He owned two homes and three luxury cars and had two servants, but he paid only $1,700 in federal taxes on an income of $160,000 in 1951 and 1952. In 1956, the government convened a grand jury to look more closely into his taxes.

The investigation seemed to stall—some suggested a political fix. On October 6, 1956, Powell told his congregation that no black person could in good conscience campaign for Dwight Eisenhower; but on October 11 he held a press conference at the White House and reversed himself, imploring all blacks to vote for Ike. Powell's most strident critic was William F. Buckley, Jr., the young editor of the conservative *National Review*. For months, Buckley demanded an indictment, even using a racist pun for a headline on one of his editorials: "The Jig Is Up for Adam Clayton Powell, Jr." (Copies of the magazine were delivered to the homes of the grand jurors.) Finally, in May 1958, a runaway grand jury defied the prosecutor and indicted Powell for income tax evasion and filing false returns.

Powell called Williams the day he was indicted, complaining that he had been set up. Williams didn't believe Powell at first, but he took the case anyway, and quickly became Powell's drinking pal as well as his lawyer. The two men were natural companions. They liked to tell tall stories and mimic each other. Powell was a well-established member of café society who, Williams joked, could "make white women jump out of their skivvies just by walking in the door." In his memoir, *Adam by Adam*, Powell returned the compliment, describing Williams as "tall, handsome, with a lower lip that makes girls swoon" and calling him the "reincarnation of Clarence Darrow." They shared a mutual loathing for the patrician William F. Buckley. "Back then, Ed thought Buckley was a snot-nosed Catholic turned into a Yankee," recalled Vince Fuller.*

---

*The feud climaxed when Buckley wrote a snide review of Williams's book *One Man's Freedom*, calling him Ed "Suffer the Guilty to Come Unto Me" Williams, and Williams retorted by calling Buckley an "Ivy League George Lincoln Rockwell" in a talk at Yale. Buckley threatened to sue for slander and Williams grudgingly apologized. But in 1968, when Buckley wanted the best possible criminal lawyer for convicted murderer Edgar Smith, whose cause Buckley had adopted, he asked Williams to represent Smith on appeal. And when Buckley himself got into legal trouble with the SEC in 1979, he again turned to Williams's firm. (Buckley's personal lawyer is still Steve Umin, a partner in Williams & Connolly.) Williams, in characteristic fashion, had turned an enemy into a client and a friend.

The jokes stopped as the trial approached. Williams became formal with Powell, no longer his fellow rake but rather his mentor and disciplinarian. As he had in the Hoffa case, Williams planned to put Powell on the stand. That meant transforming the preacher-congressman from charming roué to sober, credible witness. As the two men worked late into the night at Williams's apartment on 55th Street, Powell received a much tougher grilling from Williams than any cross-examination he was likely to get in court. One evening, Faye Emerson was up in the apartment after dinner and she watched Williams work Powell over. The lawyer was so intimidating and so mean that Miss Emerson burst into tears and begged Williams to stop.

Williams was just as hard on himself. Powell recounted in his memoir that Williams collapsed, ashen from exhaustion, one night but refused to let Powell put him to bed. The tax evasion case against Powell was technical, based on numbers and intricate calculations. Williams marinated himself in the details. Assigned to the case by Williams, Vince Fuller recalls working out the accounts to within $100. Williams would take over the accounting sheets and work them down to the cent. For hours, he sat in the apartment massaging the facts and numbers and shaping them into a compelling story. Williams had a photographic memory, and he would store in his mind whole pages of deposition transcript, right down to the page number.

Williams leavened the grind by thinking up stunts and tactics. His first move almost torpedoed the prosecution's case before it even went to trial. The government's main witness was supposed to be Powell's former secretary and business manager, Hattie Freeman Dodson. Mrs. Dodson herself had been sentenced to prison in 1956 for filing false information on her tax returns (the government tried to prove that she kicked back part of her salary to Powell, but the congressman denied it). At Powell's trial, Mrs. Dodson was supposed to testify that she had helped prepare Powell's taxes based on the figures that Powell himself had given her. For weeks, Mrs. Dodson cooperated with the prosecutors, but a week before trial, when the government called her for her last preparation, she showed up with Edward Bennett Williams on her arm. Williams announced that he was representing Mrs. Dodson. Prosecutor Morton Robson was flabbergasted. "This is highly improper!" he sputtered. "You have a conflict of interest. You can't properly represent a witness as well as the defendant! Their interests are opposed." Williams just smiled, Robson recalled, "like the cat who had swallowed the canary." Williams told the prosecutor to go ahead and ask Mrs. Dodson any question he wanted. Robson felt trapped; he couldn't question his witness in Williams's presence without giving away his case. Since Dodson had already served her time in jail, the government had no leverage over her. Frustrated, Robson realized that Mrs. Dodson had nothing to lose by refusing to cooperate— and, he strongly suspected, something to gain from Powell by not cooperating. Robson protested furiously to Judge Frederick Van Pelt Bryan. But he had no real legal authority for his objections; there were essentially no rules on conflicts of this kind. It would be years before the growth of complex, white-collar crime litigation forced the courts to set limits in the area of multiple representation. Williams's basic philosophy then—as well as later—was to represent as many people as he possibly could. "Hang together," he would tell witnesses and defendants, "or hang separately." The goal was what modern white-collar defense lawyers call "information control," or, as Williams might put it, keeping prosecutors in the dark.

Judge Bryan was not about to start writing new rules to constrain Ed Williams. He liked him too much. Though Williams privately mocked Bryan as "Colonel Blimp," he flattered and wooed the judge with little jokes and fawning remarks. "Edward Bennett Williams conceals his limitless cunning under a cloak of almost halting juvenile deference," wrote columnist Murray Kempton, who was covering the trial. "He always seems about to ask the bailiff where the defense attorney is supposed to sit." Normally, grand jury testimony is privileged and confidential. To see it, a defense attorney must make an unusually strong argument that the evidence was insufficient to indict, a very difficult task. Over Robson's strenuous objections, Bryan turned the entire grand jury transcript over to Williams. He would make very effective use of it at the trial—including the admission by one government lawyer to the grand jury that the government's case was weak.

The line to get into Judge Bryan's courtroom snaked out of the federal courthouse in Foley Square when *United States* v. *Powell* went to trial on March 7, 1960. Toots Shor was there, and so was Sugar Ray Robinson. In the first row behind Powell sat a half dozen handsome women, both black and white. The courtroom was well packed with parishioners from Abyssinian Baptist, who muttered imprecations at Robson as he walked into court. Hattie Dodson turned out to be, as Robson had feared, a useless witness. She could not recall anything that would link Powell with faulty information on his tax return. "With respect to 90 percent of her testimony," Robson complained to Bryan, "her recollection has lapsed very badly in the last two or three weeks. She recalled almost everything I asked her on the witness stand without hesitation in my office three weeks ago."

On cross-examination, Williams set about demolishing Robson's other main witness, IRS agent Morris Emanuel. The government's case against Powell had been sloppily prepared, and Williams used the transcript of the grand jury proceedings to catch Emanuel in a series of contradictions. Emanuel had given the wrong figure on Powell's earnings to the grand jury. "You don't stand by its accuracy, Mr. Emanuel, do you?" Williams asked in a soft voice as he paced back and forth before the witness. "At that time, yes, at this time, no," answered Emanuel. So, said Williams, "what you told the grand jury was inaccurate?" "As of today, not as of 1958," said Emanuel, shifting in his chair. "Do you mean the *facts* themselves were different in 1958 than they are now, or that you were mistaken about the facts then?" Williams inquired, allowing a slight edge to creep into his voice. "No, I mean and you know and I know the facts were the same. . . ." Williams cut in: "Then the grand jury did not have the benefit of a complete and accurate investigation by you. Is that right?" Squirming, Emanuel replied, "You make that sound a little difficult, Mr. Williams. The . . ." Bryan glared at Emanuel and snapped, "All right, that is a question and it deserves an answer, Mr. Emanuel. Did it or did it not?" Emanuel wiped his forehead. "I received whatever information our investigation had developed up to that point." Williams closed in: "And you know now, do you not, Mr. Emanuel, on April Fool's Day 1960, that that was not accurate information?" "That is correct," admitted the witness. Williams finished him off: "You were wrong, weren't you?" Thoroughly defeated, Emanuel answered, "I was wrong in a lot of things at that time." A murmur swept through the courtroom; Bryan had to gavel for order.

Williams had been leading Emanuel through a series of numbers, writing each down on a blackboard before the jury. Although Powell had paid low taxes in 1951 and 1952, his wife, pianist Hazel Scott, had run up heavy travel expenses that were deductible. Williams methodically led Emanuel through an accounting of each. When he had finished, he drew a line underneath and appeared to add up the figures. With a look of totally feigned surprise, he wrote down the answer. His questions had forced Emanuel to concede that Powell had failed to claim legal deductions worth over $7,000—more than wiping out his $6,700 deficiency.

As the jury watched, Williams had just proved that Powell had in fact *overpaid* his taxes. At the counsel's table, Powell turned to look at columnist Murray Kempton, who was sitting in the row behind him. Powell had a look of "utter amazement" on his face, Kempton recalled. "He was shocked to find he was innocent."

Out of the corner of his eye, Williams had been watching the clock. He knew Bryan wanted to adjourn for the weekend at noon. As the clock struck twelve, Williams ran his hand through his wavy hair and turned to walk to his seat. "I have no further questions," he declared, not even trying to conceal the triumph in his voice. As he left the courtroom, Powell joked, "They better adjourn this case. I'm making more money every day." Emanuel remained motionless in the witness chair. A spectator came up to console him. "That's a pretty good cross-examination," said John Cye Cheasty. Emanuel tried to muster a smile. "Oh, one of the alumni, huh?"

A few days later, Bryan dismissed two of the three counts against Powell. The rest, for Williams, was just showing off. Toward the end of the trial, Robson objected to a question raised by Williams on cross-examination because, he contended, the question dealt with an issue that had not been raised on direct examination. Bryan for once agreed with Robson. But Williams, without referring to the record or even his notes, called out the date on which the prosecution had covered the subject and the exact page of the four-thousand-page transcript on which it appeared. By the day of the closing arguments, Robson seemed overwhelmed. Before trial, Williams was usually good-natured and easygoing with prosecutors, but once trial began, he liked to rattle them. As Robson was preparing to enter court for his final argument, Williams came up to him and asked him to waive his privilege so Williams could sue him for defamation. "I would," said Robson, "except I wouldn't trust you." Robson said Williams only succeeded in stirring him up to give a fiery summation, but he never got over his wariness toward Williams. "I guess you could say that Ed is always working," he told a reporter in 1962. "During a case, you can sit around and shoot the breeze with other lawyers, but not with Ed. He'll take something you say and then hit you over the head with it in court."

Williams was actually disappointed with the verdict—a hung jury. The jurors voted ten to two to acquit. That was good enough for Powell, who was used to losing in committee by great margins, but the congressman noted that Williams seemed "a little crestfallen" that he had not won complete vindication for his client. Williams cheered up a month later when Powell arranged to have him named "Harlem Man of the Year." Standing on the steps of the Hotel Theresa up in Harlem, Powell heroically introduced Williams. "Abraham Lincoln freed the slaves," the parson declared, "but Edward Bennett Williams freed Adam Clayton Powell!" Williams responded by giving a powerful speech in defense of civil rights, in which he urged blacks to boycott white businesses that discriminated against them.

Standing on the edge of the crowd that day was the young woman Williams had hired out of Georgetown Law School, Agnes Neill. She watched this oratorical performance with a mixture of fascination and awe. She was no longer Williams's law associate. A few weeks before she had become Mrs. Edward Bennett Williams.

THE YEAR AFTER Dorothy's death had been a year-long stag party for Williams. *Washington Star* sportswriter Morrie Siegel recalled jumping into a limousine at 2:00 A.M. outside Duke Zeibert's to head for Williams's home in the suburbs. In the car with him were heavyweight boxer Billy Conn, professional wrestler Antonino Rocca, Hollywood producer Budd Schulberg, and Mafia don Frank Costello. As the party raucously continued in Williams's living room, Costello wandered off to the library and returned with a copy of *The Great Mouthpiece,* the biography of William Fallon, the colorful lowlife criminal lawyer. Full of Scotch, Williams asked Costello if Fallon had been a mouthpiece for him. "Yeah," replied the don in his gravelly voice, "but he wasn't as good as you, counselor. The problem was he drank too much." There was general merriment and another round of drinks.

Williams led his cronies on a three-day bender in the summer of 1959 when the Floyd Patterson–Ingemar Johansson heavyweight championship fight, scheduled for Yankee Stadium, was rained out two nights in a row. In the middle of the second night, Williams got a phone call from a desperate Leonore Lemmon. She had gone out to California with George Reeves, the television star of the "Superman" series. "Superman is dead!" cried Lemmon over the phone. She told Williams that Reeves had shot himself while they were staying in the actor's house in Hollywood. Williams told her to call the police and keep her mouth shut. Lemmon promptly told the police that she had fired the pistol while "fooling around" before Reeves killed himself. Then she held a press conference.

Williams just shook his head as he regaled his cronies with Lemmon's travails the next day. "Only Lem can turn a suicide into a homicide," he laughed. She retained Williams as her lawyer, but the police did not charge her. The coroner's report showed that Reeves had, in fact, taken his own life.

Both Lemmon and Jean Pochna claim that Williams asked them to marry him during that wild year. (Pochna says she had told Williams, "You need a baby-sitter, not a wife.") Williams's friends worried that he would marry one of the café society girls, or perhaps Faye Emerson. But Williams's former father-in-law, Duke Guider, knew better—perhaps, his daughter Betty suggests, because he shared Williams's attitude toward women. Sexy party girls were for flirting, not marrying. Williams might moon over Leonore Lemmon, but in the end, Guider predicted, Williams would seek out a solid, stable spouse, one who would be a good mother to his children.

He was right. Williams was worn out by carousing. "I need a rest," he told the *Boston Traveler* in April 1960. "And I want to spend more time with my children." There was no shortage of women desirous to take on the job of wife and mother in the Williams household. Williams joked that Rosa, his loyal housekeeper, protected him from these women by screening their calls. He dubbed the would-be Mrs. Williamses "the kidnappers" because they were always offering to take his children to the zoo. Washington hostess Gwen Cafritz led a garden club party of ladies through the house at azalea time that spring. "Such a lovely girl," she said, mournfully looking at Dorothy's photograph. "Such beautiful children!" she exclaimed, brightening when she saw Jobie, Ellen, and little Bennett. "Such a beautiful house! Such an *eligible* husband!"

For the previous six years, Williams had worked closely with his associate Agnes Neill. She was an extremely dogged researcher and able brief writer. At twenty-nine, she was shy and buttoned-up, but pretty and fresh compared to the smoky café society girls. Williams also may have sensed in her a certain resolve. At Williams's fortieth birthday party in late May 1960, Williams's partner Colman Stein sensed a more than professional bond between Williams and his female associate. Still, Tom Wadden was stunned when Agnes walked out of the office one Friday, married Williams the next day, and never returned to work. Wadden came by Williams's house to wish them well and talk about the Supreme Court case he was researching with Agnes. "I don't practice law anymore," Agnes said, sweetly but firmly. "I'm now Ed's wife."

Williams and Agnes were married at St. Mary's Church in Rockville, Maryland, on June 11, 1960. There was no reception afterward, and neither the bride's nor the groom's parents were in attendance. Williams had grown increasingly distant from his own mother and father, and his new in-laws disapproved of him. The Neills were strict, conservative Catholics. A brainy girl and something of a grind, Agnes had wanted to go to college at Swarthmore, but her parents were afraid she would be taught by a Communist or marry a Protestant. They sent her to a proper Catholic girls' school, the College of New Rochelle. Not surprisingly, the Neills were not pleased to see their daughter marry a controversial criminal lawyer, a widower with three small children on his hands. A few days after the wedding, Agnes took Williams home to meet her parents at their house in northwest Washington. Mrs. Neill started questioning Williams about how he could defend Frank Costello and Jimmy Hoffa. Williams walked out the door and did not come back into the Neills' house for almost twenty years.

On their wedding night, Williams took Agnes up to New York and out to dinner at Toots Shor's. The saloonkeeper, as usual, insulted his favorite guest. Agnes did not think Toots Shor was funny. For the rest of their long marriage, Agnes would have very little to do with the New York nightclub world that Williams savored. She didn't like saloons or the people who frequented them. But she recognized that Toots Shor and his kind were part of her husband's world, and with stoic detachment she accepted it. She was too busy raising the three Williams children to worry too much about her husband's nightlife.

Agnes came to the Williams home with more experience in the library than in the kitchen. Having faithfully cared for Dorothy's children throughout her illness and during Williams's frequent absences, housekeeper Rosa considered the children to be hers. She was not eager to turn them over to an interloper. After a few months, she quit. According to family lore, a few weeks after Rosa left, Agnes cooked what Williams described as "law book pork chops" ("made from the law book, not the cookbook"—Agnes had been reading liability cases on trichinosis from undercooked pork). The next morning Rosa was rehired. According to Rosa, she quit because Jobie resented Agnes. "I figured, if I get away, he'll learn to love his new mother," recalled Rosa. Instead, Jobie, playing with matches, set the woods on fire and tried to run away from home. One Saturday afternoon, after about a month, Williams summoned Rosa to his law office. He told her that a child psychologist had urged them to get her back, that Jobie could not bear losing Rosa on top of his mother.

Kindhearted but strict and domineering, Rosa ruled the house at Tulip Hill, and Williams did not buck her authority. "He was dependent on Rosa and intimidated by her," said Betty Killay, who was often at the house in those years. One evening, Rosa sent Ellen, who was overweight as a child, to "the penalty box"—a corner of the kitchen—for refusing to eat her potatoes. Killay said to Williams that the last thing Ellen needed to eat was another potato. The normally self-assured Williams seemed helpless to intervene. "What the hell do you expect me to do?" he pleaded with Killay. "We don't *know* what to do!" In December 1960, Agnes nearly miscarried her first baby and had to be rushed to George-town Hospital. Killay was surprised to find Williams back home mopping the floor on Sunday night, Rosa's night off. "I'll get hell from Rosa if I don't," Williams grumbled.

Williams was less intimidated by Agnes's mother. At the hospital, where Agnes lay in bed trying to avoid premature labor, Mrs. Neill confronted Williams and demanded that Agnes be sent home with her. Williams told his mother-in-law, "If you don't shut up, I'm going to throw you through the fucking window."

Agnes delivered a premature but healthy baby, a boy they named Edward Neill Williams. He was the first of four children Agnes would bear over the next eight years. Gradually, she asserted her authority over the household and the children, her own babies as well as the older children. Though she often talked about the law with Williams in the evening, Agnes had little interest in practicing law again; she was determined to be a good mother.

IV

Power

Chapter Thirteen

By THE 1960s, Ed Williams's reputation as a trial lawyer was complete. He had nothing further to gain from astonishing victories in the courtroom, and he feared he had much to lose if he failed to live up to his reputation. Moreover, the guiltier his clients, the less sense it made to bring them before a jury. More and more, Williams turned to cutting deals with the prosecutor behind closed doors. This required access, a commodity most prized in Washington by the many seeking favors from the few, and it became increasingly important for Williams to cultivate and win over Washington insiders.

Beyond the needs of his clients, however, Williams wanted to become an insider himself. "I stay close to the Throne," he liked to say to friends, by which he meant to the seat of God. He coveted proximity to secular thrones as well. It was not enough for Williams to be a celebrated figure, a great legal gladiator. Though he continued to enjoy the company of scoundrels, his craving for respectability, his longing to belong, led him to climb toward loftier circles. In the decade of the 1960s, Williams's ambition shifted, from staging spectacular courtroom upsets to penetrating and then joining the Washington elite. Where once he was satisfied with fame, he now craved power.

Williams's own contemporaries had come to power in the beginning of the new decade. John F. Kennedy was only three years older than Williams. His brother Robert, the new attorney general, was five years younger. Williams was fascinated and proud to see that these vigorous young Irish Catholics had not only been accepted, but had come to embody the establishment—the new elite, the bright young men who were making Washington exciting and full of promise. But Williams was inevitably jealous as well. He had not been endowed with boarding schools and Harvard. "The Kennedys personified what Williams wanted to be," said John Nolan, who clerked for Williams as a Georgetown law student and later became an aide to Robert Kennedy. "But Ed couldn't help but resent that he had worked so hard to get what the Kennedys had been given by their father." His unease at the ascension of the Kennedys was deepened by his personal feud with Bobby. It was bad for business, to say the least, to have the new chief law enforcement officer of the United States as your sworn enemy. Worse, without the acceptance of the Kennedys, Williams would never make it into the right social circles. He understood that power in Washington in those early Kennedy years was measured as much by the seating arrangements at Georgetown dinner parties as by the organizational tables of the federal government.

Williams, in time, became a prize for hostesses, but acceptance did not come quickly or easily. His ascension was the product of a number of different steps. While he continued to defend Mafia dons and lowlifes, he increasingly offered advice to capital worthies. He also became a leading advocate in the Supreme Court, thus enhancing his reputation as a crusader for civil liberties. At the same time, he began a pastime that would grow consuming, that of a professional sports team owner. For Williams, the years 1960–65 have to be looked at not as a steady or linear progression but as a fluid campaign advancing on several fronts. It begins with Williams seeking once again to elevate his public image.

IN THE SUMMER of 1960, writer Gay Talese came to interview Williams for a profile for the *New York Times Sunday Magazine*. He found Williams fretting about his reputation. "In occasional moments of self-doubt," wrote Talese, "Williams wonders if it isn't time to alter his image as the brilliant young lawyer who defends villains." Williams suggested that he was thinking about getting out of trial law, perhaps to run for office. But he worried about his "guilt by client" bugaboo. "I can hear it now," Williams said to Talese. "In some places they'll label me a Negro lover. In other places, they'd say, 'Here's Williams, speaker for the burglar's lobby.' And I can hear my political opponent, as he addresses the crowds, saying, 'How can you vote for the man who defended Costello?'"

Williams was especially touchy about his reputation in the fall of 1960, when JFK was elected president. Back in 1957, Mike Wallace had invited Williams on his late-night show, "Night Watch." Williams had arrived with Leonore Lemmon on one arm and Faye Emerson on the other, and he had been "irreverent, brave, and more candid than most lawyers are," recalled Wallace. A year later, after the Hoffa trial, Wallace had Williams on his show again. This time he was far more careful and "pompous" in his defense of lawyers, said Wallace, who suspected that Williams was being coached by the ubiquitous Eddie Cheyfitz. Two years after that, in November of 1960, the subject of lawyers came up in a Wallace interview with *New York Herald Tribune* TV critic John Crosby. Crosby attacked Williams for defending Hoffa and other "rather crummy people." Wallace asked Crosby if he thought Williams was immoral. "I think so . . . yes," replied Crosby. "I'd at least like to get him arguing about this. Why he picks these people to defend . . . of course, there's a lot of money in it . . ."

"And it's dramatic?" interjected Wallace. "And it's dramatic," agreed Crosby.

The next day Wallace took a call from Williams. "I'm going to sue your ass," Williams announced. "What?" asked a startled Wallace. "You called me an immoral lawyer," said Williams. The TV host thought Williams was joking—he wasn't. Wallace ended up paying him $1,000 to avoid going to court. "I was pretty mad," said Wallace. "This was huge! I was only making $400 a week and I had to write this great civil libertarian a check for $1,000." Three months later, Wallace ran into Williams at Toots Shor's. Williams stuck out his hand in greeting. Wallace just said "Fuck you" and kept walking. The two did not speak again for fifteen years.

By 1960, Williams had his explanation for representing unpopular clients down to a routine. He could both defend the principle ("the Sixth Amendment does not say everyone is entitled to a lawyer except for Frank Costello and Jimmy Hoffa") and make his clients themselves seem less threatening. Joe McCarthy, he would say, wasn't really a dangerous demagogue; he was motivated by the "glory drive" not the "power drive"—he was more interested in getting headlines than gaining control. Frank Costello was a man of his word who was actually a force for peace in the underworld. Williams did not try to defend Hoffa, but he made known his own animosity to the Teamsters boss. (As time went on, the

Hoffa jokes became increasingly crude; when Hoffa vanished in 1975, Williams cracked to friends that the Teamsters boss had been sent to the soap factory and that "we're all washing with bars of Jimmy.")

Williams was not above shading the truth to buff up his image. He wrote that "on the same day in 1954 I was referred to in a West Coast paper as the 'right-wing mouthpiece for the McCarthy fringe' and in a New York paper as the 'courtroom apologist for left-wing groups.' " But Williams kept everything written about him, and his scrapbooks show no such articles. Williams's law partners were amused when an interview with Williams appeared in a book called *Listen to Leaders in the Law* in 1963. In the interview, Williams began to describe the time he had blundered by asking if the young son of a streetcar accident victim was looking for his father's liquor bottle; the young man responded that he was bending over to kiss his father good-bye. All that was true, but then Williams got carried away and tried to put a better gloss on the incident. First he said he had been representing the young man, not the streetcar company. Then he blamed the "defense lawyer" for the mistake. The defense lawyer, of course, had been Williams.

The most effective way to defend his reputation, Williams knew, was to write a book about himself. He had been toying with the idea since the day in May 1957 when he had seen the front page of a New York tabloid taking a tally of his clients: "McCarthy Dead; Frank Costello Shot; Dave Beck Recalled Before Senate Rackets Committee." At dinner that evening with lawyer Morris Ernst, Williams had gone on about the thrill of defending these notorious men when Ernst said, "I'm going to sic Mike on you." "Mike" was Simon Michael Bessie, Ernst's son-in-law and a rising young book editor. Bessie immediately approached Williams, who wrote back that he was "very interested." At first, Williams looked for a ghostwriter. He approached Richard Condon, the author of thrillers (*The Manchurian Candidate*).

Their first outline, in the winter of 1958, seemed aimed at titillation. In a memo to Bessie, Condon listed the cases Williams wanted to write about—and for what purpose: "(1) Icardi for International Intrigue. (2) *Jones* v. *Jones*—Alienation of Affection (humor). (3) McCarthy— Garbage Disposal. (4) Costello—Cops and Robbers . . ." Condon asked Bessie, "Does your editorial board favor any particular mood?"

But Williams, frenetically busy, unsure of what he wanted to say, abandoned the book idea for a time. He later wrote that he did not feel "adequate to the task." When he picked up the project again in 1960, he had settled on a reason for writing the book. Instead of a pot-boiler writer like Condon, Williams sought out James Clayton, who covered the federal courts for the *Washington Post*.

With Clayton, Williams was explicit about his motivation for writing the book. He told the *Post* writer that he wanted "respectability." He didn't want to be remembered like Charlie Ford, the colorful Fifth Streeter. He wanted to be known as a man of moral standing and character who won cases on principle and not by trickery. Clayton agreed to take on the project, but he insisted that Williams tell him the truth. Over several evenings in the winter of 1960, Clayton tape recorded long and revealing conversations with Williams about his law practice, and Clayton drafted two chapters based on these interviews. He wrote that Williams had stopped defending insurance companies and started defending criminals because he found it more challenging and rewarding to defend human rights rather than property rights. Criminal law practice, wrote Clayton, combined "the drama of the theater, the challenge of the bullring, the excitement of the contest, and the possibility of glory and riches."

Williams showed the manuscript to Morris Ernst, who had a shrewd public relations instinct. He warned Williams that Clayton's draft overplayed the legal drama and underplayed the moral purpose. Louis Nizer, another celebrated lawyer, had just published a boastful book about his own exploits in the courtroom, called *My Life in Court*. The book was selling well, Ernst said, but Nizer had cheapened his own name. He counseled Williams to take a higher road.

Williams decided that he had better write the book himself. In the summer of 1960, he closeted himself in the pine-paneled study of a rented house on Nantucket and began to write in his distinctive looping scrawl. Clayton had described Williams's reaction to the "McCarthy Dead; Costello Shot" headline as: "Could law practice ever be more exciting than this? What was there left?"

In his own account, Williams wrote, "I had a powerful impulse to sit down and write about what I regard as the most basic principles of individual liberty guaranteed by our constitution." Gone was any mention of the exhilaration of criminal law. The emphasis was entirely on defending the Bill of Rights, which were being eroded by public apathy and ignorance.

Williams's book would be different from Louis Nizer's. He would draw on his own experiences, to be sure, but only to illustrate his larger points about individual liberty. The title would not be about Williams himself—not "My Life"—but about his cause: *One Man's Freedom*. To write the introduction, Williams went to the top: the dean of Harvard Law School, Erwin Griswold. Griswold agreed at first, but then reconsidered. Nizer's book was causing a flap in the upper reaches of the bar because Nizer had promoted himself by stretching the bounds of attorney-client confidentiality, and Griswold feared Williams would do the same. Figuring if Harvard wouldn't, then Yale might, Williams next called Eugene Rostow, the dean of Yale Law School. Rostow was less prissy than his opposite number at Harvard and wrote a glowing introduction in which he likened Williams to a young Clarence Darrow.

One Man's Freedom was published in the summer of 1962 to very respectable reviews. "A first-rate exposition, both reasoned and impassioned," commented *The New Yorker*. "Edward Bennett Williams has done the impossible," wrote Anthony Lewis in the *New York Times*. "He has managed to write a book about civil liberties without being dull, legalistic, or painfully self-righteous." In fact, the book *was* written in clear and strong language that forcefully made Williams's points about "guilt by client" and the threat to civil liberties posed by overzealous law enforcement and an indifferent public. The book climbed to number five on the best-seller list, right behind *Sex and the Single Woman* and, to Williams's great irritation, *My Life in Court*. (In a failed effort to catch Nizer, Williams plowed some of his advance into buying advertisements for the book.)

Once again, Williams's timing was right: The Warren Court was beginning to get headlines for its activities in the defense of civil liberties and civil rights, and among the educated classes, at least, reasoned liberalism was the ideology of the day. By his example and now by his writing, Williams had advanced the notion that individual rights deserved just as much protection as property rights, which long had been the top priority of the establishment bar. By his title alone, Williams had elevated the work of criminal lawyers. They did not seek to set the guilty free; rather, each time they went to court, they were defending "one man's freedom."

Williams wanted to enhance not only his own reputation, but that of the criminal defense bar as well. He scorned lawyers who were too flashy or crassly self-promoting. He particularly looked down on Nizer and F. Lee Bailey, believing them publicity hounds who went to court unprepared. He scoffed when he heard that Bailey had installed television lights over the desk in his office so he could hold impromptu press conferences. Williams was adamantly opposed to cameras in the courtroom, warning that they would only encourage showboating by defense lawyers and prosecutors. He even looked askance at the new television programs glorifying defense lawyers—"Perry Mason" and "The Defenders."

In a stern article in *Television Quarterly*, Williams wrote, "Television has taught the public through endless repetition that trial lawyers are a scheming, tricky lot." Law students are instructed "that deception may be more important than the difficult and grubby disciplines. They would like to avoid the digging that makes the law student a competent attorney." Williams castigated these shows even though they had been inspired to some extent by his own well-publicized successes. The month *One Man's Freedom* was published, "Perry Mason" star Raymond Burr asked for an audience with Williams at Toots Shor's so he could see what a real-life legal miracle worker was like. But it was precisely the fact that Perry Mason never lost that seemed to bother Williams most. In an early draft of *One Man's Freedom*, Williams had written,

> Once in a while the illusion is created, probably by an overenthusiastic press, that some great trial lawyer never loses a major case. This is pure fiction, and not harmless fiction at that. It casts the whole administration of justice in an unfavorable light. The greatest football coaches lose games. There is a limit to what a genius can do with the material with which he must work. If you turn over any given football team to the best coach in America, he may win two more games than the most incompetent coach would win with the same material. Likewise if you take a hundred criminal cases and assume that fifty of them should be won on the merits and that fifty should be lost, and then turn them over to the most able and experienced advocate in America, he will probably win sixty and lose forty. Turn the same cases over to the most incompetent trial man and he will win forty and lose sixty. The concept of a great trial lawyer who always wins has no foundation in reality. It is a television or Hollywood fiction.

Williams, of course, was writing about himself and the terrible burden of winning. He believed that he was expected to win every case. Even Vince Lombardi couldn't win if his fullback fumbled the ball. Nor could Ed Williams win with Bernard Goldfine. Williams thought that the pressure was unfair, that the television-jaded public had unreasonable expectations. The fact is, of course, that the pressure was self-imposed. It was just easier to blame Hollywood.

*   *   *

DEFENDING CRIMINALS WAS essentially the work of outsiders defending outcasts. Williams needed clients who could get him in on the inside. Ever since the Icardi case, Williams had been fascinated by espionage. This was the great age of spy versus spy in the Cold War, and Williams, a staunch anti-Communist, wanted to join the game. He loved secrets; he loved knowing what others could not, and he understood that information was power in Washington. Williams was intrigued by the secret life of his friend Robert Maheu, a private investigator who performed "off the books" operations for the CIA.* So when the U-2 spy plane of Francis Gary Powers was shot down over the Soviet Union and Powers was taken prisoner, Williams approached the State Department in January 1960 to see if he could serve as Powers's lawyer.

Williams had visions of defending the American spy in a Soviet court-room as the whole world watched. It was an interesting idea, but the Soviets balked, and in any case, Powers was later swapped for a Soviet spy. Williams kept on looking for opportunities in the intelligence world. A CIA lawyer named Mike Miskovsky was startled to find Williams roaming the hallway of the old CIA headquarters at 24th and E streets later that year. Williams explained that he was checking out one of his clients, an American businessman, to find out whether he was involved in the Communist insurrection in the Philippines. According to Lawrence Houston, the Agency's general counsel, Williams returned from Manila and was debriefed by Allen Dulles himself, the director of Central Intelligence. "Williams could not have been more cooperative," Houston recalled. "He had a keen sense of intelligence and secrecy."

WHEN WILLIAMS fiNALLY got the chance to handle a really celebrated spy case, he found himself on the "wrong" side. In the fall of 1960, Williams received a plea that would test his every-man-has-a-right-to-counsel philosophy. Igor Melekh, a Soviet spy, had been caught by the FBI trying to steal a map and aerial photographs of military installations near Chicago,

---

*It was Maheu who had hired gangsters Johnny Rosselli and Sam Giancana (who later became Williams's client) to try to assassinate Fidel Castro for the CIA. According to Jim Hougan, author of *Spooks*, Maheu's Washington-based investigative agency was the model for the "Mission Impossible" television series. Among Maheu's other missions, he once testified before Congress, was producing a phony film purporting to show a foreign leader in bed with a woman in the Soviet Union.

to be used to plan a Soviet bombing attack. The counsel at the Soviet embassy called Williams: Would he defend the Russian spy? Williams was in an uncomfortable position. A couple of the lawyers in his office argued against taking the case, saying that the office already had enough unpopular clients. Williams went home that night and talked to his new wife. She reminded him that he had spoken to bar associations and law schools all over the country on the right to counsel, and how the bar had an obligation to provide counsel within the limits of integrity. "If you turn this case down," she said, "everything you have been talking about is really a sham."

Williams took the case, after first insisting that the Kremlin give him total control of the defense. Predictably, Williams was vilified by some. When he was pictured with Melekh in *Time* magazine, he got the usual crank letters: "You must feel proud when you tip a cocktail at the country club," a Buffalo man wrote. "I'm one that hopes that you have your loved ones get seriously hurt, crippled or killed. Then you wouldn't be so anxious to protect these hoods." But Williams had an answer to his critics, and an approach that he believed could transform his defense of a Soviet spy into a blow for international justice.

Williams had been giving impassioned and high-minded speeches to schools and bar groups on the subject of "World Peace Through Law." He had dreamy notions about reviving the International Court of Justice at The Hague and investing it with real authority. His faith in the World Court seems oddly naive for someone so sophisticated and cynical about power and its uses, but Williams had a genuine idealism about the judicial process. He also knew the publicity value of appearing as a crusader for world harmony. Reviving the World Court was a favorite cause of Henry Luce, the founder of Time-Life, who had come to talk to Williams about the idea. Another outspoken fan of invigorating the World Court was Chief Justice Earl Warren, whom Williams admired and was eager to get to know.

In early December, Williams went to the Justice Department with his plan. He bypassed the attorney general, William Rogers, and asked to see the attorney general–designate, Robert F. Kennedy.

In late December, Williams briefed Kennedy on the legal issues in the Melekh case. The main question, he said, was whether Melekh, as an official of the United Nations, enjoyed diplomatic immunity from criminal prosecution in the United States. Williams proposed that both the United States and the Soviet Union agree to submit the case to the International Court of Justice. This was a great opportunity, Williams stressed. Rarely, he declared, were two lawyers given the chance to make such a contribution to the cause of world peace. It would mark the first time in history that the Soviet Union had submitted to the jurisdiction of the World Court—and set a dramatic new precedent for the settling of disputes between the superpowers. Not only that, it would be a bold stroke for the new administration.

For months, Williams heard nothing back. Then in March, Kennedy brusquely informed Williams that his proposal had been rejected. He offered no explanation. A few weeks later, Melekh was traded for a couple of American spies in a standard Cold War swap.

Williams was discouraged by his reception at the Kennedy Justice Department. "It's as cold in there as a refrigerator when I come around," he told John Siegenthaler, a Kennedy aide at Justice. Williams had a serious problem. He needed access to the upper levels of the Justice Department in order to cut deals for his clients. And the top law enforcement official in the land was a man who had compared Williams to a legal prostitute for representing Jimmy Hoffa. What's more, Kennedy had brought many Rackets Committee staffers with him to Justice, where he had created a "Get Hoffa" squad. "Bobby blamed Ed Williams for the tricks in the Hoffa case," said Laverne Duffy, a member of the "Get Hoffa" squad, "and we were suspicious of him."

With characteristic purpose, Williams had set about repairing relations even before Kennedy took office. In December 1960, he had sent the attorney general–designate a congratulatory note: "The ability and dedication which you will bring to it assures your success—and also assures Uncle Sam of the kind of representation he has long needed." At Christmas time 1960, when Agnes Williams went into Georgetown Hospital because her first pregnancy was troubled, Williams found Bobby and Ethel Kennedy there for the birth of one of their many children. The two couples had a glass of champagne together, and for the first time since the Hoffa case, when Ethel had tried to get him fired as Georgetown's counsel, they had a friendly conversation. Williams began to let it be known that he disdained Hoffa. *Time* magazine reporter Hugh Sidey, who covered the White House, recalled Williams going on about Hoffa at a boozy dinner with several reporters. "My skin crawls when I get near the guy," Williams said. His words, as planned, were reported back to the Kennedys.

In the summer of 1961, Williams took the direct approach. Visiting

RFK in his office at the Justice Department, Williams posed as a secret ally of Kennedy's against the corrupt labor leader. Kennedy recorded the conversation in a memorandum to files on August 1:

> Ed Williams told me that he was the most disliked individual at the Teamsters other than myself. He said he had broken with them and would no longer have anything to do with them. He said he understood the hierarchy was made up of gangsters and crooks and probably the only one who could save them at all was Harold Gibbons. He said he was relatively honest.
>
> He said he didn't think Hoffa was stealing money anymore but that he had lost all judgment and you just couldn't deal with him.
>
> He later told Bill Hundley [chief of the Organized Crime Division] that he was Public Enemy No. 2 at Teamster Headquarters and said that he was just waiting for the proper moment to resign. Subsequently, he said he would go down to the convention in Miami and resign.

Williams did not resign as Teamsters counsel. Instead, he gave a speech to the Teamsters declaring that he was proud to be one of them. Williams congratulated the Teamsters leaders; they had strengthened the Fifth Amendment, their lawyer said, by invoking it so often. Williams's speech was greeted with waves of applause, according to the Teamsters' newsletter. It is doubtful that the Teamsters leadership would have been so enthusiastic if they had known that their counsel had just described them to the attorney general of the United States as "gangsters and crooks."

The Teamsters were, in the end, too valuable a client for Williams to give up. But the Goldfine case gave him something to offer the new Democratic administration: the scalps of Republican lawmakers. Goldfine told Williams that he had paid off several Republican senators, and Williams saw an opportunity to do a favor for the Democratic administration and get a more favorable sentencing deal for his client (whose sentence had been delayed pending appeal). But Goldfine never delivered. Williams would set up "meeting after meeting," recalled William Hundley, the Justice Department lawyer handling the case, "but it was like Lucy holding the football for Charlie Brown: every time Goldfine said he was ready to talk, he'd pull the ball back." Goldfine demanded to see "Number One" before he would run down the list of politicians he had bribed. "Number One" was the attorney general. But when Williams brought Goldfine to Bobby Kennedy's office, Goldfine insisted on seeing

RFK's brother—the president. Exasperated, Williams gave up. Goldfine served his year in jail.

Through all these negotiations, Williams developed an easy and joking relationship with Justice's Bill Hundley. Williams impishly told Goldfine that Hundley admired the industrialist so much that the Justice Department lawyer called his son—William G. Jr.—"B.G.," the same nickname Goldfine liked to be called. So when Goldfine next saw Hundley, he smiled magnanimously and said, "So how's little B.G.? If everything works out okay, a little trust fund for B.G., heh?" Hundley pretended to be furious with Williams, and the two men laughed about Goldfine's incorrigibility for years. Hundley would turn out to be a close—and very useful—friend to Williams.

Williams's greater goal was to renew his friendship with Bobby Kennedy. Gradually, he was able to win back Kennedy's respect, but the two men never really restored their friendship, said Angie Novello, who served as Bobby Kennedy's secretary and, after Kennedy's death, as Williams's secretary. They did become "civil," recalled Arthur Schlesinger, Jr., "and Bob would use Williams from time to time."

If friendship was too much to ask, Williams was at least glad to be useful. In one case, the attorney general made use of Williams in astonishing fashion. When Kennedy was trying to decide whether to indict Roy Cohn for jury tampering, he called Williams over to his office to review the facts and get his advice. Kennedy detested Cohn, who had been his rival as junior Senate staffer investigating Communists in the 1950s. Kennedy was out to get Cohn by bringing the full weight of the Justice Department against him. It is highly unusual, to say the least, for the attorney general to make a private lawyer privy to the inner details of a criminal investigation of someone else's client, but Kennedy respected Williams's judgment, and he was brash enough to make unorthodox use of it. Williams, who hated Cohn almost as much as Kennedy did, was only too eager to help.

As he sat in the roomy, paneled office of the attorney general, Williams undoubtedly grasped the importance of this moment to his career. Here was a whole new role for him, an outlet for his skills that promised to help him realize his ambition for power. He was no longer defending some Mafia don or corrupt union leader. He was advising the most powerful law enforcement officer on a difficult question that was technically legal but, in fact, freighted with personal significance.

Bobby Kennedy would not be the last powerful official to come to

Williams for advice. Williams understood that men at the top had private problems that required discreet help. Even presidents. Williams did not have a close relationship with John Kennedy, but the president, too, made use of his legal judgment on at least one occasion. Late one night, Williams telephoned his friend Bill Fugazy, the limousine service owner, from the White House. Williams began asking the startled Fugazy questions about Roy Cohn, who had done some business deals with Fugazy. Why do you want to know all this? Fugazy asked. And what are you doing at the White House? President Kennedy asked me to find out about Cohn, replied Williams. The president, he explained, was worried that his younger brother would get burned dealing with the malevolent and elusive Cohn (indeed, the Kennedy administration indicted Cohn but failed to get a conviction).

Williams relished these peeks into the inner circle. He made it his business to learn more about the lives of the powerful, particularly the Kennedy family. He learned, for instance, that JFK was a womanizer. Williams was close to a Washington lawyer named James McInerney, a Fordham graduate and ex-FBI agent who also happened to be old Joe Kennedy's personal lawyer. One day McInerney came to Williams for advice: Joseph Kennedy had asked him to spy on Marilyn Monroe. The Kennedy patriarch was worried about his sons getting involved with the troubled star, and he wanted to find out what she was up to. McInerney didn't know what to do. Williams never disclosed what he advised McInerney, who died a few months later in a car crash, but this was just the sort of information Williams prized. He was becoming a collector of the dark secrets of Washington officialdom. The collection would grow.

IN THE WINTER of 1962, Edmund Muskie, then an up-and-coming senator from Maine, skidded off the road in a chauffeur-driven car in Delaware and hit a tree. His driver, Muskie said, "had never seen snow before." As Muskie was lying in his hospital bed nursing a badly injured leg, he was visited by Ed Williams. Muskie had never met Williams before. The lawyer warmly greeted the senator and asked if there was anything he could do. No, said Muskie, he didn't want to sue anyone. But Williams struck up a conversation with Muskie anyway, and the two soon became friends. Williams wasn't chasing ambulances, he was chasing celebrities, and Muskie was flattered by the attention. In politics, after all, there was nothing wrong with asking.

Williams's haunts—Duke Zeibert's, Toots Shor's, smoky bars and raucous sports arenas—were remote from the salons of Georgetown. But the young and vigorous men of the Kennedy era were disposed to a meritocracy, and in the early 1960s the social barriers that separated Ivy Leaguers from Holy Cross or BC men began to fall in Washington. Kennedy himself embodied a hybrid of Harvard and Irish Catholic Boston; his liege men were expected to be at home in both worlds. At the intersection of the WASP sporting set and the Irish political mafia was Edward Bennett Williams. Nancy Dickerson, a pretty television newswoman and Washington hostess, recalls slumming with Joe Alsop, the Groton-educated columnist, and Alice Roosevelt Longworth, grand-dame daughter of President Theodore Roosevelt, at boxing matches at the old Uhline Arena. There, greeting them at ringside, where the blood splattered and fighters spat their teeth, was Ed Williams. He and Alice hit it right off; she would shout "Bully!" after every telling blow.

Ben Bradlee, Williams's old friend from the criminal courts and the Atlas Club, had returned to Washington from a stint in Paris. He had become the Washington Bureau Chief of *Newsweek*, which had been bought by the Washington Post Company at Bradlee's urging. Irreverent, urbane, clever, and profane, Bradlee renewed his friendship with Williams. Bradlee was anything but ashamed of being an old-line WASP, but he liked having ethnics as friends. Aside from Williams, his best friend in life was columnist Art Buchwald, a poor Jewish boy from Queens. Bradlee drew Williams into his crowd of young journalists and Kennedy administration strivers, mostly Yale and Harvard men like columnists Rowland Evans and Phil Geyelin of the *Post*.

In Washington, where politicians come and go but journalists like Walter Lippmann, the Alsops, and now Bradlee seemed to stay forever, the most attractive and best-connected newsmen became leading social lights. By the mid-sixties Williams would be welcome in their sanctums. At a black tie party given by columnist Joe Kraft and the *New York Times*'s Tom Wicker at the Federal City Club in May 1965, the *Post* society-page reporter found Williams enjoying himself at three o'clock in the morning as he watched Teddy Kennedy and his brother-in-law Stephen Smith dance the Mashed Potato.

Although nominally still a Republican, Williams embraced the liberal zeitgeist of the times, particularly on civil rights. In a series of speeches, Williams attacked the death penalty, primarily because it fell disproportionately on blacks. At the time, it was a stand that took some courage.

Still, there were some things Williams would not do for civil rights. One of them was quit the Metropolitan Club. In 1961, Bobby Kennedy had led a revolt within the white male bastion when the club refused to admit black guests for lunch. Amid considerable publicity, thirty members quit the club. Williams was not among them. "He understood the power structure well," said Jim McCarrick, a friend from Georgetown days. "He didn't want to rock the boat. A significant number of old-time trial lawyers and judges in Washington thought the Metropolitan Club was the last, best place on earth."

Williams found his ties to the powerful useful. When Sheldon Cohen, Williams's own tax lawyer, became commissioner of the Internal Revenue Service in 1964, Williams called him with a little problem. It seemed that the IRS had seized all the assets of one of Williams's clients, a doctor who made a cancer cure from the extract of prune pits. "Christ, Sheldon," Williams complained, "I can't get paid." Cohen released enough of the medicine man's assets to pay Williams's legal fees.

But this kind of favor was small change compared to the IOUs Clark Clifford could call in. Clifford, former presidential adviser and now lawyer to the Kennedy family, had not held a government job since 1950, when he left Harry Truman's White House, but he had more power in Washington than half the cabinet. When private businessmen had problems in Washington, the smart ones visited Clifford's dark-paneled office overlooking the White House. Wavy-haired, smooth-tongued, he had great powers of persuasion and access to everyone who needed to be persuaded. Clifford said that he rarely lobbied, and he loathed the word *fixer*, but he somehow accomplished what needed to be done, with discretion and efficiency, in a city not known for either.

Williams was in awe of Clifford. He was the model of a private lawyer whose access and influence gave him real power. An invitation to Clifford's Christmas buffet was a more accurate indication of clout in the capital than membership in the Chevy Chase Club. Hugh Sidey, a close observer of Washington's greasy pole, first noticed Williams, in a soft tweed jacket, eating oysters at Clifford's Yuletide groaning board, around 1962.

Clifford and Williams had first met in 1950, when both men were just starting out on their own. "It took us a while to overcome the sense that we were cast as potential rivals in the relatively small Washington legal world of the fifties," Clifford wrote in his memoirs. But by the early 1960s, the two men had become allies.

Clifford understood that Ed Williams could be useful to him. He preferred not to handle criminal matters, but his clients sometimes came to him clutching grand jury subpoenas. So Clifford began sending them down the street to Williams. Williams was, in Clifford's estimation, a shrewd judge of character with a knack for solving problems. Increasingly, when Clifford wanted to chew over a difficult question, he gave Williams a call. Clifford flattered Williams. "How's my lawyer?" he would ask in his silky, mellifluous voice. Williams, in turn, shamelessly flattered Clifford. "I'm still young enough in spirit to have living heroes, two of them, and you're one," Williams wrote Clifford in the summer of 1967. (The other was presumably Earl Warren, or perhaps DiMaggio; the list changed from time to time.)

Williams was useful to Clifford in another small but tangible way. He could get him Redskins tickets. "I appreciate your kindness in supplying the football tickets to the Solicitor of the Interior Department," Clifford wrote on one occasion. "He is new here and he has not seen the Redskins play and is anxious to do so." In Washington, still culturally deprived in the 1960s, the hottest draw in town was the pro football team, and the man who controlled the best seats was Ed Williams.

"IF YOU WANT to have power, own a team," Williams once told a fellow lawyer, Donald Oresman. Williams understood the social force of sports, the bond it could generate between men, in the stands as well as on the field. He loved the ritual as well as the excitement of the game. And he knew that being an owner conferred status, even power. Tickets were a currency to Ed Williams; even before he could hand them out for free, he would buy them and use them as presents to men whose friendship or favor he sought. When Williams was trying to ease the chill he felt at the Justice Department in 1961, his peace offering to Walter Sheridan, Kennedy's chief investigator against Hoffa, was to take him to a heavyweight boxing bout.

Williams was not much of a football fan. He would tease his partner Colman Stein about "wasting a perfectly good afternoon" by attending Redskins games at the old Griffith Stadium. Baseball was his real passion, and his burning desire was to one day own a baseball team. In November 1960, he almost realized that dream.

Williams had become close to Bill Veeck, the maverick baseball owner of the Chicago White Sox, who was a member of good standing in Toots

Shor's society. Williams enjoyed hearing Veeck describe how he was going to shake up the stuffy major league baseball owners. As he drank beer after beer and stubbed out cigarettes on his peg leg, Veeck, who once sent a midget up to bat for the St. Louis Browns, would conjure up new gimmicks to get the fans into the park: Ladies Day, Bat Day, Ball Day, Barbecue Apron Day, livelier baseballs, home-plate raffles, exploding scoreboards. A carny hawker at heart, Veeck particularly hated the New York Yankees and constantly schemed to break the hold of the perennial champions. Williams, who was wary of Yankees in general, Joe DiMaggio excepted, would laugh and plot with him.

On November 17, 1960, DiMaggio was leaving Toots Shor's when he ran into a flushed Williams. "I'm going to buy a baseball club!" Williams exclaimed. "Can I use your name?" DiMaggio asked Williams what this was all about. Williams explained that the Washington Senators were moving to Minnesota, and that the American League was creating a new franchise in the capital. Williams had a good chance to get it. He had pulled together $3.5 million of his own money and had a couple of bankers, including his law partner Colman Stein. Bill Veeck was working to line up the other league owners to vote for him. It would help if Williams could drop DiMaggio's name at the owners' meeting now being held at the Plaza Hotel. Could he? DiMaggio said yes. Williams gave him a happy handshake and headed for the Plaza.

Williams lost. At the last minute, Cal Griffith, who was moving the Senators out to the Twin Cities, double-crossed Veeck and changed his vote from Williams to a rival syndicate. Williams was bitterly disappointed; he would have to wait almost twenty years to own a baseball team.

He was still determined to have a piece of a team, even if he had to settle for football. Almost immediately, Williams and Stein began exploring a way to buy into Washington's professional football team. Williams was intrigued by George Marshall, the owner of the Redskins. Like Veeck, Marshall was a promoter and a showman. A former chorus-line actor who had married a Ziegfeld girl, Marshall had bought the Redskins for $100 when they were the Duluth Eskimos and the fans were complaining of frostbite. He had moved them to Boston and called them the Redskins (after the more popular baseball team, the Boston Braves) and then to Washington, where they drew small, indifferent crowds. To stir up more enthusiasm, he had invented the halftime show and had even parachuted Santa Claus into the stadium one cold December day to throw little white footballs to the chilled fans. Marshall tried to broaden the Redskins' appeal by pitching them as a Southern team; the band played "Dixie" before every game. He signed up a lucrative Southern radio network, but he never fielded a winner. The reason was that he refused to have blacks on his team.

Unlike Veeck, who was funny and crude, Marshall was mean and crude, a racist and a bully. Still, Williams cultivated him, seeking him out at the night spots he frequented, joshing with him and flattering him. When Harry Wismer, who owned 25 percent of the Redskins, wanted to sell his shares in November 1960 because he had fallen out with Marshall (who refused to pay him a dividend), Williams offered to buy into the team. That winter, Williams and Stein began to negotiate with Marshall. They worked out a deal that would allow the two lawyers to buy a quarter of the team for $250,000; Williams and Stein would each agree to put down $25,000 cash, and Marshall would loan them the rest. But there were some sticking points: Stein, a tax lawyer, wanted to see Marshall's tax returns to make sure the owner wasn't looting the franchise. Marshall "looked stricken," Stein recalled, but he grudgingly opened the books. Stein discovered that "Marshall was living very well off the team." Then Williams told Marshall that the Redskins couldn't win without black players. "No nigger's ever going to work for me," replied Marshall. Williams and Stein stood up and walked out.

Williams was right, of course; an all-white team could not win in the National Football League, which had been integrated since the late 1940s. In the fall of 1961, the Redskins went 1–12–1. The season's only reward was the first draft pick in 1962. By then, Marshall was feeling the pressure to hire some blacks. The Kennedy administration offered to build a new stadium to replace dilapidated old Griffith Stadium but warned that only integrated teams could play there. Shirley Povich, the *Washington Post*'s leading sports columnist, was merciless about Marshall and his NAACP policy (Never at Anytime Any Colored Players). One day after the great Cleveland fullback Jim Brown had run all over the Redskins, Povich wrote, "Born ineligible to play for the Redskins, Jimmy Brown integrated the Redskins' end zone three times yesterday. . . ." Swallowing his prejudice, Marshall used his first draft pick in the winter of 1962 to choose Ernie Davis, the Heisman Trophy winner from Syracuse. Davis, however, had no desire to play for Marshall. Faced with paying for his sins, Marshall looked for help. He turned to Ed Williams. Could Williams enlist his client, Congressman Adam Clayton Powell, to recruit Davis?

Williams brought Powell to see Marshall over dinner at Duke Zeibert's. The dinner did not go well. "Hello, parson," said Marshall,
sullenly greeting the congressman. "You gotta talk to Davis for me,
parson." Powell drew slowly on his cigarette holder and extracted a
price. "I can help you," he said, "but you can't have only one token
nigger. You've got to have two, or three, or four." "You mean a matched
set, parson?" asked Marshall. The two men baited each other for a few
minutes, and Powell kept demanding to know when Marshall was going
to wake up and get himself a real team of good black ball players. That
morning, Marshall had read that an Italian air force pilot had crashed in
Southern Ethiopia, where, the papers luridly suggested, he had been
eaten by cannibals. Marshall replied, "When you people stop eating
Italian aviators."

Marshall ended up trading his draft pick, and Davis went to the Cleveland Browns (tragically, he died of leukemia a year later). In return for
the trade, Marshall finally got a black player: Bobby Mitchell, an all-pro
who had played in the same backfield as Jimmy Brown. The color barrier
down, Williams now felt free to buy into the Redskins.

In March 1962, Williams bought 5 percent of the team for $75,000. In
time, he would parlay that into a Washington power base roughly equiv-
alent to a seat on the House Ways and Means Committee. But his most
useful act as a new part-owner was to help Bobby Mitchell break in as the
first black player in a city that was in many ways still a Southern town.
Mitchell could tolerate Marshall, who told him, "We'll get along so long
as you stay out of jail and don't ask for money." But the fans were
sometimes abusive, yelling, "Run, nigger, run," and it bothered Mitchell that he was not allowed to eat in the whites-only restaurant across the
street from the Redskin offices at 9th and H streets.

The cruelest blow came when Mitchell was eating dinner with his wife
at Rive Gauche, an expensive restaurant in Georgetown. A well-dressed
man walked by his table and spat at him. "This got to me," Mitchell
said. He could live with the epithets from the cheap seats, but to be spat
at in a restaurant patronized by senators and members of the Kennedy
administration was too much. "My game was affected. I started to play
bad," he said. "Ed Williams sensed what had happened to me." Mitchell confided in him.

"Now, Coach," said Williams (he called Mitchell "Coach"),
"you've got to understand. There are sons of bitches in all walks of life.
Just because you're rich doesn't mean you're not a redneck." Williams

counseled Mitchell to have a thick skin, that in time the bigotry would pass. And as Mitchell scored more touchdowns and gained more yards than any player in Redskin history, it did.

The Redskins only slowly improved as a football team. But as a social event, they became a sensation in Washington during the early sixties. "To Be Seen Seeing the Redskins" headlined a *Sports Illustrated* story in October 1965. "The team is impressive socially, if not athletically, and Washington's elite turns out on Sundays," the magazine observed. Photographs showed Bradlee and Buchwald laughing it up in the owner's box, along with Chief Justice Earl Warren and Supreme Court Justice Tom Clark. The article noted that Senators Stuart Symington of Missouri and Warren Magnuson of Washington were there, together with Justice Byron "Whizzer" White, the former All-American to whom Williams had given a lifetime pass. The owner's box was Williams's box now; he was the president of the club, even though he owned only 5 percent of the team. (George Marshall had been invalided with a stroke in 1963, and his successor as president, Leo D'Orsey, died in April 1965.) Jack Kent Cooke, the wealthy media and sports entrepreneur, also owned more of the team than Williams—25 percent—but he lived out in California and let Williams vote his shares.

Williams passed out tickets to congressmen like tips to waiters. "We could get a quorum of the House anytime we ring the bell," said Dave Slattery, a Redskins official. As salve for the old Hoffa wound, Williams gave a whole box to the Robert Kennedy family. As the family grew, the eight seats were not enough; Ethel Kennedy would cram in as many as sixteen guests, requiring adults to hold children on their laps.*

---

*After Robert Kennedy was assassinated in 1968, the name of D.C. Stadium was changed to Robert F. Kennedy Stadium. Williams welcomed the name change but said it was not his idea.

Chapter Fourteen

WILLIAMS WAS KNOWN as a great trial lawyer, more comfortable dealing with concrete facts and persuading jurors with emotional rhetoric than with making abstract legal arguments in learned briefs to high court justices. But in fact, Williams was a pure lawyer as well as a great advocate. He understood that an ability to craft a novel interpretation of the law was often more important to winning a case than a clever cross-examination or a gut-wrenching closing argument at trial. It is typical of his vision and creativity that he could look at a seemingly ordinary police affidavit in a run-of-the-mill gambling case and see a chance to overturn a Supreme Court precedent that had been on the books for thirty years.

Williams had almost turned away Julius "Crippled Julius" Silverman as a client when the bookmaker came to him in 1958. Along with Meyer "Nutsy" Schwartz and Robert Martin, Silverman had been caught running an illegal gambling operation out of a row house in Foggy Bottom. Williams had long since stopped handling routine betting busts, but his interest was piqued when he glanced at the police affidavit used by the prosecutor to get a search warrant for Silverman's betting shop. The police stated that they had "overheard" conversations inside the house about betting. Figuring that the cops had used some kind of electronic eavesdropping device, Williams saw an opportunity to make constitutional law out of a penny-ante case. He agreed to represent Silverman. He boldly predicted to his client that he would lose in the trial court and again on appeal, but that he would win in the Supreme Court of the United States.

Williams sensed that the timing was right. Under Earl Warren, the Supreme Court had begun to give real meaning to the Bill of Rights. Perhaps the moment had come to establish a right of privacy in the Fourth Amendment, and to rein in law enforcement officers who were becoming increasingly quick to use wiretaps and bugs to overhear private conversations.

The law on electronic eavesdropping in the United States in the late 1950s was at once archaic and chaotic. In the landmark *Olmstead* decision in 1928, the Supreme Court had ruled that wiretapping did not violate the Fourth Amendment prohibition against unreasonable searches and seizures. In a backward-looking opinion, the court had held that a search was not illegal unless it involved some kind of physical trespass. Furthermore, the Fourth Amendment only outlawed seizures of physical property—not mere words. Williams considered *Olmstead* to be a wrong-headed decision. He favored the approach taken by Louis Brandeis, whose *Olmstead* dissent argued that the privacy right inherent in the Fourth Amendment protected a person's conversations as well as his possessions. In 1930, Congress had actually outlawed eavesdropping, but local police routinely wiretapped, and the federal government never prosecuted them, in part because federal agents were also breaking the law. In the Costello case, Williams had been appalled by the pervasiveness of wiretapping in New York—and frustrated by his inability to get the evidence thrown out.

Before he could spin a novel constitutional theory of the right to privacy, Williams had to find out *how* the police had overheard the gamblers taking bets. Compared to other departments, the D.C. police were somewhat more mindful of the law on the books. Instead of wiretapping, they had used a device called a "spike mike"—a foot-long needle drilled through the wall until it touched a heating duct. By picking up voice vibrations, the spike mike turned the heating registers of the gambling house into microphones, allowing the police next door to listen in on the bookmaking. Squeezing into the crawl space, Williams's associate Vince Fuller was able to find where the spike mike had penetrated the wall (when Fuller returned to the office, there were a lot of jokes about how he had broken his ball point pen making a dent on the duct, thus establishing a physical trespass).

As Williams had predicted, the lower court judge threw out his motion to suppress the evidence, and Silverman, Martin, and Schwartz were convicted and sentenced to jail. On appeal, as predicted, Williams lost again. But in June 1960, the Supreme Court agreed to review the case. In December, as Williams was preparing his argument, saloon owner Duke Zeibert asked defendant Bob Martin to make a line on Williams's chances of success. Martin made the government a ten-to-one favorite. Zeibert bet $100 on Williams.

The night before his Supreme Court argument, an enormous snowstorm struck Washington. Watching the drifts pile up outside, Williams predicted that the high court would not hold session the next morning. He made a batch of martinis and sat down to watch *The Wizard of Oz* with his children and Betty Killay, who was helping him mind the children while Agnes was in the hospital trying not to miscarry her firstborn. Williams guessed wrong; government offices were closed, but the Supreme Court sat anyway. (Chief Justice Earl Warren later told Williams that he felt compelled to hold court because the papers that morning had shown a picture of him cheering in the snow at a Redskins game.) Williams's sister-in-law was so hung over that she could barely move, but Williams trudged off into the snow to make his novel Fourth Amendment arguments to the Brethren.

Perhaps because of the hangover, Williams enunciated his words with particular care. His voice, which can still be heard on tapes of Supreme Court oral arguments preserved by the National Archives, sounded clear and sharp but slightly pinched. His voice was an instrument, one of his tools of persuasion. He spoke precisely and forcefully, his tenor rising as he described how the spike mike had turned the wall of the defendants' house into a giant microphone. He was deferential to the justices, careful always to address them by title and name ("Mr. Justice Frankfurter . . ."). But he let some passion creep into his voice as he extolled the right to privacy, finally lapsing into cliché by quoting the Earl of Chatham ("a man's home is his castle"). "We know that," grumbled one of the justices.

Early in his argument, Williams took the unusual step of showing the physical evidence—the spike mike itself—which caused the justices to stir in their seats and peer down over the bench. The government had overwhelming evidence in the case—betting slips, phone records—but Williams made a reasoned argument against the pernicious impact of government eavesdropping, showing how it intruded on the privacy of the innocent as well as the wrongdoer. (Hearing Williams make the same arguments in the trial court, Silverman had leaned over to Martin and whispered, "Hey, Bob, maybe we weren't guilty after all.")

As Williams predicted, he won. Spared from jail, Martin happily paid off Zeibert's ten-to-one bet at $1,000. The court's opinion was unanimous, though narrowly drawn. The Supreme Court prefers to move incrementally; reluctant to overturn precedent, it prefers to "distinguish" cases from past decisions. In the *Silverman* case, the court did not throw out *Olmstead*. It ruled that since the spike mike had actually penetrated the gambling house, there had been a physical trespass, unlike a wire tapped outside of a home. Nonetheless, "you could hear the ice cracking around *Olmstead*," said Michigan Law School professor Yale Kamisar. The court took a dig at the retrograde reasoning of *Olmstead*: "Inherent Fourth Amendment rights are not inevitably measured in terms of ancient niceties of tort and real property law," wrote Justice Potter Stewart for the court. Stewart's language echoed Brandeis's dissent in *Olmstead*: "At the very core [of the Fourth Amendment] stands the right of a man to retreat into his home and there be free from government intrusion." Williams knew he had delivered a telling blow to the court's outdated precedent, and that it was only a matter of time before it reversed outright the thirty-year-old decision. He hoped, also, that he had impressed the justices with the quality and thoroughness of his argument.

He learned that he had a few months later when the Supreme Court asked him to argue another Fourth Amendment case, *Wong Sun v. United States*. By asking him to take the case, which had been poorly argued in the lower courts, the justices were recognizing Williams as an authority on the Fourth Amendment as well as a skilled appellate advocate. He did not disappoint. In the *Wong Sun* case, a half dozen policemen looking for heroin had raided a Chinese laundry at 6:00 A.M. and chased the proprietor back into his bedroom, where his wife and children were sleeping. The laundry owner, James Wah Toy, made a confession that led to his arrest, along with another defendant named Wong Sun, for narcotics possession. The issue was whether the police had "probable cause" to make the arrest. The police had been given a tip that a man named Blackie Toy sold heroin from a Chinese laundry on Leavenworth Street in San Francisco, but the tipster gave no specific address on the thirty-block-long street. The sign on the door of the establishment raided by the police just said "Oye's Laundry."

Williams had been brought into the case after the lower courts had established the record, which is supposed to serve as the basis for the high court's decision. Nonetheless, the night before he was to argue before the Supreme Court, Williams had a hunch. If he could show that there was more than one Chinese laundry on Leavenworth Street, it would strengthen his argument that there was not probable cause to raid this particular one. Williams had to move quickly to find someone living in San Francisco who could drive down Leavenworth Street and check for other laundries. It is not often that Hall of Fame baseball players are used as private investigators, but that night Joe DiMaggio drove up and down Leavenworth Street counting Chinese laundries for his friend Ed Williams. Williams had simply called up his drinking buddy and asked him for a favor. And sure enough, in court, Justice Douglas asked the question: Were there other laundries on the street? Williams was able to say that, though the record did not disclose the number, he could assure the court that there were many Chinese laundries on the street. Officially, the court could not be bound by his off-the-record observation. But Williams's thoroughness may have been a factor in the court's five-to-four decision holding that the police had violated the defendant's Fourth Amendment rights. And although the court's decision did not deal directly with wiretapping, it dealt another blow to *Olmstead* by ruling that a man's words, as well as his home, are protected by the Fourth Amendment.

The court's majority opinion was written by Justice William Brennan. He had been enormously impressed, he later said, by Williams's precision and succinctness, his ability to zero in on an issue and get his points across in just a few words. Supreme Court justices are accustomed to windy lawyers grappling with complex issues under judicial interrogation. Williams, on the other hand, seemed totally in command of the facts and the law. "I would rate him as one of the two or three best advocates to appear before the court in my thirty-three years," Brennan said in 1989. Brennan did observe, however, that Williams was "taut. He was very intense. He might seem free and easy but he was tense as a wire. He'd be talking fluidly but you could see that his hands were clenched on the podium." Not all the justices appreciated Williams's sometimes plainspoken style. Arguing a case involving antitrust conspiracies in the movie business before the high court in 1964, Williams accused theater owners and distributors of "sophisticated economic suicide." Justice Stewart scolded, "This isn't a murder case, Mr. Williams." Pounding the lectern, Williams did not back off. "It's an economic murder case, Your Honor," he said.

Many of the justices liked Williams personally. The morning after he argued the *Wong Sun* case, he got a handwritten note from Justice Arthur

Goldberg, "Ed, I'm pleased that my maiden argument is yours." Goldberg, a labor lawyer, had become close friends with Williams before he was appointed to the court by President Kennedy in 1962. Williams made it his business to socialize with the justices. In the sixties, Williams began eating lunch from time to time at Milt Kronheim's private restaurant, a peculiar Washington institution. Kronheim, a former bail bondsman who became a liquor distributor, was a garrulous collector of legal celebrities. At his warehouse out on V Street in northeast Washington, he kept a simple dining room with unusually good food that became a kind of informal club for liberal jurists. David Bazelon and Skelly Wright, two liberal pillars of the U.S. Court of Appeals for the District of Columbia, dined there often with the liberal core of the Warren Court: Bill Brennan, Thurgood Marshall, Bill Douglas, Arthur Goldberg, and the "Chief," Earl Warren. The conversation was about sports, politics, and the law— not specific cases, but the law in general. Williams periodically joined the group. "He was a stickler never to put us in an embarrassing position," recalled Brennan. Williams was much too discreet and careful to lobby the justices on a specific case. But he made friends easily, talking about the Redskins (and handing out tickets), telling tales about his colorful clients, and talking, in general terms, about the all-too-frequent abuses of the rights of the criminally accused.

Williams grew especially attached to Earl Warren. Without knowing it, Williams had made an admirer out of the chief justice in his very first argument before the Supreme Court back in 1954. The case involved a congressman who had been convicted of taking kickbacks, and Williams had raised a novel legal issue on appeal. Incredibly, Williams failed to appear for his debut before the high court. He was eating lunch in the Metropolitan Club at about 1:45 P.M. when he received an urgent message that the justices were waiting for him: His argument had been scheduled to begin at 1:30. Williams raced up Capitol Hill to the courthouse and profusely apologized, taking all the blame on himself. Actually, the fault was the clerk's, who had given Williams the wrong date. The chief justice was enormously impressed by Williams's graciousness. The clerk was an alcoholic who often became confused, and the chief justice knew that Williams was taking the fall for him. The friendship between Warren and Williams was cemented in even more unusual fashion: on a banquette at Toots Shor's. One of Williams's drinking buddies at Shor's was television personality John Charles Daly, who was married to Earl Warren's daughter Virginia. When the Dalys came to Washington, they would invite Williams over to Earl Warren's for drinks. Williams was thrilled to go, his wife, Agnes, said. For all his worldly bemusement, Williams was a true hero worshiper, and Earl Warren was, Williams liked to say, "one of my greatest living heroes." By the mid-sixties, Earl Warren was a regular in the owner's box at the Redskins games.

It was fitting that he had a Toots Shor connection with the Supreme Court. Williams's friends marveled at his unusual mixture of high-mindedness and calculation, that he could be at once genuinely idealistic and deeply cynical. "One moment he'd be sincerely talking to you about the law and the Constitution," recalled John Reilly, a Justice Department official in the Kennedy administration, "and the next moment you'd hear that he was partying with [Mafia don] Momo Giancana."

WHEN ED WILLIAMS and *Washington Post* publisher Phil Graham met at a large dinner party at Burning Tree Country Club in the spring of 1957, Katharine Graham recalled, they "fell in love." Both men hated stuffy formal affairs. Williams was on the wagon, in training for the Hoffa trial, but he grabbed a bottle, sat down with Graham, and talked until dawn. In Graham, Williams could see an exaggerated version of himself.

Few men in Washington were funnier storytellers or better shmoozers than Ed Williams, but Graham was a raconteur and table-hopper nonpareil. Like Williams, Graham was complex, at once earnest and irreverent, edgy and easy, shy and garrulous. Both men could be moody, subject to higher highs and lower lows than ordinary people. In a city of self-important men, both were capable of pricking their own large egos with rueful self-mockery.

Graham had Williams's gift of language; it was Graham who said that a good newspaper should be "the first rough draft of history." Like Williams, Graham had married the boss's daughter—Kay Meyer, whose father owned the *Washington Post*. Just as Williams had been born an urban Irish "mick," Graham had been born a rural Southern "cracker" whose boyhood in the Florida Everglades was, if anything, more primitive than Williams's street life in Hartford. "They shared an insider-outsider bond," said Graham's son (and later Williams's law associate) Bill. "Phil was a publisher the way Ed was a lawyer." Both eagerly sought power beyond their profession.

The difference between the two, however, was that Graham already had power. He had achieved what Williams wanted: to be a kind of minister-without-portfolio in the government-law-press establishment of Washington. Graham had a head start. His father may have started poor, but he became wealthy from farming and real estate. Graham had arrived in Washington at the top, as a Felix Frankfurter Supreme Court clerk via Harvard Law School; he had come to make the New Deal work, not to argue streetcar cases. Graham had become a close friend of both Lyndon Johnson, when LBJ was the Senate majority leader in the late 1950s, and then of the young senator from Massachusetts, John F. Kennedy. It was Graham who had cut the deal that put LBJ on JFK's ticket at the Democratic National Convention in 1960.

Williams sometimes referred to himself as a "manic depressive," but Graham really was one. Aside from occasional outbursts at the office and midnight hooting with the likes of Leonore Lemmon, Williams was able to control his mood swings. Graham could not. He was sick and getting sicker. In the fall of 1962, he began to behave more and more outrageously. He would make anti-Semitic remarks about his in-laws, his wife, even his children. He took up with an Australian girl who worked as a secretary in the Paris bureau of *Newsweek*, which he owned, and told anyone who would listen that he planned to divorce Kay and marry his new twenty-seven-year-old girl, Robin Webb.

Washington, in many ways a small and gossipy soap-opera town, was both scandalized and titillated by Graham. Even President Kennedy wanted to be kept abreast of the latest developments. Georgetown society was quickly split into "Phil People" and "Kay People." Williams was in an especially delicate position. He was Phil's lawyer as well as his friend, and thus bound to do his bidding. Graham said he wanted a divorce and a new will. Graham's father-in-law, Eugene Meyer, had given Phil a controlling interest in the *Post*, explaining with the logic of his era, "You never want a man working for his wife." Now Phil wanted to cut out his wife and give her interest to Robin Webb.

Williams knew Graham was ill. When Graham loudly announced at a cocktail party his intention to marry Webb, Williams whisked both of them out the door. Still, Williams was afraid that if he refused to do what his client asked, Graham might become depressed and kill himself. Williams played for time. He told Graham that he could have his divorce, but first he would have to start behaving—no more wild binges, no more obscene outbursts at dinner parties.

Publicly, Williams was a Phil Person. Washington in those Kennedy years was a "macho place," Katharine Graham recalled, where men preferred each other or "little blondes in size-six dresses." As a forty-five-year-old housewife, she felt alienated from Williams. "When Phil hired Ed, I thought, 'Dear God, no. Now we're going to court.' I was scared." As she later discovered, she need not have been fearful. Williams knew that her husband was behaving irrationally. As a general rule, Williams did not pass moral judgment on his clients—or anyone else—with one exception: He could not understand how a man could walk out on his wife. He thought divorce was immoral, perhaps inevitable in some cases, but fundamentally against God's will.

Williams kept putting off Graham's demand for a divorce, telling him that he couldn't walk out the door one day and get divorced the next. The will was a trickier matter. In February 1963, while Williams was traveling, Graham barged into Williams's firm and demanded that another lawyer draft a will. Graham was so insistent that associate Harold Ungar agreed. Though he had never written a will before, Ungar drafted one on the spot. It was clear by now that Williams could no longer put Graham off. On February 18, Williams drafted a will that revoked all previous wills and left two-thirds of his estate to his children, one-third to Robin Webb. Kay Graham was cut out completely. At the same time, however, Williams wrote a memo to files doubting Graham's competence to make a will, and stating that he had drawn up the document only to retain Graham's confidence as a friend so he could exercise some influence over his client's conduct.

Graham was spinning faster and faster out of control. In March, he demanded a new will reducing his children's share to one-third and leaving the rest to Robin Webb. In January, he had taken the podium at a publisher's convention in Phoenix, Arizona, and made a drunken and obscene speech. Two psychiatrists had to wrestle him down and inject him with tranquilizers. Alerted in Washington, Jack Kennedy sent a presidential plane to Phoenix to pick up his fallen friend. In June, Graham took off on another manic toot, this time to Puerto Rico, where he crashed again. Flown home, he voluntarily checked into Chestnut Lodge, a private psychiatric center in Rockville, Maryland. At the hospital, Williams asked Graham, "Do you want to get rid of Robin?" "Yes," Graham answered, "but I don't know how." Williams took care of it. He explained to Webb what she already knew, that Phil was sick and that it was time to go home. Quietly, without making any money demands, she got on the plane and flew to Australia. The new wills were torn up.

Two months later, Phil Graham shot himself. Some of his friends believed that his suicide was, in a perverse way, a rational act. They thought that he had diagnosed himself and realized that he would never be able to lead a normal life, that his choice was between self-destructive outbursts and a drugged half-life.*

Before Phil died, Williams encountered Katharine Graham at the mental hospital. She thanked him for his help with Phil. Williams was warm and gentle with her; he made her understand that he felt her grief, that he understood her ordeal, and that he admired her courage. From then on Katharine Graham and Edward Bennett Williams were the best of friends; in times of trouble, she would turn to him.

In later years, after Williams became counsel to the *Washington Post*, some of Williams's detractors speculated that he had hedged his bets, that he had coldly calculated that Phil was about to self-destruct and thus switched his fealty to Katharine, who stood to inherit her father's empire. It is not hard to look at the course of Williams's career and see evidence of his playing both sides for the best angle, but Williams was a more complicated, and in some ways a better man, than some of his career moves suggest. He really did love Phil Graham and did want to help him. Williams was capable of great empathy. He did not need to feign grief and concern toward Phil; he could feel it. He was vulnerable to the same dark forces that devoured his friend, only they were less consuming and he was able to control them with his will and faith.

NOMINALLY, WILLIAMS HAD begun the 1960s as a Republican. Harold Stassen's photograph still hung on his wall, and as late as 1962 Williams was rumored to be a potential GOP candidate for governor of Maryland. He was indeed flirting with the idea of running for public office, but not as a Republican. By 1964, Washington was an overwhelmingly Democratic town. The Republicans had been routed in the presidential elections, and the Democrats controlled 67 of 100 seats in the Senate and 295 of 435 in the House.

In later years, Williams said he switched parties after the 1964 Republican National Convention in San Francisco because "the John Birchers were taking over the party." He said that he was offended when the Goldwater forces shouted down moderate candidate Nelson Rockefeller. But in fact, Williams had made the switch earlier that year. He backed

---

*Had Graham lived another six months, he might have been put on lithium, the newly discovered miracle drug for manic depressives.

Joseph Tydings, a Democrat, for the Senate from Maryland in the spring of 1964. And when Ellen Berlow, a Tydings campaign worker, came to see him that April, he told her that he was thinking of running for governor himself as a Democrat. Williams decided to test the water by giving a speech at the Montgomery County Democrats annual dinner dance at the Indian Springs Country Club that May. The speech was a "sensation," recalled Berlow, but almost immediately the doubters began murmuring. Williams wasn't a true Marylander, they said, he was a carpetbagger from D.C. And wasn't he the lawyer who defended Jimmy Hoffa and the Mafia? When Berlow told Williams she thought his candidacy would be uphill, he seemed resigned to the old "guilt by client" curse.

Still, Williams started talking again about running for office in 1966 as a Democratic congressional candidate from the 8th District in western Maryland. This time Senator Tydings cautioned him against it, warning that Williams might not get the nomination, and even if he did, the Republican incumbent, Charles "Mac" Mathias, seemed unbeatable. "What I didn't say to Williams was that he would hate being a freshman congressman, but he would have," Tydings recalled. At regular intervals until he died, Williams would entertain notions of running for office, but nothing ever came of it, and his wife and friends wondered whether he wasn't just idly fantasizing. Tydings was right; Williams would have hated being a freshman congressman. He would have been bored and impatient with sloppy staff work and the lack of real power and control. Actually, it is doubtful whether *any* elected job, short of president, would have satisfied him. Williams appreciated democracy in principle, but in practice he was authoritarian.

His friends were bemused by his switch from Republican to Democrat. "Why did he switch? Because the Democrats were incumbents!" said Peter Taft, a law associate of Williams's in the sixties and the grandson of President William Howard Taft. "That's where the power lay." But columnist George Will, who came to know Williams well, suggests that Williams's conversion was really a return to his true roots. "Williams was a natural Democrat," says Will. "He was an urban figure. There was no country club in him." Although Williams wanted to be accepted in the inner circles of the establishment, he was still by birth an outsider, whose first political memory was cheering Al Smith, the Democratic candidate for president in 1928, as he paraded past the poor Irish of Hartford. Williams, who was eight years old at the time, was told by his elders that

Smith would probably lose, but the boy was proud that a Catholic finally had a chance.

After John Kennedy's assassination, many prominent Washington Democrats were torn between personal loyalty to the Kennedys and duty to his successor, Lyndon Johnson, who regarded the Kennedy faithful as traitors. Since Williams had never fully won over the Kennedys, he was able to occupy neutral ground. Still, he was not able to avoid the cross-fire. In the fall of 1966, LBJ accepted Williams's invitation to attend a Redskins game. As Williams and LBJ watched the game, Robert Kennedy knocked on the door of the box to get in. "Let him pound," ordered the president. Williams had to apologize to RFK the next day.

WILLIAMS WANTED TO become a counselor to presidents in the manner of Clark Clifford, but he lacked Clifford's political savvy. Clifford had helped Harry Truman get reelected president by devising his "Give 'Em Hell, Harry" strategy in 1948, and in later years he had shrewdly advised a number of Democratic presidential hopefuls, including Lyndon Johnson and Jack Kennedy. Williams was still a political neophyte in the mid-sixties; in truth, he would never quite get the hang of elective politics. But there was one big favor that Williams could do for LBJ. Within a few days of Johnson's swearing-in aboard Air Force One on the long flight home from Dallas, Texas, Williams took on the assignment of defending Bobby Baker.

The son of a postman from Pickens, South Carolina, Robert Gene Baker came to the U.S. Senate as a page at the age of fourteen and never left. A bootlicker, but an agile one, he curried favor with Senate powers Lyndon Johnson of Texas and Robert Kerr of Oklahoma. Baker made it his business to know things: who owed whom a favor, who was drunk, who was on the take, who was sleeping with his secretary. By the time he was twenty-six, he was secretary of the Senate, appointed by Majority Leader Johnson in 1955. "He is my strong right arm," said LBJ, "the last man I see at night and the first man I see in the morning." The newspapers began referring to Baker as "the 101st senator." Baker thought he was more important: "On any issue, I have at least ten senators in the palm of my hand."

Baker set out to get rich and managed within a few years to make himself a millionaire twice over on an annual salary of $19,500. He sold influence and bought real estate; he bought a motel on the beach in Ocean

City, Maryland, where politicians could shack up for the weekend; he opened a lounge for lobbyists on Capitol Hill with the portrait of a naked lady over the bar. But Baker's greed finally caught up with him. In the fall of 1963, he was hired by a vending machine company to get access to a defense plant; Baker turned around and forced out his client in favor of his *own* vending company. Baker's original client, Capitol Vending, sued him for $300,000. Suddenly, the papers were filled with headlines about Baker's influence peddling. Congress announced that it would hold hearings.

Baker's lawyer at the time was Abe Fortas, a crony of LBJ's. When Kennedy was shot in November 1963, Fortas ascended to the new president's "kitchen cabinet." Neither Johnson nor Fortas could afford to be associated with Baker. On the other hand, Johnson was worried about what Baker, who knew many secrets, would say under oath about *him*. In December 1963, Ed Williams was summoned to the Oval Office to confer with the new president. Over the customary blare of three television sets and ringing phones, Williams got the usual Johnson treatment. "Only you can save Bobby," the president implored. The unstated message was that Williams would be protecting Lyndon Johnson as well.

"It was the biggest congressional investigation that this scandal-hungry city has seen since Sherman Adams tried to explain about his vicuña coat," trumpeted the *New York Herald Tribune*. Once again, Williams was sitting alongside a notorious client before the klieg lights in the Senate Caucus Room. Mary McGrory, who had covered Williams during the McCarthy censure hearings, wrote in the *Washington Star*, "That plush tenor, so often raised in behalf of human frailty, rang through the Caucus Room with its wonted suave resonance." Williams, she observed, "had grown more massive," and his curly hair was now fashionably longer. His advice, however, was the same he always gave clients dragged before a congressional committee's show trial.

"You'd have to be a complete Mongoloid idiot to do anything other than take the Fifth Amendment," he advised Baker. His client took the Fifth 120 times as the senators peppered him with lurid questions: Had Baker given Lyndon Johnson a stereo to buy his influence? Had Baker's secretary and girlfriend joined him on business trips while she was on the federal payroll? Had he used a government telephone to place bets with "one Snags Lewis, a well-known bookmaker"? Was he a friend of one Joseph Fabianich, now serving time in Leavenworth on "white slavery charges"? How many women had he referred to a Puerto Rican doctor for the performance of abortions? Had he provided "party girls" to contractors who did business with the government?

Dressed in a white silk tie and chesterfield topcoat, Baker tried to seem jaunty when the three-hour grilling was over. "Well, I took Five and I'm still alive," he told about a hundred reporters waiting outside the hearing room. At the annual Gridiron Dinner the next month, the celebrants made light of his predicament: A figure dressed as Bobby Baker came out from the curtain and declared, "What a great country this is when a poor kid from South Carolina can come up North and fleece the Yankees out of enough money to pay Edward Bennett Williams's legal fees." But in fact, Baker's ordeal was just beginning.

With the 1964 presidential elections approaching, Lyndon Johnson wanted to get Baker out of the headlines and keep him out. Abe Fortas and White House aide Walter Jenkins quietly asked Williams to settle the Capitol Vending suit against Baker. David Carliner, the lawyer for Capitol Vending, had already subpoenaed an all-star cast of Democrats— Bobby Kennedy (soon to be senator from New York), commerce secretary Luther Hodges, Jenkins, and Acting Attorney General Nicholas Katzenbach—when Williams was finally able to settle the case a month before the election. The deal—a $30,000 payment—was to be kept secret until after the polls closed in November. (Williams leaked the story to Ben Bradlee for the first *Newsweek* issue appearing after LBJ was overwhelmingly returned to office.) Williams was not through with Baker, however. He knew that a grand jury was sitting, and he was quite sure that, in time, an indictment would be handed down. A trial would be explosive; not just Baker, but many Democratic senators and the president himself would be at risk.

Chapter Fifteen

WILLIAMS'S PURSUIT OF power in Washington did not mean that he had shed his ties to the demimonde of showbiz, celebrities, fighters, and gangsters. He used his connections in that world as skillfully as Clark Clifford matched congressmen and captains of industry. Williams had become a friend of actor Burt Lancaster while representing Lancaster's movie production partner, Harold Hecht, before the House Un-American Activities Committee in the fifties. Williams also represented Robert Stroud, the Birdman of Alcatraz. When Stroud wanted to make a movie of his life in prison, Williams arranged for Burt Lancaster to play the lead. Williams had a soft spot for professional fighters, and he became a kind of legal-aid society for the punch-drunk. He also believed that boxers were exploited by unscrupulous managers. "It's criminal to see the way these leeches bleed a fighter," Williams told the *Washington Post* in August 1963. His clients included middleweight champion Sugar Ray Robinson, heavyweight champ Ingemar Johansson, and lightweight champ Carlos Ortiz. He helped them get a larger share of the purse and then fend off the IRS when they got into tax trouble.

Williams always stood ready to help glamour girls in distress. In the early sixties, his favorite cause was nightclub singer Helen O'Connell. As an air force cadet in 1942, Williams had spent hours listening moonily to her recording of "Tangerine" on the jukebox. In May 1956, he had spotted her at the next table at Christ Cella's Steakhouse in Manhattan. She was having a birthday party, and Williams sent over a bottle of champagne. Before long, he was helping win child support payments

185

from her first husband and letting her stay in his New York apartment when she returned from singing engagements on the road. Williams, she said, developed a "crush" on her. "He was full of life and he had a big heart. He was infatuated." When he was drinking, Williams flirted with her, affectionately and openly, holding hands and nuzzling her at "21" and Toots Shor's. (Shor disapproved; he didn't like married men bringing other women to his restaurant any more than he liked them bringing their wives.)

On September 25, 1962, Williams escorted Miss O'Connell to the Liston-Patterson heavyweight championship in Chicago. After the fight, a short-lived mismatch, Williams repaired to the Pump Room in the Ambassador East Hotel and began drinking with O'Connell, Bill Fugazy, and several others. He apparently had a few too many drinks, because the evening careered on from there. According to Fugazy, Williams proceeded to punch out author Norman Mailer and throw him into the swimming pool at the Playboy Mansion. (In 1990, Mailer denied there had been a fight.) After midnight, Fugazy was awakened by a call from Williams, who was hopelessly drunk and sitting in jail for assault. With Mayor Richard Daley's intercession, Fugazy said, Williams was released.

A few weeks later, he paid for his indiscretion in the gossip columns. The king of gossips, Walter Winchell, wrote that "a popular recording lark and a famed Washington lawyer were whooping-it-up [at the Patterson-Liston fight]. He's married and another baby is due at his home." The gossip buzzed through New York café society, where Williams was already known for his roistering. Even so, his friends believed that, drunk or sober, Williams would never sacrifice his marriage. Fortunately, the gossip never found its way to Tulip Hill.

If anything, Williams's clients became less respectable in the early sixties. He continued to defend Frank Costello, who had been returned to the Atlanta penitentiary pending a blitz of appeals to higher courts. Williams kept looking for new ways to attack the legality of the government's deportation order against the Mafia don, and in 1964 he found one. The Supreme Court ruled, six to two, that the law used by the immigration service to deport Costello applied only to aliens, not naturalized citizens. Although the dissenters bitterly pointed out that Costello had obtained his citizenship by fraud, he was now a free man. "This is the best Supreme Court we've ever had," the aging Mafia chieftain declared as he emerged from prison, shooting his French cuffs with diamond cufflinks. "It's a square bunch." But he said he would miss Williams, now that his services were no longer necessary. "I don't know what I'm going to do," he told *Time*. "I feel naked without a lawyer." Like the fictional Don Corleone, Costello, who was Mario Puzo's model for the Godfather, spent his last days puttering in his garden on Long Island. He died quietly of a heart attack on February 18, 1973. Only Costello's doorman, his personal lawyer George Wolf, and Ed Williams attended the funeral.

Costello's successors in the mob badly needed Williams's help. Costello had warned other Mafia chieftains to stay away from drug dealing, but the profits were too tempting. In 1960, Costello's heir as the Boss of Bosses, Vito Genovese, was convicted and sentenced to fifteen years for narcotics conspiracy. It was Genovese who had ordered Vince "the Chin" Gigante to make the assassination attempt on Costello in 1957. Nonetheless, the two top mobsters had smoothed over their differences, and in 1962, Costello asked Williams to try to get Genovese out of prison. For what was no doubt an ample fee, Williams agreed. In October 1963, as Mafia wives picketed the U.S. federal courthouse in Foley Square chanting "Free Vito!," Williams went before the U.S. Court of Appeals to make his case. He had a fairly strong legal argument: Before Genovese's trial, the prosecutor had failed to turn over to the defense lawyers the tape-recorded statements of the government's chief informer. Williams was able to show that these statements were riddled with inconsistencies that could have been used to attack the credibility of the informer when he testified in court. But the higher courts turned down Williams's appeals. "Bad defendants make bad law," shrugged Andy Maloney, one of the prosecutors, who went on to become the U.S. attorney for Brooklyn in 1986. Williams had an easier time prevailing on the legal merits when he defended relatively harmless gamblers, like Silverman and Martin, than he did when he defended murderous dope dealers like Genovese. Years later, Williams told a partner that Thurgood Marshall, then a judge on the U.S. Court of Appeals, had confided to him that the Justice Department had secretly—and improperly—informed the court that the government's chief witness had been killed. Since no new trial was possible, the judges were unwilling to overturn Genovese's conviction.

Some zealous prosecutors grumbled that Williams had become a mouthpiece for the mob. The Mafia was known for trying to control, and ultimately corrupting, its lawyers. But Williams was adamant about keeping his Mafia clients at arm's length, and he was shrewd enough and strong enough to succeed. The gangsters tried to buy him and his associates off with little favors. Peter Taft, Williams's straight-arrow young associate out of Yale, received a black cashmere coat from Costello and a television set from "Milwaukee Phil" Alderisio. ("I was always afraid to get it fixed," said Taft. "I thought it might be hot.") But Williams made sure his clients knew that he was in charge. "You need me," he told them. "I don't need you." Although Williams had never been an athlete, he was physically as well as mentally imposing, and he was not afraid to use his two-hundred-pound bulk. In 1964, Alderisio, who was the chief enforcer for the Chicago mob, went on trial for extortion in Miami. Before trial, Judith Richards, a young woman who had come to the Williams firm fresh from Harvard Law School, was preparing one of Milwaukee Phil's henchmen to testify. Unwilling to take a female lawyer seriously, the goon refused to answer Richards's questions. Williams wandered into the hotel room where they were working and asked, "How's it going?" "I can't get him to talk," Richards told him. Williams walked over to the mobster, grabbed him by the collar, and yanked him out of his seat. "Listen, you fucking son of a bitch," he said, "you stop lying to her and answer her questions or else get the fuck out of my room."

Felix Anthony Alderisio was a professional murderer. He drove a custom-made "hit car" that contained a false backseat for storing heavy artillery—shotguns, machine guns—and a fake radio grille used for hiding handguns. A special switch turned off taillights, to throw off pursuers. But he was "a good family man," according to Taft, "who grounded his son and took away his motorcycle when he smelled beer on his breath." While preparing Alderisio to testify at his trial, Taft asked the gangster's occupation. "Salvage business," answered Milwaukee Phil. He explained that he would go to train wrecks and offer $1,000 for the contents of a freight car. "What if they say no?" asked Taft. "Then I offer $900," said Alderisio.

In Miami, Alderisio was charged with extorting $300,000 from a Chicago banker by threatening to kill him. A few days into Alderisio's extortion trial, the *Miami Herald* ran a story headlined "Miami Attorneys Spellbound as Williams Argues; 'The Man' Gives a Brilliant Lesson in the Law." The jury was equally impressed. Alderisio was acquitted.

Milwaukee Phil's past exploits were front-page news in Miami, but luckily for him the jury was sequestered. As he walked out of the courtroom after the verdict, Williams smiled and said to Peter Taft, "Wait till the jury finds out who they just acquitted."

Williams had enjoyed himself in Miami. He had brought along prizefighter Billy Conn for fun. "He was our mascot," said Tom Wadden, Williams's law partner. "Ed would rub his head for good luck." Milwaukee Phil's trial team was staying at the Fontainebleau Hotel, and at the bar one night, the crowd stood six-deep to watch Williams and Conn reenact Conn's 1941 heavyweight championship bout against "the Brown Bomber," Joe Louis. Round by round they went, exchanging shadow punches, as Williams, playing Louis, reeled before Conn's onslaught. By the 13th round, Conn was ahead easily on points, but then the smart-mouthed fighter made a strategic error. He had growled at Louis, "I'm going to get you, you nigger son of a bitch." Louis knocked him out a few seconds later. As Williams, a.k.a. the great Joe Louis, wound up and threw his mock-haymaker, the barflies roared with laughter and appreciation. Conn was eager to help Williams in any way, and by day he would go around the pool at the Fontainebleau hustling cases for Williams from the hotel's flashy clientele. Williams finally stopped him. "Billy," he explained, "lawyers are not supposed to solicit cases. You can't pimp for me."

WILLIAMS WOULD TAKE virtually any client, no matter how heinous his crime. He was deeply offended by pornographers, but he resolved his qualms by hiking his fee when he represented them. In 1965, Williams defended a smut merchant named Louis Marti who had broken the law by mailing postcards and 8mm film of humans and animals of all ages performing a variety of sexual acts. Prosecutor Maloney called Williams and protested: "A Roman Catholic communicant like you! Representing that slime!" Williams told him that he had an entrapment defense. "Those were police dogs, you know," he deadpanned. Williams went on to tell Maloney that his associate, Harold Ungar, had asked Marti how he persuaded dogs to fornicate with women. "I'm only in sales, not production," Marti answered. Williams lost the case.

Williams only turned down clients if they failed to meet his demands: If they refused to pay up front or give him total control. He could sense if a potential client was going to give him trouble. "He had a sniff test," says Michael Tigar, who worked for Williams in the sixties and seventies. "He could look them in the eye and see if they were rats. He'd say, 'I'm going to get this guy out and he's going to run on me.' That would be bad for Ed's reputation, and he wouldn't tolerate it." Williams had two basic rules for clients: don't talk to the press and don't make your crime worse by compounding it, by trying to bribe a witness or a juror. Williams had been burned by McCarthy's outbursts to reporters and the shenanigans of Hoffa's henchmen; those lessons made him insist on dictatorial control. The more unsavory his clients became, the greater was Williams's detachment from them, at least publicly. "A criminal lawyer is like an eminent brain surgeon," Williams told *Newsday* in 1964. "The surgeon is concerned with technique—not the individual on the table. The patient is incidental. The stuff about a lawyer wanting to save an innocent man from the electric chair is bunk. He's worrying about technique, the same as a surgeon is concerned about where to put the knife without severing an artery. The satisfaction comes from doing the job well—not from saving the man from the electric chair." This was mostly rubbish. Williams understood that a lawyer's job was to solve his client's legal problem, whatever that might be, and his success was measured largely by the extent to which he served his client's interests.

Although a lawyer is not supposed to talk about his clients without their permission, Williams was sometimes indiscreet, using his clients' foibles and misadventures as fodder for his story-telling. Goldfine was a particularly fertile source; Williams would mimic his heavy Yiddish accent as he described the corrupt industrialist trying to buy every politician in Washington. After Williams twice got the mayor of Woodbridge, New Jersey, off for taking bribes, the mayor became a developer—and was convicted of giving a bribe. "I guess he figured it was better to give than receive," cracked Williams.

U.S. Attorney Robert Morgenthau and the other prosecutors in the U.S. Attorney's Office liked and admired Williams. They thought he was trustworthy and fair-minded. They were also beguiled by him. "Ed would take off your pants by being totally charming," said Andy Maloney, who handled a half dozen gambling and racketeering cases against Williams in the sixties. "I know it's an act now after twenty-five years, but at the time I didn't," said Maloney. "He treated me like an equal, even though I was a greenhorn prosecutor and he was already a legend." Williams would tease Maloney ("Maloney! Every morning you get up and piss on the Bill of Rights!"). But then he would go out drinking with him and tell funny stories about Frank Costello.

Williams was able to use his rapport with prosecutors to protect his clients. In 1964, while Maloney was prosecuting a bookmaker named Pasquale Borgese, stories began appearing in the tabloids that singer Frank Sinatra would be subpoenaed to testify before the grand jury. (The stories were leaked by the FBI. Hoover wanted to curry favor with Lyndon Johnson, who hoped that Sinatra's mob ties would embarrass the Kennedys.) Sinatra, like many smart celebrities faced with a grand jury, hired Williams. Williams went to see his friend Maloney. "You're killing my client, Maloney!" Williams complained. "He's got a contract to be the pitchman for Budweiser and you're gonna ruin it and cost him a lot of money." Maloney pretended to play the violin. "No, no, it's true, he needs the money, he's made a lot of bad investments," implored Williams. "It's too late, Ed," said Maloney.

Williams went down the hall to Maloney's boss, Bob Morgenthau. "My client has nothing to hide," Williams told the U.S. attorney. Williams had done some small favors for Morgenthau, like asking the New York Giants to play in an exhibition game to benefit the Police Athletic League, of which Morgenthau was chairman. Morgenthau owed Williams one. "Will Sinatra testify before the grand jury?" he asked. Williams said he would—if they could do it without the press knowing. Williams suggested that they fly out to Kansas. When that was rejected, Williams and Morgenthau worked out a more convenient arrangement. Williams and Sinatra would slip through a back door in the Criminal Court building and walk up four flights to the grand jury room. Sinatra had earlier submitted an affidavit swearing that he had never met Borgese. Maloney confronted him with photographs of the singer and the bookmaker dining together at the Copacabana. Oh, *that* Borgese, Sinatra remembered. Sinatra proceeded to answer Maloney's questions in a sincere and earnest way that convinced Morgenthau and Maloney that, while Sinatra knew mobsters, he was not involved in their rackets. The press never found out about Sinatra's secret testimony, and Morgenthau went so far as to call the Justice Department in Washington and tell them to lay off the crooner. "This was an unusual move by a defense lawyer, to volunteer his client to testify that way," said Morgenthau, "but Ed knew that we wouldn't try to set up Sinatra in some way and that we'd do it discreetly.'' Both Maloney and Morgenthau liked the way Williams carried his own bag, unlike most hotshot lawyers. ''I'll bet you ten bucks there's a football in that bag,'' Maloney said to Morgenthau, knowing Williams's obsession with the Redskins. Williams was ordered to waive his attorney-client privilege and open up; Maloney won his $10.

HOME LIFE

LEFT: As a boy, Williams would stand on a chair in his kitchen and imitate FDR's radio addresses.

BELOW: The aviation cadet (third from left) told classmates at Georgetown Law that he had been badly injured in a bomber crash during World War II. Actually, he washed out of flight school.

At high school, he "ruled with an iron hand," said the yearbook.

LEFT: Williams and his Holy Cross debating partner, Bill Richardson (right), wanted to become Washington lawyers to follow in the footsteps of Daniel Webster and Henry Clay. Richardson later became a priest.

Marrying the boss's granddaughter, pretty Dorothy Guider. He was mortified at the wedding when he realized that the shade of his blue suit was too light.

A cozy domestic scene for the cameras of *Life* magazine in 1959. Williams could be teasing and affectionate with Dorothy, but rough on her as well.

6

The poor boy from Hartford billed clients at $1,000 an hour and built this house in the wealthy suburb of Potomac, Maryland. He also bought a house on Martha's Vineyard and owned a jet plane.

7

After Dorothy died, Williams married his law firm associate, Agnes Neill. She could seem shy and prim, but she was formidable and devoted to her husband.

8

Williams's seven children: Tony, Bennett, Kimberly, Ellen, Jobie, Dana, and Ned. He was a warm and loving father who left the discipline up to his wife. He would sometimes embarrass his kids by becoming weepy over them.

9

Though he later criticized the senator's methods, Williams liked Joe McCarthy. He defended the demagogue in his censure hearings only on the condition that McCarthy give him total control.

DEFENDER

Williams thought that mafia don Frank Costello, the model for the Godfather, was an honorable man. Costello was at first reluctant to hire the controversial lawyer. ''Isn't he the guy who defended Joe McCarthy?'' he asked.

12

Williams hated Jimmy Hoffa, but he performed a legal miracle for him. Bobby Kennedy, Hoffa's nemesis, vowed that he'd jump off the Capitol if the Teamsters boss was acquitted of bribery. When he was, Williams sent Kennedy a parachute.

Felix "Milwaukee Phil" Alderisio was chief enforcer for the Chicago mob. After Williams persuaded a sequestered jury in Miami to acquit the hit man of extortion, he joked, "Wait till the jury finds out who they just let off."

13

14

ABOVE: Preparing for court with Agnes Neill and Tom Wadden. Williams would train like a fighter before trial, giving up booze. He was a chronic pessimist: "This is the w-o-o-orst case," he would moan.

LEFT: Mounting the steps of the United States Supreme Court. His friend Justice William Brennan rated him one of the two or three best Supreme Court advocates he had ever seen.

15

Defending LBJ aide and influence peddler Bobby Baker at a Senate hearing. When Baker was sent to prison in 1967 for tax fraud, Williams wept uncontrollably. He never lost another client to jail.

16

17

Winning an acquittal for Texas Governor John Connally (center) in 1975 reestablished his reputation as the best trial lawyer in America. Richard Nixon, who had put Williams on his Enemies List, called him that night to say, "I wish you were my lawyer."

18

Michael Milken believed that Williams, though stricken with cancer, would keep him out of jail. The junk bond king wept openly at his lawyer's funeral.

Joe DiMaggio was an unlikely friend. The retired Yankees star was shy and inarticulate; the courtroom gladiator was gregarious and fluent. But they shared the burden of a terrible pressure to always win.

SPORTING LIFE

Williams made the Redskins Super Bowl champs by hiring Bobby Beathard as general manager—before Jack Kent Cooke (right) squeezed him out.

20

Williams hero-worshiped Vince Lombardi, who shared his fondness for "contest living" and accompanied him to morning mass. When "The Coach" died of cancer after giving the Redskins their first winning season in fifteen years, Williams was devastated.

21

22

The players laughed when Williams joined them for calisthenics at training camp. The 'Skins president used quarterback Sonny Jurgensen as a ringer at a family touch football game. (Jurgensen's team lost; "the kids had bad hands," he said.)

The owner gets a champagne shower after the Orioles won the 1983 World Series. Williams said he had the wrong temperament for a sport where pennant winners still lost sixty times a year. His impatience helped drive Baltimore into the American League cellar.

23

24

HIGH LIFE

LEFT: "He was like a little boy reaching out to touch danger," said heiress Jeanne Vanderbilt.

LEFT: The jealous boyfriend of actress Faye Emerson threatened to kill Williams.

RIGHT: The gossip columns tittered about singer Helen O'Connell and "a famous Washington lawyer."

26

25

RIGHT: "I never met a man like Ed," said Lauren Bacall, at the party for Ben Bradlee's sixtieth birthday. "He was an upper for me."

BELOW: Party girls Jean Pochna (second from left) and Leonore Lemmon (far right) introduced Williams to café society in the 1950s. Lemmon was the model for Truman Capote's Holly Golightly.

27

28

29

ABOVE: "The Man's coming!" Toots Shor would cry out when Williams entered his saloon. "We used it as our office," said Tom Wadden.

RIGHT: "He wanted to know everyone's secrets," said *Washington Post* writer Sally Quinn.

BELOW: EBW's cronies: Art Buchwald, David Brinkley, Jack Valenti, and Joe Califano. "He'd grab you by the ass," said Brinkley. "It was a gesture of friendship."

30

31

THE INSIDER

He liked to make the powerful laugh. Here he entertains President Johnson and Judge David Bazelon (second from right) and Justice Brennan (far right) at lunch before a Redskins game.

Joking with former Defense Secretary Robert McNamara and CIA Director Richard Helms. Williams often performed favors for the Washington elite. He defended Helms against charges of lying to Congress.

34

President Ford relied on the Washington insider for his shrewd public relations instincts. With them is an old friend of Williams, singer Pearl Bailey.

Best wishes to Edward Bennett Williams — Jimmy Carter 1975

He was contemptuous of Jimmy Carter, in part because the president did not consult him for advice.

35

36

Dining by candlelight with Nancy Reagan and socialite Wyatt Dickerson. Williams was relieved when the Reagans courted the Washington establishment. His hotel, the Jefferson, was a favorite among Reagan cabinet members.

Williams was bored by Reagan's repetitious baseball stories, but he was grateful when the president asked him to be Director of the CIA in 1987. By then, he was too sick to take the job.

Williams and George Bush were longtime friends. In 1975, Williams turned down the position of CIA Director and Bush accepted it.

LAST DAYS

39

ABOVE: Ben Bradlee (with son Quinn), Buchwald, and Williams jokingly formed a club to keep everyone else out.

40

ABOVE: With his old friends Father Healy of Georgetown and Father Brooks of Holy Cross. Williams went to mass 365 days a year.

At his daughter's graduation, ravaged by cancer. "I'm about to see real power," he told one son.

41

Chapter Sixteen

AT THE JUSTICE Department in Washington, Williams was less warmly received during the Kennedy years. Herbert J. Miller, the head of the Criminal Division, remembered Williams all too well from the Hoffa trial. When Williams came to see Miller to persuade him that Milwaukee Phil Alderisio was not such a terrible hood after all, Miller greeted Williams by showing him photographs of the corpses of Alderisio's victims. Williams never befriended Miller or members of the "Get Hoffa" squad, but he did manage to win over other officials at Justice. Wadden recalled that Williams would say he was going to "toss around the football with Whizzer and Bobby in the big office"—that is, meet with the attorney general and deputy attorney general in the large office Kennedy used at Justice.

Williams was particularly fortunate when William Hundley was appointed chief of the Organized Crime Section of the Justice Department in 1961. Hundley and Williams had become great friends during the Goldfine case, trying to cajole Williams's difficult client to turn over the names of some Republican bigwigs he'd paid off. Williams and the Justice Department lawyer were so close that Hundley sometimes stayed at Williams's apartment when business took him to New York. This led to at least one interesting confrontation at the 55th Street apartment. After a late-night toot with Williams, Hundley was awakened by a knock on the door at 7:00 A.M. Still fuzzy, he opened the door. "Where is Mr. Williams?" asked Frank Costello, "and who the fuck are you?" With that, the chief of the Organized Crime Section sat down to breakfast with the aging Boss of Bosses and their mutual friend Ed Williams. Costello bragged how he fixed races so J. Edgar Hoover, who liked to play the horses, could win his $10 bets.

By 1964 and the advent of the Johnson administration, Williams was very well wired at Justice. He was close to Fred Vinson, the new head of the Criminal Division, and on good terms with Vinson's boss, Acting Attorney General Nicholas Katzenbach. Williams's access to these men— and their great faith in his judgment—was revealed by the rather extraordinary way Williams handled what seemed to be a fairly ordinary bank robbery in Evansville, Indiana, in 1965. Charles "Chuckie" Del Monico had been indicted for sticking up the bank for $22,500 in 1962. A collector for the mob, Del Monico had a special pocket cut in his suits where he kept a roll of dimes, so he could "take them out and smash you in the face," recalled Tom Wadden. "He could hit like a mule." Del Monico came to Williams and said that he had committed a lot of crimes, but not this particular one. "I don't do banks," he explained. Bank robberies were too risky ("solo hits with no getaway"). Besides, he added, what was a Miami guy doing in Indiana? Del Monico had an alibi—two witnesses who spent the evening with him in Miami the night of the robbery in Indiana. Unfortunately for Del Monico, the U.S. attorney in Evansville had ten witnesses who claimed to see Del Monico rob the bank.

Williams was intrigued with the case. He believed Del Monico was innocent, but he predicted that the hoodlum would be railroaded by a small-town jury if the case went to trial. The witnesses, he believed, were all taking their lead from the bank president, who had fingered Del Monico after seeing his picture in the newspaper. Williams and Peter Taft went out to Indiana with Del Monico, who was free on bail. The trio made an unusual road show. Williams gave a speech to the Vanderburgh County Bar Association on the evil of "guilt by client," while Taft flirted with Del Monico's girlfriend. ("She's a dead fuck," the gangster informed young Taft. "A what?" he asked. "A dead fuck," repeated Del Monico. "You fuck her and you're dead.")

In later years, Williams would give speeches attacking the lie detector as a thoroughly unreliable test of guilt or innocence. But in the Del Monico case, Williams put Del Monico "on the box." His client passed. Then Williams subjected him to "narcoanalysis"—interrogation under injections of a "truth serum." Del Monico passed again (while confessing to a dozen other crimes). Less than two weeks before the trial,

Williams called the Justice Department in Washington. He explained to his friends Vinson and Katzenbach that he had a "terrible problem. My client has been charged with a crime. I think he's going to get convicted. I can't introduce the results of a lie detector at trial. We're on the threshold of a terrible miscarriage of justice." Katzenbach asked to see the test results, then the Justice Department administered its own lie detector. Katzenbach ordered the U.S. attorney to dismiss the case. "I knew Ed socially and I liked him. My wife and I had been out to dinner with Ed and Agnes, just the four of us," Katzenbach said. "He had credibility. He told me, 'You have no idea what this guy has done, but he hasn't done this.' " Back in Evansville, the president of the robbed bank told *Newsweek*, "It stinks." But Williams was right; another man was eventually caught and convicted for the bank robbery.

Del Monico was just a small-time hood. Momo Salvatore "Sam" Giancana, on the other hand, was heir to the Capone empire in Chicago. His 1,500 Mafiosi ran gambling, narcotics, prostitution, loan sharking, and any other service the underworld had to offer in Illinois, Ohio, and Indiana. He owned mayors, police chiefs, state legislators, and a few congressmen. In the early sixties, Bobby Kennedy ordered J. Edgar Hoover to investigate Giancana. The FBI responded by following the mobster everywhere. When Giancana went golfing, he was pursued by a golf cart full of G-men. The Bureau also planted nineteen bugs and wiretaps to overhear virtually all of his conversations. When a grand jury began calling Giancana's soldiers and girlfriends to testify against him in 1965, Giancana followed the lead of the New York dons and hired Williams.

Williams's first step was to go chat up Bill Hundley and the boys down at the Organized Crime Section of Justice. Williams's basic approach was to get along with prosecutors, particularly if his client was obviously guilty. He did not want prosecutors to think of him as a hostile adversary who would stonewall or dissemble. Rather, he wanted to be regarded by them as almost a co-worker who could help resolve a mutual problem. "Ed was the best," said Hundley. "He never overstated, he never threatened." Instead, Williams would start out by talking about the Redskins, or telling war stories about his more infamous cases. Then he would start complaining about his current case, moaning about how powerful the government was, how the odds were stacked against his client. He would not pretend that his clients were choir boys; often he would complain about how irrational they were despite his best attempts to reason with them. Then Williams would shrug his broad shoulders, smile puckishly, and suggest lunch or a drink. ("Ah, c'mon, let's have a pop.")

Quite often, after a "pop" or two, the prosecutor would start complaining about *his* problems. Cases that looked ironclad on the outside could be rife with weaknesses within. Like any bureaucracy, the Justice Department has its own turf battles. In theory, the FBI and the U.S. attorneys report to the attorney general in Washington, but in fact, they often act as separate fiefdoms. Politically ambitious U.S. attorneys are notoriously independent, and the FBI under J. Edgar Hoover was a duchy virtually beyond the reach of the U.S. government. Even in cases where the defendant was overwhelmingly guilty, tensions between Hoover's men, the local U.S. attorney, and "main Justice" could bedevil a case. Williams was adept at exploiting these tensions by playing one side against the other.

In the Giancana case, Williams had plenty of internal friction to work with. Although the government was genuinely determined to bring the mobster to justice, the case against Giancana was fraught with problems. The biggest was the electronic eavesdropping used by the FBI. Having resolutely ignored organized crime for thirty years, Hoover had suddenly discovered the Mafia, or La Cosa Nostra as he preferred to call it, in the late fifties. In a hasty effort to catch up and penetrate the clannish mob, the Bureau planted scores of bugs. The legality of this electronic eavesdropping was always dubious, but by the mid-sixties, it was clearly a violation of the Fourth Amendment—thanks in no small measure to Williams.* Hoover did not make much of an effort to tell the Justice Department about his bugging campaign, and the Kennedy administration chose to look the other way. But at the Organized Crime Section, Bill Hundley was well aware that the evidence collected by the bugs was probably useless. It couldn't be introduced in court. And because of the *Wong Sun* case (also argued by Williams) any evidence gathered from the leads provided by the illegal eavesdropping was probably inadmissible as well—it would be what the high court had long called "fruit of a poisonous tree." Because of the bugs, the government's whole case against Giancana was in jeopardy.

---

*The Supreme Court finished what Williams had begun in *Silverman*, overturning *Olmstead* in 1967. In *Katz* v. *United States* the court held that electronic eavesdropping was a "search and seizure" under the Fourth Amendment. Interestingly, the court had asked Williams to argue the case, but he declined because he disliked Katz.

In Chicago, U.S. attorney Edward Hanrahan devised a novel solution. He proposed calling Giancana before the grand jury. The don would no doubt invoke the Fifth Amendment and refuse to testify. But if the court granted him immunity from prosecution, he would no longer be able to raise his privilege against self-incrimination. Immunity was usually reserved for lower level informants in order to get them to talk. On its face, it seemed self-defeating to immunize the target of the grand jury. But Hanrahan had a strong hunch. He felt sure that even if Giancana was immunized, he *still* wouldn't talk. The code of *omerta*—and the fear of winding up with cement shoes—would keep him silenced. By refusing to answer questions, Giancana would be in contempt of court, and the judge could throw him in jail indefinitely while he refused to talk. It was a clever trap. The government would win without having to prove anything. Hanrahan would be a local hero—and, perhaps, a candidate for higher office.

At the Justice Department, Hundley grudgingly went along with Hanrahan's plan, but he didn't like it. Immunizing a witness just to hold him in contempt seemed more gimmicky than smart, and it was risky. The higher courts might refuse to imprison a man without first trying him, and in any event, Giancana might fool them all and talk. Hundley had his doubts about Hanrahan, and he was exasperated as well with the overzealous G-men who had planted all those problematic bugs.

Over many hours of drinks and story-telling with Hundley and his cohorts in the Organized Crime Section, Williams was able to learn a good deal about the government's internal squabbles. He put the information to use. Armed with the knowledge that the government planned to immunize Giancana, Williams hoped to persuade Giancana to tell the government much more than it really wanted to know. If Giancana started testifying to all his varied and sensational crimes under a grant of immunity, it would embarrass the government. Grand jury proceedings are supposed to be secret, but in Chicago they leaked copiously. The papers would ridicule the government for giving Chicago's top mobster a free pass for every felony he'd ever committed. What's more, some of those crimes implicated powerful people in Chicago. Giancana had infiltrated the Daley Machine. If he started naming every alderman on his payroll, it would cause a crisis in the political machine that had appointed none other than Ed Hanrahan. Nor were Chicago politicians the only government officials who could be exposed. Giancana had been hired by the Central Intelligence Agency in 1960 in a loony and abortive scheme to assassinate Fidel Castro. Now *that* would make an interesting headline. (Giancana had told Williams all about the scheme; interestingly, the go-between hired by the CIA to approach the mobsters was Williams's old Holy Cross debating partner, Robert Maheu.) Finally, there was the most potentially embarrassing secret of all. In 1961, the head of the Chicago mob had shared his girlfriend, Judith Exner, with the president of the United States.

Williams went back to Hundley to jaw some more. He warned Hundley that he couldn't count on Giancana staying mum. The mobster might just start shoveling in all the crimes of his past under the immunity grant. That was a pretty big risk for the government to take. In 1990, Hundley said that he did not recall if Williams brought up Giancana's CIA ties or Judith Exner. (In 1976, *New York Times* investigative reporter Nicholas Gage quoted a "Giancana confidant" as saying that when Williams learned about the CIA plot, he wanted "to tell the judge about it and get Sam off the hook." Giancana refused, perhaps because he regarded himself as a patriot.) Whatever Williams told Hundley, it was enough. The Organized Crime chief agreed to work out a deal: the government would ask Giancana a few narrowly worded questions, nothing too far-reaching, about his criminal activities. If Giancana answered, that would be the end of it. He would walk free.

It was, as the gangsters say, a sweet deal for the don. Giancana told Williams that he would go along and answer the questions. On June 1, 1965, Williams's partner, Tom Wadden, walked the don to the grand jury room and said good-bye (grand jury witnesses did not have a right to have their lawyers present). Then Wadden went off to have a leisurely breakfast with Giancana's latest girlfriend, singer Phyllis McGuire. When Wadden returned to the courthouse, he found his client being led away in handcuffs. "What the hell happened?" Wadden demanded. "I couldn't make myself answer the questions," said a downcast Giancana. Wadden called his client "a dumb son of a bitch," but he understood what had happened. The code of *omerta* was too strong, and the consequences of breaking it were too great.

Giancana idled away the next year in the federal penitentiary in Leavenworth, Kansas. When the grand jury's term expired in the late spring of 1966, Hanrahan wanted to pull the stunt all over again: bring the mobster before the new grand jury, immunize him, and lock him up when he refused to talk. But Williams went back to see his friends at the Justice Department. He warned the acting attorney general, Nick Katzenbach, that repeating the gimmick would look like selective prosecution. On appeal, the courts might throw out the whole immunity statute if the government continued to abuse it. Besides, Williams argued, Giancana was finished as a don. He planned to leave the country and move to Mexico. "Ed was very good at arguing from your point of view," recalled Katzenbach. "He knew how to pitch me. He knew I was a liberal on crime issues." Katzenbach overruled Hanrahan. Giancana was set free. Hanrahan was furious. Years later, he still regretted going along with Washington's orders. "It was the dumbest thing I ever did," he said. "I should have told Justice to go to hell and let them fire me." Both Hanrahan and the federal judge who sentenced the mobster to contempt, William E. Campbell, assumed that the CIA had fixed the case when, almost a decade later, they learned about Giancana and the Castro plot.

After leaving Leavenworth, Giancana fled to Mexico, as Williams had predicted, and holed up in a walled estate in Cuernavaca. In 1975, the Mexican government expelled him, and he returned to Chicago. That June, as Giancana fried sausages in his basement kitchen, someone shot him in the back of the head seven times. He had been scheduled to appear before a grand jury the following week.

J. EDGAR HOOVER did not think Ed Williams was a trustworthy advocate or a great drinking buddy. "He hated Williams," recalled Morgenthau. "He thought he was dangerous." Hundley recalled that "Hoover's idea of a good defense lawyer was one who brought in his client, pleaded him, and cooperated with the government. To defend the client was bad. To beat Hoover was worse." Williams not only beat Hoover, he exposed his illegal means of investigation and—the greatest sin of all—held up the Bureau and its director to public scorn and embarrassment.

Williams instinctively disliked Hoover, whom he regarded as a pompous hypocrite, a homosexual tyrant posturing as a defender of morality and freedom. Long before the lawmakers and reporters caught up, Williams knew a good deal about Hoover's deceptions and petty corruption. In 1962, an FBI agent named William Turner came to Williams because he had been transferred to Alaska for volunteering information about Bureau irregularities to a congressional committee. To the consternation of Hoover and his men, Williams sued the Bureau for violating the agent's right of free speech. The suit was ultimately unsuccessful, but in the process Turner and other dissident agents fed Williams some seamy stories about Hoover's Bureau. At the time, Washington was stirring over the influence-peddling scandal of oilman Billy Sol Estes. "This Billy Sol Estes thing would be a tempest in a teapot if they started in on the FBI," agent Turner wrote Williams on May 19, 1962. "Hoover's alliances on the Hill that have made him a fortune, the chauffeuring of his friends in Govt. cars driven by agents on their free time . . . etc., etc." The dissident FBI agent told Williams about top agents using their positions for personal profit, and it is likely that he filled him in on the gossip about Hoover and his "wife," Clyde Tolson, the Bureau's number two who lived as well as worked with the director. Turner gave Williams an affidavit proving that gangster George "Machine Gun" Kelly had been convicted with perjured testimony suppressed by the Bureau back in the 1930s. And more immediately useful, he told Williams about the director's vast, secret—and illegal—electronic eavesdropping campaign against the Mafia in Chicago, New York, and Las Vegas.

The Las Vegas casinos in that era were "mobbed up." Profits were illegally skimmed and sent to Mafia bosses: the take from the Star Dust and Desert Inn was funneled to Giancana in Chicago and Moe Dalitz in Cleveland; the skim from the Fremont, Sands, Flamingo, and Horseshoe was shipped to Meyer Lansky in Miami. In 1961, Hoover ordered his men to plant bugs in bedrooms all through these casino hotels, as well as in the executive offices of the Desert Inn and Fremont. Wiretapping by the FBI may have been marginally legal at the time (the Justice Department interpreted the antiwiretapping statute to allow tapping as long as the conversations were not then publicly divulged, and the Supreme Court had not yet thrown out *Olmstead*). But bugs—microphones attached to wires—had to be installed by illegal trespass. Hoover did not want to tell the Justice Department about his bugs, and the Justice Department did not want to find out.

Nonetheless, in June 1963, Hoover sent a top secret report to the Justice Department disclosing the existence of the bugs and what they had picked up. The report went over to Justice on a Friday; by Monday it had leaked to the mob. FBI agents monitoring the Las Vegas bugs listened in horror as mobsters read sections of the report to each other over the phone. Within a day or two the owners of the Fremont had hired a private detective to find the bugs. Then they hired Ed Williams, who promptly sued the FBI for violating the civil liberties of the casino owners. Suddenly, J. Edgar Hoover's campaign to expose the mob in Las Vegas had backfired into exposure of lawbreaking by the FBI.

Where did the leak come from? William Hundley said he was one of only two or three Justice Department officials to see the report, but denied leaking it, to his chum Williams or anyone else. With the sort of Machiavellian suspicion familiar to veteran prosecutors, he speculated that the FBI sent the report over to Justice because Hoover knew the existence of the bugs had already leaked to the mob, and he wanted to pin the blame on the Justice Department.

Whoever tipped them off, Williams had little trouble making a case against the G-men. The casino bugs were attached to phone lines leased by the Henderson Novelty Co., a front so transparent that it had the same address as the FBI's office in Las Vegas. Williams subpoenaed all of Henderson's phone records from the telephone company and discovered that the bill was paid by U.S. government check. The Justice Department scrambled to get Williams's suit moved from state court to federal court, where, as Bill Hundley put it, "we had a better handle on the judges." But J. Edgar Hoover refused to sign a memorandum acknowledging that the government had authorized the bugs.

Hundley himself went out to Las Vegas to argue the case against Williams. At first, he thought he was making some progress with the local judge, John Mowbray, a progovernment Notre Dame grad. Williams was beside himself, Hundley recalled. "He thought I had a hook in the judge." When the court recessed at noon, Williams turned to opposing counsel and said, "Hundley, I'm gonna kill you. I'm going to break your fucking neck if you've gotten to the judge." But at the end of the day, the judge ruled for Williams; the case would stay in state court. "Then I was Ed's best buddy again," said Hundley. "We went out and got drunk together."

The case was eventually settled: The FBI did not have to pay any damages, but the Bureau was precluded from prosecuting the casinos. Williams made sure the matter was not hushed up. He called his crony Ben Bradlee, who had become the number two editor and heir apparent at the *Washington Post*. A top reporter, Dick Harwood, was assigned to go to Las Vegas. "Williams was an extremely cooperative, even eager source," Harwood said. Hoover was not happy with the front-page stories that began to appear in the *Post*. "That rat!" the FBI director scribbled next to Harwood's name on a clipping later found in his files.

The FBI's embarrassments continued to pile up. In a tax case involving gambler Fred Black, another client of the Williams firm, the U.S. solicitor general was forced to admit before the Supreme Court in May 1966 that the FBI had illegally bugged Black. The disclosure set off a furious round of finger pointing as the FBI and Justice Department each tried to pin the responsibility on the other.* Williams was hugely entertained by the squabbling between Hoover and the old Kennedy loyalists at Justice. At a cocktail party at his house that May, Williams regaled a half dozen guests with his description of listening to Bobby Kennedy blame Hoover for the bugs. Williams had sat next to Kennedy, now a senator from New York, on the shuttle from Washington. Kennedy told Williams that he knew nothing about the bugging; it was all Hoover's fault. One of the guests listening to Williams that evening was federal judge Edward Curran. Curran immediately reported Williams's cocktail party chatter to J. Edgar Hoover. On June 3, Hoover wrote an indignant memo to his top aides about Kennedy's assertion. He also bitterly noted the pleasure Williams seemed to take in passing it on to anyone who would listen. "Williams seemed to be particularly gleeful because he believed this placed the Director of the Bureau in a most embarrassing position and placed the entire onus for the use of the microphones on the Director of the Bureau," Hoover wrote.

J. Edgar Hoover was a dangerous enemy. In the 1960s, Williams was apparently worried that the FBI director was not only bugging casino owners and mobsters, but he also might be bugging their lawyer. He told his young assistants to be careful. "Ed would say, 'Don't do or say anything you don't want to see on the front page of the *Washington Post* tomorrow,' " said David Webster, who joined the firm in early 1967. Judith Richards Hope, who came to the firm in 1964 and worked on organized crime cases, says that delicate issues were often discussed

---

*As attorney general, Kennedy ordered Hoover to stop bugging in Las Vegas, and he never formally authorized FBI bugging anywhere else, though he knew about it. Hundley recalled listening, along with Kennedy, to an FBI tape of a bugged phone conversation between mobsters in Chicago. By playing the tape to the AG, the FBI was subtly putting him on notice about their investigative techniques. Kennedy did not want to know. He told Hundley to "get that tape out of here." Kennedy loyalists remained sensitive to the issue in 1966 when the government was forced to concede illegal bugging in the case against Fred Black. Informed that a congressional committee wanted to look into the bugging, Acting Attorney General Katzenbach said, "Oh, my God, not that! Let's don't hang this stuff out." When the government admitted the bugging in 1966, Hoover tried to curry favor with Lyndon Johnson by blaming it all on Bobby Kennedy. "The president obviously wanted to get this out, in as much as Kennedy will be seriously wounded," Bureau official C. D. DeLoach wrote Clyde Tolson. "At the same time, as the Director knows much better than I do, there are far better ways of getting these facts out than through the medium of a congressional committee." Hoover promptly leaked his version to *U.S. News and World Report*.

outside the office, on a bench in Farragut Square, to avoid being over-heard. Tom Wadden thought the Bureau might be bugging Williams's New York apartment. On the other hand, Vince Fuller, a careful and low-key lawyer, strongly doubted that the FBI had bugged Williams, and doubted that Williams really believed it either.

Chapter Seventeen

As THEY RECALLED their experiences of twenty-five years ago, the men and women who worked with Williams as young lawyers may have exaggerated the romance and melodrama. Williams himself could be hyperbolic, especially after a few drinks, and he intentionally fostered the myth of the law firm as a "band of brothers." Nonetheless, for anyone who had been insulated by law school or a clerkship, working for Williams in the early and middle 1960s was an exotic adventure, full of the sort of intrigue more commonly associated with B-movies and pulp magazines.

"It was like something out of Tom Wolfe," recalls Judith Richards, an associate in the firm from 1964 to 1967, referring to his book on the astronauts, *The Right Stuff.* "The lawyers in the firm were like fighter pilots. There was a lot of drinking and driving and shmoozing and strutting." Instead of carrying a partner's bag to a dreary corporate closing, Williams's young lawyers were thrown into court representing clients accused of grand-scale thievery and mayhem. There was, to be sure, a bit of culture clash between crude hoods and polite former Harvard Law Review editors. While trying a case in Denver, Peter Taft recoiled as one of his hitman clients nonchalantly, if greedily, bit into a whole pickled tomato (flown in especially for the mob from a New York delicatessen), splurting pulpy green juice all over his own shirt.

Williams, Wadden & Stein was not a law firm in any ordinary sense; it was a partnership in name only. Williams was in total control of the firm's dozen lawyers and everything they did. He parceled out the cases, set fees and salaries, and signed off on all strategy. Yet his colleagues were themselves pros. Wadden, in particular, was a brilliant trial lawyer, a shrewd gamesman with uncanny instincts. He was a master at obfuscation and stalling, essential qualities while defending outrageously guilty mobsters. Using schoolyard tricks, he had a special knack for rattling prosecutors: He would shoot paper planes over their heads when the judge wasn't looking. He purposefully mispronounced a prosecutor's name until the prosecutor jumped to his feet demanding, "Your Honor, direct Mr. Wadden to get my name right!" Defending a mobster named Tony Giacalone on trial for bribing a policeman, Wadden was assaulted by an exasperated prosecutor in the hallway. Wadden, who'd been baiting his opponent for days, was all wounded innocence before the judge ("Your Honor, I can't imagine what I've done . . ."). Handsome and warm, Wadden was so endearing to jurors that one sent him cookies, prompting the prosecutor to demand a mistrial, or at least equal cookies.

Tutored by Wadden, Vince Fuller was becoming an equally talented courtroom operator. Dogged, cool, always prepared, he was a somewhat better-rounded lawyer than Wadden. Fuller said he had no desire to have his name on the letterhead. "I thought anyone who put his name up with Ed would be vulnerable, would get hurt. No one was going to be able to live up to Ed's name," he recalled. "Fuller didn't care about the limelight, which made him perfect for Ed," said Corinne Metcalf, who clerked for both Fuller and Williams as a George Washington University law student. "He was content in Ed's shadow, and Ed relied on him hugely."

Williams's hiring practices were quirky and off the cuff. He hired Peter Taft after sitting across from him at a Georgetown dinner party. At the time, Taft was clerking for Williams's hero, Earl Warren, and Williams fancied employing the great-grandson of a former president and chief justice. Williams hired David Povich when his father, sportswriter Shirley Povich of the *Washington Post*, told Williams that his son had hung Williams's picture on the wall of his dorm room at Columbia and regularly cut classes to see Williams perform in court. "Really?" said Williams. "Tell that young man to come see me." Mike Tigar, who would go on to become one of Williams's most brilliant protégés, came to the firm when he was "unhired" as a Supreme Court clerk. In 1966, the Supreme Court was starting to feel the heat for its liberal decisions on race and criminal rights, and Tigar had been an outspoken student radical at Berkeley. Justice Brennan didn't want to have a Hotspur in his chambers, and Chief Justice Warren, the target of impeachment demands in Congress, did not need any more controversy. In large part to do the justices a favor, Williams took young Tigar off Brennan's hands.

"The firm was informal," said Richards. "There was only one standard: be the best." Williams was unforgiving of error. "If you didn't prepare adequately, it wasn't a mistake, it was treason—a blow to Ed's security, to what he was trying to build. He wouldn't yell at you. He'd say in icy tones, 'You've got a lot to learn, don't you?' For a couple of months thereafter, you'd be banished. No shmoozing, no martini lunches at Duke's, no trials. Then he would melt, and it would be back to Duke's, back to court."

Williams's ethics are a matter of some dispute among the lawyers who worked for him in the 1960s. In some ways he was painstakingly scrupulous. His charges were told in no uncertain terms not to hide documents or misstate the law. "It was fight until the other side begs for mercy, but do it by the rules," said Richards. But another associate in the firm at the time, Barbara Babcock, noted that the adversary system gives defense lawyers considerable leeway to make the best case for their client, even if that means shading the truth. The ethical boundaries are wide in the practice of law, and Williams was known to use the entire field. "He didn't break the rules," said Babcock, who later became a law professor at Stanford, "but he didn't always live up to the spirit of them." In her judgment, he crossed the line in preparing witnesses, subtly coaching them how to dissemble on the stand without actually putting false words in their mouths. "His only real ethic was to win," she said.

Williams was a complex and not always likable boss. He could just as easily explode in fury as be charming and soothing. He seemed to be able to laugh, cry, or rage on demand. Some admired him for his dominating qualities, others resented him, but all agreed that he was enormously manipulative. "Wadden had a kindness of spirit," said Corinne Metcalf. "Ed was more devoted to the greater glory of Ed." Williams could appear sympathetic to his clients but be "ruthless" to those who opposed him, said Richards. "He showed no compassion to people who stood in his way." He had contempt for perceived weakness. If Wadden wanted to settle a case that seemed winnable, Williams would call him a "woman."

Although Williams hired several women lawyers, including his future wife, Agnes, "he was a man's man. He liked men, not women," said

Metcalf. "He didn't trust women. He was afraid of them." Other women who worked for Williams were not quite so blunt, but they share her opinion that Williams was far more natural and easy with men. He liked to flirt and court, but he did not seem comfortable relying on a woman. "Women were good for back-room stuff, but he didn't accept that they could argue before a jury," said Babcock. "He claimed that clients wouldn't accept women, but that wasn't true. In my experience the clients were quite tolerant. Williams just didn't believe that women belonged in the courtroom."

Williams was not by nature introspective (that would be "womanly"), but he did from time to time admit to doubts and insecurities. As always, he felt dogged by the pressure to win every time he stepped into a courtroom. "I hate to try cases. I hate to lose," he would tell Richards. "I'm the most insecure guy in the world." This was an exaggeration, of course. Williams was insecure about losing cases, perhaps, but he had immense self-confidence in most other ways. He was far too restless and driven to be described as self-contented, and his moodiness verged on manic depressive. Yet unlike most borderline neurotics, he had an extraordinary sense of purpose. And when he became unhappy about the circumstances of his life, he had the capacity to change.

In the spring of 1965, Williams wearily returned from a dull trial in Denver, where he had failed to win an acquittal for Milwaukee Phil Alderisio. The facts had been stacked against Williams: A Denver lawyer named Robert Sunshine had made the mistake of selling some dry oil wells to Ruby Kolod, part owner of the Desert Inn in Las Vegas. Kolod sent hitman Alderisio to see Sunshine. "Ruby sent us," Milwaukee Phil announced to Sunshine. "We're here to kill you." Sunshine begged his way out by repaying the money, but later complained to authorities, and Milwaukee Phil was charged with conspiracy to murder, along with Kolod and two brutish-looking triggermen named Americo DiPietto and "Icepick Willie" Alderman. At the trial, Williams would "half convince the jury that Alderisio was innocent," said a Chicago newspaper reporter who covered the trial, "but then the jury would take one look at DiPietro and Icepick Willie and want marshals around the jury box."

The defeat left Williams exhausted and depressed. Drinking Scotch one night in his office, where he kept a small bar, Williams melodramatically declared to Andy Maloney, "I'm never going to try another case." He said he had to drink "double shots"—he held up two thick fingers—to get to sleep at night during Milwaukee Phil's trial. "Everyone's trying to knock me off. I'm like an old gunfighter in the Wild West. Every young gunslinger wants a shot at me." Williams said he was feeling a financial pinch as well. Criminal law, he said, wasn't nearly as lucrative as commercial law. "I've made more money than any trial lawyer who ever lived, but I've got very little to show from the practice of law."

Williams was prone to boozy overstatement. According to his accountant at the time, Austin Doyle, Williams earned in the range of $125,000 to $150,000 a year (between $485,000 and $585,000 in 1990 dollars), probably slightly less than Clark Clifford and certainly less than the senior partners of the leading Wall Street firms. Even so, Williams was a fairly wealthy man by 1965. He had inherited about $180,000 from his first wife, Dorothy, as well as valuable real estate holdings, like a half share in the building occupied by the firm, the Hill Building. He spent a good deal of time looking at real estate investments, shrewdly banking on the growth of the federal government. When Williams bought 1910 K Street in the early sixties, it was on the very edge of downtown; today the building is at the heart of the "K Street Corridor" populated by lawyers and lobbyists. Still, Williams had cash-flow problems in his firm. Aside from the Teamsters and Georgetown University (which paid him $500 a month), Williams had no institutional clients on retainer. He was dependent on whatever cases came in the door. Though he could charge Mafia dons huge fees, and even bigger fees in pornography cases, he also did a lot of work pro bono or heavily discounted for friends. Williams's billing practices were occasionally haphazard. Rather than charge by the hour, as was common practice among law firms, Williams calculated what he was worth and demanded a check. When the money ran out, he demanded another.

Wadden recalled that Williams was "very generous about sharing his fees" with the other lawyers in the firm. Every year, he gave his lawyers a Christmas bonus based on the year's profits. But in December 1965, there was no money for bonuses. Rather than admit the shortfall and deprive his troops, Williams quietly borrowed enough money to hand out his usual fat Christmas checks. The need to go to the banks shocked Williams, who had never erased the memory of his weeping father, laid off during the Depression. "My father got kicked around a lot," he would say with an edge of bitterness. Williams was absolutely determined never to be poor. He could also be a terrible pessimist about money, moaning about "all the mouths I have to feed" and the difficulty of sustaining his growing firm, which he felt was his personal responsibility. Since financial disaster seemed to beckon at every turn, he decided to take the precaution of becoming rich.

Williams, by the mid-sixties, was also growing frustrated about representing the mob. The blatancy of his clients' crimes interfered with his carefully plotted legal arguments. Maloney recalled arguing against Williams in federal court in a massive interstate gambling case involving a big-time bookmaker named Pasquale Borgese. The government had illegally eavesdropped on Borgese, and Williams was eloquent as he reminded Judge Inzer Wyatt of the law—and his own role in making it. "As I had the honor of arguing before the Supreme Court," Williams declared, citing *Silverman* and *Wong Sun*, among other cases. Maloney got up and simply repeated the facts of the case. Williams was exasperated on rebuttal. "Your Honor, Mr. Maloney never discussed the *law*." But the judge was unmoved. Once again, bad clients had made bad law.*

Williams never refused a client because of the crime he was accused of committing. Even when the mob turned from relatively tame vices like gambling and prostitution to peddling narcotics, Williams would take the case. But he would not tolerate clients who abused the judicial system or embarrassed his own lawyers. In 1961, Williams assigned Wadden and Fuller to defend a pair of mobsters, John Ormento and Carmine Galante, in a massive narcotics conspiracy case. The trial got out of hand. One of Wadden's co-counsel, Irwin "Kitty" Katz, kept stalling the trial by pretending that he was sick in the hospital. After a few days, the judge summoned Katz to court and, to the shock of bystanders, ordered the lawyer to get out of his wheelchair. When Wadden protested that his co-counsel was ill, the government disclosed that Katz had been partying for the last four days with his nurse, who was an FBI informant. As the trial progressed, the fun and games grew menacing. One of the defendants (there were nineteen of them) jumped into the jury box to scare the jurors. A juror found slivers of glass in her martini at dinner and immediately asked to be taken off the panel. Finally, just before the jury went out to deliberate, the foreman of the jury fell—or was pushed—down a

---

*The four Treasury agents who had bugged Borgese later admitted it to the court. Maloney called Williams and asked if he wanted to work out a plea bargain for Borgese. "Plea bargain? I'm going to make a citizens' arrest of those agents!" shouted Williams. But, in fact, Williams did plead Borgese to a six-month sentence. He had to: Maloney threatened to use the old Giancana trick—immunize Borgese and throw him in jail for contempt.

manhole. The judge declared a mistrial and angrily warned the defense lawyers to control their clients.

Before the retrial—at which one of the more outspoken defendants was gagged and chained to his chair in court—Wadden and Fuller withdrew from the case. "I wanted out and Ed wanted out," said Wadden. "I was afraid the judge was going to throw *me* in jail." According to Pat Wall, a lawyer who worked in Williams's office in the late sixties, Williams intended to inform Ormento himself that the firm would no longer represent him, but he was waylaid when he ran into Richard Nixon at Toots Shor's. Fuller went to see Ormento instead. When Fuller returned, according to Wall, he shakily reported that Ormento had threatened to kill "Williams and his c—— wife." (Fuller denied that Ormento made this threat, although he says the mobster reacted "very explosively.") Whether or not Ormento threatened to kill Williams, the gangster did threaten to kill the judge, Lloyd MacMahon, whom he referred to in open court as a "son of a whore." (At the second trial, a witness threw a chair at the prosecutor, and the judge found the head of a horse on his front porch one morning. The defendants were nonetheless convicted.)

Frank Costello had been a gentleman; his successors were not. Giancana had the "face of a gargoyle and the disposition of a viper," according to *Time* magazine. Galante was "scary. He had a wild look," said Paul Curran, who prosecuted him. "The mob usually just killed witnesses, but Galante went after policemen, prosecutors, and judges." Williams liked rogues, but these men were ogres. What's more, clients who threatened judges and jurors were bad for the firm's reputation. Williams did not abandon his defense of Mafiosi, but gradually the firm's "vowel practice," as his young lawyers dryly referred to the defense of Sicilians, faded out in the late sixties.

IN THE FALL of 1965, Williams became involved in a case that opened his eyes to a new and extremely lucrative side of the law. Herb Siegel, a rough-edged self-made multimillionaire, decided to buy Paramount Pictures. The movie company resisted by hiring Louis Nizer. The celebrated lawyer quickly sued Siegel on antitrust grounds, arguing that since Siegel already owned a large talent agency, General Artists Corp., he would gain the power to tie up the movie business. If Paramount was to have Nizer, Siegel wanted his own top gun.

Bypassing the Wall Street lawyers more familiar with corporate struggles, Siegel went to Ed Williams. Eager for a change of pace—and for an opportunity to face off against Nizer, whom he regarded as a superficial self-promoter—Williams took on the case. He was surprised by how much he enjoyed it. This was long before the era of hostile takeovers, but the Paramount proxy struggle had all the elements that would make the merger-and-acquisition business so appealing to lawyers in the 1980s: high rollers, high stakes, and high fees. Williams was an extraordinarily quick study unfazed by the intricacies of securities and antitrust law. He particularly relished outfoxing Nizer with checkerboard tactical moves.

When Nizer held a press conference to denounce Siegel, Williams sued him, saying that Nizer was improperly soliciting shareholder votes. Williams baited Nizer in court, accusing him of "niggling and pettifoggery," and openly laughed at the pomposity of Nizer's closing argument. Williams won; Nizer's suit failed, opening the way for Siegel's takeover bid. (Paramount ultimately brought in Gulf + Western's Charles Bluhdorn as a white knight to buy the company.)

Before going to trial in the Paramount case, Williams had recruited an old friend, Paul Connolly, to represent a Broadway producer who was Siegel's partner in the takeover attempt. Connolly had been Williams's student at Georgetown after the war, and Williams had persuaded Howard Boyd to hire him at Hogan & Hartson. It was Connolly who had defended Williams against the personal injury suit stemming from his 1953 car crash. Williams was enormously impressed by Connolly's performance in the Paramount case. Connolly's cross-examination of Paramount chairman Barney Balaban was so tough and so effective that Balaban literally wet his pants in court. Connolly and Williams had talked idly from time to time about practicing law together, but after the Paramount case, the conversation became more meaningful. "Before, Ed had always wanted Paul to work for him," recalled Mary Connolly, Paul's wife. "Now Ed wanted Paul to work *with* him."

Connolly, by this time, was managing partner of Hogan & Hartson. With almost fifty lawyers, the Hogan firm was second only to Covington & Burling in size and power in the capital. Williams told Connolly that he wanted to move away from criminal law, and that he wanted a more stable base from which to work. Connolly saw an opportunity for his firm. "Paul realized that Ed would be a great civil litigator, that he could scare the hell out of all these innocents who try civil cases but can't find their way around the courtroom," recalled David Webster, a Hogan & Hartson lawyer. Connolly made a proposal: He suggested that Williams come to Hogan & Hartson. Williams was intrigued. He made a counter-proposal: He would come if the name of the firm was changed to Williams, Hogan & Hartson. Connolly took the proposal back to his partners. They were not enthusiastic. "What will our corporate clients say about Ed?" asked E. Barrett Prettyman. Nelson Hartson, the surviving name partner, was more blunt in private conversation with some of his colleagues in the firm: "I'm not going to turn this firm over to the Roman Catholics."

Instead of Williams coming to Connolly's firm, Connolly went to Williams's. On December 7, 1966, the name Williams & Wadden was dropped. The firm was now Williams & Connolly. Connolly brought with him corporate clients—General Motors (and the Corvair case) and El Paso Natural Gas. He introduced law firm rituals, like an annual dinner dance, and law firm business practices, like billing by the hour instead of by flat fee. Williams never did like the dinner dance (he disliked dancing and having to be sociable in a formal setting), and at first he balked at billing his hours. "If I wanted to charge by the hour, I'd be a plumber," he complained. But when he discovered that the firm could charge more that way, he eagerly embraced the practice. "I thought I knew how to charge until I saw Ed's bills," Connolly remarked to a mutual friend, Jim McCarrick. For his part, Connolly accepted the gamier clients still trooping into the firm, like Milwaukee Phil Alderisio. A somewhat vain man who was always perfectly tailored, Connolly insisted on traveling first class and staying in luxury hotels. On a trip to Chicago to represent Milwaukee Phil in the late sixties, Connolly was denied the suite he asked for at a hotel. Milwaukee Phil's bagman, Irwin Weiner, leaned over the desk and said to the manager, "Do you want water tomorrow?" Connolly got the suite.

Tom Wadden, meanwhile, was driven out of the firm. Williams had become increasingly worried about Wadden's drinking. All the lawyers in the firm drank heavily at times, but Wadden, in Williams's opinion, drank more heavily more often. Although Wadden was always sober when he went to court, Williams began to eye him critically. In 1965, Andy Maloney was sitting next to Williams, watching Wadden try a case, when Wadden paused for a moment looking for an exhibit. Williams was visibly angered. At lunch, Williams asked Maloney, "What do you think of Wadden?" and tore into him for being unprepared and for shooting from the hip. Maloney, who had high regard for Wadden, was taken aback. "It was the first time I ever saw a mean side to Ed," he said.

When Connolly came over, Williams simply informed Wadden that the name of the firm had been changed. (Colman Stein, the other name partner, had retired to Florida earlier that year.) "Tom was broken-hearted," said Peter Taft, who had been coached by Wadden and was close to him. Williams disliked unpleasant confrontations, and he avoided Wadden for weeks. A few months after Connolly arrived, Wadden left to go out on his own. "It wasn't the right place for me," Wadden said. "I didn't want the firm to grow or bill by the hour."

Chapter Eighteen

LESS THAN A month after the firm became Williams & Connolly, Williams went to court to try his most important case in a decade. Although he had done his best to delay and avoid trial, the Bobby Baker case finally went to trial on January 9, 1967. Baker had been indicted a full year earlier, after a grand jury spent eighteen months hearing 170 witnesses. Baker was charged with nine counts of fraud and tax evasion. According to the indictment, a group of savings and loan owners in California had given Baker $100,000 to buy influence in Washington with well-placed "campaign donations" to needy senators and congressmen, and Baker had simply pocketed the money.

Williams had taken the case because President Johnson had asked him to, but from the first he had misgivings. Williams liked colorful mavericks, and he tried to like Baker. He was amused by Baker's well-publicized skirt chasing. After reading in the *Washington Post* that the average male has sexual intercourse seven thousand times in his life, Williams turned to Baker and said, "Bobby, you've got four thousand of mine." Williams tried to bond with Baker with the usual male rituals. At their first dinner out together at Duke Zeibert's, the two men had a friendly drinking contest. Each consumed ten martinis. Williams went to his car, which was parked in a private garage, and proceeded to drive right through the garage door. Although he was amused by Baker, Williams never really trusted him. "Bobby is a big bullshitter," Williams would say ruefully. He knew that Baker's slipperiness could be fatal when he took the stand.

214

In the Baker case, Williams could not follow his usual practice of cozying up to the prosecutor and the judge. The trial judge, Oliver Gasch, was an old foe. As a young city attorney, Gasch had aggressively cross-examined one of Williams's witnesses while defending the city of Washington in a slip-and-fall case. In open court, Williams had called Gasch a "character assassin." Promoted to U.S. attorney, Gasch had been highly critical of Williams's gimmicky defense of Jimmy Hoffa. On a more personal level, Gasch tried to hire away Agnes Neill from Williams in the late fifties. Williams stopped Gasch on the street and growled, "Next time you want to talk to Agnes, talk to me first." When Williams heard that Baker had drawn Gasch as a judge, he was typically apocalyptic. "This man hates my guts!" he told Baker. "He is the worst judge in America for you. He will rule against you on every motion I make." Baker turned down Williams's offer to withdraw from the case.

Williams was just as unhappy with the prosecutor, Bill Bittman. "He pisses on the Constitution," Williams groused. Bittman, whom Bobby Baker described as a "Midwestern shitkicker," grew up in Milwaukee, the son of a tombstone salesman. He was assigned to the case by the Justice Department as a reward for convicting Jimmy Hoffa of stealing from the Teamsters' pension fund in the spring of 1964. Grimly determined and humorless, Bittman "had the zeal of a crusader, a grand inquisitor," recalled Mike Tigar, who worked with Williams in the Baker case. "His rule was 'kill them all, God will recognize his own.' " Bittman arrived in Washington with an armor of hostility and wariness not only toward Williams but also toward his superiors in the administration. Before he left Chicago, a federal judge there cynically advised him to "rent, don't buy" in Washington. Bittman shared the widespread suspicion that Lyndon Johnson would order the case dropped. Bittman didn't even trust the FBI to handle his investigation, figuring (correctly) that J. Edgar Hoover would connive with LBJ. Instead, the prosecutor used IRS agents who he believed were more independent.

"My dealings with Williams were very cautious," Bittman said. "I had been told that he couldn't be trusted, that he would charm the pants off me and have me for lunch." Because he was "intimidated" by Williams, Bittman "overprepared." He remained wary all through the trial. "I got nervous watching the jury watch Williams. Their eyes followed him around the courtroom. I knew if I made a mistake he'd shove it right up my ass." At first Williams did try friendly persuasion. "Ed was very charming and disarming,'' said Austin Mittler, Bittman's assistant. "But the blarney didn't work with Bittman."

The two lawyers tangled openly over Williams's relations with the press. Williams's first line of attack against the government was to try to get the case thrown out for illegal bugging. The same bugs that had been used to eavesdrop on the Las Vegas mob had picked up some of Bobby Baker's conversations. The secretary of the Senate had ties to big-time gamblers as well as to influential lawmakers. "The utter disregard for law exhibited by the agents [who planted the bugs] almost defies belief,'' Williams railed as he dragged a three-foot-high stack of recordings into court and tried to subpoena J. Edgar Hoover.

Bittman was willing to acknowledge that the bugs had been illegal, but he argued that they were irrelevant: The government had not used Baker's bugged conversations to make its case against him. Bittman wanted to avoid a full-blown public hearing on the matter, so he offered Williams a deal. In the judge's chambers, Bittman agreed to stipulate that Baker had been illegally bugged. But in what he believed to be an off-the-record conversation, he told Williams that he did not want any publicity about the government's admission.

Two days later, he saw Williams showing the transcript of the stipulation to reporters and claiming that the government had violated Baker's constitutional rights. "I went crazy,'' Bittman recalled. "I called him every name in the book. I said I would never have another conversation with him without a court reporter present." Bittman went to Judge Gasch and asked for a gag order. He protested caustically that both *Time* and *Newsweek* were preparing cover stories on Williams that would be "puff pieces." Gasch refused to invoke the gag, but Williams was forced to cut off his cooperation with the newsmagazines.

As Williams predicted, Gasch ruled against him on every pretrial motion to suppress the evidence or dismiss the case. "It was my first big case as a judge,'' Gasch later said. "I had been appointed by President Johnson, and Baker was close to Johnson. I wanted it well documented that we were objective."

Having failed to persuade the court to dismiss the case, Williams tried to do just what Bittman feared: get the case dropped by the Justice Department, or at least cut a favorable deal. "There was a lot of talk about making the case go away,'' recalled Tigar. Texas oilman Clint Murchison, who was close to both Baker and LBJ and helped to bankroll Baker's legal fees, tried to persuade the president to spare Baker. In a clear breach of judicial propriety, Supreme Court Justice Abe Fortas, who had once been Baker's lawyer, spoke to Williams almost every night about the progress of the case. Presumably, Fortas relayed Williams's reports on to the White House, where Fortas remained a member of Johnson's kitchen cabinet.

Lyndon Johnson was paranoid about the Baker case. "He was tormented by 'guilt by association,' " said Ramsey Clark, Johnson's attorney general. Publicly, he tried to put some distance between himself and the man he once called his "strong right arm." Baker was "nobody's protégé," the president insisted. He was just another Senate employee. Privately, Johnson wanted to know exactly what was happening in the case. Sitting with Williams in the owner's box at D.C. Stadium a few months before the trial, the president—in his one and only appearance at a Redskins game—bluntly told Williams, "This is the most important case of your life." Johnson was terrified that Bobby Kennedy's loyalists in the Justice Department would use Baker to blacken the White House. A memorandum from J. Edgar Hoover's personal files, released under the Freedom of Information Act, reveals the high level of Johnson's interest and concern about the case—as well as Hoover's desire to accommodate him. In January 1967, on the eve of the trial, the memo states, the president became "quite exercised" to learn that the Bureau of Narcotics had loaned Bittman a secret recording device to tape a conversation with a potential witness. Hoover had assured the president that the FBI had refused to help Bittman with this eavesdropping. Johnson ordered Hoover to do—"as discreetly as possible"—a "name check" on the Bureau of Narcotics officials who had authorized the recording device in order to see if they were "close to Robert F. Kennedy."

What did Johnson not want Bittman—or the dreaded Kennedys—to find? Williams liked to insinuate that Baker had bombs to drop at trial. "This case will bring down the White House!" Williams declared to Bill Hundley. "Ed would hint that Baker was a flake and a madman, and that you never knew what he was going to say at trial." Some of the lawyers working with Williams suspected that some of the money given to Baker by the S&L owners had found its way into Lyndon Johnson's wallet. But Baker had denied this. His longtime tax lawyer, Boris Kostelanetz, also said that he knew of no secret payments to Johnson. Prosecutors Bittman and Mittler said the same thing. History may show that Baker was a bagman for Johnson when LBJ was majority leader. (In his memoir, *Wheeling and Dealing*, Baker described himself as "the official bagman" for Senate Democrats.) But the Baker case concerned events that happened after Johnson had become vice president and had distanced himself from his Senate protégé. If Williams did know about a bribe to Johnson, he took that story to his grave. Peter Taft, who also worked on the Baker case, was doubtful. "Ed had a big mouth," he said with a laugh. "He would have told us."

Williams did try to bluff. "Ed would hint to the feds, 'you've got a lot of guts to let this guy on the stand,' but he didn't have anything to back it up," said Taft. The officials at the Justice Department were worried that the trial would be politically embarrassing to the Johnson administration, and that it could also damage Democratic congressional leaders who were supposed to be on the receiving end of the money Baker took from the S&L owners. But "making the case go away" entailed far greater risk. The White House and Johnson knew that Bittman was a stubborn, fiercely independent prosecutor who would bitterly complain to the press and the Hill if any attempt was made to drop the case. Wide-open congressional hearings would be more dangerous than a criminal trial, where the administration could exercise at least some control over the evidence just by the way the prosecutor framed the charges.

As it was, Bittman was "a little paranoid. He didn't trust us," said Ramsey Clark. Twenty years later, Bittman was still suspicious. "In my opinion, there were certain efforts, there were a number of things done, direct and indirect pressure on me to get rid of the case," Bittman said, speaking slowly and choosing his words carefully. "There was not a fix, but, no question, certain moves were made." He said he had overwhelming evidence that Baker took a $5,000 payment to arrange a national bank charter for a California bank. "It was a dead-bang, lay-down conflict-of-interest case," he insisted. But his superiors at Justice dropped the charge from the final indictment. Bittman would not speculate why. His assistant said that the prosecutorial team had presented their bosses at Justice with a number of illegal acts by Baker. He suspected that Justice steered the ultimate indictment away from areas that might be politically embarrassing to congressmen or officials in the Johnson administration. Nick Katzenbach, the acting attorney general who had signed off on the indictment in late 1965, denied this. His only interest, he said, was in bringing a case they could win at trial. "I felt if we went after Baker, we'd better have a good case," he said. He was not unmindful of political considerations. "I always thought the Baker case would be my downfall," Katzenbach said. He was afraid that he would be pilloried by the press for doing too little or fired by Johnson for doing too much. But, in fact, he said he never heard from the White House about Baker. He speculated that Johnson did not trust him enough to talk to him because of his Kennedy ties. Johnson didn't need Katzenbach to know what was going on in the case, since J. Edgar Hoover was only too eager to feed the president.

In his memoir, Baker wrote that he was offered a deal by the Justice Department: If he pleaded guilty to a single count, the Department would recommend leniency in sentencing, and at the most Baker would go to jail for a few months. Baker said he turned down the offer because he believed he was innocent. Bittman and his Justice superiors all denied that any deal was offered. Tigar added that Baker would have copped a plea "in a New York minute."

As usual, Williams was obsessive in his preparation for trial. Munching on bags of hamburgers from a White Tower greasy spoon down the street, he fenced and parried with his associates. Tigar once cited Wigmore, a well-known legal authority, on a point of evidence, and Williams growled back, "What circuit does Wigmore sit on? He's a fucking law professor. You got any cases?" As usual, Williams wanted to exercise complete control over the case, even to the point of refusing to let his associates put their names on the pleadings. "Wadden saw this as a plot to deny credit to anyone in the world except Ed," Tigar said, "but the rest of us said, 'It's just Ed.' " Williams was characteristically pessimistic. "Every ten years or so Washington needs to burn a witch," he explained to his secretary, Lillian Keats. "This year it's Bobby."

Baker did have a defense. Although the government claimed that Baker had stolen the $100,000 that the S&L owners gave him to buy influence, Baker claimed that he had given the money to Senator Robert Kerr of Oklahoma, a power on the Senate Finance Committee. Kerr, in turn, had loaned back $50,000 to Baker to help the overextended wheeler-dealer repay his debts. Williams had evidence that at least some of the S&L cash had made it into Kerr's safe-deposit box, which had been opened after Kerr died in 1963. A multimillionaire (owner of the Kerr-McGee Oil Co.) who believed that his interests and Oklahoma's interests were interchangeable, Kerr had been well known for his fondness for cash. "Money is the most powerful substance known to man," the senator had declared more than once. It was entirely plausible that he did take a payoff from the S&L industry through Baker—a suspicion reinforced by the fact that Kerr dropped his bill to increase taxes on the S&Ls the day after Baker arranged a meeting between him and the chief S&L lobbyist.

There was, however, a big drawback to Baker's defense. "We could prove that the money went to Kerr," explained Peter Taft, "but then the jury would convict him of that crime—bribery! It didn't matter to the jury that he was guilty of a crime different from the one he was charged with. We didn't say bribery, of course, but it was. Ed knew this was a lousy defense and that the jury would see through it. The guy was guilty of bribing a senator. What kind of defense is that?"

Williams was not encouraged by jury selection. Over his objection, Judge Gasch announced that the jury would be sequestered. That cut out all the upper-middle-class whites who wanted to go home to their families at night. Williams was left with a jury of retired government employees, who, he knew, would not be forgiving about official corruption.

Williams's opening argument was brilliant, a fifty-five-minute oration to a rapt jury, delivered without notes—as always—clearly and directly pointing the finger at the dead senator. Listening at the government's counsel table, Austin Mittler, Bittman's chief assistant, was "awed. I felt we had lost," he said. "I was embarrassed even being in the same courtroom trying a case against Williams." But Williams's defense strategy ran into trouble as soon as the government began putting on witnesses. The S&L owners testified that they had given the money to Baker to pass along as "campaign contributions" to key lawmakers. The government then trooped seven senators and a congressman, House Ways and Means Committee chairman Wilbur Mills, into court to testify that they had not received a nickel from Bobby Baker. On cross-examination, Williams tried to ask one of the senators if he had received any of the money from Senator Kerr, but Judge Gasch cut him off. The judge said that the answer would be irrelevant; Baker, not Kerr, was on trial.

Williams, of course, believed that it was almost always necessary to put a defendant on the stand, as failure to testify was as good as an admission of guilt to most jurors. But he put Baker on the stand with great trepidation. Preparing his client for trial, Williams had become impatient with his rambling and evasiveness. "Shut up, Bobby," Williams snapped. "Don't remember so much." Williams was afraid the jury would see Baker as he really was: a sleazy influence peddler who lived high while ordinary government employees—like the members of the jury—droned away at low-paying jobs. Williams also worried that Baker would come across as a smart aleck and a cracker to the jurors, eleven of whom were black. (Baker wanted to call black character witnesses, like

Adam Clayton Powell, but Bittman trumped him by warning that, in retaliation, he would call witnesses to testify about Baker's adultery with his secretary.)

Williams did his best to clean up Baker's life-style for the jury. Deals were referred to as "business transactions," influence peddlers were "corporate spokesmen," and the lobbyist's bar that Baker owned, The Quorum Club, was deemed a "cocktail facility." Baker was earnest and polite, answering questions, "Yes, sir," and "Yes, Mr. Williams." Baker testified that when he had run into financial difficulties in 1962, he had gone to "the best friend I ever had around the Capitol"—Lyndon Johnson. The vice president had told him to go see Kerr, who gave him a line of credit in an Oklahoma bank and a $50,000 loan. His eyes misting over, Baker told how Kerr had forgiven the loan at Christmas time, a week before he died, "for the many wonderful things that you have done for me." Baker tried to be emotional and sincere.

But the true Baker came out on cross-examination. He seemed arrogant, preening too much about having flown on Air Force One, and Bittman caught him in small lies, placing him in Las Vegas when Baker testified he had been in Los Angeles. Bittman was completely ready for Baker; he did not repeat the mistake Edward Troxell had made in the Hoffa case and assume that Williams would not put his client on the stand. When Baker finished testifying, Williams was unsparing with his client. "Bobby," he said, "you're the worst witness who ever appeared on a witness stand."

Bittman also picked at Williams, in exactly the way Williams had baited prosecutors in other trials. Late in the proceedings, Williams complained that he had not been shown the prior statements his witness had made to the IRS. Bittman responded, "That's right, you don't. Otherwise, he probably . . . well . . .." The clear insinuation was that if Williams had seen the witness's prior statements, he would have encouraged him to testify differently—he would have suborned perjury. Williams rushed to the bench, demanding a mistrial. "It was a low blow, it was a foul blow. I resent it bitterly," he protested.

For once, Williams was bested in a closing argument. Just as Williams had used biblical injunctions against lying to destroy John Cye Cheasty in the Hoffa case, Bittman summoned up the Bible to damn Baker's greed. He zeroed in on Baker's "one great defect of character. The Old Testament describes it best, 'The love of money is the root of all evil,' and he loved it in cash. The feel of it. The power of it. Through his office and through his hands there constantly flowed huge amounts of cash. Why? Because Robert Baker consciously chose to trade on his position of trust for his own pecuniary profit.''

Williams had agreed to move the closing arguments to the ceremonial courtroom. It was a tactical error. The cavernous, circuslike aspect of a room filled with the press and other lawyers gave the impression of a show at which the jury was not the true audience. Williams's words flowed without the help of notes, and he moved easily about the court (for a big man, he was remarkably light on his feet). But to one of the young lawyers in his firm, Barbara Babcock, he looked ''too expensive and too white.'' His frequent biblical quotations seemed patronizing, as if the Bible was not a resource he regularly drew on to live, or even argue, by. When Williams had not quite finished, Judge Gasch broke in. ''Mr. Williams. We have all enjoyed what you said. Two hours and fifteen minutes. It hardly seems that long,'' he commented dryly. Williams visibly sagged, but he did not object. Babcock suspected that Gasch's remark was intended to signal the jury that they had just seen a very professional show that should entertain and delight, but not raise doubt about the prosecution's case.

In his rebuttal, Bittman shrewdly conceded that the jury had heard ''the greatest argument by the greatest lawyer,'' but added, ''All I have is the facts.'' Listening in the packed courtroom audience, Judith Richards ''knew it was all over. It was like someone putting a pin in the Goodyear Blimp.''

After a day of deliberation, the jury convicted Baker on all nine counts. ''Baker had nothing to go on other than he had a good lawyer,'' a juror told the *Washington Star*. The jurors told the newspapers that they thought Baker had lied on the stand. Privately, Judge Gasch blamed Williams for using a ''dead man's defense'' in trying to blame Kerr for taking the cash. ''Black juries don't like you to lay it off on the dead,'' he said.

Williams looked as if he had been ''hit by a brick'' when the verdict was announced, Baker wrote. An hour later, when he arrived at Baker's house on Van Ness Street, Williams had ''red swollen eyes. The instant he attempted to speak to me he started crying again. He did not cry a silent, gentlemanly stream of tears; his thick body shook and jerked almost convulsively as he sobbed.'' Baker made Williams a stiff drink and said, ''Ed, you worked your ass off.'' But Williams was inconsolable.

"Ed was down for days," said Vince Fuller. But once the tears dried, he blamed everybody but himself. On the night of the verdict, Williams telephoned Lyndon Johnson and blamed the press; if it hadn't been for the pretrial publicity, he told the president, Baker would have been acquitted. At his office, Williams blamed the jury for failing to understand the complexity of the case and the judge for ruling against his motions. Williams started telling biting stories about his imagined afflicters. According to Williams, one juror was overheard asking another juror, "Who's this Captain Gains?" The other juror replied, "I think he's going to testify tomorrow." Williams spun a complicated tale about how Judge Gasch had had it in for Williams because his new law partner, Paul Connolly, had defended a dance studio sued by the judge's mother after she tripped doing the Lindy. (Connolly had argued that the woman was lonely and neglected by her son.) Williams blamed his young associates Taft and Tigar for inadequately preparing Baker for trial. He never said so, but privately Williams may have also blamed himself for losing his first showcase trial in seven years.

Baker was sentenced to a maximum of three years in prison. He served sixteen months at Allenwood Federal Penitentiary, where he played on the tennis team and befriended another inmate, Jimmy Hoffa. Williams fruitlessly appealed Baker's conviction again and again. Over twenty years later, even after Williams's death, lawyers in the firm continued to try to help Baker get his convictions overturned, and they uncovered some evidence that would have been useful in the winter of 1967. Under the Freedom of Information Act, Baker obtained a document showing that the Justice Department had learned from an unidentified informant that Senator Kerr had, in fact, received an S&L contribution from Baker. If Williams had been able to put that information on the stand, he might have been able to bolster his case substantially.

Yet for all the work Williams had done on the case—and his grief over losing—one wonders if he really did do all he could have on Bobby Baker's behalf. The case appears to have been well suited to the "gray-mail" tactics Williams would later use to defend public officials who had damning secrets to tell. True, while Williams hinted to prosecutors that Baker would "tell all" in open court, he may not have had concrete evidence of Baker passing bribes to Lyndon Johnson. Bobby Baker said that Williams never suggested to Baker that he expose LBJ or any U.S. senators in order to defend himself. If he had, Baker added, he would have refused. "I'm not that kind of guy," said Baker in 1991. Nonetheless, is it possible that, in the end, Williams was unwilling to launch a frontal attack on the White House because he was afraid of alienating the occupant? The fact that Williams talked every night to Abe Fortas, LBJ's informal legal adviser, and reported on the progress of the case is not reassuring about Williams's ultimate motives.

Chapter Nineteen

LOSING THE BAKER case made Williams itchy again. "I'm sick of this shit. We've got to get out of this business," he told Bill Hundley over lunch after the trial. "My clients are discriminated against. I don't need it. I'm going to run for the Senate." He was irked when *Newsweek* ran a cover story that spring on F. Lee Bailey, calling him "the hottest mouthpiece since Perry Mason." Williams complained that Bailey was always hustling to the courthouse steps to try his cases in the press. Williams's irritation was compounded by the fact that *he* was originally supposed to be the subject of cover stories in both *Time* and *Newsweek* that winter. His defeat in the Baker case had knocked him off.

In the *Newsweek* story on Bailey, Williams was relegated to a mere sidebar, lumped in with two other trial lawyers, Percy Foreman and Melvin Belli. Williams knew that he no longer had exclusive claim to the title of "best trial lawyer in America." In the 1960s, a new generation of courtroom lawyers had come along, winning highly publicized cases and then trumpeting their achievements. With some justification, Williams felt that he had cleared the way for Bailey by making the defense of criminals a respectable profession, and he believed that he was at once less showy and more substantive than the newcomers. Bailey was gracious enough to tell *Newsweek*, "If I ever got in trouble, Ed Williams is the one I'd want representing me." Williams growled to sportswriter Morrie Siegel, "I wouldn't take the case."

The presence of competition for the spotlight that was once solely his own made Williams look for new arenas. Increasingly, he talked about running for office. After the Baker case, he had a drinking bout with John Reilly, a former Kennedy aide at Justice and a shrewd political operative. Williams tried to persuade Reilly to run his campaign for governor of Maryland, but Williams's friends did not take these flights of political fancy too seriously. What Williams really wanted was to be named attorney general. He already regarded himself as the number one lawyer in the nation; he wanted to make it official. He knew that his standing was high at the White House.

Clark Clifford had been talking up "his lawyer" to the president, and Johnson had started asking Williams over to the White House from time to time for a chat. Williams's advice was always the same: fire J. Edgar Hoover. Williams told Johnson that Hoover was wiretapping and bugging in flagrant disregard of the law. Williams had picked up through his sources that Hoover was bugging Martin Luther King, Jr., as well as the mob, and he warned the president that Hoover's obsession with the civil rights leader was politically dangerous as well as morally wrong. Johnson responded by telling the story of his Uncle Hud's fishing trips on the Pedernales River. Uncle Hud, said Johnson, always tented with a fellow who was a sleepwalker. Why? Because he'd "rather have him inside the tent pissing out than outside the tent pissing in."

Johnson thought Williams would make "a great attorney general," he told his aide Jack Valenti, but he couldn't give him the job. His hands were tied by Williams's defense of Bobby Baker. Confirmation hearings for Williams would turn into another Baker trial, Johnson said. Before the cameras and the press, some senators might want to probe more deeply into what Williams knew about Baker's past—and his ties to the former majority leader. Though Williams could invoke his attorney-client privilege, the questions alone would be embarrassing. Then there were all those other controversial clients, like Jimmy Hoffa and Frank Costello. Williams was just too risky a choice. A month after the Baker trial, Johnson picked Ramsey Clark, who had been "acting" AG, to be the new attorney general.

In June 1967, a rumor circulated through Washington, surfacing in the *Washington Post*, that Williams would be named U.S. ambassador to the United Nations. The idea had some appeal to Williams. He had not shed his idealistic notions about "world peace through law," and he fancied that his negotiating skills would be well suited to a global stage. The truth is that Williams would have been bored and exasperated by the endless and often pointless debate at the U.N.; nonetheless, Williams's desire to escape the bitter memory of the Baker case made almost any alternative seem attractive.

His escapist fantasy seemed more real when LBJ called him in July 1967. "I have something very important I want you to do for your country," Johnson drawled in his unctuous, insistent way. The president asked Williams and his wife to dinner at the White House, where he would tell him what he had in mind. After dinner, Johnson summoned Williams into his bedroom and began to give him the Johnson treatment. Agnes Williams, strong minded and dead set against her husband going into public life, followed Williams and the president right into the bedroom. (As Williams later told the story, he could see, over Johnson's shoulder, Agnes shaking her head and mouthing the word *no*; Agnes attributes this version to her husband's hyperbole.) Johnson did have a job offer to make, but it wasn't what Williams had in mind. He asked Williams to become the mayor of Washington. Thinking fast, Williams responded that he was deeply honored, but really, the city was racially tense and the president would be wiser to appoint a black. For once, Johnson did not press; he was astute enough to see that Williams was right. Instead, Johnson fished around in a box of papers and pulled out a plastic bust of his own head. Disappointed, Williams returned to the dinner table, awkwardly bearing the president's bust.*

By 1967, Williams had made it into Washington's inner circle, and was welcomed by the new order. He was even a regular at Nancy Dickerson's dinner parties at Merrywood, dubbed by *Washington Post* gossip columnist Maxine Cheshire as "the Secret Society—the inner elite of the Great Society." Bobby Kennedy, too, had softened his grudge. A Redskins fan who watched games from the box provided by Williams, Kennedy wrote his old nemesis to congratulate him on an exciting Redskins victory over the Dallas Cowboys in December 1966. At the end of his note, Kennedy couldn't resist scrawling a P.S. to remind Williams who had ultimately won the greater game of incarcerating Jimmy Hoffa. "I noticed Hoffa lost his appeal," wrote RFK (Hoffa had been convicted

---

*Johnson appointed a black, Walter Washington, as the capital's mayor. In this pre–home rule era, D.C. had been essentially run by Congress. There had been some internal debate at the White House over the best choice for the city's first mayor. Jim Rowe, Tommy "the Cork" Corcoran's law partner and a wise old hand, had recommended Williams. He wrote Johnson, "For some reason, [Williams] has always had standing among the Negroes, probably because he is a defense counsel with tremendous 'guts' and therefore in some way, they 'identify' with him. The fact that he recruited a lot of Negro football players for the Redskins also has not hurt a bit." However, another Johnson adviser— Joe Califano, who would become one of Williams's law partners—pushed for a black.

of jury tampering in 1964). "I guess I can climb back on the Capitol which I jumped off of about ten years ago. Just maybe this time Hoover will push me off." Williams was now included in various Kennedy rituals, like the annual Hickory Hill pet shows, where spoof awards were made for categories like "longest nose." The behavior of Bobby Kennedy's dog, Brumus, provoked this rather heavy-handed attempt at humor in a letter to RFK from Williams on August 7, 1967:

> I have been retained by Mr. Art Buchwald to represent him in the matter of the vicious and unprovoked attack made on him Wednesday, July 25, by the large, savage, man-eating coat-tearing black animal owned by you and responding to the name Broomass (phonetic).
>
> Mr. Buchwald has been ordered to take complete rest by his physician until such time as he recovers from the traumatic neurosis from which he is suffering as a result of the attack. He will be in isolation at Vineyard Haven, Martha's Vineyard, Massachusetts, for an indefinite period at a cost of $2,000 a month.
>
> He is concerned about the effect of exposing this ugly episode on your political future. . . . Since Broomass is black, the case is fraught with civil rights undercurrents.

Washington in the late 1960s, like the rest of the country, was roiled and chaotic. Lyndon Johnson's decision in March 1968 not to run for reelection and Robert Kennedy's assassination in June stunned the establishment. The push for civil rights, the women's movement, and particularly the Vietnam War turned once dull or tittery cocktail parties into shouting matches. Congressmen did the frug and political pundits experimented with marijuana. "Swinging Washington" may seem like a contradiction in terms, but that is what the gossips called it in the late sixties when the *Washington Post* started a new section called "Style" to chronicle the fervid social antics of the powerful and the wannabes.

Williams hated the sixties counterculture—the music, the dress, the mores—and made no effort to understand it. He was unsympathetic to feminism and against the sexual revolution. When his friend Rene Carpenter displayed a birth-control diaphragm on her television talk show, "Everywoman," Williams told her, "That's the most disgusting thing I ever saw." For much of the late sixties, he was a hawk among doves in the mostly liberal crowd in which he moved. "Hang tough," he counseled Lyndon Johnson on Vietnam. Only when Williams's political mentor Clark Clifford turned against the war in March 1968 did Williams come around after him, along with the remaining hawks of the Demo-cratic establishment. Yet, curiously, Williams was a beneficiary of all the unrest and assaults on authority. Williams had always been a maverick, an outsider, and now rebels were ''in.'' The Chevy Chase Club and its ilk were in retreat in the late sixties. Defending the unpopular seemed raffish and radically chic. Williams was not only invited to the ''best'' dinner parties, he was regarded as a prime catch.

Williams did not like large, formal parties, and he refused to go to impersonal galas. ''I never saw him at a charity ball,'' recalled Nancy Dickerson. He enjoyed holding forth at the cocktail hour, and he liked sitting at small, round tables where he could dominate, recalled Sally Quinn, who was writing for ''Style.'' ''But he hated long tables or noisy parties where he had to talk the whole time to the women on his right and left. He got impatient when women pulled him out of the table conver-sation to ask about his kids.'' He dreaded making polite conversation with the wife of a government official, said Betty Killay. ''He didn't understand why he had to sit next to women. He regarded Washington as a town full of powerful men and the women they married when they were young.''

But hostesses learned how to take care of Williams. ''In Washington dinner parties, hostesses follow a rule,'' said Barbara Howar, a socialite of the Johnson era. ''Everyone is supposed to get a good partner and a bad partner—a dog and a pony. Ed only got ponies.'' Williams may have been bored by the dowdy wives of aging cabinet secretaries, but he loved the company of beautiful women, especially intelligent ones, and they liked him. ''He made you feel like a woman, which in this town is rare. He made you feel like he wanted to talk to you,'' said Pamela Harriman, the handsome British wife of Governor Averell Harriman. ''He never looked over your shoulder,'' said Barbara Howar. ''He gave you total attention.''

He was always sympathetic to women in distress. Once a lady-in-waiting for Lyndon Johnson's daughters, Howar was ostracized by the White House when she danced a few nights too many on tabletops and took up with a married White House aide. Howar was married herself at the time, and her Iranian husband threw her out of the house and tried to take away her children. She came to Williams for help at a time when other lawyers in town wouldn't touch her. ''Ed saved me,'' Howar re-called. ''He saved my children.''

Williams could also render more short-term assistance. At a dinner party given by prominent media socialites Dick and Shirley Clurman in New York, Williams walked up to Barbra Streisand, who was feeling unlucky at love and looking morose as she sat by herself on a couch in the corner. "If you let me sit next to you, I'll give you a free cry," Williams said. The two spent the next hour huddled together in soulful conversation.

At a small dinner in the residence of the White House in 1967, Williams sat next to Mrs. Alfred Vanderbilt. A radiant blond, Jeanne Murray had been a celebrated debutante in the 1930s, a member of the Catholic *jeunesse dorée* of Southampton society. She had married and divorced a Vanderbilt and had a well-publicized affair with British Minister of State Anthony Nutting. When he resigned during the Suez crisis, the gossips wrote that the Right Honourable Mr. Nutting's real motivation was to spend more time with Mrs. Vanderbilt.

At a fancy party thrown by the Kennedys at the St. Regis Hotel in 1961, Jeanne Vanderbilt had been the only one polite enough to talk to the lonely and resentful outsider standing on the balcony, Lyndon Johnson. LBJ was forever grateful; when he became president, he regularly invited Mrs. Vanderbilt to small dinners at the White House.

Williams talked to Mrs. Vanderbilt about his desire to become attorney general. He said that he did not dare ask because of the Baker case. So Mrs. Vanderbilt asked for him. She delivered the president's negative reaction at a breakfast at the Hay Adams Hotel. "He seemed disappointed but not surprised," she recalled.

Williams began calling on her when he came to New York, as he still regularly did on business. "He was marvelous company," she remembered. She called him "Edward," and he took her out to dinner with boxing champion Sugar Ray Robinson, whom she called "the Shug." "Edward liked to be the lion, but he wasn't insistent. He wasn't domineering," she said. She found him strangely reticent in some ways. He always insisted on seeing the guest list before coming to dinner parties at her apartment, and he did not want her to come see him argue in court. When she went downtown to see him argue a case on behalf of some black militants accused of shooting Malcolm X, he told her, "Don't do that again."

"He was like a little boy reaching out to touch danger," Jeanne Vanderbilt said. "I felt he was searching for something, but that he never was going to find it." Williams was romantic and flirtatious, but he did not seem interested in an affair, nor did he indulge in the kind of wild declarations of love he had bestowed on Leonore Lemmon and Jean Pochna. He did not want to betray his wife, Agnes, and he certainly was not about to abandon the institution of marriage.

Williams could be a moral purist. He was critical of Jacqueline Kennedy for asking Cardinal Cushing to bless her remarriage to Aristotle Onassis. (Jackie had come to Williams for advice as well; he had warned the president's widow against marrying the Greek shipping tycoon.) Williams complained that only the rich could buy their way in and out of matrimony, and he chastised the Church for selling annulments to wealthy Catholics. Yet Williams, with his strong sense of the essential sinfulness of man, often chose to forgive. The night after Teddy Kennedy drove off the bridge at Chappaquiddick—and failed to call the police until morning—Williams said he was sympathetic to the youngest Kennedy brother. "I can understand it," he told Jeanne Vanderbilt, meaning he could empathize with Kennedy's weakness of flesh and fear of damnation. Vanderbilt could not understand how Williams could be so accepting of behavior that she regarded as murderous. "I didn't like him [Williams] so much after that," she said. "I didn't think he was so funny."

A month earlier, on the first anniversary of Robert Kennedy's assassination, Williams had met Lauren Bacall at RFK's grave. She was on the road in Baltimore, in rehearsal for her Broadway hit *Applause*. She was overwhelmed by Williams. "He was a powerhouse, a man of gigantic personality and panache," she said. "I never met a man like him. He was always an upper for me. He made me sit up. He was fun and fascinating."

Williams saw her often on his trips to New York. Like Mrs. Vanderbilt, Bacall thought Williams was torn by conflicting impulses. Although Williams was never reflective about himself in the company of men, he appeared to do some soul searching with Lauren Bacall. "He was a split personality. He used that term," she recalled. "He called it his internecine struggle. He was very much a family man, a total lawyer who wanted to be a Supreme Court justice. Yet he had flair, he loved representing colorful characters. I thought there was a war between the two sides, the half that wanted to live dangerously and the half that wanted to live safely."

This may have been a pose by Williams, an effort to make himself seem like a more romantic and tortured figure. Williams was conflicted all right. But the description he gave Bacall of the forces pulling at him is a little disingenuous. The "danger" to Williams was not hanging around with mobsters—that was fun, even comfortable. For Williams, real risk would be the exposure that comes with seeking public office. A confirmation hearing at which Williams was the nominee, not merely the lawyer, was a far riskier place to be than Frank Costello's table at the Copacabana.

Bacall disliked his drinking. "He was a sloppy drunk," she said. "He drooled. You'd want to say 'sober up,' but then he'd recover." At a dinner party at the Clurmans' in 1972, Bacall made the mistake of publicly scolding him. Williams did not see her much after that.

Chapter Twenty

AT FIFTY, WILLIAMS no longer had, as Gay Talese had once described it, the "face of a young Jesuit." Liquor and contest living had taken their toll; the wavy reddish-gray hair was growing gray and thin, and the massive body was beginning to run to fat. The smooth, soft cheeks had become fleshy and furrowed, and the nose looked as if it had been on the losing side of a bar fight. But Williams retained his remarkable ability to change expression and demeanor in an instant to suit his audience and purpose. He could be Edward Bennett Williams, courtroom warrior, overawing and intimidating, his anger held just shy of physical violence. Or Edward, pious and humble, innocent of all the sins he had known and forgiven.

The man his male friends flocked to was Eddie, the Irish boyo, puckish and bemused, twinkling and brimming with fun and machismo. "Washington is a man's town, and men were attracted to Ed," said Sally Quinn. "He'd walk into a room and he'd be immediately surrounded by men— admiring, eyes glistening. It was almost a sexual thing, like perfume. Men of great rank were drawn to him." They came to banter and talk about politics and the Redskins, to hear him tell stories, to bask in his masculine aura.

Williams had a wide circle of male friends devoted to him; during the writing of this book, at least a score of men declared, with complete sincerity, "You know, Ed was my best friend." But his true best friends were Ben Bradlee and Art Buchwald. Bradlee and Buchwald had befriended each other in the fifties in Paris, where Bradlee was a foreign

233

correspondent for *Newsweek* and Buchwald a humor columnist for the *New York Herald Tribune;* when Buchwald came to Washington in 1962, he fell in with Bradlee and Williams, who had renewed their earlier friendship. The threesome began having lunch at least once a week. Half-mocking men's clubs, they formed what they called "the Club," the sole purpose of which, like all good clubs, Buchwald explained, was "to keep others out."

Writing three times a week for 230 newspapers, Art Buchwald was the most widely read humor columnist in America in the 1960s. His deadpan parodies poked gentle fun at self-important Washington. Puffing on his six-inch cigar, the short, roundish Buchwald could even publicly tease Williams about the touchy subject of his clients. Williams, Buchwald liked to say in his speeches to law students, "has made a career of defending the scorned, the degraded, the oppressed—no matter how rich and powerful they are." A poor Jewish foster child from Queens, Buchwald was a natural ally for Williams, who liked all self-made ethnics and had a particular kinship with Jews. Williams knew a little Yiddish, and he sprinkled colorful Yiddishisms into his conversation. He loved expressive words like "gonif" (thief) and "bupkes" (slang for "nothing").

Williams's affinity with Bradlee dated back to their late nights at the Atlas Club. While Bradlee was a proud Brahmin with enormous social grace, he disdained (or pretended to) thin-blooded WASPs and snobs as much as Williams did. Bradlee's table manners may have been perfect, along with his French, but he could be as earthy and profane and raucous as a South Boston saloon on Friday night. Bradlee had affectionately called Williams a "primitive" because he was a man "of primary colors and strong feelings." Bradlee also liked to say that Williams "didn't have to read books, because he already knew what he thought." Bradlee may have been describing himself; as he grew older, Williams began reading widely on politics and history, though he affected an anti-intellectual bent. But the fact that Bradlee could mistake Williams for his own self-image is the point. Despite their vastly different backgrounds, they saw themselves in each other. The two formed a kind of aristocracy of personality: In a city of outsized egos, no two men dominated a room quite as completely as Ben Bradlee and Ed Williams.

The room they often chose to dominate at lunch was Duke Zeibert's. "There was nothing subtle about Duke's," wrote Lynn Rosellini in the *Washington Star.* "Kosher dills on the table. The chair covers are tan plastic, the lights are bright—the better to spot celebrities." Spouting sports talk, sopping up the stew gravy with crusts of pumpernickel, the con men, construction kings, gamblers, lawyers, lobbyists, and politicians would "yell and wave at each other" across the room. When Bobby Baker got out of jail, his first stop was Duke's for bourbon and corned beef. Duke himself was so blithely antifeminist that he told Rosellini, "Women? Let 'em stay home and make babies and take care of the house."

The Club's other meeting place was the tonier Sans Souci. The principal purpose of the restaurant with gold brocade walls and heavy French food was to see and be seen. Discovered by the Kennedy White House and embraced by the more sociable of the Great Society strivers, the Sans Souci was designed, on purpose or not, so that every table had a view of every other table. The maître d' seemed to take reservations by political and social standing, not by the order of calls, and Bradlee, Buchwald, and Williams were never kept waiting.

Entertainment at the Club consisted of teasing. "In shifting twos we'd pick on the third," said Bradlee. Williams and Buchwald would go to great lengths to trump each other. Both men had a tendency to gain weight, and looked for an incentive to take it off. Williams suggested "greed" because "greed has been the motivating force in both our lives." They decided to have a diet contest. At the end of three months, the winner would collect $100 for every pound he took off.

The two immediately resorted to psychological warfare. Buchwald sent Williams a tray of French pastries at noon one day; Williams retaliated by sending Buchwald a large chocolate layer cake with a card, "Always thinking of you. Eddie." Knowing Williams's predilection for cocktails and desserts, friends began making side bets on Buchwald.

At first it did not appear they would be disappointed. Trying a case in New York, Williams actually gained six pounds, while Buchwald lost ten in six weeks. Williams demanded a summit and tried to call off the bet, but Buchwald refused. He suggested instead that they donate the proceeds to charity. When Ambassador Yitzhak Rabin of Israel walked by their table, Buchwald told him that Williams was going to buy Israel a new fighter plane. At the end of the three months, Buchwald had lost sixteen pounds. He was so confident of victory that for the weigh-in ceremony at the Metropolitan Club, he hired a violinist to play "Hearts and Flowers" as Williams waddled from the steam room to the scales, and "Let a Winner Lead the Way" for his own triumphal procession.

The weigh-in was scheduled for the day before Thanksgiving, 1972. At

10:00 A.M. that morning, Williams appeared in the office of Brendan Sullivan, a young associate in the firm. Williams commanded Sullivan to come play squash with him at the Metropolitan Club. As they crashed around the court, Sullivan noticed that Williams was unusually bundled up, encased in a rubber suit, like a diver's, underneath a sweat suit. After an hour, Williams refused to stop playing. "It was an unbelievable marathon," recalled Sullivan. "I thought Ed was going to die. He turned red and finally sat on the floor. Then he said, okay, we're going to the steam room. You're supposed to be in there for three minutes. After ten minutes, I asked him what the hell he was doing. He said, 'I've got to weigh in.' He stayed in there for forty minutes, which is medically unsound. It could have killed him."

It was, Buchwald recalled, "the greatest upset in diet history." Williams had lost twenty-one pounds, much of it fluids in the last two hours. Buchwald's own violinist broke into "Hail to the Redskins!" when the results were announced. Williams nearly fainted before he collected his $500, which he donated to Cardinal O'Boyle's Right to Life Committee for unwed mothers.

When they ran out of jokes on each other, the trio would turn on their friends, wives, and colleagues. The teasing could be a little rough. Williams would complain, albeit with mock seriousness, about Agnes's straitlaced view of life. All three began calling her "Agony" and "Agoness," mimicking Williams's voice and his habit of drawing out syllables, "A-a-a-goness."

For Joe Califano, who was notoriously cheap, they took up a collection to buy him a new suit. Their friends' vanity was an easy target. If Nancy Dickerson and her equally well-coiffed and tailored husband, Wyatt, were coming for lunch, the Club would dryly wonder if the happy couple planned to arrive wearing matching blue blazers. Much of the joking revolved around blackballing friends who were eager to join the Club. When Katharine Graham, Bradlee's employer, came to lunch, Buchwald would say, "I'm for you, but Ben's against you."* (Buchwald, she said,

*Williams went to elaborate lengths to prolong this jest. On April 2, 1970, he reported to Graham on her candidacy for admission. "I, as a committee of one, reported the matter out favorably a long time ago. But a motion for recommittal was unexpectedly made by an alleged friend of yours, and that motion is now pending. Our poll shows the vote now to stand one for, one against, and one undecided. It would be an obvious betrayal of confidence for me to tell you who is against you and who is undecided. But I do think it is fair to say that we should concentrate all our efforts in the next 24 hours on Buchwald. I know that you will keep this message in confidence. If it ever becomes

also gave her a "ghastly purple orchid," and, after Attorney General John Mitchell threatened during Watergate that "Katie Graham's gonna get her tit caught in a wringer," he gave the chairman of the board of the Washington Post Company a golden tit.)

A favorite target of the Club was Joseph Alsop. Williams and Buchwald thought the patrician columnist was effete, imperious, and insufferably arrogant. (Bradlee, tugged by class loyalty and Mrs. Graham's fondness for Alsop, was more forgiving.) In the winter of 1970, Buchwald's play *Sheep on the Runway* began a Broadway run. The central figure was "a poisonously stupid and arrogant columnist . . . who has prejudices where his brains ought to be."

Buchwald called the columnist "Joseph Mayflower," but everyone in Washington knew he was Joseph Alsop. The town was happily scandalized. Alsop told Rowlie Evans that anyone who went to the opening in New York was no friend of his, and *Post* gossip columnist Maxine Cheshire gleefully printed the announcement. Alsop hired a lawyer who demanded that Buchwald change the columnist's name, as well as write *Time, Newsweek, The New Yorker, Life,* and the *New York Times* stating that he intended no resemblance between Joseph Mayflower and Joseph Alsop. Buchwald went to Williams, who was elated by the threat to the play, which had opened to bad reviews in Philadelphia. "Alsop might save your show after all!" Williams declared. "This is great. A two-day deposition! We'll agree to have announcements before every show! We'll take out ads stating that we're being sued!" Buchwald anxiously inquired, "Does he have a suit?" "No chance," Williams responded. "But if he wants to sue we must not look a full house in the mouth." Buchwald told Alsop's lawyer that he had retained Edward Bennett Williams; the lawyer immediately scuttled back into the shadows. The gossip helped sell seats. Bradlee, his loyalty torn, did halfheartedly ask Buchwald to change the name, but the humorist ignored him.

Not everyone thought the Club's jokes were funny. "The locker room stuff could be a bore," said Sally Quinn. "It could seem too macho, these guys grunting, insulting each other, never completing a sentence." Other journalists were put off by the "Benjy-Artie-Eddie" camaraderie and in-joke exclusivity of the Club. But in some ways the hairy-chested front of the Club was a facade. For all their one-upsmanship, the three men

---

known to the others that I have communicated with you in this vein, I must, of course, deny it. Love, Ed." On her seventieth birthday, the Club finally admitted Mrs. Graham—but informed her that members faced mandatory retirement at the age of seventy.

probably spent more time worrying together about what to do with their wayward children, who, like other adolescents in the late sixties, were in full rebellion. The frenetic late sixties shook families throughout the ruling circles of Washington. David and Ann Brinkley gave a last New Year's Eve party and split up. Bradlee's marriage was on the rocks; his wife, Tony, announced, after the Bradlees celebrated Williams's fiftieth birthday with a large bash, that she was sick of giving parties and with increasing frequency retreated to her sculpture in the basement. Buchwald himself was having a difficult spell of depression despite the success of his play.

For all the macho and tomfoolery, the joking between Williams, Bradlee, and Buchwald had an almost rueful quality at times. There was an unspoken awareness among the three of the enormous pressure each felt to remain preeminent in their fields. The Club was hardly group therapy; introspection and self-analysis would have been too touchy-feely for these men. Yet the bond between them went far beyond diet contests and making fun of snobs. Buchwald's joke that he and Williams got on so well because neither man wanted anything from the other was said only half in jest. In a city where most friendships are based on what one can get from another—information, power, favors—the freedom from having to hustle and pay court is an enormous relief. Bradlee and Williams did, to be sure, use each other to swap tips and information, and Williams sometimes accused Bradlee of feeding his indiscretions right back to the editors of the *Post*. (If Williams complained that he was going to fire the Redskin quarterback at lunch, by 3:00 P.M. his phone would be ringing with a call from the *Post*'s sports desk. "That goddam Bradlee!" Williams would roar. "He's a fucking sieve! Goddam press! You can't trust 'em! They have no friends!") But these rants were mostly for show, to let off steam. The fact is that Williams and Bradlee depended on each other for solace as well as advice. Bradlee is know known for his sentimentality. But in thinking about his best friend after he died, Bradlee compared him to his father. Bradlee's father had been an all-American football player at Harvard, and he had an enormous chest. As a little boy, Bradlee recalled, he liked to curl up in his father's lap and lean on that enormous chest as it heaved and sighed. It made him feel secure and safe. "When I was with Ed," Bradlee said, "that's how I felt."

Chapter Twenty-One

WILLIAMS'S OWN CLUBHOUSE was his box at RFK Stadium. It may seem peculiar that the Washington Establishment would so devotedly trek out to a stadium in the middle of a slum to watch a poor-to-mediocre team grunt and huff seven Sundays a year. But in the mid-sixties, watching the Redskins became, for the nation's capital, a ruling-class ritual on an emotional, if not esthetic, par with Wimbledon and Ascot for the British. The appeal of the Redskins can be partly explained by Washington's obsession with the art of winning and losing in all its incarnations. Former CIA director Richard Helms, who got his tickets from Williams, offered a more high-flown theory: "Rooting for the Redskins was the one thing that united Washington," he said. "It was a healing ground." During Vietnam and Watergate, the Washington elite wanted something they all could cheer for, and the Redskins sufficed.

Though Williams used the twenty seats in his box, and scores more throughout the stadium, to curry favor and stroke the powerful, he also used his box for his friends and minions. Alongside Earl Warren and Averell Harriman sat several Catholic priests from the various schools attended by the Williams children. As the number of children increased (Agnes had two girls and two boys in addition to the one girl and two boys adopted by Williams and Dorothy), so did the number of priests. To make room, Buchwald was moved from the first to the second row of the box. "Hey Eddie, do you have to be Catholic to sit in the first row?" Buchwald teased. "Hey Benjy," he yelled to Bradlee, who had retained his front-row seat. "Can you see anything down there?"

The regulars in the box, which included Williams's old pals from Georgetown as well as Bradlee and Buchwald, made fun of new entries and hangers-on around the box. They mocked the "star fuckers," the advertising directors, TV station managers, and auto dealers who lined up in Williams's office behind the box to glimpse celebrities. They ogled the tight white sweater of Duke Zeibert's date, Elizabeth Ray, the blond "secretary" who ended the career of her boss, the influential House Rules Committee chairman Wayne Hays, when she admitted that she couldn't type. And they turned thumbs down when Williams invited Nixon's new national security adviser, Henry Kissinger, to the box. Kissinger at least got into the spirit. "Bad call!" screamed Williams after an interference penalty on a Redskins defensive back. Kissinger shook his finger at the referee and demanded, in a stentorian tone, "On what theory?"

Williams rarely sat still in his seat. He would pace, fret, yell, sulk, pound his fists, and denounce his players. When his field-goal kicker was a little shaky, Williams muttered, "That guy puts the thrill back into the extra point." Williams expected his guests to be as serious about winning as he was. When Barbara Howar made the mistake of confusing a Redskins game with a cocktail party and got up to leave before the half, Williams said to her, "Keep on going." She was never invited back.

Williams became as consumed with the Redskins winning on the field as he was with his law firm winning in court. In the sixties, he managed to improve the Redskins from the worst team in the league to a slightly below average team, mostly by opening the door to black players and ponying up the money to trade for quarterback Sonny Jurgensen and veteran linebacker Sam Huff. At the beginning of every season, Williams would brim with hope. "Titletown!" he'd exclaim. "Washington's gonna be Titletown!" Then, as the Redskins began losing again, anger and despair would set in. Tom Wadden learned to avoid Williams the Monday after a Redskins defeat. Earl Dudley, a Williams associate, recalls his anxiety when Williams simply refused to focus on a Supreme Court argument on the Monday morning after the Redskins lost to Dallas, their hated rival, 35–0. "It was almost impossible to get Ed into the car to go up to the court. He was beside himself," recalled Dudley. (Williams did manage to pull himself together for the argument, representing the United Mine Workers on the question of whether labor is exempt from the antitrust laws, but he lost the case.)

Though Williams only owned 5 percent of the team, he acted as if he owned 100 percent. And he was continuously embroiled in legal disputes that threatened his control. When George Preston Marshall, the curmudgeonly majority owner, was incapacitated in December 1963 with a host of diseases, including cerebral arteriosclerosis, a damaged heart, diabetes, and emphysema, he made Williams a conservator of his estate, along with two other minority owners, Leo DeOrsay and Milton King. Marshall's two children, Catherine and George Jr., immediately objected. They claimed that Williams and the other conservators had a conflict of interest, since they could represent their own interests over Marshall's in handling the estate, which consisted mostly of Redskins stock. Marshall, however, had been estranged from his children for years, and he indicated in his lucid moments that he did not want his affairs placed in the hands of his children. The children's next move was to try to get Marshall to change his will, which cut them out. The children insisted, despite evidence to the contrary, that Marshall wanted to leave his money to them. As the old man lay speechless and motionless in his house, the children read him a new will leaving them the estate, and signed it for him.

The family feud rattled through the courts for most of the 1960s. Williams was pestered and threatened by the attempts of the Marshall children to take away what he considered rightfully his. He was unforgiving of the young lawyers in his firm who worked on the Marshall litigation if they produced anything less than perfection. Judith Richards made a mistake researching a question of law and Williams barely spoke to her for months. David Webster, a lawyer who had come to the firm with Paul Connolly, recalled struggling to write a brief defending the lower court judge's decision to throw out the Marshall children's challenge to Williams as a conservator of the estate. Judge Alexander Holtzoff had dismissed the suit without a hearing or discovery, and Webster did not see how he could defend this before the Court of Appeals. "It just won't write," Webster told Williams. "I think we're going to lose." Williams exploded. "Lose! Lose! God damn you! You *can't* lose!" Webster, who could be as temperamental as Williams, shot back, "I didn't think you could lose the Bobby Baker case either. . . ." Then, Webster recalled, Williams "really blew."

When Marshall finally died in 1969, his will left his estate to care for the poor children of the District of Columbia—the poor white children, that is. He specifically instructed that the money not go to blacks. Williams realized that the discriminatory will would never stand up in court, and he feared that the Marshall children would be provided with a basis for interminable litigation. To buy them off, he had the Redskins purchase a chunk of stock from the estate and retire it, with the proceeds going to the children in settlement of their dispute. Ultimately, the Redskins bought up all of Marshall's stock from the foundation established to help poor boys (black and white) of Washington. As a result, Jack Kent Cooke ended up owning 85% of the team (he bought out the other minority owners) and Williams boosted his share from 5% to 15% without spending a nickel of his own. Cooke had to give Williams voting control of his stock, because as the owner of professional basketball and hockey teams in L.A. he was barred from active management by the "cross-ownership" rules of the National Football League. So, for a personal investment of less than $100,000, Williams in effect acquired total control of the team.

Williams had an apparent conflict of interest in handling Marshall's estate. How could he properly represent the interests of the estate when his own interests were so entangled in the disposition of Marshall's stock? By voting to sell Marshall's stock back to the Redskins, he was giving himself more control over the team and increasing the value of his own investment. "I would have ruled there was a conflict," said D.C. Superior Court Judge Paul McArdle, who was an old friend of Williams as well as a former head of the D.C. Bar. Williams's defenders argue that he did not hurt anyone by helping himself. Marshall had no use for his children and no desire to leave them the team. The foundation for poor boys set up by Marshall's will received a fair market value for the Redskins stock, according to outside appraisers. Still, the Redskins did have to raise ticket prices to pay the interest on the debt incurred through the buying of the stock. Of course, Williams could charge whatever price he wanted, since there was overwhelming demand for Redskins tickets by the early seventies. But the fact is that Redskins ticket prices were the highest in the National Football League.

Without question, Williams had gone overboard in his determination to take and keep control of the Redskins. Marshall may have been indifferent to his children, but when it had come time to provide the court with a medical opinion as to whether further visits by his children would impair Marshall's health, Williams arranged to have his own friend and family doctor, Steve Jones, deliver the opinion. Marshall's children complained that they were barred from the house by Redskins employees. One of them, Leroy Washington, was Williams's chauffeur. Williams remained a bitter enemy of the Marshall children, whom he disparaged with cutting stories. When Catherine Marshall tried to claim the visiting team's owners' seats at a Giants game at Yankee Stadium in the mid-sixties, Williams was already sitting in them. As Williams told the story, Catherine, who had married a Russian nobleman and whom Williams referred to as "the Princess," loudly objected. "I don't know this woman," Williams said to the stadium ushers who were drawn to the contretemps. "She's drunk. Have her arrested." ("It never happened," said Catherine Marshall. "Untrue and outrageous.") When Williams came to view Marshall's body at the funeral home after he died, Catherine greeted him at the door by screaming. "You're a murderer! A murderer!"

Williams's dealings with the players and the staff were more pleasant, though no less intense. The Redskins were surprised and amused when Williams appeared at training camp in Carlisle, Pennsylvania, in July 1965, his first year as president of the club, dressed in shorts, a Redskins T-shirt, and rubber-soled coaches' shoes. He then proceeded to do calisthenics with the team and catch passes. Williams had been too busy studying or pumping gas to play sports in high school and college, but he was not above fabricating his athletic bona fides. He told reporters that he had played "a little bit of end" in high school, as well as "some right field" for the baseball team, and that he had been cut "trying out for the Holy Cross nine" in college. None of this was true, but he had played so much law firm touch football and softball that he was a passable middle-aged jock. Williams told reporters that he had taken the field because he heard that Jerry Wolman, the owner of the Philadelphia Eagles, was practicing with *his* team in nearby Hershey, Pennsylvania. "Anything Wolman can do, I can do better," declared Williams.

The Redskins went out and lost their first five games that fall. Williams was frustrated by his inability to control the team's fate. As the Redskins lost their third straight, Williams came down from his box to pace the sidelines. After he started shouting obscenities at the referee, he wisely reconsidered his position and withdrew to the box. "I'm accustomed to winning or losing because of something I do," he told reporters. "Here I don't even know what's wrong. I wake up nights trying to figure out what's wrong." The banners that began appearing in the stadium did not help him sleep. One read, "We Want Louis Nizer."

After the fifth loss, Williams went to the locker room and gave an inspirational speech. He "talked to pride," recalled halfback Bobby Mitchell. "You're doing this for yourself, not for me or Mr. Marshall," Williams said. He saw football as a stepping-stone for players, not as the be-all and end-all of their lives, and he stressed this in a way that would seem quaint to modern million-dollar players. "Play well and maybe some executive in the stands will want to hire you," Williams told the team. Not everyone appreciated his earnestness. When Williams asked the players why they were having problems, Ed Quinlan, a tackle with a Boston Irish accent, piped up, "Because we don't *pah-ty* enough!" Still, the team won its next game (and gave Williams the game ball) and then two more before resuming its losing ways.

Williams thought the coach, Bill McPeak, was a loser, so he fired him at the end of the season. Williams wanted a proven commodity, a famous name as his coach, and he fruitlessly pursued a pair of great college coaches, Ara Parseghian of Notre Dame and Bud Wilkinson of Oklahoma. He finally settled for a "name brand" former quarterback, Otto Graham, the Cleveland Browns star of the 1940s and 1950s who had gone on to coach at the tiny Coast Guard Academy. Williams had misgivings about Graham as soon as he arrived in Washington. It bothered Williams that Graham chose to eat at Scholl's cafeteria, where tourists filled their trays with mashed potatoes and steamed vegetables and booze was not on the menu. "A bad sign," muttered Williams, and he wasn't joking. The players also wondered about their straitlaced new coach. When he heard that Williams had hired the Coast Guard coach, Sonny Jurgensen, a free spirit, asked Williams, "Hey Ed, what do we do now? March to practice four abreast?" More disturbing, Graham did not share Williams's obsession with winning. "I would rather lose two or three games and have every score 35–28 than win every game 3–0," Graham told *Sports Illustrated*. "I would rather lose a few ball games that are entertaining—a lot of excitement—than win all games that are very dull to watch." To Williams, this was heresy; how could losing possibly be entertaining?

Williams supported Graham by spending money on draft picks, but the players that were chosen were not always the best investments. The Redskins used their number one choice in 1966 to sign Charlie Gogolak, a placekicker from Princeton, to a $1 million contract. Gogolak was studying at law school three years later. Williams overruled his coaches the next year to draft a big slow fullback from Idaho named Ray McDonald, who stutter-stepped every time he arrived at the line of scrimmage. Williams traded for an able but wacky running back aptly named Joe Don Looney, who had once punched out a coach at Oklahoma. Looney ended up playing for the U.S. Army in Vietnam and then worshiping a Buddhist monk. (Williams, who had been having car trouble with his Lincoln, wrote William Clay Ford, the owner of the Detroit Lions, who sold him Looney, "I thought you were my friend, Bill, but you sold me two lemons in one year.") Although Williams knew it was a poor idea to second-guess the coaches, Mitchell said that Williams began to subtly undermine Graham by coming down to the sideline in the second half of losing games, where he would stand silently, like an undertaker.

Williams had better relations with the players, whom he cajoled and clucked over. In an effort to get wide receiver Charlie Taylor to quit smoking cigarettes, Williams gave him a pipe every time he scored a touchdown (Taylor's pipe collection grew to seventeen by the time Williams gave up). Williams got on especially well with Sonny Jurgensen, his party-boy quarterback, though he enjoyed carousing himself too much to play the scold. He drank with his star quarterback and challenged him to paddle ball matches at the YMCA that Jurgensen described as "bloody."

On Thanksgiving, the Williams family played the Buchwald family in an annual touch football game. One year Williams brought Jurgensen to quarterback his team. When Buchwald protested against the ringer, Williams insisted, "He's family." To Buchwald's amazement, the Williams team lost because his children kept dropping Jurgensen's passes. "He threw the ball too hard," complained Williams. ("Kids had bad hands," said Jurgensen.)

Jurgensen could be a difficult player to handle. When the team got off to a poor start in 1965, Williams called Jurgensen into his office at the Hill Building and declared that he was going to do something to make the team win. "We gotta shake the team up," he said. Jurgensen suspiciously asked what Williams was getting at. "I'm going to bench you," Williams replied. "You can't do that!" Jurgensen retorted. "It's not my fault the team stinks." That Sunday, Jurgensen sat on the bench while the Redskins fell behind St. Louis, 37–0. Williams sent word down from his box to send Jurgensen in. Jurgensen refused to go in the game—but he started again the next week. Coach Graham was helpless to control his quarterback. When the Redskins fell behind the Detroit Lions, 7–0, in a meaningless game at the end of the 1968 season, Williams asked Graham at halftime why the backup quarterback, Harry Theofilides, was in the game. "Sonny won't play," replied Graham. "He says it's too cold." Williams told Graham to order him. "*You* order him," said Graham. Jurgensen remained warm on the bench.

Williams was more generous and sympathetic to his players than most owners. "He was a good owner," said Brig Owens, the players' representative on the Redskins. "His door was always open. On other teams, if you were player rep you got traded. But Ed respected me." (When Owens retired in 1978, Williams helped Owens get into law school, just as he did for at least three other players.) Most pro football owners regarded Williams as a dangerous radical. "Except for [Cleveland owner Art] Modell and [Pittsburgh owner Art] Rooney, the NFL owners were in fantasy land. They thought they owned the players like slaves," recalled Bill Hundley, who left the Justice Department in 1966 and worked for a year as the NFL's head of security.* Washington's own George Marshall had been so high-handed that according to one (probably apocryphal) legend, he shipped an injured player home from an away game in a boxcar. But Williams argued for more generous benefits for players and was generally a peacemaker in any contract negotiations with the players' union.

Williams had a low opinion of most of the owners, especially Dallas Cowboys owner Clint Murchison, whom he called a "pissant," and he feuded constantly with NFL commissioner Pete Rozelle. (Williams endorsed the attacks on Rozelle made by radio commentator Howard Cosell. "You've got that snake pinned," he told Cosell.) But despite their strained relations, Williams could win over his fellow owners with lawyerly logic. When the NFL merged with the AFL in 1966, the old-guard NFL owners wanted to maintain the ratio of sixteen NFL teams to ten AFL. Williams pointed out that the AFL owners had paid $27 million to merge the leagues (and their valuable television markets). "They didn't pay $27 million to play with themselves," Williams noted dryly. "His common sense carried the day," recalled Cleveland's Modell.

Otto Graham's teams struggled up to a 7–7 record in 1966, then slipped to 5–6–3 in 1967 and to 5–9 in 1968. The team lost faith in the coach. The players asked Jurgensen to call a closed meeting with Williams to voice their complaints about Graham. "Well?" asked Williams when he entered the locker room. The players lost their nerve; Williams was greeted with shuffling feet, averted eyes, and silence. It didn't matter; as

---

*Williams got Hundley the job with the NFL. In his book *Interference: How Organized Crime Influences Professional Football*, Dan Moldea relates how Williams called in the IOU when a federal grand jury began looking into allegations that several Redskins were involved with professional gamblers. Hundley was able to persuade his former employers at the Justice Department that the players were clean. The investigation was dropped before any subpoenas were issued.

far as Williams was concerned, Graham had already hung himself that summer when he told the newspapers, "I know what they mean when they say winning isn't everything, it's the only thing; but I disagree with it."

Williams wanted to hire the man who had coined that phrase. He had first met Vince Lombardi in 1963 in Miami, where Williams was defending Milwaukee Phil Alderisio, and Lombardi was vacationing after his Green Bay team won the NFL championship by beating the New York Giants 37–0. The two driven men had quickly fallen into Williams's favorite subject, "contest living." "Success is like a narcotic," Lombardi said to Williams. "One becomes addicted to it, but it has a terrible side effect. It saps the elation of victory and deepens the despair of defeat." These, of course, were Williams's sentiments exactly. "The betrayal of success," Williams called the feeling. "It never brings you the kind of satisfaction that you hope for when you're trying to get there."

Williams began working on Lombardi in November 1968 when Green Bay arrived in Washington and rolled over the Redskins 27–7. Lombardi had stepped down as coach the year before to become Green Bay's general manager, but he missed the sidelines. He had breakfast with Williams that Sunday and sat with him in the owners box. "Washington is really a great place isn't it?" Lombardi was overheard to say. "This is where it all happens." The stroking continued in Tony Sweet's restaurant in Miami the night before the 1969 Super Bowl. Williams was practically lovesick over Lombardi. "You know you're the only one I want," he told him. Lombardi felt uneasy about leaving Green Bay, which treated him like a deity. But Williams was able to offer him shares of stock in the team, something publicly owned Green Bay could not. Lombardi finally said yes. (He also told Williams to "bet the Jets." The next day quarterback Joe Namath and the New York Jets staged their historic upset over the Baltimore Colts.)

Williams was "shaking with pleasure" after he had recruited Lombardi, Bobby Mitchell said. "The Coach! The Coach!" Williams exclaimed, cautioning Mitchell, "We can't tell the world about this yet." Williams "thought he had just taken care of every problem that ever existed," Mitchell said. When the deal was announced in February, most of Washington shared Williams's sense of elation. Wherever Lombardi went people would stand and applaud. Attorney General John Mitchell confided to Williams that President Nixon had considered making Lombardi his running mate in 1968. Some pundits thought Lombardi had moved beyond that job by becoming coach of the Redskins. "Lombardi Calling Shots in What Was Nixon's Capital," wrote *Washington Post* political columnist David Broder.

Lombardi gave Williams a new punch line to his Slobodkin story after he watched the Redskins practice in the summer of 1969. "Ed, I'm sorry, but we don't have a defense," Lombardi told Williams. "If we had a defense," Williams responded, "we'd still have Otto Graham coaching." That fall, Lombardi gave Washington its first winning team since 1955. Williams rated Lombardi's 7–5–2 record as "the greatest coaching year that Vince Lombardi had in his whole career" because he took "a bunch of rinkydinks, total rinkydinks" and made them winners. Williams worshiped Lombardi, whom he saw as not just a football coach but as a kind of philosopher king who had a "covenant with greatness." (It is not too much of a reach to say that Lombardi may have been as well a romanticized father figure, a stark contrast to Williams's own father, the floorwalker who "got kicked around a lot.") Lombardi was equally respectful of Williams. When Lombardi's wife, Marie, interrupted Williams at lunch at Duke Zeibert's, Lombardi gave her an elbow. "Shut up," commanded the coach. "He's talking." Both devout Catholics, Williams and Lombardi began going to morning mass together.

The idyll did not last. In the winter of 1970, Lombardi was diagnosed with cancer of the rectum. Williams spent hours by Lombardi's bedside that next summer as his "living hero" died a slow and very painful death. For years, he had difficulty talking about Lombardi without choking up. "Lombardi was the first man that Ed ever told he loved," recalled Ben Bradlee.

Lombardi's funeral was excruciating for Williams. His grief was turned to anger by the appearance of a drunk and sloppy Toots Shor at the pro football owners' dinner after the wake. Bill Fugazy, who was close to both Williams and Lombardi, brought Shor to the owners' dinner, a sober and gloomy affair at the Starlight Roof of the Waldorf-Astoria in New York. Shor had become a pathetic figure by the late sixties. His saloon had been attuned to the rhythm of day baseball games, which allowed the writers and ball players to while away their evenings at the bar, but night baseball ended that. Shor had money problems, exacerbated by his generosity (when an auditor saved Shor $4,000 by stopping liquor leakage by the staff, Shor celebrated by throwing an $8,000 party for his friends). Like many of his patrons, Shor was an alcoholic who became increasingly dissipated. Joe Namath, the toast of New York after the 1969 Super Bowl, was asked if he liked going to Shor's. No, he answered matter-of-factly. Why not? "Because the owner spills drinks on you," Namath answered.

When Shor, quite drunk, arrived at the Waldorf, Williams took one look at him and said to Fugazy, "Get him out of here." But Shor was determined to make a scene. He stood up and starting berating the owners. "You're a bunch of shitheels," he began. "None of you knew Vince Lombardi. He was *my* friend. . . ." As Shor slurred and rambled on, NFL commissioner Pete Rozelle nudged Fugazy and whispered, "Do something. Get him out of here." Fugazy managed to get Shor down the elevator and into the street, where he promptly began urinating. A policeman arrested him for indecent exposure. Shor started clamoring, "Get my lawyer! Edward Bennett Williams!" A few minutes later, Williams had Shor in tow at P. J. Clarke's, where the saloon owner proceeded to lose his false teeth in a bowl of chili. Disgusted, Williams said to Fugazy, "You find the teeth." Fugazy wrestled Shor home; Williams, restless and sick with mourning, wandered off into the night.

Williams wound up at an apartment at 975 Park Avenue where Jean Pochna was staying with her sister. He was "drunk and exhausted," Pochna recalled. Though their affair had long since ended, Williams had stayed in touch with his old party-girl friend. She recalled that he was marginally coherent. He looked at her, standing before him in a long white dressing gown, and asked, "Did you ever think of becoming a nun?" She laughed, but understood that he was completely serious; his grief, the liquor, the funeral mass, had opened up his long-buried memories of the nuns back at St. Augustine's in Hartford. All done in, Williams staggered to a bedroom and passed out.

Chapter Twenty-Two

THE ANTIWAR MOVEMENT and the student revolution of the late sixties and early seventies presented a host of new constitutional questions on the limits of civil disobedience and free speech. The efforts of the Nixon administration to crack down on dissent called for lawyers willing to defend the dictates of individual conscience against the power of the state. Throughout his career, Williams tried to elevate his defense of unpopular clients by wrapping it in the mantle of civil liberties and the defense of human freedom. The great civil liberties cases, he said in 1977, often "involve prostitutes, bootleggers, narcotics pushers and other people who espouse a political philosophy that is anathema to the public at the time." Williams was remembering his Holy Cross debating tricks here. Prostitutes, bootleggers, and pushers are not known for having political philosophies, but he lumped them with undefined "other people" who do. The fact is that Williams had no qualms about defending lowlifes accused of crimes of vice, but he generally refused to defend activists who embraced political causes, and he had an outright antipathy to student protesters.

When Dr. Spock, Marcus Raskin, and several other antiwar activists were criminally indicted for inciting students to burn their draft cards, the American Civil Liberties Union asked Williams to defend them. Mike Tigar, who had been a student radical leader at Berkeley before coming to the firm, urged Williams to take the case. "I'd have to be out of the office for months," grumbled Williams. "Would they pay expenses?" Tigar could see that Williams did not want to take the case. His irritation

250

and resistance rising, Williams demanded, "Well, I suppose they'll have press conferences right? Will they agree to shut up for me? And at trial won't they talk about Lyndon? Talk about the war? Fuck them! They don't need a lawyer! They need a toastmaster!" Williams turned down the case. ("He didn't like the free speech crap," recalled Tigar.) Instead, Telford Taylor, a Nuremberg war crimes prosecutor, represented Raskin, and Leonard Boudin, the leftist lawyer, represented the others. They won an acquittal.

Tigar also tried to get Williams to defend the editors of *Ramparts* magazine when they faced criminal prosecution for burning their draft cards. In January 1968, Tigar trooped the *Ramparts* editors into Williams's office. Emboldened by the prospect of having the great Edward Bennett Williams by his side, one of the *Ramparts* editors enthused that he would "hold a press conference that will rock the Department of Justice!" Williams told him to get another lawyer. Tigar was furious. "You've got a bad case of the generation gap," he accused his boss. Williams relented. One of his associates, Peter Taft, went with the editors to the grand jury, which did not hand down indictments.

Williams did not care for Tigar's clients, who included black militant Angela Davis, but he liked Tigar, and he protected him. He admired Tigar's fertile brain, and he was amused by his radical macho swagger. (Williams liked to boast that Tigar was sleeping with Bernadine Dohrn, the tempestuous leader of the Weather Underground, though it was untrue.) When Tigar incorporated the local headquarters of SDS (Students for a Democratic Society), the student radical organization, using Williams & Connolly letterhead, Williams faced a revolt of the firm's other lawyers, many of whom were conservative Catholics. Since Williams had been the one vote for Tigar, he was kept on. Williams tried to accommodate Tigar's wish to defend radicals. When Tigar asked Williams if he could defend a militant accused of sabotage in Denver, Williams responded, "Couldn't you find a commie closer to home? Look, I'll find you a bomber in Maryland." But he went along, and Tigar spent seven weeks in Denver to win an acquittal.

In January 1970, Williams was appointed by a federal court to defend one of nine antiwar protesters—the so-called D.C. Nine—charged with vandalizing the Dow Chemical offices in Washington. The protesters, mostly members of Catholic religious orders, had poured blood in the offices of the napalm manufacturer. They claimed that they had been "obeying another law in another book," damning Dow's "programmed destruction of human life.'' Williams was assigned to defend a Father Robert Begin. Remarkably, Father Begin fired the most able defense counsel in America. The priest explained to reporters that Williams "would look at it from the legal viewpoint. He simply could not see the moral context. I really think I'm better off without him.''

Williams was a man of the Old Church, obedient to authority, temporally and spiritually close to the throne in the Jesuit tradition. He had no use for radical Catholics who threw off their Roman collars and took to the streets to dispense social justice and challenge the regime. He was equally critical of student radicals; indeed, he was hostile to the younger generation in general. Williams blamed "the breakdown of religion" and "permissive parents" for letting their children "grow fat and indolent.'' Williams, the striver for perfection who had to work his way up from nothing, was bothered that "kids don't care anymore about attaining excellence in anything. They don't care about being the best they can be in light of their talents because they're getting a free ride,'' he told *U.S. News & World Report* in September 1970. "They can live on a beach and throw rocks at the system and know that we're going to take care of them.''

As urban crime became a political issue and student strikes closed campuses, Williams the civil libertarian could sound as pro–law-and-order as Richard Nixon. Calling for more police and a "West Point–type academy" to train law enforcement officials, Williams declared, "You've got to have order to have progress.'' When Nixon made law and order a campaign issue for the Republicans in the midterm elections of November 1970, Williams, now a good Democrat, moderated his rhetoric, calling for "both liberty *and* order.'' He was, of course, careful never to publicly criticize the legacy of the liberal Warren Court. The notion that the court's "turn 'em loose'' decisions, as they were termed by the right, had contributed to the crime wave was "pure hokum,'' said Williams. But his private views on civil liberties were becoming more conservative in the early seventies. Bob Weinberg, a liberal constitutional authority and prolific brief writer in Williams's firm, lamented Nixon's attempt to fill the Supreme Court with conservative justices who seemed bent on rolling back the great liberal decisions of the Warren Court. If Hubert Humphrey had been elected, Weinberg suggested, then he would have put Williams on the Supreme Court—and this turn to the right would have been averted. "Don't be so sure,'' Williams had replied.

Williams was particularly offended by the circus atmosphere of the

Chicago Seven trial, where black militant Bobby Seale had to be bound and gagged to stop him from shouting obscenities at the judge. "Speaking as the father of seven children," Williams told the *Washington Post,* "I'm embarrassed by the defendants. . . . I think they desecrated the courtroom." If Seale, Abbie Hoffman and company had "behaved themselves" they would have been acquitted, said Williams. It wounded him to see the judicial system spat upon. "I love the system," Williams told a TV interviewer that winter of 1970. "Everything that I have in the world comes from it. I want the courtroom to be a place of dignity and decorum, and I bitterly resent what has happened in some of the courtrooms of the country. . . . I think it's symbolic of the breakdown of respect for authority that seems to be taking place all through the country, and it sickens me to see that it has seeped into the courtroom. . . ."

Williams's law-and-order jeremiads made him some unlikely fans. "Your TV interview on dealing with crime published in today's *Post* makes you my hero for life," wrote Dean Acheson, the high WASP Covington & Burling partner and former secretary of state. "If the President would fire that old fart [John] Mitchell and make you Attorney General I would become a Republican."

Williams's unwillingness to take on radicals as clients was only partly based on his contempt for their unruliness and their disrespect for the system that had so generously rewarded him. What disturbed Williams even more was their attempt to use the courtroom as a soapbox. They were less interested in winning an acquittal than in having their views heard. That would make them very difficult for Williams to control. The real reason Father Begin had fired Williams was that the lawyer had insisted that he do all the talking. Williams was not about to be the "toastmaster" for some long-haired hippies, any more than he had let Joe McCarthy conduct his own defense in a Senate hearing. "For Ed, the most important thing was that he had control over all aspects of his life," said Tigar. "It was his bottom line. His successes came when he was in control, and all his frustrations had to do with lack of control."

Williams's most publicized case during the antiwar era was defending a man whom the protesters would regard as a war criminal. In the late summer of 1969, Williams represented a Green Beret accused of murdering a Vietnamese double agent. On assignment from the CIA, Col. Robert Rheault and his men had taken the renegade spy out on a barge in the South China Sea, where the Vietnamese had been "terminated with extreme prejudice"—shot in the head and thrown to the sharks. Such summary justice was not especially unusual for special forces units, but the new commander of U.S. forces in Vietnam, Gen. Creighton Abrams, wanted to put an end to the practice and needed to make an example. A former tank commander, General Abrams disapproved of the more rakish Green Berets, who were always getting themselves in trouble and needing to be rescued by heavy units of the regular army. The general may also have been hearing the murmuring back home about "war crimes" trials (he knew the story of the My Lai massacre was just about to break). Colonel Rheault and his men were charged by the army with murder.

An athletic, blond Brahmin who had graduated from the elite boarding school, Phillips Exeter, as well as West Point, Colonel Rheault was from a prominent Boston family. The family lawyer, Daniel Mahoney, called Williams, who flew to Martha's Vineyard to see Rheault's wife at the family summer house. Caroline Rheault recalled that she took "an instant dislike" to Williams, who told her that the colonel was "guilty as hell," but reassured her that he would get her husband out of jail. Williams then flew to Saigon to see his new client. Williams was apprehensive when he arrived in the city, which was still reeling from the Tet offensive that spring. "What do I have to look out for?" he anxiously asked Robert Kaiser, the *Washington Post*'s Saigon correspondent. Visiting Rheault in his spartan cell in Long Binh, Williams told the Green Beret colonel that he had "contacts" in Washington who would "take care" of the charges against him.

Williams's plan was to use a tactic he had used before and would use again. He would warn the administration that if they persisted in prosecuting Rheault, his client would be forced to reveal embarrassing secrets in open court. Rheault would have to show that his alleged crime was in fact a commonplace necessity of war. The Green Beret would have to testify as well that he had participated in illegal cross-border operations into Cambodia. The White House would choke on these disclosures, Williams predicted, and drop the case.

The White House did drop the case—but before Williams had a chance to threaten his "graymail" defense. According to Stanley Resor, who was secretary of the army at the time, the intervention of Congressman Mendel Rivers of South Carolina saved Rheault. Rivers, the chairman of the House Armed Services Committee, persuaded the White House that it would have to drop the case if the administration expected Congress to pass a defense authorization bill that year. Congressman Rivers was a loyal supporter of the Central Intelligence Agency, and CIA officials were not eager to see their agents forced to testify in open court.

The news of the administration's about-face in the Rheault case came only three days after Williams had arrived in Saigon. Williams had flown first class and dined at La Cave, Saigon's best French restaurant, where he entertained Bob Kaiser with colorful stories about his career. After Rheault was released, Williams sent him a bill for $25,000. The Green Beret was angry about paying it. "Williams didn't do anything," said Rheault, "and I was only making $14,000 a year. We shouldn't have hired him, but my family hit the panic button."*

Williams did defend one prominent figure of the Protest Generation, but the case had nothing to do with political activism. Peter Yarrow, a singer with the popular folk singing trio Peter, Paul and Mary, was arrested for having sex with a fourteen-year-old girl at the Shoreham Hotel in Washington in the summer of 1969. Yarrow was married to a niece of Senator Eugene McCarthy of Minnesota, the Democrats' antiwar candidate in 1968. McCarthy and Williams were old friends; they liked to drink together and argue about the Catholic church and McCarthy's bad poetry. (McCarthy thought so highly of Williams that he said he would have made him FBI director in his administration, so he could purge Hoover's files.)

As a favor to McCarthy, Williams agreed to represent Yarrow. The folk singer had the bad luck to draw Judge Edward Curran, a strict Catholic and moralist. Fortunately for Yarrow, however, Curran and Williams were old friends. Yarrow had no defense on the merits—he had greeted the girl, a groupie who called him from the lobby, stark naked. But Williams thought he could plead for leniency at sentencing. He asked Jim Rowe, a lawyer who was also close to Curran, to lean on the judge for the shortest possible jail term. (This ex parte foray did not work very well: Rowe reported back that he had gotten the sentence down to two years. "Nice work, Rowe," said Williams. "Last time I heard it was one year.")

Williams went to see Judge Curran himself in chambers. Curran was

---

*Rheault was not the only army officer accused of war crimes who was represented by Williams. When Gen. Samuel Koster was charged with "dereliction of duty" for failing to investigate the My Lai massacre, he came to Williams for help. Williams turned the case over to a young lawyer in his firm, Brendan Sullivan, who years later would gain fame defending Oliver North in the Iran-Contra scandal. Sullivan succeeded in getting the charges against Koster dropped.

sympathetic to Williams, but not to his client's crime. "Eddie, I love you, I want to help you, but *this* . . ." the judge told Williams, shaking his head over the sinfulness of teenage sex. A young lawyer in Williams's firm, Tom Patton, watched these "two old Catholics"—who called each other "Eddie"—arguing about sin and repentance. In his formal, forty-five-minute plea in open court, Williams described his client's "deep-seated inferiority feelings" about women, and the "sexual problems" he suffered as a result. He played to Judge Curran's disapproval of modern mores by portraying the groupie as "the end product of an upbringing in jungle morality," and noted that her parents were divorced. Curran was a hard sell; Williams had to spell the word *groupie* and define it for the judge. "I hate to think that morality is going out the window," Curran said. "What he did is bad." He sentenced the folk singer to three months in jail. Yarrow's twenty-three-year-old pregnant wife wept as Williams tried to comfort her.

This was the sort of crime Williams could understand and forgive: a lonely young man, ashamed of sexual impotence, succumbing to weakness of the flesh. It can be fairly guessed that Williams saw some of his own frailties in Yarrow. Moreover, while not interested in defending draft card burners, Williams was sympathetic to the lost and alienated children of the times (one of whom was his eldest son, Jobie, who had dropped out of high school in 1970).

In 1971, Williams represented Heidi Fletcher, the daughter of the deputy mayor of Washington, when she was charged with felony murder for driving the getaway car in a bank robbery. Fletcher's boyfriend fatally shot a policeman in the holdup, and when police caught the getaway car, they found it loaded with a variety of shotguns and revolvers. In a heart-felt, truly affecting argument before the court, Williams managed to persuade the judge that his client was not a premeditated criminal, but rather a sad, overweight girl who loved teddy bears and desperately needed to be loved in return. The judge sentenced her to a girls reformatory under the Federal Youth Corrections Act, which allowed her to be released at any time. The lenient treatment caused some grumbling in the press. Columnist Nicholas von Hoffman of the *Washington Post* wondered if Heidi would have gotten the same treatment if she had been black and poor and not the deputy mayor's daughter with Edward Bennett Williams standing by her side.

When Williams helped the poor and weak, he was often helping the rich and powerful at the same time. In late 1970, a group of Native

Americans seized Alcatraz Island and attempted to turn the abandoned prison into their own colony. The Alcatraz Indians became radical chic. Ethel Kennedy complained that they were suffering on the island because they had to watch football games on a small black-and-white television set. As a favor to Ethel, Williams made sure they got a big color one.

Williams was sensitive to the demands of Native Americans. Some were even demanding that he drop the name "Redskins" from his football team because it was demeaning. At first Williams brushed them off. Calling their demands "silly," he asked, "Suppose blacks got together and demanded that Cleveland's football team stop calling itself the Browns?" But then a delegation of Native American militants visited Williams's office. They denounced the lyrics to the Redskins fight song, which went "Scalp 'em, swamp 'em / We will make 'em big score / Read 'em, weep 'em / Touchdowns we want heap more!," as "Tonto-ism." When one of the Indians literally put a gun to Williams's head, he agreed to change the lyrics to something less offensive.

Williams was not generally shaken by violent confrontation. The night after Martin Luther King, Jr., had been shot in April 1968, and Washington had erupted in looting and arson, Williams had flown into National Airport, back from business in Chicago. He could see the flames and smoke from the plane as it landed. He was met at the airport by his faithful driver, Leroy Washington. "What the hell is going on here, Leroy?" Williams asked. "A little misunderstanding," answered Washington. Williams and Washington had a close relationship. Williams was always cursing his driver for being late or getting lost, but he enjoyed his company, generally preferring to sit up in the front seat with Washington unless he had a client in the car.

When Williams and Washington arrived at the Hill Building that April night, they found chaos. The rioting was occurring only three blocks away, along 14th Street, and the lawyers and staff understandably feared it would spread west into the white business district. Lawyers and secretaries were rushing about, trying to find a safe place to put files in case the rioters descended on the firm. Williams took in this frenzied activity and called a meeting of the firm in the conference room. To his chauffeur, he whispered, "We're going to have a little fun, Leroy." When everyone had anxiously assembled, Williams solemnly made an announcement. "The name of this firm," he intoned, "is now Washington, Williams and Connolly. And Washington here is the boss." As anxious faces began to smile and nervous titters became hearty laughs, Williams put on Leroy's chauffeur's hat. "Ready to go, Mr. Washington?" he asked. On the way to Williams's house, Washington recalls, he sat in the back and smoked a cigar while Williams drove. It took someone with Williams's panache (and gall) to disarm a tense scene with a stunt like that. He could be patronizing to Washington—their relationship reminded some in the firm of Jack Benny and his butler Rochester. ("Where did you get your license, Leroy?" Williams would demand. "Sears?") But their friendship was genuine.

Williams occasionally cracked racial jokes. In the 1970s, after Williams had become counsel to the *Washington Post,* Ben Bradlee came to him with an awkward problem: The *Post* had run a picture of Los Angeles Rams linebacker Isaiah Robertson over a picture caption identifying an accused rapist. Robertson was threatening to sue. Williams's considered legal advice (delivered with a wink) was: "Fuck 'em. They all look alike." Williams still called blacks "shines," and worse. But in the crude Toots Shor tradition, he was equally insulting to other ethnic groups, including his own. He called Irish Catholics "harps" and Italians "dagos." He joked that the onion rolls at Duke Zeibert's "killed more Jews than Hitler." Yet he was not antiblack any more than he was anti-Italian or anti-Irish. As an admirer of the underdog, he had early on rooted for the civil rights movement. Significantly, black athletes like Bobby Mitchell, whom Williams installed in the Redskins front office after his playing days ended in 1969, swore by him. And while Williams refused to represent whites in politically charged cases, he did defend black militants.

In 1967, he brought an unsuccessful appeal for several black men convicted of murdering Malcolm X. To Williams, the appeal was just another case, but it was a case that many "reputable" lawyers would not touch. Williams's attacks on illegal eavesdropping by the FBI in the 1960s benefited black militants and radicals as well as Williams's Mafia clients. In 1968, his legal efforts to free Milwaukee Phil Alderisio had the ancillary effect of setting free boxing champion Muhammad Ali. The Supreme Court reversed Alderisio's conviction for extortion because the FBI had not allowed the Mafia hitman to inspect the records of federal investigators who had illegally eavesdropped on his phone conversations. Ali's lawyers—with some help and advice from Williams—were able to use the precedent to throw out the boxing champ's 1967 conviction for draft evasion.

The one institution Williams always stood ready to help was the Catholic church. When priests were caught in embarrassing situations or crimes large or small—getting a parishioner pregnant, dipping into the alms box—they would turn to Williams. "He would help any Jesuit," recalls Father James Connor, who was the order's Provincial Superior in Maryland in the 1970s. "He was very realistic. He never seemed shocked, but he didn't condone either. He was so worldly. It was easy to panic, but Ed would calm you down. He'd seen it all, and he was absolutely discreet." Williams was able to use his many connections to police, prosecutors, and judges—many of them Catholic themselves—to keep the indiscretions of the local priesthood out of the papers.

The Church also turned to Williams on larger constitutional questions. In 1971, Williams represented a group of Catholic colleges whose federal grants were under legal challenge as a violation of the separation of church and state. Williams was asked to handle the case by the president of Fairfield College, a Jesuit institution in Connecticut, after the school had awarded Williams an honorary degree. Williams took the case, *Tilton* v. *Richardson,* to the Supreme Court and won. But he did not do it for free. Williams's law partner Jeremiah Collins recalled Williams pestering him after he had taken the Catholic college administrators out to lunch. "Did you set the fee? Did you set the fee?" Williams demanded. Collins had: $250,000, which he said was the largest ever charged by the firm at the time.

That spring, Williams commuted to Yale every weekend to teach a course on how to argue constitutional issues before appellate courts. His law firm colleagues joked that there was unusual emphasis on church-state questions in the course that year. It greatly pleased and honored Williams to teach at Yale, the school he could not afford as a young Holy Cross grad. Williams may have disdained snobs, but he coveted an Ivy League pedigree. When author Norman Sheresky asked Williams to review a highly flattering chapter on him before publication of his book *Masters of the Courtroom,* Williams made sure the long list of his achievements included teaching at Yale. After Sheresky had written "lectured at numerous universities and colleges" Williams penned in "including guest lecturer in constitutional litigation at Yale Law School."

IN THE LATE sixties and early seventies, Washington lawyers came under attack for representing large corporations against "the public good." In October 1969, law students working for consumer activist Ralph Nader picketed Lloyd Cutler's prominent Washington law firm because he represented the Automobile Manufacturers Association in an air pollution case in California. Lawyers like Cutler were accused of using their political connections on behalf of narrow business interests. By hiring a Lloyd Cutler or a Clark Clifford, Ralph Nader charged, a corporation could get special favors and breaks from the federal bureaucracy.

Fortune magazine strikingly illustrated the political role of Washington lawyers by portraying an antitrust hearing before the Federal Trade Commission (FTC) during the Johnson administration. The article noted that Thomas "Tommy the Cork" Corcoran and James Rowe, two New Dealers who had stayed on to become enormously influential Washington lawyers, merely sat at the counsel table while another lawyer from another firm presented the case. Corcoran and Rowe never said a word. But one of the FTC commissioners was up for reappointment, and everyone knew that Rowe was an intimate of President Johnson. An FTC official told *Fortune,* "You had to feel their mere *presence* was a signal of some kind."

Williams was untroubled by charges of "influence by association." "What are you supposed to do—stop practicing law whenever one of your friends becomes president?" he asked. The idea that one of his friends could become president did not seem remote to Williams. Getting your friends into office, and then asking them for favors, was the way the world worked, his world anyway. Clark Clifford, the ultimate Washington insider, was his "hero."

Flying on the private jet of Phillips Petroleum on the way to handle a case with Clifford in the mid-seventies, Williams gleefully acted out a pantomime of a delegation of Arabs visiting Clifford in his office. Williams, a perfect mimic, imitated Clifford gravely telling the visiting sheiks, "You understand, of course, that I can only get you access." Then Williams imitated the Arabs winking and grinning as they shoved a bag of gold across Clifford's desk. Clifford watched this performance with some distaste. "Now, Ed," he interrupted, "you know it doesn't work that way." Williams just laughed. He didn't really believe that Clifford was a bagman, but he had enormous regard for Clifford's connections and his ability to use them to solve problems. He was even more admiring when the problem Clifford solved was his own. In 1972, Clifford rescued Williams from the revenge of his old nemesis, J. Edgar Hoover.

Hoover blackmailed his foes, from Martin Luther King, Jr., to John F.

Kennedy, by bugging their private conversations. There are no publicly available records to prove that Hoover bugged Williams, but Williams suspected he did. In the mid-1960s, Williams's name had begun turning up in the logs of FBI agents who were secretly tape recording the phone conversations of Milwaukee Phil Alderisio. Williams's successful appeal of Alderisio's extortion conviction had enraged Hoover. The legal challenge, with its attendant publicity, was one more blow to Hoover's campaign of illegal bugging. The FBI director decided to pay Williams back.

In 1969, the FBI leaked to *Life* magazine investigative reporter Sandy Smith the logs of bugged telephone conversations between Alderisio and one of his henchmen that showed the mobster bragging about his control over Williams. In the logs, Alderisio boasted that Williams would "stand call"—that is, stand up for Alderisio or do whatever the Mafioso wanted. He further bragged that he had placed the son of Frank Balistieri, the mob boss of Milwaukee, in Williams's law firm, and that he had been paying Williams "under the table." He discussed going in on a real estate deal with Williams in Towson, Maryland, and remarked that he often talked to Williams's wife.

It is highly doubtful that any of what Alderisio said about his relationship with Williams was true. Gangsters liked to boast that they "owned" their lawyers, but in Williams's case, they definitely did not. The idea that Williams would hire the son of a Milwaukee mobster as a lawyer in his firm simply because Alderisio told him to was preposterous; no son of Balistieri ever worked for him. Equally incredible was the depiction of Agnes Williams as a telephone pal of Milwaukee Phil. Although Alderisio paid Williams well—about $180,000 all told—Williams reported the earnings to the IRS. As for the real estate deal, there is no evidence of it anywhere, and Williams claimed never to have seen Towson, Maryland.

Nonetheless, the phone logs of a gangster discussing his secret deals with the great Edward Bennett Williams would be a sensational story for the 6 million readers of *Life* magazine. According to a memorandum-to-files, Williams had been tipped off about the *Life* story by one of his many friends in the press, David Kraslow of the *Los Angeles Times*. Williams's memo describes the steps he took to kill the story.

First, he called the attorney general, John Mitchell, whom he had befriended when Nixon was elected president. Williams told Mitchell "that while his Solicitor General, Erwin Griswold, was up in the Supreme Court arguing that logs of illegally obtained conversations should not be made available to defense counsel because they often contained 'errant gossip damaging to innocent third person,' his FBI director was busily leaking this errant gossip so that it would be published as widely as possible." Williams reported that "Mitchell went into action forthwith." Next, Williams called his old friend Bill Hundley, who, fortuitously, was doing some legal work for Time-Life. According to the memo, "when *Time* and *Life* were alerted to the fact that they were about to publish dangerously libelous stories they ordered the plates smashed and withheld the story."

Williams was not home free yet. Three years later, a pair of *Reader's Digest* editors appeared in his office waving the same leaked phone logs. This time Williams turned to Clark Clifford. By further small-world good fortune, Clifford was an old friend of Hobart Lewis, the editor and publisher of *Reader's Digest*. Quietly but surely, Clifford drove a stake through the heart of the *Reader's Digest* story. The depth of gratitude Williams felt is clearly not feigned in his letter to Clifford:

> It is too hard for me to tell you face to face how much it means to me that you have made my trouble your trouble. But I must express to you how deeply Agnes and I appreciate what you have done for us. You must also know that I have so much admiration, respect and affection for you that I could never have asked you to undertake this for me unless the suggestions and accusations were absolutely false and without semblance of foundation. Of course, I'm troubled that there is someone abroad who is attempting to traffic in the destruction of something I have spent a whole lifetime trying to build and preserve, but the fact that you are with me when I need you almost makes the whole experience worthwhile.

Clifford responded by reaffirming their alliance in mock chivalric terms: "Rest assured that we shall man the ramparts together, and I assure you that this constitutes a formidable force sufficient to cause the boldest of malefactors to tremble."

LIKE CLIFFORD, WILLIAMS wanted to play kingmaker in Washington. In 1968, he had given $5,000 to the losing candidate, Hubert Humphrey. Beginning in 1970, he methodically began meeting with candidates he deemed worthy of preventing Richard Nixon from winning a second term. He dined with Senators Edmund Muskie, Eugene McCarthy, Walter Mondale, Fred Harris, Birch Bayh, Ted Kennedy, and George

McGovern, and importuned potential Republican renegades John Gardner, HEW secretary under Johnson and author of a book that Williams prized called *Excellence,* and John Lindsay, the popular mayor of New York. Williams flattered these men with letters (he wrote Mondale after an unsuccessful Senate debate against John Stennis of Mississippi, "I thought your advocacy in a losing but righteous cause was superb . . ."). And he did not hide his ambition: "I want to help elect the next president of the United States," he declared to reporters. Late at night, he amused his law partners by announcing that he was thinking of running for president himself. They would mimic his cry: "We're going to New Hampshire!"

More concretely, Williams wanted to have political influence. He knew that his firm would never be considered truly powerful unless it could open doors in federal regulatory agencies as well as win battles in court. There was less excitement in door opening, to be sure, but greater profit. Williams did not want to be an influence peddler himself. He thought the work too boring and somewhat demeaning. (Vince Fuller recalled watching Williams turn red in the face as a New York corporate lawyer asked him over the phone if he could get his client in to see a senator. "I'm not a goddamned doorman!" Williams exploded, slamming the phone down.) But he wanted to find a partner who could pull levers in the manner of Clark Clifford.

Abe Fortas had been well connected in the Democratic establishment since the New Deal. When he was forced to resign from the Supreme Court in 1969 because he had arranged to receive $20,000 a year for life from a foundation set up by financier Louis Wolfson (a convicted felon and a client of Ed Williams), Fortas approached Williams about joining his firm. Williams liked Fortas and had worked closely with him on the Baker case, but Williams's associates balked at bringing him into the firm. They were worried about the taint of scandal, as well as Fortas's domineering personality.

Then a younger partner at Fortas's old law firm, Arnold & Porter, began to catch Williams's attention. At forty, Joe Califano had already been chief domestic adviser in the Johnson White House. He had excellent connections on the Hill from the glory days of the eighty-ninth Congress that passed LBJ's Great Society legislation. The son of a Brooklyn schoolteacher, Califano had gone to Holy Cross, and like Williams, he had tremendous drive and ambition. The matchmaker who put them together, according to Califano, was Katharine Graham, who would sit the two near each other at her dinner parties. Williams began inviting Califano to Saturday lunches with Bradlee and Buchwald.

"Joe was awed by Ed," said Ben Heineman, a lawyer who worked with Califano. "He thought he was a nice LBJ." Califano was not comfortable at Arnold & Porter. Fortas had brought him into the firm at a high draw, and that had created resentment among the other partners, which Califano's lack of humility did little to smooth over. When Williams began feeling out Califano about joining Williams & Connolly, Califano was receptive. In May 1971, Williams, Connolly and Califano had lunch at the Georgetown restaurant Rive Gauche, shook hands, and added Califano's name to the letterhead. In a large *Washington Post* story (Bradlee flacking for Williams, Califano suspected), Williams declared that he and Connolly would be the "War Department" while Califano would be the "State Department."

OF ALL THE institutional clients in the capital, the one that Williams and Califano coveted most was the *Washington Post*. It was by far the most powerful private organization in Washington, as powerful as any public agency of government. Under Phil Graham, the *Post* had gobbled up much of the competition in the city, and under the ownership of his widow, Katharine, it was on the verge of becoming a truly national paper. The editor making this push for greatness was Williams's best friend, Ben Bradlee. When Katharine Graham had made Bradlee the editor of the *Post* in 1965, staffers still joked that "the *Post* is a lot like Brazil; they both have potential." Bradlee was determined to make the paper a legitimate competitor to the *New York Times*.

Bradlee naturally wanted Williams as the paper's lawyer, but the more conservative Post Company management had favored first Covington & Burling, the city's old-line firm, and then William Rogers, Eisenhower's attorney general and a pillar of the legal establishment. Rogers had the additional virtue of being a Republican; he was seen by some as a hedge against the *Post*'s liberalism. "The *Post* hired Bill Rogers to be close to Nixon," Bradlee later said, "to correct our *Daily Worker* image."

In June 1971, Bradlee and the *Post* were presented with an opportunity to make the final jump into national prominence. Several months before, Daniel Ellsberg had leaked the Pentagon Papers, the government's secret study of the roots of U.S. involvement in Vietnam, to the *Times*. When the *Times* began publishing them on June 13, Bradlee was beside himself.

He would later say that every word of the Pentagon Papers appearing in the *Times* was printed in his blood. The *Times* had a giant scoop, and the *Post* editor was desperate to catch up. On Wednesday, June 17, the *Times* suddenly stopped its series: The U.S. government had obtained a court order restraining publication. The *Post* redoubled its efforts to get the Papers, and on Friday morning, the *Post*'s national editor Ben Bagdikian arrived on Bradlee's doorstep with a cardboard box containing all 4,400 pages of the top-secret document. Bradlee immediately put together a team of writers and editors racing to get a story ready by deadline that night.

The *Post*'s lawyers, however, were adamantly opposed to publication. Two of Bill Rogers's partners, Roger Clark and Tony Essaye, warned Bradlee that the paper would run an unacceptable risk by defying the government. By publishing after the *Times* had been enjoined, the *Post* would be deliberately flouting the court, knowingly breaking the law. The *Post* was a large media conglomerate dependent on the goodwill of government. If the *Post* was indicted, the Federal Communications Commission (FCC) might move to strip the company of its three lucrative television stations (indeed, the networks all refused to touch the Pentagon Papers). An additional complication was that the *Post* had "gone public" only two days before with an offering of 1.35 million shares of common stock. There was a clause in the legal agreement for the sale of stock that provided for cancellation should a "disaster" or "catastrophic event" strike the paper. A criminal injunction, warned the lawyers, could be catastrophic.

Bradlee turned gray listening to the lawyers. He had already told Bagdikian that he would resign if the *Post* failed to publish the Papers. As the lawyers droned on about impending calamity, Bradlee excused himself and went to a telephone to call Ed Williams. He knew Williams was in Chicago in the middle of a fraud trial, and he had to get his friend Jim Hoge, the editor of the *Sun-Times,* to send a copy boy over to the court to ask Williams to demand a quick recess. Williams called Bradlee back twenty minutes later.

"I explained the situation," recalled Bradlee. "I didn't load it." For fifteen minutes, Bradlee outlined the dire warnings of the *Post*'s lawyers. "That's bullshit, Bradlee, pure bullshit," Williams said. Williams seemed to be downright jovial about Bradlee's predicament, teasing him about being a losing football team late in the fourth quarter.

Bradlee began to feel better. What about the law? he asked. "Bradlee,

I've been in this city for thirty years and for thirty years I've watched respectable and responsible journalists tell the Congress and the executive branch to go fuck themselves. What's Nixon going to do? Put every major editor and publisher in jail? Nixon doesn't have the balls to go after you, Bradlee.''

The *Post* editor felt an enormous sense of relief. "I felt alive for the first time in days," he said. He went back and told the lawyers he was determined to publish. That evening, he made the same argument to Katharine Graham. Overcoming the qualms of her closest business adviser, Fritz Beebe, Kay Graham told Bradlee, "Go ahead.''

Williams advised the *Post* to publish the Pentagon Papers, said Bradlee, "because his balls told him to. He didn't have to look at the law books. There was no *Plessy* v. *Ferguson,* no *Marbury* v. *Madison.* He felt the paper's history, our politics, our aspirations. He knew that at this moment we had to publish, or fall back to being second rate." Bradlee was right about Williams's boldness. But he underestimated Williams's knowledge of the law. Williams did not have to consult any law books because he already knew what they said. In 1955, he had represented a smutty gossip sheet called *Confidential Magazine* when the post office refused to mail it out. Williams had argued that the First Amendment does not permit "prior restraint." If the government couldn't censor *Confidential,* it wasn't going to be able to stop the *Washington Post* from publishing materials of enormous historic significance.

The government was not able to stop the *Post* from publishing the Pentagon Papers, but it tried. The case went to the Supreme Court on an expedited appeal. Bradlee wanted Williams, not the timid lawyers in Bill Rogers's firm, to argue the case before the high court. Surprisingly, Williams turned him down. He told Bradlee that he could not drop everything and rush back to Washington. He was in the middle of a difficult trial, and he could not abandon his client. Bradlee pleaded with him to find a way, but Williams was stubborn. "I can't forsake one case for another," he insisted. "Can't you just ask for an adjournment?" asked Bradlee. "The judge is already pissed at us," said Williams. "I can't do it." Williams was "in agony," said Tom Patton, a young lawyer in the firm who was assisting Williams at trial. "The Pentagon Papers was the case of a lifetime, and he called it a laydown winner." But he was loyal to the client who had already hired him.

The case Williams was trying in Chicago was hardly as significant as the Pentagon Papers. His client, Harry Sonneborn, was the president of McDonald's, the hamburger chain. When he divorced his wife, the property settlement left her $1 million. A few weeks later, McDonald's went public and Sonneborn was suddenly worth $44 million. Claiming she had been the victim of fraud, his ex-wife sued for half of the money.

Williams did not even like Sonneborn. He was a conservative, humorless businessman who could not tell funny stories or, worse, fully appreciate the ones Williams told. But his case was lucrative to the firm, and more important, it was Williams's first jury trial since the Bobby Baker case. For four years, Williams had shied away from juries. Now he felt he needed to prove that he hadn't lost his knack.

Before trial, he inspired himself as usual by being completely pessimistic. "Oh, Jesus! God! Why the hell did we get stuck with this case!" he would moan, recalls Patton. "This is the worst case. The wo-o-o-orst case. Nobody's going to believe that Harry didn't know he was going public before the divorce. No one is going to bel-i-e-e-e-ve this!"

At trial, Williams sought every conceivable advantage. Every morning, he insisted on getting to court early. It bothered him that the plaintiff's counsel sat close to the jury box, while he sat across the courtroom. So every morning, Williams, Patton, and David Webster, another member of the trial team, would lift the defendant's table and move it an inch or two toward the jury box. Then they would lift the plaintiff's table and move it an inch or two away. (By the time trial ended, said Patton, the two tables were only about six inches apart.) To rattle opposing counsel, a short man named Arnold Shuer, Williams placed his podium directly behind Shuer's chair. When Williams addressed the jury, his voice would boom over and through Shuer. Finally, Williams's exasperated opponent could take no more. "Would you mind moving? And not shouting?" he demanded. "I'm not shouting," replied Williams, in a calm, soft voice.

It is questionable whether Williams's little tricks made any real substantive difference, but they had an important psychological effect on Williams and the lawyers with him. It made them feel they were a little smarter and a little tougher than the opposition. Even though the odds were stacked against them, Williams always conveyed a sense of confidence and destiny to his young lawyers. He was like Henry V before Agincourt: His men might be outnumbered and weary, but by sheer grit and moxie they would triumph over the softer, duller enemy. To be on a trial team with Williams was to have the feeling of "we happy few, we band of brothers.'' The analogy was explicit for Williams. "We're *brothers*," he'd exclaim, reaching out with his meaty hand and grabbing a startled young associate by the arm.

Williams won the case, and saved his client $20 million, a small percentage of which he took back as his fee. He missed the opportunity to argue the Pentagon Papers case, but within a few months he won the greater goal: Katharine Graham fired the Rogers firm as counsel and hired Williams, Connolly & Califano to represent the paper. The Rogers firm had prevailed in the Pentagon Papers case, but the high court's decision was narrowly drawn and muddy, and many legal observers believed that the case had been poorly argued. (The joke at the *Post* was that their lawyer ''read the First Amendment for the first time on the way down on the shuttle.'') Bradlee was able to convince Graham that the next time the paper got into a tight spot—and those times were coming—it needed a lawyer who understood not only the law but the use and abuse of power.

Chapter Twenty-Three

AMONG THE CLIENTS that Joe Califano brought with him when he joined Williams & Connolly was the Democratic National Committee (DNC). A phone call at 5:00 A.M. on the morning of Saturday, June 17, 1972, awakened Califano with some startling news. A few hours earlier, five men had been arrested breaking into the offices of the DNC at the Watergate. The burglars had been caught copying files and bugging telephones. Califano hung up and called another of the firm's clients, the *Washington Post*. Califano suggested to Howard Simons, the managing editor, that the Watergate burglary might be a good story. Later in the morning, Califano was told that the police had found the phone number of the Committee to Re-Elect the President on one of the burglars. At their usual Saturday lunch at Duke Zeibert's, Williams and Califano idly speculated about the break-in. "What if this goes into the White House?" wondered Califano. The next evening, Sunday, Califano decided to file a suit for the Democrats against the CRP, better known as "CREEP." With the presidential elections approaching, the Democrats needed help.

Williams had wanted Califano to use his political connections to bring business to the firm, but he was unhappy with his partner's representation of the Democratic party, and the reason was that Califano wasn't being paid for it. Devoting almost half his time to the DNC, using other lawyers in the firm as well, Califano had run up about $500,000 worth of free work for the Democrats. When Califano went off to Cape Cod for a long weekend at the end of June, Williams groused about having to represent the Democrats against CREEP in a preliminary hearing before federal

District Judge Charles Richey. CREEP's lawyer, Kenneth Parkinson, charged in court that the Democrats' suit was a publicity stunt aimed at "destroying the presidential chances of President Nixon." He also pointedly noted for the record that Williams represented both the DNC and the *Washington Post*. Parkinson's aggressive tone aroused Williams's ire. As Parkinson was leaving the court, Williams loudly declared, "Until you made your argument, I thought you guys were innocent." One of the CREEP lawyers snarled back, "We don't have to take your shit."

A month later, Williams was marching the Watergate burglars and various CREEP officials into the Hill Building for depositions. By now, he was happy to be representing the Democrats. A small army of reporters waited on the street outside his building, thrusting cameras and microphones at the impassive Republicans as they entered and left the Hill Building. Williams liked the attention and the skulduggery: It amused him that G. Gordon Liddy, one of the Watergate burglars, slipped in a back entrance and walked up eight flights of fire stairs to evade reporters.

When CBS correspondent Daniel Schorr breathlessly appeared in Williams's office trying to find E. Howard Hunt, Liddy's confederate, Williams suggested that the former CIA agent was probably hiding in the bathroom. Hunt, wearing dark glasses and a hat, finally emerged and put his hands over his face as photographers pounced. (Hunt's lawyer was Bill Bittman, Williams's antagonist in the Baker case, and the two old adversaries picked up where they had left off five years before. Williams accused Bittman of "trying to impugn my motives," and Bittman shot back, "I will not let you intimidate me.")

Williams's questions in these early depositions were remarkably well informed. He knew about the secret unit set up by the Republicans to catch administration leakers. "Was there a group over there at the committee known as 'The Plumbers'?" he asked Liddy. After whispering with his lawyer, Liddy responded, "No. Not that I know of, unless there were some plumbers in the basement working on the plumbing." In fact, Williams knew about the existence of the Plumbers unit because Democratic investigators led by Walter Sheridan—an old nemesis of Williams's from Bobby Kennedy's "Get Hoffa" squad—had tracked down a former FBI agent named Alfred Baldwin, who had served as a lookout for the Watergate burglars and was now secretly talking to the Democrats.

For the most part, the CREEP officials stonewalled in their depositions. But after deposing an extremely evasive John Mitchell, Williams was convinced that a scandal was in the offing. Williams thought that Mitchell, who had been friendly as attorney general, was now terrified of him. "He walked in with brown shorts," Williams crudely boasted to an associate. By coincidence, Williams was visited that afternoon by Lee Iacocca, then a rising executive at Ford Motor Company. The lawyer was flushed and agitated, Iacocca said. "This is going to be huge!" Williams happily exclaimed. "I can tell when a guy is lying and these guys are lying and covering up."

That same afternoon, Williams called Califano, who was still on the Cape, and repeated what he had said to Iacocca. "I'm no politician," said Williams. "You're the politician. But I know when people are lying, and this guy is lying. We've got a real case here." Califano was bemused by the sudden enthusiasm of his partner, who had been so grumpy about representing the DNC. "We?" asked Califano.

On September 21, Judge Richey decided that the suit could not be resolved before the November elections, and put a halt to the depositions. Suspecting that Richey was trying to win an appointment to the Court of Appeals out of the White House, Williams was furious. "I was within an eyelash of blowing Watergate wide open," he told author Robert Pack. "I would have gotten the whole story before I was through."

Williams did succeed in getting the attention of Richard Nixon. Less than two weeks after Williams deposed Mitchell, Nixon sat sulking and fuming with his chief of staff, H. R. Haldeman, and White House counsel John Dean. They were thinking of ways to use Williams's old foe, the FBI, against the muckraking lawyer. "Perhaps the Bureau ought to go over—" Nixon began.

Haldeman cut in: "The Bureau ought to go into Edward Bennett Williams and let's start questioning that son of a bitch. Keep him tied up for a couple of weeks."

Nixon stopped the conversation to take a phone call. He asked the caller, "Did you put that last bug in? . . . And don't, don't bug anybody without asking me. Okay?"

Nixon then held forth on how Haldeman and Dean and everyone who worked for him should recognize that this

> is war. . . . Don't worry. I wouldn't want to be on the other side right now. Would you? I wouldn't want to be in Edward Bennett Williams's position after this election.
>
> DEAN: No. No.

NIXON: None of those bastards—

DEAN: He, uh, he's done some rather unethical things that have come to light already, which in—again, Richey had brought to our attention.*

NIXON: Yeah.

DEAN: He went down—

NIXON: Keep a log on all that.

DEAN: Oh, we are, indeed. Yeah.

NIXON: Yeah.

HALDEMAN: Because afterwards that's the guy.

NIXON: We're going after him.

HALDEMAN: That's the guy we've got to ruin.

DEAN: He had, he had an ex parte—

NIXON: You want to remember, too, he's an attorney for the *Washington Post.*

DEAN: I'm well aware of that.

NIXON: I think we're going to fix the son of a bitch. Believe me. We are going to. We've got to, because he's a bad man.

DEAN: Absolutely.

NIXON: He misbehaved very badly in the Hoffa matter. Our— some pretty bad conduct there too. . . .

At this point, Nixon instructed Dean to begin taking "the most comprehensive notes on all those that have tried to do us in."

NIXON: They're asking for it and they are going to get it. And this, this— We, we have not used the power in this first four years, as you know.

DEAN: That's true.

NIXON: We have never used it. We haven't used the Bureau and we haven't used the Justice Department but things are going to change now. . . .

DEAN: That's an exciting prospect.

---

*Judge Richey did not recall Williams doing anything unethical. Without defense counsel present, Williams did see Richey in chambers to apologize for a late filing by his firm in the suit, but a record of the conversation was made for the defense counsel to see.

NIXON: It's got to be done. It's the only thing to do.
HALDEMAN: We've got to.

Nixon forecast that the *Washington Post* was "going to have damnable, damnable problems" when the time came for the Post Company to renew the FCC licenses for its television and radio stations. A week later, CREEP head John Mitchell told *Washington Post* reporter Carl Bernstein over the phone, "You fellows got a great ball game going. As soon as you're through paying Ed Williams and the rest of those fellows, we're going to do a story on all of *you*." It was then that the former attorney general made his infamous threat to Bernstein's publisher. If the *Post* printed a story that Mitchell personally controlled a Republican slush fund to gather information on the Democrats, Mitchell warned, "Katie Graham's gonna get her tit caught in a big fat wringer."

Indeed, the licenses of two of the Post's TV stations were challenged by "citizens groups" organized by prominent Nixon supporters, sending the price of Post stock plummeting by 50 percent. Nor was Nixon just bluffing about Williams. In January 1973, after drinking alone one night in the Oval Office, the president asked his aide Chuck Colson to figure out a way to have Williams removed as president of the Washington Redskins. Colson never made a move to deprive Williams of his cherished team, but he did steal away one of Williams's oldest and most lucrative clients, the Teamsters Union. That December, Teamsters president Frank Fitzsimmons had called Williams and warned him that unless his firm dropped the Watergate case, the Teamsters would take their legal business elsewhere. Although seven of Williams's twenty-five lawyers were kept busy with Teamsters litigation, Williams told Fitzsimmons to "go to hell." The Teamsters account moved to the law firm Chuck Colson had joined when he left the White House that winter.

Williams's taxes were audited down to the last nickel for the next three years. Fortunately for Williams, his wife, Agnes, was a meticulous bookkeeper, and the IRS never found any irregularities. But Williams's suspicions were confirmed when his friend and tax lawyer, former IRS commissioner Sheldon Cohen, learned from IRS insiders that the agency was ordered to "zing" Williams. More ominously, Williams's house was broken into in October 1973, and the burglars rummaged through his files, including some dealing with Watergate. At the time, Williams feared that the Plumbers had been revived, but Agnes later concluded that the burglary was an "inside job" by some local workmen. Always fearful of electronic eavesdropping, Williams had his offices swept for bugs several times before Nixon was finally driven from office in 1974. Still, Williams could joke about the climate of fear during Watergate. At a dinner honoring Joe DiMaggio in 1974, he told the audience, "If I'm nervous it's because I am a Washington Democrat and this is the first time in two years that I have talked to a microphone I can see." But Williams did not take Nixon lightly. Before he died, Watergate special prosecutor Leon Jaworski told Robert Pack that he had been "very much disturbed over what Nixon might undertake to do to Edward Bennett Williams," and conveyed his anxieties to Williams.

Republicans were wary of a cabal between the Democrats and the *Washington Post,* with Williams as the pointman. "Does it not seem strange that Mr. E. B. Williams, the Democrats' unpaid attorney in the Watergate civil trial, is also the attorney for the *Washington Post?*" Senator Bob Dole of Kansas had asked on the eve of the 1972 election. In fact, Williams had a potential legal conflict of interest that became a real one when CREEP subpoenaed the *Post*'s sources for its Watergate stories in the winter of 1973. Califano managed to get the subpoena quashed, but at the end of his argument, Judge Richey summoned him to the bench. "Pick a client," said the judge. "The *Post* or the DNC." Califano chose the *Post,* and the firm dropped out of the Watergate suit (later settled by CREEP for $750,000). Williams was irritated about being forced to choose. Determined to control as much as he could, regarding himself as an impartial umpire as well as an advocate, Williams had fairly relaxed notions about what constituted a conflict of interest. "Ed used to say that we don't have a conflict until our lawyers meet in court," laughed Califano. "But in this case *I* was the lawyer for both sides. So we had to drop out of the case."*

---

*The firm also ran into a conflict when Vice President Spiro Agnew was charged with taking bribes. In the summer of 1973, Brendan Sullivan came to Califano and told him that he had been approached by a Maryland businessman who confessed that he had given Agnew cash in a brown paper bag. The man wanted the firm to represent him if the bribes came to light. At the same time, a young reporter named Richard Cohen began breaking the Agnew story in the *Post.* Agnew subpoenaed Cohen's notes, which the *Post* refused to produce. (Williams shrewdly advised Cohen to turn the notes over to Kay Graham, on the theory that the judge would be more reluctant to put her in jail than Cohen if he found the *Post* in contempt.) So the firm was in the awkward position of potentially representing both the reporter writing about Agnew's bribes as well as one of the men who bribed Agnew. Califano was standing outside court with a motion to quash the subpoena for Cohen's notes when Spiro Agnew suddenly emerged to announce that he had accepted a plea bargain and resigned as vice president.

One conspiracy theory about Williams and Watergate deserves close inspection. Because of his connections and his vast store of inside knowledge, some observers speculated that he was Deep Throat, the legendary source for Bob Woodward and Carl Bernstein, the resourceful *Post* reporters who broke the story tying the White House to the break-in. In later years, Williams's children would demand, "Dad, c'mon, please, just one question. No kidding around. Just tell us this. Were you Deep Throat?" Williams would enigmatically respond, "You all know Deep Throat." It pleased and amused Williams that not only his children but reporters and politicians suspected that he was the ultimate source of the Watergate revelations.

Woodward and Bradlee both insist that Williams was not Deep Throat. "I didn't get anything out of him," says Bradlee. "I thought, 'Holy God, we'll get everything. Ed is finally going to pay off.' " According to Bradlee, Williams refused to give the *Post* any inside information from the DNC suit. Bradlee said that he joked with Williams about being unforthcoming. When he thought the *Post*'s telephones were being tapped, he would sarcastically say to Williams over the phone, "Thanks for the grand jury minutes and all, Ed."

But, of course, if Williams *was* a good source, the *Post* editor could never admit it. Whether or not Williams gave Bradlee hard information, he certainly gave him real encouragement at a time when most of the rest of the press was ignoring the story, and the *Post* was feeling vulnerable and exposed. Woodward and Bernstein were brash young metro desk reporters, not yet experienced enough to be on the national desk. Bradlee trusted them, but it helped when his shrewd friend reassured him. According to Bradlee, Williams said, "Ben, the kids have got to be right because otherwise why are the Nixon people lying to you so goddamn much? If they're clean why don't they show it? Why are there so many lies? I'll tell you why. Because you've got them." Woodward also acknowledged that Williams encouraged him to keep on the story. "This is all about pressure, from the Democrats, from the press," Williams told Woodward. "There are too many people involved. This is going to blow." Indeed, within a few days of the Watergate break-in, Williams publicly told any reporter who would listen, "Forget about the burglaries. The story is the money. Keep your eye on the money."*

---

*In the movie version of *All the President's Men*, Woodward and Bernstein's dramatic account of breaking the Watergate story, it is Deep Throat who tells Woodward to "follow the money."

Williams's advice turned out to be prophetic. At the time, Williams said he was relying on his intuition and years of experience with liars and crooks. But, in fact, he was relying on something more concrete. According to a lawyer in his firm, Williams knew that Nixon's White House was corrupt *before* the Watergate break-in.

In the spring of 1972, his client Robert Vesco had told him that he had given $200,000 in one-hundred-dollar bills in a briefcase to the Committee to Re-Elect the President. Bobby Baker had brought Vesco to Williams when the Wall Street speculator was under investigation by the SEC for looting several mutual funds of some $200 million. Vesco had hoped his bag of cash would help persuade the Nixon administration to drop its prosecution against him. In fact, the White House had put the money in a slush fund to pay for burglarizing and bugging the Democrats' headquarters at the Watergate. It is unlikely that Williams knew exactly how Nixon's operatives spent Vesco's money. But the mere fact that his client was delivering a suitcase full of hundred-dollar bills to the White House alerted him to the possibility of scandal.

It cannot be known whether Williams told Bradlee about Vesco's payoff. Telling the *Post* editor about his client's activities would have been against the code of legal ethics, although Williams could say that he had followed a higher moral law by exposing the abuse of executive power. Certainly, Williams was able to advise his friend to press forward with the Watergate story with a high degree of confidence that, in the end, the *Post* would not be proved wrong.

For all his encouragement, Williams was a bit wary of the *Post* reporters. He was not a believer in absolute freedom of the press. The Supreme Court's *Sullivan* decision protecting the press against libel suits from public officials was "Earl Warren's one great mistake," Williams said. He believed the decision had given reporters a license to be irresponsible and had made the press "a more dangerous element" in society. "Ed thought Woodward and Bernstein were undisciplined," said Bradlee. Williams would demand of the *Post* editor, "Who are these guys? Why can't you control them? I'm always saving their ass."

In fact, Williams did have to move fast on one occasion to keep "Woodstein" out of jail. In December 1972, Woodward and Bernstein took the questionable step of approaching the Watergate grand jurors to ask them about the case. One of the grand jurors complained to the prosecutors, who in turn complained to Judge John Sirica. Williams was dispatched on a mission to pacify the angry judge. Known as "Maximum

John,'' Sirica was of a mind to jail the two reporters for contempt. Fortunately, Williams and Sirica were old friends, fellow Catholics and criminal lawyers from the fifties. Williams was godfather to one of the judge's children. Williams took the tack of agreeing with Sirica that reporters were irresponsible nuisances, but he argued that the grand jurors had not actually leaked anything, so there had been no breach of grand jury secrecy. He promised that the two young reporters would behave in the future. Sirica agreed to let them off with a verbal reprimand.

Woodward and Bernstein were summoned to Williams's office. "I saved your wiseass necks,'' he told them. "Sirica was some kind of pissed.'' The two reporters were contrite. But Woodward was secretly amused by this show of scorn. He believed that Williams had known all along that the reporters were talking to grand jurors and had approved of it. According to Woodward, Bradlee had checked with Williams before "Woodstein'' went out to knock on the doors of the grand jurors. Woodward quoted Bradlee as exclaiming, "Fast Eddie says it's a go!''

Califano strongly disputed that Williams gave any such go-ahead. He said that, typically, Bradlee would call both Califano and Williams for advice, and if he didn't like what he was hearing from one, he'd ask the other. Moments after Bradlee called to ask if his reporters could talk to grand jurors, said Califano, "Ed and I met on the stairwell going to each other's offices. We both said 'I told him no!' '' Bradlee's recollection is more ambiguous. "I recall asking them if there was a law against going to the grand jury,'' Bradlee says. "They said it violated no law, but they didn't say go ahead and do it either. My guess is that Ed blurred it, and I blurred it.''

Recounting, in *All the President's Men,* the decision to contact the grand jurors, Woodward and Bernstein wrote: "Everyone in the room had private doubts about such a seedy venture. Bradlee, desperate for a story, and reassured by the lawyers, overcame his own.'' When he saw the galleys of the book, Williams was furious. He felt the alleged "reassurance'' by the lawyers made him look sleazy. He was also upset about a scene in the book describing him drunkenly arguing with White House speechwriter Pat Buchanan. He told Califano to call the publishing house, Simon & Schuster, and get the offending passages excised.

Califano warned Dick Snyder, the new head of Simon & Schuster, that the passage would hurt the *Post* as well as Williams and "cause legal difficulties.'' Snyder felt "young and intimidated,'' he said. "I had never played in this league.'' The books were scheduled to go out to the bookstores in only three days, so Snyder tried to buy time. "Gee, Joe, I'm not sure of the status of the books," he fibbed to Califano. "I'm not sure they haven't been printed. I'll get back to you." The books were shipped before he called back. "There was a lot of talk about 'see you in court,' but it was all a bluff," said Snyder. For a few years afterward, Woodward and Bernstein were on Williams's blacklist.

THE POST IN the early seventies was really more Califano's client than Williams's. There was a division in the firm between Califano's lawyers, who were pro–free press and handled the Post's libel work, and Williams's criminal lawyers, who "believed wholeheartedly in the Sixth Amendment [guaranteeing the right to counsel] but weren't so sure about the First Amendment," said Ben Heineman, a Califano protégé. Still, Bradlee would always turn to Williams for advice on matters large and small, and so, from time to time, would Kay Graham. "He had great common sense," said Graham, "and more than that, judgment."

Chapter Twenty-Four

IT FRUSTRATED WILLIAMS that his parents could not comprehend the extent of his success. When neighbors and friends told May Williams that her son was making $500 an hour, she would scoff, "Don't listen to that, it's just talk." Williams's parents had lived modestly and frugally for so long that they did not know what to do with the money Williams sent them. In the mid-fifties, Williams had sent his parents $40,000. The money just sat in a bank. Thereafter, Williams bought them things instead of giving them cash. His parents almost never came to Washington, and he rarely went to Hartford. Once, Williams brought his mother to a Redskins game, to sit in the owners box. The woman who had been a busy-body on the front stoops of Adelaide Street was meek and silent; Williams looked pained. She called him Edward, and he self-consciously mimicked her Hartford accent—"Ed-wood"—to his sophisticated friends.

Williams was even harder on his father. A newspaper reporter, Tom Kelly of the *Washington Daily News,* who had come to know Williams while covering the courts, was struck by the contempt in Williams's voice as he described his father's "total lack of ambition." Williams "almost sneered," said Kelly. He wondered whether Williams fit the pattern of other famous men whose drive had come from the tension between a resentful, ambitious mother and a weak, defeated father. May Williams was in no way a domineering grand dame in the mold of the mothers of Franklin Roosevelt or Douglas MacArthur. She was never more than a gossipy and not terribly bright housewife. But as a younger woman, she

279

had resented her husband's passivity, his monotonous habits and lack of zest. It is likely that Williams sensed his mother's anger as they sat in painful silence at dinner in the dim house on Adelaide Street. "Ed must have gotten the same message from his mother," surmised Kelly. "It was, 'Don't be like your father.' "

Williams's father, who had become senile, died in 1965 at the age of ninety. After he died, his wife, too, became a little dotty. Twice she was hospitalized for "mental problems," according to the Williams family doctor, Steve Jones. Williams ended up spending $50,000 a year to put her in an expensive nursing home outside Hartford. Williams would become irritated and embarrassed when she rambled on in the garrulous way he remembered from his childhood. "Where is this story going, Ma?" he'd demand. "What's the point?" After returning from brief visits to Hartford, Williams would recount to his friends, with a mixture of hurt and humor, his conversations with his mother. " 'Hi Mom,' Ed would say, 'Who is it?' she'd say. 'It's your son, Eddie.' She'd say, 'Are you studying? You ought to be married,' " recalled a friend in whom Williams confided. "He'd tell these stories to make himself feel better about her dying. His mother was never going to say, 'Oh, Eddie, you're so successful.' " Near the end of her life, he was upset that she would mistake him for his cousin John when he came to visit. "I came all the way to see her and she doesn't recognize me!" he stormed at his cousin Gerry Ray. "Why bother?" Williams's mother died in November 1973 at the age of ninety-two. His secretary, Angie Novello, said that she had never seen Williams so depressed as he was in the ensuing weeks.

As a father himself, Williams began to improve in his second marriage. To be sure, his frequent travels and six-day workweek still made him an absentee parent much of the year, and he remained uneasy with the basic tasks of child rearing. He couldn't bear medical crises of any kind, and would drive a child to the emergency room before putting a Band-Aid on a cut finger. He also lacked an essential skill of parenting, patience. "He was a disaster trying to teach you to ride a bike," recalled his daughter Ellen. One day, Williams took her on a carriage ride through New York's Central Park. After about a half hour, Williams got bored. He gave the carriage driver a twenty-dollar bill and told him to drop his daughter, who was then about nine years old, back at the apartment. Then he disappeared in a cab.

But when Williams was home, he was playful and affectionate. On Sunday mornings, as his wife slept late, Williams would appear in the children's rooms wearing boxer shorts and, at times, a gorilla mask. Leading choruses of "When the Saints Go Marching In," he would muster the children to the kitchen, where he overcooked toast and eggs, "speckled eggs" and "toasties," burned bread with slabs of butter. He liked to laugh at the Three Stooges and wrestle with his boys, who could only win by putting their toes on his nose. "He was like a little kid," said his son Tony. "He liked dirty jokes and bathroom humor." In the afternoons, he led expeditions to the zoo, where they went to see the seals and bears, and to Glen Echo amusement park, where he refused to go on scary rides. (Williams was afraid of heights; he would not allow his children to look down from his tenth-floor office.)

One afternoon in the mid-sixties he was feeling neglectful and impulsively he told Ellen to grab a football and hop in the car. As Williams told the story, they spent the afternoon at Silver Spring Park, where father taught daughter pass patterns—down and out, hook and go, post. Exultant and sweaty, they finally climbed back into the car and headed home. Williams joked to Ellen, "One day you will have children and you'll tell them I taught you how to run a post pattern." Ellen, who was eleven, replied, "I'm going to tell them that there was a day when my father taught me the post pattern, and I'm going to tell them it happened on October 13, 1967, the happiest day of my life." Williams began to cry.

In his public remarks, Williams stressed the need for disciplining youth. Pontificating about the lack of moral fiber in society to the *National Observer* in December 1972, Williams declared, "As for discipline, I've only known two real disciplinarians in my entire life: Vince Lombardi and my wife. My wife has more rules for kids than the Internal Revenue Service. Discipline is the only way your kids are ever going to know you love them." But in his home life, Williams was a "friend, not a disciplinarian," said his daughter Dana. The really strict person in the house was Rosa, the strong-armed housekeeper. Williams teased Agnes about her attempts to discipline her children. "When you get old, the kids are going to like me, not you, because you're too strict," he told her. "It was pretty immature of him," said Dana, who, like most of her siblings, saw her father not as a fearsome courtroom warrior but as a funny, sentimental man they called "Big Bear."

The younger Williams children "never acted up or tested him," said Dana. "We were just so glad to be with him." Williams was able to convey his joyousness and good-heartedness to most of his children; their sunny dispositions reflect his lighter side. The oldest boy, Jobie, did not have such an easy time with his father. In an attempt to instill some discipline, Williams and Agnes sent Jobie to a military academy from fifth to eighth grades. The freedom of high school was too much for him. At the age of fifteen, he ran away from home; the police found him in New Orleans. Inevitably, he discovered drugs. By the age of seventeen, he was in angry revolt against his parents. His father finally threw him out of the house.

Like other disaffected teenagers in the early seventies, Jobie wandered around the country, alighting in Texas, Florida, and finally in California. He was not entirely cut off from his parents, however. Williams's secretary, Angie Novello, recalls that Agnes kept after Williams to write Jobie every week and send him money. "You have to keep a light in the window," said Williams, who was heartbroken by his inability to reach out to his eldest boy. Williams also got Jobie jobs with a series of former clients, including Louis Wolfson, who owned a ranch. Finally, after several years of drifting, Jobie became a charismatic Catholic. He weaned himself from drugs and alcohol, reconciled with his parents, and worked as a computer programmer. Years later, he did not seem bitter, saying that his father had little choice but to kick him out of the house.

ON THE SURFACE, Williams's marriage to Agnes in the 1960s and 1970s did not seem especially close. He was not demonstratively affectionate with her. At social events, while he was loud and boisterous, she was prim and sober, rarely drinking more than a glass of wine. "It seemed like an old-fashioned Catholic relationship," said a friend. "The husband goes out with the boys, and the wife is loyal and long-suffering." Even the Williams children acknowledged that Agnes was publicly self-effacing. "He had been literally her boss, her professor," said daughter Dana. "When they first met, Dad told me, she was shy and would stand by him at cocktail parties." Unlike Dorothy, who would come back at Williams when he baited her, Agnes would just smile blandly, or say, "Oh, Ed."

But the appearances were deceiving. Agnes was certainly old-fashioned in the sense that she was content to stay at home while her husband worked. She was ambitious for him. She felt that her father, a modestly successful engineer, had been held back in his career by her mother, and she was not going to repeat the mistake. But she was hardly a pushover. She could be stubborn and relentless when she wanted something. Her children teasingly called her ''Hurricane.'' With a mixture of respect and admiration, Williams called her a ''mule.'' He respected her intelligence and spent hours talking with her about the law, arguing over cases. He found her a useful sounding board, because she was theoretical and logical while he was earthy and intuitive. He liked to tell friends that Agnes was one of the three smartest lawyers he ever met and he meant it: She had written his winning briefs in *Icardi* and *Silverman*.

In private, Williams had a teasing and affectionate relationship with Agnes. He spent hours talking to her on the beach in Nantucket or Martha's Vineyard, and called her often on the phone from work. One morning, he greeted his son Ned by telling him that he and Agnes had just stayed up all night talking about the past and the future. ''It was one of the nicest conversations I've ever had,'' he said.

Williams never told Agnes about his flirtations with other women. She believed he loved her, and she was right. ''Ed didn't want Arlene Dahl or Ginger Rogers. He wanted Agnes,'' said Art Buchwald. ''She was perfect for him.'' Williams loved the idea of being a ''family man.'' He considered it a high compliment to be called one. He hated divorce, and he loved the mere sight of a pregnant woman. He knew that Agnes was a source of stability for him. ''He was black Irish and he knew he was on the edge and needed a restraining force,'' said Buchwald. Agnes brought order and limits to a life-style that Williams sometimes feared would spin out of control.

Williams was a man of lusty appetites. He bolted his food, usually cleaning his plate before anyone else at the table. Before lunch he could empty a bowl of rolls, lavishly buttering them and then salting the butter. He loved junky and greasy food: He far preferred sausages and hash browns at a luncheonette to haute cuisine at a fancy restaurant. ''His favorite foods were fried baloney, Cheez Whiz, peanut butter, and soft ice cream,'' said Dana. Not surprisingly, Williams was always struggling with his weight. His closet contained two sets of suits: prediet, for a man of about 220 pounds, and postdiet, for a 190-pounder.

His taste for liquor made dieting hard. Williams himself documented just how hard when he went on the Georgetown Diet Management Program in 1979. As required, Williams wrote down everything he ate. His lunch the first day was: ''gin and tonic and crackers.'' For dinner he had three gin and tonics, one light beer, and roast chicken with stuffing. For lunch the next day he had two gin and tonics, two beers, and a tuna sandwich. After having five gin and tonics and a beer with dinner the next night, Williams wrote down his calorie total for the day: 2,990, more than twice as much as his "modified diet plan" allowed. He scrawled the word *Disaster!* across the page. By the fifth day, he had taken to skipping lunch in order to drink his calories: five vodka tonics and a beer for dinner, five martinis and a beer the next day. The day after that he gave up, not having lost a pound.

His diets were effective when he went on the wagon, as he usually did every year at Lent, but his mood suffered. David Brinkley recalled hosting a party at which Williams declined to drink and instead sat silently on a couch, "his chin on his chest." Williams's exuberance could lift a party, and his despondency could sink one. Brinkley began to feel a pall settling across his living room as the other guests were subdued by Williams's brooding presence. "Finally, I said to him, 'For God's sake, I can't stand you sober! Please drink some whiskey!' " Brinkley recalled. "Booze made him happy. He'd put his arms around you. He was really a pleasant, likable drunk."

Not always. One evening at Duke Zeibert's during the 1960s, Williams had been drinking heavily with sportswriter Morrie Siegel and his wife, Myra McPherson, a tart-tongued *Washington Post* "Style" section writer. Williams was going on about how his father was a lowly department store floorwalker who got pushed around a lot. "Ed," interjected McPherson, "you make a lot of money. Why don't you retire him?" In one violent heave, Williams turned over the table, spilling drinks and dinner all over Siegel and McPherson. Williams called McPherson the next day and apologized, as he often did after a drunken outburst. "I have it on good authority that I was a shithead last night," he told McPherson.

In 1968, at the wake for Dorothy Williams's father, Williams got belligerently drunk and began insulting Dorothy's family. The next morning, massively hung over, he methodically apologized to everyone staying at the Guiders' house. When he got to Betty Killay, Dorothy's sister, she told him that he didn't have to apologize to her, that he had said nothing rude to her. "Well, then, you're the only one I wasn't rude to," he sighed. He told Killay that Agnes had ordered him to make amends with his victims of the night before.

Williams's drinking was something of a family joke. Ellen woke up Jobie one night at Christmas time at Tulip Hall and pointed outside. There, lying on his back in a snowdrift holding the plug to the outdoor Christmas tree, was their father, passed out. It was such a ridiculous sight that both children giggled. Agnes Williams did not think her husband's drinking was quite so funny. After a New Year's Eve party at the Brinkleys', Ben Bradlee saw Williams's chauffeur, Leroy Washington, shovel his drunken boss into the backseat of the limousine. Bradlee peeked inside and could see Agnes stern with anger. "She chewed his ass," said Bradlee. "He understood it. You paid for your sins. If it wasn't God, it was Agnes."

Williams's drinking was as hazardous to his driving as it was to his dieting. Williams was notoriously reckless in an automobile. He was oblivious to the road as he told stories, and when he told a punch line, he had a disconcerting habit of stomping on the brakes, as if for emphasis. After liquid dinners, other lawyers took turns driving him home; Ellen woke up screaming one morning when she found a strange man in the next bed. It was her father's partner Peter Taft, who had been too drunk to drive home himself. Williams's correspondence shows him paying off fender-benders in 1970 and 1971 that were clearly his fault. By then, however, he was generally driven by Leroy Washington, who had begun as a driver for the Redskins but increasingly became Williams's personal chauffeur.

Judged by the standards modern clinicians use to measure drinking habits, Williams may have been an alcoholic. Certainly, he often needed liquor to give him a lift in social settings, and his consumption, particularly in his early days, could be prodigious. In his cups, Williams was sometimes maudlin or irrational. But if he was addicted, he was hardly dysfunctional. According to his partners and clients, he never allowed drinking to interfere with his work ("he cared too much about control for that," said Jack Vardaman). And his family says that he did not drink heavily in the evening when he was home relaxing with Agnes and the children. His friends generally shrug off his drinking by saying, "Ed was Irish." Everyone agrees that, aside from an occasional bender, his drinking gradually tapered off in later life.

Eventually, Williams's hard living began to affect his health. He was legendary among his friends and colleagues for subsisting on almost no sleep. But according to his doctor, Steve Jones, Williams suffered from insomnia. Jones told Williams that he would sleep better if he drank less, but Williams did not pay him much heed. More serious, and not surprisingly given his frenetic life, Williams had high blood pressure. Beginning in 1969, Jones put Williams on a diuretic to control his hypertension.

In January 1972, Williams was forced to bed, exhausted, with pneumonia. He told reporters in Chicago, where he was defending former

Illinois governor Otto Kerner on bribery charges, that he had not had a vacation in eighteen months. Williams still didn't like vacations, at least the kind spent lying on a beach or reading a book under a palm tree. When Agnes took him to a remote resort in the Virgin Islands in the mid-seventies, Williams complained that it was his "idea of hell: no air-conditioning and no telephones." Peter Taft said that when Williams went to Nantucket in the summer of 1963 he got sick after three days; as soon as he returned to Washington, he miraculously recovered. Nantucket, with its quiet beaches, bored Williams, although swimming in the ocean relaxed him. (He called rough ocean waves "nature's Jacuzzi.") He liked to play with his children in the surf, and inveigled Agnes into the water by promising to go to the opera for every four times she went swimming. Williams would often invite his law firm protégés to Nantucket. Brendan Sullivan recalled a pell-mell weekend of watching Ed cavort in a raging surf while his children, several of them quite small, tossed about on rafts. Sullivan, a former lifeguard, anxiously wondered how Ed was going to explain to Agnes that he lost one to the undertow. But at the end of the day the whole group piled happily into the car and careered home down the winding island roads, singing cowboy songs. Williams would occasionally go fishing, which also bored him, and he hated sailing. He was frustrated by having to beat against the wind. There was too much zigzagging, he complained; why couldn't the boat go straight ahead?

Williams felt particularly relaxed sitting around a casino in Las Vegas. Although he didn't play dice or cards himself (too difficult to control), he liked shmoozing with the gangsters, hookers, and bookmakers, swapping stories that were amazing—and sometimes even true—about the underworld. Before the Holmes-Cooney fight, he sat contentedly at a casino table with Bob Martin, who had become the top legitimate odds-maker in Las Vegas after Williams got him off in the "spike mike" case. Martin was working the phones, making bets, while Williams jawed with Howard Cosell and Joe DiMaggio and checked out the showgirls in their pancake makeup and skimpy spangles.

Williams was less comfortable with what he called "the green pants set," the preppy men with lockjaw accents and Pucci-dressed wives who populated Nantucket and Martha's Vineyard in the summer. Williams had little use for thin-blooded WASPs whose summer homes had been paid for with grandfather's trust fund. But he did enjoy the company of self-made men, the journalists and powerbrokers who bought up gray-shingled houses on the sandy islands off Cape Cod in the sixties and seventies. Of the two islands, Martha's Vineyard was more of a power base than Nantucket, where Williams had summered from 1960 into the mid-seventies. The Vineyard had become a summer outpost of the liberal establishment. Kay Graham had a house there, as did Jacqueline Onassis, Art Buchwald, and Walter Cronkite. Sensing Williams's boredom with Nantucket, Agnes bought a house on the Vineyard in 1977 so Williams could be closer, as she put it, "to the action." The rambling white clapboard house was in the middle of Edgartown, not off on an isolated beach, and Williams enjoyed poking about the town, checking in at the sheriff's office and the local newspaper (owned by his friend, *New York Times*man James Reston). Williams bought a piece of the local radio station, which was a financial loser but gave him something to do so he could avoid relaxing. The remoteness of the island made Williams uneasy. When bad weather or fog grounded the flights back to Washington, he would explode at the airline clerks. "I'm gonna sell my goddamn house!" he yelled at Art Buchwald during one outburst.

To provide more space for his seven children, Williams moved the family in 1972 from Tulip Hill to a mansion in Potomac, Maryland, complete with stables and horses and a few cows. He jokingly called his 13-acre spread "the Ponderosa," and was even sighted one day wearing a cowboy hat and a suede jacket. He rode his horse Randy a few times but then lost interest. Averse to normal suburban pursuits like leaf-raking, Williams had not much to do with the farming side of his estate—that is, until his cows got loose one day and one was hit by a car. A doctor rushing to an emergency struck the cow and totaled his car. Perhaps not realizing just whose cow he had struck, the doctor sued. "Kids," said Williams, "I'm going to give you a lesson in life. Always be the aggressor. I'm going to sue this guy's ass off for killing my cow." The doctor dropped the suit.

For Williams, athletic activity was not so much recreation as hand-to-hand combat. Golf was too slow, but racquet sports brought him face-to-face with his opponent and allowed him to use all his wiles. (He preferred singles to doubles; singles was *mano a mano,* and he didn't have to depend on his partner.) Large, slow, and somewhat ungainly, Williams was hardly a smooth tennis player, but he was adept at finding his opponent's weak spot and making him choke. Williams particularly enjoyed playing with Walter Cronkite on Martha's Vineyard because Cronkite was just as uncoordinated and guileful as Williams. The TV anchorman faked a back injury to hustle Williams, and taunted him about using an oversize metal racket, challenging him to a match with his "teensy weensy but manly" wooden racket. Williams's tennis matches with his son Ned became almost too intense; Williams refused to lose to his son and Ned refused to lose to a fat old man. Finally, Ned broke his racket and stopped playing his father.

Williams would play any racquet sport: tennis, racquet ball, paddle ball, squash, or Ping-Pong. After his neighbor Thomas Taylor trounced him at Ping-Pong during the 1950s, Williams took lessons for several months from an instructor at the Metropolitan Club. He invited Taylor to a showdown—and still lost. He switched instead to squash. Played on a narrow, four-wall court with two bodies constantly jostling for position, squash was ideally suited to Williams's powers of physical and psychological intimidation. By cunning and by throwing his body around, by dominating the "T" at the center of the court, Williams could often win the first few games with superior players. (It particularly delighted Williams when he showed up a far better player, Senator John Warner of Virginia, in front of his new wife, Elizabeth Taylor.) A frequent opponent, Brendan Sullivan, described Williams's psychological warfare: "He'd make you believe that you treated him unfairly," said Sullivan. "He wouldn't call a 'let' [demanding the point be played over for interfering with a shot], but he'd let it be known that he *should* have called a let. So you'd think that he thinks that you've cheated, but that he is showing great forbearance. He'd curse and yell, 'You're cheating me! I'm not going to play with you anymore if you do that again!' It was all theater; he wasn't really mad. But it worked."

One of Williams's bonding rituals with the young lawyers in his firm was to play softball and touch football with them on the weekend. Williams was just as competitive about winning these games as he was about winning a court case. His shows of competitive spirit became legendary in the firm. Once, when his daughter Ellen was pitching, he drilled a shot off her leg. He ran over to make sure she was all right—but only after running safely to first. Williams felt a particularly urgent need to defeat Hogan & Hartson at interfirm softball. Trailing 5–0 one year after an H&H batter had hit one of his pitches about three hundred feet, Williams produced a special, soggy ball he had brought just in case. When Williams pitched to Hogan & Hartson's next batter, he threw his "doppus ball," as he called it in his mock-Yiddish, while the Williams & Connolly batters continued to hit away against a normal ball.

Williams's team won, leaving the senior partner exultant about his sub-terfuge. Williams was a better winner than a loser. Up by four runs in the last inning of a game, Williams pitched to a small boy who hit a grounder to second. The throw to first was just in time, but the umpire called the boy safe anyway. Williams exploded. "The kid was out! He was *out!*" he ranted. The opposing team went on to score five runs and win. Williams welled up with tears and began to cry like a Little Leaguer who had dropped the game-losing fly ball. His law partners, who were accus-tomed to his moods, gaped in wonder at the rawness of his emotional drive.

WILLIAMS WAS AS DESPERATE as ever to make the Washington Redskins winners. He was so quick to see defeat lurking in every dropped pass or fumbled snap that the players and coaches started calling him "Panic Button." After Lombardi died in September 1970, the Redskins had resumed their losing ways under an interim coach. Williams was deter-mined to find a coach who was just as driven to win as he was, and he finally found one in George Allen, the coach of the Los Angeles Rams. In January 1971, Williams lured Allen away from the Rams with a seven-year contract, worth a reported $875,000, exorbitant for the time. Williams announced enthusiastically, if not accurately, "This is the last coach I'm ever going to hire."

Williams had met Allen on the beach in Waikiki at an owners' meeting in 1966. Humorless and self-important, Allen drank milk and smiled through clenched teeth. But, like Williams, he was single-minded about the task at hand. Allen spoke in inspirational clichés that Williams mim-icked to his friends but, in fact, believed. "Winning is being totally prepared," Allen liked to declare to the players and coaches (Williams would nod). "Every day you waste you can never make up" (Williams would nod again). "The achiever is truly alive" (more nods). "The future is now" (Williams reached for his checkbook).

Allen quickly made nineteen trades for older, more experienced, more costly players. He insisted on building a new $700,000 state-of-the-art training facility that the *Washington Post* described as the Caesar's Palace of practice fields. Allen himself did not come cheap: $125,000-a-year salary, a chauffeured car, and a new house were all in his seven-year contract. "I have given him an unlimited budget," Williams declared, "and he has exceeded it."

Although the Redskins sold out every game and enjoyed increasing television revenues, Williams pleaded that the Redskins were money losers. He constantly complained that the stadium was too small (53,000 seats) and his payroll too high. As a result, the Redskins had to charge the highest ticket prices in the league. What neither he nor the sportswriters who covered the Redskins mentioned was the team's heavy debt burden. In order to secure control of the team for Williams and Jack Kent Cooke, as well as boost the worth of their own stock, the Redskins had borrowed about $7 million to buy up George Marshall's shares when he died. The debt service, as writer Joe Nocera pointed out in the *Washington Monthly* in 1978, was over $500,000 a year.

Allen may have been expensive, but his "Over-the-Hill Gang" won. After the Redskins had won five in a row, including a 20–16 thriller against hated Dallas, *Sports Illustrated* found Williams on the flight home, standing in the front of the plane and leading the team in a chorus of "Gimme that Old-Time Religion." President Nixon, in a pre-Watergate show of support, sent Williams a telegram congratulating him on smart trades and predicting a championship in 1972. The self-proclaimed First Fan was an accurate forecaster. The Redskins defeated Dallas in December 1972 (Henry Kissinger served Williams Russian caviar before the game) to win their league, and went to the Super Bowl that January in Los Angeles.

They jokingly called the chartered 727 the "People's Plane," but the passenger manifest was strictly inside the Beltway. Williams brought along Earl Warren, Ed Muskie, Carl Rowan, Nancy Dickerson, Ben Bradlee, and David Brinkley, among other Washington heavyweights, on the flight out to the West Coast from Washington. (The plane was delayed half an hour because Ethel Kennedy was late.) On the way out, Williams could not stay out of the aisles, where he hugged everyone in sight. Jack Kent Cooke, the absentee owner of the Redskins, took the crowd on a tour of his art collection, provoking mockery and ridicule from the owners box regulars like Bradlee and Buchwald. Williams just shook his head and refused to join in the kidding; Cooke, he reminded others, owned 85 percent.

The Redskins played poorly in the Super Bowl. At the half, with the team trailing the Miami Dolphins 14–0, Phil Geyelin, editor of the editorial page of the *Washington Post,* tried to buck up Williams by reminding him that the Redskins had been a strong second-half team. Red-faced and tense, Williams had already given up. "You've got to come to the

Super Bowl twice to win,'' he said. "You never win the first time.'' The
Redskins' fans had a brief moment of hope when Dolphin kicker Garo
Yepremian "played Armenian roulette,'' as Williams put it, and threw up
a wobbly pass that a Redskin intercepted and returned for a touchdown.

But the Redskins offense was pitiful, and Williams fell into a deep and
wordless gloom as the clock ran out. On the way out of the stadium,
Agnes reminded Williams that they were supposed to go to a postgame
party at the Los Angeles Forum. "You have got to go,'' she said. "Why
the hell should I?'' he asked. That night, he flew to Las Vegas instead,
where he had a court hearing in the morning. In one of his last mob-
related cases, he was entering a guilty plea for Morris Lansburg, owner
of the Flamingo, in a profits skimming case. "Ed couldn't get it over with
fast enough,'' recalled Bill Hundley, who was a co-counsel with him in
Las Vegas.

Chapter Twenty-Five

WILLIAMS NO LONGER HAD any interest in defending mobsters and gamblers. He wanted a big role in the main event, the emerging Watergate scandal. As the Watergate Special Prosecutor's Office began rummaging through the dark closets of the Nixon administration, the indictments spilling out provided employment for about forty defense lawyers around Washington. Since Williams had been virtually a prosecutor himself in the DNC case against the Committee to Re-Elect the President, he could not defend the principal Watergate defendants. But he did have some gratuitous after-the-fact advice for Richard Nixon. "I would have burned the tapes on the White House lawn at a press conference," Williams told reporters, who listened incredulously to this ethically dubious plan. "Then I would have apologized." Nixon should have explained that while his intention had been to "record history," he could now see that releasing the tapes to the public carried too great a risk of "embarrassing foreign leaders" to whom the president had talked—and talked about—in the Oval Office. Privately, Williams added with a smile, "then I would have put my nose down and my ass up and hunkered down."

Many of the cases emanating from the Watergate Special Prosecutor's Office in 1973 and 1974 involved illegal campaign contributions to the Republicans' vast slush fund. Not surprisingly, the wealthy donors accused of giving these illegal contributions queued up to hire Ed Williams. The first in line was also the most shadowy, fugitive financier Robert Vesco. In May 1973, Vesco was indicted, along with former attorney general John Mitchell and CREEP chairman Maurice Stans, for obstructing an investigation into whether he had given the Republicans $200,000 to make his problems with the SEC go away. After hiring Williams, Vesco never had to set foot in a U.S. courtroom. Williams and his associates managed to block attempts to extradite Vesco from his island holdout in the Bahamas by arguing that the crimes Vesco stood accused of were not covered by extradition treaty.

One of the bankrollers of American politics was Dwayne Andreas, a soybean magnate who ran an agribusiness conglomerate out of Minneapolis, Minnesota. Andreas covered his bets by giving some to Republicans, but he gave most of his money to the Democrats. He was a natural target for Special Prosecutor Leon Jaworski, who wanted to show that he was a nonpartisan corruption fighter. In December 1973, Andreas was indicted for making $100,000 in illegal campaign contributions to Hubert Humphrey's 1968 presidential campaign.

Andreas was eager to avoid a messy public trial. He told Williams to "just get rid of" the case by pleading guilty to a single count. There was little risk of jail, since judges were not sentencing CEOs to prison for illegal corporate contributions. Williams, however, told Andreas that he could win. He wanted to avoid a jury trial; jurors, he believed, would regard Andreas as a fat cat trying to buy political influence and find him guilty no matter what the law said. But he believed that he could convince a judge that Andreas had done nothing legally wrong. He was even willing to accommodate the prosecution by stipulating—agreeing before trial—to the facts. The government argued that Andreas had tried to circumvent the law prohibiting corporate contributions by writing a personal check to Humphrey and then reimbursing himself with corporate funds. But Williams argued that the corporate funds were a legitimate loan, and that Andreas had paid the money back.

Chuck Ruff, the government prosecutor, realized that the government had made a mistake by not demanding a jury trial as soon as he walked into the judge's chambers. The judge, Edward J. McManus, shook Ruff's hand, but he was looking over his shoulder at Williams, who had walked in behind the government lawyer. "Mr. Williams!" exclaimed Judge McManus. "What a pleasure to have you here! I've brought my son with me; he's a second-year law student and wanted so much to meet you!" With that, the young man who had been standing over in the corner came forward to be introduced, "wide-eyed with wonder at the very thought of shaking Ed Williams's hand," Ruff said. "I had the feeling it was going to be a long day, and it was."

The government had filed voluminous briefs on a number of complex legal issues, but the judge never said a word about them. The only words he uttered at the end of the one-day trial were "Not guilty." The young government lawyers working on the case were flabbergasted. "It was a stunning display of judicial irresponsibility," said Roger Witten, who was working on his first case fresh from a judicial clerkship. "The judge acted as if he was a jury, and not a judge." (Of course, in a non-jury case, the judge is supposed to act as both judge and jury.)

Witten bore no ill will toward Williams, however. "He treated us like grown-ups," said Witten. Most of the young lawyers in the Watergate Special Prosecutor's office were just out of law school. To try a case against the great Ed Williams was an honor. But Williams never condescended to them. "He was a joy to deal with," recalled John Koeltl, who, with another young prosecutor, Tom McBride, handled a third Watergate-related case against Williams. The client was George Steinbrenner, owner of the New York Yankees and a Cleveland ship-building company. Steinbrenner was charged with illegally funneling over $100,000 of corporate contributions to political candidates, including the Nixon campaign.

In every meeting with McBride and Koeltl, Williams would spend the first half hour or so talking about the Redskins and recounting colorful cases he had argued. He told them the Slobodkin story, both to warm them up and to subtly remind them that he kept his clients at arm's length. As always, Williams was not confrontational in these meetings. And as usual, the prosecutors came to feel comfortable with him, to trust and like him. At night, they would go home, proud to have rubbed shoulders with the legendary lawyer, and tell Williams's funny stories to their friends and wives.

All this goodwill, of course, had a purpose. Williams told Jack Vardaman, a lawyer in his firm, that he always treated young Koeltl, who was not yet thirty, with as much respect as Leon Jaworski. "The youngest guy is just as important," Williams counseled. "You never undercut him." The line lawyers wrote the prosecutorial memorandum—the "pros memo"—that would be the basis for the indictment. Young prosecutors also had the power to leak to the press. It was vital not to antagonize them.

Williams was trying especially hard to get along with the government lawyers in the Steinbrenner case because his client was in deep trouble. Not for the corporate contributions; no one went to jail for that. But

Steinbrenner had funneled the corporate contributions through his employees in the disguise of "bonuses" that the employees then contributed to political candidates. Steinbrenner's employees had admitted to the government that their boss had instructed them to lie to the grand jury in an effort to cover up the crime. This was subornation of perjury and obstruction of justice—and people found guilty of those crimes usually wound up in jail.

The records of government prosecutors are usually sealed from the public. But the law setting up the Watergate Special Prosecutor's Office also provided that the records of the office later be made available to the public under the Freedom of Information Act. The prosecutor's file on the Steinbrenner case provides a revealing insight into Williams's defense strategy. Williams started off by offering up other wrongdoers—including Williams's former client, the Teamsters—if the government agreed to go easy on Steinbrenner. After Williams and Vardaman met with McBride and Koeltl on October 18, 1973, Koeltl wrote, "Steinbrenner could provide us with more than a dozen companies which had been involved in 610 [illegal corporate contribution] violations. . . . Williams indicated that Merrill Lynch had substantial difficulties in the campaign finance area. . . . Williams indicated that Steinbrenner had heard that the Teamsters had given more than a million dollars, that the million dollars had been kept at the Hotel Pierre, and that someone from the Teamsters had then stolen it back again." Williams and other lawyers in the firm came across like honest brokers, just trying to work out the best deal for everyone. Vince Fuller, who was also working on the case, told Koeltl that Steinbrenner was "paranoid" about the ongoing investigation.

The government started out demanding a tough deal: charging Steinbrenner with both illegal campaign contributions and obstruction of justice and recommending a jail sentence to the judge. The government would insist on bringing the case in Washington instead of Cleveland, because of "the political influence we believe Steinbrenner to have in Ohio," McBride wrote. But over time, the government slowly backed down. Meeting followed meeting; Williams amiably stalled and jawed.

Meanwhile, the lawyers back at the firm were delivering "shopping carts" of legal briefs to the overworked Special Prosecutor's Office, said McBride. One of Williams's secret weapons was a prolific brief writer, Bob Weinberg, who could think up dozens of different arguments, many of them obtuse and arcane, on any single point of law. It was standard procedure at the Williams firm for Williams to pleasantly waste the time of government lawyers with entertaining small talk, and then keep them up all night trying to respond to Weinberg's multitudinous motions and briefs. Implicit was the threat that if the negotiations did not work out, Williams would be compelled to go to trial. Then the prosecutors would see a different Ed Williams. The happy hour chitchats would suddenly become twenty-four-hour-a-day total warfare. "It made you more willing to cut a deal," said McBride. "You knew that if you went to trial against Williams, it would be intense labor. We didn't have the resources. It was just two or three guys out of law school."

Finally, after a score of meetings, Williams showed the fist in the glove. He threatened that if the government insisted on charging Steinbrenner with obstruction of justice, he would recommend to his client that they go to trial. The government promptly backed down. On the obstruction of justice charge, the prosecutors agreed to allow Steinbrenner to plead to being "an accessory after the fact," a misdemeanor. The disposition of the case would not be in Washington, all astir over corruption, but back in Steinbrenner's friendlier hometown of Cleveland.

At least, McBride thought, the government had drawn a tough judge in Cleveland. Leroy Contie had once imprisoned a twenty-two-year-old woman bank teller who was a mother with small children on embezzlement charges. But Contie was all-merciful with Steinbrenner. He refused to impose a jail sentence, and only fined Steinbrenner $15,000—less than Williams charged him for the week. The government lawyers were shocked. "It's unbelievable," one of them told the *New York Times*. Special Prosecutor Jaworski told his staffers that he was "incensed."

Pressed by a reporter to explain his leniency, the judge asked why the government, if its obstruction of justice case was so strong against Steinbrenner, allowed him to plead to a misdemeanor instead of a felony. The judge also noted that he was merely following the recommendation of the probation office, which had argued against a jail sentence. "We got a lot of letters from quite prominent people—the people you read about in the newspapers," said Dominick Lidoi, who wrote the presentencing report. "My understanding is that Steinbrenner has done a lot with deprived kids. The public sentiment has to be taken into account." The "public sentiment," of course, had been carefully orchestrated by Williams, who persuaded seventy of the rich and powerful to write the parole office. The letters included a telegram signed by the entire New York Yankees baseball team.

Williams found Bowie Kuhn, the commissioner of baseball, to be less forgiving than Judge Contie. Meeting with the commissioner six days after Steinbrenner walked free in Cleveland, Williams was "politely threatening," Kuhn later wrote. "Perplexed by the court's leniency," Kuhn suspended the Yankees' owner from major league baseball for two years. Although he could have easily gone to jail, Steinbrenner was not grateful to Williams. "I paid him $100,000," he told Bill Fugazy, "and all he did was cop a plea."

HUGH HEFNER, THE owner of *Playboy*, believed that he had been personally targeted by the White House. In December 1974, grand jury subpoenas were raining down on the Playboy mansion, the price of Playboy stock was plummeting, and the company's board of directors was threatening to quit. Hefner's personal secretary, Bobbie Arnstein, had been charged with running cocaine, and the U.S. Attorney's Office was said to be after Miss Arnstein's boss. Prosecutors told Playboy's in-house lawyer, David Rubin, that they had evidence that Hefner was the leader of a ring transporting cocaine from the Playboy Club in Jamaica to Chicago. The contraband was supposedly hidden in a hollowed-out compartment in the *Big Bunny*, Hefner's DC-9.

Hefner interviewed other leading defense lawyers, including F. Lee Bailey, but chose Williams. "He was impressed that Williams was treasurer of the DNC [Williams's friend DNC chairman Bob Strauss had given him the job earlier that fall]. Hefner loved name droppers and Ed was the best name dropper around," recalled Rubin. Hefner says he hired Williams because "my friend Warren Beatty told me to. Warren said, 'Get Ed Williams. This is a political case, and Ed can go to the Justice Department for you.' "

Before Christmas, Williams flew out to the Playboy mansion in Los Angeles, and Hefner gave him the tour: the exotic zoo, the entertainment center with bedrooms conveniently located off the game rooms, the grotto. "This is paradise," Williams told Hefner. Actually, he was uncomfortable. For all his fascination with sin and fondness for racy company, Williams had a prudish streak. At RFK Stadium, he ordered the cheerleaders, the Redskinettes, to cover their bared navels. "Ed didn't like to be seen courting pleasure," said Steve Umin, a lawyer in his firm who accompanied him on the trip. "A casino was okay, that's the sporting life, but the Playboy mansion was a step too far forward. It was like paying for sex." Williams had never read *Playboy,* Umin said. "He thought it was porn."

Williams and Hefner had a few things in common. Both were on Nixon's enemies list and both kept every word ever written about themselves (though Hefner was way ahead of Williams, with 353 scrapbooks to Williams's 48). But they were fundamentally different. Hefner never rose from his famous circular vibrating bed until 3:00 P.M., and he preferred to do business wearing black silk pajamas. Where Williams was wry, Hefner was earnest. He described himself as "the most moral millionaire I know." Williams never returned to the mansion after that initial meeting, much to Hefner's irritation, because the Playboy czar refused to leave his pleasure palace. The lawyer and his client had to communicate by telephone.

Hefner's in-house lawyers flew to Washington to visit Williams. Rubin was overwhelmed as he was led past Williams's enormous, three-sided desk, into the inner sanctum, Williams's conference room—decorated with numerous plaques and honorary degrees and autographed photos of celebrities and storied clients. "It was like a throne room," said Rubin. "You thought you were in the presence of God." Williams told the Playboy team that the case against Hefner was "politically inspired. Nixon was a shithead and his aides were terrible guys." The U.S. Attorney, "Big Jim" Thompson, wanted to run for governor by scalping Hefner. But not to worry. Williams knew the right people at Justice; he'd take care of it. Leaving the office, Rubin wondered if Williams was just showing off to justify a big fee. Still, the man, like his office, was imposing. When Rubin had inquired about the fee, Williams had cut off any discussion of how his work would be itemized or recorded. "I'll send you a bill," he said.

Back in Chicago, the rumors intensified. The prosecutors told the Playboy lawyers that they had testimony that Hefner kept a large cup of cocaine on the table at business meetings, with little spoons at every place. Thompson called in Bobbie Arnstein and told her that there were death threats against her. She was to trust neither friend nor foe, and certainly not Hefner. A few weeks later, Arnstein killed herself. Hefner was understandably distraught. He held a press conference to accuse Thompson of a politically motivated witch hunt.

Meanwhile, Hefner and Rubin heard nothing from Williams. Hefner called him in Washington, and Williams assured his client that he was talking to the right people. Finally, in March 1975, Williams called Hefner with good news: There would be no indictments. Hefner asked Williams if he could get the new U.S. Attorney, Samuel Skinner, to make a statement exonerating Hefner. Williams said that such statements were not the normal practice of prosecutors, but he'd try. Skinner was amenable to Williams's request. He told reporters that the investigation had found no drug use in the Playboy mansion.

"After that, we thought Williams really *was* God," said Rubin. "He implied to us that he killed the indictment by talking to the attorney general. We were convinced that he had fixed the case." Hefner was immensely gratified. "Ed had access to people in Washington who wouldn't even talk to our people," said Hefner.

What, exactly, did Williams do in Washington to save Hefner? "Not much," said Steve Umin, who worked on the case. "The charges were all B.S. There was some pot smoking but not much else. The government finally found a couple of housemothers in the Bunny dorm falsifying prescriptions for Hefner's uppers, but that was it. Really, it had nothing to do with Washington." After Umin examined documents and interviewed witnesses, "we sat down in Chicago and asked the prosecutors what they had," he said. "They didn't have anything, so they dropped the case." Former U.S. Attorney Skinner confirmed Umin's account.

Williams sent Hefner a bill for $250,000. It was not itemized, said Rubin. It just said, "For services rendered." Hefner gladly paid.

Chapter Twenty-Six

In the mid-seventies, Williams was increasingly preoccupied with the growing pains of his law firm. When Califano had come to Williams & Connolly in 1971, he was taken aback at the informality of the place. "Nobody kept records over there. There was no budget, no hiring committee, no administration, no nothing. Just Ed," recalled Califano. He told Williams, "We've got to run this place like a business." That meant billing hours and recruiting stable long-term clients, instead of living from one case to another. Williams already understood that the Mafia practice had to go. "He saw that U.S. Steel is not going to want to come to the firm that represents Milwaukee Phil," said Califano. But Williams resisted becoming more businesslike, which he regarded as a threat to his personal control. "In the beginning, Ed bitched every inch of the way. That is, until the financial returns came in. Then he liked it."

Paul Connolly had actually introduced the idea of billing by the hour to the firm, but it was Califano who suggested that clients pay unusually high fees for the unique services of the firm. Williams became a convert. He told Connolly that his hourly rate, about $200 an hour in the early seventies, was too low. "The clients won't pay," Connolly protested. "They'll pay," said Williams. He told David Webster that, for his part, he was "billing twenty-four hours a day." When Califano arrived at the firm in 1971, Williams was making about $200,000 a year. When Califano left in 1976, Williams was making $1 million a year.

Williams's hiring practices had remained highly personal and haphazard. He once hired a lawyer, the son of a judge, at a cocktail party in

Honolulu. In 1971, he hired a young lawyer who had studied to become a priest at the University of Louvain, the Catholic seminary in Belgium. The lawyer lasted two days at the firm and vanished. "But he had studied at the Louvain! Everyone who goes to the Louvain is a genius!" Williams protested when his partners asked him why he had hired the young ex-seminarian.

As the firm expanded and diversified, Williams needed lawyers with skills other than trying cases. "I need a tax lawyer," he told Steve Porter, when he hired the CPA away from Hogan & Hartson in 1969. Williams persuaded Porter to come to the firm by asking him to "take care of Sonny Jurgensen's tax problems." Actually, Porter discovered, Jurgensen had no tax problems, but by dangling the name of the Redskins' quarterback, Williams had gotten across the point that law practice at Williams & Connolly was more interesting than at other firms. Porter soon discovered that "tax work" for Williams meant any work that taxed his patience—property settlements, uncontested divorces, business plans, representing Johnny Carson's second wife. Williams did handle some big tax cases himself, but the cases often required no special expertise in handling tax returns, because, as Porter said, "there usually were no tax returns."

Williams liked to take on lawyers who struck his fancy by winning a celebrated case or showing they were "tough," Williams's highest accolade. In 1971, he hired Aubrey Daniel, the army captain who prosecuted Lt. William Calley for the My Lai massacre, when Daniel wrote a letter to President Nixon protesting his decision to release Calley from an army jail. Brendan Sullivan, another army captain, caught Williams's attention by successfully defending twenty-seven soldiers accused of mutiny when they linked arms and sang "We Shall Overcome" at an army stockade.

Califano, however, wanted to make hiring more systematic. "I said, 'Let's get the best and the brightest,' " Califano recalled. He pushed Williams in the direction of hiring lawyers with impressive academic credentials—law review editors at Harvard and Yale who had gone on to clerk for Supreme Court justices. Williams, predictably, turned this into a competition: He boasted that his firm had *more* Supreme Court clerks than any other. As law students at the top schools heard that the firm's young lawyers were able to work on exciting cases for high pay—a rare combination in the law, especially for young associates—the competition to be hired by Williams, Connolly & Califano became intense.

By the late seventies, one thousand applications would flood in for only five or six jobs. Williams always saved a place or two for the sons of the powerful: in the seventies he hired Chuck Robb, LBJ's son-in-law, and Bill Graham, Katharine's son ("Billy should ride sidecar with me for a year," Williams advised his mother, who was wondering what to do about her somewhat rebellious son). Williams also liked to hire attractive women. He wanted to hire Elizabeth Hanford, a vivacious brunette out of Duke and Harvard Law School, but the hiring committee decided her grades were too low. As the wife of Senator Robert Dole, Elizabeth "Liddy" Dole later became a cabinet secretary in the Reagan and Bush administrations.

As the bright stars recruited by the firm got a little older and more experienced, they inevitably wondered when they were going to make partner. In theory, the firm had always been a partnership, but in fact, the partnership was no more than names on a letterhead. "I think Ed told me that I was a partner," said Peter Taft, who worked with Williams through most of the 1960s, "but how would you know? Ed controlled everything." Williams's autocracy was a limitation on growth. When he asked Sheldon Cohen, his personal tax lawyer and former IRS commissioner, if he would like to merge his small firm with Williams's, Cohen responded, "Your guys treat you as God. I can't deal with that. I believe in democracy."

By the early seventies, Williams, Connolly & Califano was nominally a troika, run by the three name partners. Most of the day-to-day business decisions, however, were being made by Califano, who was a more efficient administrator than Williams and more power-driven than Connolly. Many of the younger lawyers began to suspect that Califano wanted a "politburo with himself as top apparatchik," as one of them put it. In the ranks, there was growing resentment against Califano. He was credited with modernizing the firm, but his brusque style undermined the camaraderie that Williams had so exuberantly nurtured.

Gone were the Saturday lunches at which the whole firm could take a couple of tables at Duke Zeibert's and while away the afternoon listening to Williams tell the same funny stories over and over again. There were fewer softball and touch football games. Instead, there were Califano's flow charts tracking associates' time. He would tell partners, "you can have 50 percent of this associate, 20 percent of that one. . . ." Califano seemed to enjoy keeping the junior lawyers waiting outside his office for an hour. The older lawyers, particularly the Georgetown Catholics like

Vince Fuller and Ray Bergan, admired Califano's hard-nosed approach. But to two of the brighter associates, Steve Umin and Paul Wolff, Califano seemed like a "Darwinian monster" who favored adjusting salaries to differentiate between productive and less productive lawyers. "He said he wanted to encourage competition, but really he wanted to show the power he had over our lives," said Wolff.

In early 1973, Umin and Wolff began talking to other associates, including Jack Vardaman, Earl Dudley, and Bill McDaniels, about the firm and their place in it. It was time to do something, they all agreed. The name partners were the only ones who knew what was going on in the firm. Vardaman and McDaniels nervously approached Williams and said the time had come to create a true partnership. Williams surprised them by saying, "I agree with you." Then, typically, he stalled. Finally, in early 1974, he created eight general partners—the old-guard employees like Fuller and Bergan—and seven "special partners"—the "Young Turks." The younger partners were still not satisfied. They felt they had not been given their share of power and wealth. They tried to hold a few firm-wide meetings to discuss matters, but attendance was spotty. "Some people were afraid; some liked the benevolent dictatorship," recalled Umin. Finally, with some trepidation, Earl Dudley was nominated to draft a memo to present to the name partners.

In December, ten young lawyers went to Williams's office. Fuller, who had been with Williams nearly twenty years, did not take part, nor did Bergan and several of the older lawyers. Ostensibly, Dudley's memo was about the structure of the compensation system, but really, Umin recalled, it was about the future of the firm. As the Young Turks laid out their concerns and desires, Williams "looked like he was going to explode," but didn't, according to Wolff. Califano attacked the "minutiae of the memo," and Connolly said nothing.

Tense conversations between the young lawyers and the name partners continued over the next few weeks. Dudley's memo called for "lock-step" compensation, the practice then common on Wall Street, that rewarded lawyers by seniority in the firm, not by hours billed or business generated. Publicly, Williams derided lock-step compensation as "socialism." Did Dudley want to create a "civil service"? he asked contemptuously. "There was a lot of macho talk about 'you eat what you kill,' " recalled Umin. But Williams would sometimes speak one way and act another. Gradually, sensing that the time for change had come, he acceded to the demands of the Young Turks. The result was a compromise that awarded partners points based on seniority as well as productivity. "This really wasn't a dispute about money," said Umin. "We were warned that if you made little gradations, lawyer would be set against lawyer, and that would threaten to destroy the firm."

In the Dudley memo, the young lawyers strongly urged "one lawyer–one vote" governance of the firm. Making every partner equal—even if only in theory—was hard for Williams to accept. At lunch at the Metropolitan Club, he asked Lloyd Cutler, the senior partner of one of the city's major firms—Wilmer, Cutler & Pickering— "Lloyd, do you mean to tell me you have one lawyer–one vote?" Cutler allowed that he did. "He looked pretty skeptical," recalled Cutler. Even so, Williams grudgingly went along with the one man–one vote proposal for the sake of peace in the firm.

Williams, Connolly & Califano became a genuine partnership that winter. By the end of 1975, all the Young Turks had been elevated. All, that is, except Paul Wolff.

Califano could not abide Wolff, whom he thought insolent and a little too hip. The young lawyer made fun of Califano, giving him a pink flamingo to put on his lawn at the annual Christmas party (Califano had criticized Wolff, who had funky tastes, for keeping a pinball machine in his office) and asking, "Hey, Joe, how's your pizza truck?" Years later, Wolff said, "I tried to deflate his ego and show him that this wasn't Arnold & Porter. I was overly harsh." Califano was dead set against making Wolff a partner.

Wolff had won three cases that year. But in December 1975, after a month of intense meetings among the partners, Califano told Wolff that the firm had voted not to make him a partner. Umin told Wolff that the older partners in the firm had outvoted the younger ones. Wolff was crushed. He was popular among the young associates, and several bitterly complained about the decision. Pierce O'Donnell, a respected young lawyer as well as Williams's squash partner, actually quit the firm in protest. Richard Cooper, another highly regarded lawyer and former president of the Harvard Law Review, refused to interview job applicants.

Wolff heard nothing from Williams for a week. Finally, the firm's founder called him on the phone and asked him to lunch. When they sat down in Williams's regular booth at the Palm, Williams said there had been a mistake. He was sorry. Williams asked Wolff if he would think about staying with the firm, that there would be another partners' meeting, and that the earlier decision to deny Wolff would be reversed. But he wanted to know: If, after all this, he was offered a partnership, would Wolff accept? With that, Williams began to cry, first sniffles, then real tears streaming down his face. Wolff began to cry as well. The two men sat there in the crowded restaurant at lunch weeping wordlessly. Neither looked up from his plate. "I couldn't stop," Wolff recalled. Finally, Williams said, "Let's go back to the office." As he stepped out of the limousine, Williams said to Wolff, "It's a deal?" Wolff responded, "It's a deal."

Williams's grief over the pain that Wolff had been put through was genuine. But the "deal" that Williams struck with Wolff was not the first one he made that day. That morning, unbeknownst to Wolff, Williams had met over breakfast with several of the young lawyers pressing to make Wolff partner. "Wolff will never be a partner as long as we have one partner–one vote in this firm," declared Williams. So they struck a deal: They would abandon pure democracy in the firm if Williams would vote to make Wolff a partner. Thereafter, the firm was a weighted partnership, with voting power tied to seniority and earnings. Califano drafted the agreement. Williams called it "bastardized democracy."

For all his macho talk about "eating what you kill," Williams was fundamentally a conciliator in the firm. He disliked confrontation with friends and employees, and he hated putting hard issues to a vote. Rather, he preferred to work around dicey problems. "There was a lot of patsy in Ed," said Wolff. Williams could not bring himself to fire lawyers. "Guys would hang on too long. He wouldn't cut the string. He wanted to be loved too much," said Umin. Williams cared deeply about the firm because it was a monument to him and because it was a unique institution that he had built. For a lawyer to leave the firm seemed a personal affront to Williams, an act of betrayal. Despite his loyalty and generosity of spirit, Williams sometimes showed a sulky, vengeful side. When Judy Richards told Williams that she was leaving to get married and move to California, Williams was icy to her. He had promised to stand up beside her when she was sworn in to the Supreme Court bar that month, but the day of the ceremony, he called her and said he was too busy. She had to scramble to find another sponsor.

Perhaps because his own children showed no interest in the law, Williams would adopt young lawyers as his surrogate sons. There was, over the decades, a long line of Williams acolytes: Fuller, Taft, Tigar, Umin, Sullivan, and in later years Greg Craig and, in particular, Larry Lucchino. These young men not only worked with Williams on cases, they lived with him, sharing hotel suites when cases were tried on the road, playing sports with him, dining with him, and drinking with him (a hollow leg was a helpful attribute when traveling with Williams). They saw him in all his changeable states, from joy to deep depression and every mood in between. The first time Williams went on a crying jag while reminiscing about Earl Warren or Vince Lombardi, the young lawyer across the booth at the Palm would feel embarrassed and awkward. Thereafter, he would feel flattered to be on such intimate terms with the great man, and then, after a decade or so, bemused or perhaps bored by his sentimentality.

Some lawyers less favored by the boss grumbled that he surrounded himself with sycophants. In offices around the firm there were almost as many portraits of Williams by Karsh of Ottawa as there were Harvard Law School degrees. But Williams could be brutal to yes-men. "If you agreed with him he'd try another argument," recalled Brendan Sullivan. "He'd say, 'Do you agree with *that*?,' as if you were a sap who'd buy anything." After listening to Williams rehearse his Supreme Court argument in the *Tilton* case, Earl Dudley told him, "Ed, you deserve to lose this case. Your position is wrong." The loyal Catholic, Williams was arguing that the First Amendment separation of church and state did not bar Catholic colleges from receiving federal funds. Dudley, a liberal WASP, thought it did. "For the next three weeks, my phone rang every half hour," Dudley recalled. "It would be Ed asking, 'What about this? What about that?' He would look for a point of resistance and head right for it."

From the time Califano arrived in 1971 to the time he left in 1976, the firm had more than doubled in size from eighteen lawyers to thirty-eight. By the end of the decade, it would nearly double again. Williams was ambivalent about growth. To be sure, he was happy to have the reputation as the hottest trial firm in Washington, if not the country. The Williams firm practiced civil litigation the way Williams had always practiced criminal law: flat out, relentless, unyielding. Williams, Connolly & Califano was tougher and more resourceful than other firms. It wasn't afraid to go to court, like the stuffy old-line firms. The Slobodkin story was the firm's motto: If you had a defense, you could use Slobodkin (or, by implication, Covington & Burling or Sullivan & Cromwell). If you didn't, if you were in really deep trouble, then you came to Williams, Connolly & Califano.

"We were hot. We were celebrities," recalled Califano. "We had the greatest partnership and great work and we were growing like crazy. Ed would say, 'We're alive! We're alive! Look! Williams, Connolly, and Califano! Where's Covington? Where's Arnold? Where's Porter? Where's Hartson? Where's Hogan? They're dead. We're alive!' "

But at other times, the burden and responsibility of running a large and increasingly bureaucratized organization weighed on Williams. He was so determined to maintain control over every aspect of his life that he wanted to know every detail, every wrinkle. At times, he felt overwhelmed, and he would become cranky. When Mike Tigar returned to the firm in 1974 after five years of teaching law on the West Coast and practicing in Paris, Earl Dudley said to him, "You've got to watch Ed, he's not like he used to be. He's really mercurial. He's really bitchy."

Williams was the firm's rainmaker. Clients came because he was there, and they expected Williams to personally handle their cases. Williams became adept at palming off their problems to other lawyers in the firm. At the initial meeting with clients, he would give the impression that he personally would take care of them, all the way to the courtroom if necessary. But then he would lateral them off to another, more junior lawyer, promising the client that the young lawyer was brilliant, forceful, and energetic. Not every client bought this bait-and-switch.

When Williams tried to pass off one client to his protégé Brendan Sullivan the client balked. "I want the Edward Bennett Williams of today, not tomorrow," he said. Armed with powers of instant absorption and total recall, Williams was able to skillfully drop into a case at the last minute when he had to. When Sullivan was assigned by Williams to represent Gen. Samuel Koster in the My Lai massacre case, Williams still handled a final meeting with the army brass charged with deciding whether to press charges. Williams was very busy at the time, and Sullivan only had the thirty-five-minute drive out to Fort Meade to brief Williams. As Sullivan talked the whole way, Williams just seemed to be staring out the window, paying no attention. At the meeting, however, Williams was able to come across as if he had been working on the case for months. A few months later, after a hearing handled by Sullivan, the charges against General Koster were dropped.

Within the firm, some lawyers felt that Williams passed off cases he thought were losers. The most infamous example was the bribery trial of former Illinois governor Otto Kerner. A liberal hero for his work as chairman of a presidential commission—the so-called Kerner Commission—on racial unrest in the cities in the 1960s, Kerner was a federal judge when he was indicted in May 1971 in a complex scheme to buy stock in a racetrack cheaply in return for certain official favors. Kerner sought out Williams, who agreed to defend him and appeared for him at preliminary hearings.

But Williams never really got on with Kerner, who had an imperious manner. Williams asked Paul Connolly to take the case, despite the fact that Connolly was a civil litigator unfamiliar with criminal trials. Connolly was eager to take on such a high-profile case, but it was a very difficult one: Kerner had perjured himself before the grand jury prior to hiring Williams. Also, Williams knew that Kerner, with his clipped, almost British accent, would seem too lordly to a blue-collar jury. Connolly was unable to humble the former governor and judge before trial. Kerner was convicted and sentenced to prison.

There was sympathy for Connolly among his colleagues, but there was a feeling that the firm, accustomed to miraculous results, had lost face. Connolly was being overshadowed by Califano, who insisted on getting a higher percentage than Connolly in the new pay scale—just to show, some of his partners suspected, that he had the upper hand. Connolly was not enthusiastic about Califano's empire building. In 1973, when the resentment toward Califano was beginning to fester, Connolly made a toast at a firm dinner. He said that he hoped the firm would never get too big, that it was the ideal size, just like a British barrister's office. Earl Dudley noticed Williams impassively watching Connolly. "Ed wasn't buying that rhetoric," said Dudley.

Williams did not like to be associated with defeat or any controversy that could blacken his reputation. In the early seventies, he was irritated by the bad publicity resulting from the firm's aggressive representation of the United Mine Workers (UMW). In the late sixties, the corrupt leadership of A. W. "Tony" Boyle came under attack from UMW dissidents led by Joseph A. "Jock" Yablonski. In December 1969, Yablonski and his family were murdered by gunmen who broke into their house. Suspicions centered on Boyle and the other UMW leaders. The UMW dissidents were represented by Joe Rauh, a liberal labor lawyer. In May 1970, Rauh went to court to try to disqualify the Williams firm from representing both the union and the union leaders, saying there was a potential conflict of interest. A few days later, Rauh asked Williams out to lunch and made a case against Boyle and the union leadership. Williams told Rauh that the UMW was not his client, but rather Paul Connolly's, and that he was unfamiliar with the case. According to Rauh, Williams nonetheless promised to go back to the firm and make the case that Boyle should step down so the union could hold another election.

Williams later said the lunch with Rauh "never happened," though Rauh's appointment calendar shows that it did. Jerry Collins, who was doing most of the work on the case with Connolly, said, "It's entirely possible that Ed would go along with Rauh to make peace." In any case, there was no talk of Boyle stepping down, and the firm continued to represent the union and Boyle at the same time. When a federal court of appeals ordered the firm to represent one or the other, the firm chose to stay with Boyle and the other officers. The firm, in a letter signed by Jerry Collins, also advised the union leadership that it could continue to pay the salary of one of Boyle's henchmen, Albert Pass, even though Pass was under indictment for murdering Jock Yablonski.

When a federal judge ruled against that as well, Rauh went on the attack. His target was Williams. He persuaded a West Virginia congressman to insert into the Congressional Record a scathing attack on Williams for allowing the union to pay "hush money" to the murderer of Jock Yablonski. Arnold Miller, who succeeded Boyle as head of the UMW after Boyle was finally convicted of murdering Yablonski, refused to appear on the same platform with Williams in 1974 when he won an award from Antioch Law School for making the practice of criminal law respectable. In a letter drafted by Rauh, Miller accused Williams of being "unethical." The press picked up on all this finger-pointing, and John Herling, a leading labor writer for the *Washington Daily News*, began sniping at Williams in his columns by dredging up his representation of Jimmy Hoffa. Rauh, meanwhile, was telling any newspaper reporter who asked that Williams was a "hired gun" who had the "ethics of a pigsty."

All of this incensed Williams. "I never had one frigging thing to do with that case," he grumbled to Robert Pack. Williams began throwing darts at a board covered with a photograph of Joe Rauh. But he also grumbled about Jerry Collins, who wrote the letter authorizing what Rauh called "hush money." Williams couldn't very well blame Collins for being overly zealous in the defense of his client—after all, aggressive defense was a Williams & Connolly trademark. But he blamed Collins for stirring up unfavorable publicity that ended up on Williams's doorstep. For a time, Collins fell out of favor with the boss.

Connolly himself was no longer regarded as a ruling power in the firm.

Williams loved Connolly as a brother, but he relied on Califano to run his firm. Because of his hypertension, Williams's doctors had suggested that he get a fish tank for his office. They claimed it would be soothing and relaxing for Williams to watch fish swim lazily about. Predictably, Williams enjoyed watching the big fish chase the little fish. He named the biggest fish "Califano."

Chapter Twenty-Seven

HIS FIRM WAS thriving, his team was winning, and his insider status was secure. But Williams had not won a big highly publicized criminal trial since he had saved Adam Clayton Powell from jail in 1960. His defeat in the Bobby Baker trial in 1967 still gnawed at him. He had made his reputation as a great trial lawyer, and he wanted to prove that he had not lost his touch, that he could still dazzle the public by successfully defending a notorious client against stiff odds. Watergate was the great legal as well as moral spectacle of the day, but Williams felt excluded from the main arena. He could not very well defend the same Nixon White House he had sued as counsel to the Democratic National Committee. So Williams was left to represent corporate fat cats who had been caught making illegal campaign contributions. The defense work required Williams's skill at manipulating prosecutors, but it was mostly behind the scenes.

John Connally put Williams back on the front page. Connally's highly publicized trial in the spring of 1975 would reestablish Williams as the nation's preeminent trial lawyer. To his law partners—and to Williams himself—the defense of John Connally would be remembered not just as a successful day in court but as a work of art. At the very least, it was a how-to guide to the defense of politicians accused of corruption.

John Connally, former secretary of the treasury under Nixon, former governor of Texas, Lyndon Johnson's right-hand man, was not known for humility. The first time the Watergate special prosecutor asked him to testify before the grand jury, he "didn't pay a hell of a lot of attention to it," Connally recalled. The prosecutor was probing political payoffs to the Nixon administration from the milk producers, one of the most generous lobbies in Washington. Had Connally been offered $10,000 by a middleman named Jake Jacobsen to help the milk lobby? Connally dismissed the question. He couldn't recall "a dang thing" about any such conversation. A few months later, however, when he was called again before the grand jury, his memory improved. He had discussed such a contribution with Jacobsen, he conceded, but he swore that he had turned down the money.

The Watergate Special Prosecutor's Office had become omnivorous, but Connally was too busy plotting his own political future to notice. Connally was on a thirty-six-state speaking tour, a warm-up for a presidential run in 1976, when the grand jury leaks began. Columnist Jack Anderson and Dan Schorr of CBS reported that Jake Jacobsen was singing to the grand jury, testifying that he had given Connally a $10,000 payoff. It began to dawn on Connally that the relaxed standards common in Texas did not apply in Washington. Watergate had "poisoned the atmosphere," he said.

Connally had been poorly prepared for his grand jury testimony, using only a lawyer from his old firm in Houston for counsel. Now he needed a real lawyer. One of his advisers, Mickey Gardner, suggested Edward Bennett Williams. Gardner was thinking not only of Williams's legal skills but also of the fact that he was Katharine Graham's lawyer. A bit naively, Gardner believed that Williams would be able to stop the leaks just by picking up the phone and calling the publisher of the *Washington Post*.

Williams took Connally's call late on a Friday night in June 1974. "I'm at the Mayflower Hotel," Connally told him. "You've got to come over right *now*." Taking the first subtle step in his minuet of control, Williams told Connally he would see him—the next morning in Williams's office. Accustomed to lawyers who groveled for their clients, Connally did not realize that Williams would insist on reversing the roles. Instead, when Williams agreed to take the case, Connally was impressed that Williams didn't bother to check first with Kay Graham. "You know, he didn't hesitate," Connally marveled to Gardner. Williams, he said, seemed "calm and dispassionate." After the briefest consideration, Williams set his fee: $400,000.

Before Williams became Connally's master, he became his friend. The two men enjoyed swapping tales of their rise to prominence—Connally from a Texas dirt farm, Williams from the double-decker on Adelaide Street. They shared political gossip and jokes, laughing sardonically about how their mutual friend, the garrulous Democratic party chairman Bob Strauss, was so "humble and self-effacing." Williams was comforting to Connally's family. He reassured Connally's wife, Nellie, who was shaken when crowds outside the courthouse hissed at her husband. Williams told her, "It's just the atmosphere of Washington," another of the capital's periodic spasms of self-righteousness.

Over time, almost without realizing it, Connally found himself becoming dependent on Williams. A Democrat-turned-Republican, Connally was really a corporate statist. He believed in the power of government to help business. The rights of the poor and the downtrodden had not been of much concern to the Texas millionaire. Lyndon Johnson, his onetime mentor, once said, "Connally hasn't been worth a damn since he started wearing $300 suits." But during their long hours of preparing the case, Connally became a good deal more humble as Williams lectured his client on "human liberty." A few months after Connally's trial, Williams would tell a reporter, "I don't think he had thought seriously about the problems of civil liberties. I don't think he had thought in depth about them. But by golly," said Williams with a smile, "he has now." A man with a dramatic sense of himself, Connally felt his well-publicized legal woes had reduced him to the status of *ida*, the Japanese class of garbageman. He looked at Williams, with his enormous brooding head, his hair swept back from his wide brow, and called him Simba—the East African word for lion.

On July 29, 1974, Connally was indicted for taking a $10,000 illegal gratuity from Jacobsen and then lying to the grand jury about it. A week later, on the day that Richard Nixon succumbed to the Watergate onslaught and resigned as president, Williams accompanied Connally to the federal courthouse, where he was arraigned and fingerprinted. Afterward, the two men sat in Williams's office watching television as Nixon awkwardly waved from his helicopter and flew off into exile and disgrace. "You could feel what everyone in the office was thinking but nobody was saying," said Mike Tigar, the associate who was helping Williams on the case. Had it not been for the milk fund and the aggressive Watergate prosecutor, Connally believed, he would have been sworn in that day as president of the United States. Before the grand jury called him, Connally had fully expected Nixon to ask him to be his vice president, to succeed Spiro Agnew, who had resigned to avoid bribery charges in 1973. Now Connally faced a jail term, and only Williams could save him.

Williams's initial strategy was the same one he invariably employed in major criminal cases: delay. To mute the reverberations of Watergate, Williams wanted to put as much time as possible between Richard Nixon's resignation and Connally's trial. Williams knew that he could not make the case quietly go away by cutting a favorable deal with the prosecutor. His cagey charm was useless with the prosecutor assigned to the case, Frank Tuerkheimer, an upright and wooden law school professor who was wary of his famous opponent. The judge, however, was a more promising target. Frail and slight, with wispy hair, a pinched face, and arthritic hands, Judge George Hart was a Nixon appointee and Republican hard-liner. A few years before, he had sent Williams a friendly note praising him for his pro–law-and-order remarks during a TV interview.

In pretrial conferences, Williams shamelessly played to Hart's prejudices against the press. "I wouldn't talk to these people [reporters], Judge," Williams said at one session in Judge Hart's chambers. "Tell you what I do. I found the best way not to have a problem is not to talk to them, not to take their calls." Williams asked Hart to impose a gag order on both the prosecution and the defense. "The one person I can't put any restriction on is Connally," said Judge Hart. Williams replied, "He hasn't talked to anybody. *I* put a restriction on him." Warming up to the spirit of press bashing, Judge Hart remarked, "These newspaper reporters . . . ever since *Sullivan versus New York Times* . . . have got a license to lie." "That's right," agreed Williams, ignoring, for the moment, his representation of the *Washington Post*.

In the fall of 1974 and the winter of 1975, Williams's firm flooded the prosecutors with the usual tide of pretrial motions. Many were simply to buy time, but one was critical. Connally had been indicted for taking the payoff as well as for lying to the grand jury. The prosecutor vigorously argued that perjury counts should be tried together with the illegal gratuity counts, since the lying was intended to cover up the payoff. It was all part of the same crime.

Viewed from the perspective of common sense and logic, Tuerkheimer had a good case. But jury trials turn on evidence, not inference. To protect the rights of defendants, jurors are shown a squinty-eye view of reality. They are supposed to see only those facts that are susceptible to proof and directly relevant to the crime charged. Thus, the jury might be interested in knowing that a defendant charged with murder had been convicted of murder before. But the fact of the first murder conviction will generally be kept from them lest they become prejudiced in deciding whether the defendant had committed the second murder. Williams argued that the payoffs and perjury were separate crimes and should be tried separately. If the state wished to try a man for crime *A*, he argued, it could not introduce evidence of crime *B*—and allow the jury to convict the defendant of that. The jurors should not be permitted to reason that the client is charged with so much that he must be guilty of *something*.

Despite the restrictive rules of courtroom evidence, the legal precedent was mostly against Williams on the question of severing charges that were as closely intertwined as taking a payoff and then lying about it. Indeed, Williams was vexed to discover that the D.C. federal court case most strongly supporting the prosecutor's position was Judge Oliver Gasch's opinion refusing to sever the tax and fraud counts in the Bobby Baker case.

Nonetheless, in the Connally case, Williams was able to persuade Judge Hart to sever the perjury counts. In the judge's chambers, the prosecutors grumbled that if Connally had been a Mafia don, the link between the charges would never have been cut. Tuerkheimer remained bitter about Hart's decision. "Williams's argument was casuistic, but beguiling," he said years later. "Hart thought really highly of Williams. He didn't give a shit if he pissed off Frank Tuerkheimer, but he sure wasn't going to alienate Edward Bennett Williams. I've never seen a lawyer interact better with a judge than Williams."

In retrospect, Judge Hart's action may have been decisive. The government had much stronger evidence of Connally lying than taking the payoff. In his second appearance before the grand jury, Connally had flatly contradicted his initial testimony. At first he had said that he never discussed the payoff with Jacobsen; then he had admitted that he had. Here was demonstrable perjury. But as to whether he actually took the payoff—the proof essentially rested on Jacobsen's word against Connally's. And Connally would prove to be a much better witness than Jacobsen.

As he almost always did in a federal case, Williams planned to put Connally on the stand to testify in his own defense. He was determined that Connally would be well prepared—better prepared than Bobby Baker or Otto Kerner. Williams faced a difficult task. Connally *was* arrogant.

He also had left a trail of contradictions in the grand jury room. In order to repair the damage he had done before the grand jury, Connally had to be carefully coached. Because the basic question—Did Connally take the payoff?—boiled down to Connally's word against Jacobsen's, Williams did not have to cook up an imaginative new theory of the case, as he did for Jimmy Hoffa, who had been filmed by the FBI taking a bribe. But he did want to make sure that Connally would not get tripped up by small factual inconsistencies. Bobby Baker had been ruined by his petty lies on the stand. Williams was determined that Connally would not suffer from the same sloppiness.

For hours, Williams and his associates worked over Connally in Williams's conference room. (Mike Tigar, with typical mock-heroic swagger, had renamed the blue-walled chamber "the Situation Room" to convey a more warlike atmosphere.) No fact was too small or seemingly insignificant to go unmassaged. Aided by Tigar, who had returned to the firm in 1974 specifically to help on the Connally case, Williams collected every call slip, every phone bill, every bank statement, every scrap of evidence that the prosecutors could possibly use to catch Connally in a lie. In the "Situation Room," Williams played prosecutor, setting small traps for the witness. Connally had told the grand jury that he had met with Jacobsen at five o'clock in the afternoon one day at the Sheraton Crest in Austin, Texas. But a hotel waiter had told the prosecutors that he had served Connally and Jacobsen breakfast. Remembering how Bill Bittman had made Bobby Baker squirm by placing him in Las Vegas on a night Baker had said he was in Los Angeles, Williams bore into Connally about this seemingly minor inconsistency. Williams was earthy with Connally. "Remember when that shine came into your hotel room with the poached eggs? Right now that shine has got it—he's got you!" Williams put himself right in Connally's face, demanding an answer. Connally spluttered that he couldn't remember any damn waiter. No! said Williams. You can't just say you don't remember. It will seem like you're being evasive, that you're hiding something. You have to be positive, he told Connally. His client got the message. "Yes, I *do* remember that waiter," the defendant replied, with a pleasant smile. "Such a nice man. You know what, now that I think about it, I do recall. . . ."

Williams intentionally tried to provoke Connally, to get him to lash back. He used Richard Keeton, a lawyer in Connally's firm, to play prosecutor, asking needling questions that irritated Connally. "Why did you hang around with sleazebags?'' Keeton would demand. Jut-jawed and upright, Connally was full of righteous indignation about his predicament. He continued to feel that he was the victim of Watergate morality, that the rules had changed on him after the fact to make criminal what was once merely business as usual—at least in Texas. ''To be accused of taking a goddamned $10,000 bribe offended me beyond all reason,'' Connally later protested. Among cynics in the firm, there was a sneaking suspicion that Connally's indignation stemmed from the fact that he had been indicted for taking such a *small* payoff. The joke around the firm was that if the bribe had been $200,000, Williams would have believed the government, since, in Texas politics, $10,000 was a mere tip. Williams joined the laughter, though he was always careful to maintain his belief in Connally's innocence.

With rising indignation, Connally demanded that Williams subpoena Nixon's attorney general, John Mitchell, to support him. ''No!'' Williams insisted. ''No Watergate! We don't even want to *mention* Watergate to the jurors. They'll blow up the courthouse.'' Connally worked himself up into a state. ''They have spent five million dollars if they've spent a dime to ruin me! Let them blow up the courthouse!'' To defuse the moment, Williams used Mike Tigar as a foil. Tigar, who liked to boast about all the militant radicals he had defended, joked, ''You're the second client I've represented who wanted to blow up the courthouse.'' Williams cracked, ''Yeah, but the first one did it before the indictment.'' All three men had a good chuckle. ''Okay,'' said Williams, ''you can look at your family from the stand once during your testimony and say that you would never lie. But that's it. No matter how unjust you think this is, the jury won't. So don't be arrogant.''

Not all of the facts facing Connally could be easily explained away. As part of the cover-up, the prosecutors contended, Connally had given the $10,000 back to Jacobsen and told him to put the money away in a safe-deposit box. Jacobsen would then testify that he had been given the money by the milk fund, but when Connally refused to take it, he had put the cash away to be used for someone else's ''campaign contribution.'' But there was a catch, Jacobsen would testify. The first batch of bills that Connally gave him were too new. They came into circulation *after* Jacobsen received $10,000 from the milk producers. Just before the prosecutors were scheduled to open the safe-deposit box to see if the money was there, Connally had hurriedly substituted a new stack of *old* bills.

According to Jacobsen, he had moved very fast, finding the money in just a few hours. Naturally, the prosecutors wanted to know where Connally had come up with $10,000 in old bills in such a hurry.

Suspicion centered on a millionaire rancher named Rex Cauble, an old friend and frequent contributor to Connally's past campaigns. Connally's phone records showed a number of calls to Cauble on the day in question. Furthermore, bank and travel records showed Cauble withdrawing $7,500 and flying to Houston just as Connally was arriving there. Questioned about the bank draft by prosecutors, Cauble maintained that he had heard a female friend complain that she had never owned a Lincoln Continental. To surprise her, he had bought her a Mark IV. Not believing this tale for a minute, the prosecutors hoped to refresh Cauble's memory and use him as a witness against Connally. "Cauble was potentially dynamite," said Tuerkheimer. But five days before the trial the Texas high-roller suddenly clammed up and refused to cooperate. There wasn't enough time to take him before a grand jury and use the leverage of a perjury indictment. So the prosecution never called him to the stand.

What had happened? A basic Williams rule is to get as many witnesses as possible under the defense tent. Usually, this is accomplished by paying their lawyers (perfectly legal), or at least arranging for their representation. In this case, Williams got his old buddy William Hundley. The former Justice Department lawyer was now a criminal defense lawyer, renting space in Williams's building and taking many of his cases as referrals from his landlord. Hundley was as accommodating as ever. He told Cauble to keep his mouth shut.*

A week before trial, Connally noticed that the jokes had stopped in the "Situation Room." The easy camaraderie with his associates, the foolishness with Tigar, had given way to a kind of purposeful gloom. Williams was in his pretrial trance. To his friends as well he had become increasingly remote. They recognized the symptoms. "He's gone into training for the past eight weeks," Art Buchwald told *Time* magazine. "He's surly, he won't drink, and he won't go to parties. He's miserable."

---

*Connally was deeply grateful for Cauble's silence. In 1982, Cauble, who had been appointed a Special Texas Ranger by Governor Connally and often declaimed against drugs, was convicted of smuggling 108 tons of marijuana from Mexico. Before Cauble was sentenced to prison, John Connally appeared as a character witness. He described Cauble as "a man . . . who would sacrifice anything for his loyalty to his friends." Some fifteen years after the Connally case, Hundley told the author, "Cauble could have sunk Connally. But Ed sent him to me."

Trial began on April Fool's Day, 1975. Sitting in the crowded court-room, writer Larry L. King observed that Williams "appears a little glum, as if maybe his feet hurt, or he'd rather keep his next appointment." Williams was worried about the jury. He had tried to get the venue changed to Texas because, he argued, the massive pretrial publicity had polluted the jury pool. Williams had run into Spiro Agnew on the street, who bluntly told him, "I think you are going to lose. That's not saying anything against your client—I was innocent, too—but I couldn't go to trial before a bunch of black people. They wouldn't have understood." Williams shared Agnew's fears, though never publicly. In the privacy of Judge Hart's chambers, he argued that the mostly black juries of the District of Columbia would not give Connally a fair trial. Hart was not unsympathetic, but he refused to move the case.

Williams liked to scoff at lawyers who tried to choose a jury scientifically. "I take the first twelve in the box," he told reporters. "That was a lot of B.S.," said Tigar. "He carefully chose jurors. But he used his gut. We were looking for jurors who had a stake in the process, who believed in the system." Williams had his own crude demographic rules: strike Scandinavians (too pro-government) and keep Irish (pro-underdog). But these were in short supply in the District. The real issue was what type of black. He used his peremptory challenges to strike "anyone who looked like a street dude or a revolutionary—anyone who might like to see a rich white establishment type marched off in chains," observed King.

The remaining pool "looked like they could be found in a choir on Sunday mornings. Aging or aged black ladies, given to decorous dress and fruit hats and random shouts of Amen." King wrote in his notebook, "Williams will not hesitate to quote the Good Book." Williams particularly wanted a black woman who carried a Bible to court every day. He was pleased with the jury foreman, a librarian with a Ph.D. named Dennis O'Toole, who he felt confident would understand the notion of "beyond a reasonable doubt." In order to avoid flaunting Connally's wealth, he bluntly told his client to keep his gaudy, rich Texas friends out of the courtroom. For his part, Williams wore, as always, his shapeless "basic suit."

Williams did his best to play the expectations game. With reporters he went on in his usual way about the awesome power of the government overwhelming his frail and lonely client. "Doors open everywhere to the majesty of the government," he intoned. The doomsaying had some effect: The reporters covering the trial had to abandon their pool when everyone predicted a guilty verdict. Columnist William Safire noted that Watergate prosecutors had won every case before a D.C. jury, who uniformly saw prosecutors as "good guys" and Nixon as "evil." But some shrewd observers saw through Williams's game. *Newsweek* quoted a "longtime colleague" as saying, "Williams wouldn't take the case for himself unless he thought he could win it. If he didn't, he'd give it to some younger guy who needs the money."

The press sized up Williams, against his opponent, prosecutor Tuerkheimer, and pronounced a mismatch. A *New York Times* profile gushingly described Williams as "a criminal trial lawyer of the classic mold . . . in a nation where the criminal trial is a native form of drama, Edward Bennett Williams may be the consummate leading man. He does not raise his voice; he aims it. He does not so much address a jury as woo it." The press noted that Tuerkheimer's most recent trial experience consisted of representing the Sierra Club in environmental cases. Tuerkheimer was brainy (Bronx High School of Science, Columbia and New York University Law School) but utterly lacking in flair. Reporters called him "the Undertaker" and offered a $5 bounty to the first person to see him smile. The *New York Times* reported that he was once seen raising an eyebrow. Williams arrived in court in his Lincoln Continental. Tuerkheimer rode a bicycle.

Williams seemed oddly subdued when he stood to give his opening statement on April 3. He began by trying to inoculate the jury. "This is *not* a Watergate case," he stated. Connally "did not stonewall it," he said, using the Watergate term to describe Connally's otherwise unavoidable compliance with subpoenas. Williams wanted none of the drama—or stench—of Watergate to attach to the Connally case. Indeed, he was intentionally dull. He rambled on for several hours about milk price supports, baffling the jury and putting reporters to sleep. By being boring, Williams was "brilliant," Tuerkheimer later observed. "He took the sizzle out of the tape."

The "tape"—an essential accoutrement of a Watergate trial—was a recording of Connally beseeching President Nixon to raise price supports for the milk producers. The conversation had been picked up by Nixon's fatal Oval Office tape recorders on March 23, 1971. The tapes threatened Connally by bringing the recently deposed president's whiny voice into the courtroom as the two pols discussed the need to placate the powerful farm lobby.

There was no mention of payoffs on the tapes, however, no "smoking gun"—at least not on the tapes that the jury heard. The jury was not allowed to hear a recording of a far more damaging conversation that took place between Connally and the President. After the formal meeting on milk price supports broke up that day in March 1971, Connally had asked to speak privately with Nixon. "It's on my honor to make sure there's a very substantial amount of oil in Texas that will be at your discretion," the treasury secretary said. "Fine," said Nixon. "This is a cold political deal," Nixon continued. "They're very tough political operators." "And they've got it," Connally said. "They've got it," Nixon agreed. "Mr. President," Connally concluded, "I really think you made the right decision."

Within a few days, the dairy lobby had coughed up a pledge of $2 million to Nixon's reelection campaign—and the administration had come out in favor of milk price supports. Before trial, Tuerkheimer had strongly argued that Nixon and Connally were discussing the quid pro quo for the President's support of the milk producers. The words were coded and cryptic, but the meaning was clear in light of what was said before and what happened after. Tuerkheimer translated "oil" as Texas-speak for money. But Williams just as strongly objected to admitting the tape into evidence. The tape was of poor quality and hard to hear. It was confusing and ultimately irrelevant, he said, since any payoffs mentioned were not for Connally but rather for Nixon. Once again, Judge Hart sided with Williams. He ruled that the tape was inadmissible.

The prosecution did have some strong circumstantial evidence—bank records supported Jacobsen's account of making and withdrawing deposits of money before and after his meeting with Connally. But ultimately, the case boiled down to Jacobsen's word that Connally had taken the money. It was necessary, therefore, for Williams to destroy Jacobsen as a witness.

In many ways, Jacobsen was just like Bobby Baker, a slick and ubiquitous hanger-on to Lyndon Johnson. He had been a "high-rent valet" for LBJ, picking out the right music to play on the presidential yacht, making sure Johnson's tailor arrived on time. Jacobsen himself was always tanned and carefully groomed. He was honey-voiced, quietly smarmy. "He looks like a guy who has just had his fingernails polished," wrote the *Washington Star*. He wanted to be seen as a Texas wheeler-dealer, but he had grown up a poor Jewish boy in New Jersey. His first name was really Emmanuel, but when he moved to Texas he changed his name to E. Jake Jacobsen; "Manny" had become "Jake." In 1973, Jacobsen went bankrupt, unable to pay $12 million in bills. The same year he was charged with defrauding a savings and loan in San Angelo. Faced with up to thirty-five years in jail, Jacobsen had made a deal: In exchange for leniency, he would testify against John Connally.

The spectators began lining up at 4:00 A.M. to see Williams cross-examine Jacobsen. Six hundred people—lawyers, law students, Watergate buffs, a smattering of the rich and famous—patiently vied for ninety seats. The press had played the cross-examination as the critical show-down of the trial, if not the most dramatic courtroom confrontation of the decade. "It was supposed to be the great face off, the cobra versus the mongoose," wrote Mary McGrory in the *Washington Star*.

Williams looked "a little pale and puffy" as he paced the courtroom before Jacobsen took the stand, wrote McGrory. After getting only four hours of sleep a night for weeks, he had succumbed to the flu. Williams was chronically apprehensive before trial, but his partners had never seen him so nervous. He was so preoccupied that when spoken to, he just stared back, lost in thought.

But Williams's anxiety at the prospect of cross-examining Jacobsen was nothing compared to Jacobsen's at being questioned by Williams. A *Texas Monthly* article described the government's star witness "peering warily, cowering almost," his mouth "tightly pinched." Writer Larry L. King likened Jake to "an astonished lizard." Williams started in by leading Jacobsen to admit that he faced thirty-five years for fraud and conspiracy in Texas. Hadn't Jacobsen turned on his friends to save himself? Hadn't he even offered evidence against Lyndon Johnson to curry favor with the prosecutors? In a small voice, Jacobsen answered, "No." The courtroom audience stirred at the mention of the former president. Here, surely, came a bombshell from the Great Defender. . . .

But the mention of Lyndon Johnson was the only drama of the day. Williams did not follow up. Rather, he merely read from Jacobsen's copious testimony to the grand jury. "It was Sominex from the spell-binder," wrote McGrory. "Visiting lawyers dozed off and reporters worked on crossword puzzles hidden in their notebooks."

In fact, Williams was once again dull by design. He did not want to have a confrontational square-off against the government's witness. "There was a tremendous temptation to show off for the press," recalled Brendan Sullivan. "Instead, Ed was a bore. Jake was a terribly dangerous witness. One false step and you're dead. So before the trial, Ed said, 'I'm going to put a bridle on him.' '' The "no" Jacobsen gave Williams in response to his question about LBJ was about the only negative answer Jacobsen gave Williams in two days of cross-examination. Mostly, Williams asked leading questions, and Jacobsen answered in the affirmative. "It was a study in tedium," Williams later recalled. "Tedium! Because I never let him give me any answer except yes. Yes, yes, yes—all through the cross-examination, I never let him get out of control. I was slowly chipping him to death, and he knew it.''

Like every move he made during the trial, Williams's methodical questioning of Jacobsen was aimed at building a foundation for closing argument. Williams had drafted the notes for his summation *before* trial. The draft would change during the course of the trial, but it served as a road map to the evidence Williams sought to elicit. Williams disdained cross-examiners he called "truth seekers—they just shake the Christmas tree and hope something good falls off. Usually more bad stuff comes off than good." Instead, Williams put a bridle on witnesses "so taut that all they can do is follow your lead, answering your questions, yes or no." Like a pointillist painter, Williams was putting small dots on a canvas that would, in the end, paint a devastating portrait of the witness.

Williams's mastery and control can be illustrated by his questioning of Jacobsen on the seemingly insignificant question about the gloves John Connally had worn, specifically, the rubber gloves—or glove—that Connally wore when he gave Jacobsen $10,000 to put back in his safe-deposit box to conceal the crime. Was the glove beige or yellow? Jacobsen could not recall. It might have been white. Where was the glove?

JACOBSEN: I believe the rubber glove or gloves was on the side of the money, not on top of the money.

Williams pointed out that Jacobsen had testified before the grand jury that Connally wore only one glove. When did he change his mind and decide that Connally might have worn two gloves?

JACOBSEN: Between the time I testified before the grand jury and the time I testified here.
WILLIAMS: (Pause) What was it that changed your recollection?
JACOBSEN: Just the logic of it. . . .
WILLIAMS: (Another pause) It was the logic of it, is that right?

A slight edge of sarcasm had crept into Williams's voice. Yes, replied Jacobsen.

> WILLIAMS: Was that because, Mr. Jacobsen, the prosecutors pointed out to you that nobody could count money with one glove on one hand and a big pile?

Having shown that Jacobsen would tailor his testimony to "logic"—or presumably anything—Williams asked Jacobsen to count the $10,000 himself. The jurors—none of whom had ever seen so much cash in their lives—were treated to the sight of a self-confessed bagman sorting through large stacks of cash, in piles of twenties, fifties, and hundreds. The impact was devastating. "Williams made Jake seem like a lowlife, sleazy and slippery," said Dennis O'Toole, the jury foreman.

Williams himself came across as "natural and easy," recalled O'Toole. Williams was always careful to seem low key and affable in the courtroom. He rarely hectored witnesses or showed off, and he saved his histrionics for closing arguments. "He had a human touch," said O'Toole. "His face was mobile, expressions crossed it easily. He didn't seem at all coached."

In fact, of course, Williams was completely rehearsed. He was working twelve hours a day. He ate one meal—a steak at the Palm at 5:30—and headed back home to work some more. He had a drink with his meal but no more—until Thursday night. Judge Hart did not sit on Fridays, so Williams treated Thursday night as "Saturday night," recalled Richard Keeton, the Houston lawyer who had helped prepare Connally. Keeton remembered watching boxing movies with Williams in his basement one Thursday night after trial. After polishing off a pitcher of martinis, Williams leaped to his feet and starting throwing punches at the flickering figures on his screen, looking for all the world like he was ready to rip off Jake Jacobsen's head.

One day during a court recess, Williams found himself standing next to Jacobsen at a row of urinals, a vulnerable place, thinking that he would have to destroy this weak and vain man beside him. He told his children that evening that he lamented this necessity. Any man's character, he said, is fragile.

John Connally came to the stand on April 15, elegantly dressed and coiffed as always, strong-jawed and resolute. As he walked across the courtroom, he looked like "a two-million-dollar shipment of silver," wrote Larry L. King. Jacobsen had stared down at the floor and mumbled. Connally sat straight up and spoke crisply. Williams led him through a rapid-fire exchange, asking directly if the accusations against him were true. Did he ask Jacobsen for money? "I did not!" Connally declared, his voice ringing across the packed chamber.

Connally was, his biographer James Reston, Jr., wrote, "a dream witness: coherent, succinct, immensely impressive. His denial was total and it was spoken unhesitatingly, as if from the heart." In the jury box, Foreman O'Toole believed that his task had been made simple. He had been instructed about the standard of "beyond a reasonable doubt." As O'Toole understood his instructions, he was not to guess at what really happened, but only to consider the evidence presented. It was the difference between truth and *legal* truth. Whatever the real truth, O'Toole knew, when he heard Connally's testimony, that he had "reasonable doubts."

Williams knew Judge Hart would instruct the jurors that testimony of good character could, by itself, create a reasonable doubt. Williams was eager to sow those doubts by putting on a stunning parade of character witnesses to testify for Connally. One by one, they took the stand: LBJ's widow, Lady Bird Johnson; former secretary of defense Robert McNamara; former secretary of state Dean Rusk; presidential advisers James Rowe and Robert Strauss. . . . They were all Democrats, speaking of "Mr. Roosevelt" and Harry, Jack and Lyndon. No one ever mentioned Richard Nixon. Particularly effective with the mostly black jury was Congresswoman Barbara Jordan of Texas, whose husky eloquence had helped to impeach Nixon when she served on the House Judiciary Committee in the Watergate summer of 1974. (In 1968, Jordan had responded to Connally's favorite son presidential candidacy by remarking, "Why that son of a bitch. How does he think he can be anyone's favorite anything?" Jordan agreed to appear as a character witness for Connally as a political favor for Democratic party chairman Bob Strauss.)

Williams had been a little apprehensive about putting on another witness, Reverend Billy Graham. A white preacher and a black jury? A Southern Baptist? Graham's "a little flaky isn't he?" Williams had asked his associates. Didn't he say that Richard Nixon had been brainwashed in Red China?

Williams was still feeling uneasy when Graham, wearing pancake makeup and a rub-on suntan, climbed into the witness box.

"What is your work at the present time, sir?" asked Williams.

"I am an evangelist, preaching the gospel of Jesus Christ all over the world," replied Graham.

From the jury box came a distinctly audible "A-a-men." It was the elderly black lady who had come to the jury voir dire carrying a Bible. Williams had to turn away from the jury to hide his smile. "I thought that 'A-a-men' was a good sign," he later deadpanned to reporters. Eugene McCarthy told Williams, "You ought to put that show on the road. You wouldn't lose a case."

Tuerkheimer was a beaten man. His closing argument was apologetic, almost pleading. He asked the jury to "understand that this is not a contest among lawyers. It is your job to determine the facts of the case, not to decide whether Edward Bennett Williams or any of us is a better lawyer. I don't think there'd be much contest on that point. I hope you don't hold any inadequacies on our part against the government or prosecution in this case." The judge had to ask him to use a microphone so the jury could hear him.

Williams dropped his measured tone for the summation. He roared and whispered and turned red in the face. He attacked Tuerkheimer: "The prosecution's case is in a shambles! A wreck!" He took a last swipe at Jacobsen: "Sordid, despicable, mendacious, noxious, heinous . . . spewing forth a litany of lies. . . ." Echoing his assault on John Cye Cheasty in the Hoffa trial, he declared, "The words *lie* and *liar* do not flow easily from my lips. They are ugly words. . . ." He was solemn: "Have we reached the point in our society where scoundrels can escape their punishment if only they inculpate others? If so we should mark it well. Today it is John Connally. Tomorrow it may be you or me." As he usually did, he quoted from the Bible, likening his cross-examination of Jacobsen to the story of Susanna and the Elders in the Book of Daniel—the "first recorded cross-examination," as he put it. His final plea was straight out of thirty years of closing arguments: "I ask you to lift at last the pain and anguish, the humiliation, the ostracism and suffering, the false accusation, the innuendo, the vilification and slander for John Connally and his family. And if you do, the United States will win the day."

Williams maneuvered for advantage to the end. "Stand in front of me!" he commanded Tigar as they walked into the judge's chambers to deliver the exhibits that would be sent to the jury room. Williams was busily putting paper clips on Jacobsen's bankruptcy statement, which showed that he had kept the $10,000 payoff. By this point, it was all overkill. The jury deliberated six hours. The first vote was nine to three to acquit; by day's end, the jury was unanimous.

As Foreman O'Toole read the verdict, Williams grabbed Tigar's leg under the table. "This makes up for the last time," he said in a fierce whisper. The shame of Bobby Baker had been expunged; Williams was, in his own phrase, "numero uno" again. Nellie Connally hugged Williams; her husband thanked the jury and began discussing his political future with reporters.

That night, Williams got gloriously drunk at the victory party, held at Bob Strauss's apartment at the Watergate. Nixon's successor, President Gerald Ford, called to congratulate Connally; then Richard Nixon called. He asked to speak to Williams. "I wish you were my lawyer," he said. "It's too bad you represented the *Post*." Nixon invited Williams to come visit him in exile in San Clemente. Williams thanked him, not pausing to inquire if Nixon had removed his name from the enemies list. Then he hung up and stumbled over to his host, the chairman of the Democratic party.

"Fuck you, Strauss," he said, "I'm representing *Richard Nixon*." To Tigar, he said, "You know, I *should* be Nixon's lawyer." Tigar, still the dissident, responded, "Ed, when was the last time you went out to try a case alone?" It was a few weeks later that Williams made his remarkable assertion that if he had been Nixon's lawyer, he would have advised him to burn the Oval Office tapes on the White House lawn.

Williams's children had never seen him so gleeful, laughing and shouting. "I can't believe it!" he exulted. *People* magazine came out to Williams's stately new house in Potomac and photographed him surrounded by his happy family. The magazine pronounced him "the greatest criminal lawyer of his time," and said that the Connally verdict had put to rest the doubts of "old admirers in the legal fraternity" who had wondered if "he could still win a really Big One." The magazine quoted Thomas "Tommy the Cork" Corcoran on Williams's performances. "Pure opera, boy," said the old fixer.

The inevitable post-trial blues set in after a few days. "At the end of every case like this, I feel I've shortened my life another notch," he told *People*. To other reporters, he hinted that he was thinking of leaving the law. "I'm going to take sixty days to canvass all the options I have open to me," he said. He was thinking of running for the U.S. Senate.

Chapter Twenty-Eight

WILLIAMS HATED WORKING with other lawyers, at least those whom he could not control. To him, working with co-counsel on a case was "like watering down fine wine," said Brendan Sullivan. "He thought other lawyers just got in the way. They were Slobodkins! They were just going to screw up his artistry." But as Williams's clients became increasingly wealthy, they inevitably brought along their own high-priced counsel. Their presence helps explain Williams's episodic disaffection from the law in the mid-seventies.

The billionaire oilman Armand Hammer was swept up in the Watergate net in 1975, charged with trying to disguise a $100,000 personal contribution to the Nixon campaign by giving it under another name. Hammer hired Williams, who set about cutting a deal with the Special Prosecutor's Office, as he routinely did in these campaign contribution cases. But in court, as he stood up to plead to a minor felony, the irascible old entrepreneur balked. Hammer wanted to be assured that the sentence would not carry jail time. Williams watched in dismay as the judge threatened to throw out the whole plea bargain Williams had carefully concocted with the prosecutor. Hammer and his lawyers retired to discuss the matter. Hammer had brought along Louis Nizer, Williams's old nemesis. When Nizer sided with Hammer on rejecting the plea, Williams exploded. The shouting was so loud that it could be heard out in the hallway. A clerk of the court had to ask the feuding lawyers to be quiet. In a huff, Williams quit the case.

In the fall of 1975, Williams was offered a starring role in the most

328

overexposed trial of the decade. The parents of Patty Hearst asked Williams to represent the fugitive heiress, who stood accused of robbing banks with her kidnappers in the Symbionese Liberation Army (SLA). The case, with all its lurid trappings of sex and revolution, would hold the nation's attention for months. Williams turned it down. The Hearsts had already hired Vincent Hallinan, a leading radical lawyer. Worse, they were also talking to F. Lee Bailey. "I won't work with those lawyers," Williams told his partners. "You can't control them." He heaped scorn on Bailey for appearing on late-night TV shows, publishing *Gallery* magazine (a knockoff of *Playboy*), and getting divorced twice before marrying a stewardess. Williams was delighted when Bailey lost.

Williams also turned down a celebrated case closer to home. Marvin Mandel, the governor of Maryland, was indicted for racketeering, and he naturally wanted the man who had rescued John Connally. "We begged Ed to take Mandel," said Bill Hundley, who was representing a co-defendant. "But he thought the case was a loser. He hated cases with multiple defendants. There'd always be a defense lawyer he couldn't handle who'd go off on a little photo op of his own. Ed would never come into a case without total control over everyone." Williams's partners cite another drawback to representing Mandel: They weren't sure Mandel could pay his legal fees.

Williams didn't want to represent politicians anymore. In his more manic moments, he wanted to be one. After a few drinks, he sometimes wanted to be the president of the United States. He was constantly being pushed by one of his wealthy clients, Louis Wolfson, to run for the White House. Wolfson offered to raise money for him and pay for a national poll to show that he had high name recognition. In New York, a longtime court watcher named John Kennedy (no relation to the president) was gathering letters from various media luminaries, ranging from Norman Mailer to James Reston of the *New York Times*, supporting the idea of a Williams-for-President candidacy. Having personally come to know presidential candidates, Williams not unreasonably thought he could do a better job. He was particularly fed up with Ed Muskie, his candidate in 1972, for weeping during the New Hampshire primary and then quitting the race. At a private meeting at his home, Williams had angrily lectured Muskie: "You never pull out! You never give up! You never accept defeat!"

With his friends and partners, he liked to fantasize. Can you run for president, he'd wonder, without ever having run for office before? The other lawyers had learned not to take this sort of question too seriously. Steve Porter, a lawyer in the firm assigned to drive Williams home from the Christmas party in 1971, recalled Williams carrying on about how Muskie had promised to make him attorney general. Williams was on one of his extreme highs, and he turned to Porter, a young tax lawyer, and said with a straight face, "And you! You've done such a good job, we're going to make you secretary of the treasury!" The next morning Porter cheerfully said hello to Williams. The senior partner, hung over and moody, rudely ignored him. As Williams turned his back, Porter demanded, "What the hell kind of way is that to treat your secretary of the treasury?"

Williams's dream of running for the Senate from Maryland was not so implausible, and there were some who thought he might give it a go. As early as 1973, Williams had been rumored as a candidate for the seat held by J. Glenn Beall, a feckless Maryland Republican. David Brinkley was taken aback one day in early 1975 when Williams asked him if he would quit his job as network anchorman to become Williams's campaign press secretary. Brendan Sullivan did his best to discourage Williams from running. "You want to see what it's like?" he asked. "Go to the Safeway and spend thirty minutes shaking hands at the end of the aisle. You want to do that for two years?" Williams sheepishly said no. In June 1975, at the end of the sixty days Williams had set aside after the Connally trial to consider his "many options," he put out the word that he would not run for the Senate after all.

Williams had been pushed to run by Bob Strauss, the Democrats' national party chairman. The two men had met at a New Year's Eve party at Duke Zeibert's in 1971 and become natural allies. Strauss was noisy, funny, and outspoken in a gravelly southern voice that always held the promise of inside information. To him all women were "darlins" and all men were "sumbitches." Like Williams, he had been socially snubbed in his early years. He complained to Williams that for years he had lived three blocks from the Dallas Country Club and never been allowed to join. Williams, the Chevy Chase Club reject, understood the feeling.

Strauss had persuaded Williams to serve as the party's national treasurer in 1974. "I made him do it," recalled Strauss. "His partners were against it." The party was $9 million in debt after George McGovern's landslide loss in 1972, and Strauss thought that Williams would be a good fund-raiser. "He could put on a good act," said Strauss. Williams, always ready with a favor for the powerful, had helped soothe Strauss's strained relations with the labor unions. He courted Al Barkan, the AFL-CIO's political director, who had been denigrating Strauss as a Texas yahoo. Barkan started complaining about the union's lack of seating and parking at RFK Stadium; Williams took the hint, and relations between the party chairman and organized labor improved thereafter.

Williams had performed a more important favor for Strauss during Watergate by saving him from a criminal indictment. Eager to show their nonpartisanship, the Watergate prosecutors had begun to investigate a $50,000 contribution to the Democrats from Ashland Oil that Strauss, as party head, had failed to properly disclose. Williams went off to see Leon Jaworski, the special prosecutor, and his staff. Williams complained that Strauss was vulnerable to prosecution because of a mere technical error that Congress had made drafting the law. Pacing back and forth, Williams gave a high-minded speech to the assembled lawyers, most of them graduates of Harvard and Yale, about equal protection and due process. Watching this show, Harry McPherson, another lawyer representing the Democrats, decided to chime in. He adopted Williams's manner and tone of high indignation and righteousness. It was morally unjust, McPherson insisted, to hang Strauss on a "mere lacuna of the law."

In the elevator down, Williams looked over at McPherson. "Lacuna," he said. "Fuck." The two had a good laugh. Then Williams went over to the Justice Department, which was also considering a criminal case against Strauss. The Justice Department lawyers were a different crowd from the young law review editors at the Special Prosecutor's Office. Most were Irish Catholics whom Williams had known for years. With them, Williams was "all Harp," said McPherson, "salty and funny and profane. It was Mozart in one hall, rock 'n' roll in the other." Strauss was never charged.

Williams was a better criminal lawyer then party operative. The endless political meetings were boring and frustrating. His three years as Democratic party treasurer "soured him," said Bill Ragan, a friend from Georgetown days. "He wasn't in control, he wasn't in the limelight, he wasn't accomplishing anything." Pamela Harriman, the new and politically ambitious wife of Democratic gray eminence Averell Harriman, watched Williams pace uneasily about at a Democratic National Committee meeting at his house in Potomac in 1974. "He seemed uneasy, restless. I think he didn't really like politics because he couldn't manipulate them."

Williams was an avid player when it came to arm twisting in smoke-filled rooms, but he had no patience for the slow and cumbersome business of putting together electoral majorities. "To succeed in politics, you have to build networks of boring people," said R. W. Apple, the *New York Times* political correspondent. "Running for office is nothing but the institutionalization of cocktail parties, and Ed hated that."

At a midterm meeting of the Democratic National Committee in 1974, Williams had accosted Apple in the hallway of the Mayflower Hotel. The McGovernites were seizing control of the party and changing the rules. They wanted to take power away from the insiders—like Williams—and give it instead to "the people," mostly by setting quotas for women and minorities at the 1976 Democratic convention. "This is a fucking disaster," Williams told Apple. A few months later, Strauss and Williams stayed up all night at the Muehlebach Hotel in Kansas City, Missouri, trying to beat back the move for quotas. They lost.

Williams had bitterly watched the nomination of George McGovern in 1972. He was sitting with Bob Strauss as the convention droned on into the wee hours of the morning. A major contributor to McGovern stood up in the seat in front of Williams. "If McGovern gets elected, which I doubt," Williams told Strauss, "I'll make a million. That"—he pointed to the man in front—"will be the first SOB who gets indicted for stealing, and he'll come to me." In disgust, Williams got up and left the hall before McGovern arrived to make his acceptance speech.

By expressing his disgust with the Democratic party to the chief political writer of the *New York Times*, Williams was not exactly being discreet. Among those interested to read about Williams's disenchantment was the president of the United States, Gerald Ford. "I decided to woo him a bit," said Ford. Despite the fact that he was still the treasurer of the Democratic party, Ed Williams began to receive invitations to White House functions. Williams was even less circumspect with the president. "He told me the McGovernites were ruining his party," Ford said.

Ford had begun calling Williams just to chat—about football and politics at first. "He relaxed me," said Ford. As time went on, Ford would enlist Williams's help in protecting the national security establishment, which had come under siege after Watergate. Williams genuinely liked Ford, according to Agnes Williams. "He resented all those jokes impugning Ford's intelligence," she said. Williams liked the fact that Ford called him by his full name—"Edward." Only his mother had called him Edward before. He was very pleased and proud when Ford gave him a

White House pass. He liked to show the laminated badge to his children. "Can you believe it?" he'd ask with a kind of wonder that, to his children, seemed childlike. His family was struck by his reverence for the institution of the presidency. Even after Ford left office, Williams remained "awed by him," said his son Bennett. For all his worldliness, Williams would throughout his life hold a certain reverence for positions of great authority. In the mid-1970s, he set about to collect the signatures of every president and chief justice, paying as much as $15,000 for a letter signed by an ancient chief executive (he tried as well to collect a letter from Al Capone, but never found one). Cardinals and presidents caused Williams to bow. While he represented the rights of the accused, he never lost the regard for hierarchy and power that the Jesuits had instilled in him.

The abuse of power was the predominant political issue in America in the mid-1970s. Few prominent men were exempt from public scrutiny. Henry Kissinger, Ford's secretary of state (and a frequent visitor to the owners box at RFK Stadium), was embroiled in lawsuits for bugging government officials he suspected of leaking to the newspapers. Although Kissinger was defended in these suits by the Justice Department, he began to consult Williams informally. "Henry always used to talk to me because he thought the lawyers at Justice were so bad," Williams told Robert Pack. Williams enjoyed describing how Kissinger would call Edward Levi, the attorney general, and tell him, "I'm sitting here with Edward Bennett Williams, and he says . . ." Levi was irked at the second guessing from Kissinger's hired gun. (In fact, Williams was not paid.) "You haven't committed murder, have you, Henry?" the attorney general would ask. Kissinger was so impressed with Williams that he began talking to him about "other matters," ranging from personnel questions to dealings with Congress. "Williams had a great PR sense, and he knew how to cut to the chase," said Kissinger. "He had great insights into how Washington really works."

Having deposed a president, congressional investigators and prize-hungry reporters turned to other bastions of heretofore entrenched authority, like the CIA. The headlines in 1975 promised sensational stories about the Agency's "Family Jewels"—two decades of CIA assassination plots against foreign leaders and illegal spying on U.S. citizens. Watergate had changed all the rules: Skulduggery that had once been winked at under the doctrine of "plausible deniability" was now the subject of congressional hearings and indignant editorials.

At the White House, Ford listened to the baying and worried about the future of the CIA. Congressmen were talking about creating a special committee to probe the Agency. With columnists inveighing against the "Imperial Presidency," the balance of power was swinging back to Capitol Hill. What should the president do? Ford asked Ed Williams. Appoint your own commission, Williams answered. Get ahead of the curve. Ford responded by creating the Rockefeller Commission, under his vice president, Nelson Rockefeller, to propose reforms in the intelligence community. The commission was not able to entirely dull the sting of congressional investigations, but at least it showed that the White House was not on the defensive.

"The Rockefeller Commission was a great idea," said Ford. "Edward had great intuitive ability to analyze public and press reaction." Ford decided to ask Williams to help the intelligence community on a more permanent basis. On November 1, 1975, he asked Williams to become the director of the Central Intelligence Agency.

Williams told Ford that he was "surprised and flattered" by the offer. Williams hated surprises, even flattering ones. He was given only one day to make up his mind; Ford wanted to announce a cabinet shuffle on November 3. At the law firm, Joe Califano urged him to take the job. The Democrats were sure to win in 1976, Califano said, and Williams would be a shoo-in for secretary of state. Williams listened warily. He suspected that Califano wanted him out of the law firm so that *he* could take over. At home that night, Williams told his children that to take the job would mean selling the Redskins. "No!" they chorused. Agnes told her husband that he'd never be able to keep secrets.

The next morning, Williams declined the president's offer. (Ford's second choice, U.S. Ambassador to China George Bush, instantly accepted the job, and began signing notes to friends, "Head Spook.") The reasons he gave were numerous and varied. To former CIA director Richard Helms, Williams was flip. "I can't keep my mouth shut," he said. Helms didn't believe him. Years later, Williams told Helms he did not want to sell off his real estate holdings. Williams told Buchwald and Bradlee that he couldn't afford to take the CIA job. Mike Miskovsky, an old friend of Williams's and a longtime lawyer for the CIA, probably comes closer to the real reason: "Ed knew he'd be a bad bureaucrat. He'd be too impatient. He didn't want to get caught doing anything illegal. He had a cautious streak, and the Agency was a lousy place to be after those Hill investigations."

As a consolation prize, Williams was given a seat on the President's Foreign Intelligence Advisory Board. One of the steps taken by the president in the wake of the CIA scandals was to create a board of prominent citizens charged with keeping an eye on the intelligence community. There had been such advisory panels in the past, but they had been weak watchdogs. Ford made sure this one would have some force by stocking it with prominent citizens, including Edward Teller, the nuclear scientist; former defense secretary Melvin Laird; and Edward Land, the chairman of Polaroid. Williams was pleased to be put in the company of these men, and even happier to be made privy to the deepest secrets of all, the most highly classified operations of the intelligence agencies.

The CIA and FBI scandals had exposed massive wiretapping and eavesdropping on American citizens. At the Justice Department, Attorney General Edward Levi was charged with cleaning up the abuses. He set about drafting guidelines and procedures under which the National Security Agency (NSA) could listen in on American phone calls. Drawing the proper line was not easy. Although domestic wiretapping had been banned by the Supreme Court, the court had ducked the issue of whether warrants were required for wiretaps aimed at catching foreign spies. Levi and his men tried to strike a balance, allowing certain eavesdropping to continue, but only after high-level approval. The Justice Department also wanted to sharply limit the dissemination of names and information picked up by eavesdropping. The Department did not want a national security tap that picked up the voice of, say, a senator, sent over to the White House where it could be used for political blackmail.

These new rules had to be cleared by the President's Foreign Intelligence Advisory Board, which had become known in the alphabet soup of Washington by its acronym, PFIAB (pronounced Piff-ee-ab). A delegation from the Justice Department, led by Solicitor General Robert Bork, presented their proposals to this august panel in a secure conference room in the Old Executive Office Building in July 1976. Bork was particularly worried about the reaction of Edward Bennett Williams. He was afraid the great civil libertarian would say the new rules did not go nearly far enough to protect the privacy rights of American citizens.

Sure enough, as Bork outlined the new rules, he could see Williams growing agitated at the other end of the long mahogany table. Williams was the first to speak up. The delegation from the Justice Department stirred uneasily. "Uh oh, here it comes," thought one of Attorney General Levi's special assistants.

"These guidelines," said Williams, growing red in the face and banging the table, "they *gag* and *shackle* the intelligence gathering of the United States! They are excessive and legally unwarranted!" Williams went on to insist that the intelligence community must have a free hand to counter the Soviet threat. The *Soviets* spy and steal our secrets. The U.S. government cannot just sit back helplessly and let them. Williams was particularly incensed by rules that prohibited the government from listening in on what the Soviets were picking up with their own electronic surveillance devices in the United States. A vast web of Soviet listening devices was monitoring calls from Washington and New York. The Soviet eavesdropping, known as "the Waldorf link," presented a real threat to U.S. security, said Williams. It made no sense to him that the Soviets could tap our phones but we couldn't even listen in to check on what they were hearing.

Across the table, Bork and the other Justice Department lawyers were dumbfounded. Here was the man who just a few years before had appeared before the U.S. Supreme Court arguing against the use of warrantless wiretaps to catch foreign spies. Williams had been representing two Soviet spies, Igor Ivanov and J. W. Butenko, who had been convicted of stealing national security secrets. Williams wanted their arrests thrown out because they had been caught by illegal wiretaps. Williams had been unequivocal: "The Founding Fathers," he had told the high court, "did not make any exception in the Fourth Amendment with respect to spy catchers or subversive hunters." True, he was acting as an advocate, but surely these views were his own as well. He had made countless speeches defending the right to privacy against wiretapping. Indeed, in his book, *One Man's Freedom*, Williams had specifically denounced the use of electronic eavesdropping to catch spies. "We defeat our own ends if we adopt the techniques of totalitarianism in security cases," he wrote.

Trying to explain this contradiction years later, some of Williams's law partners just smiled. "Ed had a remarkable way of drawing lines," said Greg Craig, who worked with Williams on national security cases. Mike Tigar, who wrote the brief in *Ivanov*, insisted that Williams drew a distinction between electronic eavesdropping that is used to spy on the Russians, and eavesdropping that is used to convict spies in court. Williams believed that the former was unfortunate but necessary. The Cold War was a jungle; if the Russians played dirty, then the United

States had to fight back with the same low blows—but *not* in the courtroom. The courtroom was a sacred place, Williams believed. It should never be sullied by such things as bugs and taps. It was one thing to spy on someone—even a U.S. citizen. But the fruits of that spying should never be used to send someone to jail—even a Russian spy.

This is too clever by half. The main reason illegally obtained evidence is excluded from the courtroom is to discourage law enforcement from breaking the law. It is not to keep the courtroom somehow "pure." It is certainly not to spare the criminally accused from going to jail. Rather, it is to protect the underlying right—in this case, privacy, which is guaranteed by the Fourth Amendment's freedom from "unreasonable search and seizure." The law recognizes that sometimes the guilty must go free to serve a broader purpose, such as protecting the sanctity of the home. But the end is safeguarding privacy, not sparing the guilty.

In fact, of course, Williams was not always the civil libertarian he appeared to be. The liberty he really cared about was that of his clients. He was mostly interested in keeping his clients out of jail by winning cases, and the Bill of Rights was a useful tool toward that end. When they conflicted with some other goal—for example, fighting communism—Williams was willing to sacrifice civil liberties. As he grew more conservative in the 1970s, Williams became increasingly hawkish on foreign policy, a complete skeptic about the so-called "detente" between the United States and the Soviet Union.

Agnes Williams believes that her husband changed his mind about electronic eavesdropping as a result of his PFIAB experience. "He would come home from those meetings and tell me how concerned he was about the extent of Soviet eavesdropping in this country," she said. "He believed that we had to fight fire with fire."

Attorney General Levi was shocked when he was informed of Williams's opposition to the new restrictions on national security eavesdropping. "I was surprised to find this great liberal opposing what I thought was a reasonable approach," he said. Hearing of Williams's objections, President Ford asked him to make his case to the cabinet. Williams made an impassioned plea against fettering the CIA in its struggle against the Kremlin. He quoted Justice Robert Jackson: "The Constitution is not a suicide pact."

Williams was hostile to Levi, whom he regarded as a prissy law professor, and he was particularly cross at Levi for firing some of his Irish cronies in the Internal Security section. Ford listened with bemusement. After the debate, he asked Williams to stay behind in the Oval Office. The former Michigan center wanted to talk football. But when it came time to sign off on the new eavesdropping rules, Ford went along with his attorney general.

Chapter Twenty-Nine

RICHARD HELMS WATCHED the investigators move in on the CIA with growing trepidation. For almost thirty years, he had worked for the Central Intelligence Agency, eight of them as director. He was, to use his biographer's words, the "Man Who Kept the Secrets." Helms knew all there was to know about the Agency, and he was increasingly worried that he would be made an example of by zealous reformers.

In early 1976, Helms learned that the Justice Department was probing the 1971 CIA break-in of a photo shop in Alexandria, Virginia. The black-bag job had been intended to recover secret documents that, the Agency feared, were being fed by a low-level CIA employee to her live-in boyfriend, a Cuban agent. Helms had authorized the break-in. Now he feared that he would be charged with a criminal civil rights violation. At the suggestion of Clark Clifford, Helms called Ed Williams from Tehran, where he had gone as ambassador after retiring from the Agency in 1973. What should he do? Williams did not hesitate. He liked Helms, and he wanted to protect the CIA. "Stop worrying about all this," he said. "If they go after you I'll defend you personally."

Williams paid a visit to Harold "Ace" Tyler, the deputy attorney general. Williams knew Tyler, a former judge. He had argued before him in New York federal court and socialized with him at judicial conferences. (Williams offered his services to hold seminars on criminal law for the judges; it was an excellent way to get to know them.) Williams argued to Tyler that the CIA had a right to protect itself—even to the point of violating the Fourth Amendment. In the defense of national security, it

339

was perfectly permissible for the Agency to do what the police could not do to solve an ordinary crime. "Williams was astute. He knew how to play me," recalled Tyler. "He knew what was worrying me: How could you expect an American jury to believe that the CIA could not order its troops to bust in on an employee who was giving secrets to her commie lover?" The Justice Department decided not to indict. The *Washington Post* quoted Williams praising the Justice Department for "an unusually smart decision." He told Bob Woodward, "If the government has a right to conduct electronic surveillance, then it has the right to make surreptitious entry." Thus did Williams, the civil libertarian, bootstrap government break-ins on top of bugging.

Despite Williams's persuasiveness, Helms was still not home free. Congress was putting tremendous pressure on the new Carter administration to offer up some heads in the CIA scandals. In early 1977, Helms was informed that he was under investigation for lying to the Senate Foreign Relations Committee in 1973 about CIA involvement in the 1970 Chilean elections. Weighing his oath of secrecy to the Agency, Helms had denied that the CIA had worked with a multinational corporation, ITT, in a failed effort to prevent leftist candidate Salvador Allende from winning. The Justice Department was preparing an eight-count perjury indictment. Once more, Helms went to Williams for help. If what Williams did for John Connally serves as a textbook for advocacy in open court, what Williams did for Richard Helms is a model for maneuvering behind closed doors.

Williams prided himself on inside knowledge. He knew exactly what CIA witnesses were telling the grand jury because he had his own network of informers in the Agency and on Capitol Hill, old hands still loyal to Helms. One Helms friend went a little further than most, however. Summoned to go before the grand jury, Senator Stuart Symington offered to show a copy of his testimony *before* he testified. He was clearly offering Williams the opportunity to shape the testimony.

Symington, a former secretary of the air force and pillar of the national security establishment, was adamant about doing whatever was necessary to protect Helms. "If they prosecute Dick, the whole temple will come down," he warned Greg Craig, the young lawyer working with Williams on the case. Craig wasn't sure what to do. Was Symington offering to perjure himself? The copy of the testimony Symington had given Craig was garbled and confused. Showing it to Williams, Craig tentatively offered that he could "straighten it out a little. . . ." "No!" said

Williams. Craig stopped, embarrassed to have even suggested such a thing. But Williams wasn't thinking about ethics. He was thinking about tactics. After reading Symington's tangled statement, Williams slyly remarked, "It's perfect. The prosecutor will be completely confused."

Williams's basic defense strategy was not to argue that Helms was innocent, but to discourage the government from bringing the case to trial. The former CIA director knew enough scandalous secrets to make Watergate seem like a peccadillo. He knew much more than the congressional committees and investigative reporters had been able to dig up. He knew secrets about senators and cabinet officers, Republicans and Democrats alike—many of whom were still serving on the Hill and in government. If the government persisted in prosecuting Helms, it would be only fair that he be able to defend himself by calling some of these men to account for their own actions. "Graymail" was the name for Williams's strategy. Williams had been using the same basic techniques for years, since at least 1957, when he defended an army security officer who had been charged with giving government secrets to the House Un-American Activities Committee. Subpoenaing the attorney general to produce the documents, Williams threatened to expose the secrets in open court. The Justice Department backed off and allowed Williams's client to plead guilty to stealing pieces of paper worth a few cents.

Williams began his campaign the Washington way: by leaking to the press. "It's going to be like a Shakespeare play, Bobby," he told the *Washington Post*'s Bob Woodward at a cocktail party that summer of 1977. "Dead bodies all over the stage! If Helms tells what he knows the government won't be able to function. We won't be able to have an embassy in any South American capital. It'll raze the presidency, the judiciary, and the intelligence establishment if this comes out!"

Williams never did tell Woodward exactly what Helms was going to say. He was just trying to pique Woodward's interest, to get him to poke around a little. The truth is that Williams did not *know* all of Helms's secrets, or even many of them. Faithful to the old Agency rule of compartmentalizing information, Helms never told his lawyer more than he needed to know. Shrewd as well as discreet, the veteran spymaster understood that Williams could be just as threatening with bluster as with the facts.

At Williams's first meeting on the case with Justice Department prosecutors that July, he began by sounding reasonable. "You can understand how Ambassador Helms feels," he told the prosecutors. "Here he has served his country for twenty-five years, serving in that part of the government that has never been scrutinized before. You can imagine," he went on, "what is going on in his mind now that his government is turning against him after all these years. If the government persists, if the administration insists on trying this case, there will be . . ."—Williams grew hard, the genial expression vanished, his eyes narrowed, and he slammed his hand on the table—". . . no more secrets!"

Helms's legal position was that "of a man wrapped in the flag, with a derringer peeping out between the folds," wrote his biographer, Thomas Powers. In September, Williams aimed Helms's derringer at the attorney general, Griffin Bell. Bell pretended to be unfazed. "Come on, Ed," replied the attorney general. "You must be joking. This guy is so patriotic that he lied to a congressional committee. He's not going to tell secrets in open court." Williams did not argue. He sensed this was not the time to be confrontational. Indeed, the attorney general was in a magnanimous mood. He had talked it over with President Carter, Bell said, and the government had decided to make an offer. If Helms would plead, he would only be charged with two counts—not of perjury, but of "misleading" the congressional committee. Williams mulled it over for a moment. "No jail," he demanded. "We can't promise," said Bell. "It's up to the judge." Well then, said Williams, why don't we go see him? Bell, a folksy Atlanta lawyer comfortable with judicial informality, agreed to call Judge William Bryant, the chief judge of the U.S. District Court for the District of Columbia.

This was the sort of backroom conniving that delighted Williams. He joked that Judge Bryant would be all "on his tippy-toes" when he saw the attorney general, thinking that he was about to be offered a place on the Court of Appeals. Judge Bryant seemed eager to accommodate, but he was wary of getting caught. "If you get seen coming over here to work a deal, it will be the biggest story of the year," he warned. Nor could Bryant guarantee which judge would sit on the case. Ever since Judge Sirica had hogged all the Watergate cases, he explained, judges were assigned by lot.

Williams decided to go ahead and take the Justice Department deal, but first he wanted a few more concessions from the government. The plea had to be "conditional"—Williams wanted the chance to withdraw it if the judge insisted on jail time. Helms must not lose his government pension. And he wouldn't plead "guilty" but rather nolo contendere—"no contest."

It remained to sell the deal to his client, who was in a defiant mood. Feeling betrayed by his government, Helms was angry and half inclined to fight it out in court. For reinforcements in persuading Helms, Williams turned to Clark Clifford. As they had so often in the past, the smooth and urbane Clifford and the earthy, blunt Williams played carefully rehearsed roles. They met Helms in Clifford's dark-paneled office overlooking the White House. "Dick," began Clifford in his mellifluous voice, as he fingered a paperweight on his desk, "if you take this deal you'll be unscathed. This will be remembered as but a small pimple on the backside of humanity." Williams was more to the point: "If we go to trial, you're gonna get a black jury," he warned. "They're not gonna get it. You're a honkie, and you're just sitting there." Helms agreed to the deal.

Williams needed to move quickly. The press was beginning to sniff around; Fred Graham of CBS and Ron Ostrow of the *Los Angeles Times* were calling his office every day. Williams and Ben Civiletti, the deputy attorney general representing the government, went to see Judge Barrington Parker, who had been assigned the case, on Monday, October 31. Parker agreed to accept the plea that afternoon, but then he threw in a hooker. He wouldn't make any promises about jail time. Sentencing would be on Friday.

Williams and Civiletti repaired to the hallway outside Parker's chambers. Civiletti warned Williams that if he backed out, the government would reinstate the original eight-count indictment. Williams was in a bind. Parker was a flinty, independent judge and hard to predict, but he decided to take the chance. His reasoning, he later explained to Greg Craig, was political. Judge Bryant was close to Judge Parker; they were both black. Bryant was politically ambitious. He wouldn't want to embarrass the president or, for that matter, Ed Williams. Williams said to Craig, "Bryant will help us on this."

Helms was brought down from Williams's law firm, where he had been instructed to wait, and taken to the courthouse. On the way in, Helms walked right by Fred Graham of CBS. Surprisingly, Graham did not follow them to the courtroom. But that night, after Helms had taken his plea, Graham went on the nightly news to announce that the courtroom proceeding had been pulled off "with all the secrecy of a covert operation." Watching the news in his office, Williams exploded. "The lazy goddamn asshole! He was standing right there!" (Actually, Graham was stuck on the courthouse steps, waiting for Judge John Sirica to emerge from the courthouse to give his first TV interview after Watergate. Graham was surprised to see Helms walk by; normally the Justice Department alerted reporters to major court appearances beforehand.)

On Friday, the courtroom was jammed with reporters. Dressed for court in his "basic suit," the nondescript blue sack, Williams paced nervously, hands thrust in his pockets. Slowly, Judge Parker, who had lost a leg in a traffic accident, made his way to the bench. As he pronounced sentence, the judge spoke severely: "You now stand before this court in disgrace and shame," he lectured Helms, who tightly gripped a podium and set his jaw. Parker then fined Helms $2,000—the maximum—and imposed a two-year jail sentence. The sentence, however, was suspended. Helms would go free.

Outside on the courtroom steps, Williams vigorously defended Helms to a gaggle of reporters and cameras. He announced that Helms would "wear this conviction like a badge of honor." Then he turned on Fred Graham, who was standing there with a microphone in his hand. "I want to say something to you, Mr. Graham," said Williams, seething. The October 31 hearing had been held in "open court. . . . It was a wide-open procedure which you opted not to attend and you covered your own inertia and your own indulgence by recklessly and irresponsibly attacking the system."

Williams stalked off to the waiting limousine and climbed into the front seat with his chauffeur. Helms and Craig got in the back. Williams was remorseful. "You think that was a little rough back there on the steps?" he asked. He worried that Judge Parker would drag him back into court for giving his little "badge of honor" speech and throw out the plea.*

Back at his office, Williams was still stewing about the judge and "that fucker Fred Graham," as he persisted in calling the TV reporter. Helms was in a hurry to leave for a lunch of former CIA agents at Kenwood Country Club (they would give him a standing ovation and pay the $2,000 fine by throwing checks and $20 bills into a plastic garbage can). During the course of the case Williams and Helms had never discussed a fee. "What do I owe you?" asked Helms. Craig alone had run up $67,000 worth of billable hours on the case. "You don't owe me anything," said Williams.

---

*Parker accepted the plea, but he did not forget Williams's outburst. A few years later, Williams's partner, Vince Fuller, appeared before Judge Parker to plead Westinghouse Corp. guilty to making payments to foreign officials. Judge Parker imposed a million-dollar fine. "That's your badge of honor, Mr. Fuller," the judge said.

Chapter Thirty

JIMMY CARTER'S ELECTION in 1976 had been a personal blow to Williams. His candidate had been Senator Henry "Scoop" Jackson of Washington, whose hawkish anticommunism he admired. Jackson had flattered Williams by asking him to manage his presidential campaign. Actually, Williams would have been content with any of the candidates put forward by the Democratic establishment, Walter Mondale or Hubert Humphrey. So he had watched with growing gloom in February 1976 as the early television returns projected Jimmy Carter to be the winner of the New Hampshire primary. Williams had been sitting in the Georgetown drawing room of Averell Harriman that night, flanked by Bob Strauss and Clark Clifford. George Stevens, the filmmaker and Georgetown insider, recalled the consternation of these men of the Washington establishment as an obscure governor from Georgia knocked off the party favorites. The Democrats would finally win the White House. But it would be the wrong Democrat.

Unlike his more flexible friend, Bob Strauss, Williams was never able to accept Carter. He thought the peanut farmer from Plains, who was trying to abolish the (tax-deductible) three-martini lunch, was a prig. On abortion, Carter was pro-choice. When Archbishop Joseph Bernardin of the Conference of Bishops spoke out in the summer of 1976 against the pro-choice plank in the Democratic platform, Williams warned Carter that Bernardin spoke for the Catholic hierarchy, and it spoke for the rest of Catholic America. "Carter is in trouble with forty-five million Catholics," Williams told the *Washington Post*. Carter had vaguely promised

Williams that he would "do something," but his staff brushed Williams off.

What really bothered Williams about Carter was that the Democratic nominee did not ask him for advice. Carter barely knew who Williams was. At the Democratic convention in New York that July, Williams offered to take Art Buchwald to a party for Carter thrown by Bob Strauss. In the receiving line, Strauss fulsomely introduced Williams as the party treasurer who was doing so much to ensure victory in November. Carter just gave Williams a limp, wet handshake—"like picking up a flounder," Williams recalled. Buchwald, however, was warmly greeted by the nominee. "Mr. Buchwald! I'm so happy to see you! Rosalynn, Billy, look here! Miss Lillian! It's Art Buchwald!" Williams was furious. "You son of a bitch," he said to Buchwald. "I've been working for the party for two years. I get a wet flounder and you get the big hello!"

Williams suggested to Strauss that he resign as party treasurer. The Carter camp seconded the suggestion, but Strauss asked Williams to stay on. In fact, the most useful political work Williams did during the 1976 campaign was for the Republican nominee, President Ford. In September, the press heard that the Watergate special prosecutor was looking into allegations that Ford had received illegal contributions from the maritime unions. While the investigation dragged on, stories about it began appearing every night on the network news. Locked in a tight race for reelection, Ford was in anguish as he waited for some word from the prosecutor, Charles Ruff. In the puritanical post-Watergate era, the president could hardly afford to pick up the phone and call the Justice Department to hurry things along, so Ford called Williams. The president got canny public relations advice from the criminal lawyer. Call a press conference, said Williams. Say that "justice delayed is justice denied. That'll get Ruff off his ass." The advice worked. Ruff quickly responded by clearing the president of any suggestion of wrongdoing.

The Democratic party treasurer voted for Jerry Ford. Carter returned the favor by abolishing the President's Foreign Intelligence Advisory Board. Williams was discharged with an unsigned form letter. He also received a "Notice to Federal Employees about Unemployment Compensation." In later years, as the Carter presidency self-destructed, Williams took mordant pleasure in waving the unemployment form at friends.

Carter's final blow was to steal away Williams's partner Joe Califano, who left the firm to become secretary of health, education and welfare.

"Williams didn't want me to go," said Califano. "We had a great partnership, the firm was growing like crazy, we were celebrities." Califano suspected Williams was a little jealous of his plunge into public service. Williams was certainly irritated when Califano's income from the firm for 1976 appeared in the newspapers: $550,000. That was an enormous salary for a lawyer in 1976. (Cyrus Vance, the secretary of state who had been the senior partner of a distinguished Wall Street law firm, Simpson, Thacher, made half as much.) Williams, who had paid himself $850,000, did not like to see the firm's finances in print. Asked by reporters if the stories about Califano's salary were true, Williams growled, "Yeah, we had a bad year." Califano wanted more money as he went out the door. "What's my present?" he asked Williams. "Your draw," grumbled Williams. Califano protested that when Abe Fortas went on the Supreme Court, he "got a big wet kiss from Federated Department Stores." Williams retorted, "But I'm not sure it was legal." Nonetheless, Califano was awarded a handsome bonus, based on the client business he had "in the pipeline" to the firm. "Just remember," Williams wrote Califano, "when they write your obituary they won't remember anything you did at HEW. They will just remember that I got your income up to $550,000 in 1976. No telling what I could have done in 1977."

After Watergate, newspaper reporters were becoming more of a nuisance to Williams. No longer could he count on lazy courthouse scribes and establishment-friendly columnists to print what he told them. A new generation of self-styled investigative reporters were trying to follow Woodward and Bernstein into glory. "These kids look at your ass and see a Pulitzer Prize," Williams complained. And for the first time, Williams himself became a target.

In the fall of 1976, Williams began to hear that a reporter named Paul Kaplan was talking to his friends and other lawyers around town, asking about his past. Kaplan had been commissioned to write a profile of Williams for *Washingtonian* magazine, one of the new "city magazines" that had popped up in the 1960s and 1970s. The magazine could be frothy, but some of its pieces had a hard edge. On the morning of October 4, Williams got a phone call from Katharine Graham. She was distraught. Kaplan had been in her office asking unpleasant questions about Williams's role in drafting the wills left by her late husband. According to Graham, this young reporter seemed to be insinuating that Williams had acted improperly—either by first drawing up the wills that cut Mrs.

Graham out of the *Washington Post* in favor of her husband's girlfriend, or by then destroying the wills in order to curry favor with Mrs. Graham.

Williams was furious. Kay Graham was a friend, as well as his most prized client. Now some rude reporter was making her relive some very trying times, and smearing Williams to boot. In a memorandum to files, Williams wrote that it was "perfectly clear" that Kaplan was on a "hatchet mission." Noting that he had refused to talk to Kaplan himself, Williams said the reporter was "slandering" him in interviews with his former associates and clients. Williams called the publisher of the *Washingtonian*, Laughlin Phillips. In another memorandum to files, William dryly noted that he told Phillips he would "hold him responsible for any defamatory statements. That concluded the conversation." Phillips recalled the conversation more forcefully. "He told me he would use every recourse," said Phillips. "He was very intimidating." The article was spiked.

With more accommodating reporters and authors—those who agreed to show him their work before publication—Williams did not hesitate to use a blue pencil. When he was interviewed by author Norman Sheresky for a fawning book called *Masters of the Courtroom* in 1976, Williams bragged about offering to represent Henry Kissinger if he became a victim of post-Watergate morality. When Sheresky sent him the manuscript, Williams drew a line through the paragraph discussing his potential representation of Kissinger.

Williams was unhappy about his inability to control authors who went ahead and published. In April 1977, Laurence Leamer published a book called *Playing for Keeps in Washington* about power games in the nation's capital. The chapter on Williams hinted, for the first time in print anywhere, that Williams might be a more complicated man than the public image he liked to project. The book said that Williams was moody and restless. Leamer also quoted Williams as telling friends that he was "leaving the Church." Williams was apoplectic. He called Leamer at home at 8:00 A.M. "You little shit. You're not going to make one damn cent on this book." He made a point of addressing Leamer, who pronounces his name "Lamer," as "Leemer."

Williams wanted to sue Leamer for defaming him by questioning his faith. "Leemer! Leemer!" Williams bellowed at John Kuhns, a libel lawyer in his firm. "We've got to do something! This is the worst thing ever written about me!" Kuhns finally got Williams to calm down and take his own advice, which in cases like this was to do nothing, since a libel suit would only attract more attention to the book. Instead, Williams wrote a letter to Abe Rosenthal, the editor of the *New York Times*, asking him to make sure Leamer's error was never repeated in his newspaper.

In fact, Williams was not about to leave the Catholic church. But he was feeling low and dispirited that May of 1977. The day before he wrote Rosenthal, he wrote to Madison Square Garden president Mike Burke, who was asking Williams to help with a charitable cause, "I am going through the most difficult period of my professional life." Williams told Burke that the Carter administration had lured away six of his lawyers, including his partner Califano. "I am strung out so thin at the moment that I cannot take on any extracurricular activity."

Williams had just agreed to take on the case of John Kearney, an FBI agent who was accused of bugging the headquarters of the Weather Underground in the early 1970s. (Kearney was Holy Cross '43; Williams agreed to defend him for half price and eventually got the charges dismissed by arguing that Kearney was taking the fall for his superiors at the Bureau.) Williams told Kearney that he was tired, that he had been working too hard. He didn't feel right, he said. He felt like a pregnant woman with morning sickness. Williams said the same to his friends, who told him that he worked and played too hard. His doctor, Steve Jones, thought he was suffering from nervous exhaustion and put him on tranquilizers.

In early June, Williams flew out to Las Vegas to advise his Redskins partner, Jack Kent Cooke, in a messy divorce. (Cooke's wife had tried to run him down with her car and now wanted $43 million, $1 million for each year of their marriage.) Williams was sharing a suite in Las Vegas with his old friend Joe DiMaggio. "We went out for a few drinks and went to bed," said DiMaggio. "In the morning, he asked me, 'Joe, did you get sick last night? I spent the night with my head in the bowl. You don't suppose that bartender slipped me a mickey, do you?' "

Williams was not suffering from a "mickey." He was suffering from cancer. His digestion was poor because a malignant tumor was obstructing his colon. Back in Washington, Williams went for a lower GI (gastrointestinal) X-ray at Georgetown. He met with Dr. Jones and another old Georgetown friend, Jim McCarrick, a surgeon at Suburban Hospital, to get the results. McCarrick told Williams that cancer had invaded the wall of his colon near his spleen. Williams looked at the floor and shook his head. Later, at lunch with television newswoman Nancy Dickerson, Williams made light of the scene. He described a pair of technicians arriving before the doctor to examine his X-rays. "Ooh, look at that," said one technician to the other, "Ooooh, look at *that*." Laughed Williams, "It was as if they were looking for gold."

According to McCarrick and Jones, Williams was terrified. He told his doctors that he had sat beside Vince Lombardi while "the Coach" had died a very painful death, and he was afraid that was going to happen to him. The doctors told Williams that Lombardi had died of rectal cancer. Williams's case was different; it could be completely cured. "I was optimistic," said Dr. McCarrick. "I was a little concerned about the operation because of his drinking history, but he got through that okay."

Williams quietly entered Georgetown Hospital on July 7, 1977. His daughter Ellen was shocked at the sight of him lying, gray and in pain, after the surgery. She left in tears. Paul Connolly had difficulty entering the hospital room; he was so overcome when he did that he couldn't talk. Vince Fuller never made it. He went to the hospital chapel to pray instead.

Slowly, Williams overcame his depression and set his will to overcoming his disease. He went back to work. Only his close friends and partners were told that he had cancer, and he told them that both his parents had suffered from colon cancer—and lived to be ninety. The newspapers printed only that he had suffered from an "intestinal disorder." But every few months, Williams quietly checked back into the hospital to make sure that his cancer had not returned.

BY THE SUMMER of 1977, Williams was fed up with George Allen. He had never really liked the Redskins coach, whose idea of a good time was dinner at the Marriott and who was notorious at Duke Zeibert's for the cheapness of his tips. It offended Williams that "Allen was always the most important person in every anecdote he told," said Ben Bradlee. Williams was willing to tolerate Allen's ego and humorlessness when he was winning, but the Redskins had not enjoyed a championship season since they had gone to the Super Bowl in 1973. Allen liked to say the "future is now," but the press described his philosophy as "trade now, pay later."

The Redskins coach and general manager had traded away all the Redskins' future draft choices to get proven veterans. Now the so-called Over-the-Hill Gang really was. The players were tired of Allen's ceaseless rah-rah, his insistence that every game was "the biggest game of your life." Even Williams thought Allen placed too much emphasis on the old college try. He preferred Sonny Jurgensen, the quarterback who didn't train very hard but at least threw spirals, over Allen's choice, the combative but graceless Billy Kilmer. Williams joked that Kilmer threw the football "end over end." It bothered Williams to see the highly paid Jurgensen sit on the bench. "George," Williams pleaded, "we've got a half-million-dollar air force. When are you going to use it?"

Williams thought Allen was getting increasingly erratic. In a game against the Philadelphia Eagles, Allen refused to identify his own son to the referee in order to avoid a fifteen-yard penalty. The referee wanted to throw a flag when Allen's son, Bruce, came on the field to hector the Eagles quarterback. Allen insisted to the official that the young man must be a ball boy for the Eagles. Williams told his friends that Allen had taken to patrolling the woods near the Redskins' practice field, hoping to surprise spies from opposing teams. Allen, whom Williams mockingly called "Herbert," his middle name, had become "Nixon with a whistle" to reporters who covered the team.

Williams and Allen haggled constantly over money. The Redskins payroll—$3.6 million—had become the largest in professional football after Allen's expensive trades, and Williams was, as ever, worried about the team's finances. The team lost $500,000 in 1976, $750,000 in 1977. Jack Kent Cooke, the team's absentee owner, was thinking about selling his controlling interest in order to pay for his divorce. If Cooke went, Williams, who only owned 15 percent of the team, would have to give up day-to-day control to a new owner. The players were no longer docile in the 1970s, demanding more and more pay and benefits and threatening to strike if the owners balked. "I don't understand it, I just don't understand it," Williams, the paternalist, complained to Joe DiMaggio over dinner in New York on the eve of the 1975 NFL strike. Williams became so exercised about the disloyalty of his players that he spilled his martini over his steak and had to order another meal.

Williams had a hard time saying no—to Allen or the players. The Redskins went into training camp in 1976 with twenty-five players still unsigned, but then Williams promptly coughed up $1.8 million to sign four new stars. Allen was constantly badgering Williams for new equipment and gadgets. "Allen would never let go," said Bobby Mitchell, the Redskins' Director of Scouting. "George would say, 'Ed, you know on the field today Manny Sistrunk couldn't even move that guy. We need that new weight machine to make Manny strong!'' Williams would get out the Redskins checkbook. He even agreed to build a forty-yard field on a slight incline because a physiology professor had told Allen that running uphill would improve his players' speed.

Williams lost patience, however, when Allen began spending Redskins money on himself. Williams bitterly complained to friends that Allen's children were making phone calls on a Redskins credit card and that Redskins groundskeepers were mowing his lawn. In 1972, Williams had saved Allen from serious punishment from the league when the team's general manager was caught trading away draft choices he didn't have. At an early-morning owners' meeting, Williams, who had been up until 4:30 A.M. drinking with Miami Dolphins coach Don Shula, had made an eloquent plea on Allen's behalf (''Williams spoke English, which confused some owners,'' joked Cleveland's Art Modell). Now Williams thought Allen was out to chisel the Redskins.

When Williams emerged from the hospital after his cancer operation in July 1977, he was in no mood to dicker over Allen's latest contract demands. At a press conference a week after his surgery, looking wan after his reported ''intestinal disorder,'' Williams said he was extending Allen's contract for four more years with a generous salary increase. But Allen wanted more, including stock options. (*Sports Illustrated* reported that his contract demands included a maid for his wife.) Williams was beginning to covet another coach—Ara Parseghian, perhaps, or the Dolphins' Shula. Allen, for his part, had begun flirting with other teams as well. The contract negotiations stalled when the team failed to make the play-offs in the fall.

The day before the Super Bowl, Williams delivered an ultimatum to Allen: sign or else. Allen said he had to talk to his wife and lawyer. But on Monday, Allen still had not decided. Williams told Allen he was withdrawing the offer. A few years before, Williams had joked that he had given Allen ''an unlimited budget and he had exceeded it.'' Now he told the *Washington Post*, ''I gave Allen unlimited patience and he exhausted it.''

Williams later worried that he might have been a little too outspoken with the *Post* reporter. At about 10:00 P.M. that night, he called Bradlee. When does the first edition come out? Williams asked, and Bradlee read him the *Post*'s banner headline: ''Allen Fired by the Redskins.'' ''Jesus!'' said Williams. ''Jesus! I better come over!'' At Bradlee's house in

Georgetown, Williams insisted that the headline was wrong. He had not fired Allen. "Of course, you fired him," scoffed Bradlee. "What the hell else do you call it?"

In fact, Williams hadn't given up on Allen. Indeed, he met with Allen the next day, still thinking the coach might sign the contract. "Ed didn't fire Allen. The newspaper did," said Bobby Mitchell, who was in the middle of the negotiations. "Ed hated to fire people. He was just waiting for George to say what he wanted to hear and ask for the job. But [the coach's] pride wouldn't let him."

Allen was enraged. He called Williams "deceitful, devious, a Jekyll and Hyde. One day he calls you up and he's ranting and raving; the next day he's meek as a kitten. That's his training. He's an actor. He's a cold-blooded fish. He uses people." But no one was listening. In Washington, Allen was the heavy, villain of the piece. Two months after Allen departed, accusing Williams of bugging his phone and changing the locks on his office, the *Post* ran a blow-by-blow account of the coach's demise, called "The Final Plays" (after the title of Woodward and Bernstein's best-seller on Nixon's collapse).

Allen was portrayed as devious and cheap; Williams as noble and long-suffering. In describing Williams's 1972 intervention to save Allen from being punished for cheating the league owners, the article stated, "He had built a reputation in the legal and political circles of Washington and the nation as an honorable, ethical man. And here was the coach he had hired charged with penny-ante chiseling." A few weeks later, the pesky *Washingtonian* magazine concluded that Deep Throat for "The Final Plays" was undoubtedly Williams. The author of the article, Tom Dowling, pointed out that the real drain on the team's coffers was not Allen's petty self-dealing, but the half-million-dollar debt service on the loans Williams and Cooke had taken to retire Redskins stock and increase their own control.

To replace Allen, Williams hired Jack Pardee, a former Redskins linebacker who was coach of the Chicago Bears. Williams liked the fact that Pardee went to church every day—and had overcome a bout with cancer. Allen went on to coach the Los Angeles Rams, though he was fired before the season began. Carroll Rosenbloom, the Rams owner, "has told all his confidants that he concluded Allen was a fruitcake," Williams wrote Joe Califano in August 1978.

Allen remained the butt of jokes for Williams. After Allen left, Williams was talking to Bobby Mitchell in his office about the Redskins, and he bent down on his knees to get a coffee cup out of a cabinet. "He was kneeling down," Mitchell recalled, "and all of a sudden, he looks up at the ceiling, puts his hands together and starts saying, 'Lord, there are hungry people, people starving all over the world, and here I tried to force $250,000 down a man's throat and he wouldn't take it. Lord, I wish somebody would do that to me.' " Mitchell fell to his knees beside him. "Me, too, Lord," he said. Williams roared with laughter.

Chapter Thirty-One

ON JULY 13, 1978, Paul Connolly died of a sudden and unexpected heart attack. He was 57. Williams was shocked and bereft. Califano had elbowed Connolly aside in the running of the firm, but Williams had always felt close to Connolly, a gentler soul. Now both Connolly and Califano were gone. Califano's name was dropped from the firm which he left to go into government, but when Connolly died, Williams kept his name in the firm, which remained Williams & Connolly. "I've got no one to talk to," Williams mourned to Califano, who was still serving in Jimmy Carter's cabinet. The burden of administering the firm, now almost sixty lawyers, fell again to Williams alone. He was lonely, worried about how he would keep the firm growing to "feed all these mouths," and whether his health would hold up. But the only child had overcome loneliness with ambition before. Williams resolutely set out to find clients who could pay high fees.

He did not have to look far. There was no shortage of rich men in deep trouble in 1978. The government's focus on white-collar crime, begun by U.S. Attorney Robert Morgenthau in Manhattan in the 1960s, had picked up momentum after Watergate. White-collar crime convictions had doubled since 1972. Jimmy Carter had vowed in his presidential campaign to go after "big-shot crooks," and his Justice Department had declared white-collar crime and public corruption to be the top priorities of federal law enforcement. Their targets, at least the ones who could afford him, routinely turned to Edward Bennett Williams.

Dominic Antonelli was Williams's kind of self-made man, a former parking lot attendant who now owned most of the parking garages in Washington. Rough-edged, vaguely sinister in the dark-tinted sunglasses he always wore, Antonelli rewarded his friends. In 1977, federal prosecutors began to suspect that Antonelli had been too generous with his friends in government. At the same time Antonelli leased one of his buildings to the D.C. Department of Human Services, he had provided a home mortgage through a straw man to the director of the city agency, Joseph P. Yeldell. In April 1978, after a sixteen-month investigation of public corruption in the District of Columbia, Antonelli was indicted for bribery.

Williams's associates were a little surprised when he agreed to take the case. Williams came to the case too late—at the end of the grand jury process—to work out a favorable deal with the prosecutors, so he had to go through an exhausting and time-consuming trial. Plus, the case would not get the kind of front-page attention that the Connally trial had brought—Antonelli was a metro section story. Larry Lucchino, one of Williams's protégés, asked the senior partner why he was taking the case. "The guy's worth $100 million," replied Williams. "When this case is over, he'll be worth $98 million." Besides said Williams, Antonelli could give him good real estate tips.

Court watchers assumed that Williams would not take a case unless he was confident he would win. To be sure, there was no "smoking gun" in *United States* v. *Antonelli*. The facts were complicated and ambiguous but not really in dispute. Antonelli had leased a building to the city, and he had given a city official a $35,000 second trust on his home through a bank he owned. The critical question was what Antonelli intended by his actions. This was the typical pattern in a white-collar case. As the *National Law Journal* put it, "Cases frequently turn solely on the state of mind of the defendant—whether he *knowingly* put false information on a balance sheet, whether he *intentionally* misrepresented company sales to raise the price of stock."

What was Antonelli's true intent? The prosecutors claimed it was to bribe a city official to give him a favorable long-term lease on a building, located in a decaying area of town, that could never find a commercial tenant. Williams, however, came up with a different "theory of the case." This wasn't a case of bribery, he insisted. It was friendship. Antonelli was just doing a favor for his old friend Yeldell, who was financially strapped. In fact, Williams likened Antonelli to the Good Samaritan in the Bible.

In his early years, the prosecutors Williams went up against tended to be faceless GS-14s or Irishmen with whom he could drink. But the pro bono spirit of the early 1970s and the televised celebrity of the Watergate prosecutors had made a stint in the U.S. Attorney's Office more attractive to the brightest graduates of the best law schools. Rick Beizer, one of the prosecutors in the Antonelli case, was a former Harvard football player who wore bow ties and sported a modish Afro. Hank Schuelke, his partner, was a wisecracking former army prosecutor in Vietnam. Both men were on to Williams's gamesmanship, which by now was legend among prosecutors.

During pretrial discovery, Williams tried his usual jive. He told George Allen stories ("The guy was a nut! He threw big galvanized garbage cans around the locker room before Dallas. These guys weren't Rhodes scholars, but they're not that stupid . . ."). He blustered that prosecutors were "playing needle in a haystack" by forcing him to examine all 1.4 million documents they had collected during the investigation. "You've been doing this for eighteen months and I've been doing it for two weeks! Give me a break!" protested Williams. "Just tell me what you're gonna use against us."

The prosecutors were amused and fascinated by Williams's jocular theatrics, but not moved. "Why don't you just ask Antonelli?" asked Schuelke. "He was present at the creation." ("I'm dealing with wiseasses," Williams sighed when he returned to the firm.) "Ed would do his Joe Palooka routine, then ten minutes later he'd be educated and urbane, making references to Aeschylus and Doonesbury," said Schuelke.

After Schuelke's opening argument, Williams came over to the counsel's table to congratulate him. "Now you really ought to think about moving over to the other side," Williams said. Schuelke wondered to himself, "Is he offering me a job? Or just jerking me around?" Schuelke decided to dish back. A few days after the trial began in October 1978, the *Washington Post* ran a large photograph of President Carter sitting with Williams in his box at RFK at a Monday night football game. "Some people will stop at nothing to influence jurors," said Schuelke. "I don't even like the guy," Williams responded. If the Redskins lost on Sunday, Schuelke would sidle up to Williams and casually ask, "Hey Ed, I've been busy. What happened? Skins win?" Williams would glare back. "You little cocksucker."

Williams had as much trouble from Judge Gerhard Gesell as from the prosecutors. The judge, a former partner at Covington & Burling, was accustomed to dominating the courtroom. After a day of being repeatedly overruled by Gesell, Williams told Lucchino, "This guy thinks only one person can be in charge in the courtroom. Unfortunately, he thinks it's him." Gesell, of Andover and Yale, had an old-boy way of referring to people by their last names. Schuelke and Beizer were "lads" but Williams was just "Williams." To be patronized by a preppy was more than Williams could bear. "That SOB!" Williams ranted. "I don't care if he calls me 'Ed' or 'Mr. Williams,' but just not goddamned *Williams.*" In private, Williams started calling Gesell a "miserable Dutchman" and a "Prussian."

Williams's final burden was Antonelli's co-defendant, Joseph P. Yeldell. "The 'P' stands for power," boasted Yeldell, a political figure in the mold of Marion Barry, who was running for mayor that fall. At first, Williams enjoyed Yeldell, whom he called a "bad dude" who "lives by his mouth." But then Yeldell took the stand. "We had spent days with Yeldell, preparing him to testify, but he came unglued," said Greg Craig, who worked with Williams on the case. At one point, Yeldell admitted to the jury that he had lied seventeen times on his public disclosure forms. For two and a half days, Yeldell twisted in the witness box. Williams tried to keep a straight face at the counsel's table, but he was miserable. He turned to David Kendall, who was also assisting him with the case, and made an attempt at black humor to show his feelings. "Would you rather be you right now, or Paul Connolly?" he asked. Back at the firm, Brendan Sullivan saw that Williams had sweated through his shirt. "Now I know what Hell is like!" Williams exclaimed. "It's like God saying, Eddie, I want you to watch the cross-examination of Joseph P. Yeldell for two hours!"

Two days later, Williams trotted out his Good Samaritan theory to the jury in closing argument. He held up the Bible. "Have we reached the point in our history when if a man reaches out to help his brother who is in trouble, it is to be viewed with suspicion and doubt and distrust and accusation? Because if we have reached that point in our history, this Book has no place in the courtrooms of America." Schuelke watched this performance without surprise. "I had read all his closing arguments. His stuff was canned. He did it the same way every time. I could tell you what the next sentence was going to be," he said. When it came time for rebuttal, Schuelke told the jury that he, too, remembered the Good Samaritan story. He just didn't recall the part where, after the Samaritan bandaged the wound, he came back two weeks later and said, "Okay, now it's my turn."

The jurors chuckled. Williams had lost touch with black juries. "Ed's summation was hokey and overblown," said Greg Craig. "Ed thought it would work with a black jury used to hearing black preachers. But he ran into an ethnic gulf. He was better off with the Rosas and Leroys [his longtime maid and chauffeur] than with these street dudes."

The jury took three hours and forty minutes to convict. Yeldell's secretary ran from the courthouse shouting "dirty bastards!" Williams was speechless. He did not congratulate the prosecutors, nor did he speak to his own lawyers. "He was very depressed," said his daughter Dana. "When he got down like that, he'd get very quiet and just go to bed." At the firm, other lawyers were afraid to go into his office. Inside, Williams sat silently, brooding.

Williams didn't emerge from his despondency for two weeks. Then his associates turned up an interesting fact: The father of the jury foreman had once been fired from his job at one of Antonelli's garages. Could that have prejudiced the juror against the defendant? Judge Gesell agreed to hold a hearing on the issue on the Wednesday before Thanksgiving. But the defense move nearly backfired when the juror's father suddenly disavowed the affidavit he had given Williams's law firm. He claimed that the defense lawyers had put words in his mouth. "It was a put-up job," said Schuelke. "The affidavit had been written by some associate. It read like *Black's Law Dictionary*." Greg Craig countered that the prosecutors "got to the guy and made him change his story." Whatever the truth, Williams was suddenly forced to take the stand himself to defend his integrity, much to Judge Gesell's barely concealed delight. As Williams left the courtroom, he joked, "I don't know if we won a new trial, but at least we beat the obstruction of justice charge." In fact, he was shaken. At the Palm that night, Mike Tigar baited Williams, "Hey, Ed, Gesell really tucked it to you." Williams swung heavily into Tigar's booth. "I will meet that son of a bitch on any field of his choosing," he declared. "Any contest! Any weapons! Just so long as that bastard isn't the referee!"

Over the weekend, Gesell told another judge that he planned to deny Williams's motion for a new trial, but on Monday, Williams's ever-resourceful associates revealed that the juror had also failed to disclose that she had had an account at Antonelli's bank. That was too much for Gesell. "Not in my courtroom," he said. He ordered a new trial.

The prosecutors remained suspicious about the sudden revelations of juror prejudice. "When did Williams become aware of all this?" asked

Schuelke. "I think they knew all about the juror during the trial, but they were just holding it in reserve, a trump card if they lost." Williams's associates strongly denied this. "We brought forth the information as soon as we learned it. We were not using it as an insurance policy," said David Kendall. The legal ethics are murky in this area. A lawyer who knows of evidence that would cause a mistrial is supposed to bring it to the court's attention right away to avoid the time and expense of a wasted trial. But a defendant has a right to be tried by the jury that has been empaneled. "Williams played the game with a little chalk on his shoes," said Schuelke, "but he's no different from any other lawyer in a hotly contested suit. You take advantage wherever you can get it."

The retrial was to be held in Philadelphia, where a neutral jury could more easily be found. Williams was pleased with the new venue. "In Philly, they know corruption," he said. "A bribe is cash in an envelope. It's not a loan paid off with interest pursuant to a note." The jury was middle-aged, mostly white and ethnic, and female—Williams's ideal. At the first trial, hoping to appeal to black jurors, Williams had allowed Yeldell's lawyer, who was black, to question witnesses. In the second trial, neither Yeldell nor his lawyer was allowed to say a word in court. "Yeldell sat so far from Antonelli at the witness table that he was practically in the next courtroom," joked Beizer. The trial was short and uneventful. Williams made no mention of the Good Samaritan. The jury acquitted after a brief deliberation. "Too bad I didn't pay Yeldell's lawyer by the word," joked Antonelli as he walked, a free man, down the courthouse steps.

Williams's partner Brendan Sullivan learned the outcome while he was driving down Highway I-95 back from another case. In his rearview mirror he saw a large black limousine "going ninety miles an hour." The car flew past him, and Sullivan saw Williams and the trial team, driven by Leroy Washington. They were waving champagne bottles and giving the "V" for victory sign.

Despite the celebration, it was not a famous victory. "Victory?" Williams said to a woman who stopped to congratulate him. "All we did was split a double header." With New York lawyer Peter Fleming, an old buddy, Williams was less modest about his performance. "Hall of Fame," he called it. But the newspapers hardly took notice. During the Connally trial, columnist Mary McGrory had written that Williams was "the great lawyer to whom the great repair." But there was nothing monumental about Antonelli, save the legal bills that Williams sent him.

In his early years, Williams had made his name defending the notorious—Joe McCarthy, Frank Costello, Jimmy Hoffa, Adam Clayton Powell. Now he found himself defending rich men who preferred privacy.

He felt he had no choice. He said he was held down by his obligations to the law firm. In fact, he was trapped by his obsession with maintaining control. The night at the Palm when Mike Tigar had teased him about Judge Gesell, Williams had become gloomy. "I build myself a magnificent building," he said about his law firm, "but it's like a prison. I've got all these brilliant lawyers, but suppose I got the Dreyfus case. Could I go and leave the firm to these law review editors? No, they've got no judgment. . . ."

Still, there had to be a better way to make a living than going to trial—twice—to save a parking lot magnate from his indiscretions. Williams hated the grind of trials. He still prepared for them as if he was arguing for his own salvation. Larry Lucchino recalled watching him refile every bit of paper in the Antonelli case just to make sure it was all properly organized in his mind. He wasn't sure he could do it any more. "Fighters don't quit because they get tired of fighting," he said. "They quit because they don't want to train." Williams was sick of training. He wanted to find a less exhausting way to make a million dollars a year.

V

Wealth

Chapter Thirty-Two

IT WAS INEVITABLE that Stanley Sporkin, a self-styled enforcer of corporate morality in the post-Watergate era, would come up against Williams. Sporkin saw himself as a crusader. Disheveled, intense, with dark circles under his eyes, the enforcement chief of the SEC played Grand Inquisitor and Confessor to Wall Street in the late 1970s and early 1980s. Watergate had exposed the underside of corporate America as well as the abuse of public power. Federal investigators and probing reporters discovered slush funds to pay off U.S. officials and foreign governments alike, enmeshing blue-chip corporations like Westinghouse and McDonnell Douglas in a tangle of foreign bribery scandals. To the newspaper-reading public in the sour atmosphere of the time, executive suites began to seem like sinister places, dens of connivance and deceit.

Mucking out the boardroom stables was a large undertaking, even for someone as driven and egotistical as Stanley Sporkin, and the SEC enforcer had to ration his limited resources. Like Ed Williams, Sporkin wanted to pace himself by avoiding full-blown trials—going to court was too costly and time-consuming for the SEC's small staff. He wanted publicity. He believed that exposure had a purifying effect. He wanted to force corporations to police themselves by embarrassing them with bad press. Typically, when the SEC caught businessmen manipulating the stock market, Sporkin would settle the case with a consent decree, by which the malefactors would have to disgorge their ill-gotten gains and agree not to break the law in the future. The guilty executives, Sporkin hoped, would be fired by their companies. At the least, they would have to admit they had done wrong. Sporkin believed that confessing—to him—was good for the soul. "He wanted you to say yes, you had been screwing widows and orphans, and then he'd forgive you," said Don Oresman, the general counsel of Gulf + Western Corp.

Sporkin's investigation into Gulf + Western was regarded at the time as the most complex securities case ever. It was heralded with a three-part series in the *New York Times* in 1977 by investigative reporter Jeff Gerth (who happened to have attended the bar mitzvah of Sporkin's son), and it would drag on for four years.

Gulf + Western was the creation of Charles Bluhdorn, a World War II immigrant who had arrived in America with $15 and leveraged himself into a huge conglomerate with two hundred subsidiaries that produced everything from movies to cement. Bluhdorn was one of the first on Wall Street to use what was known in the 1960s as "Chinese paper," long-term commercial debt instruments that offered very high interest rates and little security. (Two decades later, they would be called junk bonds.)

In November 1979, the SEC filed a civil suit accusing Bluhdorn of manipulating the stock price by swapping assets between subsidiaries to create artificial gains. Gulf + Western's outside counsel, Arthur Liman, worried that the SEC would "go criminal" against Bluhdorn. "We better get the best," Liman told the company's in-house lawyer, Oresman. They called Ed Williams.

Bluhdorn was high-strung, shy, and volatile. He was uncomfortable with outsiders until they earned his trust. At the initial meeting with Williams at a company apartment on Central Park West, Bluhdorn sat across the room from his new lawyer, eyeing him warily. It was clear to Oresman that Bluhdorn was not ready to open up in any way. After a desultory discussion of legal matters, Williams began to tell his signature Slobodkin story ("if I had a defense, I'd have Slobodkin!"). At first, Williams was low key and easy, familiar in an almost intimate way with his standoffish new client. But as Williams went on, warming to his tale, building toward the punch line, Oresman noticed that Williams seemed to be growing, to be filling the large and formal room with his magnetism and robust presence. "He grew like a genie out of a bottle," said Oresman, "until Charlie was enveloped in confidence." Bluhdorn visibly relaxed and smiled weakly for the first time. Like other powerful but frightened men who had come to Williams in times of trouble, he felt safe.

Williams's air of assurance was partly bluff. He did not know the first thing about securities law. He had to hire a law professor from George-town, Don Schwartz, to teach him two hours every Saturday morning. Jerry Shulman, a lawyer in Williams's firm, assembled a master case book describing some twenty different Gulf + Western transactions that were under investigation by the SEC. Shulman tried to educate Williams about the case, "but it seemed we were making no headway," said Shulman. "He didn't seem to be getting it at all." One morning, before Bluhdorn was scheduled to come to lunch to be briefed on the case, Shulman lectured for hours "without a flicker of recognition from Ed," he said. But when Bluhdorn arrived, Williams walked him through the case without ever glancing at a piece of paper. "He knew all the nuances and facts, and he picked up intuitively what was key," said Shulman. "He had been sorting key words and phrases in his mind."

Not only did Williams have a near photographic memory, he had a "tape recorder for a brain," said Lewis Ferguson, a lawyer for the firm. Williams once refused to read a ninety-five-page memo that Ferguson had written on international law in a complex oil rights case. But after Ferguson briefed him orally, Williams convinced the client he was an expert in international law, a subject about which he had little knowledge an hour before. (Williams threw in his usual touches, telling the client, "Well, I could go see [Secretary of State] Cy Vance, of course.")

Williams's show of securities expertise was more for Bluhdorn's behalf than the SEC. Williams really did not need to be an expert in securities law, because his strategy had little to do with the law, or even the facts of the case. Williams's approach was simply to delay. The longer the case lasts, the more circumstances will change, Williams said. Recollections will dim. Sporkin will get tired and want to move on to the next corporate villain, the next headline. Williams called it "putting age on the case."

Sporkin, despised on Wall Street, was called Attila the Hun for his aggressive tactics. Sporkin-bashing was a sport among securities lawyers. But Williams "never brought any animus to the table," said Arthur Liman. "He leveled with Stan, which was refreshing. Sporkin was used to posturing lawyers. 'The SEC is bad! My client is innocent!' There was none of that cant with Ed." There didn't need to be. Sporkin knew Williams's reputation as a relentless adversary. "Williams spoke softly but carried a big stick. He didn't have to tell you he'd beat your brains out, because you knew he would," Sporkin said. Williams's aim was to lull Sporkin, not provoke him. "Ed was great at defusing things, at lowering the tempo,'' said Liman. ''Sporkin would get all inflamed by staff lawyers, but Ed would just stall him.''

At negotiating sessions, Williams preferred to talk about anything but the case. Many negotiations were devoted to Sporkin offering advice to Williams on how to get along with the players union in professional baseball (Williams had just bought the Baltimore Orioles). After an hour or two of baseball chatter, Williams would knee Oresman under the table. Taking the signal, Gulf + Western's in-house lawyer would say, ''Gee, Stan, Arthur and I have to catch the shuttle back to New York.'' Sporkin would splutter, ''But we didn't talk about the settlement! When are we going to meet next?'' Outside Sporkin's office, Williams would smile and say, ''Well, we got another ten days.''

When he wasn't talking baseball to Sporkin, he was trying to persuade the SEC enforcer that his client was not a crook. This took time, because Bluhdorn came across as furtive and slippery. Williams tried to paint him as a corporation builder, a master entrepreneur, maybe not the sort who came from Harvard Business School, but a man of integrity nonetheless, even if he didn't always dot all his i's and cross all his t's. ''Charlie's a force of nature,'' Williams explained. ''He makes corporations the way volcanoes make islands. There's got to be room in this world for unconventional people.''

Personally, Williams had little use for Bluhdorn. As the negotiations with the SEC dragged on, Williams began to tire of his client. ''Bluhdorn was addicted to the phone,'' said Liman. ''He could talk for two hours straight and never ask if you were still there.'' During one of these harangues, Williams got up from his desk, lay down on the floor, and pretended to take a nap.

Having won Bluhdorn's confidence, Williams now kept his distance. When Sporkin took Bluhdorn's deposition, Williams almost never objected or interceded. Williams considered lawyers who constantly jumped up to object to be insecure showboaters. Most objections, he believed, just served to irritate the judge and jury. But Bluhdorn was furious at him. He wanted his lawyer to object, to make speeches, to express outrage, not to just sit there.

Commenced in 1979, the SEC's suit against Gulf + Western was still unresolved two years later. Sensing that Sporkin was ready to let Bluhdorn off with a slap on the wrist, Williams was finally ready to settle. He wanted Bluhdorn to take a harmless consent decree and get the case over with. To Williams, an investigation that did not end in a jail sentence for his client was a victory. But when Williams made his settlement proposal to the board of Gulf + Western, Bluhdorn balked. It was a matter of honor to this proud immigrant to appear innocent. To settle with Sporkin would be un-American, Bluhdorn argued to his board of directors. Bluhdorn got so worked up that he succeeded in stirring his board as well. By the end of the meeting, the board members were insisting that they be named in the suit along with Bluhdorn. Williams turned to Liman and said, "Arthur, we were paid to keep these people out of a lawsuit. Now we're supposed to go to the SEC and tell them to name not one, but twenty!"

In fact, Bluhdorn was wise to hold out. The SEC eventually dropped its suit against him. Williams had over $1 million in legal fees but not much satisfaction. "He didn't like this case," said Oresman. "It didn't have intensity. It was just about delay." Williams missed the very intensity he had wanted to flee by avoiding the grinding pressure of trials. He was, as ever, restless and seemingly discontent. "He was full of anger," said Oresman. "He could keep it under control professionally, but it was always there."

AT A DINNER party at Kay Graham's in the mid-seventies, Williams had stood in a circle of friends excoriating one of his firm's clients, Otto Kerner, the former Ohio governor who had been convicted of fraud while serving as a federal court of appeals judge. "That dumb bastard," exclaimed Williams, "wouldn't resign from the bench before the trial. So he gave the jury no choice. Do you find him guilty? Or do you send him back to judge other people?" Ben Bradlee smiled at his friend and said, "The fact that Kerner was guilty might have had something to do with it."

"Not much," shrugged Williams.

The group laughed. Bradlee, in mock seriousness, had played the journalist, demanding the truth. Williams, playing the lawyer, had answered, what does truth have to do with it? The moment was lighthearted; the old friends went back to teasing and swapping gossip. But the banter masks a serious and difficult question about Williams's character and outlook.

Some lawyers believed that as he grew older and his clients grew at once wealthier and more anonymous, Williams became increasingly dissatisfied with his life in the law. "Ed always had a larger ambition to do more positive things. As a young lawyer, he argued that he was protecting the system. But I think he grew cynical about this,'' said Henry Ruth, a former Watergate prosecutor who knew Williams in the seventies. "Criminal defense is a deeply cynical world." Williams did have a deeply pessimistic view of human nature, perhaps from long association with his clientele. But his very pessimism, together with his strong Catholic faith, made him forgiving of human weakness. Williams could seem deeply cynical, a moral relativist, at the same time he could be almost saintly in his sense of redemption.

Williams was an emotional and elemental man, not introspective or reflective. He would moan and grumble about his yearnings with friends and family (and, after a few drinks, with just about anyone who would listen). But there is no outward sign that he ever engaged in any kind of serious self-examination. He may well have searched his soul while kneeling down at morning mass, but publicly he never questioned the contradictions of his life. When others did—like Eunice Shriver, who had asked him after church, "How can you defend evil?"—Williams had his stock answer. He was an advocate. He didn't defend the morality of his clients. He protected the legal rights of the accused. Moral judgments he left to God.

The contradictions, of course, cannot be so loftily—or easily— explained away. There are too many of them: the outsider who longed to be on the inside, the would-be candidate for public office who never served a day in government. Williams clearly wanted to be more than a hired gun. It did not satisfy him to merely keep rich men out of jail, not even when he dressed up the cause as "one man's freedom."

One simple explanation for the path he took, of course, is economic. Having been poor, Williams always wanted to be rich. "His background," Brendan Sullivan said, "helped him understand that he couldn't live on $60,000 a year." Certainly, there were deeper forces that drove him—a fear of failure and need for love unmet in a lonely childhood. Power motivated him as much as greed. After all, he defended Richard Helms for free. Even so, a desire for wealth was without question a factor that kept him working for rich men instead of the taxpayer. The huge legal fees that Charlie Bluhdorn paid may not have brought him ultimate fulfillment, but they put more distance between his affluent present and his penurious past.

Chapter Thirty-Three

RICHARD HELMS NEVER had to pay Williams for keeping him out of jail in 1977, but he was able to repay Williams in a way that some Washington insiders prize more than money. He nominated Williams for president of the Alfalfa Club. Founded in 1914, the Alfalfa Club takes its name from a plant that has deep roots and a great thirst. The club exists to give one dinner a year, a boozy love-in for the permanent Washington establishment. Helms describes Alfalfa's five hundred members as "the top people in the government and in the military industrial complex." At the annual dinner, "the patriotic overtones are strong," said Helms. "There are no guys here disposed against the flag." Or women at all: Alfalfa prided itself as a last bastion of male chauvinism. Typically, large Washington dinners salute the flag with the Marine Corps color guard. At the Alfalfa dinner, the entire Marine Corps band plays (the director is a member).

Alfalfa presidents are usually drawn from the Senate club or the inner circles of the Executive Branch. Alfalfa presidents in the 1980s included Vice President George Bush, Senate Finance Committee Chairman Lloyd Bentsen of Texas, and Senate Armed Services Committee Chairman Sam Nunn of Georgia. Williams joined this lofty group in 1983. In 1987, he described the Alfalfa dinner to Tony O'Reilly, a leading Irish businessman and political figure, as "the best dinner we have in this town. The president, most of the cabinet, congressional leaders, and the Supreme Court inevitably attend." It offended Williams that President Carter refused to attend the Alfalfa dinner while he was in the White House.

"Carter's a candy ass," said Williams to Father Tim Healy, the president of Georgetown University. It bothered Williams even more that Carter still wasn't asking him for advice. Nor were any of the Georgia mafia who surrounded the president and prided themselves on being outsiders.

Carter's aides felt they had no need for Williams—that is, until muck-raking columnist Jack Anderson informed Chief of Staff Hamilton Jordan that he was about to publish a column claiming that Robert Vesco tried to bribe Jordan to drop charges against the fugitive financier. Jordan was enraged. On the advice of Bob Strauss, he went to see Williams in August 1978, on the day before the story was scheduled to appear in the Sunday papers. Williams was only too happy to help. He immediately shot off a letter to every newspaper with syndication rights to Anderson's column threatening a libel suit if they published the false and defamatory charges.

It apparently did not concern Williams that he had a three-way conflict of interest. He already represented the *Washington Post*—one of the papers he was threatening to sue—as well as Robert Vesco. But Williams's attitude toward conflicts was, as always, relaxed. He simply assumed he could represent everyone's interests. The more control he had, the better, and representing all sides in a case gave him total control. Furthermore, he didn't want to miss a chance to warm up to the White House that had so far frozen him out. "He wanted to get back in the game," said Strauss. "He missed it."

Jordan eventually cooled down and decided not to sue, and Anderson backed off the story in later columns. Relations warmed briefly between Williams and the Georgians. Williams was invited to a state dinner and Carter sat in Williams's box at a Redskins game. But the distrust on both sides lingered. It was exacerbated a year later when Carter fired Califano as HEW secretary. "The president had a push-button line to the deity," sulked Williams. "He didn't need us mortals."

Williams couldn't wait to see Carter defeated in 1980. He plotted with oil man Marvin Davis to bring their friend Gerald Ford out of retirement to seek his old job. In the summer of 1979, Davis and Williams flew to Vail, Colorado, to have lunch with the former president. "The two of them tried to talk me into running again," said Ford. "Ed said he'd head a group of Democrats for Ford and Marvin said he'd write the checks." Ford was tempted and secretly gave them permission to "float a trial balloon."

In February 1980, Nicholas Lemann, then a young *Washington Post* reporter, attended a press conference of a committee that had been formed to draft Ford. The press conference didn't seem very newsworthy to Lemann, but he noticed that one of the members of the committee was Williams. Lemann was taken aback. Hadn't Williams been treasurer of the Democratic National Committee? Lemann called Williams, who angrily refused to comment. A few minutes later, Lemann, who was brand new on the job, was summoned to the office of the paper's editor, Ben Bradlee. Williams called me, said Bradlee. It was all a misunderstanding. The editor instructed his reporter to leave Williams's name out of the story.

The Ford trial balloon fizzled. Williams had to find another way to stop Carter. He was not enthusiastic about Carter's principal Democratic challenger, Edward Kennedy. He thought Kennedy was spoiled and weak, and had failed to live up to his family name. "They gave Teddy the ball on the one-yard line and he still couldn't score," said Williams.

As Carter rolled over Kennedy and amassed enough delegates to guarantee his nomination, Williams desperately cast about for a way to unseat the president. A couple of young congressmen, Michael Barnes of Maryland and Thomas Downey of New York, convinced him that Democratic rules permitted Carter delegates to bolt to another candidate on the first ballot. Never mind that Williams had opposed this interpretation in 1974 because it threatened to weaken the control of the party hierarchy. Now he enthusiastically embraced the movement to "free the delegates . . . from being held hostage." Williams called Bob Strauss in California to say that he had just been appointed the chairman of the Committee to Continue the Open Convention. "We can stop Carter!" Williams exclaimed. "Are you out of your fucking mind?" Strauss inquired. "For a guy as smart as you, this is the stupidest thing I've ever seen." Williams insisted that the Open Convention movement could win a majority of the delegates. "I don't think you'll get a single delegate," said Strauss.

Williams still needed to find someone to replace Carter. Arnold Picker, a wealthy Florida businessman who had written a check to Ed Muskie for $250,000 in the days when that was still legal, pressed Williams to recruit Muskie. Williams agreed to meet with Muskie for dinner at the Palm.

It was not much of a plotters' cabal that squeezed into a booth at the steakhouse that July evening. Williams had been lukewarm about Muskie ever since the senator from Maine had wept on the campaign trail in 1972. Muskie said almost nothing during the dinner. Since he had just been made secretary of state by President Carter, he was in an awkward position to be conspiring against him. Leon Billings, a Muskie aide, asked Williams, "Will Kennedy drop out? Can you get him to withdraw?" Williams replied, "Listen, Ted Kennedy has never committed a selfless act in his life." "Well," said Billings, "you can't expect Ed Muskie to commit an act of political suicide." Williams had another drink. "Who's with me?" he demanded of another Muskie associate, Berl Bernhard. "I'm in the goddamned Kentucky Derby and I don't have a horse." Williams was nervous about challenging Carter alone. "Who's with me?" he asked. "I don't want to get my neck chopped off."

His courage rose again in New York. The Democrats' mood the week before the convention was tindery. The press was feeding the anti-Carter movement by predicting a revolt on the convention floor. Williams had appeared on "Face the Nation" the previous Sunday, so absorbed by his cause that he ran three red lights in his rental car on the way to the studio. Now, in one of his old haunts, P.J. Clarke's saloon, he hooked up with New York's governor, Hugh Carey, who gave him a police escort. Barreling past the traffic, sirens wailing, Williams began to believe he had a chance to pull off a political miracle, single-handed.

On the opening night of the convention, Williams was scheduled to address the delegates. He pictured himself delivering another Cross of Gold speech, stunning a jam-packed Madison Square Garden with his eloquence. He had watched old films of his friend Eugene McCarthy causing a near-riot on the convention floor with his nominating speech for Adlai Stevenson in 1960. He thought he could do the same against Carter. The party would rise up against the feckless Georgian and nominate someone reliable instead, Ed Muskie or Scoop Jackson. Maybe even Ed Williams.

Williams spoke into a wall of sound. The delegates, jawing with each other and reporters down on the floor, didn't pay any attention to him. "Ed had to shout, but you couldn't hear him more than six feet away," said John Nolan, an old friend who was up on the platform with him. "The speech was hokey and old-fashioned, more like a courtroom argument."

Williams was humiliated. "Even you didn't listen to me," he growled at Strauss as he stalked off the podium. The Open Convention movement flopped. Williams later claimed that the Carter forces had "played hardball" and stolen his prepared speech just before he went on, forcing him to wing it. "And then afterward we found the notebook in a garbage can in a backroom of Madison Square Garden," Williams told Robert Pack. It is unlikely that Williams or his associates went fishing in the garbage after the speech. Williams did repair to "21" with his young associate, Greg Craig, to drown his sorrows. He was slugging gin when the Democrats' aristocratic eminence Averell Harriman and his wife, Pamela, entered the room. The barroom crowd stood and applauded. "Ed almost puked," said Craig. "He hated Harriman. No balls and too much Groton."

Williams was low that summer. In August, he flew his teenage son Tony up in a private plane to have dinner with him in New York. Over steaks at Christ Cella's, he told Tony that he was down and lonely and working too hard. He was defending a shady businessman named Victor Posner in a grand jury investigation, and he was "sick of it." The father and son relaxed over gin and tonics. The next morning he told Tony that hiring the private jet to fly him up had "cost ten grand, but it was a lot cheaper than other ways to get me cheered up."

Williams cheered up some more later that month when he had lunch at "21" with Jacqueline Kennedy Onassis. She had become a book editor and wanted Williams as an author. Williams was intrigued to see that Frank Sinatra, sitting at the next table, was ignoring them. The attention from Jackie and the lack of it from Sinatra titillated Williams and eased some of the pain of bombing on national television at the Democratic convention.

Williams's friends found him strangely naive about politics. "He never backed winners," said Buchwald. "I'd ask Ed's advice about a lot of things—life, sports, law," said R. W. Apple, political correspondent for the *New York Times*. "But I'd never ask him about politics." Williams was "great at the retail level, at human dealings, but he was terrible at the pulse of the electorate," said Williams's old associate Peter Taft, who had moved to Los Angeles where he was active in Republican politics. "Washington's not the best place for developing political judgment. It's so isolated. What the hell did Ed know about farmers?" Williams tended to back establishment figures whom he knew. In 1980, he placed bets on six Democratic candidates for the Senate, all incumbents: Frank Church, John Culver, Warren Magnuson, George McGovern, Alan Cranston, and Birch Bayh. Five of the six lost.

Williams was not without political beliefs. His hawkish anticommunism led him to join the Committee on the Present Danger with Paul Nitze and Gen. Matthew Ridgway to warn that if the U.S. arms control negotiators sold out with SALT II, they would open a "window of vulnerability" to Soviet attack. Williams offered to represent Soviet dissidents persecuted by the Brezhnev regime. When the Kremlin refused to give him a visa, he held a press conference with Scoop Jackson to denounce the Kremlin for human rights abuses. He "practically declared war," said *Time* magazine correspondent Strobe Talbott, who was watching with a Williams & Connolly lawyer. To conservative columnist William Safire, Williams wrote, "it seems to me that the older we get the more we agree on basic issues. The question is—is it wisdom or senility?"

But for the most part,"Williams put personal loyalties before politics," said Safire. "It was all ad hominem. But that's better than just putting your finger up in the air." Williams was "people-, not policy-oriented," said Vicki Radd, a politically active young lawyer in his firm. During the Carter administration, Williams wrote the president suggesting that he nominate Robert Bork for the Supreme Court. Williams's endorsement of an archconservative for the high court may seem startling, but it had more to do with Williams's personal liking for Bork than with Bork's judicial philosophy. When R. W. Apple began talking political theory to Williams, the lawyer scoffed, "Aw, that shit doesn't matter." Asked by a politically innocent doctor to explain the difference between a Republican and a Democrat, Williams said the terms were "meaningless."

Williams was no particular fan of Ronald Reagan's, but his attitude improved when Reagan asked him to serve on his transition team three days before he was elected in November 1980. Williams agreed to counsel him on foreign policy, but asked that the news not be announced until after the election, lest it be "misconstrued as an endorsement." Within two weeks, Williams and his wife were among fifty Washington luminaries invited to a dinner with the president-elect and his wife at the F Street Club. "Obviously, he's reaching out," said Williams, "which is more than the current president ever did." Reagan swapped sports stories with Williams, who was glad to see that the drink trays included something stronger than the white wine Carter served. "Make it a Scotch and soda," said Williams. "The Carters are gone." Reagan completed his seduction of Williams by reconstituting the President's Foreign Intelligence Advisory Board and appointing Williams, along with his cronies like John Connally and Clare Boothe Luce.

Williams returned the favor by housing half of Reagan's cabinet in a hotel that he owned, the Jefferson. Secretary of Defense Caspar Weinberger and his wife booked a suite at the hotel, as did Attorney General William French Smith, Secretary of Transportation Drew Lewis, Secretary of Labor Raymond Donovan, and CIA director William Casey. Vice President George Bush also stayed at the Jefferson during the transition, as did Walter Annenberg, Reagan's ambassador to England. The Annenbergs brought their housekeeper, the Weinbergers brought their dog. "It's the service that's so wonderful," said Jane Weinberger.

In 1976, when Williams had bought the Jefferson, the small, fifty-year-old hotel was fading toward seediness. He hired Rose Narva, who had impressively restored the Sheraton Carlton nearby, to create what he called "the Connaught of America." Williams had picked the venerable London hostelry as his model, Narva said, "because it wasn't fussy, and you had to know someone to get in there." Narva promptly banished frozen food, installed a twenty-four-hour butler service, and put fresh flowers in every room. Laundry was delivered in a little wicker basket and shirts were ironed by hand. Guests did not need to stop at the desk; the bellman had the key. At breakfast, Williams would come into the dining room and admire his hospitality. The attorney general would be munching a croissant in one corner, the director of the CIA slurping coffee in another. Williams beamed. They were his guests! It was his club! He would shake hands, chat a bit, and go back to the office to keep his other clients out of jail.

Chapter Thirty-Four

IN THE 1980s, as the get-rich Reagan era arrived, Williams increasingly took on clients who were, in the new superlative, "super-rich." One of the most ostentatiously wealthy was oilman Marvin Davis. Staked by his father, a former boxer who had made a fortune on Seventh Avenue in the garment industry, Davis cashed in on the global energy crisis of the 1970s. He was smart enough to sell the bulk of his holdings for more than $600 million before the price of oil plummeted in the '80s. He was luckier to escape a criminal indictment. In 1979, a federal grand jury had investigated whether Davis had cheated the government by a practice called "daisy chaining," a shell game that transformed cheap oil from old wells into expensive oil from new wells. Williams talked the prosecutor out of bringing criminal charges, and Davis settled for a small civil fine.

A six-foot-four, three-hundred-pound pile of a man, Davis enjoyed the ambience of Toots Shor's and boxing arenas just as much as Williams. And like Williams, Davis liked to be surrounded by celebrities. It pleased him to have a famous lawyer; he was impressed when, while having dinner at Chasen's, Frank Sinatra (who had an on-again, off-again friendship with Williams), Lew Wasserman, and Mrs. Cary Grant all stopped by Williams's table to pay their respects. Conversation between Davis and Williams was straight out of the Toots Shor manual of greeting friends by insulting them.

Williams called Davis a "star fucker" and a "fat son of bitch," and Davis called Williams "a two-bit ambulance chaser." Davis, who also counted Gerald Ford and Henry Kissinger as friends (they invested in his wells), liked to ask Williams why he never went into government. "You cheap bastard, it was the money, wasn't it?" Davis taunted. "Yeah, that was part of it," said Williams. "Yeah, about 96 percent," said Davis.

Ben Bradlee watched Williams's budding friendship with Davis and "didn't get it. Davis was not Ed's kind of guy," said Bradlee. "He was pretentious and flashy. I could see Ed with a rogue like Robert Vesco, but not Marvin Davis. But Ed loved all the money it produced." The relationship between Davis and Williams did generate a great deal of money for Williams's firm, fees well into seven figures. Even Davis was shocked by the size of the bills. "I love Ed Williams," Davis cracked to Jay Emmett, a mutual friend. "I'm a billionaire. I wish I could afford him."

Davis himself was tired of making money just for money's sake. He announced he wanted to buy a business that was "fun." He loved movies and had built a private screening room in his house in Denver. Then, when he couldn't get the first-run movies he wanted, he bought the movie theater down the road. In 1981, he decided to buy 20th Century–Fox. Davis asked Williams to recommend "the best merger and acquisitions lawyer in the business." Williams, who had done only one takeover in his life, an unsuccessful venture fifteen years earlier, recommended himself. Davis demurred. But "Ed screamed and ranted and raved, and I just couldn't say no to him," said Davis. Ira Harris, the Solomon Brothers M&A specialist who had suggested the deal, scoffed at the idea of Williams and told Davis that he should retain a firm with experience in takeovers. Williams disarmed the investment banker. "Pretend this is high school, and you're the teacher and I'm the student," Williams told Harris. "You've got fifteen minutes to teach me." By the first meeting, "you would have thought Williams's specialty was corporate and securities work," said Harris. Williams "never became a technician," said Jerry Shulman, who practiced corporate law in Williams's firm, "but he had a businessman's mind. He understood the bottom line. He wasn't interested in nuances of accounting or accrual or earnings per share. He cared about cash, how much was coming in and how much was going out."

More importantly, Williams knew how to negotiate. He told Davis that if he really wanted the studio, "don't be cheap. Don't pussy foot. Make a rational bid to preclude a bidding war." He helped persuade Davis to up his bid from $58 to $60 a share. "You're gonna get there anyway," said Williams. Williams also helped win the acquiescence of Herb Siegel, the chairman of Chris-Craft, who owned 20 percent of Fox. There was in the go-go 1980s a fraternity of new-money high-rollers that was every bit as cozy as a club of old-money WASPS. The members were sometimes opponents, sometimes allies in business, but they all knew each other and each other's tastes and habits, which they tended to share. Williams's dinner with Siegel at "21" was like a lodge meeting of the brotherhood of the self-made. Williams had represented Siegel, a former talent agent for Jimmy Gleason and a Toots Shor regular, back in 1966 when he had tried to take over Paramount. The white knight who rescued Paramount at the time was one of Williams's current clients, Charles Bluhdorn. Siegel's lawyer was Arthur Liman, who had worked with Williams on the Gulf + Western case. There was the usual joking and joshing until Siegel finally asked, "Okay, what's the price?" He agreed to it almost instantly.

With the management of 20th Century–Fox, Williams played the heavy. He scheduled an appointment with Dennis Stanfill, the Fox CEO, for a Friday afternoon (the timing was designed to minimize leaks). When Stanfill canceled, claiming flu, Williams sent the message that if Stanfill was too sick to see them, he was going to lose his company. When Stanfill arrived, Williams appealed to greed: by selling out, Stanfill personally stood to make $7 million. Stanfill accepted the offer.

The deal almost fell apart when Siegel and Davis started bickering; Williams and Liman had to physically stop Davis from walking out. But in March 1981, Davis bought Fox for $730 million (using only $50 million of his own money). Williams was ecstatic. He had loved the wheeling and dealing and the size of the numbers involved. Drinking at the Beverly Hills Hotel bar after the signing, he exclaimed "Mergers! I love 'em!" (He pronounced it "moy-jahs," mimicking the New York accents of his confreres at the bargaining table.) "Moy-jahs! This is for me! No more trials, no more courtrooms. Moy-jahs!"

Williams relished his trips out to the coast, the chance to joke with Walter Matthau and flirt with Loretta Young at the Brown Derby. "Look at all these girls!" Williams exulted at Davis's parties in the palatial Beverly Hills house he had bought from singer Kenny Rogers for $21 million. "You can be my casting director," Davis joked. Williams bought the Beverly Hills Hotel for Davis from Ivan Boesky, whom Williams described as a "pig," and sold it to the Sultan of Brunei for a $65 million profit. Davis gratefully showered gifts on Williams: a pair of silk pajamas, a stretch limousine, even $300,000 toward refurbishing the football stadium at Holy Cross—a school that Davis, a Jewish graduate of

NYU, had never seen. Davis was effusive about Williams. "One of the greatest guys I've ever known. The one guy I defer to," he said. The feeling was not entirely mutual. In private, Williams could be cutting about Davis for waffling on deals.

Still, he was genuinely fond of Davis, whose bluster masked a shy streak Williams understood. Williams liked it that Davis had been "married to the same woman for forty years," said one of Williams's partners, Jack Vardaman, and that Davis was generous to charity. In 1985, Davis was sued for fraud, and Vardaman handled the case. Before trial, Williams urged Davis to settle. He feared that a jury would not be forgiving to the multimillionaire. When Vardaman and Davis brushed aside Williams's doubts, Williams burst out, "But Marvin, I care about you!" Davis went to trial anyway and won. "Last time I'm taking your advice," he groused at Williams.

He was kidding, of course. Williams continued to advise Davis on his deals and defend him against the lawsuits they sometimes spawned. He helped Davis sell Fox to Rupert Murdoch in 1985 and to stage an unsuccessful takeover attempt on CBS in 1986. (Davis proposed that Williams be appointed "trustee" of the CBS News Division to "guarantee its integrity.") Davis talked to Williams on the phone every day; he especially valued his Washington lawyer for his ability to "get intelligence," and not just about the latest doings on Capitol Hill. "If you needed something on someone," said Davis, "Williams could get it—all the personal details." Williams briefly considered opening an office in Los Angeles to service Davis, but he abandoned the idea. Despite the glitzy lure of Hollywood, Williams was not a creature of show business, and despite the big money and his newfound love of "moy-jahs," Williams was interested in more than "doing deals." His natural center of gravity was in Washington. He understood that celebrities in New York and Los Angeles turned over faster than new restaurants. In Washington, Williams was always in power.

WILLIAMS WANTED TO be a full-service favor bank to his friends and the prominent, who were usually one and the same. He liked to play the role of wise counselor, although he pretended to be burdened by it. Dropping by the office of a young associate on a Saturday morning, he might start by complaining, "I just got a call from Clare Boothe Luce, and she wants . . ." His face would wrinkle in vexation and perplexity, as if this was one more cross he had to bear, another intrusion on his otherwise peaceful existence. His associates came to understand that, in fact, he wanted to be bothered, that he would be disappointed not to be asked to perform some favor, large or small, for the mighty.

They came first and foremost for his "gypsy instinct," his ability to "spot the paving stone that would trip you," as Father Healy put it. Williams was enormously empathetic and shrewd with people who brought him their problems. "You felt he understood your problem more completely than you understood it yourself. He was so wise in the culture of Washington," said Ben Bradlee. "His solutions to problems would be so right they seemed obvious," said Bill Graham. "It was so simple that you'd say, 'Why didn't I think of that?' " Williams exuded quiet confidence that no matter how difficult the problem, he could find a way out. "He had a way of saying, 'I'll take care of that, don't worry,' that put you at ease," said Jack Valenti, the former LBJ aide and longtime Washington lobbyist for the Motion Picture Association. Handing off his friends' minor legal matters to junior associates in his firm, Williams would blithely command, "Take this case and proceed to victory."

Williams took care of all manner of legal problems for the rich and powerful. He negotiated Valenti's salary from the Motion Picture Association, which helps explain why it was higher than any trade association lobbyist's in Washington. He negotiated Lee Iacocca's severance pay from Ford Motor Co., and a year later defended the Ford family from a frivolous lawsuit brought by Roy Cohn. He jokingly offered his friends' wives free divorces from their husbands, though he generally disapproved of divorce. "If you ever leave your wife," he told Valenti, "I'll personally represent her and strip you of every dollar you have."

Williams dispensed personal advice as well as legal help. He was especially good at delivering bad news. "I'll tell it to you cold and true," he would begin. "Co-o-old and tru-u-e." When Bill Graham seemed to be unlucky at marriage, divorcing his first two wives, Williams took the *Washington Post* scion aside and said, "Billy, there are just some things that people don't do well. Some people shouldn't drink. Some people shouldn't gamble. You," he said, "shouldn't marry." (Graham is now happily remarried.) When Senator John Warner asked Williams's advice about marrying Elizabeth Taylor, Williams answered, "Screw her but don't marry her."

Williams could be supportive and upbeat as well as blunt and crude. In 1986, George Bush's son Marvin was bedridden with ulcerative colitis at

Georgetown Hospital. "I was lying there with five tubes running through my body feeling pretty worthless," Bush recalled. "Ed called me out of the blue and told me that it was young people like me who have limitless opportunity. He didn't try to sympathize like other people. He was feisty. He said, 'We need you. You've got a lot of friends who need you.' It worked. He gave me a sense of hope when there wasn't a lot of hope in the air."*

Williams could be threatening when he needed to be. He didn't shout; he didn't need to. His voice had a way of turning cold and flat, as if he were repressing a great fury. "There was a terrible *evenness* in his delivery," wrote the *Washington Post*'s David Remnick, who came under cross-examination from Williams for nosing around in his personal health matters. Physically, he was very intimidating. "He'd lean right into you with that enormous head," said Father Healy. "It was like being accosted by Il Commandatore in the last act of *Don Giovanni*." It often took Williams but a single phone call to accomplish what he wanted. Paul Nitze's former son-in-law was threatening an alienation-of-affection suit against Nitze for breaking up the marriage of his daughter. Nitze came to Williams after the staid and cautious lawyers at Covington & Burling urged him to settle. Williams made a phone call and the lawsuit vanished. R. W. Apple's divorce was turning messy after his wife hired a "bomber." One phone call from Williams made the lawyer back off. Pamela Harriman was upset when *Haywire,* her stepdaughter's book that accused her of breaking up Leland Hayward's first marriage, was being made into a movie. Williams called the lawyers at CBS, and Mrs. Harriman's name was cut out of the script entirely. An hour had to be cut from the four-hour production. "It was massacred," said the producer, Michael Vine. It amused Williams that Brooke Hayward had accused her stepmother of stealing her mother's pearls. "The pearls!" Williams chortled. "The pe-e-e-e-a-rls!"

Often, Williams's advice was to do nothing. Sally Quinn ran into legal complications when she tried to buy a house in Kalorama, an exclusive

---

*Williams was constantly performing favors for the children of friends, giving them summer jobs and writing letters of recommendation. He had a form letter for college recommendations: "I have known _____ since he was an infant, and I have known his family for___ years. I regard him as an outstandingyoung man of sterling character and impeccable integrity. He is bright, personable and industrious. He enjoys the respect and attention of his peers. I unqualifiedly recommend him for your favorable consideration." (Williams had an explicit agreement with Georgetown and Holy Cross: If he sent a handwritten note, it meant admit; if he sent this form letter, ignore it.)

neighborhood in Washington. "Drop it," said Williams. "But it's my dream house!" said Quinn. "Sally," said Williams, "it's just a fucking house." Williams would almost invariably discourage his friends from suing for libel. Typically, he would spend an hour or so letting the aggrieved celebrity ventilate about the vileness of reporters, usually chiming in to agree.

Henry Kissinger once came to Williams fulminating about the "slimy lies" spread about him in books by William Shawcross and Seymour Hersh. Williams nodded sympathetically and said, "But don't sue. It degrades you to get down in the gutter with them. Anyway, the law is against you." To win a libel case, public figures have the difficult burden of proving that the statement was published with knowledge that it was false or reckless disregard of the truth, Williams would explain, citing past Supreme Court decisions aimed at protecting the First Amendment. Williams also talked Gerald Ford out of filing a defamation suit against Los Angeles businessman Justin Dart, who had told a reporter that Ford was a "dumb bastard." (Williams did, however, extract an apology and a contribution from Dart to the Betty Ford Center.) When actress Angie Dickinson came to him complaining about a story in *Ladies' Home Journal* alleging that she had slept with John F. Kennedy, Williams listened for a while and said, "Angie, want some advice? Come have a drink with me." They had a drink and Dickinson cooled off. "I was all fired up when I went to see him, but he convinced me I'd draw more attention to the story," she recalled.

It was a standing joke in the firm that no matter how busy he was, Williams always had time to listen to women in distress, particularly young pretty ones. He was forever rescuing Barbara Howar, the writer and flamboyant party girl of the Johnson era, from one predicament after another. When the publishing house of Stein & Day was slow paying Howar her royalties for her memoir, *Laughing All the Way,* he called the publisher, Sol Stein, and threatened. "Sol, I'd hate to have to deep-fat fry your balls, but if she doesn't have an accounting by Thursday, I'm going to have to start heating the oil. . . ." He saved Nancy Dickerson's husband from a criminal tax investigation and inscribed a copy of his book, *One Man's Freedom,* to her: "Nancy, if you ever get in trouble, read this until I get there." Williams was delighted to help Dale Hadden, a model and actress who had appeared in *Sports Illustrated*'s annual bathing suit issue, when her husband, a CIA agent, was mysteriously slain in Paris. For different reasons, Williams always stood ready as well to help out judges. The firm handled a variety of small legal matters for members of the bench, and even defended the son of a chauffeur of a Supreme Court justice in a murder case.

Williams almost never sent a bill for any of these services. He regarded them as acts of friendship. His partners grumbled occasionally when he used up the time of young associates to help his friends free of charge, but they did not complain loudly, and never to Williams. They understood that his pro bono work for the powerful was good for business, that favors beget favors. It was a loss leader: Word of Williams's indispensable talents went out from his influential friends to clients who could pay. Henry Kissinger, for instance, referred a lucrative foreign technology transfer case to the firm after Williams listened so patiently to his problems.

By no means were all of Williams's legal services calculated to ingratiate the firm with the powerful. Father Healy recalled Williams stepping in to help "a mutual friend whose foolish liaison with a woman had led to a criminal action. Ed used a chit with a prosecutor for no reason other than friendship," said Healy. "This was someone who couldn't help him—someone who wasn't part of his world." On at least one celebrated occasion, Williams was, to his credit, willing to jeopardize his standing in the inner circle by obeying his first and greatest duty: the right to counsel.

When John Hinckley shot President Reagan in March 1981, his parents came to Williams & Connolly for help. Vince Fuller, who had been approached by the Hinckley family, went to Williams's office to talk about taking the case. Williams was uncomfortable. He was pleased with his ties to the newly elected Reagan administration, and he knew that defending the man who had tried to kill the president would not sit too well at the White House, particularly with Nancy Reagan. But he told Fuller to take the case. "This is what the firm was built on," he said. Williams commiserated with the father of the deranged boy, John Hinckley, Sr., telling him that he understood troubled children.

After a brilliant defense, Fuller won an insanity verdict for Hinckley, but the phlegmatic Fuller lacked Williams's PR touch. Meaning to downplay his achievement, Fuller told reporters, "Another day, another dollar." There was much mirth in the firm when the Soviet newspaper *Isvestia* translated Fuller's remark as "This will bring me great wealth." (In fact, the firm was well compensated by the Hinckley family.) Williams winced at Fuller's remark, but he was proud of his performance, and he went over to Fuller's house to celebrate. To his friends who asked how his firm could defend an assassin, Williams shrugged, "Look, we get a lot of nuts and fruitcakes."

On the prime-time television show "60 Minutes," CBS's folksy commentator Andy Rooney answered Williams's critics: "So why does this nice Catholic boy who graduated from Holy Cross College and loves all-American games defend these people whose crimes seem indefensible to the rest of us? Well, he has this silly respect for the law. He believes every man has a right to a fair trial and a defense lawyer, just the way the law says he should have."

Unlike other big firms in Washington, Williams & Connolly had no formal pro bono publico program to help indigent clients. Nonetheless, Williams would, from time to time, help out the poor. He would personally read the hundreds of letters pouring into his office, many from crackpots, seeking his help. He could be moved by a good sob story. Ordering a lawyer in his office to represent a penniless old lady, he declared, "I want to show her there's justice in the world." On Christmas Day, 1979, the baby boy of Jack and Betty Ross died in his mother's arms after a pediatrician had prescribed the wrong medicine. Distraught and enraged, the couple called Williams's office at midnight and left a message saying that they had lost their son. Williams called back the next morning; he then instructed a young lawyer to handle the case. The couple won $250,000.

Williams's charm was not reserved for the well connected. He was capable of showing great warmth and generosity to what he called, with unintended condescension, the "little people," the whole panoply of support staff that served him. Chatting up courthouse personnel was partly for tactical advantage, of course; making allies out of the bailiffs, clerks, and stenographers was his attempt to get the last extra edge over his adversaries. But Williams was equally solicitous of restaurant waiters and pool lifeguards. He once spent a day helping the Siasconset Beach Club lifeguard get into law school, and he flirted with the plump woman behind the desk at the Edgartown Tennis Club as though she were Lauren Bacall. For every story of Williams being rude to other lawyers in his firm, there is another story of his showing some small kindness, particularly to their spouses. Jerry Shulman, who had just joined the firm, recalled watching Williams at a firm cocktail party put Mrs. Shulman at ease by commiserating with her about lower-back pain. Dropping to the floor, Williams showed her his favorite back exercises. Larry Lucchino's mother, a Pittsburgh housewife, came to a Williams party that was studded with celebrities from government and the sporting world. Sensing her unease, Williams put his arm around her and guided her around the room "like she was his date," recalled Lucchino.

Williams was able to share his feelings in a way that bathed others in sympathy and fellow-feeling. When limousine magnate Bill Fugazy lost his teenage daughter to suicide, Williams made him feel as if she was his daughter, too. Listening to Williams eulogize her late husband, Robert Schulman, who had been a partner at Williams & Connolly, Betty Schulman felt that "it was like Ed adored Bob, and that he was his only friend."

It was difficult to reconcile the calculating Williams, who carefully compartmentalized his emotions, with the man who showed such openness of heart. Williams always had both selfish and generous sides to his nature, but as he achieved his deep ambition for fame, power, and wealth, the balance of these forces subtly shifted within him. He remained restless and determined to dominate, to be sure, yet in the 1980s, in the last decade of his life, he showed his kindness more often. He postured less; his self-effacement became more sincere. His fight with cancer may have been one reason for this mellowing. Confronted with mortality, he more often stopped to ask himself what really mattered. The answer, as the end neared, was his family, his friends, and his faith. Williams believed that people were not static, that they were capable of change. "Life is a moving picture,"he was fond of saying. He was speaking about himself.

Williams's faith was absolute. He believed in Heaven and Hell, in damnation and resurrection. His Church was the Old Church, simple and certain; he had no use for the questioning reforms of Vatican II. "Subtleties bored him," said Father Tim Healy. "He accused me of having a schoolmarm mind." Williams had always attended mass on Sunday and very often on weekdays, but he began going 365 days a year after he was stricken with cancer in 1977. "He believed in the power of prayer," said Father John Brooks of Holy Cross.

Williams's mass-going followed a set ritual. He would invariably arrive eight or nine minutes early for the seven o'clock service at Holy Trinity in Georgetown and wander back to the altar to light the candles. Father Jim Connor, the pastor, would watch Williams fumbling with the matches and wicks and wonder how someone so worldly could still seem as innocently devout as an altarboy. Connor was glad to have Williams as a lay reader a couple of mornings a week at mass. There was a great temptation for the first generation wealth in Connor's parish to become agnostic and secular, and it was good for them to hear Williams intoning the New Testament's denunciation of greed.

As the mass began, Williams would hunch over in his customary seat in the third row and open his missal, his own, well-thumbed recital of the Holy Sacrament. He always carried his missal in his litigation bag, the large black briefcase that lawyers use to carry papers and documents to court. Williams liked the stillness in the church, the familiar incantations, the brief respite from the telephone. To those sitting alongside, it seemed that he drifted off into a reverie. When the congregation responded to the readings of the mass, Williams would be out of sync, rising and sitting down after everyone else. Sometimes he was just a beat or two off; other times he seemed to be following his own, inner, text.

Williams was warm and solicitous toward his fellow parishioners. When one of the hard core of fifteen or so daily attendees was absent, Williams would miss him or her. "Where's Margaret?" he would ask Bob Flanagan, his financial adviser and fellow reader at the services, worrying that she was sick. Williams did not know the last names of most of the parishioners, unusual for a man who kept a mental Who's Who of Washington. When it came time to exchange the "kiss of peace," he would cross the aisle to enthusiastically shake hands (though he "hated the huggers," said Flanagan).

Williams was truly generous to Catholic charities. He gave away about 10 percent of his salary, a significant amount when he earned more than $1 million a year, and he often gave anonymously. Georgetown and Holy Cross, as well as Agnes's alma mater, the College of New Rochelle, and his children's schools, Georgetown Prep and Georgetown Visitation, received fat checks every year.* He raised millions more as chairman of the board of trustees at Holy Cross. Williams was proud of his old school. "Ed loved to say, 'the Col-lege of the Ho-ly Cross,' " said sports announcer Howard Cosell. But he felt the Jesuit school needed some sprucing up. It bothered Williams that a college building facing the street had unsightly air conditioners sticking out of the window. He demanded that they be removed. He wanted Holy Cross to build. "I don't see any holes in the ground," he scolded the president, Father John Brooks, who con-

---

*Various priests charged with educating the Williams children were rewarded as well with Redskins tickets (among the letters congratulating Williams on firing George Allen were two from priests to whom he had given season passes). Williams believed football should defer to religion: He asked the NFL to move a Redskins game from RFK Stadium to Philadelphia so it would not conflict with a mass to celebrate Pope John Paul II in October 1979.

sidered placating Williams by "buying a bulldozer to move dirt around."
At board meetings, Williams kept repeating one of his pet maxims,
"You've got to keep moving or you're standing still." Believing that a
winning football team was essential to the school's reputation, he got the
canny general manager of the Washington Redskins, Bobby Beathard, to
find the Crusaders a new coach who could win. Not every effort paid off.
Williams always tried to draw big-name graduation speakers, but Philadelphia mayor Wilson Goode arrived a week after his police force had
burned down several city blocks in a botched effort to roust an extremist
group. "It was the shortest graduation speech on record," Williams
observed.

Williams heavily discounted his legal fees for Georgetown University,
a client for forty years. Although he was usually quick to settle cases he
could not win, he was oddly stubborn when it came to defending the
rights of the church. In the 1980s, Georgetown was embroiled in a protracted legal struggle that pitted the university's religious freedom against
the rights of student homosexual groups. By refusing to recognize gay
groups, the university was charged with violating the D.C. Human Rights
Law. With a suit threatening to disrupt university life, Father Tim Healy,
the school's president, wanted to settle. Normally, Williams would be
found on the side of pragmatism, but in this case he wanted to take the
case to the Supreme Court.

"Ed thought homosexual conduct was a sin," said Bob Flanagan, a
Georgetown grad. (Williams routinely referred to homosexuals as "fags"
and "poofters.") Williams was widely criticized for his stand by the
more liberal Georgetown law school faculty. "Ed was a fool on this one.
He was on the wrong side of the law," said Sam Dash, a Georgetown law
professor. "This was just him fulfilling his own ego, not Georgetown's
interests." The case was settled despite Williams's objections.

Williams was equally hard-line against antipoverty activist Mitch Sny-
der, who went on a hunger strike to protest that Holy Trinity Church in
Georgetown was spending $4 million to refurbish the church instead of
feed the poor. The church elders worried that Snyder would die, but
Williams told them not to give in. "The guy's a hot dog," he said.
Snyder quit his strike.

Williams's proudest Catholic cause was the Knights of Malta, an ancient order that in the United States has become a service organization
composed largely of wealthy Catholics. Williams revitalized the local
chapter, changing its name from "Southern" to "Federal" and admitting

women ("Dames"). He arranged to send some $30 million worth of food and medical supplies to Catholic relief organizations in Central America and Africa.

Williams could be irreverent about the church; at Ethel Kennedy's sixtieth birthday party, he went as a friar accompanied by Eunice Shriver as a pregnant nun. But he was deadly serious about the Knights of Malta, who wore black robes and carried crosses to their ceremonial meetings. Membership in the order was the highest honor a Catholic layman could have. Williams brooked no teasing about it from his friends. "Sinatra is in the Knights of Malta, isn't he?" jabbed Jay Emmett. "No!" exploded Williams. "He is *not*." (In fact, Williams blackballed Sinatra, despite the singer's promise of a large donation.) When Williams's lunch pals offered to take up a collection to buy him a new robe, Williams sternly said, "That's enough."

Williams had a hard time saying no. In 1986, Mother Teresa came to his office in the Hill Building to ask for a contribution from the Knights of Malta to a hospice for AIDS patients. "AIDS is not my favorite disease," Williams told Paul Dietrich, a fellow member of the order who helped him raise funds. Williams and Dietrich rehearsed a polite refusal to Mother Teresa. Her head peeking over Williams's enormous desk, the diminutive nun made her pitch, and Williams apologetically, but firmly, declined. "Let us pray," said Mother Teresa and bowed her head. Williams looked over at Dietrich, and the two men bowed with her. When she was done, Mother Teresa gave exactly the same appeal. Again, Williams politely demurred. Once more Mother Teresa said, "Let us pray." Williams looked up at the ceiling. "All right, all right," he said, and pulled out his checkbook.

Williams's daughter Ellen tried to make her father's charity a little more hands-on by persuading him to work in a soup kitchen on Christmas Day, 1984. The whole family piled into two cars and headed downtown after lunch. Williams was "shy and uncomfortable at first," Ellen recalled, but he warmed to the task. He got interested trying to find out who in the soup line was "really down and out" and who was "just freeloading."

The auxiliary bishop of Washington, Eugene Marino, also tried to get Williams to take a more personal role by asking him to record an inspirational television spot. He wrote Williams in April 1978 that he was "seeking to capture on film your personal relationship with Christ." Williams's subject was to be "Jesus is Lord, He is our Hope, our Salvation.'' After trying to record a homily, Williams wrote the bishop that he couldn't bring himself to do it; his faith was ''too private.''

As he got older, Williams began to talk increasingly about devoting more of his time to charity and public service. ''The last quarter of my life is going to be pro bono publico,'' he declared to a Williams & Connolly associate, Sarah Duggin. Williams was especially expansive on this subject with his friend Ben Bradlee. Both men were restless with the grind of their professional lives, and they fantasized about quitting their jobs in order to join forces, seek adventure, and do good. As a boy, Bradlee had read Upton Sinclair novels about a character named Lanny Budd who was a dashing secret agent and troubleshooter for the president. Was there a revolution brewing in Urubaduba? A hostage crisis in the Levant? Lanny was the man for the job. Let's be like Lanny Budd! Bradlee would exclaim. The two men dreamed of setting up a consulting firm. Not the usual kind, the Beltway Bandits who leech off the government, but a combination of Lord Castlereagh and ''Mission Impossible.'' They would negotiate hostage crises in far-off lands or ''solve the Boston School strike, whatever,'' Bradlee said. ''They weren't thinking small,'' said Bradlee's wife, Sally Quinn. It was a wonderful idea after a martini or two.

Chapter Thirty-Five

WILLIAMS WAS BETTER able to realize his fantasies in the sporting world, where he was rich enough to buy his dreams. His love of contest had always found an outlet in the athletic arena. He would compete at almost any sport except golf (too slow) and sailing (too preppy, too tippy). Though fierce, he was a mediocre athlete. His record against Larry Lucchino at "winter tennis"—played every Sunday at 8:00 A.M., wind and ice notwithstanding—was "two and eighty-four," recalled Lucchino. But as his wealth accumulated, he found another path to victory: He could buy the best athletes in the world. His judgment of talent was sometimes lacking, and his impatience stood in the way of dynasty building. Nonetheless, in the 1980s, Williams became even better known as a sportsman, as a high-profile big-league owner, than as a Washington lawyer.

Boxing remained his first love. Williams was a ringside regular at championship bouts. He liked to be as close to the fighters as possible, to feel the concussion of the punches and the spray of sweat and blood. He said he wanted to "taste the fight." Actually, Williams would watch any fight, including staged ones. On Saturday mornings, when he was supposedly laboring away at the firm, he could be found in front of his television set at 11:30 watching professional wrestling. (He liked the showmanship; he was a particular fan of "Hulk" Hogan.)

Williams talked often on the phone to heavyweight champion Muhammad Ali, whom he counseled on legal and personal problems, and his firm successfully defended Don King, the flamboyant fight promoter, against tax evasion charges. Williams asked King if he could help him find a fighter to back. King suggested a then-unknown teenage slugger named Larry Holmes. Williams, who preferred "brand names," wasn't interested. Instead of backing the future heavyweight champion of the world, Williams bought a middleweight named "Irish Mike" Baker, who had been an amateur champion. In 1976, Williams had paid Baker $10,000, plus expenses, in return for two-thirds of his purse. Baker "reminds me of a light Billy Conn," Williams said, optimistically. His friends scoffed that Baker was a "slow white guy who led with his head." Baker turned out to be a bleeder as well. He quickly fell out of the rankings, and his only real value to Williams was as a house-sitter in the summers when the Williams family went to Martha's Vineyard.

Williams was not a heavy gambler. The roulette wheel and the black-jack dealer were too far beyond his control, but he often made small wagers, usually on the outcomes of ball games. After looking for Holy Cross's gridiron opponent on a Saturday, Williams would shout at his Ivy League–educated partner Larry Lucchino, "You take the girls from Harvard. I'll take the Crusaders." Williams also used betting to lose weight. His children observed that it was the only method that worked.

Williams did not frequent the track, but in the late seventies he was given a racehorse by Pittsburgh Steelers owner Art Rooney. Williams was a novice at raising thoroughbreds. "How's he doing?" Williams would ask the horse's trainer. "Well, he's eating good," would come the reply. In 1979, Williams took two of his sons, Ned and Tony, to watch the horse, Amadon, run at Charles Town, West Virginia. Williams's silks were burgundy and gold—Redskins colors—and the PA system at the track played "Hail to the Redskins" in Williams's honor. Amadon was lagging in seventh place at the first turn. "Boys, we're out of here!" said Williams. "We were in the tunnel before the horse finished," recalled Ned. The horse spent his career out of the money.

Williams's greatest sporting ambition was to own a major league base-ball team. The boy who had sold "ice colds and red hots" for the minor league Hartford Senators wanted to own the big league Washington Sen-ators. He had bought into the football Redskins only after he failed to win a baseball franchise in Washington in 1961. In 1972, he had tried again to get a team in Washington but failed in an attempt to move the San Diego Padres. Undaunted, he kept searching for weak franchises that might want to move to the nation's capital.

Baseball commissioner Bowie Kuhn was also interested in bringing baseball back to Washington. In the mid-1970s, the commissioner began to eye the Baltimore Orioles, who won on the field but lost at the gate. Even though the team had had the most successful record in baseball over the previous decade, the Orioles had never drawn more than 1.2 million fans in a season. The Los Angeles Dodgers, by contrast, regularly drew over 3 million. Financially strapped, Orioles owner Jerry Hoffberger was looking for a buyer. In the summer of 1978, Kuhn urged William Simon, the former treasury secretary, to enter the bidding. Simon said he wanted a partner. The baseball commissioner suggested he try Ed Williams.

Williams did not hesitate to join up with Simon. His constant wrangles with George Allen had wearied him of the Redskins. He also sensed that the football team might not be his private plaything anymore. Having sold his professional hockey and basketball teams in Los Angeles to pay for his divorce, Jack Kent Cooke was moving back to the East Coast. It was inevitable that the 85 percent owner of the Redskins would want to take back some of the control over the team that he had left to Williams for the past fifteen years.

Cooke's switch from the West to the East Coast sporting scene was a problem for Williams, but it was also a solution. Despite his expensive divorce, Cooke was still wealthy and financially liquid. When Simon approached Williams about buying the Orioles, Williams decided to share the opportunity—and the cost—with his Redskins co-owner. In August 1978, Williams and Cooke joined forces with Simon to bid Hoffberger's asking price of $12 million. That month, Cooke wrote Williams expressing satisfaction with the beckoning Orioles deal: "I am grateful, indeed, that you wish to expand our partnership into this exciting new project which, I predict, will be a source of uncommon satisfaction to all of us. And I am not unmindful of the inevitable contribution to our respective exchequers."

A proud and cantankerous man, Hoffberger was wary of the carpetbaggers who wanted to buy his team. He rightly suspected that Simon and Williams wanted to move the Orioles out of Baltimore and down the road to Washington. A civic booster for his home city, Hoffberger began fishing for local buyers. After months of on-again, off-again negotiations, Simon lost patience. In February 1979, he denounced Hoffberger to the *Baltimore Sun*. "I've never seen such duplicity in my life," he said. "It's like dealing with the Scarlet Pimpernel." The deal was off.

Williams, who often observed that "nothing is often a good thing to do and always a brilliant thing to say," quietly watched through the spring and early summer of 1979 while a group of local businessmen tried and failed to come up with the $12 million. Then, without fanfare, he approached Hoffberger with his own offer—$11.8 million. He carefully stroked the Orioles owner, telling him that he was essential to the franchise, that he was the soul of Baltimore while Williams was a mere outsider. He offered to give Hoffberger the title of president of the team if he sold ownership to Williams. In July 1979, Hoffberger agreed. Williams became a major league owner. Hoffberger became a figurehead whom Williams eventually eased out.

Williams was rich, but not as rich as most baseball owners. He was able to put up $500,000 in cash, but the rest of the $11.8 million was borrowed, mostly by leveraging his real estate holdings—the Jefferson Hotel and an office building on 18th Street. Williams also borrowed $3.5 million from the Redskins, which as a practical matter meant mostly from Cooke. What Cooke expected in return for that favor was to become a matter of bitter debate in later years.

"Take me out to the ball game," sang the waiters in Joe and Mo's, a Washington restaurant, when Williams arrived there for dinner the night the deal was announced. The waiters, like nearly everyone else in the capital, assumed that the Baltimore Orioles would soon become the Washington Orioles. Resentful of their powerful neighbors forty-five miles away on I-95, insecure about losing their status as a "major league city," Baltimorians were downcast about the sale. "Baltimore to Williams: The Orioles Belong to Us" headlined the Sunday *News American*. A Baltimore columnist caustically described the new owner as "a smooth professional from the high-powered D.C. martini set." Williams was apprehensive as he went to his first press conference in Baltimore on August 2. As usual, he had carefully rehearsed his answers. He would stay in Baltimore, he announced—so long as the team was well supported by the fans.

The newspapers did not believe him. They continued to report that a move to Washington was imminent. When the *Washington Post* quoted "sources close to Williams" as saying the new owner would move the Orioles to Washington within three years, Williams blasted the story as "the nadir of irresponsible journalism . . . totally and absolutely without foundation." Williams's denials damped down the press speculation. And to save the team, the fans responded by turning out in record numbers. When a sell-out was announced at a late-season series against the

Red Sox, the crowd roared and turned to look up at Williams's box in the second deck behind home plate. The new owner waved and gave a thumbs-up signal.

Meanwhile, he had told Larry Lucchino to cruise up and down I-95 in a helicopter, looking for new stadium sites close to Washington. "Dad *did* intend to move at first," said son Tony. "But he came to love Baltimore." The love was highly conditional. Williams could not afford to own a financial loser. The year Williams bought the team, the Orioles drew 1.6 million, a record. After losing over $200,000 in 1978, the Orioles made $1.5 million in 1979. Williams was able to pay generous new salaries for his stars, pitcher Jim Palmer and infielder Doug DeCinces. But the next summer, he put Baltimore back on notice. "This was to be a trial year for Baltimore attendance," he warned, "and the trial is just about to begin." The fans came through again, setting a new attendance record of 1.8 million.

By 1983, the team was drawing over 2 million a year. Shrewd marketing by Williams accounted for much of the surge.* He set out to make the Orioles a regional franchise, signing broadcast contracts that would bring the team into homes in seven states, and dropping the word *Baltimore* before *Orioles* in promotional materials. His real target was Washington and its affluent suburbs. When Williams bought the team, 10 percent of its fans came from the Washington area. Within five years, the team drew 25 percent of its attendance from the capital. In the end, Williams did not need to move the Orioles to Washington. In effect, he moved Washington to the Orioles.

Williams found himself spending more and more time on the Orioles and less and less on the Redskins. When Jack Kent Cooke bought a horse farm outside Washington, he told reporters that Williams would remain "the dominant force" in the Redskin organization, but Williams knew better. Asked about his relationship with Cooke at the Redskins annual homecoming lunch in 1979, Williams invoked "the golden rule: He who has the gold, rules." Although he pretended otherwise at first, Williams did not like Cooke, whom he found pretentious and overbearing. A multimillionaire who had started out playing the clarinet for a nightclub band in Canada and selling soap, Cooke was easy to mock. Vain and effusive, he called men "darlings" and women "pets." But he was a

---

*Throughout his ownership of the Orioles, Williams was advised by Jay Emmett, a former client and Paramount executive with smart promotional instincts, and Williams's young law partner Larry Lucchino, who became the Orioles' president.

shrewd operator, and he set about to undermine Williams almost as soon as he arrived.

After George Allen's departure in 1978, Williams had hired Bobby Beathard, a then-obscure Miami Dolphins assistant coach, as general manager. It was an inspired move. Beathard would go on to create a Super Bowl champion. (Howard Cosell claims to have persuaded Williams to hire Beathard, who had an uncanny knack for finding talented players. "He can find 'em in the trees," Cosell told Williams.) Beathard soon discovered that he was serving two very different masters. "Cooke bragged, Williams never did," he said. "Williams would blow and then forget it. Cooke never forgot. Williams was first class, Cooke was nickel-and-dime cheap." Cooke was jealous of Williams and his immense clout in Washington. The former owner of the Lakers and the Kings and builder of the Los Angeles Forum was big-time in L.A., but in Washington, he was just "out there," as Williams indelicately put it. Williams meant out in Upperville, the Virginia horse country, but he might as well have meant Mars. The majority owner of the Redskins wanted to take back what he felt was rightfully his. He began with the general manager. "From the beginning, Jack tried to turn me against Ed," Beathard said. "He told me not to talk to Williams, not to tell him anything."

In January 1980, Williams read in the newspapers that Cooke was looking for a new coach. Williams wanted to stick with Jack Pardee, whom he regarded as a paragon of small-town virtue, despite the fact that George Allen's successor had won six and lost ten that fall, the Redskins' worst record in a decade. Williams gave Pardee a vote of confidence in the newspapers. Two days later, Cooke fired Pardee. After the new coach, Joe Gibbs, lost his first five games in 1980, a sign went up in the end-zone seats that read: "Go Back Cooke. We Want EBW." The *Washington Post* ran a front-page picture of the sign, over the caption, "Sign of the times: Redskins fans let team owner Jack Kent Cooke know their feelings during loss to 49ers. . . ." What the *Post* did not know was that the sign had been hung there by EBW's sixteen-year-old son Tony.

The owners box at RFK Stadium, Williams's private preserve before Cooke arrived, became less congenial. Under the Williams regime, the guests might have sat on the Supreme Court during the weekday, but the ambience on Sundays was hot dogs and beer. A determined social climber, Cooke brought in waiters in black tie, pink tablecloths, and matrons from Upperville draped in furs. Cooke argued against Williams inviting the same guests every week, urging him to make more "political" use of the seating. "But these are my friends!" Williams protested, forgetting for the moment how he had used the box to secure his own social and political standing a decade earlier.

Williams retreated to the other owners box, the one at Memorial Stadium in Baltimore. It was all his, and he felt reasonably welcomed by the fans, despite all the talk of moving to Washington. "Ed-die! Ed-die!" they chanted on opening day 1980. Williams thought the cheers were for him (they were for Eddie Murray, the Orioles' new $1 million-a-year first baseman). Baseball, after all, had always been his first love. "Football was no good," Williams declared to his old Georgetown Law School friend Bill Ragan. "This is the sport, this is the sport."

Football gave Williams only sixteen chances a season to work himself into a state over winning. The baseball season ran 162 games. Williams found himself attending almost every home game. He arranged to have a telephone number he could call that would allow him to listen to radio broadcasts of Orioles games from anywhere in the country. When the Orioles played away, Williams would drive around for two hours listening to the car radio, which got better reception than the radio in his home. His children would accompany him, cringing in the backseat as Williams, as ever an awful driver, careered around the back roads of Potomac, Maryland, his mind off in Fenway Park or Yankee Stadium. If the Orioles won, Williams would superstitiously instruct his children to sit in the same places the next night.

Williams hung on every pitch. On the opening day of the 1980 season, the Orioles' starting pitcher, Hall of Famer Jim Palmer, began by throwing a pair of balls. Williams began banging on the window separating his box from the seat occupied by Hank Peters, the general manager. "What the hell is the story with Palmer?" Williams demanded. Peters, a calm man gaited to baseball's long season, stared back in disbelief. Sportswriter Morrie Siegel, seated behind Williams, leaned over to his old friend and said, "Hey, Ed. They play 162 of these things." With a rueful smile, Williams told his friend Jay Emmett, "I'm emotionally unsuited to own a baseball team. What kind of sport is it where you can lose sixty times a year and be a roaring success?"

Williams's anxieties about winning on the field were matched by his worries over money. In 1976, the courts had ruled that players were no longer chattel but free to bid their services to any team. In the new era of "free agentry," salaries tripled between 1975 and 1980, from an average $52,000 a year to nearly $150,000. With a smaller media market than the big-city teams, the Orioles struggled to stay in the running for top players. The average Oriole salary, $116,000, stood eighteenth out of the twenty-six teams in baseball. The bidding war was "crazy," declared Williams. "It's outrageous. I can't believe it. It's got to come back. It can't work, and in the end, it'll blow up. It's just madness."

Baseball commissioner Kuhn shared his concern. He feared that baseball would divide into two classes. The wealthy teams would corner the best players, and the teams in smaller markets would be perennially stuck in the second division. Kuhn advised the owners to come up with a new rule requiring any team that hired away a free agent to compensate the club losing the athlete with a player of roughly equal ability. The effect, of course, would be to slow the bidding race, since owners would have less incentive to steal away high-priced talent.

The players, naturally, felt the owners were conspiring to threaten their newly won freedom to earn as much as they were worth. A strike loomed. Williams once more resorted to hyperbole. "It would be like a nuclear war and cause permanent damage to both sides," he warned.

Certainly, a strike risked permanent damage to Williams's own pocketbook. When the players walked out on May 22, 1981, Williams was beside himself. He had borrowed to buy the Orioles at two points over prime—20 percent at that time of swollen interest rates. Without a steady stream of income, he risked failing to meet his interest payments. At home, the humor turned black. "We're going to have to sell the house, kids," he announced, and his children weren't entirely sure he was kidding. At Williams's sixty-first birthday party in May, Art Buchwald stood and announced to guests, "This is the last time we'll ever eat meat in this house."

Williams was determined to get a settlement, and quickly. But most of the owners, particularly the wealthy ones from big markets, were suspicious of him. Williams believed in revenue sharing: He wanted team owners to share broadcast and ticket receipts on a more equitable basis, as they already did in football. (The American League split the gate 80–20, compared to 60–40 in the NFL.) "I'm basically a capitalist, but I think baseball needs a quasi-socialist system to survive," Williams had said at an owners meeting in December 1980. "Revenue sharing, hell, that's communism!" retorted Buzzy Bavasi, the general manager of the California Angels. Now, in the summer of 1981, the owners did not listen to Williams's pleas to compromise with the players.

Nor did Bowie Kuhn give Williams much help. The baseball commissioner preferred to stay on the sidelines and let the owners work things out themselves. Williams was furious with Kuhn. "What does he mean it's not his business?" Williams ranted to sportswriter Morrie Siegel. "What the hell do we pay him for?" On the phone every morning to sportscaster Howard Cosell, Williams complained that Kuhn was too weak to stand up to the players' union chief, Marvin Miller. "Ed thought Bowie was a little too Princeton, a little too corporate law," said Larry Lucchino. "He wasn't a street fighter." At a dinner in New York in June, Williams shocked the commissioner by announcing, "Our friendship is over."

Williams told reporters that he was "down and depressed. This is the worst year of my life," he declared. His strike insurance was about to run out. He was keeping up interest payments, but if the season was canceled, he feared he'd have to sell the team. Williams worked to cut a deal. He kept a back channel open to the players through the Orioles' representatives, Doug DeCinces and Mark Belanger. He called on President Reagan to intervene. Violating a "gag" rule imposed by the owners, he held secret early morning meetings with federal mediator Ken Moffett at the Jefferson Hotel throughout August, searching for a way out.

Finally, on the verge of canceling the season, the owners settled. Players' representative Miller gave the credit to Williams. "He wanted to settle any way possible, by binding arbitration, this way or that." The owners were less happy. One stated: "The scars that Williams left are very deep . . . and they won't heal easily." Moffett added, "A lot of people don't like to give Williams credit . . . they think he was trying to do them in, and he was, because he was trying to get this thing settled."

The strike had lasted fifty days and canceled 713 games. Even after collecting $44 million in insurance benefits, the owners lost $72 million. But Williams had survived.* Moreover, his conciliatory role, his determination to save the season, won him important points with the fans and players. "His moderation reinforced his club's sense of unity, helping pave the way for the team's 1982 and 1983 success," wrote James Edward Miller in his history of the Orioles, *The Baseball Business*. In 1982, the Orioles came within a game of winning the pennant, and in 1983, they swept into the World Series with the best record in baseball. The team won more by teamwork than the performance of individual stars. Williams began calling the Orioles a "band of brothers," his highest accolade.

---

*Despite his poor mouthing, Williams ended up *making* money on the strike. Insurance more than made up for the shortfall, since he did not have to pay salaries.

The Orioles achieved a kind of mystique in those years. "Are the Baltimore Orioles the Best Team in Baseball, or Just the Best Run?" asked the *Wall Street Journal* in October 1983. The story noted that the team had made it to the Word Series without "big salaries and big jealousies." "Nobody's going to beat Baltimore," wrote New York Yankees' third baseman Graig Nettles. "Baltimore is perfect. Everyone knows his role and is comfortable and happy in that role. They get along with their manager . . . and they've gone out and beaten the hell out of everybody."

Williams basically let the Orioles run themselves. He paid close attention, to be sure. In the middle of discussing a legal matter at the firm, he was known to pull out a yellow pad and start writing down Orioles lineups. But he never used the phone from the owners box down to the dugout, and he did not second-guess the general manager, Hank Peters, or their veteran field manager, Earl Weaver. He was more generous at salary time than Hoffberger, who had been notoriously cheap. (Hoffberger had let Reggie Jackson and Ron Baylor slip away; Williams paid tens of millions to keep stars like Jim Palmer, Al Bumbry, and Eddie Murray.) And he rarely showed up in the clubhouse to inspect his investments. It was a formula for success. Roger Angell wrote in *The New Yorker:* "The Orioles are the dominant American League team of our time. . . . The heart of it, clearly, is that the Orioles always cling to and personify the idea of a team."

With two out in the bottom of the ninth in the fifth game of the 1983 World Series, the Orioles led the Philadelphia Phillies 5–0. One more out and Williams would own a world champion. Pete Rose was batting for the Phillies. The Orioles pitcher, Scott McGregor, who had given up only five hits, threw a ball. "Fuck!" Williams cried. Talk-show host Larry King, who was sitting nearby, shouted, "Are you crazy? You're gonna win." Williams replied, "You never know, man. Pessimism is a way of life." Rose hit a soft line drive to Cal Ripken at shortstop and Williams leaped up, hugging his box-mates and shouting. In the clubhouse, he called an old lady in Hartford who had once taken him to baseball games at Bulkeley Stadium. She was blind and dying in a nursing home. "We won! We won!" Williams shouted into the phone. He threw his arm around Orioles designated hitter Ken Singleton. "This is the happiest I've ever been," he said. Singleton was startled to see that Williams was on the verge of tears.

General Manager Peters came up to Williams, who by now was dripping with champagne. "Are you happy now?" he asked. Williams sobered. "I'm worried about next year." On the flight home, King noticed that Williams seemed to be drifting off, oblivious to the beautiful October night. "Where are you?" King asked. Williams answered, "I've got a trial Wednesday."

Chapter Thirty-Six

In fact, Williams did not go to trial the Wednesday after the World Series. He went to court to ask for a postponement of the scheduled trial in a complex white-collar crime case that had been dragging on for four years—and would drag on for four more. Williams did not go to trial anymore, not if he could possibly help it. His aversion was based partly on fatigue: He could no longer stand the grind of preparing for trial. But in the secretive world of white-collar crime, Williams understood that, win or lose, just going to trial was a defeat.

When Williams talked to young associates who had come to the firm hoping to be great trial lawyers, following in the footsteps of the firm's founder, he scoffed. "Trying cases! That's all you guys talk about," he growled at them. "I'll tell you what a great trial lawyer is. He keeps his client from going to trial. He keeps his client from getting indicted in the first place. That's victory. Don't give me this crap about trial law."

Wealthy businessmen investigated by the U.S. attorney or the IRS or the SEC did not want their business affairs spread out in open court. They did not want to endure the ignominy of a long and highly publicized trial. They wanted their well paid lawyers to make the case "go away." Criminal investigations were best strangled in the crib, at the grand jury stage or even before. The perfect case was the investigation that no one—outside the offices of the prosecutor and the potential defendant—ever even heard about.

No one was better at making cases just "go away" than Ed Williams. In the late seventies and early eighties, he invented and perfected many

403

of the techniques of white-collar defense. "He was the model and the seed," said former Watergate special prosecutor Chuck Ruff. "In the 1970s, he *was* the white-collar bar. When someone got in trouble, there's one name they knew. They'd say, 'I'm going to the best, I'm going to get Ed Williams.' " Williams was the best. His defenses were tenacious and brilliant. But they raised difficult and troubling questions of legal ethics and the functioning of the judicial system, questions that most white-collar lawyers would just as soon not examine too closely.

In an "ordinary" or street crime—a murder, a robbery, a rape—there is usually overt evidence of the crime—the bloody shirt, the broken window, the suspect's fingerprints. Defense lawyers usually don't get involved until the police have been along to sweep up this evidence. White-collar crimes are different. As Kenneth Mann points out in his thoughtful study *Defending White-Collar Crime,* they are "frauds whose very design seeks to leave no traces." Prosecutors are forced to put together "bits and pieces of evidence that are hidden, dispersed or seemingly innocuous."

The most critical role of a white-collar defense lawyer is to keep the prosecutor from getting the evidence. It is, in Mann's dry terminology, "information control." In some senses, it is no different from what courtroom lawyers do when they object to evidence on the grounds that it is irrelevant or prejudicial. There is a crucial distinction, however. The courtroom rules of evidence seek to discard *irrelevant* information. A good white-collar lawyer seeks to stop the prosecutor from finding information that is directly relevant to the guilt of his client. At a certain point, "information control" can become obstruction of justice. But in the murky world of legal ethics, that point remains ill-defined.

Before he can keep information from the prosecutor, a criminal lawyer has to learn it from his client. This is not always easy, given that clients have selective memories. "Clients never come in and admit guilt," said Brendan Sullivan. "It's always, 'the prosecutor's after me.' " Williams had little patience with clients who came in protesting their innocence. A state official facing a bribery investigation came to Williams insisting that he had an "ironclad case" for acquittal. Williams examined some documents and remarked that the case looked difficult to him. The official was cocky and sneered that "a second-year associate could do it." Williams stared at him from the end of his long conference table. Then he cross-examined the official for an hour. When he had finished, "the guy looked like he had gone through World War III,'' said a lawyer who was in the room. ''He was in tears.''

Williams let his clients know that he was in control, not them. He would pointedly tell them the story of Faye Emerson crying because his questioning of Adam Clayton Powell was so harsh. ''He was saying to clients, you may be guilty,'' said Mike Tigar. ''But this is all about evidence. No one is going to jail unless the government has the evidence. But first I've got to find out. I'm not going to buy into your feeling that the system is fucking you over.''

As a rule, Williams didn't bother to take notes in the initial interview because he knew the client was lying. Slowly, he'd probe for the truth. Some clients would ''embrace the wrongdoing,'' in the delicate phrase of defense lawyers, but most would not. ''I've always demanded the truth,'' Williams joked to Joe Califano, ''and I've never gotten it.''

The fact is, however, that Williams did not always want the truth—at least the whole truth. If he thought there was any risk of the client testifying—and Williams always put defendants on the stand if he could not avoid trial—then he did not want to be in the position of suborning perjury. He would—as we have seen in the Hoffa, Baker, and Connally cases—help the client come up with a plausible theory to explain away incriminating facts. This was done subtly, through leading questions and a certain amount of winking and nodding. White-collar cases usually turned on questions of intent—did the client *knowingly* perform some action, like juggling the accounts, with the *intent* to commit fraud.

When Dominic Antonelli loaned money to Joseph P. Yeldell, did he intend to bribe him? Or just help him? ''Williams did not have to demand total candor,'' said Steven Brill, the editor of the *American Lawyer* and a student of the white-collar bar. ''He demanded the best possible story. People don't admit criminality. Human contact doesn't work this way. People don't say, 'I stole $400,000, now what do you want me to do?' They put the best gloss on the facts. If they say, 'I stole $400,000,' Ed would say, 'What kind of pressure were you under? Did you steal it or borrow it?' Well, the client gets the picture. Yeah, sure, that's right, I returned the money!''

The issues get trickier—and the ethics grayer—when the prosecutor seeks to find out not only what is in the mind of the defendant but in his filing cabinets as well. Some lawyers greet subpoenas for corporate records with more nods and winks. Telling a client to withhold or destroy evidence is clearly obstruction of justice. But some white-collar practitioners see nothing unethical in looking the other way. They tell the client what the subpoena is looking for, and why the evidence would be significant to the case. But they leave it up to the client to actually produce the evidence. If the client reports that the drawer was empty, well, it's not the lawyer's job to enforce compliance with the law.

The ethical issues here are ambiguous—at least in legal terms. Lawyers believe in the adversary process. Their client has a right against self-incrimination, and to confidentiality with his lawyer. Lawyers are not required to reveal that their clients committed a crime. If the lawyer learns that the client did not turn over information in response to a subpoena, he is not required to report it to the court. On the other hand, a lawyer cannot *knowingly* engage in a plot to conceal information or defraud the court. The question then is what does the lawyer *know*. The Code of Professional Responsibility gives little guidance, except to say that doubts should be resolved in favor of the client. Lawyers naturally tend to take a legalistic view. They are not "legally knowledgeable" even though they may be in fact.

In his book, Mann distinguishes between "probers" who actively force their clients to reveal the truth to them and obey government subpoenas, and "nonprobers" who take a more passive—and ethically dubious—approach. To his credit, Williams was in the "probers" camp, at least where the production of documents was concerned. Lawyers from Williams's firm would round up all the documentation, incriminating and exculpatory, and take charge of producing it to the prosecutors. Everything was carefully logged. The firm might narrowly interpret subpoenas, of course, but documents were never destroyed. "It's not because Ed was boy scoutish," said Vince Fuller. "It's to keep the client from hurting himself. Clients panic. They are their own worst enemy. The best favor you can perform is to get control and not let them destroy documents. The prosecutor will piece together the missing stuff and draw the worst possible inference."

Prosecutors generally agree that Williams played clean. "There was no venality about him," said Mark Richard, a career Justice Department prosecutor. "I never felt he distorted the facts. He made the most of what he had." Williams was as always protective of his reputation. Clients who destroyed evidence would reflect badly on him. "I think Ed produced documents," said Bill Hundley. "You could say it was out of fear—that they were all gunning for him. He had to be very careful."

The defendant's knowledge and state of mind, the documentary evidence—these were critical, but not the prosecutor's only source of information. White-collar cases were typically complex conspiracies, involving multiple defendants and witnesses. A prosecutor's best hope was to divide and conquer: to pick off individual defendants and "flip them" against their co-conspirators, or to find low-level employees who would testify against their bosses. It was critical for Williams to get to these potentially lethal witnesses before the prosecutor, and, if possible, keep them quiet. This was not a new imperative for Williams; recall how the government's main witness in the Powell case, Hattie Dodson, suddenly experienced a memory loss when she became Williams's client on the eve of trial. Or how Rex Cauble refused to help the prosecutors in the Connally case after Williams arranged to have him represented by Bill Hundley. "It's better to have the camel in the tent pissing out than outside pissing in," said one of Williams's partners, quoting the old LBJ aphorism. "You want the firm to represent as many as possible, and farm out the rest to people you can work with."

Naturally, prosecutors bitterly object to this sort of stonewalling. They argue that it is a conflict of interest for a lawyer to represent more than one party in a case. The theory is that the lawyer will sacrifice the interest of one to protect the other—for example, that he will order the secretary to lie to protect her boss, thus exposing the secretary to a perjury charge. Williams dismissed this argument. As we have seen, he had a highly paternalistic view toward conflicts; he believed that he could serve everyone's interests at once. His partners point out that no low-level employee ever went to jail for perjury in a Williams case. Williams believed in full disclosure and obtained waivers from witnesses and defendants giving him the right to handle their defense. If the other side didn't like it, then the prosecutor was free to immunize the witness and make him testify for the state.

The conflicts area is another ethical fogbank. Appearances don't necessarily reflect reality—either for better or for worse. Despite the appearance of a conflict, Williams was often able to serve many clients at once without sacrificing any of them. The only losers were prosecutors who were boxed out of a case. Yet the risk was real that the small fry could get stepped on. Typically, if Williams was representing a corporation or its CEO in a white-collar case, he would arrange to have separate counsel represent the employees. There would be no appearance of conflict; the employees now had their own independent counsel.

But how independent? Typically, the lawyer's fee would be paid by the corporation, not by the employee. The employee's lawyer himself was often a friend of Williams's and dependant on Williams for referrals in the future. He felt both personal and marketplace pressures to do exactly what Williams told him to do. "The way it works is that the corporation comes to Ed, and he hands out the business," said a former federal prosecutor in Baltimore who now specializes in white-collar defense. "The unwritten rule was if you cut and run on Ed, you're off the list."

If Williams could not stop a prosecutor from obtaining information about his client, he could at least slow him down. As Stanley Sporkin learned in the SEC's protracted case against Gulf + Western, delay was one of Williams's favorite weapons. "Ed always believed that time was on your side, that a witness might die or the prosecutor would quit or get sick of it," said Peter Fleming, a New York defense lawyer and frequent co-counsel of Williams's. "He would say, 'You know what's the greatest thing a lawyer can accomplish? It's when the judge told you eighteen times you're going to trial April 1, it's docketed, you'll be in contempt if you're not ready—and you go down and get a continuance.' " Williams's skills at stalling were legendary in his firm. At a Christmas dinner, Mike Tigar regaled the other lawyers by picturing a long line of the recently departed queued up outside the Pearly Gates. He described St. Peter with his staff, intoning, "You're in, you're out, you're in, you're out—you! Williams! Thirty-day continuance."

Williams could slow down a case simply by overwhelming the prosecutor with paper. Williams liked to elicit sympathy for the plight of his poor, lonely client, cowering against the awesome power of the U.S. government. It is true that clients sometimes came to him shaking from a knock on the door by FBI agents. But thereafter the "lonely client" was surrounded by a phalanx of well-paid and superbly trained Williams & Connolly lawyers. The "powerful government" often consisted of an overworked junior prosecutor with a poor support staff. The quality of the legal arguments churned out by Williams & Connolly was high, and the volume was massive—motions and pleadings on any and every conceivable procedural point. "I'd read the papers coming from Williams's firm, and think, 'Oh my God.' I'd be resigned to defeat," said the Justice Department's Mark Richard. "Then I'd read them again and realize it was all bullshit." Winning or not, the papers had to be responded to, and that took time. Not surprisingly, prosecutors sometimes wearied and decided to move on to the next case.

Over the years, Williams & Connolly became famous—or infamous—
for their aggressive tactics. The firm's approach was variously described
as "scorched earth" and "take no prisoners." The terms may describe
some of Williams's more zealous partners. But his personal approach was
more subtle—a mixture of good cheer and implied threats, of forthright-
ness and deception. To prosecutors, Williams always seemed detached
from his clients, and hence more credible than more partisan advocates.
He never demeaned prosecutors, never belittled the government's case.
What's more, he was fun to talk to. Still, behind the jokes was the threat
that war might break out at any moment. Prosecutors naturally wanted to
put off the day of reckoning. "It was fun to talk about the Redskins! It
was horrible to go to court!" said Fleming.

Williams would not hesitate to charge prosecutorial misconduct against
the same prosecutors who had been laughing so heartily at his jokes the
day before. In 1978, Williams represented Velsicol Chemical, accused of
lying to the Environmental Protection Agency (EPA) about the cancer-
causing properties of its pesticides. The young prosecutor handling the
case told the grand jury that the company official testifying before them
had hired Williams & Connolly because he realized the seriousness of his
crimes. Williams exploded when he found out. "Never in thirty-five
years have I seen anything so outrageous!" he fulminated to the judge,
charging prosecutorial misconduct. The case was dismissed.

Williams's ability to outperform the prosecution was never more vividly illustrated than in the case against Abel Holtz. In 1981, the federal
government began "Operation Greenback," an investigation into Florida
bankers suspected of laundering drug money. A prime target was Holtz,
president of Miami's Capital Bank. Men identifying themselves as
"Javier," "Carlos," and "Hector" were depositing millions in $20
bills—stuffed into cardboard boxes, suitcases, flight bags, and paper
sacks—into Holtz's bank. A grand jury began hearing evidence against
Holtz. He was within days of being indicted when Williams had an idea.
He offered to let the prosecutor interview Holtz, to ask him any question
he wanted, to decide if he was really guilty. "I'm going to do something
I've never done in my whole career," Williams told the prosecutor,
Charles Blau. "I'm going to give him to you. The only condition is that
you can't use this interview against him." Blau immediately agreed.
Williams's move, of course, broke all the rules of information control.
But with the grand jury on the verge of indicting his client, he had to try
something bold.

Holtz told the prosecutor that he had no idea that his bank was being flooded with crumpled $20 bills of suspicious origin. The prosecutor did not believe him, but he did not indict him either. Holtz's testimony had turned up some new leads, raised some new questions. The investigation continued. Meanwhile, however, the prosecutor was transferred to Washington. A new prosecutor took over, and once more the grand jury began to hear evidence. Now Williams struck. He accused the new prosecutor of violating the agreement with his predecessor not to use Holtz's testimony against him. It would be prosecutorial misconduct, Williams threatened. Complaining that the government had been "hoodwinked" and "mousetrapped," U.S. Attorney Leon Kellner dropped the case. Williams was pleased with his trick. "You play Dizzy the Dunce," he told a lawyer working on the case with him. "Then you kick the shit out of them."

If Williams could not manipulate the prosecutor, there was always the judge. Over the years, Williams carefully ingratiated himself with members of the bench. In 1977, Steve Truitt, representing the pressmen's union striking against the *Washington Post,* came up against Williams. Truitt was shocked to find that the *Post*'s counsel had represented the judge in the case, Leonard Braman of D.C. Superior Court, in an earlier court proceeding. Truitt wanted the judge disqualified. Williams was irked. "They don't understand," he complained to his partners. "This is the way I've been doing business in this town for twenty years." Williams pretended to hardly know the judge when he met with Truitt at the courthouse. "Is this where his chambers are?" Williams asked. Inside, however, the judge spoiled the act by giving Williams a warm hello. By threatening to ask for an order from a higher court, Truitt was finally able to get the judge to recuse himself.

Not all of the ploys Williams used worked. Nor would it be fair to say that he was always on the "wrong" side of a case. Prosecutors are often overzealous. They go on fishing expeditions and concoct imaginative charges against flashy businessmen who, they assume, must be guilty of something, even if it isn't the charge listed in the indictment. Some U.S. attorneys are more concerned with headlines than justice. But as a practical matter, clients did not come to Williams unless they were in serious trouble. Guilty or not, they always came to the right place. For the last decade of his career, Williams never lost a client to jail—and it wasn't because they were all innocent.

Chapter Thirty-Seven

WILLIAMS'S SKILL AT defending white-collar clients, as well as the pitfalls he faced, can be illustrated by an examination of his strategy and tactics in four major criminal cases during the late seventies and early eighties. These cases show that he was able to manipulate the system to a remarkable degree. But not every prosecutor and judge could be rolled, and Williams was sometimes faced with prickly ethical issues. He did not emerge unscathed.

In the winter of 1976, Williams received a call from the corporate lawyers for Phillips Petroleum, the Oklahoma oil giant. Watergate had spawned a criminal tax investigation of the oil company's political slush fund. The federal judge who was hearing the case in Tulsa, Allen Barrow, seemed hostile. Could Williams help?

Williams looked into Barrow's background. He learned that Barrow was a political hack who had been appointed to the federal bench in 1961 by Bob Kerr of Oklahoma, over the objections of President Kennedy. Kerr, the most influential lawmaker on the Senate Finance Committee, had called Bobby Kennedy at the Justice Department and warned him, "If you and your brother want to get any legislation through my committee in the next four years, my friend is going to be a federal judge."

Working with his old friend Clark Clifford, whose political cunning was well suited to the cause, Williams fashioned a strategy for winning over the judge. Local lawyers regarded Barrow as on the dim side, which he was. But Williams treated him "as if he were Oliver Wendell Holmes," said a Williams & Connolly lawyer involved in the case. "The judge just needed a little respect.'' In chambers, Williams swapped stories with Barrow about Kerr and Bobby Baker. The judge became so enamored that he asked Williams to speak to immigrants at naturalization ceremonies. Barrow told the new citizens what an honor it was to be addressed by such a famous lawyer who had flown all the way from Washington (on the Phillips company plane). In return, Williams went on about how lucky these new Americans were to be sworn in by such a respected federal jurist. The prosecutors watched this spectacle and felt ill.

Out of earshot, Williams mocked Barrow. Sitting at a lawyers' conference in chambers, he whispered to Jack Tigue, one of his co-counsel, ''Barrow is the kind of asshole who would wear his watch around his ankle. Look . . .'' Williams dropped his pen on the floor and Tigue and Williams bent over under the table. Sure enough, Barrow had something that looked like a watch strapped to his ankle. (It was a pedometer; the judge had a heart condition and had been ordered to walk a mile a day.) ''Ed was like a kid, always pulling pranks,'' said Tigue. One of Williams's in-jokes with Clark Clifford showed that Williams believed that the judge was in his pocket. Williams sent Clifford a photograph of himself shaking hands with Barrow, both men wreathed with grins. Williams had drawn bubbles over their heads, like characters in a comic strip. The bubble over Barrow's head read: ''You're my main man, Mr. Edward.'' In the bubble over his own head, Williams had written, ''Now, Allen, my boy, you just stick with me. I'll always tell it to you true—and you and me together, why we'll give those government bastards a good country screwing.''

In theory, grand juries are supposed to be a check on prosecutorial abuse, but prosecutors generally regard the grand jury as a tool. Rare was the grand jury during Williams's time that refused a prosecutor's request for an indictment. The grand jury room was the domain of the government; other lawyers were generally not allowed in. Not surprisingly, prosecutors could become lax about the procedural niceties designed to ensure the neutrality of the process. Part of Williams's all-out defense of his clients was to make sure those rules—no matter how insignificant they seemed—were strictly enforced.

On February 12, 1976, the government's chief witness, an accountant named James Akright, testified before the grand jury. He had not quite finished his testimony when it was time to send the jury home for the evening. The witness's lawyer, John Martin, needed to catch a plane back to New York. So the prosecutors decided to let Akright complete his testimony back in their office with his lawyer present. The witness's final hour of testimony was "innocuous," said the prosecutor, Chad Muller, and he did not bother to read it to the grand jury the next day. Williams demanded a hearing before Judge Barrow when he found out. He insisted to the judge that the prosecutors had withheld exculpatory information from the grand jury and violated the secrecy rules by allowing the witness to be accompanied by his lawyer. Williams demanded that the judge dismiss the indictment for prosecutorial misconduct. He was full of righteous indignation before Barrow.

Privately, to one of his partners, Williams conceded that his argument was a pretty weak reason for throwing out the whole indictment. "If I win on this point," he whispered to his partner Jack Vardaman, "you get to argue in the court of appeals." Barrow came through for his new friend. He dismissed the indictment. The case was settled in November 1977 with a wrist-slap nolo plea and a $30,000 fine. The next April, Barrow nominated Williams for an award as "an outstanding jurist" from his alma mater, Fordham Law School. A month later, Barrow wrote Williams to ask a favor: Would he please lobby Congress for more federal judges to ease the caseload in Oklahoma?

Muller, the prosecutor, still marvels at Williams's performance. "He was approachable, easy to talk to, and nonconfrontational with me. His suit was rumpled and his fly was down most of the time. He could have been practicing in Bexar County," said Muller, a lawyer from San Antonio. "But he wargamed this whole thing. I guess he set me up pretty good."

WILLIAMS'S OWN CLIENTS could be more difficult to control than the judge and the prosecutor. In 1979, the U.S. attorney in Ohio began an investigation into Home State Savings and Loan of Cincinnati. The S&L was selling mortgage commitments that were so full of escape clauses that, as one Williams & Connolly lawyer put it, "they might as well have been insuring fire under water." The government wanted to charge the thrift with fraud. The real target, however, was Home State's owner, Marvin Warner. "We thought Warner was behind the whole thing," said James Cissel, one of the prosecutors. An immigrant's son who had made $100 million selling mortgages and raising racehorses, Warner had bought his way into Democratic politics, giving more money to the party in Ohio in the mid-seventies than anyone else. He was rewarded with a seat on the Democratic National Committee and the ambassadorship to Switzerland, where he offended local sensibilities by holding an auto show of American-made cars on the embassy's front lawn. Warner naturally came to Williams when the grand jury began looking at the worthless paper being peddled by his thrift. He assumed, not unreasonably, that Williams would make the investigation "go away." To Warner, this was no different from the scrapes he had gotten into as a fraternity brother down in Alabama. Williams mimicked his client's drawl, "Why mah daddy would just go see the sheriff's daddy." Williams was now "daddy" and the sheriff's daddy was the Criminal Division of the Department of Justice.

Williams took complete control of the case. The prosecutors hoped to divide and conquer by turning employees who participated in the scam into government witnesses. But before they could, Williams flew the potential grand jury targets back to Washington, where they were served lunch in Williams's conference room. As the waiters dished out the filet, Williams rose to deliver his familiar speech to frightened grand jury targets. "You can hang together," he said. "Or we can hang separately." They decided to hang with Williams and signed conflict waivers allowing him to control the defense. Then they took the Fifth Amendment before the grand jury.

Williams's defense was that there was no fraud: The escape clauses were all there in the contract, albeit in very fine print. The local prosecutors, however, wanted to indict. Williams went over their heads and beat his familiar path to the Criminal Division over at Justice. He proposed a deal: a nolo plea with restitution to the customers who'd lost money. Overruling the local prosecutors, the Justice Department agreed.

"It was a great deal," said one of the defense lawyers involved in the case. "But Marvin always wanted to renegotiate every deal." A brash hustler who bragged to Williams that he made love to girls in the backseat of his diplomatic limousine, Ambassador Warner ordered his lawyer to go back to the Justice Department and cut a better deal.

In his most even, measured voice, Williams responded, "I can't do that." Warner demanded to know why not. "For two reasons," said Williams. "One, I never do anything fatal to my client. Two, I have given the government my word. Now if you really want to do this, you take young Culverhouse here . . ." He pointed to Hugh Culverhouse, Jr., a young Miami lawyer Warner had brought along, ". . . and you go down to the Justice Department and do it yourself.'' The roomful of lawyers grew very quiet. Culverhouse, who was thirty years old, looked, according to one witness, ''like he had been shot through the heart'' (a description Culverhouse does not dispute). Then Williams turned to the president of Home State, Burt Bongard, and said, in the same even voice, ''I can understand why Marvin doesn't want to take the deal, because it's his money. But if I were you, Burt, I'd take my fat little ass down to the synagogue and *pray*,'' he said, allowing his voice to rise for the first time, ''that Marvin takes this deal.'' The defendants took the deal. The case never received any publicity. Five years later, Home State collapsed in a massive case of fraud and almost took down the Ohio banking system with it.

FOR WILLIAMS, THE Marc Rich case was all about control—and losing it. Commodity traders called Rich ''El Matador'' because he liked to kill bull markets by selling short. Secretive and intensely shy, Rich would trade almost anything with anyone. ''If you've got tomatoes,'' Rich would tell customers, using his term for testicles, ''we can do a deal.'' During the Iranian hostage crisis in 1980, according to federal prosecutors, Rich continued to broker deals that allowed the Ayatollah to swap oil for West German arms. Rich was so successful at trading that he needed a tax shelter for the $1 billion in cash he was earning every year.

In 1981, he found a shelter in 20th Century–Fox. Marvin Davis, who had joined with Rich in earlier oil ventures, asked him to be a silent partner in purchasing the movie company. That same year, however, some of Rich's employees began talking to federal prosecutors about Rich's shady trading practices. Among them was daisy chaining— evading federal pricing regulations by changing cheap ''old oil'' into expensive ''new oil.''

Williams had saved Marvin Davis from a criminal indictment for ''daisy chaining'' the previous year when Davis's company had paid a $20 million civil fine, and the case had gotten almost no publicity. Davis suggested to Rich that he hire Williams to perform the same service. Williams agreed, confident that he could make any criminal case against Rich ''go away,'' provided Rich was willing to pay a relatively small fine. ''I can get rid of it for $30 million,'' he said.

He went to see Sandy Weinberg, the assistant U.S. attorney handling the investigation in Manhattan. Williams put his feet up on the desk and said, "Let's settle this." Weinberg, who was thirty-two years old and feeling intimidated by the legendary figure sitting across from him, bravely said, "We're not interested." Williams was taken aback. Casually, he asked Weinberg, "What are you thinking about?" Weinberg spelled it out for him: "J-A-I-L."

Weinberg's boss, Rudolph Giuliani, the U.S. Attorney for the Southern District of New York, wanted a RICO indictment. The Racketeer-Influenced and Corrupt Organizations statutes had been passed by Congress to help prosecutors go after Mafiosi and drug dealers. Giuliani, who was zealous and politically ambitious, wanted to use it against white-collar criminals as well. The penalties under RICO were huge—prison terms and forfeiture of assets. It was a powerful weapon, and Williams had never seen it before in a case like this. "Williams underestimated the seriousness of the prosecution at first," said a lawyer who worked with him on the case. "They wanted Rich to do time. This was going to be the biggest tax case ever." Weinberg informed Williams that the case was about "people, not money." He was concerned that Williams's client would flee the country when he realized that he faced a prison term. "You don't have to worry," Williams replied. "My clients don't flee."

Williams, as usual, had advised his client to stonewall. Rich refused to obey a grand jury subpoena to turn over documents that were being held in Switzerland. His lawyer argued that as a Swiss company, Marc Rich AG was immune from any U.S. court order. The case stalled for a year as Williams fenced and parried over issues of international jurisdiction. But in June 1983, the U.S. Supreme Court refused to overturn the lower court judge's decision to hold Rich in contempt—and fine him $50,000 a day—until he surrendered the documents. Williams decided the time had come to comply. His appeals were exhausted, and any further refusal would come close to obstruction of justice.

But Rich refused to listen. Instead, he hired a new raft of lawyers who told him what he wanted to hear, that he did not have to comply with the subpoenas. Courtroom 128 in the federal courthouse at Foley Square was soon awash with lawyers, all representing Marc Rich. "Face it, Marc Rich is a golden tit," one lawyer told writer Craig Copetas, commenting on a story that a third-year law student could telephone Rich, say he was interested in the case, and be sent a retainer for $25,000. Judge Leonard Sand watched the confusing swirl of lawyers at the counsel table and said, "I will take a five-minute recess to enable counsel for Marc Rich, incoming, outgoing, or whatever, to confer with each other."

Without Williams's participation, Rich's new legal advisers came up with a stunt. On June 29, they created a corporate shell, called Clarendon Corp., to put Rich and his personal assets out of reach of the court. Judge Sand exploded, angrily calling the scheme "a ploy to frustrate the implementation of the court's order." Worse, in August, federal agents intercepted a team of Rich's new lawyers smuggling two steamer trunks of documents out of the United States.

Williams was mortified. According to lawyers on all sides, he had known nothing about the corporate shell or the attempt to secrete documents out of the country. Yet he was sitting before Judge Sand in his courtroom, being publicly castigated like the mouthpiece of a drug dealer. His discomfort turned to rage in September. The government handed down a fifty-six-page, fifty-one-count indictment charging Rich with a wide array of criminal violations, laced with juicy details like descriptions of his dealings with the Ayatollah. Rich responded to the warrant for his arrest by refusing to return from Switzerland.

Williams was standing in the office of Marvin Davis in Los Angeles when he heard the news that his client was on the lam. According to Davis, Williams shouted in the phone, "You know something, Marc? You spit on the American flag. You spit on the jury system. Whatever you get, you deserve. We could have gotten the minimum. Now you're going to sink."*

Back in New York, Rich was hiring still more lawyers. Williams reacted bitterly when prosecutor-turned-defense-lawyer Thomas Puccio came onto Rich's payroll, no doubt because he was a friend of Giuliani's. In a transatlantic speakerbox conversation with Rich held in the offices of tax lawyer Boris Kostelanetz, Williams exploded again, according to Jack Tigue, who was there. "Listen Marc, you don't know what the fuck you're doing. I've got lots of clients," he said. "I don't need this bullshit. If you want another lawyer, get him," Williams declared, and hung up.

Rich asked him to fly to Switzerland. The fugitive trader lived in the village of Zug, in a villa stuffed with objets d'art—a Picasso, a Braque, a Miró. Rich still was puzzled as to why Williams couldn't just fix the case. For his fiftieth birthday party, *Fortune* magazine reported, Rich had staged a mock boxing match between a clown wearing a Marc Rich AG logo and one dressed as a New York cop. A clown in judge's robes was the referee.

---

*Rich denies this account. "There is not a shred of truth in it," Rich said. Williams "never asked me to return to stand trial—in an atmosphere he called unstable and inflamed."

Williams was in a surly mood when he arrived there. After several drinks at dinner he announced, "I'm resigning. You don't trust me. Fuck you." In the Mercedes on the way back to the hotel, Peter Fleming, one of his co-counsel, told Williams that he couldn't resign, that he was the "glue" that held the defense together. Williams glowered. After a quarter hour of silence, Williams said, "You don't think I can resign, do you?"

Whether out of professional responsibility or, more likely, a desire for Rich's fees, Williams remained in the case. He pressed for a settlement, but Giuliani proved to be more resistant than most prosecutors with whom Williams had dealt. For days the defense team dickered with the U.S. Attorney's Office. When they hit a sticking point, Giuliani would "come in and posture," said Fleming. Williams would think he had an agreement, but then Giuliani would back out. Williams thought the U.S. attorney, who had once wanted to be a priest and was now planning to run for governor or the Senate, was a publicity hound. It irritated Williams to read that Giuliani had refused to defend Mafiosi when he was a criminal defense lawyer. "Rudy Giuliani is the toughest negotiator I've dealt with since Tom Dewey," Williams told Fleming in a mock-stentorian voice. "What's this Dewey bullshit? You were fourteen when Dewey was busting rackets," said Fleming. "The man is consumed with raw power," Williams groused.

Williams wanted to get the case over with, but the ransom was high. On October 10, 1984, Rich and his companies pleaded guilty to thirty-eight counts of tax evasion, $50 million in illegal oil profits in 1980 and 1981, and making false statements to the U.S. government. He paid over $170 million in fines—more than any criminal defendant ever had at the time. His legal fees to Williams were over $2 million. Williams wearily told Weinberg, "I hate this case. This is a bad case. The only good thing about it is the fee."

WILLIAMS WAS WILLING to take on difficult clients if the price was right. Victor Posner was a very difficult client. A grade-school dropout, he built a pyramid empire in the seventies buying and selling corporations. Critics charged that he was looting and plundering them as well. While his companies began to sink in red ink in the early eighties, Posner was paying himself as much as $10 million a year in salary. His corporations shelled out another $1 million or so a year for his perks: yachts, limousines, airplanes. "How Posner Profited Even Though His Companies Didn't" was the headline in *Forbes* in April 1985. The magazine compared Posner to a Latin American dictator bailing out to Switzerland before he was lynched by an angry mob. Posner's pursuers in real life were government prosecutors who had been after him for years. The SEC was able to force Posner to pay back $1.3 million in perks that he had failed to disclose to stockholders in 1977, but the fine was a pittance. The feds wanted to find a way to nail Posner—to put him in jail if possible. In 1978, a federal grand jury in Manhattan began hearing evidence.

"I'll defend him, but he's going to pay," Williams told his partners when Posner came to him. Williams knew that he would have a hard time cutting a deal with the prosecutors; the government had invested too much time and money trying to make an example of the corporate raider. A hard-edged man with a well-known taste for teenage girls, Posner would make an unsympathetic defendant. If they could just get him before a jury, the prosecutors were hopeful they could get him into jail. The government's problem, however, was a familiar one. They were sure that he was guilty of some crimes, but they were not sure which ones, or if they could prove it. Like the G-men of the 1930s who finally jailed Capone for income tax evasion, the federal prosecutors tried to fashion a criminal tax case against Posner. They focused on his perks: Had Posner ordered his companies to pay for the condos and limos and speedboats as a way of evading taxes?

The U.S. attorney in Manhattan was eager to indict, but tax cases had to be approved by the Justice Department in Washington, Williams's home turf. At Justice, Williams argued that prosecuting Posner would be unfair; after all, other executives got lavish perks. As usual, Williams was persuasive. Justice ruled against an indictment. But in Manhattan, the U.S. Attorney's Office came up with a new angle. They claimed that Posner had conspired to inflate the value of some real estate that he had donated to a small college in Miami in order to take a big tax write-off. They wanted to indict Posner for defrauding the government of $1.2 million.

This indictment Williams was not able to head off, but he *was* able to delay it. He pulled out all his old tricks to get the indictment dismissed twice on technicalities. Williams was so aggressive about accusing the prosecutors of misconduct that the assistant U.S. attorneys on the case began referring to the lawyer writing Williams's motions as "Worse Yet." After every paragraph alleging some unpardonable act of prose-

cutorial misconduct, the next paragraph would begin, "Worse yet . . ."
"He almost papered us to death," said Chris Todd, the prosecutor.
Williams's associates staked out the grand jury room to quiz the government witnesses as they came out, so Todd put a garbage bag over the head
of one key witness. A Williams & Connolly lawyer, Greg Craig, chased
the witness down several flights of stairs to corner him.

By forcing the prosecutor to reindict Posner, and by demanding a series
of evidentiary hearings to determine if the government was following
proper grand jury procedure, Williams bought time. Again and again, he
managed to stall the case. When his young associates impatiently pushed
to go to trial, Williams quoted his cracked version of Confucius: "He
who seeks justice may catch it." Williams was almost obsessive about
winning continuances. Returning to a Williams & Connolly Christmas
party in 1982, he was delighted to report to his associate William Murphy
(who was the feared "Worse Yet") that he had won yet another delay.
He goosed Murphy. "Whoa!" Williams cried, giddy as a teenager who
has just been given the keys to his father's car.

But Williams couldn't avoid trial forever. After over four years of
procedural fencing, *United States* v. *Posner* finally went to trial in federal
district court in Miami on July 26, 1984. Williams was going to have to
expose his unsavory client to a jury after all. He was not at all happy to
be back in a courtroom. As he stood in the courthouse lobby on a hot July
day on the eve of trial, a television reporter approached him. "Say, I was
wondering," the reporter asked, "aren't you . . . ?" Williams cut him
off. "Keep wondering," he said, and stalked out of the courthouse.

Still, Williams always had "one more card to play," said his associate
Greg Craig. Indicted along with Posner was a real estate appraiser named
William Scharrer. It was Scharrer who had given Posner the appraisal
inflating the value of his land so he could get a generous tax write-off. As
usual, Williams wanted total control of the defense, which meant defending Scharrer as well as Posner. Williams picked Scharrer's lawyer, Hugh
Culverhouse, Jr., and indicated that Posner would pay for Scharrer's
defense. Scharrer was skeptical. He worried that his interests would be
sacrificed to Posner's. But Williams assured him that it was common
practice for the wealthier defendant to pay for a unified defense, and that
it was always wiser to "hang together than hang separately."

The government's most damaging evidence was a letter from Scharrer
to Posner admitting that he had put a high value on the real estate "for tax
purposes." But this "smoking gun" could only be used against Scharrer,

not Posner. Under the rules of evidence, the words of one conspirator cannot be used against another without independent corroborating evidence. On the fourth day of trial, the prosecutor introduced the smoking gun. Williams immediately moved to sever Posner from the case, saying the letter would unfairly prejudice the jury against his client. Judge Eugene Spellman granted the severance. Williams, with a sigh of relief, disappeared and went swimming. Posner had slipped away again, postponing once more his day of judgment.

Scharrer, however, still faced the jury. And his lawyer, Culverhouse, was totally unprepared. So far, Culverhouse had done exactly what Williams had told him to do, which was very little. By his own account, Williams had picked him for the trial team not for his forensic talents but "because I was a good local spy. Ed loved it that I could ex parte the judge," said Culverhouse, whose father was a close friend of Judge Spellman's. When Culverhouse reported to Williams on his private conversations about the case with Spellman, Williams's eyes would widen. "You called the judge?" Williams asked. "There was real appreciation in his voice," said Culverhouse. During the trial, Culverhouse's role was to sit at the counsel's table. He did rise once to make an objection, but Williams, in open court, grabbed him by the tail of his jacket and yanked him into his seat. "Sit down!" Williams commanded.

Now, suddenly, Culverhouse faced the prospect of standing up all alone to defend Scharrer. He was not very effective. Scharrer was convicted on four counts and sentenced to jail. Furious, feeling betrayed, Scharrer hired a new lawyer and tried to get his conviction reversed for "ineffective counsel." He claimed that he had been sacrificed by Posner's lawyers. The motion produced some embarrassing publicity for Williams. The *National Law Journal* ran a picture of the famous lawyer looking shifty-eyed under the headline, "Williams' Role in Case Questioned." Among white-collar defense lawyers, there was considerable clucking. "Williams treats co-counsel like children," Peter Fleming remarked. "But when the crunch comes, suddenly we're all grown-ups." There was a strong suspicion that Scharrer had been set up, left to "do Posner's time." Williams was uncomfortable with the headlines and the chatter. When the prosecutor in the Posner case teased Williams by cracking, "I hear Scharrer's hired Joe Rauh," Williams just frowned at the mention of his old nemesis. More embarrassing, Williams was forced to take the stand in his own defense in a hearing on Scharrer's "ineffective counsel" motion.

Ultimately, Williams was vindicated by Judge Spellman's opinion. Scharrer was not a sacrificial lamb, the judge found. "The record fails to show any specific instance in which Scharrer's attorney was forced to choose between divergent interests of Posner or Scharrer," states the court's opinion. Culverhouse later insisted that Williams did not forsake him. To be sure, at the time he expected to be abandoned. In the hallway after the severance, Williams had said to him, "You think I'm going to walk out of here and leave you stranded, don't you?" "Yeah," said Culverhouse. "I'm not," said Williams. "You better get ready to work." Williams himself headed for the beach, but he left behind three Williams & Connolly lawyers to back up Culverhouse in court. So careful was their coaching that Culverhouse read his summation aloud from notes that had been written by Bill "Worse Yet" Murphy. It was the only time the jury saw Culverhouse wear glasses.

Scharrer never got over his bitterness. "They didn't give a shit about me," he said six years later. "They were just trying to defend Posner." Culverhouse and Williams's associates claim they did not intentionally sacrifice Scharrer. An acquittal in the *Scharrer* case, they say, would only have benefited Posner at his retrial. Nonetheless, Scharrer would have been much better off if his lawyer had been prepared and truly working for him. He undoubtedly could have cut a deal to testify as a witness for the prosecution. After all, the government's true target was Posner, not a small-time real estate appraiser. When the case did go to trial, it was obvious to the jury that Culverhouse was a tool of the Posner defense. "No matter how well you support someone, it usually doesn't come off as well," said Atlee Wampler, who represented Scharrer after he fired Culverhouse. For Williams, Scharrer's public bitterness was an embarrassment, but he had bought more time for his client.

Chapter Thirty-Eight

WHEN WILLIAMS SPOKE of a case now, he often used medical analogies. He compared himself to a surgeon. "I have to have absolute control over the operation," he told clients. "You can't put your hand on the scalpel and hope to survive." His partners understood that his obsession with winning delays, with buying time, was not just about serving clients. Williams wanted to win a continuance himself. His cancer had returned.

After his operation for colon cancer in 1977, Williams had become a "bit of a hypochondriac," he said. He went to Sloan-Kettering in New York every few months to have a colonoscopy, a procedure to detect polyps in his bowel. "I think I'm a pervert," he told his family doctor, Steve Jones. "I like having that thing up my rear end." But the crude jokes masked his growing anxiety. In the summer of 1980, while Williams was flailing vainly at Jimmy Carter and trying to head off the grand jury pursuing Victor Posner, tests showed a disturbing rise in his CEA—carcinoembryonic antigen—an index that measures blood chemistry associated with cancer cells. The colonoscopies remained negative, but by December 1981 his CEA was up to forty—about twenty times normal. On February 24, 1982, the doctors found a tiny lesion—the size of a pencil point—on Williams's liver. It was malignant. The next day, he underwent major surgery that removed two-thirds of his liver.

For most people, metastatic colon cancer that reappears somewhere else in the body is a death sentence. The usual life expectancy is twelve months, and many doctors in a general hospital won't bother operating. But Sloan-Kettering, internationally famous for cancer research and treatment, was not an ordinary hospital. "They have a license to do heroic things," said Dr. Jones. And giving up was not an option for Williams. His cancer doctor, Jerome DeCosse, told him he had a 35 percent chance to live more than five years after an operation to remove the malignancy in his liver. Williams chose to believe that he would be in the 35 percent.

Williams announced to his family that he had declared war on cancer. "Cancer was the enemy. He was going to fight it and beat it," said oldest daughter Ellen. Williams was determined to show that he could shrug off major surgery. The first request he made to his son Ned was to ask him to go over to Second Avenue and buy him a Big Mac. To his friend Jay Emmett he said, "Get me a steak and a baked potato." Williams was out of bed walking after a day and back in his office after a week. "He insisted on driving back to Washington through a big snowstorm," said Dr. Jones. "The pain must have been incredible."

At the firm it was business as usual. He informed his partners that the doctors had told him that there was no reason why he shouldn't make a full recovery. His prognosis, he said, was normal life expectancy. "The first thing I did was get my actuarial tables," he announced. "I've got another 18.7 years to go." The *Baltimore Sun* reported that Williams had "minor surgery" for a "small tumor." Williams resumed his usual chaotic schedule, traveling out of town eighty-nine times in 1982. It was all "proof" that he had beaten the disease. On Martha's Vineyard that summer, he boasted to Kay Graham that he had been up and walking after a day. It had taken Ronald Reagan three days to get up after *his* operation, Williams said.

On November 1, 1983, two weeks after the Orioles won the World Series, the doctors discovered a half-inch malignant nodule in his lung. Williams shrugged it off. He would just cut it out and keep going. He had turned down his doctor's recommendation that he follow up his liver operation with chemotherapy. The evidence that chemotherapy might help was iffy, and Williams did not want to be slowed down by the side effects. He preferred surgery. The way to deal with cancer was to go in and dig it out. He viewed surgery in the same way he did going to trial, as a necessary ordeal. "I'm ready, I'm prepared," he told Dana before going under the knife a third time. By awful coincidence, Williams's partner and protégé, Larry Lucchino, was stricken with cancer as well in 1984. One afternoon at the office, Lucchino was moping about, depressed, fatigued by chemotherapy. "Let's go have some real chemotherapy," said Williams. He took Lucchino to the Metropolitan Club, where they sat drinking gin at three o'clock in the afternoon. Worrying and resting was not the solution, Williams insisted. Work was.

Williams never complained of pain or illness. He told reporters that he never felt sick from his cancer. His public front was brave and resolute, and it remained so until the end. His private feelings were another matter. In March 1984, his CEA jumped up again. This time the tumor in his lung—the other lung—was the size of a baseball. Surgery was scheduled for March 13.

His partners sensed that Williams's courage was flagging slightly when he informed them of the recurrence. "I know this is getting tedious for you," he said, "but I'm going into surgery again. I don't know if I'm ever going to come back to the firm." The room became very quiet. "If I can't come back full steam, I'm not going to come back at all." In New York for the operation, Williams called Peter Fleming for dinner. The two had become fast friends during the Marc Rich fiasco.

"I'm just not going to do it," Williams said. Fleming didn't know what he was talking about. "Do what?" he asked. Williams told him about the scheduled operation. "You can't imagine the pain," Williams said. In lung surgery, the doctors have to pry open the patient's ribs. Williams spoke of limping around the hospital, trailing catheters and tubes and dragging a lung-pump behind him. Realizing that Williams was looking for a hand from his brother lawyer, Fleming answered, "You're a competitor. You'll do it." Williams needed some bolstering from his family, too. At dinner at the Palm that March with daughter Ellen and son Bennett, Williams said, "This is the last time. I'm tired of taking this crap. It's too painful."

It was by now obvious to Williams that this was not the last surgery, that he would have to keep on visiting the surgeon's table to survive. He wasn't going to "beat" cancer. He could only hope to stave it off, to delay its lethal progress through his body. Slowly, Williams accepted reality. He adjusted his philosophy. "I understand this disease," he told Lucchino. "I will be at war with this disease for as long as I live. The point of this war is not to wipe out the other opponent, but battle it to a stalemate."

Williams's faith helped heal him emotionally. He believed in the power of prayer, that God could heal him physically as well as spiritually. Faith was "the best insurance policy there is," he told Barbara Howar. "Oh, Ed, that's bunk," replied Howar, a lapsed Catholic. "But suppose it isn't?" he replied. Williams also accepted the notion of God's will, that

"Thy will be done" could mean life *or* death. "This was hard for him," said his daughter Dana, who understood that her father hated to cede control to anyone, even to God.

Williams never missed morning mass, even if he was traveling. His address book now included the addresses of Catholic churches within a walk or short ride of luxury hotels all over the United States and Europe, and he liked to scout out new ones. "Hey, I found a great little Italian church for you," he told Larry Lucchino on a trip to Boston. He took Lucchino to the church, where Lucchino dryly noted to Williams that the mass was being conducted in French, not Italian. "French, Italian, what's the difference," said Williams. "I got you here." Going to mass "is the most important thing I do all day," Williams told his wife, Agnes. He was comforted by the miracle of his faith, a belief that in death there is life, and that God would receive him despite his imperfections. The Catholic mass, with its faith in the Resurrection, is about hope, and Williams wanted to hope.

Williams could never stand still. He kept repeating his adage that "Life is a motion picture." Once more, he returned to the firm and plunged back into work. His sense of humor returned. He told his partners that he would just keep on cutting out the tumors whenever they appeared. "I'm going to have zippers installed," he said.

At home, Agnes pleaded with him to slow down. She was frustrated when he threw himself into preparing for the Posner trial in Miami that July. "Ed, why are you doing this?" she demanded. Williams said he had no choice. But he did not brush off his wife or ignore her advice. Agnes had always been a sober and strong-willed helpmate to her husband. Williams may have made fun of her stolid style with his friends, but at home, he listened to her and respected her. More than anyone else, Agnes had helped Williams accept the reality of his disease. It's like diabetes, she explained. You don't beat it; you live with it.

As Williams became sicker, his friends sensed that his marriage was becoming closer, more intimate. He had always relied on Agnes as an adviser in difficult moments. Brendan Sullivan recalled watching Williams stare moodily out the window of his office while he pondered a "problem to which there was no readily apparent right or wrong answer." After a long silence, Williams said, "I'll ask Agnes about it. She's the only one I really trust anyway." Now, as he became needier and physically weaker, he also became more openly affectionate with her. At a small dinner to celebrate their twenty-fifth wedding anniversary,

Williams dispensed with his usual story-telling and joking and raised his glass in a simple toast: "To Agnes, whom I love very much." There was no doubt among anyone at the table that he really meant it.

Williams, however, was still an incorrigible flirt. In 1982, he teasingly wrote Nancy Dickerson, "Thanks for the picture. I have it in a dark closet and peek at it every night when Agnes isn't looking. I hope she does not find it." Clare Boothe Luce, a legendary coquette, wrote Williams as he lay in bed recovering from his second operation, "Get well or move over." Williams wrote back in the same mock-seductive tone, "Why can't I have both? I am getting well and ready to move over. Hurry! Hurry! Love, Ed." In his cups, Williams could be truly shameless. At a particularly liquid evening to celebrate Ben Bradlee's sixtieth birthday, Williams was seated between Lauren Bacall and Nora Ephron. With a gleeful leer, Williams signaled Bradlee, who was on Bacall's right. "Lookee here!" Williams said, and nodded down toward Bacall's lap, where he had placed a large and groping hand. "Lookee here!" said Ephron, who lifted Williams's other hand from her lap.

But Williams's nocturnal prowling was long since over by the 1980s. To be sure, he could still drink hard. After watching the 1984 elections with Dr. Jones, Williams asked him to stay for "one more pop," and proceeded to demolish a fifth of Scotch. But such bouts were less frequent, and usually in tamer company than his late-night toots of early years. Although Williams claimed that he never felt sick, he increasingly complained of fatigue to Dr. Jones. His great pleasure now was not knocking 'em back at the Palm but rather going home, putting on his pajamas, and crawling into bed. He often went to bed as soon as he came home, lying in front of a roaring fire (even in summer, when he turned on the air-conditioning full blast). He liked to have his children join him in the bedroom, talking or reading or just being there.

Williams saw far more of his children now than he had as a younger man. His older children were grown and gone, but his children by Agnes were still teenagers or of college age in the early eighties. His approach to parenting, and Agnes's as well, had been changed by his bitter experience with Jobie. In the early seventies, Williams had pontificated about the need for discipline. But with his younger children, he was loving and forgiving. "After Jobie, we understood that you have to accept the children that God gave you and not try to remake them in your own image," Agnes said. With Jobie, Williams struggled, with mixed success, to find a common bond. At Jobie's wedding in 1975, Williams had been sullen at first. The reception, held at a VFW lodge in southern Maryland, was dry. But then Williams paid to have the bar open, and his spirits improved. He danced with the bride and embraced Jobie. "I love you, son," he said. "Have a good life for me."

Most of the children were not stellar students, and none showed much interest in following their father into law. Williams never pushed them, and never seemed to mind if their grades were less than perfect. "He was a realist and tolerant," said Father Healy. If Williams had any ambitions for a son who would follow in his path, they were fulfilled by his protégé, Larry Lucchino. From a modest background in Pittsburgh, Lucchino had gone on to Princeton, where he played basketball with Bill Bradley, and to Yale Law School. Lucchino had a filial devotion to Williams, who trusted his young lawyer to represent his interest with the Redskins and later the Orioles. Surprisingly, perhaps, Lucchino was not resented by the Williams children, who seemed to have their father's generosity of spirit without his relentless ambition. Williams was proud of his children's honesty and decency. When Ellen, the oldest girl, turned down a car from her parents because it would give her an unfair advantage over her siblings, Williams boasted to his friends, "Didn't Aggie raise them right?" Agnes, whom Williams had described as having "more rules than the IRS" in the early seventies, was still the family disciplinarian, but a less rigid one. It was a family joke that one of Dana's friends couldn't understand why she never got in trouble with her parents for breaking the rules. "We don't have rules," she explained. That was not entirely true. Williams finally grounded Tony for a month for staying out most of the night with some friends, but then he discovered he enjoyed having his sixteen-year-old boy around the house. "Agnes," he said, "we're grounding Tony for six more months."

With seven children, Williams had to ration his time with each one. Sometimes, his children even had to make appointments to see him. But he was careful to make time, often taking his boys on trips to boxing matches or ball games. He even volunteered to drive his teenagers to a Grateful Dead concert in Baltimore, though he insisted on wearing a necktie and grimaced at the marijuana fumes and raucous music. When Dana complained that the boys got all the trips, he took her to Yale Law School to watch him judge a moot court and then down to Atlanta to watch a Redskins game. "He always made you feel like you were the most important one," she said, a feeling the other children echoed. His partners observed that Williams could be chewing them out, pause to take a phone call from his daughter Ellen that was all sweetness and light, and then resume his angry tirade.

Ellen and the younger children regarded their father with bemusement and affection. "He didn't get mad at us," said Dana. "When he did, we'd accuse him of acting like an only child." The children teased him for his vanity. Williams was indignant after watching a made-for-TV movie about Bobby Kennedy and the Hoffa hearings in which the role of EBW was played by the actor José Ferrer. "He's seventy-four and Cuban!" Williams protested to Betty Killay, who was over for cocktails. At that moment Ellen walked in the front door. "Hi Betty, hi José," she said. When Williams was drinking, he'd get "sloppy and sentimental," said Dana. " 'Oh-h-h, I love you kids,' he'd say. It made us a little uncomfortable, embarrassed."

Williams did not spoil his children financially. Declaring that inheritance taxes should be confiscatory, he warned them not to count on a legacy (a stand that he predictably softened as death approached). Williams liked rich men who were self-made, but he voiced contempt for scions who lived off family money. It was an almost obsessive point of pride to Williams that he had come up from nothing. "We were both in the *gutter*," he'd exclaim, throwing his arm around David Brinkley in poor-boy fellowship, ignoring Brinkley's protest that, really, his own parents had been perfectly well off. With Marion Javits, wife of Senator Jacob Javits, he played a peculiar parlor game called "Top This Poor." Standing together at fancy parties, they recounted their wretched childhoods, his poor and Catholic in Hartford, hers poor and Jewish in New York. Ever competitive, Williams dared the other dinner guests to best these tales of woe. Speaking to a class of Harvard students, Williams went on about how important it was to grow up poor, how it builds character and "makes you tough." A proper young man stood and asked him, "Tell me, sir, how does one overcome the lack of the privilege of being poor?" Afterwards, Williams asked his host, Harvard professor Martin Peretz, "Who was that guy?" "Dickie Rockefeller," answered Peretz.

WILLIAMS DID NOT look like a rich man. In his baggy, shapeless "basic suit," he dressed more like an insurance adjuster than a successful litigator. Partly, he dressed for effect—he did not want to appear flashy to prosecutors or juries. As a young man, he had affected an Ivy League look, wearing Brooks Brothers button-downs and flannels, but as he got older, he stopped paying so much attention to his attire. He once looked down at his feet at morning mass and noticed that he had put on one black shoe and one brown shoe. On Martha's Vineyard, amid the pink-and-green yachting set, he wore stretch pants with an elastic waist and a velour shirt. "That looks awful," sighed Agnes, sending him back to get a blue blazer. When Ben Bradlee began wearing boldly striped Turnbull and Asser shirts bought for him by Sally Quinn, Williams accused his best friend of being "pussy whipped."

Williams did have an interest in acquiring objects of value: He collected the autographs and letters of famous men, and he developed a taste for early twentieth-century American painting, particularly urban landscapes by Guy Wiggins. But he resisted the entreaties of Rose Narva, the manager of the Jefferson, who was constantly trying to get Williams to spend more on furnishings for his hotel. Oriental rugs? They don't even cover the floor, he protested. He preferred wall-to-wall carpeting.

Williams did not know or care much about finery, but he did care about amassing wealth. It was a measure of his success. He wanted to live as well as his rich clients. If Marvin Davis could have a Boeing 727, then Williams at least deserved a little business jet. In 1986, he bought a $2 million, four-engine, nine-seat Jet Star II, and couldn't resist telling friends that the former job of his pilot, a retired air force colonel named Bob Lazaro, had been flying the president of the United States on Air Force One. Still, Williams tried not to appear too ostentatious. When Davis gave him a stretch limousine, he sent the vast automobile over to his hotel, for the use of guests, and kept his less showy black Lincoln Town Car.

With a mansion and a stable in Potomac, a rambling summer house in Edgartown, and a winter condo in Key Biscayne, Florida, Williams lived very comfortably. He could well afford to. Billing clients at the rate of $1,000 an hour, he paid himself more than any lawyer in the country, with the possible exception of personal injury lawyers who reap windfalls from huge damage awards. In 1976, Williams's salary was $850,000; in 1978, $1.25 million; in 1985, $1.7 million; and in 1988, the year he died, $1.9 million. He was personally generous, always grabbing for the check, contributing heavily to charities, giving panhandlers five-dollar bills, and tipping 20 percent. He was also generous with his clients' money. "It's like toilet paper," he winked to his partners at billing time. "If you run out, go and get another roll."

He was more conservative investing his own money. He distrusted the stock market and stayed out of it. He bought real estate, but all of his land and buildings were within walking distance of his home or office. Determined to maintain control at all times, he did not believe in absentee ownership. "I work too hard making money to give it to someone else," he said. He did buy shares of stock in American Security Bank and Giant Food because "I bank at American Security and I shop at Giant." But Williams did not let his money just sit. He was a smart businessman who invested in a growth city and profited from its postwar boom.

"He didn't like the status quo," said his financial adviser, Bob Flanagan. "He told me, 'You're either moving ahead or falling behind.' " His investment decisions, like his moods, were deeply affected by the progress of his cancer. "When things were on the upswing, he'd have vision, he'd look down the road and buy something," said Flanagan. "But when he called me and started asking about his liabilities, I'd know something was wrong. It meant he was going back into the hospital. No more deals, no more vision."

THE DEMANDS ON Williams's time continued to grow, even as his health declined. From eight in the morning to six at night, he held court. Businessmen one step ahead of the grand jury, professional athletes, senators and cabinet members, attractive widows, Knights of Malta—all trooped in and out of his 1,500-square-foot, three-room suite of offices on the eighth floor of the Hill Building.

"Visitors sit before him in puny armchairs like nervous petitioners before the throne of Louis XIV," wrote David Remnick of the *Washington Post*. Williams's throne room was dominated by a custom-made desk that looked like "the prow of an aircraft carrier," wrote Remnick. A model of Williams's private jet stood as if ready to launch down one runway. To Posner prosecutor Chris Todd, the desk looked like a "Darth Vader console." Williams described it more benignly, and perhaps more revealingly, as his "womb." Enclosing him on three sides, the massive piece of modernistic furniture had a television, a tape recorder, and the latest in office telephone technology (Williams's speed dial included the private numbers of the cardinal's residence at St. Matthew's Cathedral and fugitive Marc Rich's Swiss villa).

Neatly arrayed before him at all times was a row of thick, soft-leaded Black Hawk Number One pencils. Beyond the desk was a small cozy study with a couch, where he could snatch brief naps. Visitors with really important business were summoned through the study, where they were shown photographs of Williams and Lombardi and DiMaggio, Gerald Ford and LBJ, into a vast, royal blue conference room hung with dozens of citations and honorary degrees and mementoes of Williams's colorful past, including a transcript of the White House tape in which Richard Nixon threatened to "fix the son of a bitch." Prosecutor Todd called the inner sanctum the "Hall of Impressions." The effect—and the intent—was to awe the visitor.

Guarding the gate to Williams's suite was his secretary, Julie Allen. An attractive forty-ish divorcée, she knew how to banter and flirt with Williams and not to take his rages too seriously. He could be harsh to her, chiding and berating her, and she would roll her eyes and wait for him to calm down. She understood his mood swings. On her desk was an old elevator register with an arrow that pointed to floors one-to-ten. She called it a "mood meter." When Williams was jolly, she pushed the arrow up toward ten, and when he was silent or angry, she plunged it toward the basement. When the arrow rested on the lower floors, the lawyers in the firm knew to stay away.

Williams made no attempt to disguise his moods within the firm. "When he was bored, he was boring," said partner Jerry Collins. "He would shift his feet, look at his big watch, shoot his cuffs." After he had made his point and wanted the discussion over with, "he'd just turn and stare out the window. That was it," said Brendan Sullivan. He was abrupt to the point of rudeness on the phone. There was never a "hello" or "good-bye." His partners knew the conversation was over when they heard a click at the other end of the line. "He was impatient. He hated to waste time, maybe because he knew he didn't have much time left," said one. "He'd just leave the room or pick up the phone to make a call in the middle of a conversation. He was totally rude. It was his place and we were pleased to be there."

Then, for no apparent reason, the mood would change. The open-hearted Williams would reemerge, full of life and fun and warmth. He would be accessible and easy, as if he had time to shoot the breeze with almost anyone who walked in his door. He would discuss highly confidential matters with the lowliest associate. "Ed couldn't keep a secret if he wanted to," said partner Kevin Baine. He rarely stayed angry. "He could be rough and tough, but it would pass," said partner Jack Vardaman. "He'd put his arms around you and tell you he loved you. He had a way of treating you as an equal, of listening to you, to your hopes and desires and fears.''

Because he wanted to be liked, and because he genuinely believed in second (and third and fourth) chances, Williams never shed his extreme reluctance to fire anyone. In the early eighties, when he had to let go one of the managers at the Jefferson Hotel, he was effusively complimentary and reassuring to the man. The confused employee had to ask Bob Flanagan, ''Have I been fired?''

Williams was obsessively punctual. Lawyers in his firm learned to be on time or be left behind. ''If he said, 'Meet me in the lobby at 8:30,' he'd be gone by 8:32 with or without you,'' said Larry Lucchino. Williams brooked no excuses. The morning of an eighteen-inch snowfall in Washington in February 1981, he had a breakfast meeting with Lucchino and Redskins general manager Bobby Beathard. All three men arrived at the empty dining room at precisely 7:30 A.M. In a strong-and-silent display of business meeting macho, no one made any mention of the storm raging outside. To get home, Beathard had to abandon his car and walk the last two miles through the drifts.

Williams wanted to do things his way. He saw life as an endless series of foul-ups, and he did everything he could to avoid them. One reason why he bought his own plane was because he did not trust commercial airlines to get him where he wanted to go. He saw even the simplest act, like ordering a cup of coffee, as a snafu in the making. After dinner at the Jefferson one night, Williams ordered regular coffee, while Lucchino, Flanagan, and Jay Emmett ordered decaffeinated. Williams insisted that the waiter bring everyone regular. What are you doing? protested his tablemates. ''He'll screw it up,'' Williams said, gesturing to the waiter. ''I'll get stuck with decaf.'' So Williams made the waiter bring everyone regular coffee. When he had what he wanted, then he permitted the others to order what they wanted.

It was the refrain of his existence: He had to be in charge, and he would brook no challenge to his control. In court, if an associate whispered in his ear, the young lawyer would never make that mistake again. If Williams was giving a dinner, he would spend hours doing the place cards and reviewing the guest list. He wanted to know everything that was happening in his law firm, his charities, his ball club, and in the city he regarded as his domain. If someone was coming to see him, he wanted to know why. He could not stand to be away from a phone for more than a few minutes. At Holy Cross, Father Brooks had to install a phone in the

football stadium at commencement just so Williams could stay electronically tethered to the greater world.

Yet as Williams's law firm grew in the seventies and eighties, it became increasingly difficult for him to stay abreast of every aspect of the
firm's practice. "He was ambivalent about what he had created. It bothered him that he didn't recognize every lawyer in the firm," said Vickie
Radd, one of the younger lawyers whom Williams befriended and used as
an information source. When Connolly was alive and Califano still at the
firm, Williams had been able to delegate much of the management tasks.
Now it was a struggle to keep a handle on the seventy-odd lawyers who
filled all ten floors of the Hill Building and spilled into another building
Williams partly owned down the street.

For a time, it appeared that Califano might come back to the firm.
Williams watched with a certain perverse pleasure as President Carter lost
faith in his HEW secretary. "You think Califano's going to get canned?"
Williams gleefully asked Bob Strauss. "He's scared shitless." Williams
had warned Califano not to go into government, and now, fired by Carter
in July 1979, Califano was back looking for a job. Williams was glad to
have him. The younger partners, however, were not. They objected to
Califano's demands, which included a car and driver and, over five years,
a salary equal to that of Williams himself. "I'm going to have a fuckin'
revolution on my hands if Joe comes back," Williams told Art Buchwald. Califano, sensing the resentment and eager to write a book and start
his own firm, decided not to come back after all. The decision made, both
men wept.

Williams disliked running the law firm, but he wasn't willing to let
anyone else do it. Indeed, he felt his partners already had too much
power, and he pretended to long for the days when the firm was a sole
proprietorship. Califano came to see Williams while he was lying in bed
at Sloan-Kettering in March 1984. Agnes told Califano that he looked
tired. Califano responded that he'd been to an acrimonious all-day partners meeting at his new firm, Dewey Ballantine. Williams rose up, shaking the tubes that were sticking out of him, and roared, "You SOB, you
deserve every minute of it. You drafted that partnership agreement and
then left me with it!" Williams reminded Steve Umin of a proposal Umin
had made at a firm meeting at the Metropolitan Club in 1970 proposing
that the firm never grow larger than fifteen lawyers. "I wish we'd done
it," said Williams. "I wish I'd been a solo practitioner. You know what

the different is between a solo practitioner making $2,000 a year and this firm?'' he asked. ''Just a whole bunch of zeros.''

The young lawyers now coming to the firm had impressive résumés, but they lacked the street savvy of the older partners. Sought after by the best schools and law firms, the new recruits often brought large egos and a sense of entitlement. Williams disdained the name-droppers and braggarts among them. ''I don't want to hear about their cases,'' he complained to Sarah Duggin, a senior associate. ''My cases are more interesting than their cases.''

In 1980, the associates met with Williams to discuss how the firm was run. A few associates complained about the lack of a formal policy for creating new partners. ''For example,'' piped up Kevin Baine, ''Murphy over here asked me . . .'' Williams cut in. ''Murphy? Who the hell is Murphy? You think we need to explain to you guys?'' After that, when the subject of an associates meeting came up, the senior partners would say, oh, yes, we had a meeting—once. Williams only grudgingly attended the firm's annual dinner dance, or ''prom'' as he called it, and he left as soon as he could.

Certain associates would strike Williams's fancy because they were not only brainy but quick and imaginative, as well as fun to drink with. Williams could not bear losing them. When Bill Murphy, a mordant Irishman and skilled advocate, left the firm in the fall of 1983, Williams told him that he regarded his departure as a ''divorce.'' Greg Craig, Williams's able sidekick in the Helms, Antonelli, and Posner cases, announced that same morning that he was going to Capitol Hill to take a job on Senator Edward Kennedy's staff. Williams stared out the window after receiving this second blow and said, ''This is the greatest professional betrayal and personal disappointment of my life.''

Every January, Williams gave the same speech to his partners. He told them that he was worried, that he didn't know how they would possibly bring in enough business to ''feed all the mouths.'' Lucchino called it ''Ed's Henny Penny the-sky-is-falling speech.'' Upon making new partners, he slapped them on the back and said, ''Now you can share all the losses.'' Since Williams & Connolly partners made more money on average than any other law firm partners in Washington, this seemed unduly pessimistic, but Williams never shook his Depression mentality, his fear that what he had made in a lifetime he could lose in an instant. ''I'm Sisyphus!'' he declared every New Year. ''The rock is at the bottom of the hill, and I've got to push it up again!'' By nature, he looked at the dark side. Flying over Baltimore in Williams's private plane on a bright winter's afternoon, George Will said to his host, "Look, Ed, there's a fine view of the Orioles' stadium.'' Williams peered out the window. "No parking,'' he said.

Williams's younger partners wanted the firm to grow at faster rate—15 percent a year versus the firm's growth rate of 8 to 10 percent—but Williams was cautious. He resisted a move to open an office in Los Angeles, and he did not recruit aggressively to expand the firm's corporate and tax practice. He was indifferent to normal big law firm benefits, stalling for a decade before instituting a pension plan and scoffing at the idea of sabbaticals. Retiring or taking time off wasn't contest living, it was giving up.

Williams focused on the money going out and coming in. He was fanatical about not wasting electricity, sending out memos and driving by the Hill Building late at night to make sure the last one out of the library had turned off the lights. He was paranoid about getting sued, fearful that pedestrians walking by the firm would slip on an icy sidewalk or be struck by a falling windowpane. When it came to billing clients, he was expansive, telling associates to bill for the time they spent in the shower. Williams's own billing practices were guaranteed to generate high revenues.

At the end of 1984, he told reporters that he had billed 3,200 hours that year, over 60 hours a week—despite the fact that he had undergone surgery twice that year. He had worked "more hours than anyone else at a firm known throughout the Washington legal community for its endless workday,'' wrote the *Washington Post*. Williams used his 3,200 hours as proof that he could work hard despite his disease. "I needed to find out myself,'' he told the *Post*. "Maybe I was testing myself.''

The fact that he *billed* 3,200 hours, however, did not mean that he *worked* 3,200 hours. In fact, Williams sometimes billed for all twenty-four hours in a day. The way Williams figured out how many hours to bill on a given case was to figure out what he was worth—an arbitrary figure—and divide by his hourly rate, which at the time of his death was $1,000 an hour.

Williams was the chief "rainmaker" for the firm, as well as top biller. In the mid-eighties, he was responsible for bringing in roughly 30 percent of the firm's business. Naturally, lawyers in the firm worried about what would happen to the business if Williams died, and he himself understood that he had to prepare the firm for this eventuality. But the younger partners had trouble persuading him to "turn over the reins," said Lewis Ferguson, one of them. "He's not been particularly anxious to do so," Ferguson told the *American Lawyer* in May 1985. "He still has his hand in every pie." Williams could not let go. He felt his firm needed him too much. And in the case of *Tavoulareas* v. *The Washington Post*, he was right.

Chapter Thirty-Nine

WILLIAM TAVOULAREAS, THE president of Mobil Oil Corp., was a proud and stubborn man. When he read the *Washington Post* article on November 30, 1979, accusing him of "setting up" his son with a job in a shipping firm, he was outraged. His oil company had been cuffed about by the press for the past five years, and now the *Post,* a particular tormentor, was going after his family name. Tavoulareas wanted to get even.

He went to Ed Williams for help. The problem, of course, was that Williams represented the paper that Tavoulareas wanted to sue. Normally, a lawyer with an obvious conflict would just refuse to see his potential adversary. Taking his usual casual view of such matters, Williams ushered Tavoulareas into his office. He gave the oil company executive the same advice he invariably gave public figures who want to sue the press. Yes, he agreed, the press is irresponsible and untrustworthy, but libel trials are expensive and messy. And because of the difficult standard of proof that a plaintiff must overcome to win, the press almost never loses. So, he advised Tavoulareas, forget about it.

Tavoulareas did not take Williams's advice. A few weeks later, Williams found himself refereeing a shouting match between Ben Bradlee and the Mobil executive. Tavoulareas called the *Post* editor a "dickhead." Bradlee threatened to investigate Tavoulareas's past "back to the basinet." Williams jokingly suggested that the two "go eight rounds." But when the *Post* refused to print a retraction or identify the source of the story, Tavoulareas filed suit.

Unable to settle the case between two prideful antagonists, Williams was expected to defend the *Post* in court. But before the case went to trial in 1982, Williams's cancer returned. Compelled to undergo surgery that March, Williams had to turn the Tavoulareas case over to one of his law partners, Irving Younger. In 1980, Williams had recruited Younger, a flamboyant law professor well known to the bar for his lectures on trial advocacy. The Tavoulareas case was Younger's first big test in the real world, and, in Williams's estimation, he flunked.

After a two-week trial, the jury awarded the Mobil chairman $1.8 million. Williams was disgusted with his new recruit. He felt that Younger had gone into trial inadequately prepared and that his style had been too flip and shoot-from-the-hip. Worse, Younger had told reporters that he could have "played the judge like a violin." Williams always ordered his lawyers not to talk to reporters (a rule from which he excepted himself). Williams was furious with Younger and ordered him to grovel before the judge with a letter of apology. A few days later, Judge Oliver Gasch—Williams's old nemesis in the Baker case—wryly began, "Mr. Younger, you may begin playing when ready."*

At the *Post,* Kay Graham was also unhappy. She was even more concerned when the *Post* lost the first appeal. She wondered aloud whether the paper should bring in another big name First Amendment lawyer, Floyd Abrams perhaps, to argue the second appeal. The *Post* was perhaps Williams & Connolly's most prized client, and Williams could not bear failing it. He assured Graham that he would personally argue the case.

In September 1985, less than a month before Williams was scheduled to argue the Tavoulareas case, X-rays showed yet another cancer tumor in his liver. When his surgeon, Dr. Joseph Fortner, opened Williams up, he was unable to cut the tumor out. The malignancy had wrapped around the vena cava, a major artery. Instead, the surgeon implanted radiation isotopes in the hope of shrinking the tumor and sewed Williams back up. The procedure was a long shot.

Williams always tried to be upbeat after operations, but his son Tony noticed that his father seemed despondent after this one—the sixth (one colon, two liver, and three lung) in nine years. As Williams left Sloan-Kettering in New York on Saturday, September 21, his wife Agnes watched him pause and stand still in the early fall sunlight. She told her

*Williams was a little unfair to Younger, who was able to persuade the judge to throw out the jury's verdict because it was not supported by the evidence. An appeals court reinstated the jury verdict.

daughter Dana how unusual that was; her husband didn't believe in "stopping to smell the flowers."

The argument before the court of appeals was now only two weeks away, but Williams told Tony that he couldn't let anyone else in the firm take his place; he had to appear himself. So he began to prepare mentally and physically. "The problem with Irving Younger," Williams told his colleagues after his partner had "blown" the trial in *Tavoulareas,* "is that he doesn't have an iron butt."

For two weeks, Williams shuffled about his study, working over his argument with two young lawyers from his firm, Kevin Baine and David Kendall. Williams looked weaker and thinner, Kendall observed. Usually, he would stride around, his powerful body rolling and rocking as he wrestled with some slippery argument. Now, favoring the fresh six-inch incision in his right side, he moved stiffly and gingerly as he set about convincing himself of the rightness of his client's cause.

"I've been thinking," he told Baine and Kendall, "in a civilized society, we can get along without every liberty—except free speech." The two young lawyers looked at each other. This was the same Ed Williams who liked to say "the press is the only institution with a license to screw up." Who said, "I don't like fucking journalists. They sit in the trees and shoot people." Who called reporters "pygmies with dart guns." "Gee, Ed," Baine said with a smile, "you sound like a new man."

The "license to screw up" that Williams had sardonically referred to was a case called *New York Times* v. *Sullivan.* To protect the press when writing about public officials, the U.S. Supreme Court in 1964 ruled that libel plaintiffs must prove that the defendant acted with "actual malice." Defined by the court as "knowing falsity or reckless disregard of the truth," actual malice is very difficult to prove.

Williams was fairly confident that he could show that the *Post* had not acted with actual malice. But in this case, he wanted more than a legal victory. It wasn't enough to get his client off on a technicality. He did not want to admit that, yes, maybe the story was wrong, but that the *Post* should be let off the hook because it had not "knowingly or recklessly" printed a falsehood. For the sake of his friend Ben Bradlee, for Graham, and for the reputation of the paper, he wanted to vindicate the *Post.* He was determined to prove that the story was true.

Normally, such questions of fact are left to juries to decide, and in the *Tavoulareas* case, the jury had already decided that the story was false. But in order to protect newspapers from vindictive local juries, the Supreme Court in the *Sullivan* case had instructed appellate judges to review the facts de novo—to second-guess the jury. So, for Williams, this would not be an airy and abstract legal debate in the court of appeals. He would approach the judges as if they were jurors.

There were a couple of tricky legal questions that Williams would have to dispose of along the way. One involved the question of whether evidence of ordinary malice, as opposed to constitutionally defined "actual malice"—knowing or reckless disregard of the truth—was relevant and hence admissible at trial. The distinction sounds legalistic, but it was important, because Tavoulareas claimed that the *Post* was out to get him, and thus he wanted to show the *Post*'s malicious intent. Kendall thought such evidence should be inadmissible, but Baine argued that they probably couldn't get away with contending that the evidence of malice should be excluded altogether. Instead, they should suggest that while relevant, evidence of malice was not probative. Williams listened to this rather abstract debate for a while, and then he put the proposition a different way.

"You mean," he said, "that the evidence has a ticket of admission, but only to the cheapest seats in the house?" Baine and Kendall smiled. In a single sentence, Williams had cut through a knotty problem that had tied Kendall up when he had unsuccessfully argued the case before a three-judge appellate panel in 1984. Williams, as always rehearsing his spontaneous quips, committed this one to memory, for use at the right moment.

Williams had one more legal issue to resolve. The *Sullivan* case had been extended to apply to public figures as well as public officials. There was some question as to whether Mobil president Tavoulareas qualified as a public figure. What, Williams wondered, should he tell the court if the judges turned the tables and asked if he, Edward Bennett Williams, was a public figure? You have to say yes, said Kendall. "God," said Williams, "I don't want to do that." He didn't want to give the press a license to shoot at *him*.

ON OCTOBER 3, 1985, the line outside the fifth-floor courtroom at the United States Courthouse on Pennsylvania Avenue began forming two hours before arguments were scheduled to begin in *Tavoulareas* v. *The Washington Post*. Supreme Court clerks, lawyers, reporters, and a smattering of Georgetown socialites stood patiently in the somber marble hallway. They had come to see the judges explore the critical First Amendment issues posed by the case, but mostly they had come to see Edward Bennett Williams give what many thought would be his last great courtroom performance.

Ben Bradlee, who never appeared to be worried about anything, concealed his anxiety with jokes and small talk. It had been bad enough to give back a Pulitzer Prize earlier that year that a *Post* reporter, Janet Cooke, had won for a story about a five-year-old heroin addict who turned out to be fictional. Losing the Tavoulareas suit would leave another black mark on the paper. The press critics were starting to say that the *Post* had grown cocky and sloppy after Watergate, that it went overboard in its relentless search for what one *Post* editor indelicately referred to as "holy shit!" stories. Bradlee was counting on his best friend to step off the operating table and vindicate the paper. As Bradlee later described his situation, "I was waiting for Eddie to ride in on a white horse and pull my balls out of the fire."

Bradlee sat down on a newspaper on the floor to wait. There, he later recalled, "sitting on her ass beside me, amid the coffee cups and cigarette butts, was the most powerful woman in America," Katharine Graham, the sixty-eight-year-old chairman of the board of the Washington Post Company. She looked worried. She was nervous about Williams—that he was too sick to argue, that he had to appear too soon after the operation, that he was really a trial lawyer, not an appellate lawyer, that criminal law, not the First Amendment, was his forte.

She was not reassured when Williams emerged from the elevator on the fifth floor of the courthouse, lugging his black legal bag, shortly before 9:00 A.M. To Bradlee, his old friend looked pale and puffy, fleshy and sweaty. To Patrick Tyler, the *Post* reporter who had written the story about Tavoulareas, Williams "looked like an old Mafia hitman in a black raincoat." Bradlee and a few reporters shouted encouragement: "Let's go, Eddie! Go get 'em, Eddie!" Williams just stared at them. "Jesus Christ," the lawyer muttered, and pushed by into the courtroom.

After taking the time to chat with the bailiffs and court reporter, he amiably greeted his opponent, John Walsh, who was representing Tavoulareas. In the flat neon light of the courtroom, Walsh thought Williams looked shabby and haggard. He was, in fact, in some discomfort: The night before he had popped one of his stitches. When it came time to argue, however, Williams was forceful and theatrical. He roamed from the podium, defending freedom of the press with fervor and passion. At one point he apologized for his emotionalism; it was "difficult," he told the judges, "to discuss a liberty this precious without getting excited." Williams looked "leonine and assertive," Kendall wrote in his diary that night. To other observers in the courtroom, however, the aging courtroom lawyer just seemed overbearing and overwrought, his rhetoric quaint and a little hokey. "It was a stump speech. It lacked texture and finesse," said Michael Tigar, Williams's old protégé who was now a University of Texas Law School professor. Some of the younger lawyers in the audience found Williams surprisingly rude to the judges. He so quickly brushed past one question from Judge Ruth Bader Ginzburg that the *National Law Journal* reporter wondered if Williams was hard of hearing.

Williams was impatient with Ginzburg because she had asked a technical, legalistic question about appellate review. Williams was concentrating instead on Judge Kenneth Starr, a young jurist on the court who was something of an unknown but who seemed to be asking the right questions: Was the story true? Was it fair? "It was clear that Williams's intent was to cut through the mumbo jumbo and get down to what the case really was in terms of right and wrong, and in my view, it was that kind of case," Judge Starr later recalled. He thought Williams that day was a "fabulous presence, full of vigor and righteous indignation. He was much more than the proverbial hired gun."

Three seats to Starr's right, however, Judge Antonin Scalia began to close in. Williams knew that his most difficult sell would be Scalia, an archconservative notably unsympathetic to the press. Scalia wanted to ask about the evidence of malice—that reporters at the *Post* felt under pressure to produce "sensationalistic stories." Yes, Williams was willing to concede, that evidence was relevant. But not very. Seemingly offhand, he quipped, "It has a ticket of admission, but only to the cheapest seats in the house."

In the courtroom, there was a ripple of laughter. Several judges smiled. Then Williams grew stern. To say that reporters *were* under pressure to produce these stories, he thundered, would be "a distortion and abortion of the record!" No, the story was totally fair, totally truthful. Tavoulareas's son had been a $14,000-a-year clerk at the Atlas shipping company. After Tavoulareas intervened, his son suddenly became a 75 percent owner of the company. "I say to you," Williams instructed the court, "that anyone who would believe a $14,000-a-year clerk went to a 75 percent owner of Atlas on the theory of meritocracy has to believe in the tooth fairy.'' The courtroom audience burst into laughter. This time, several judges joined them. At the counsel's table, reported the *National Law Journal*, Tavoulareas's son Peter looked ''like he had been punched in the gut.''

After the argument, Patrick Tyler, the *Post* reporter, came up to Williams to congratulate him. He clapped Williams on the shoulder and was shocked when Williams staggered slightly. Tyler reached for Williams's arm; the old lawyer was trembling.

When the decision came down several months later, Williams called Bradlee. ''Benjy!'' he cried. ''We win, 7–1!'' The court's opinion had been written by Judge Starr. It was a total vindication of the *Post*. ''The tooth fairy line really got to me,'' Judge Starr later said.

Chapter Forty

WILLIAMS WAS "NOT much fun to watch a game with," said George Will, his frequent companion in the owners box at Memorial Stadium in Baltimore. If the game was close, Williams would be tense, "looking for the cracking ice around his feet." The Orioles would have to be ahead by about eight runs before Williams could relax, and if the team was losing, he was "miserable." "Ed, it's not a game you can play with your teeth clenched," the columnist told his friend, who glowered back. The seat next to Williams in the box was usually empty because to sit beside the owner was to risk physical injury. "He'd whack you in the ribs, wham!" said his son Bennett. Williams told Jack Valenti that it "was literally painful to lose." If the team was on a losing streak, he'd say, "I can't go to another game, I can't stand it." Losing, he told Lucchino, made him "physically sick."

He felt increasingly ill in the summer of 1984 as he watched his World Champion Orioles slide into fifth place. His ace pitcher, Jim Palmer, had lost his touch, and the team's designated hitter, Ken Singleton, could barely get his batting average above .200. In October, Williams informed General Manager Hank Peters that he was going to become a "hands-on owner." He wanted to spend some money to buy established stars in the free-agent market. "What do you need to win?" he asked field manager Joe Altobelli. Altobelli shrugged and suggested a center fielder. The Orioles had always "grown their own," and Peters had some reservations about fiddling with this formula for success. He thought there were some promising young outfielders coming up through the farm system. But the

445

coaches couldn't promise that they would be ready to produce by the next season. Williams couldn't wait. The Orioles went out and spent $11 million over five years to sign two veteran outfielders, Fred Lynn and Lee Lacy and a relief pitcher, Don Aase.

The moves were a gamble. Lynn was a star, but already past his prime at the age of thirty-four. Aase had undergone major back surgery. Williams took an even greater chance by buying second baseman Alan Wiggins of the San Diego Padres for $2.8 million after the Orioles' regular second baseman made three errors in one inning. Wiggins tested Williams's faith in redemption. A two-time drug loser, the infielder never kicked his habit and was suspended from baseball two years later. To sign these high-priced free agents, the Orioles were required to give up three top draft picks, further weakening a farm system that was showing serious signs of decay.

Peters thought Williams was impatient because he was dying. He also believed that Williams was reacting to the jibes of his winners-only circle in Washington. He was not far wrong. "I can't let go," Williams admitted in 1986. "Even if you start without an ego," the media "make you into a genius or an idiot every morning. Your ego becomes involved for self-protection, for survival." Williams hated to let down the ordinary fans, much less the well-heeled regulars in his box. Walking out of Memorial Stadium one night after the Orioles had blown a game in the ninth inning on an error, Williams and his chauffeur, Leroy Washington, were accosted by three irate fans. "Which one of you bastards is Williams?" one beery rooter demanded. Williams pointed to Washington.

Williams preferred to stay out of the players' clubhouse, but he couldn't resist as the losses mounted. One night in 1984, after a long slide, he gave the team an inspirational speech in Boston ("if you can look inside yourself and give yourself an inner 'V' for victory, you'll be surprised how many 'W's' that will put on the scoreboard"). The players were a little intimidated by the great courtroom orator. "When Williams gave a pep talk, I always felt like shouting 'Guilty!' " said outfielder Larry Sheets. Williams did not interfere with Altobelli's decisions on the diamond, but he second-guessed him constantly in the owners box. When Altobelli signaled for a bunt, Williams would leap to his feet and rant, "Goddamned worst play in baseball!" Williams thought bunting was feminine, a "pussy play," he called it.

Williams was contemptuous of Altobelli, who had won the World

Series in 1983 but once bragged that he had read only one book in his life, the biography of a hockey player. When Altobelli came out of the dugout during a game to change a pitcher, Williams shouted, "Don't think, Joey! Don't think!" Williams began calling Altobelli "Cement Head." In June 1985, as the Orioles headed back toward the second division, Williams fired his manager. To replace him, Williams brought the legendary Earl Weaver, who had led the Orioles in the late sixties and seventies, out of retirement. Weaver was more interested in bowling than baseball at this stage of his life and lasted little more than a season.

In 1979, Williams had given Hank Peters a five-year contract as general manager and told him, "You're the rock on which I'm going to build the church." After the World Series in 1983, he signed Peters to another five-year contract. But losing seasons in 1984 and 1985 soured the relationship. Williams accused Peters of coasting, of becoming a "nine-to-fiver." He began referring to the general manager's office as "Sleepy Hollow." Peters thought Williams had entered "a dangerous period when owners learn the language of baseball without knowing what the hell they are talking about. Williams didn't know as much as he thought he did," said Peters. George Will offered a more neutral opinion: "Peters had a lower metabolism than Ed. He took the long view, that things come and go."

The press watched all this turmoil in the front office and mourned for the good old days. "The Orioles as we have known them for the last quarter century—placid, excellent, hermetic, slow to change, tasteful, and conservative—are gone," lamented *Washington Post* columnist Thomas Boswell. The *Post* and the *Baltimore Sun* began comparing Williams to George Steinbrenner, the mercurial owner of the New York Yankees who constantly fired managers. The comparison galled Williams, who disdained his old client (while at the same time envying the Yankee owner's deep pocket for buying talent). Williams was thin-skinned about the press anyway, seizing on the smallest slights in otherwise flattering articles. As always, he tried to seduce reporters. "He could be a teddy bear, creating a sense of intimacy that was very alluring but very deceiving," said Mark Hyman, who covered the Orioles for the *Baltimore Sun*. But he could also be withering with reporters who "betrayed" him. "How can they accuse me of meddling with the team when I own it?" he demanded.

Despite its woes on the field, the team thrived at the box office. The Orioles drew over 2 million fans in 1984 and 1985 while finishing fifth and fourth in the American League East. Still, Baltimoreans remained fearful that Williams would follow the example of the football Colts and abandon the city. In 1980, Williams had vowed that "baseball will never leave Baltimore," but he negotiated a very favorable lease that he renewed only year to year. "Birds Owners Shows He's a Taker, Not a Giver" was a headline in the *Baltimore News American* in February 1984. Underneath was a crude cartoon of Williams standing on the mound, spitting at the baseball in his hand.

After losing money throughout the seventies, the Orioles were now profitable. Season tickets had multiplied almost tenfold, to over twelve thousand, and radio and television revenues had doubled and tripled. Then, in the summer of 1984, Williams was suddenly presented with a demand from Jack Kent Cooke to share in the profits. The Redskins majority owner informed Williams that he was exercising his "option" to buy half the Orioles—at the original price of $12 million, a fraction of what it was now worth. Williams was "shocked and outraged," said his financial adviser, Bob Flanagan. When Williams insisted that Cooke's contract to buy half the Orioles was a figment of his imagination, Cooke threatened to sue.

Cooke was not entirely dreaming. In 1978, the two Redskins owners had indeed discussed buying the Orioles together and moving them to a new stadium, to be shared by the Redskins and Orioles, off I-95 between the two cities. The cross-ownership rules of the NFL made it difficult for Cooke, who owned 85 percent of the Redskins, to take an active ownership role in a baseball team. Instead, according to Cooke's lawyer, Milton Gould, Cooke agreed to loan Williams $3.5 million. Williams promised he'd get the football league to ease the rules so that Cooke could come in as a full partner at a later date. (In fact, Williams did argue strongly against the cross-ownership restrictions at league meetings.) Cooke's lawyer points out that the loan was at 6 percent—less than half the going interest rate at the time. The money was actually loaned to Williams by the Washington Redskins Inc., but Cooke considered the loan to be personal, since he owned most of the team. Williams, however, argued that he was simply borrowing against his own investment in the team, which by now was worth at least $5 million. Who was right? There was no proof, only some unsigned option agreements with the costs and percentages left blank. But Cooke's real aim, Williams suspected, was not to buy into the Orioles. It was to drive Williams out of the Redskins.

Cooke had been gradually squeezing Williams out of the football team ever since he had moved back to the Washington area from the West Coast in 1978. Williams still had the title of president of the Redskins but no operational control. When Williams flew with Marvin Davis out to the Super Bowl in 1983, Davis asked him why he was sitting in the stands instead of in the owners box with Cooke. "Because the prick didn't invite me," replied Williams. After the game, Williams was pleased that the veteran players embraced him and ignored Cooke. Cooke responded by refusing to invite Williams up to the television platform to receive the championship trophy from NFL commissioner Pete Rozelle.

In his own mawkish way, Cooke tried to repair the relationship by sending Williams a poem that June. "What mother or father hasn't experienced the vague, disturbing impression so tenderly put by Galway Kinnell," wrote Cooke, quoting Kinnell's poem, "Your cry, waking from a nightmare / when I sleep walk / into your room / pick you up / and hold you in the moonlight / and cling to me / hard / as if clinging could save us. I think / you think / I will never die. I think I exude / to you the permanence of smoke or / stars / even as / my broken arms heal themselves / around you." Williams replied, "I am crying from a nightmare, how come you don't come to my room and pick me up?"

Instead, Cooke presented Williams with a real nightmare: the threat of a public lawsuit over control of the Orioles. Throughout that summer the two antagonists skirmished. The socially ambitious Cooke badly wanted to join the Metropolitan Club, and Williams had agreed to propose him back in 1981. When Williams withdrew his recommendation that June just as the members were about to vote on Cooke's candidacy, Cooke protested, "Oh, no, I have waited so long for this." Williams said his membership in the exclusive club would have to wait. In a "suppliant" voice, Williams recorded in a memorandum to files, Cooke pleaded, "I really want to stand for election at the Metropolitan Club right now." Williams let him dangle.

Cooke retaliated by pulling Williams's postseason tickets to the owners box and parking passes at RFK Stadium. In August, he began to float the idea of buying his own baseball team and bringing it to Washington, where it would siphon off the Orioles' large Washington following. In September, Williams drove out to see Cooke at his farm in Virginia, but the conversation quickly degenerated into a shouting match. Finally, that winter, the two men agreed, in effect, to a divorce. Cooke dropped his claim on the Orioles. Williams sold his own 14 percent of the Redskins to Cooke for $5 million. That was less than half what it was worth, but Williams just wanted out. He didn't want a high profile lawsuit with reporters digging into the past, examining how Cooke and Williams had come to gain control of all the Redskins stock from the George Preston Marshall estate. ("Hey, Leroy," Jay Emmett teased Williams's chauffeur. "Was it you or Ed who put the pillow over Marshall's face?")

Williams nurtured a bitter hatred of Cooke for the rest of his life. "I want to flush that piece of shit out of this city once and for all," he vowed. Grabbing Larry King as he headed up the ramp to Cooke's box one Sunday, Williams demanded, "Where are you going? You don't go there. You are either on his side or my side."

Chapter Forty-One

JUST AS WILLIAMS held deep resentments against some men, he could develop almost romantic attachments to others. "He would fall in love with doctors" who held out the hope of a cancer cure, said Art Buchwald. "Then, when the cure didn't work, he'd get pissed. 'That fucker!' " Williams was very fond of his oncologist at Sloan-Kettering, Jerome DeCosse, a fellow Roman Catholic and Vince Lombardi fan. "I have a haunting fear that I shall never be able to repay you," he wrote DeCosse after his fourth operation in March 1984. "You are our numero uno hero." The hospital found a way to be repaid by not sending Williams a bill, on the assumption that he would make an even more generous donation. Williams grumbled about the cancer center's expectation ("I never should have let Marvin Davis visit me in the hospital"), but he did not disappoint. Williams donated $100,000 to cancer research and even persuaded his client Victor Posner to kick in $35,000.

But when the surgeons at Sloan-Kettering sewed Williams up in September 1985 without cutting out the tumor, Williams had to find a new hero. He looked first to Dr. Steven Rosenberg at the National Cancer Institute. Rosenberg was on the cover of *Time* that fall for his innovative research into Interleukin-2, which the magazine billed as a possible miracle cure for cancer. Although Williams had avoided chemotherapy so far, surgery was no longer the answer. He had to try a different approach, and IL-2 was the one getting the most favorable publicity.

Williams began treatment in January 1986. Unaccustomed to public hospitals, he was disgruntled when Rosenberg refused to let him have a phone and put him in a ward with other patients. The treatment itself was excruciating. Williams shook, his skin burned, and, most terrifying, he hallucinated. "I had never defined the phrase 'going through hell,' but now I can," he told Jack Valenti. Williams walked out of the hospital without completing the course of treatment.

His next stop on the search for medical salvation was the Dana Farber Cancer Institute at Harvard. He learned of the institute's work through Larry Horowitz, a senior aide to Senator Ted Kennedy. Dana Farber had saved the life of Kennedy's oldest boy, Teddy Jr., who had lost a leg to cancer. With his belief in "brand-name players," Williams signed on with Dr. Emil Frei of Harvard for a nine-week course of a new chemotherapy, leucovorin. Every week in the spring of 1986, Williams flew to Boston on Sunday night, stayed at the Ritz Carlton, and spent two hours in a chair the next morning watching leucovorin drip into his bloodstream. In the "infusion room" at Dana Farber, he whiled away the time chatting with the other patients, particularly a bookie named Sol Smith, with whom he swapped gambling stories.

Williams was a great favorite with the nurses. "He was impatient if you fudged, and he could be hard on the staff, but people became very fond of him," said one of his early caretakers, Ann O'Donnell. "He'd come in and say, 'I'm back, the bad penny has returned.' " Williams flirted with the nurses and gave them baseball tickets. He became especially close to Joyce McKenna, an RN in the infusion room, writing gentle and funny letters to her eighty-five-year-old mother, thanking the old woman for her prayers. The nurses banded together to give Williams a plaque inscribed with Dickens's words from *Nicholas Nickleby*, "Among men who have sound and sterling qualities, there is nothing so contagious as pure openness of the heart." Presented with the plaque, Williams mumbled a thank-you and turned away to cry.

Joyce McKenna is a tough-minded nurse who has seen many patients die, yet when talking about Williams two years after his death, her eyes still filled with tears. Williams's "openness of heart" touched many patients and professionals during his many visits to the grim precincts of a cancer ward. To the children at Sloan-Kettering, he sent Orioles baseball jackets and tickets. For one particular little friend, he arranged special seating at Yankee Stadium where he could bring his oxygen tank. He exchanged a lively and sweet correspondence with the sick boy for a year until his letters stopped coming.

Williams's spirits rose in the infusion room as he watched his CEA, the

index monitoring his cancer cells, fall from a high of 400—an astronom-
ical figure—down to 30 by October 1986. "The results were spectacular," said Dr. Frei. A CAT scan that fall showed no sign of the tumor in
his liver. Williams was ecstatic. Frei was his new "numero uno" hero.
"The tumor is *gone!*" Williams exulted to his daughter Dana. "Can you
believe it?"

WILLIAMS HAD BOUGHT more time for himself, but he had run out of time
for Victor Posner, his client charged with criminal tax fraud. He had
fended off the government for more than seven years, but this was one
case that he could not just make "go away." The prosecutors were
determined to put away the rapacious corporate raider. Trial was set for
late June in Miami.

Williams did not want to try the case. "I can't do this anymore. Why
am I here?" he complained to a young lawyer from the firm who had been
assigned to assist him. "I'm never going to do this again," he told
another member of the trial team. "This is the last trial. I'm too old for
this." Williams had discussed the possibility of Vince Fuller handling the
defense if he was too sick, or possibly even going outside the firm to
another trial lawyer. To some extent, Williams's grumblings were ritual,
his usual pretrial moaning and groaning. He had been declaring that he
was "too old" to try cases for twenty years, but he was still a prisoner of
duty. He may have thought of himself as an aging fighter who could no
longer face the ordeal of training, but he could not walk away from a
fight.

Williams did not like his client very much. He respected Posner's raw
energy and envied his genius for reading balance sheets, but he disapproved of his client's rude manners—snapping his fingers at waiters and
calling them "boy"—as well as his taste for teenage girls. Posner boasted
about his sixteen-year-old girlfriend. "Who wants an old bag when you
can get one of these?" he asked at a dinner with his lawyers, gesturing at
his date. "Stand up, honey, and show them what I get every night."
Williams told Marvin Davis a story—probably apocryphal—that Posner
had begged off preparing for trial one night because he had another
engagement. "Where are you going?" asked Williams. "The prom,"
said Posner, who was sixty-seven years old.

The government's case against Posner was strong but not airtight. In
1975, he had donated sixteen acres of land to Miami Christian College

and taken a charitable tax deduction of $125,000 an acre. In 1972, however, he had sold the same land to a Miami real estate firm for $38,000—and they had given the property back three years later because they couldn't find a buyer. In 1978, he gave the college six more acres and took a tax deduction of $175,000 an acre. The appraiser, William Scharrer, had already been convicted (in 1984) for telling Posner in a letter (the "smoking gun" of the first trial) that the valuation was "probably unrealistic, in as much as it was developed for tax purposes."

As in most cases of white-collar crimes, the critical legal question was Posner's intent. Did he "knowingly and willfully" file false tax returns? Williams, as usual, looked for a "theory of the case" that would make Posner's intent seem benign to the jury. Williams examined Posner's career and decided that his client was a "visionary." He had built his empire by being bullish. Where other people saw a weedy plot of land, he saw a shopping center. In fact, Posner *had* wanted to build a shopping center on the land. The problem was he knew that it was very unlikely that he could get it zoned for commercial use.

Williams did not exactly put words in Posner's mouth. But according to Hugh Culverhouse, Jr., who participated in the witness preparation, Williams was not particularly subtle about communicating his "theory of the case" to Posner. "Victor, this is the way I see this case," Williams began, outlining his theory. "There's no other explanation. This is what I think you were doing. Now, Victor, what were you doing?" "The startling thing," said Culverhouse, was that "Victor was doing just what Ed thought." Posner told Williams, "I thought the land was a shopping center. I thought it the day I looked at it."

For days, Williams prepared Posner at his office tower on Miami Beach. He wanted to smooth Posner's rough edges, to clean up his language, and to try to make him sympathetic—or at least presentable—to a jury. "He really worked Victor hard," said Tony Williams, who had accompanied his father to Miami and sat in on some of the witness preparation. Mimicking the Texas accent of the prosecutor, Chris Todd, Williams came at Posner with a full range of emotions—tough, cloying, mad, funny. When Posner stumbled, Williams said, "Victor, watch!" and played the witness himself as another member of the trial team, Richard Cooper, took the role of prosecutor. When Posner learned his part properly, Williams shouted encouragement. "You got 'em, Victor!" Posner, who was five feet six, would "stamp his little feet," said one of the lawyers preparing him.

Williams worried that Posner would not be a good witness in his own defense. The grind of preparing him, and mastering the details of Posner's real estate machinations, drained Williams. He had always hated hot, muggy weather, and Miami in late June suffocated him. "Where's the air? Air! Air!" he demanded of drivers as he climbed into stuffy limousines. At the little Catholic church where he attended mass in the morning, Williams turned down the thermostat while the priest was putting on his vestments (the priest turned the thermostat back up when he came out). Williams went through three chauffeurs before he found one who could get him to morning mass on time—and who always made sure that the air conditioner was blasting at the right temperature when Williams stepped into the car.

Williams ate his normal pretrial diet: assorted junk food, crackers, Cheez Whiz, and milk. At a restaurant, after he and Tony had consumed foot-long hot dogs and a beer, the waitress asked what he would like for dessert. "Your mother would want us to have something healthy," Williams told his son. "We'll have some fruit." He ordered two pieces of apple pie, topped with slices of cheese.

Working day and night in his apartment on Miami Beach, Williams wore the same gray stretch pants and purplish velour shirt until Tony protested that his father's clothes were beginning to smell. Knowing how much swimming relaxed him, Tony made his father buy a bathing suit and swim in the ocean. Although he complained that the water was too warm, it did unwind him a little. On Wednesdays, Williams went to a hospital in Miami and received his weekly dose of chemotherapy. For two hours, he would talk on a mobile phone while heavy doses of leucovorin dripped into his arm. To prosecutor Chris Todd, Williams "seemed like a bull." But one day he found his opponent lying on a couch in the court reporter's office, groggily fighting off the side effects of his treatment.

This was Edward Bennett Williams's last trial, and everyone sensed it. "It hung over all of us," said Culverhouse. "You'd say, 'Are you okay?' And he'd get mad as hell at you." He was, in the kind of melodramatic metaphor Williams liked to use, a wounded old lion, swiping and growling at his predators, readying himself for a last kill before he was killed himself.

The hunting ground was not sweeping or grand. The small Miami courtroom, built in 1980, was of cheap government construction, with molded furniture and sand-blasted walls. The counsel tables were fixed, so Williams could not scheme for small advantage by moving them about. It all felt a little too up-to-date to the old warrior as he performed his ritualistic pretrial survey, pacing off the distances between the witness stand and the jury box. Although Williams disdained another modern invention, hiring consultants to help gauge jury reaction, Posner had insisted, so the firm had hired a woman psychologist. "I've been analyzing the jury pool . . ." she told Williams, who cut her off. "Let's pick the first twelve," he said, winking at Culverhouse. Williams enjoyed the macho show. While the psychologist wanted to use questionnaires, Williams relied on body language. "I don't want 'Yessir' stiffs," he said. During voir dire, the prosecutors referred to the jurors by their numbers; Williams, with his photographic memory, addressed them by name.

Williams, as always, had carefully cultivated the judge, Eugene Spellman. Spellman was a good Catholic and a sports fan, and he enjoyed Williams's ribald jokes and tales from the arena. Dealing with Williams, Spellman later said, "was the most delightful experience I've ever had." Williams flirted outrageously with the judge's secretary, whom he called "Glorious Gloria." The judge and his staff were sensitive to Williams's illness, scheduling court appearances around his chemotherapy treatments and giving him a couch where he could rest during the afternoon.

In his customary fashion, Williams was at once intimidating and avuncular toward the prosecutors, Chris Todd and Neil Cartusciello. "I've never enjoyed being knocked around so much in my life," said Todd. "It took me a while to figure out that Williams orchestrated his anger, that he was like a kid who cried not because he was really hurt but because he wanted attention." During the endless pretrial maneuvering, Williams held court, telling war stories about Hoffa and Bobby Kennedy, Frank Costello and the mob. "He was bored by our stories," said Todd. "He knew his stories were better, and he liked hearing them more."

At the trial, Williams treated Cartusciello, a precise, earnest young philosophy major from Harvard, like a junior associate in his firm, correcting his syntax and suggesting ways to tighten his sentences. "Who was the force behind the decision?" Cartusciello asked a witness. Williams grumbled. "Force behind the decision. What is that?" Cartusciello corrected himself: "All right, who made the decision." When the young prosecutor asked to "tender the evidence," Williams sighed theatrically. "I'll object unless you tell me what 'tender the evidence' means." Judge Spellman cut in, "I think he means he wants to submit the evidence." Cartusciello seemed rattled, which was Williams's intention.

After the judge upheld one of Williams's objections, Cartusciello sheepishly said, "Thank you, and I apologize." Every time he wanted to approach the witness, the prosecutor clasped his hands prayerfully, and asked, "Your honor, may I . . ." Williams, who had not hesitated to wander about the courtroom as if it were his living room, asked Spellman to give Cartusciello blanket permission to approach the witness so he wouldn't have to ask every time. Williams was "getting permission for his opponent to feel at home," observed the *Miami Herald,* noting that Williams's act was less a "magnanimous gesture" than a "demonstration of control." Williams was so in control that as he stood to object to another prosecutorial misstep, Judge Spellman remarked, "Mr. Williams, you're winning. Sit down."

Spellman and Williams appeared to be allies as they took turns correcting the prosecutor. "They play the commonsensical, almost folksy examplars of age and experience to Cartusciello's and Todd's prototypical uptight attorneys," wrote the *Miami Review,* a legal journal covering the trial. When Williams began referring to the prosecutors as "Howdy Doody," the judge wanted to know which one was Howdy.

"It was a crushing mismatch between one of the country's foremost trial attorneys and two relatively young assistant U.S. attorneys," wrote the *Review* on June 27. The article went on, however, to intimate that Judge Spellman was under Williams's thumb as well. That was unfortunate for the defense. The day after the article appeared, Spellman ruled against almost all of Williams's objections. Williams knew he had overplayed his hand. "Never get your picture in the papers," he muttered to his trial team as they left court that day.

Williams seemed restless, almost bored. He had always been careful to respect courtroom etiquette, to defer to the judge and the formalities of trial procedure. But for the first time in a courtroom, he allowed his impatience to get the better of him. Williams began to ignore the rule that requires opposing lawyers to direct their comments to the bench, rather than addressing each other directly. Failing to formally object to Cartusciello's mistakes, Williams simply told the prosecutor what to do. Worse, he usurped the bench's prerogative to instruct the witness. When a witness responded to a prosecutor's question by simply nodding, Williams commanded him to respond orally. Spellman had to remind Williams that he was the judge.

In court after receiving his chemotherapy on the first Wednesday of the trial, Williams became unusually testy, berating the prosecutors in front of the jury. Spellman sent the jurors out and told the lawyers to see him in chambers. "I was afraid they were going to come to blows," the judge recalled. Williams paced the hallway outside the judge's chambers, trying to regain control of himself. Finally, he poked his head inside. "Judge, you know how the Italian army marches?" he asked. He walked into the room backward, with his arms up.

Williams played his usual courtroom tricks on Todd. After leaving the podium, he turned off the microphone, in the hopes that the jury would have trouble hearing Todd, who had a soft voice. Yet Todd had his own ploys, and they were perhaps more effective with the jury. Presenting an exhibit, Williams placed himself between the prosecutor and the jury, so the jury would focus only on him. Todd got up from the counsel's table and walked over to the corner of the jury box, where he crouched down, ostensibly to get an unobstructed view of the exhibit. He sat cross-legged, Indian-style, looking up at Williams. "The jurors saw him like a five-year-old boy, his mouth slightly agape, watching a wizard," said Culverhouse, who was sitting at the defense counsel's table. "I thought to myself, you SOB, you know exactly what you're doing." Williams, off-balance for once, rushed through the presentation. "You couldn't duke it out with Todd, he was like the Pooh boy," said Culverhouse. "It was like trying a case against a woman. He seemed so vulnerable, sitting there cross-legged. Ed did much better when he was up against the Big Bad State."

As Williams had feared, Posner hurt his cause when he took the stand. Williams had hoped to portray the corporate raider as a grandfatherly sort who had generously tried to help a struggling little Christian college. But in three days on the stand, Posner came across the way he truly was—"a gutsy street fighter," reported the *Miami Review*. The defendant battled Todd all the way through the cross-examination. In a high-pitched nasal voice, he answered, time and again, "totally untrue," "absolutely no," "completely incorrect." He disputed incontrovertible facts, like the depressed value of Miami real estate in the mid-seventies. He was both the tough guy, beginning his sentences, "I told him, I says . . ." And the rich man: "I have the ability, through money or whatever, to purchase anything of value anyone offers me, whether it's land or stock. And I'm paid a handsome salary to do it." Todd paused in his questioning. "A handsome salary?" he asked. Posner, who earned $12 million in 1985, more than any executive in the nation, replied, "Satisfactory." The jurors burst out laughing.

During the worst moments of Posner's cross-examination, there was an audible pounding sound. It came from the defense table, where Williams was slamming his palm on the arm of his chair, helpless in rage and frustration at his client's arrogant tone. Williams may have been hoping that Posner would hear his signal to shut up. Todd had to suppress a smile. "Here Posner was lecturing me before the jury and I heard this sound. Whap! Whap!" Todd knew of Williams's reputation for totally preparing witnesses, yet "it was as if Posner had just decided to be himself," said Todd, "as if he was defying the instructions of his lawyers, to show them that he was a multimillionaire who could do what he pleased."

After the first day, Posner's claque of personal lawyers congratulated their boss on his bravura performance. Williams said to his client, "You think you're doing well? Bullshit. You're doing lousy." To the Williams & Connolly lawyers, Williams despaired: "He was the wo-o-orst. . . ."

For the final argument, Judge Spellman ordered loudspeakers placed outside the courtroom so the overflow spectators could hear Williams's last oration. Without notes, Williams spoke for two hours, thirty-nine minutes. He flailed against "prosecutorial barbarism," muttered that "the case was lying here dying of anemia, then we began to hear some things not worthy of the government. . . ." He was bombastic and physical, slashing and punching the air with his hands. He trotted out his old bromides for the jury from earlier arguments, going on about the inscription above the Supreme Court that promised "equal justice under the law." When he was done, he challenged the jury to convict Posner of everything, all fourteen counts, or nothing.

The jury convicted Posner on all fourteen counts. The courtroom spectators, mostly lawyers, had been awed by Williams. "He's only the second man I've ever seen who's lived up to his reputation," said one, Harley Tropin. "The other was Sandy Koufax." But the jury had been overawed. For the most part, they were in their thirties and forties, raised by television, a cool medium. Williams seemed too hot to them. They told the *Miami Herald*'s John Dorschner that they were put off by the way Williams had approached the jury box, even leaning in to speak to them face-to-face. One juror had been embarrassed that Williams might notice that her shoes were off. Williams liked to flirt with women jurors, and during the trial he thought that one in particular, Bertha Blanco, might be receptive. But the jurors disliked the way Williams stared at them. They teased Blanco, "Bertha, it looks like he's going to swallow you." The jury felt more comfortable with the prosecutors. One juror compared Todd to Mork, the gentle TV alien played by comedian/actor Robin Williams. While the courtroom audience thought Cartusciello was prissy, the jurors regarded him as sweet and polite.

The facts had been confusing and the jurors had been hesitant to peer into Posner's state of mind, to convict him for his intentions. It was all very abstract. But every evening, as the jurors stepped into the steam bath of the Miami night, they saw something that stuck in *their* minds. There stood a line of three black limousines waiting for Posner and his lawyers. As they trudged off to their hot little cars sitting in a parking lot a block away, the jurors observed the limousines idling and knew the air-conditioning was on high. The temperature would be just right for the defendant and his team of high-priced lawyers.

Williams was downcast. He told Culverhouse that he could no longer relate to juries, that he had lost his touch. He knew that he had been too impatient and angry in the courtroom. True, he had been as totally pre-pared as ever. He had even foreseen the impact on the jury of seeing Posner drive away in a stretch Cadillac limousine. "You might as well carry a big sign that reads 'Shit,' " he told Posner, instructing his client to drive in a smaller-sized car—an Oldsmobile—to the courthouse. Williams could not be blamed for failing to anticipate that his demand for instant air-conditioning would alienate the jury as well. This was a trivial detail, of course. But it underscored a truth about the trial that Williams could not overcome. In the end, the jury saw the case as a question of special privileges for rich men. One juror noted that he could live for a long time just on one of Posner's tax deductions. Posner's lawyer, the legendary Edward Bennett Williams, had come across to the jury too much like the rich and powerful man he was defending.

"Never give up" was more than a trite maxim for Williams. In his trial strategy, there was always one more line of defense, even after the verdict was in. A week after the trial ended in late July 1986, the *Wall Street Journal* reported that several of the jurors had broken the rules by reading about the trial in the newspapers. Specifically, they had learned about William Scharrer's conviction, which had been kept out of evidence during the trial. Williams immediately flew down to Miami and de-manded a hearing. The jury, he argued, had been fatally prejudiced.

What the jurors read or heard about Scharrer was probably not a critical factor in their verdict. Nonetheless, Williams asked Judge Spellman to order a new trial, and the government did not oppose the motion.

Williams, however, was not about to go through another trial. Instead, he worked out a deal. After six years of conferences and phone calls with Williams, Spellman held the great defense lawyer in high esteem. He had become his friend as well, and Williams was able to easily talk and reason with him. Although Posner faced up to forty years in prison, Williams was able to propose an alternative sentence that Spellman embraced. By doing a little research, Williams learned that Spellman was concerned about the rise of Miami's homeless population. He also found that Spellman and his wife were close to Catholic relief workers who were pushing for better housing for the city's poor. Williams proposed that Posner could better pay his debt to society by working twenty hours a week for five years to solve the problems of the homeless. Over the strong objections of the prosecution, Spellman agreed.* Posner was sentenced to devote five thousand hours and give $3 million to helping the homeless, under the supervision of a Catholic shelter, Camillus House.

Williams may have lost his touch with juries, but he had not lost his ability to sway the judge, nor had he lost his indefatigability. After a decade-long quest to put Victor Posner in jail, the government had been thwarted less by Williams's moxie than his sheer relentlessness.

---

*U.S. Attorney Leon Kellner remained bitter about the deal. ''I was extremely upset. It sent the message, 'If you're rich you don't go to jail.' ''

Chapter Forty-Two

WILLIAMS WOULD NEVER go to trial again. But he could still be persuasive behind closed doors, and not just with judges and prosecutors. His knack for evoking the empathy of ordinary people helped save Charles "Lefty" Dreisell from a criminal indictment in August 1986, only a month after the Posner trial.

A flamboyant coach, Dreisell had built a winning basketball program at the University of Maryland. He earned $335,000 a year for his efforts and walked onto the court before games to the strains of "Jesus Christ Superstar." But he treated his players, whose verbal SATs averaged 330—about 150 points below the university average—like young children. In June 1986, one of Dreisell's stars, Len Bias, died from a cocaine overdose. When called by phone a few hours after Bias was rushed to the hospital, Dreisell instructed his other players to clean up the room before the police arrived. The case became a symbol of the rot in intercollegiate athletics, and a local prosecutor, who was running for reelection, decided to try to indict Dreisell for obstruction of justice.

Normally, Williams did not let his clients testify before the grand jury, but in this case he felt that, as a public figure, Dreisell would be damaged if he took the Fifth. He had gambled and won before by letting his clients talk. He told the prosecutor, Arthur Marshall, that he was "leaning toward" letting Dreisell testify. Magnanimously, and inexplicably, Marshall responded by offering to let *Williams* testify before the grand jury as well. Trying not to look like Br'er Rabbit on the way to the Briar Patch, Williams coolly replied, "Sure, I'll go in there."

462

At the Prince George's County Courthouse, Williams got the celebrity treatment. While other witnesses sat in a waiting room, Williams was allowed to wait his turn in an empty judge's chamber. One by one, the judges of the county filed in to pay their respects, telling him how honored they were to host a legal legend. Williams, who had just heard that his CEA was down again, was happy and talkative, and he held forth. "He was like the pope, giving audiences," said Lon Babby, a lawyer in the firm assisting him on the case.

In the grand jury room, Dreisell was just as cordially received by the jurors, who called the famous coach by his nickname. One juror waved. Dreisell was all folksy, down-home country charm. Williams, who followed, freely admitted that his client had done a "stupid thing." But you can be stupid without being criminal, he said. He told the grand jury about five mistakes that *he* had made in his life. Then he asked them to take thirty seconds to think of mistakes they had made in their own lives. Rather than indict Dreisell, the grand jury should demand an investigation into the problems of intercollegiate athletics. "I'll help you," he promised.

The grand jury, in a rare show of independence from the prosecutor, refused to indict. Marshall was furious. "We had overwhelming evidence that Dreisell knew drugs were involved. He met with two of the players but didn't come forward. That's obstruction of justice in my book. But the grand jury didn't believe it," he said. Two weeks after Dreisell was cleared, Marshall lost his reelection bid. A few weeks after that, a citizens committee asked Williams to help them clean up college sports. A lawyer at Williams & Connolly inquired if he was interested. Deadpan, Williams answered, "Are you crazy?"

EVEN NOW, WILLIAMS worried about his public image, fretting to Larry Lucchino that he did not want to be regarded simply as a baseball owner, or even as a brilliant lawyer. He wanted to be seen as a man who was concerned with the great events of the day—a "wise man" who counseled the powerful even if he did not hold public office himself.

Jesse Jackson certainly saw him that way. "No matter who was in, Williams was never out," said the black political leader. "You came to him." Jackson would call Williams to chat about politics and power in Washington at least once a month, and often once or twice a week. Once, at a party thrown by Donald Trump before a heavyweight boxing championship, Jackson had amused the glittery fight crowd by dropping to his knees before Williams and kissing his hand. "Godfather," said Jackson.

The two men had become friends during a boycott Jackson had led against Anheuser-Busch in the early eighties. Jackson had organized the boycott to force the beer company to give more distributorships to minority owners. Since many of its customers were black, Anheuser-Busch was worried about the boycott, and called on Williams to help end it. (Williams had long ties to the Busch family, which owned the St. Louis Cardinals.) "Young August Busch III was a pretty buttoned-down guy and he was scared to death of the boycott," said a lawyer at Williams & Connolly. "Williams treated Jackson with respect, unlike the beer companies," said the lawyer. Meeting at the Beverly Hills Hotel with the civil rights leader in September 1983, Williams had been able to work out a quiet settlement that included generous donations to the United Negro College Fund as well as an increase in the number of minority-owned beer distributorships.

Jackson was taken with Williams. "You could trust him. He was a mediator, a matchmaker. He won no matter who lost," said Jackson. Williams told the minister, who had been born poor and illegitimate, about his own struggle to climb out of the Irish ghetto in Hartford. "He had an acute sense of poverty," said Jackson. They talked about their sons as well. (Williams's son Ned played football at Georgetown Prep; Jackson's played for the more exclusive Episcopal school, St. Alban's.) "The message was that Ed and Jesse were soul brothers, taking on the establishment together," said a lawyer who participated in the Anheuser-Busch negotiations.

When the establishment turned on Jackson, he came back to Williams. In 1977, Senator Hubert Humphrey had seen a piece on "60 Minutes" describing Jackson's attempts to motivate inner-city youths to get an education. Humphrey urged HEW Secretary Joe Califano to fund the program. Jackson gratefully asked Califano for $25,000. Califano told him he needed "a million" and gave the black leader grants that ultimately totaled $6 million. When federal auditors asked to look at Jackson's books early in the Reagan administration, they found chaos. Jackson's organization, PUSH-Excel, was unable to account for over $1 million of the money. The matter was referred to the Justice Department.

Jackson came to Williams claiming that he was a victim of a vendetta by the Republicans. The case was dragging on, producing unflattering newspaper stories at a time when Jackson was trying to raise money for his 1988 presidential campaign. Could Williams help at Justice? This was just the sort of high-level favor Williams relished doing. He asked to meet with Justice Department officials, anticipating that he would need all his wiles to head off a criminal investigation. In fact, he discovered, at a private meeting in September 1987, that the department had no intention of prosecuting Jackson or his organization. The officials said they had no evidence of fraud. Williams was able to push along a half-million-dollar settlement, and the insinuating headlines went away.

A grateful Jackson came back for more. Would Williams agree to run his 1988 presidential campaign? This time, Williams begged off. He also instructed his minions not to allow Jackson and his entourage to stay at the Jefferson Hotel. He was afraid they would "stiff us on the bill," said Williams's business adviser, Bob Flanagan. Williams was less admiring of Jackson than Jackson was of him. He told his partners that he regarded Jackson as a "lowlife," "a medicine man," and "a charlatan."

Williams's opinion of President Reagan was not much higher. He told talk-show host Larry King confidentially that Reagan was "the dumbest man he ever met. He tells baseball stories in the morning and repeats them in the afternoon as if no one had ever heard them." Reagan was Williams's guest at opening day at Memorial Stadium in Baltimore in April 1986. Williams grumbled to Jay Emmett about the delays caused by the secret service and the hardship of making small talk with a deaf man. "But it's good for getting clients," Emmett responded. Williams just smiled. In the dugout before the game, Orioles catcher Rick Dempsey asked Reagan what he was going to do about Libyan strongman Muammar Qaddafi. "I'll tell you, Rick," replied the president, "what I'd really like to do is nail his testicles to the bench there and push him over backward." (A week later, Reagan sent a dozen F-111s to bomb Qaddafi's tent.)

Williams was more admiring of Reagan's vice president, George Bush. "He's an Alfalfa kind of guy," said Williams, referring to the all-male insiders club that Williams held in high esteem. But Williams was still nominally a Democrat. As usual, he picked the wrong one for 1984, backing John Glenn. Williams was still capable of sounding like a liberal. He surprised his Democratic friends in early 1981 by telling the *New York Daily News,* "We've got to stay the liberal party, the party of labor and the minority groups, the party most sensitive to individual liberties, the party that exalts human rights over property rights." He congratulated Georgetown president Tim Healy for boosting minority enrollment from

3 percent to 22 percent, despite restlessness among the alumni. "Don't quit," said Williams. "We've got to train our kids to live in a two-color America." He could even be dovish on foreign policy. He was wary of the Reagan administration's intervention in Central America, fearful it would provoke an anti-American backlash in the region. "He knew what was going on down there and he didn't like it," said Jesse Jackson.

WILLIAMS "KNEW WHAT was going on down there" because he was a member of the President's Foreign Intelligence Advisory Board and because he had become a close confidant of the Director of Central Intelligence, William Casey. Williams and Casey had served together on PFIAB during the Ford years, and when Casey was appointed CIA director by President Reagan in 1981, he naturally came to stay in Williams's hotel, the Jefferson.

Williams gave the new CIA director a pep talk. Banging the air with his large fist, he told Casey that U.S. intelligence had been "dismantled" by Ford and Carter. Williams recalled his battle with Attorney General Levi back in 1976 over U.S. wiretapping practices. It was against Williams's vehement objections at PFIAB that the Justice Department had stopped the National Security Agency and the FBI from reading the Soviets' "take" of phone calls in the United States in order to protect the privacy of U.S. citizens. This was ridiculous, Williams had said. The Soviets could tap calls, but U.S. intelligence agencies could not. "They were stealing and we couldn't look in our pockets to see what had been taken," Williams exclaimed to Casey. To win in any contest, said Williams, "you've got to have good intelligence. You've got to know. If you don't, you're dead." As Bob Woodward recounted the conversation in his book *Veil,* Williams went on to say, in classic overstatement, "The CIA is like a great dog that got hit by a truck. You can only say, 'He was a great dog until he got hit by a truck.' He threw an arm around Casey," wrote Woodward, "as if to say, 'Go get 'em, boy.' "

Williams had always been fascinated by the spy world, and he relished the ringside seat afforded him by PFIAB and Casey. He had strong opinions on how to play what the Victorians sportingly called the Great Game. Williams saw the KGB as a powerful and sinister rival of the CIA. After hearing a CIA review of the evidence surrounding the shooting of Pope John Paul II in 1981, Williams concluded, "There is no doubt in my mind that the KGB did it. I don't know why we don't use this for propaganda purposes.'' Williams urged Casey and the FBI to beef up counterintelligence. He also urged the intelligence agencies to use information swept up in the net of electronic surveillance to prosecute Americans at home, especially drug dealers. (As a criminal defense lawyer, of course, Williams would have bitterly fought such government intrusion.)

Williams was glad to be back in the clubby male world of foreign intelligence. When John McMahon, Casey's deputy, reported to PFIAB on the progress of an interagency group dealing with the question of whether to hire homosexuals, McMahon asked the all-male gathering, ''How many of you guys want to hire cocksuckers?'' One of the ''guys'' piped up, ''Only if they're women.'' Williams, who made no attempt to hide his animus against gays, laughed hardest.

PFIAB had some forceful members, including the former chief of naval operations Adm. Thomas Moorer; former Marine Corps commandant Gen. Robert Barrow; Robert Six, the founder of Continental Airlines; arms control negotiator Eugene Rostow; Texas tycoon H. Ross Perot; and economist Alan Greenspan. Their approach to oversight of the intelligence community was ''tough love,'' wrote former Reagan administration official Martin Anderson. They skeptically questioned CIA officials about security at the U.S. embassy in Moscow. ''KGB agents *worked* in the U.S. embassy,'' said Rostow. ''We thought that was crazy. The State Department liked it because they could get theater tickets.'' Williams was willing to challenge the intelligence establishment, including his friend Casey. After it leaked out that the CIA was secretly mining harbors in Nicaragua, Casey demanded that PFIAB form a committee to find the leak. ''You're a master of diversion,'' Williams accused Casey. ''You declare a war secretly, mine the harbors, and then say the worry is leaks. You were caught with a smoking gun and you yell robbery!'' The CIA director backed off. When Casey came to brief PFIAB, he usually mumbled incomprehensibly. The members pulled their chairs closer to him and finally installed a microphone. Williams was not fooled. ''Casey's mumbling grows in direct proportion to the toughness of the question,'' he told his PFIAB colleagues.

Although PFIAB was a boys' club, it was headed by a woman, Anne Armstrong. She was a heavy GOP contributor from Texas who had served as U.S. ambassador to Britain for Jerry Ford but who knew nothing about intelligence. Many of the PFIAB members, including Williams, were disdainful of Armstrong behind her back. Ostensibly because the board was too large and unruly, she purged it on Halloween 1985. All the tough questioners—including Williams—were asked to resign. Some suspected that Casey was behind the housecleaning. In his memoir of the Reagan years, *Revolution*, Martin Anderson alleged that Casey wanted to drive the most aggressive interrogators off PFIAB to give the CIA director a freer hand with some of his more dubious activities—like illegally funding the contras in Nicaragua.

A couple of weeks after he was fired from the board, Williams suddenly rejoined—as "general counsel." Noting Williams's close relationship with Casey, Anderson suspected that Casey had bought Williams by putting him back on the board. Like LBJ and J. Edgar Hoover, Casey may have figured it was better to have Williams inside the tent than outside. "I wouldn't want him as *my* enemy," Anderson said. Columnist William Safire endorses this conspiracy theory. At a dinner party, Safire accosted Casey for cleaning out PFIAB. The director adamantly denied that he had played any role in the purge. As proof of his innocence, Casey exclaimed, "They even threw off Ed Williams." Surely Casey wouldn't purge his own friend and ally EBW. "That's a cover," Safire shot back. Casey couldn't suppress a smile. "Is it that transparent?" he asked. Safire's suspicions were confirmed when Williams was back on the board less than a month later.

Young associates at Williams & Connolly would sometimes be startled to find the director of the CIA riding the elevator in the Hill Building on his way up to Williams's office. This made Casey uncomfortable; ever the covert operator, he began asking Williams to meet him at a private dining room in the Jefferson. Casey used Williams occasionally for private missions, tapping into the lawyer's wide network of business contacts. For instance, he asked Williams to talk to the CEO of one American company in order to persuade the company to stop selling high technology to the Eastern Bloc countries. Casey preferred this nonbureaucratic approach to problem solving. Williams was the CIA director's own "off-the-shelf" legal troubleshooter.

The suspicion naturally arises that Casey sought Williams's advice on far more nefarious activities than simply appealing to the patriotism of CEOs. Did Casey tell Williams about his other "off-the-shelf" operations, like illegally funneling arms to the Contras? Those in a position to know say no. "I don't think Casey ever told anyone outside the Agency except Oliver North," said Richard Helms, the former CIA director and Williams's friend. Brendan Sullivan, who was North's lawyer and

Williams's partner, said that Williams knew nothing of the secret arms network.

It is unlikely that Casey, who believed in strictly "compartmentalizing" information, told Williams his darkest secrets, but it is impossible to know for sure. In any case, when the scandal did blow up in November 1985, Williams was, as usual, on the inside. As investigators and reporters closed in that Thanksgiving, Oliver North did not need to look very far for a lawyer. He came, like so many notorious figures before him, directly to the firm of Williams & Connolly.

Brendan Sullivan has a prosaic explanation. Tom Green, a lawyer who was advising both North and his confederate, Gen. Richard Secord, referred the marine colonel to Sullivan because he could not represent both men. Sullivan and Green were friends and had worked together on other cases. Bob Flanagan adds a more intriguing dimension to the story. When the scandal first broke, Williams received a phone call from H. Ross Perot, the billionaire entrepreneur who had been a PFIAB member. Perot asked Williams to "take care" of North—and assured him that when it came time to send the impecunious lieutenant colonel a Williams & Connolly–sized bill, there would be enough money in the kitty to pay for it.

For Williams to defend North himself would have been a potential conflict. Williams was too close to Casey, who might have become an adversary of North's had the CIA director lived more than a few months after the scandal broke. But then again, for Ed Williams, conflicts were relative and virtually unavoidable since he had advised so many powerful people. The players in Iran-contra were all familiar names in Williams's Rolodex. Williams was a close friend of the lawyer chosen by the Senate to lead the Iran-contra investigation, Arthur Liman. At the time, Liman was Williams's co-counsel in the defense of junk bond king Michael Milken. Williams represented the *Washington Post,* a newspaper with a score of reporters devoted to uncovering the secret acts of Williams's friend, Bill Casey, and the firm's client, Oliver North. To make matters even more incestuous, Williams was an old and useful source to the *Post*'s top investigative reporter, Bob Woodward.

Williams had iced Woodward for a couple of years after the publication of *All the President's Men* in 1974. He had even tried to stop publication of the book until Woodward deleted the claim that Williams had given the journalists permission to quiz Watergate grand jurors. But in the late seventies, as Woodward sipped a drink at the Georgetown Club, he suddenly felt Williams's meaty hand on his shoulder. "Bobby! How are you?" asked Williams, all smiles. "What are you up to?" Woodward said he was working on a book about the secret doings of the Supreme Court. "Come see me," said Williams. "I'll help you with Brennan."

Woodward wasn't sure how to explain this sudden show of hale fellowship, but the reason was simple enough. Woodward was no longer a scruffy Metro desk reporter. He was a Pulitzer Prize winner, a "brand name." Williams had decided to be his friend—and sometime source. He would not feed him much in the way of new secret information, but he would confirm what Woodward had dug out from other sources. Woodward's notes show him meeting Williams on November 10, 1984, at Duke Zeibert's, where, over two martinis and a Duke's hamburger, Williams confirmed to Woodward that the United States was increasing covert aid to the mujaheddin resistance in Afghanistan. "We're having a PFIAB meeting on that," said Williams. On November 23, after a classified PFIAB briefing from the CIA, Woodward's notes show him getting confirmation of more details of the Afghanistan operation. As Woodward began to write *Veil*, his book on Bill Casey and the Agency, Williams was able to offer useful guidance.

At the *Post*, Bradlee felt uncomfortable about the fact that the *Post*'s lawyer was also a member of PFIAB. "We saw a conflict there," said Bradlee. "We were always screwing around on the edge of national security and the government was always trying to find leaks." Even Williams, normally oblivious to such niceties, realized he was in an awkward position. At one of his lunches with Woodward, the *Post* reporter told Williams an important fact that Casey had failed to divulge in his briefing to PFIAB. Woodward planned to publish the information— and Casey was in the process of trying to get the *Post* to withhold publication. Williams was caught in the middle of a three-way collision, trying to serve the interests of PFIAB, Casey, and the *Post* all at once. "I know one thing," Williams sighed. "I've just resigned as PFIAB general counsel."

But he didn't. Nor did he give up the *Post*, needless to say, or his friendships with Casey and Woodward. He chose, as he had so often before, to play the role of mediator, representing all sides. ("I'm representing the *situation*," he liked to say.)* The information Woodward had

---

*During the Connally case, Williams became angry when the *Washington Post* began printing stories leaked by the government's witness, Jake Jacobsen. Williams summoned the *Post*'s reporter Richard

given Williams at lunch that winter of 1986 involved a top secret operation, code-named Ivy Bells, that allowed the United States to intercept the Kremlin's undersea cable traffic to Soviet submarines. Casey was threatening to get a court order to bar the *Post* from publishing the information. Williams went off to have breakfast with the CIA director on May 8 to see if he could work out a compromise. He reported back to Bradlee that Casey was still threatening to prosecute under the espionage laws prohibiting disclosures of secrets to the enemy. Williams thought the government was bluffing. "I have lots of experience with their cowardice," he said. Nonetheless, he advised the *Post* to hold off publication. Grudgingly, Bradlee agreed. But then NBC News went ahead and ran their own version of the story, and the *Post* had to hurry into print to catch up. Once again Williams called Casey. Sitting in his conference room with one of his associates, Kevin Baine, Williams told the CIA director, "I've looked at this story. This story is no problem. Believe me." Casey agreed not to prosecute. "I don't want a pissing match," the CIA director told Ben Bradlee.

Bradlee was not happy with Williams's role as the middleman. "I thought Ed was a little too protective of Casey. He would say, 'You've got to talk to Casey,' then he would go over there and they would feed each other antipress prejudices," recalled Bradlee. But Williams apparently believed that he was serving a higher calling than his client. Williams may have encouraged Ben Bradlee to print the Pentagon Papers back in 1971, but at this stage of his life, he was more protective of national security than he was of the First Amendment.

As WILLIAMS FELT his mortality, he became increasingly bothered that he had never served the government in a real job. In January 1987, he was given the opportunity to serve his country in the area that interested him the most. He was offered the job of Director of Central Intelligence.

That Christmas, Bill Casey had been felled by cancer of the brain. He lay close to death in Georgetown Hospital as the Iran-contra scandal enveloped Washington and threatened to expose Casey's carefully concealed network of off-the-books operations. Knowing that Casey's days were numbered, the White House began to cast about for a successor.

Cohen to his office, and tried to threaten him. "What would you say if I were to subpoena you and ask your source?" Williams demanded. "Well, normally, I'd say that I wanted to call my lawyer," said Cohen, "but you *are* my lawyer, so I'm not saying anything."

George Will, who was Nancy Reagan's close friend as well as Ed
Williams's, had lunch with Williams and sounded him out about the CIA
job. The columnist knew of Williams's restless longing to serve and his
deep interest in intelligence. Williams was very receptive. "He wanted
the job," said Will. The columnist communicated Williams's eagerness
to Mrs. Reagan.

At the White House, the First Lady was "bugging" Chief of Staff Don
Regan about Casey, Regan recalled. Protective of her husband, appalled
at the storm enveloping the White House, she wanted to ease out the
ailing CIA director and replace him with someone who had high credibility among the press. "I was resisting her," said Regan. It was the
Christmas season, and the chief of staff felt that shoving aside the em-
battled CIA director would be unseemly, even if he was terminally ill.
"But Nancy told me that if we tried Ed Williams, the answer would be
yes." So Regan, who was beginning to worry about his own job, sent for
Williams. The two men met in the West Wing on January 19.

Regan, who knew about Williams's own battle with cancer, asked him
about his health. "Ed was very forthcoming about his disease," said the
former chief of staff. "He said he was determined to conquer it. 'I'm
going to lick this,' he said. But he said he had to wait. His doctors were
just about to hold a conference on his health. He told me he wanted to
take the job, but he'd have to get back to me." Regan responded, "Take
your time," explaining that he did not want to rush the transition, out of
"concern for Mrs. Casey."

At the firm, Brendan Sullivan tried to discourage Williams from taking
the CIA job. "I gave him an easy out. I told him that it would look
strange to the world if the firm defending Oliver North had as its lead
partner the new Director of Central Intelligence." It was Sullivan's belief
that Williams did not really want the job. "He latched on to this appearance problem," said Sullivan.

Williams's real problem was not a conflict of interest, it was his cancer. He had received a bad jolt when his friend from the infusion room at
Dana Farber, Sol Smith—Smitty the bookie—died that November. The
two men had been on the same track, taking leucovorin and gaining hope
as their CEAs steadily declined. "Smitty's death was like the canary in
the mine," said Ned Williams.

Williams himself had been feeling poorly that January, suffering from
diarrhea and general weakness. When he arrived at Dana Farber on January 20, the day after his meeting with Don Regan at the White House,

he was in very poor shape, vomiting and running a high fever. He was examined by Dr. Frei. The diagnosis was ominous.

Back in the fall, when Williams's CEA was dropping so encouragingly, Dr. Frei had told Williams that there was a chance that his tumor would shrink to the point where an operation could cut it out altogether. Instead, the tumor had grown. Now it was obstructing his bile duct. On January 22, Williams was operated on at New England Deaconess Hospital by Dr. Glenn Steele. The surgeon found the tumor still hopelessly entangled with a major artery running into Williams's liver. He was only able to run a bypass through the obstruction and into the bile duct to keep the liver functioning.

Agnes Williams told Don Regan that her husband really wanted the job, but he was in no shape to take it. On February 9, Williams wrote the president's chief of staff formally declining the offer. "I could not enter into any new task running at full speed," he told Regan. Williams had missed his last shot at public service. From now on, his principal occupation would be staying alive.

Chapter Forty-Three

IN LATE JANUARY, two days after his surgery, Williams was sitting up in bed, a tube sticking out from his stomach, leaking bile. "What a goddamn mess," he told Dr. Robert Mayer, a young attending physician. Williams, however, did not seem particularly angry or frustrated. In the corner of his hospital room sat a stack of boxes marked Drexel Burnham Lambert. "Why are these here?" asked Mayer. "Beats me," shrugged Williams. "They just send them."

The boxes were full of documents detailing the financial transactions of Michael Milken, the junk bond broker whose creative financing had set Wall Street roaring through the 1980s. Trying to save himself from a long jail term, stock manipulator Ivan Boesky had begun singing to the federal government in the summer of 1986 about his shady dealings with Milken. Subpoenas from the SEC and the U.S. Attorney's Office began arriving at Milken's brokerage firm on the morning of November 14. The junk bond king had called Ed Williams by evening.

Williams had agreed to represent Milken, but as usual he wanted control. "If you get your appendix out you only want one person holding the scalpel," he told Milken's personal lawyer, Richard Sandler. Williams exploded when he learned that Drexel Burnham's outside counsel, the firm of Cahill, Gordon, had already begun negotiating with the U.S. attorney. "What's going on?" he bellowed to Sandler. "If there's no control here I don't want to be involved." Milken's lawyers were taken aback at this outburst. They wondered if Williams was too temperamental. Milken was worried that his new lawyer didn't seem to know much about securities law. But a trip to the SEC in Washington, familiar turf to Williams, reassured the junk bond trader. "You can't believe how they treated Ed Williams," Milken said to Sandler. "They were so deferential!"

Williams liked Milken. Here was a billionaire who ate in his kitchen and gave $200 million a year to charity. He was a more complex and refined personality than Victor Posner, and he would be far easier to sell to a jury. Williams had no difficulty constructing a romantic persona around the renegade financier, whom he regarded not as a crook but as a visionary. The fact that the stuffed shirts on Wall Street resented Milken made him more appealing to Williams. While the press and prosecutors described Milken as greedy and above the law, Williams preferred to see him as creative yet modest. The fees further increased Williams's enthusiasm for his client. Understanding that Milken would be charged under the harsh RICO statutes, which threatened to confiscate his assets, Williams asked to be paid up front. Milken sat down and wrote Williams a personal check for $2 million. Williams carried the check around in his wallet and gleefully waved it at his partners.

Williams had taken on Milken in November while his CEA was still dropping and he was beginning to hope for a real recovery. He told Milken that he had been fighting cancer for years, but that the disease had never interfered with his work. The severe setback in January forced Williams to level with Milken about the seriousness of his condition. He offered to drop out of the case, but Milken wanted him to stay. "You're the captain of the ship," he said. Milken had grown attached to his lawyer; he felt safe and secure in his presence. At a private dinner at the Jefferson that summer, Williams raised a glass to his new client. "We will win," he vowed. Milken believed him.

WILLIAMS'S CANCER DOCTOR, Emil Frei, was apprehensive as he watched his patient plunge back into work. "I have some concern over the magnitude of the patient's activities, which if anything are greater than in the past," Dr. Frei wrote on Williams's medical chart on March 4. "I cautioned him that there was a possibility he would continue to do well for months, but that the possibility exists that he could get worse rapidly and that he should plan his activities accordingly."

Williams's moods, always changeable, became more so. He could be tender with Agnes. Flying back from the Orioles' spring training in late

March to attend the funeral of his partner Bob Schulman, he noticed that his wife was shivering a little in the plane's air-conditioned cabin. "Aggie, are you cold?" he asked, getting up to wrap her in a blanket. He hugged her and she flirtatiously cocked her eye at him. To Betty Killay, sitting in the next seat, Williams and his wife of twenty-five years seemed like newlyweds. Yet driving back from Baltimore with his family in Sunday traffic a few weeks later, he became almost uncontrollably angry. He ranted and whined, slammed the side of the car, cursed and carried on. Attempts to tease him out of his tantrum failed. His friends and family sat in silence as he raged and flailed at the stalled cars and his own helplessness.

To Dr. Jones he increasingly complained of fatigue. In January, the surgeon had repositioned his bowel in order to insert the bypass in his liver, and Williams now suffered from severe bouts of flatulence. He dealt with his rumbling bowel by ignoring it, but the discomfort and embarrassment must have been considerable.

In June, the bypass through the tumor in his liver became infected. He checked into Dana Farber with a temperature of 103 degrees, "sure that this was the end," said Dr. Frei. "He was mad at me, he was mad at the world. He didn't want to go back into the hospital. 'You can't help me,' he said." Dr. Frei pumped him full of antibiotics and the fever came down. His CEA, however, was soaring. The cancer was spreading again; another tumor appeared in his lung.

Having fallen in love with Dr. Frei, Williams now fell out. "Cancer doctors are all the same," he grumbled. "They poison you, they burn you, they cut you. The only thing that changes is the order." Agnes Williams had a more sober view. In her deliberate, meticulous way, she had always sifted through the sometimes conflicting and confusing medical advice, keenly aware that the doctor's interest was not always her husband's. "Agnes always seemed so prim, while Ed was folksy, but she could be very outspoken, and she didn't hesitate to disagree with us or Ed," said Dr. Mayer of Dana Farber.

Swimming in the ocean had always been Williams's one true relaxation. But in the summer of 1987, he was too sick to swim much. On the beach, passersby recoiled if he took off his shirt. His chest and stomach were now crisscrossed by angry purple and blue welts and lumps, the scars of a half-dozen major operations. "What are we doing here?" he demanded as he sat morosely on the beach. That June, he went grudgingly to the wedding of Maria Shriver and Arnold Schwarzenegger in

Hyannis Port, Massachusetts. "I'm up to my ass in Kennedys," he complained to Jay Emmett. At the wedding dinner, Emmett rose to make a toast, and in an enthusiastic if unthinking way, tried to honor his old friend. "There's a guy here who can do this better than anyone—Ed Williams!" Emmett declared. Williams was furious. He was not prepared to make a toast. Emmett tried to make amends, stammering, "Eddie . . ." "*Eddie!*" Williams shot back. Williams would tolerate being called "Eddie" by Bradlee and Buchwald, but he disliked the nickname and its longer version, "Fast Eddie."

At a dinner at Kay Graham's on the Vineyard that summer he had too much to drink and weepily lamented that he had never served in government. But to Pamela Harriman a few weeks later he said he had "no real regrets" that he never entered public life. So much of it is "counterproductive and messy," he told Harriman's widow, who was herself an active force in Democratic politics. His own life, he said, had been under control.

Mrs. Harriman had found Williams in his house in Edgartown, sitting in a small, dark study with the air conditioner on high. The day was bright and sunny, the harbor sparkled nearby, but Williams was watching television intently. He was closely and critically scrutinizing the performance of his protégé, Brendan Sullivan, as he defended Oliver North in the nationally televised Iran-contra hearings. Williams shook his head at North's soulful invocation of God and country. "No one has ever had a witness like that," said Williams.

Mrs. Harriman suspected that Williams was jealous, and he was. He had been crotchety about Sullivan's high-profile defense of North. He thought Sullivan had come on too strong in the client's defense on the first day of the hearings. Williams had said nothing when his partner had returned to the firm that evening, but Sullivan sensed his disapproval. There were no pleasantries, no words of encouragement. Sullivan had been surprised and a little wounded, but then the headlines began: The press called Sullivan's defense "brilliant" and lawyers everywhere began aping his crack to the committee investigators that he was "not a potted plant." Suddenly, Williams was proud of the young lawyer he had trained so well to carry on in his own tradition. He was pleased as well when the checks began flowing in to the firm from all over the country to pay for North's defense. "Thank God that's the end of this pro bono shit," Williams said to Father Healy.

Williams's jealousy returned when the press continued to praise Sullivan without mentioning his mentor. Williams told his friend Arthur Liman—the chief counsel of the committee investigating North—that Sullivan had become too close to his client. He grumbled about North's omnipresence in Sullivan's office, which adjoined Williams's. "Fucking guy, all he does is hang around here, getting you coffee," said Williams, complaining about "all these Naval Intelligence guys hanging around the hall. . . ."

North regarded Williams as an elder statesman, and came to him for his political advice. "They want me to run for the senate in Virginia," North said, proclaiming, "I can win!" Williams skeptically reminded North, "Your senator, Trible, is a Republican." North insisted, "That doesn't matter. I'll win." Williams offered some personal advice: "The day you run for office will be the end of you." Williams had more advice when he learned the identity of the judge who would hear the criminal charges against North—Gerhard Gesell, the stiff-necked jurist who had refused to be dominated by Williams in the Antonelli trial. Williams greeted North with the news as he stepped out of the elevator on the eighth floor of the Hill Building. "Run!" he said.

WATCHING THE ORIOLES lose, always grim for Williams, had become almost unbearable. "This team is helping me die," he told Jay Emmett. The owners box at Memorial Stadium became a bunker. Jim Miller, the director of the federal government's Office of Management and Budget, made the mistake of paying Williams a friendly courtesy call in his box on "OMB–Orioles Night" in July 1986. Failing to recognize President Reagan's budget director, Williams exploded in rage when the stranger was admitted to his box. The next day, Williams contritely wrote Miller, "I am deeply sorry if you were offended at your reception at the ballpark. My friends know and understand that I use the games to unwind. There is nowhere else I can unwind during the frustration of defeat. And, unfortunately, that's just what I was doing when you arrived. For that reason, there is usually a guard at the door, who is to admit visitors only after I've been 'warned.' In any event, no offense was intended."

Williams had become fed up with the Orioles coaching staff. He had been grumbling about his general manager, Hank Peters, for several years, describing Peters's indecision as "hanking around." He began to prepare a case against him. In February 1987, the Orioles owner arrived, unannounced, to watch Peters and his personnel director, Tom Giordano, pick players in the amateur draft. "He didn't even say hello," said Giordano. Williams had reason to doubt the judgment of his coaches. Not a single Orioles first-choice draft pick had graduated into the majors during the 1980s. The trade publication *Baseball America* rated the club's farm system as the second worst in baseball.

In April 1987, Williams suddenly discovered that only 5 percent of the Orioles' minor leaguers were black. He blamed Peters and Giordano for racial prejudice. If the two baseball executives were insensitive to race, they had plenty of company in front offices around the major leagues. That same April, the Los Angeles Dodgers' general manager, Al Campanis, embarrassed himself and all of professional baseball with his remarks about black abilities ("I truly believe that they may not have some of the necessities to be, let's say, field managers or perhaps a general manager . . .").

As the public storm engulfed Campanis, Williams announced that he was placing two prominent black athletes, former Orioles great Frank Robinson and Yale and professional football star Calvin Hill, in front office jobs. At the time, the Orioles had no blacks in management positions. Williams saw himself as a liberal on race in sports, as the man who had integrated the Washington Redskins. Nonetheless, Peters later pointed, with some bitterness, to the timing of Williams's discovery of bias in the front office. "The only time Ed ran up the flag on race was after Campanis," said Peters. "He never said a word to me about it before then." After the Campanis incident, Williams became outspoken about baseball's failure to promote blacks, and he encouraged Jesse Jackson to keep the pressure on major league owners. At an owners meeting that spring, Jackson appeared and performed his little mock-ritual of kissing Williams's hand. (Privately, Williams admitted to Baseball Commissioner Pete Ueberroth that he was "guilty" for not hiring more minorities. Williams was also honest with the Baseball Commissioner about his feelings towards the other owners. He first greeted Ueberroth at an owners meeting by throwing his arm around the new commissioner and declaring, "Welcome to the den of the village idiots!")

Williams generally got along with the players, black or white, but his caustic remarks sometimes got back to the clubhouse. He called overweight third baseman Floyd Rayford "Fatso," and he offended the Orioles' best and highest-paid player, Eddie Murray. At a rain delay during the 1986 season, Williams criticized Murray, who was black, for lack of hustle and for setting a poor example for other players. Murray, who was hobbled by injuries, was angry with the owner and refused to be mollified by his apology. At spring training the next season, the moody star turned his back on the owner when he came into the clubhouse to address the team.

Williams's comments about Murray "poisoned an already unhealthy clubhouse atmosphere," wrote Orioles historian James Edward Miller. The team finished last in 1986 and second to last in 1987 with a 67–95 record, the worst since Williams bought the team. Williams hated to fire people, but on the Monday after the final game of the 1987 season, he made his move on Hank Peters. "I hope this doesn't affect our friendship," Williams said to Peters as he showed him the door.

"MR. WILLIAMS LOOKS very well indeed and feels well on all counts," wrote Dr. Frei after seeing his patient on September 21, 1987. "He is fully active having traveled to some six different cities in the last seven days for work." Williams was tolerating his increased dosage of chemotherapy; his bouts of diarrhea and gas had subsided, but his CEA continued to rise—170, 200, 230, 340 in November. The leucovorin was not working; as Dr. Frei noted with clinical detachment on Williams's chart, "the patient is refractory to such treatment."

Williams had always hoped that he could be healed by faith. One of his nurses, Ann O'Donnell, saw him coming from a healing service at Holy Trinity in Georgetown and asked whether he believed that he could be cured by the power of prayer. "What do I have to lose?" he answered. During the healing service, the sick and lame would sometimes fall back as they felt the release of evil spirits. "Catchers" stood behind to cushion their fall. Williams was cheerfully cynical about this miracle of faith. "You know, I could tell who was going down, I could tell," he joked to Larry Lucchino, who was in the midst of his own (successful) battle against cancer. Williams also visited a faith healer in Worcester, Massachusetts, Father Ralph DiOrio, on his trips to preside over the Holy Cross board of trustees.

Williams's faith did not cure him, but it did comfort him. At Holy Cross, he slept in a simple, bare room set aside for him in the Jesuit community. He began reading more theology, especially the work of Teilhard de Chardin and the homilies of Walter Burghardt, a theologian at Georgetown. ("Dear Numero Uno," Williams had written Burghardt after hearing him give a homily in December 1984, "You are still the only man alive who can get a jaded old fart like me to write a fan letter. . . .'') Williams's faith was literal and unquestioning; he had no use for abstract philosphical debates. Yet, as he became more ill, he seemed more curious about the nature and meaning of faith. Williams was as ever private about his piety, but his close friends suspected that he was preparing for death the way he did for trial—studying with the priests, as if readying himself to argue before the ultimate court.

At a dinner in New York with some lawyers from the firm, Kevin Baine asked Williams, ''What would you do today if you had to do it all over again?'' Williams said he was not sure. ''When I was younger,'' he said, ''I really thought there was a great need to show that everyone was entitled to legal representation. But now this is commonly accepted. The needs of the world today are more spiritual. If I were a young man starting out today, I think I'd become a priest.''

With his family and, after a few drinks, with his old friends, he sometimes wondered if he had chosen the wrong vocation. ''We should have been priests,'' he told Peter Fleming, who was helping him defend Michael Milken. Williams would not have been just any priest, of course. ''I know I would have made cardinal,'' he boasted, half in jest. ''Then I would have gone for the big one.'' Williams's fantasies of running for the White House were replaced with even grander visions of the Vatican. He was drawn by the ''regalness and power'' of the robe, said his daughter Dana, and also by the ''monkish life. When he was sick of everything, this was the better way, the retreat from the world.''

Posterity was, naturally, on Williams's mind, and he thought more and more about writing a book. He was flattered that ''my friend Jackie'' Onassis had been after him for almost a decade to write a memoir. Over the years, various authors and journalists had approached him about an authorized biography. In 1982, he had been the subject of an unauthorized biography by *Washingtonian* writer Robert Pack, to whom he had given several long interviews, but he was ''not happy'' with the book, which he described in a letter to a friend as ''poorly written and generally unsuccessful.'' (Williams's judgment may have been colored by the fact that Pack included some critical anecdotes about him, though the tone of the book was generally favorable.) Williams was torn about writing an autobiography. He wanted to tell of his exploits, but he did not wish to appear boastful, ''like Louis Nizer or F. Lee Bailey.'' He wanted to mine his rich vein of stories, but he worried about violating the attorney-client privilege. He may have also realized that writing a book would force him to dredge up some unpleasant memories that he had chosen to forget or papered over with myth.

In June 1986, Williams had approached *Washington Post* reporter Bob Woodward about helping him write a book. He had told Woodward that the Holy Cross commencement speaker that spring, Governor Mario Cuomo, had "harangued" him "thirty-five times" to write a book. He had gone to see Jackie Onassis for advice, and she had delicately suggested that he needed some "exterior discipline"—that is, a ghostwriter. Williams tried to tempt Woodward with some titillating stories from his past, but the reporter was too busy with projects of his own. At about the same time, Simon & Schuster sent Robert Sam Anson, the author of an insightful profile of Williams in the *American Lawyer,* to talk to him about an authorized biography. The conversations never went anywhere, although Williams admired Anson's *Exile,* his portrait of Richard Nixon in the years after Watergate.*

Williams considered letting his daughter Dana, a journalist herself, try her hand at a memoir. She began reading old newspaper clips and interviewing her father. But when she asked him about his childhood, she observed that his answers were "flat. He didn't want to talk about it," she said. "Growing up, he just wanted to get out of Hartford." Dana moved on to a newspaper job. Williams next hired Michael Scully, a freelance writer, to ghostwrite a memoir. But that project, too, was abandoned when Williams became too consumed by his illness.

Williams knew he was dying, that his long battle was coming to an end. "This is the last round," he had told Vince Fuller in late 1987. Williams worried that he was becoming a curmudgeon, that he was becoming too disagreeable even by his own moody standards. He snarled at his ever-patient secretary, Julie Allen. He rarely bantered with his fellow lawyers. "There was no joy left," said his partner Paul Wolff. Lucchino and Flanagan sadly concluded that Williams could not find the energy to be funny or engaging. All his strength was reserved to fight his disease.

---

*Williams was moved by Nixon's dogged climb back from disgrace. After reading *Exile,* Williams wrote the former president a warm and conciliatory letter. In June 1987, Williams and the man who had once threatened to "fix" him had a nostalgic lunch at Le Cirque in New York. Williams told Nixon of going to see Mayor Richard Daley of Chicago on his deathbed. "Hizzoner" had told Williams that his one great regret in life was stealing the 1960 election from Richard Nixon. Mellower, but still the practical politician, Nixon pointed out that he would have just lost the electoral vote even if Daley hadn't thrown the Illinois vote. Nixon picked up the tab for lunch.

On December 7, 1987, on his way back from a baseball owners meeting in Dallas, Williams had become violently ill. By Christmas, he was yellow with jaundice. The growing tumor in his liver had obstructed his bile duct again. A drainage tube hanging outside his stomach worked imperfectly. He was wracked with fevers and hospitalized for dehydration. His weight began to drop.

VI

Glory

Chapter Forty-Four

As THE ORGAN piped up the bridal march, the congregation turned to watch Williams escort his daughter Dana down the aisle of Holy Trinity Church on January 9, 1988. Many of Williams's old friends, who had not seen him since he had entered the hospital in December, recoiled. At the back of the church, Kay Graham looked "stunned, beside herself," recalled Bob Flanagan. "I was shocked," said Ed Muskie. "He looked fragile and wasted." Jack Valenti flinched to see that his old friend's "collar gaped" from all the weight he had lost. Valenti began to weep. "I knew he was dead," he said. "I had always thought Ed Williams was the one guy who was going to beat cancer, and now I knew it wasn't true." Ben Bradlee turned in the pew to Larry King and asked, "What are we going to do when he goes?" Bradlee's wife, Sally Quinn, thought Williams looked "bright yellow and shrunken." The bride, she observed, "seemed to be carrying him down the aisle."

"His friends were reaching out and grabbing him as we walked by," recalled Dana. "He was startled and shy." At the altar, Father Brooks of Holy Cross thought Williams might collapse. "I gave up on him," he said. "Ed made it to the pew, but his head slumped down." But then, after Williams slowly wobbled to the altar to read from the scripture, "he sounded like Saint Paul," said Brooks. In a clear and resonant voice Williams read the passage his daughter had chosen for him from the Book of Isaiah: "Fear not, for I have redeemed thee. . . . When thou walkest through the fire, thou shalt not be burned." A few feet away, Father Jim

487

Connor, the pastor of Holy Trinity, could not help but smile and think to himself, "That sucker is ready."

At the reception at the Metropolitan Club, Williams said to David Brinkley, "I'm going to get through this and go home and croak." After dancing haltingly with the bride, he grabbed Sally Quinn. "Get me out of here." They went into the hall. "Sit with me," Williams commanded. They talked for half an hour. "I was desperate. Funny stories, anything," said Quinn. "He didn't want anyone to know how bad he felt, he was so proud." That night Williams checked into Georgetown Hospital. Father Thomas Gavigan of Holy Trinity appeared and asked Williams if he wanted extreme unction. Williams seemed relieved. He said yes, and the Jesuit priest gave Williams the Last Rites.

But once again, he rallied. Ann O'Donnell, his longtime nurse, found Williams a few days later, hooked up to an IV, frustrated and angry at the other nurses, chafing to get out. Williams asked O'Donnell to nurse him through his death. He told her that he did not want to die in a hospital. But first, he said, he had to save Mike Milken.

THE JUNK BOND king, who was now a grand jury target, was just as interested in saving Williams. In late January, Milken gave Harvard Medical School $1 million to help establish a chair for Williams's doctor, Emil Frei (Marvin Davis kicked in another $1 million and Williams himself donated $500,000). "Mike didn't want to believe Ed was going to die," said Milken's lawyer, Richard Sandler. "He could see what was happening, but he kept hoping for a miracle. Ed was the Messiah. He was going to take us through it."

Williams had shed some of his romanticism about Milken. He was astounded to learn that Milken had made a half billion dollars in a single year. "What are they doing to *earn* this?" he wondered to his partners. "He knew it was a giant Ponzi scheme," said one. Saving Milken was clearly going to require all of Williams's savvy and finesse. Public revulsion was growing against the excesses and greed of the eighties, and Milken was a natural target. In early February, Milken was subpoenaed to testify before the House Commerce Committee and its influential chairman, John Dingell. Williams thought he had fended off Dingell with a phone call. He had offered to send a sworn affidavit from his client explaining that he could not answer the commitee's questions without incriminating himself. The committee staff had agreed, but Dingell insisted that Milken appear anyway. Williams was furious; he complained that he had been "double-crossed" by the chairman. Dingell had a reputation for making the CEOs of major companies quail before his questioning, but to Williams, Dingell was just a former student (at Georgetown Law in the fifties) who had grown up to become a publicity hound. He decided to teach Dingell a lesson in media manipulation.

As the flashbulbs popped in the Commerce Committee hearing room on February 11, Williams invoked an old rule to clear the room of television cameras. There would be no nightly news scenes of Milken repeatedly taking the Fifth like a gangster. Then he smoothly chided Dingell on his heavy-handed tactics. By the end of the hearing, even Dingell's committee members were questioning the chairman's fairness. "Williams Turns the Tables: Milken Counsel in Control of Dingell Hearings" was the headline the next week in the *Washington Legal Times*.

Williams was relaxed and happy as he rode back to the Hill Building with Milken after the hearing. He knew he had outmaneuvered Dingell. As he shook hands with Milken, Williams coolly said, "If you have another problem, just call me."

But holding off Rudy Giuliani, the aggressive U.S. attorney in Manhattan, was proving more difficult. The balance of power had subtly shifted between prosecutors and white-collar lawyers in the late eighties. Impatient with the gamesmanship of the defense bar, judges were increasingly siding with the prosecutors to reject defense motions. It was harder to get an indictment dismissed using Williams's old standby, prosecutorial misconduct. Any errors committed at the grand jury stage could be cured at trial, the judges were ruling.

The prosecutors were also having more luck attacking Williams's "hang together" strategy. Judges were beginning to rule that it was a conflict of interest for one lawyer to represent a number of potential defendants and witnesses. Williams was impatient with these attacks, which went to the heart of his desire for control. "If I see one more conflicts memo I'll throw up," he told his partners. But the law was changing with the public mood, and Williams was powerless to stop it.

In its investigation of Milken and his brokerage house, Drexel Burnham, the government's strategy was to divide and conquer—to make potential defendants accuse each other. Williams had given his usual speech to Milken's colleagues at Drexel, many of whom were potential grand jury targets. "If you go down the road together, you look like a solid wall," Williams had told them in the winter of 1987. "But if you start to crumble, you'll become like a Greek tragedy. The U.S. attorney will sit in the front row. There will be dead bodies all over the stage and he'll never have to lift a finger.'' When Giuliani wrote Williams that he could not represent multiple parties in the case without creating a conflict of interest, Williams wrote back huffily that *he* would be the one to decide if he had a conflict.

Eventually, the government succeeded in dividing Milken from Drexel Burnham, but by then, Ed Williams was out of the case. He was too sick. In the spring of 1988, Williams used one of his coach's clichés to tell his co-counsel, Arthur Liman, ''Arthur, you're going to have to carry this one to the goalpost yourself.''

ALONG WITH HIS natural exuberance, Williams lost his vast appetite. No longer could he inhale a couple of martinis and a Duke's hamburger for lunch. Unable to properly digest food, he began literally to starve. He became obsessive about his weight, forcing himself to eat. He hated fruit, but he would dutifully eat cut-up fruit at his desk, closing his eyes and wincing as if he were imbibing medicine. Even more distressing—to him—he lost his taste for liquor. He no longer pretended that he felt fine. ''How are you?'' Dr. Mayer asked him on his trips to Dana Farber. ''Not good, Bobby, not good,'' he said.

Still, he kept casting about for new cures. That winter, he began a new course of radiation and chemotherapy at Johns Hopkins in Baltimore, but it only made him feel sicker. He became depressed. On Easter Sunday, he insisted on driving his family to brunch at the Jefferson. Behind the wheel, Williams had always struck fear in his passengers, but now he got angry when his children began grasping the handholds. Two blocks from the hotel, he rear-ended a parked car. ''He was really down and really sick. He knew he was losing the fight,'' said his daughter Ellen. ''He was furious.'' He blew up at Ned for being late, and the family tried to make the best of a sad meal.

Yet Williams was able to find some solace that spring in the productive lives of his children. He cried when Ben Bradlee showed him a story by his daughter Dana on the front page of the *Boston Globe*. He watched his son Tony, an aspiring newscaster, on television in Baltimore. He was particularly proud when his son Ned was admitted to Harvard's School of Education. On his sixty-eighth birthday, his daughter Ellen had a boy, whom she named Edward. That May, he saw his youngest child, Kimberly, graduate from college.

Williams gave the commencement speech, a serious and moving talk about religion in which he portrayed Jesus Christ as a criminal defendant with the law, the judge, and the jury all stacked against him. Standing on the podium of Spring Hill, a little Jesuit college in Alabama, his thin gray hair flying in the wind, he looked "like death," said Tony. The speech drained him, and he never gave another.

THE ORIOLES WERE worse than ever that spring, setting a new league record by losing their first twenty-one games in a row. Williams had been terribly sick on opening day, a 12–0 debacle, and he stopped coming to the ballpark. He wanted to sell the team, but first, he gave the city of Baltimore a farewell present. Williams abandoned his hardball tactic of signing stadium leases year to year. When Maryland agreed to build a new stadium in the winter of 1988, Williams signed a fifteen-year lease. Financially, this step was a sacrifice, since it limited the options of a new owner and thus reduced the price that Williams could get for the team. But Williams felt genuinely grateful to the city's loyal fans.

Williams's voice began to slow and slur. "Do you understand me?" he impatiently asked a young partner, Lon Babby, in April. "People say they can't understand me. Do you understand me?" He began to lose his mental edge. At a partners' meeting in May, he confused names and fell into a dull silence. He told his partners that he was trying a new cure—a pump attached to his waist that could keep a steady stream of chemotherapy flowing into his body. But they knew from his slow, weary voice that he didn't believe the cure would work.

His secretary, Julie Allen, tried to find ways to boost her boss's flagging spirit. In April, she called Bob Strauss and asked him to set up a lunch with Clark Clifford. It was to be a last laying on of hands between the men who could fix any problem, except their friend's mortality. "There are a number of domestic and worldwide problems that need to be solved and I am confident that we can dispose of them in an hour or so," Clifford jauntily wrote Williams on May 2. In Clifford's private dining room, Strauss tried his bluff Texas humor, but the laughter was thin. Clifford, the silver-tongue persuader, never at a loss for words, sat silent and morose. Williams constantly had to visit the men's room. Clifford took him gently by the arm. Returning to the table, Clifford looked at Strauss and dissolved in tears. Strauss shook his sobbing friend, pleading, "You've got to pull yourself together."

Ben Bradlee was afraid to call Williams. "I got all hung up," he said. "I was afraid to bother him, and the result was that I barely talked to him." But with Julie Allen, Bradlee hit on the idea of a reunion of the old lunch club. Bradlee, Buchwald, and Califano flew up with Williams to the Holy Cross graduation at the end of May. The trip cheered Williams. He smiled wanly as the priests fussed over him ("God love ya, Eddie, yer lookin' fine!") and managed a laugh as Buchwald mildly shocked the Catholic audience by telling an old story about the condom he kept in his wallet as a teenager. ("It's still here!" he exclaimed, displaying the moldy tin foil packet to the assembled graduates and their proud families.) In the commencement tent, however, Williams grew silent. "I've got to go," he said.

His friends knew that the time had come to say good-bye. Marvin Davis insisted on seeing Williams. "He didn't want to," said Davis, "but I called Agnes." Walking to the door, Davis tried to steel himself to keep smiling and not cry. He needled Williams in the old Toots Shor style. "Your firm stinks. I'm pulling out," he deadpanned. Williams didn't take the joke. "What do you mean?" he demanded in a weak flush of anger. Then he saw Davis was kidding. He said to Davis, "I'm bored, Marvin. I'm so fucking bored."

On the July 4 weekend, Williams went to Martha's Vineyard for the last time. He was upset that passersby no longer recognized him on the street; he had grown too gaunt. When he returned, he went downtown to his bank and emptied out his safe-deposit box. At his office, he sat silent and alone for a time and went home, never to return.

At home, the phone still rang occasionally. Bradlee called to tell Williams that he loved him. Barbara Howar called on him to get her out of one last jam. She was being sued by her publisher, Simon & Schuster, for the advance on a book she had failed to deliver. Williams told her to inform the publishing house that he was representing her. He figured, correctly, that the invocation of his name would win a settlement.

The Society of Jesus needed a last favor as well. The Jesuits owned a garbage dump in Montgomery County that was, its neighbors claimed, full of toxic wastes. Williams made a phone call to scare off their lawyers.

A final bit of unpleasantness remained with Jack Kent Cooke. In 1986,

Williams had foolishly agreed to represent Cooke's girlfriend, Suzanne Martin, who wanted to sue the Redskins owner for forcing her to have two abortions. She had married Cooke instead, but now the threatened lawsuit had surfaced in a messy divorce proceeding. Cooke's lawyer, Milton Gould, publicly accused Williams of "extortion" and a conflict of interest for representing Martin against his former client and business partner. The story appeared in the *Washington Times* and the *Legal Times* as Williams lay ill that August. Williams asked Bradlee to keep it out of the *Post,* and his old friend agreed ("It was a nothing story," said Bradlee). Cooke angrily wrote Williams, "I hope you get what's coming to you." The tawdry affair saddened Williams, said his daughter Dana. "He wanted to die gently," she said.

With his children, Williams was especially affectionate and solicitous. "He didn't want to upset anyone," Dana said. Softening his objection to inherited wealth, he changed his will to leave each child $1 million.*

He wanted his children to sit with him in the evenings as he rested under his "Baa," a soft blanket given to comfort him by his friend Jay Emmett. "Let's take a little nap," Williams said to his son Tony, who lay down beside his father. Mock-macho to the end, Williams called these sweet respites "power sleeps."

In the winter of 1988, Williams had undertaken to head a capital campaign for the Catholic Archdiocese of Washington. In August, Cardinal Hickey came to the house to bless him. Williams and Agnes knelt before the cardinal as he made the sign of the Cross. Williams believed in life after death, he had told Larry King. He had often discussed the hereafter with Father Healy at Georgetown. There was "nothing domestic" about his vision of heaven, said Healy. "He didn't see golden thrones or make jokes about seeing old judges up there."

On a hot August afternoon, Tony Williams found his father lying under his Baa, chilled and nauseous. Williams roused himself to show Tony a copy of the August *Regardie's* magazine, which had touted Williams as one of the most powerful men in Washington. "They don't realize what power really is," said Williams. "I'm about to see true power. Fighting death is selfish. It's time to let go and see what real power is."

---

*Williams left $2 million each to Holy Cross and Georgetown; $1 million to the Archdiocese of Washington; $150,000 apiece to his sister-in-law Betty Killay and his secretary Julie Allen; and $50,000 to his chauffeur, Leroy Washington. His estate amounted to well over $100 million after the sale of the Orioles and the Jefferson Hotel in 1989. Williams trusted Agnes, who inherited the rest, to dispose of the fortune.

On Sunday night, August 7, Agnes and Ned were eating dinner when they heard a crash upstairs. They found Williams lying on the floor, babbling. They tried to put him to bed, but he kept struggling up again. Though wasted by his disease, he still had power left in his body, and Agnes was unable to comfort and pacify him. Finally, Tony arrived home. He crawled into the bed and held his father.

Williams had wanted to die at home, but Agnes and the children needed help, and they called an ambulance in the early hours of the morning. Williams protested, but he was too weak to resist. At Georgetown Hospital, he drifted in and out of a semi-coma, slowly regaining lucidity as he was rehydrated with intravenous fluids. After a couple of days, he was able to take a phone call from Governor Mario Cuomo. "I'm not going to make it, Mario," he said. Cuomo tried to joke with him about his old clients. "They're going to build a statue to you, Ed. In Sicily," he teased. Williams laughed weakly. Joe Califano came and chatted a bit about the presidential race. Williams muttered that the Democratic candidate, Michael Dukakis, was too weak on defense. In the evening, Williams drew close to Ann O'Donnell, who had nursed him since the first tumor had appeared eleven years before. "You smell so good," he said in a barely audible voice. "I never thought this day would come."

On Friday, Agnes was told that Williams might not last the night. She asked to have a bed made up beside him. In the morning, Dr. Marc Lippman, the director of the Lombardi Cancer Center, came to see the patient. Williams was alert. He startled Lippman by asking, with a kind of boyish earnestness, "Have I put up a good fight? Have I tried?" Lippman answered that he had. "Do I have to keep fighting?" Williams asked. "Can I quit?" Lippman nodded and said yes. The two men sat quietly for a while and Williams drifted off.

Williams woke and began giving Agnes instructions. He told her who should give the eulogies, which priests should stand at the altar, and who should carry his casket to the grave. In the afternoon, Father Gavigan came over from Holy Trinity. Williams told the priest that he wanted to make a last confession and that he wanted the Last Rites. "He seemed peaceful and realistic," said Gavigan. "He was not scared or upset."

By 4:00 P.M., Williams was having difficulty breathing. His hands were swollen; his body was filling with fluids. He shifted uncomfortably in bed. A nurse gave him a shot of morphine. He told his son Jobie that he was in pain, and fell silent. Agnes and Ellen came back from five o'clock mass and sat beside him. His breathing became labored and shallow, and the great body, scarred and tortured by its long ordeal, finally gave out. At 6:15, on August 13, 1988, he died.

A wake was held at Gawler's Funeral Home on Sunday evening amid a furious electrical storm. "It's Ed," said Peter Fleming to Vince Fuller, pointing heavenward. Vice President Bush came to view the body on his way down to New Orleans to accept the GOP nomination for president.

In the end, Williams had finally been able to let go. Agnes believed that his faith had calmed him, that his "restless heart" had "found rest in Thee." Before Williams died, Agnes chose a passage from the Bible, Paul's letter to Timothy, to be carved on her husband's gravestone: "I have fought the good fight, I have finished the race, I have kept the faith." Her husband "thought he had earned the right to have those words on his tombstone," Agnes said. "In spite of all his human weaknesses and imperfections, he had labored to follow the dictates of his faith through a long and often tempestuous life."

Williams may well have found peace in God, but his spirit was too restless to be easily fulfilled. He was throughout his life a victim of what he called the "betrayal of success." Addicted to winning, he could never quite satisfy his yearning. He had accomplished a great deal in his life, but not, he believed, as much as he could have. Indeed, his great gifts of persuasion and passion do seem wasted on the likes of Victor Posner. His ambition made him strangely cautious; he would not risk what he could not control.

Yet if lives are measured by those they touch, Williams lived fully and well. He had dozens of "best friends" who truly believed they were. With politicians and gangsters, churchmen and "little people" alike, he had an ability to convey the sense that they mattered at that moment to him more than anyone in the world. In a real sense, he was not deceiving them. If he was often calculating, he possessed as well a true openness of heart.

AFTER THE FUNERAL service, the pallbearers—who included Bradlee and Buchwald, Sullivan and Fuller, Lucchino and Flanagan, Valenti and Califano—struggled to carry the mahogany casket up a little hill to a knoll in St. Gabriel's Cemetery, not far from Williams's home. Magnificent in his vestments, wearing a miter and carrying a gold-encrusted shepherd's staff, Cardinal Hickey read prayers for the dead. Williams's body was lowered into the grave as family and friends stood by in the August heat, staring at the coffin. For several minutes no one moved, as if they could not accept that someone so vital lay lifeless in the ground.

No one spoke. After the tumult of the service, the small cemetery seemed pastoral and tranquil. "So unlike Ed's life," thought his friend Jay Emmett. Slowly, the pallbearers made their way down the hill, lost in separate thought. Larry Lucchino, whom Williams had fathered through his own bout of cancer with love, admonitions against self-pity, and "real chemotherapy" (martinis), felt "completely alone." At the foot of the hill, Ben Bradlee shooed away a gaggle of photographers.

In years after, in times of trouble, Bradlee would reflexively reach for the phone to call Ed Williams. His heart would break as he came to remember that his old friend was no longer there.

Appendix

Appendix

EBW AND J. EDGAR HOOVER

THE ANIMOSITY between Williams and FBI Director J. Edgar Hoover is amply demonstrated in the files that the FBI kept on Williams, released to the author under the Freedom of Information Act on June 7, 1991. During Hoover's reign, the FBI kept close and improper tabs on Williams and tried to damage his reputation with the press and the President of the United States.

The FBI first opened a file on Williams in January 1953, when he was angling unsuccessfully for an appointment as U.S. attorney for the District of Columbia. But the Bureau didn't show any real interest in Williams until he began denouncing illegal wiretapping by the FBI in 1957. In press interviews and speeches, Williams pointed out that the Justice Department could hardly prosecute local police forces for violating the federal antiwiretapping law when the FBI was flouting the very same law. At first, Williams was careful to state his "respect and admiration" for the Bureau and its director. But then in May 1961, Williams crossed Hoover. In testimony before the Senate Judiciary Committee, Williams tweaked the FBI Director for his hypocrisy by quoting an old speech of Hoover's that condemned illegal wiretapping by law enforcement agencies. An FBI official duly reported the jibes to Hoover. In the margin of the report, the Director noted, huffily and ungrammatically, that he had given his antiwiretapping speech in 1940, "21 years ago in which world conditions worsened."

The report to Hoover went on to state that Williams was accompanied by an "entourage" and that Williams was interested in putting on a "show." "The group with him included three young, attractive girls who obviously hung on every word that was uttered and clustered around him following the testimony. He obviously enjoyed the limelight of publicity." A few days later, an FBI agent spotted Williams at the White House press photographers' annual dinner, talking to a group of reporters from *Time-Life*. "Williams had been drinking considerably," the agent observed. Williams confronted the agent and said that he wanted to meet Hoover but complained that the Director "won't see me." Williams added boastfully, "I can walk into Bobby Kennedy's office to see him any time I desire." Williams demanded to know if Hoover was "afraid" to meet with him. Reading the report, Hoover underlined the word "afraid" and wrote in the margin, "I would avoid him as I would a skunk and for no other reason. H." The FBI agent who encountered Williams at the dinner went on to state, "Williams seems to thoroughly dislike Mr. Hoover and the FBI. Williams is a very conceited, tricky, evasive, and opinionated individual." Hoover underlined the word "dislike" and wrote, "and I reciprocate it."

Hoover promptly opened up a new file on Williams. The file is heavily blacked out by FOIA censors, but the reader can pick up whiffs of the sort of raw gossip and unsubstantiated allegations that often filled the "Bufiles" that Hoover kept on the powerful in Washington. There is, for instance, a charge that Williams tried to "buy off" an unnamed lawyer in 1959, though the informant observes that "Williams was too smart and shrewd to become involved in such a fraud." Memos to Hoover began referring to Williams as "Washington, D.C., attorney and Bureau antagonist." Hoover decided to get even in the usual way. He instructed his minions to contact "friendly news media" to report that Williams was becoming "a mouthpiece for the Cosa Nostra." In August 1966, Hoover was incensed to learn that President Lyndon Johnson had sat with Williams in the owners box at a Redskins exhibition game. Hoover had his White House liaison, C. D. DeLoach, write presidential assistant Marvin Watson, "I thought the President might be interested in knowing that Edward Bennett Williams, well-known Washington, D.C. attorney, during the past few years has represented individuals comprising the elite of the hoodlum hierarchy in the United States."

As Williams socialized with his mob clients, he was watched by the FBI. On October 21, 1964, while Williams was defending Felix "Milwaukee Phil" Alderisio on extortion charges in Miami Beach, an FBI agent reported on Williams and a group of mobsters leaving a Miami Beach restaurant to return to the Eden Roc Hotel. "All appeared to be under the influence of alcohol, particularly Williams," the report stated. Spotting the agents, Williams confronted them for harassing him. He was informed that the Bureau had no "investigative interest in him."

That was true in the sense that Williams was not under criminal investigation. But in the Hoover era, the FBI did not need much of an excuse to pry. As the FBI spied on Alderisio, they also spied on his lawyer. The Williams files—at least those portions that have not been blacked out by the censors—do not reveal any attempt at electronic eavesdropping on Williams, but it is very likely that the wiretaps on Alderisio picked up conversations with Williams. Whether by use of informants or electronically, the Bureau clearly violated the attorney-client privilege between Williams and Alderisio. After the mobster was convicted of extortion in Denver in April 1965, an FBI report states that "Alderisio was in constant contact with Williams in connection with this conviction and other matters. During a meeting in approximately June 1967, Williams reportedly informed him that he had an excellent contact with the Justice Department and felt that they could get to the recently appointed Supreme Court justice." The report offers no evidence that Williams tried to "get to" the "newly appointed justice," who was Thurgood Marshall. (Alderisio's conviction was overturned in 1969, Marshall voting with the majority.)

The FBI's vendetta against Williams seems to have ended with Hoover's death in 1972. The White House taping system recorded President Nixon ranting against Williams, who was representing the Democratic party in its Watergate suit, and threatening to "fix that son of a bitch" in September 1972. But a year later, the FBI reported to Watergate Special Prosecutor Henry Ruth that the White House had not ordered any special investigation of Williams or "adverse treatment." By 1979, Williams had made peace with the Bureau hierarchy. On April 17, Director William Webster invited Williams to speak at the Bureau's "Distinguished Lecture Series." Afterward, Williams joined Webster for a pleasant lunch in the Director's dining room.

Notes

Notes

CHAPTER 1

13 *church too small:* Agnes Williams; Bennett Williams
13 *funeral scene described: Washington Post*, August 17, 1988
14 *Milken stricken:* Robert Litt
14 *gypsy's instinct:* Agnes Williams
15 *Bradlee misses EBW; Pentagon Papers advice:* Benjamin Bradlee
15 *"why it was such a good friendship":* Art Buchwald
15 *rehearsing jokes:* Larry Lucchino; joke file ("Humor" and "Anecdotal material") is in Williams Papers (hereafter WP)
15 *"breath sucked out of you":* David Remnick, "The Ultimate Trial of Edward Bennett Williams," *Washington Post*, April 9, 1986
16 *"never crossed his arms":* Barbara Howar
16 *"grab you by the ass":* David Brinkley
16 *"think he was nutty":* Robert Flanagan
16 *"give an endowment":* Barbara Howar
16 *"Priests." "Tickets":* Larry Lucchino
16 *obituaries:* EBW's obituaries are in a privately printed memorial "Edward Bennett Williams," courtesy of Williams & Connolly
17 *"Dad would have loved this":* Dana Williams
17 *"magic mouthpiece":* Paul O'Neil, "Star Attorney for the Defense," *Life*, June 22, 1959
17 *"hottest lawyer":* Gay Talese, *New York Times Magazine*, September 25, 1960
17 *"top criminal lawyer":* "The Winning Loser," *Time*, February 10, 1967
17 *couldn't be like him:* Steve Urbanczyk

19 *"no errors, only conspiracies"*: Arthur Liman
19 *"loved the power"*: William Graham
19 *"Whaddya know?"*: Sally Quinn
20 *"defend evil?"*: Eunice Shriver
20 *"not entitled to* you*"*: Stephen Jones
20 *"put up with it"*: David Povich
20 *"toastmaster"*: Michael Tigar
20 *EBW and press:* Larry Lucchino; Kevin Baine
21 *"loved liberty"*: Peter Fleming
21 *"world of Caesar"*: Arthur Liman
21 *"reaffirmation of self"*: Michael Tigar
21 *"going to New Hampshire"*: Steven Umin
21 *not chosen for Supreme Court:* Lauren Bacall
21 *"public life was so intrusive"*: Brendan Sullivan
21 *"living hell"*: Michael Tigar
22 *"primitive"*: Benjamin Bradlee
22 *"convenient marketing device"*: Confidential interview with author
22 *EBW and Vince Lombardi:* EBW interview with Kenneth Adelman, *Washingtonian* magazine, May 1988
22 *"Ed . . . done in"*: Michael Tigar

CHAPTER 2

EBW's childhood is based on interviews with Geraldine Ray, Mrs. Jacques Brignac, Dorothea Fricke, Charles Buck, Muriel "Jerry" Waterhouse Davis, Joseph Spillane, David Rosen, Charles Arthur, Marshall McGuire, William Hickey, William Cullina, and Peggy O'Neill.

25 *Joe and May Williams:* Geraldine Ray; Mrs. Jacques Brignac
25 *"better kisses"*: Dorothea Fricke
25 *"fun stops"*: Mrs. Jacques Brignac
26 *"break out"; sneaking out:* EBW interview with Michael Scully, WP
26 *Chapman trial:* Robert Pack, *Edward Bennett Williams for the Defense* (Washington, D.C.: National Press Books, 1983), p. 111–12 (hereafter Pack)
26 *"great man"*: EBW interview with Michael Scully, WP
26 *dutiful child:* David Rosen
26 *soft-spoken and bashful:* Peggy O'Neill; Dorothea Fricke
27 *"little numbers racket"*: David Rosen
27 *"premeditated"*: Charles Buck
27 *"ran the place"*: EBW interview with Michael Scully, WP
27 *high school years:* Bulkeley High School Yearbook, 1937, pp. 128, 141, and 187
27 *"Herbie Hind"*: William Hickey

27   *dress:* Muriel "Jerry" Waterhouse Davis

28   *father laid off:* Geraldine Ray; Mrs. Charles Arthur

28   *gas station job:* Williams, E.B., *"The Summer Job I Had as a Boy,"* *Esquire,* June 1958

28   *"Ed was cheap":* Muriel "Jerry" Waterhouse Davis

28   *Hartford described:* John Gregory Dunne; J. G. Dunne, *Harp* (New York: Simon & Schuster, 1989), pp. 27–28

29   *EBW's college decision:* Muriel "Jerry" Waterhouse Davis; Joe Spillane

29   *"never looked back":* Victoria Radd

29   *"Forget it":* Mrs. Jacques Brignac; Geraldine Ray

29   *Holy Cross described:* EBW's Holy Cross experience is based on interviews with Brother Brutus Clay, Tom Doherty, Joe Fahy, Arthur Garrity, Robert Maheu, Matthew McCann, Father Ray , Father William Richardson, John Ryan, and Robert Scully

29   *Holy Cross rule book:* Courtesy of Holy Cross library

30   *Section A and "Tiger" Dwyer:* Father William Richardson; Father John Brooks

31   *Holy Cross curriculum; "swallowed dogma whole":* Father John Brooks; "Educational System" Holy Cross Catalogue, 1936–37

32   *debating and Father Dolan:* Robert Maheu; Father William Richardson

34   *Jesuit training and casuistry:* Father William Richardson; Father Timothy Healy; Father Robert J. Harvanek, "The Jesuit Vision of a University," Loyola University of Chicago

34   *"Towards the True Norm of Morality":* Holy Cross *Tomahawk,* March 11, 1941

34   *EBW and Waterhouse:* Muriel "Jerry" Waterhouse Davis

35   *Irish Catholics in New England and Joseph Kennedy:* Doris Kearns Goodwin, *The Fitzgeralds and the Kennedys* (New York: Simon & Schuster, 1987), pp. 249–54

35   *"sons of firemen":* Father William Richardson

36   *"power and influence":* Ibid.

36   *Decision to go to law school:* Ibid.

37   *angry scene with father:* Peggy O'Neill

CHAPTER 3

38   *Georgetown Law School described:* William Ragan

38   *EBW bored:* Pack, p. 119

38   *"beer money":* Baltimore News American, August 5, 1979

38   *rejected by FBI:* D. M. Ladd to A. H. Belmont, July 14, 1953. From Williams's FBI file, released to author through Freedom of Information Act, June 7, 1991.

39   *joins air corps at Maxwell Air Force Base:* Fen Seton; Robert Safton

39   *told friends he crashed in a bomber:* Stephen Jones; Peter Maxson; Frank
     Waldrop (EBW told Waldrop he felt guilty that he had been the sole sur-
     vivor)
40   *Williams told his first biographer:* Pack, p. 118
40   *Williams's discharge:* Baltimore Field Office to F.B.I. Director, December
     2, 1975, quoting proceedings of academic board, Air Force Training De-
     tachment, Bennettsville, South Carolina, June 2, 1942. According to the
     F.B.I., this report was "deleted and destroyed" sometime between 1975
     and 1981
40   *résumé:* WP
40   *"still can't fly":* EBW to Fen Seton, January 15, 1981, courtesy of Fen
     Seton
40   *seemed depressed:* Muriel "Jerry" Waterhouse Davis, James McCarrick
41   *"lonely place at the time":* Pack, p. 118
41   *dropping out:* Paul Jacobs, "Edward Bennett Williams, Courtroom Virtu-
     oso," *Coronet,* December 1957
41   *"Silver Buck":* William Ragan
41   *watching real cases, reading Darrow biography:* Alvin Toffler, "Get Me
     Ed Williams!" *Saga Magazine,* July 1960
41   *wandering around city:* Pack, p. 119
42   *"People from real cities":* David Brinkley, *Washington Goes to War* (New
     York: Knopf, 1987), pp. 24–25
42   *"black cloud":* Ibid., p. 78
42   *Irish in Washington:* Thomas Kelly; Lewis Carroll
43   *"brightest student":* Howard Boyd
44   *Hogan & Hartson described:* Ibid.; Lester Cohen, *Frank Hogan Remem-
     bered* (Washington: privately printed, 1985), passim
44   *Ella Thomas case:* Tom Kelly, "The Chief," *Washingtonian,* July 1967
45   *"kiss him good-bye":* Pat Wall
45   *chair trick and "died for his country":* Washington Star, January 29, 1948;
     Howard Boyd
45   *not accept defeat:* Howard Boyd
46   *"drank a little too much":* Ibid.
CHAPTER 4
48   *engaged to Dorothy:* Betty Killay
48   *Guider/Hogan family described:* Ibid.
49   *wedding:* Ibid.
49   *Dorothy described:* Ibid.; Frank Waldrop; Robert Scott; James McCarrick;
     Stephen Jones; Father William Richardson
50   *phenomenally successful; "squarely in the great American middle class":*
     Albert Blaustein and Charles Porter, *The American Lawyer* (Chicago: Uni-
     versity of Chicago Press, 1954), p. 1

51   *William Fallon:* Gene Fowler, *The Great Mouthpiece* (New York: Grossett & Dunlap, 1941)

51   *Fifth Streeters:* Lewis Carroll; Frank Stickler

51   *"Are you ready . . . Mr. Miller?":* Leonard Melrod

51   *Lofton case:* EBW interview with James E. Clayton, WP (hereafter EBW with JEC)

52   *no criminal rights:* Edward Bennett Williams, *One Man's Freedom* (New York: Atheneum, 1962), pp. 72–205 (hereafter OMF)

52   *truncheoned college student: Washington Post,* June 12, 1947

52   *dragnets:* OMF, p. 144

52   *"Lord Haw Haw": Washington Daily News,* August 27, 1946

53   *"flesh and blood . . . person":* EBW with JEC

53   *vomit:* Ibid.

53   *leave Hogan & Hartson:* Howard Boyd; Betty Killay

53   *Hogan described:* Cohen, *Frank Hogan Remembered,* pp. 63–68

54   *"The ideal client": New York Mirror,* July 3, 1951

CHAPTER 5

55   *Chase described:* Nicholas Chase; Paul McArdle

56   *"He's mean":* Howard Boyd

56   *firm name:* John Parker

56   *wanted fees:* Leonard Melrod

56   white-collar crime *coined:* Kenneth Mann, *Defending White-Collar Crime* (New Haven: Yale University Press, 1985), p. 1

56   *"just a bunch of hoodlums":* Stephen Fox, *Blood and Power: Organized Crime in 20th-Century America* (New York: William Morrow, 1989), p. 296

57   *Charlie Ford:* Benjamin Bradlee, "D.C.'s Great Mouthpiece," *Washington Post,* May 15, 1949; Jacob Stein

57   *hoochie-goochie:* William Beckler

57   *Ford and Barrett:* Bradlee, "D.C.'s Great Mouthpiece"

57   *bottle club investigation: Washington Star,* February 22, 1950; *Washington Times-Herald,* February 22, 1950

57   *Judge admonishes jury in Quinn case: Washington Post,* May 6, 1950

58   *EBW at Atlas Club:* Shirley Povich; Eugene Gott

58   *Bradlee described:* David Halberstam, *The Powers That Be* (New York: Knopf, 1979), pp. 537–38

59   *dull town:* Brinkley, *Washington Goes to War*

59   *seven sins:* John Buckley

59   *"The nuns":* Michael Tigar

59   *Sergeant Blick:* Frank Waldrop; Brinkley, *Washington Goes to War,* p. 229

60   *MID:* Betty Killay

60   *"certain feelings":* Frank Waldrop

60   *"trashy and sentimental"*: Ibid.
60   *"shots from his id"*: Benjamin Heineman
61   *"plush tenor"*: *Washington Star*, February 25, 1964
61   *"whored and . . . felt guilty"*: Frank Waldrop
61   *Madonnas and prostitutes:* Betty Killay
61   *Ambrose case: Washington Star,* June 30 and July 1, 1950; January 8 and 29, 1951
62   *EBW and Ambroses at Atlas Club:* Eugene Gott; Gott to author, September 11, 1989
62   *Ambrose sentenced: Washington Star,* January 29, 1951; *Washington Times-Herald,* January 29, 1951; *Washington Post,* January 30, 1951
62   *"big fights"*: Betty Killay
62   *Chase and EBW:* Nicholas Chase
63   *"get involved in causes célèbres"*: Laurence Leamer, *Playing for Keeps in Washington* (New York: Dial Press, 1977), p. 247
63   *Metropolitan Club:* Nicholas Chase
63   *Luciano dispute:* Ibid.
63   *"shouldn't have taken that case"*: Robert McChesney
64   *Congressional Club blackball:* Thomas Wadden
64   *Senator Young: Washington Star,* May 14, 1948
64   *Lafayette Park: Washington Post,* December 22, 1950
64   *"alienation of affections"* case: *Washington Times-Herald,* April 5, 1951
64   *EBW goes to 1948 Republican National Convention:* Betty Killay; EBW with JEC
CHAPTER 6
67   *Pearson and McCarthy:* Luvie Pearson; David Oshinsky, *A Conspiracy So Immense: The World of Joe McCarthy* (New York: The Free Press, 1983), pp. 179–80
68   *EBW solicits McCarthy:* William F. Buckley, "The Unexamined Side of Edward Bennett Williams," *National Review,* July 31, 1962
68   *EBW denies:* Pack, p. 51
68   *Sirica's account:* John Sirica
68   *EBW represents McCarthy in Benton case: Washington Post,* August 20, 1952; *Washington Times-Herald,* September 4, 1952
68   *McCarthy and the IRS: New York Times,* December 3, 1954
69   *EBW and Jonkel: Washington Post,* March 2 and 16, April 22, 1951; *Los Angeles Times,* March 7, 1951
69   *EBW thinks McCarthy is not really dangerous:* EBW with JEC; Pack, p. 162
69   *EBW says nothing:* It is interesting that EBW attacked abuse of congressional investigating power to win a new trial for a gambler, Charles Nelson, in 1952 (*Washington Daily News,* July 2, 1952), but never publicly questioned McCarthy for the same abuse.

69   *Spellman praises McCarthy:* Oshinsky, *A Conspiracy So Immense*, p. 305

69   *"anti-Harvard, anti-sissy":* Murray Kempton

70   *"Television!":* Paul McArdle

70   *Red Scare:* See Richard Fried, *Nightmare in Red: The McCarthy Era in Perspective* (New York: Oxford University Press, 1990)

70n   *Madden and Russian security risk:* Murdaugh Madden

71   *"less courageous":* OMF, p. 139

71   *"Don't name that many":* Victor Navasky, *Naming Names* (New York: Viking Press, 1980), pp. 317–18

71   *"panicked":* Ibid., pp. 229–30

71   *"Williams insisted":* Ibid., p. 85

71   *"didn't have a feeling":* Pack, p. 137

72   Red Channels *and Aware, Inc.:* Fried, *Nightmare in Red,* pp. 157–58

72   *"Williams . . . a good friend of Scott McLeod's":* Navasky, *Naming Names,* p. 162

72   *"chicken shit and chicken salad":* Ibid., p. 303

72   *Rossen names names: New York Times,* May 8, 1953

73   *"Sought New Gods": Washington Daily News,* May 9, 1953; Williams scrapbook No. 1, WP

73   *"the next day":* Howard Koch, *As Time Goes By* (New York: Harcourt, Brace, Jovanovich, 1979), pp. 210–11

73   *Carl Foreman and Harold Hecht cases:* Pack, pp. 139–41; *Los Angeles Herald Examiner,* March 24, 1953; *Los Angeles Times,* March 24, 1953

73   *McCarthy's fall:* Oshinsky, *A Conspiracy So Immense*, pp. 314–26

74   *"dishonest"; "brains or guts"; "senile"; "half bright": New York Times,* September 2, 1954

74   *McCarthy asks EBW to help; "You don't need me":* EBW with JEC

75   *EBW attacked by Shor and Spigelgass:* Ibid.

75   *"100 percent witch hunter":* William F. Buckley

75   *Jean McCarthy and EBW:* Buckley, "The Unexamined Side of Edward Bennett Williams"

75   *Dorothy Williams and McCarthy: Washington Post,* September 19, 1954

75   *Williams consults McCarthy:* EBW with JEC

76   *"Have you no decency?":* Oshinsky, *A Conspiracy So Immense*, p. 463

76   *"If one case doesn't work . . .":* Ibid., p. 133

77   *"peed in the lemonade":* Ibid., p. 477

77   *censure motion:* Ibid., pp. 472–78

77   *"fresh in my mind":* OMF, pp. 62–63

77   *"get off the front page":* Oshinsky, *A Conspiracy So Immense*, p. 478

78   *"The Senator is out of order":* Ibid., p. 479

78   *"most unheard of thing":* Ibid.

78   *"McCarthy Drama Is a Turkey": Washington Star,* September 2, 1954

78 *"McCarthy's Counsel Jousts":* Ibid., September 8, 1954

78 *"smooth-tongued young man":* Ibid.

78 *"take off":* Washington Post, September 2, 1954

78 Tu Quoque: Ibid., September 10, 1954

79 *EBW "shocked":* Ibid.

79 *"No one blames . . .":* Washington Star, September 8, 1954

79 *"handmaidens"; "book Joe didn't write":* Time, November 22, 1954

79 *plan to save McCarthy:* Pack, p. 158

80 *"threw the pen":* Barry Goldwater, *Goldwater* (New York: St. Martin's Press, 1988), p. 163

80 *"I don't crawl":* Neil McNeil, *Dirksen: Portrait of a Public Man* (New York: World Publishing, 1970), pp. 125–26

80 *"scarlet C"; "McCarthywasm":* William Manchester, *The Glory and the Dream* (New York: Bantam Books, 1975), p. 718

80 *EBW depressed:* EBW with JEC

80 *"Rated Tops":* Hartford Courant, August 19, 1954

80 *"Tough Battler":* Washington Star, August 20, 1954

81 *"boyish air":* New York Times, August 23, 1954

81 *"most capable":* The New Yorker, September 18, 1954

CHAPTER 7

82 *"those press clippings":* Frank Waldrop

82 *Cheyfitz described:* Associated Press profile December 27, 1958; "Hoffa's Deal Maker," *Fortune,* April 1958

83 *"natural born watercarrier":* Frank Waldrop

83 *"cold and calculating":* Thomas Kelly

83 *scene at Arthur Krock's:* Rowland Evans

84 *salary:* Nicholas Chase

84 *"affidavit face":* Howard Boyd

84 *Dudley case: Washington Times Herald,* June 6, 1953; Pack, pp. 168–69

84 *Pearson case: Washington Post,* May 7 and 16, 1953

84 *"we've lost":* Luvie Pearson

85 *"cut the bo-o-olsheet":* Pat Wall

85 *backbiting:* Lewis Carroll

85n *vetoed for U.S. attorney:* EBW with JEC

85 *"Do you require your students":* William Beckler

86 *helping Pearson, became a source:* Luvie Pearson

86 *saving Joseph Welch:* EBW with JEC

86 *hated vacations:* Betty Killay

86 *Icardi calls in New Hampshire:* Aldo Icardi

87 *True account:* Michael Stern, "The Case Against Aldo Icardi, Murderer," *True,* May 1956

87 *Pentagon press release:* OMF, pp. 32–33

87   *case background; "sentenced to infamy":* Ibid., pp. 30–35
87   *"dago murderer":* Aldo Icardi
87   *"really exciting trip":* Robert Maheu
88   *finding Moscatelli:* OMF, pp. 47–48
88   *Williams's strategy; trip to Press Club:* Aldo Icardi
89   *memorized jurors' names:* Anthony Lewis
89   *Williams's cross-examination of Cole:* OMF, pp. 52–53
90   *Keech's decision; Icardi collapses: Pittsburgh Press,* April 19, 1956 *New York Times,* April 20, 1956
90   *"Who reached the judge?":* William Hundley
90   *"Go back to your family":* Aldo Icardi
90   *"Sixth Amendment Lawyer": New York Times,* April 20, 1956
91   *"brilliant attorney in action": Life,* May 7, 1956
91   *first reported case in seventy-five years:* OMF, p. 57
91   *"shook the curse":* EBW with JEC
CHAPTER 8
92   *Costello described:* Fox, *Blood and Power,* pp. 298–302
92   *Wolf looks for lawyer:* George Wolf with Joseph Dimona, *Frank Costello, Prime Minister of the Underworld* (New York: William Morrow, 1974), p. 249
92   *"Tell Wolf to call me":* Irving Ferman
92   *"Isn't he the guy who defended Joe McCarthy?":* Joseph Califano, "In Memoriam: Edward Bennett Williams," *Georgetown Law Journal,* October 1988, p. 1
92   *"He'll come high":* Wolf, *Frank Costello,* p. 249
93   *EBW consults Father Lucey:* Phil Condon
93   *"Is this a good career move?":* Thomas Wadden
93   *"sky's the limit":* Ibid.
93   *EBW meets Costello:* EBW with JEC
94   *Costello; manners and vocabulary:* Fox, *Blood and Power,* pp. 300–301
94   *Costello hearings:* Ibid., p. 302
94   *"not very familiar"; "overmodest":* Murray Kempton
95   *Aurelio wiretap:* Fox, *Blood and Power,* p. 300
95   *Costello wiretap; "atom bomb":* OMF, pp. 108–109
95   *Wadden's investigation notes:* Costello file, Williams & Connolly (courtesy Vincent Fuller)
95   *Williams wins case:* Pack, p. 272
96   *"sick man"; "dying man"; "feel better already": New York Mirror,* September 29, 1956
96   *Costello released: Washington Post,* March 11, 1957
96   *"Ed's the champ": Life,* June 22, 1959
96   *"very pleasant fellow":* Pack, p. 264

96 *EBW and Costello at Copacabana:* Thomas Wadden
96 *C-note under plate:* Leonore Lemmon
96 *Theater tickets story:* Michael Bessie
97 *Runyon's characters:* Fox, *Blood and Power*, pp. 113–17
97 *Shor's described:* David Halberstam, *Summer of '49* (New York: William Morrow, 1989), pp. 123–24
97 *EBW and Shor drinking contest:* Duke Zeibert
97 *"used it as an office":* Thomas Wadden
98 *"The man's coming":* Leonore Lemmon
98 *"I'm always for the underprivileged":* New York Post, September 30, 1956
98 *Costello and McCarthy objected:* Ibid., October 15, 1956
98 *"blanket the town":* Ibid., December 6, 1956
98 *DiMaggio; "touch the bright lights":* Halberstam, *Summer of '49*, p. 58
98 *"40 percent of the time":* Washington Post, October 19, 1958
99 *Leonore Lemmon described:* Shirley Povich; Thomas Wadden
99 *"I called him 'Freshman' ":* Leonore Lemmon
99 *infatuation with Lemmon:* Ibid.; letter from Joan Dreyspool to author, undated, received August 1989; Jewel Baxter
99 *"worst lover":* Leonore Lemmon
100 *"hit the rail":* Ibid.
100 *"Daddy's in New York":* Life, October 21, 1957
100 *"sadness in her life":* Betty Killay
100 *"scared of babies":* Ellen Williams
100 *"Jobie's got big problems":* Betty Killay
100 *Tulip Hill cost; described:* Andrew St. George, "His Defense Never Rests," *Pageant*, January 1958
100 *"like a motel":* Betty Killay
100 *"secondhand furniture":* Ibid.
100 *EBW finances:* Ibid.
101 *ask neighbor for help:* Thomas Taylor
101 *"Where's the furnace, bud?":* Betty Killay
101 *EBW home life:* Ibid.
101 *EBW and Dorothy's relationship:* Ibid.
101 *"she was jealous":* Ibid.
101 *EBW abusive to Dorothy:* Robert Scott
101 *Dorothy and EBW at Zeibert's:* Duke Zeibert
102 *Toys from Anastasia:* Ellen Williams
102 *Dorothy sick:* Stephen Jones
102 *"pouring down the booze":* Ibid.
102 *"We can't talk about it":* Betty Killay
102 *car crash described; lawsuit: Grant v. Williams*, case book no. 4838-54

D.C. Court records, Suitland, Md.; letter to author from Robert Pack, August 22, 1989

103   *"I knew a lot of cops"*: Thomas Wadden

103   *"Wadden was very smooth"*: C. William Tayler

103   *Pack and EBW:* Robert Pack

CHAPTER 9

104   *"Hoffa's been arrested"*: "When in Trouble Call Ed Williams," *New York Post Magazine,* March 24, 1957

104   *push-ups: Time,* March 25, 1957

104   *"very exciting": Parade,* May 5, 1957

104   *"You'll find out"*: Laverne Duffy

104   *early Robert F. Kennedy–EBW relationship:* Angela Novello

105   *"very close friends"*: Pack, p. 254

105   *EBW asks RFK to become law partner:* John Nolan

105   *Cheyfitz and Beck:* "Hoffa's Deal Maker," *Fortune,* April 1958

105   *Teamsters "mobbed up"*: Arthur Schlesinger, *Robert Kennedy and His Times* (Boston: Houghton Mifflin, 1978), pp. 137–39

106   *Cheyfitz switches to Hoffa:* Leamer, *Playing for Keeps in Washington,* p. 259

106   *Hoffa described:* Ibid., p. 140

106   *Kennedy investigates Teamsters:* Fox, *Blood and Power,* p. 321

106   *"make your hair curl"*: *U.S.* v. *Hoffa,* trial transcript, WP, pp. 515–17

106   *patriotic duty:* Pack, p. 210

107   *Kennedy sets trap:* Clark Mollenhoff, *Tentacles of Power* (Cleveland: World Publishing, 1965), p. 147

107   *"bullet-proof vest"*: Robert F. Kennedy, *The Enemy Within* (New York: Harper & Row, 1960), pp. 40–43

107   *"spoiled little jerk"*: Schlesinger, *Robert Kennedy and His Times,* p. 154

107   *Hoffa arrested: Washington Post,* March 14, 1957

107   *"bright new star"*: *Newsweek,* March 25, 1957

108   *"in a class with Darrow"*: Mollenhoff, *Tentacles of Power,* p. 188

108   *"when in trouble, get Ed Williams"*: *New York Post,* March 24, 1957

108   *May 2 described:* William Slocum, "Legal Cover: Keeping Costello Free," *New York Mirror,* May 24, 1957

108   *complains of overwork: Washington Post,* May 19, 1957

108   *Beck refuses to identify son: New York Times,* May 9, 1957

108   *Costello shot:* Leonard Katz, *Uncle Frank: The Biography of Frank Costello* (New York: Drake Publishers, 1973), p. 29

108n   *EBW angry at Cohn for fleecing McCarthy:* Murray Kempton

109   *tabloid headline: New York Mirror,* May 3, 1957

109   *What other lawyer:* EBW with JEC

109   *"not the end of the world"*: Robert Maheu

109 *"wo-o-orst case":* Ibid.

109 *"I really need this, Your Honor":* Washington Star, June 15, 1957

109 *reason to delay trial:* Ibid., June 14, 1957

109 *"Can you type?":* Agnes Williams

109 *"trial will start Monday":* New York Daily News, June 15, 1957; Agnes Williams

110 *Williams in training:* Thomas Wadden; Vincent Fuller

110 *"going to the candles":* Robert Scott

110 *Maheu investigates Cheasty:* Robert Maheu

110 *Jencks case break:* OMF, p. 176

110 *fears for Cheasty's health:* Mollenhoff, *Tentacles of Power,* p. 197

110 *"narcotics"* . . . *"disgraceful":* Hoffa trial transcript, WP pp. 937–39

110 *"sidekick"* . . . *"Disgraceful":* Ibid., pp. 955–58

111 *"still"* . . . *"No":* Ibid., pp. 1011–12

111 *"investigate the National Association"* . . . *"avoided the whole thing":* Ibid., pp. 1000–1038, 1485–86

111 *"pretending to work"* . . . *"moral to lie":* Ibid., pp. 1880–87

112 *Cheasty deteriorates; "taken up drinking again":* Washington Star, July 2, 1957

112 *"Kennedy's a friend of yours":* Schlesinger, *Robert Kennedy and His Times,* p. 155

112 *Kennedy routinely leaked:* Hoffa trial transcript, WP, pp. 2219–25

112 *baiting Troxell:* Vincent Fuller

113 *"might as well take his toothbrush":* New York Post, March 24, 1957

113 *Williams prepares Hoffa to testify:* Thomas Wadden; William Hundley; David Previent

113 *Hoffa testifies:* Hoffa trial transcript, WP, pp. 3008–23

113 *Troxell surprised:* David Webster (Troxell told this to Webster)

113 *Fuller shocked:* Vincent Fuller

114 *"army of supporters":* Pack, p. 234

114 *"ganging up":* David Previent

114 *"pert" and "widely known" Miss Jefferson:* Washington Afro-American, July 6, 1957

114 *"They had Jefferson; we had Alexander":* Oliver Gasch

114 *"darkest day":* OMF, p. 221

114 *Hiring Miss Jefferson:* William Bufalino

115 *"punch you in the nose"; Hoffa and Louis:* Mollenhoff, *Tentacles of Power,* p. 206

115 *"never happened!":* Pack, p. 230

115 *it did happen:* Oliver Gasch; David Previent; John Cye Cheasty

115 *Fuller version:* Vincent Fuller

116 *Pearson blames Cheyfitz:* Washington Post, August 1, 1957

116 *Baker and Monsignor Higgins:* Pack, p. 232
116 *Baker and Louis:* In his book, *The Fall and Rise of Jimmy Hoffa* (New York: Doubleday, 1972), Walter Sheridan, Kennedy's chief investigator for the McClellan committee, asserted that Baker and another Teamster, Paul Dorfman, "arranged" for the appearance of Louis in court
116 *"totally plausible":* Father Richardson
116 *"Does he really deny?":* Benjamin Bradlee quoted by Pack, p. 233
116 *"He was ranting":* Thomas Wadden
116 *"second guessing":* Clark Mollenhoff
116 *Williams's summation to jury:* Hoffa trial transcript, WP, pp. 3294–95
117 *"essential superiority of free enterprise":* Murray Kempton, "The Mercenary," *New York York Post,* July 14, 1957
117 *"He's a jumper":* Murray Kempton
117 *Williams prays at verdict: Coronet,* December 1957
117 *"If . . . ever drives a truck . . .":* Washington Post, July 19, 1957
117 *Costello on Hoffa ("no gentleman"):* Albert DeStefano
118 *Costello wagers on Hoffa:* Pack, p. 239
118 *"deathly sick":* Mollenhoff, *Tentacles of Power,* p. 213
118 *"send him a parachute":* Robert Scott; Jimmy Hoffa, Jr.
118 *Cheasty ruined:* John Cye Cheasty
118 *"dazzling": Time,* July 29, 1957
118 *Robert F. Kennedy deletes unflattering references:* Arthur Krock, *Memoirs* (New York: Funk & Wagnalls, 1968), p. 342
118 *"Halo Tarnished": New York Mirror,* July 3, 1951
118 *"Joe Louis and I beat the Hoffa rap":* "New York Confidential," *New York Mirror,* July 31, 1957
118 *"enough to make me dizzy":* "Star Attorney for the Defense," *Life,* June 22, 1959
CHAPTER 10
119 *"our sympathy goes out to Mr. Kennedy": America,* August 3, 1957
119 *"no right to ask . . . questions":* "The Struggle to Get Hoffa," *Saturday Evening Post,* June 27, 1957
119 *"overcompensated":* Schlesinger, *Robert Kennedy and His Times,* pp. 154–55
119 *Ethel Kennedy pressure on Georgetown:* EBW with JEC
119 *"You ruined your life":* Ibid.
119 *Fordham rejection:* Andrew Maloney
120 *"effervescent young Edward Bennett Williams": Washington Star,* June 24, 1957
120 *"You will get slaughtered":* Thomas Taylor
120 *"Country clubs":* EBW with JEC
120 *"rejected by that place":* Dr. Benedict Duffy

120   *blackballed by Lawyers' Club:* Paul McArdle

120   *"got angry about it":* EBW with JEC

120   *Babcock article:* Barbara Allen Babcock, "Defending the Guilty," *Cleveland State Law Review,* 33, no. 2, 1985

122   *"insidious identification":* Washington Star, January 27, 1957

122   *speaking tour: New York Post,* September 25, 1957

122   *"convinced me that I was unethical": The Georgetown Hoya,* October 24, 1957; Benedict Duffy

122   *"I wanted Floyd Patterson": New York Daily News,* November 4, 1957

122   *"just wonderful": Washington Daily News,* November 5, 1957

122   *joins ACLU: New York Times,* March 11, 1957

122   *"never came to any meetings":* Irving Ferman

123   *"just a front":* Paul McArdle. Mike Miskovsky and Bernard Nordlinger also say EBW was not active in integrating the bar, but Charles Rhyne says he was.

123   *"conspicuously absent":* Howard Westwood

123   *"shines"* and *"spades":* Benjamin Bradlee; Michael Tigar

123   *liberal on race:* see OMF, pp. 299–308

123   *consulting Kefauver: New York Post,* July 30, 1957

123   *represents young black in dragnet:* OMF, pp. 146–47

123   *"We were the dregs":* Samuel Dash

124   Life *spread:* "Defending the Unpopular," *Life,* October 21, 1957

124   *"elevated the whole system":* Mario Cuomo

124   *"respectable and most aren't":* Yale Kamisar

125   *"Ed put on a show":* Samuel Dash

125   *Burger impressed:* Warren Burger

125n   *"the institution would last longer":* Frank Waldrop

125   *"legal prostitutes": New York Journal American,* July 17, 1960

125   *Teamsters election rigged:* Allen Friedman and Ted Schwartz, *Power and Greed Inside the Teamsters Empire of Corruption* (New York: Franklin Watts, 1989), p. 149

126   *O'Donoghue turns out to be reformer:* Raymond Bergan

126   *"needs . . . a moral czar":* St. George, "His Defense Never Rests"

126   *"Ed didn't push for reform":* Raymond Bergan

126   *"Don't yell at your attorneys, Jimmy!":* Joseph Konowe

126   *"Not me":* Ibid.

126   *EBW resigning from Teamsters?: Newsweek,* January 5, 1959

126   *EBW turns over Teamsters work:* Raymond Bergan

127   *Schmidt background: Newsweek,* July 27, 1959; Pack, pp. 246–51

127   *"it is the truth": New York Herald Tribune,* July 24, 1959

128   *"I have a reputation": Washington Star,* July 14, 1959

128   *"but I hope the lawyers . . . will":* Raymond Bergan

128   *scene in Frankfurter's office:* Pack, p. 251
128   *Crum's alcoholism:* Ibid.
CHAPTER 11
129   *"weary sense of strain":* Sol Pett, "Lawyer Williams Looks at Success,"
       Washington Post, October 19, 1958
129   *Goldfine hires EBW: New York Times,* December 10, 1958
129   *Powell hires EBW: Washington Post,* May 11, 1958
129   *EBW's hectic schedule:* Toffler, "Get Me Ed Williams!"
130   *"scarcely a gangster now alive":* Leonore Lemmon. According to Vin-
       cent Fuller, Williams composed this ditty himself.
130   *Mock trial of Toots Shor:* Pat Wall
130   *"Because you don't charge me":* Morris Siegel
130   *Faye Emerson described:* Leonore Lemmon; Morris Siegel; Jack Walker
131   *"I'll kill the son of a bitch":* Jack Walker
131   *Pochna background:* Jean Barry Pochna; letter from Pochna to author,
       January 19, 1990
132   *"too tacky":* Jean Barry Pochna
132   *"he'd do anything":* Ibid.
132   *fight at bottle club:* Duke Zeibert
132   *"didn't have a big drive":* Jean Barry Pochna
132   *"I can't get to him":* Leonore Lemmon
133   *"He was crazy":* Ibid.
133   *"it went into her lungs":* Betty Killay
133   *Dorothy becomes fatally ill:* Betty Killay; Stephen Jones
133   *Williams defends Goldfine: New York Herald Tribune,* April 29, 1959
134   *EBW offers deal to Pearson:* Tyler Abell, *Drew Pearson Diaries* (New
       York: Holt, Rinehart and Winston, 1974), p. 510
134   *asks wrong question of Anderson:* Jack Anderson
134   *exposes confidential file:* Pack, p. 283
134   *"pecking away . . . at the hospital":* Ibid., p. 282
134   *Williams in a panic:* Robert Maheu
134   *"can't say good-bye":* Betty Killay
134   *"last two weeks were sheer terror":* Ibid.
134   *"karate chop":* Ibid.
134   *broke down and wept:* Paul McArdle
134   *"get my hands on him":* Betty Killay
134   *drunk; Joe DiMaggio:* Ellen Williams
135   *"I'm here":* Ibid.
135   *"I only did it for Dorothy":* Betty Killay
135   *lure EBW back to work:* Thomas Wadden and Colman Stein
135   *Goldfine background: Time,* June 23, 1958
135   *Slobodkin story:* Williams told this story regularly. For one rendition see

EBW's introduction to Gerald Ford, *Humor and the Presidency* (New York: Arbor House, 1985)

136n   *Slobodkin's bar admission:* Paul Wolff

136   *"only . . . if he pleads insanity":* Thomas Wadden

136   *EBW versus Richardson:* Elliot Richardson; *Boston Globe,* February 10, 1961

137   *Goldfine pleads: New York Times,* June 6, 1961

CHAPTER 12

138   *Powell described: Time,* May 2, 1960; Will Haygood, "Keeping the Faith," *Boston Globe Magazine,* November 2, 1986

139   *Powell's flipflop on Eisenhower:* Buckley, "The Unexamined Side of Edward Bennett Williams"

139   *"The Jig Is Up": National Review,* February 22, 1958

139   *"jump out of their skivvies":* Thomas Wadden

139   *"reincarnation of Clarence Darrow":* Adam Clayton Powell, *Adam by Adam* (New York: Dial, 1971), p. 181

139   *"snot-nosed Catholic":* Vincent Fuller

139n   *Buckley and EBW in later life:* William F. Buckley and Steven Umin

140   *makes Faye Emerson cry:* Leonore Lemmon. Williams himself told this story to clients to warn them about the rigors of preparation. Vincent Fuller believes it is apocryphal.

140   *Powell put him to bed:* Powell, *Adam by Adam,* pp. 174–75

140   *preparing for trial:* Vincent Fuller

140   *Mrs. Dodson herself: New York Times,* March 19, 1960

140   *"This is highly improper!":* Morton Robson

141   *"Colonel Blimp":* Pat Wall

141   *"limitless cunning": New York Post,* January 1, 1960

142   *"recollection has lapsed very badly":* Pack, p. 299

142   *Emanuel cross-examination:* Ibid., pp. 294–95; Vincent Fuller

143   *"shocked to find he was innocent":* Murray Kempton

143   *as the clock struck twelve:* Murray Kempton, "On the Beach," *New York Post,* April 1, 1960

143   *"making more money every day": New York Herald Tribune,* April 26, 1960

143   *"one of the alumni":* Pack, p. 296

143   *exact page of the four-thousand-page transcript:* Gay Talese, "Counsel (Extraordinary) for the Defense," *New York Times Magazine,* September 25, 1960

143   *"wouldn't trust you":* Morton Robson

143   *"Ed is always working":* Bill Davidson, "Defender of Wrongo's Rights," *True,* January 1962

143   *"crestfallen":* Powell, *Adam by Adam,* p. 181

144   *EBW "freed Adam Clayton Powell"*: *Sports Illustrated,* October 4, 1965
144   *Agnes Neill:* Agnes Williams
144   *"drank too much"*: Morris Siegel
145   *"Only Lem can turn a suicide into a homicide"*: Ibid.; *New York Post,* June 26, 1959
145   *"baby-sitter, not a wife"*: Jean Barry Pochna
145   *Guider predicts steady wife:* Betty Killay
145   *"I need a rest"*: Charles Ball, "E.B. Williams, Nation's Busiest—and Weariest—Attorney," *Boston Traveler,* April 29, 1960
145   *"the kidnappers"*: Betty Killay
145   *"Such an* eligible *husband"*: Ibid.
145   *EBW's courtship of Agnes Neill:* Boris Kostelanetz; Colman Stein; Thomas Wadden
146   *Neills displeased:* Michael Miskovsky
146   *Agnes Williams' background:* Agnes Williams
146   *EBW walks out of Neills':* Stephen Jones
146   *wedding night at Toots Shor's:* Dana Williams Fulham
146   *"law book pork chops"*: Tony Williams
146   *"learn to love his new mother"*: Rosa Peltway
146   *EBW and Rosa:* Betty Killay
147   *"throw you through the . . . window"*: Stephen Jones
CHAPTER 13
152   *envies Kennedys:* John Nolan
152   *"How can you vote for the man . . ."*: Talese, "Counsel (Extraordinary) for the Defense"
153   *Wallace and EBW:* Mike Wallace
153   *McCarthy's "glory drive" . . . "power drive"*: Pack, p. 162
153   *makes known animosity to Hoffa:* Hugh Sidey
154   *"washing with bars of Jimmy"*: Pat Wall
154   *"same day" headlines:* OMF, p. 22
154   *changes defense lawyer story:* Albert Love, ed., *Listen to Leaders in the Law* (New York: Holt, Rinehart and Winston, 1963), p. 123
154   *"sic Mike on you"*: EBW with JEC; Michael Bessie
154   *approaches Condon:* Richard Condon
154   *Condon's outline:* Richard Condon to Michael Bessie, undated (Bessie believes winter of 1958), Harper & Row papers, courtesy of Harry Ransom Collection, Univ. of Texas, Austin
155   *"respectability"*: James Clayton
155   *"possibility of glory and riches"*: Clayton's drafts are in the Williams papers
155   *Ernst counsels a higher road:* James Clayton
156   *Dean Griswold backs out:* Michael Bessie; Eugene Rostow

156   *"first-rate exposition"*: The New Yorker, June 23, 1962
156   *"done the impossible"*: New York Times, June 24, 1962
156   *spent advance on advertising:* James Clayton
156   *EBW belittles Nizer and F. Lee Bailey:* Morris Siegel
157   *"Television has taught"*: E. B. Williams, "The High Cost of Television's Courtroom," *Television Quarterly,* Fall 1964
157   *Raymond Burr asks to meet EBW:* New York Journal American, May 7, 1962
158n   *Maheu's career:* Jim Hougan, *Spooks* (New York: Bantam Books, 1979), p. 292
158   *offers to help on Powers case:* Newsweek, June 20, 1960
158   *defending American businessman:* Michael Miskovsky, *Manila Chronicle,* April 10 and 12, 1962 (businessman was Harry S. Stonehill; Philippine government wanted to deport him for alleged smuggling)
158   *EBW debriefed by Dulles:* Lawrence Houston
158   *Melekh case background:* OMF, pp. 308–309
159   *"everything . . . is really a sham"*: EBW with JEC; Agnes Williams
159   *"You must feel proud"*: anonymous, undated letter in WP
159   *EBW and "World Peace Through Law"*: OMF, pp. 311–18; Charles Rhyne
159   *Williams meets with Robert F. Kennedy:* OMF, pp. 319–21
160   *Melekh case dropped: New York Times,* March 25, 1961; *Time,* March 31, 1961
160   *"cold as a refrigerator"*: John Siegenthaler
160   *"suspicious of him"*: Laverne Duffy
160   *"assures Uncle Sam"*: EBW to Robert Kennedy, December 19, 1960, courtesy John F. Kennedy Library, Boston
160   *champagne at the hospital: Washington Star,* February 6, 1961
160   *"My skin crawls"*: Hugh Sidey
161   *"most disliked individual"*: Robert F. Kennedy, memo to file, August 1, 1961, courtesy John F. Kennedy Library, Boston
161   *speech to Teamsters: The International Teamster,* August 1961; *New York Times,* July 6, 1961
161   *dickering over Goldfine:* William Hundley
162   *EBW and Hundley:* Ibid.
162   *EBW and Robert F. Kennedy:* Angela Novello, Arthur Schlesinger, Jr.
162   *Robert F. Kennedy solicits EBW's advice:* William Hundley; William Fugazy
163   *EBW counsels John F. Kennedy:* William Fugazy
163   *EBW learns of JFK's womanizing:* Bob Woodward (EBW told Woodward in 1986 in hopes of tempting the *Washington Post* reporter to help with his memoirs)

163 *EBW and Muskie:* Edmund Muskie

164 *EBW and Alice Longworth:* Nancy Dickerson

164 *EBW at Federal City Club: Washington Post,* May 24, 1965

165 *refuses to quit Metropolitan Club:* James McCarrick

165 *"I can't get paid":* Sheldon Cohen

165 *EBW and Clifford:* Hugh Sidey

165 *"potential rivals":* Clark Clifford with Richard Holbrooke, *Counsel to the President* (New York: Random House, 1991), p. 271

166 *"How's my lawyer?":* Clark Clifford

166 *"living heroes":* EBW to Clark Clifford, August 1967, courtesy of Clark Clifford

166 *"I appreciate your kindness":* Clifford to EBW, November 11, 1969, courtesy of Clark Clifford

166 *"own a team":* Donald Oresman

166 *peace offering to Sheridan:* Walter Sheridan

166 *"wasting a perfectly good afternoon":* Colman Stein

166 *Veeck and EBW:* David and Shirley Povich

167 *"I'm going to buy a baseball club!":* Joe DiMaggio

167 *fails to buy Senators:* Bill Veeck, *Veeck—as in Wreck* (New York: G. P. Putnam's Sons, 1962), pp. 354–59

167 *Marshall described:* Bernard Nordlinger; Shirley Povich

168 *"No nigger's ever going to work for me":* Colman Stein

168 *EBW and Marshall:* Morris Siegel; Shirley Povich; *Washington Star,* September 20, 1970

169 *"don't ask for money":* Bobby Mitchell

169 *EBW helps Mitchell:* Ibid.

170 *Redskins become social event:* "To Be Seen Seeing the Redskins," *Sports Illustrated,* October 4, 1965

170 *"We could get a quorum":* Ibid.

CHAPTER 14

171 *Silverman case background:* OMF, pp. 93–105

171 *predicted success in Supreme Court:* Duke Zeibert

172 *wiretapping history:* Samuel Dash, *The Eavesdroppers* (Rutgers, N.J.: Rutgers University Press, 1959), passim; E. B. Williams, "The Wiretapping-Eavesdropping Problem: A Defense Counsel's View," *Minnesota Law Review* 44, pp. 835–871

172 *Fuller's ballpoint pen:* Michael Tigar

173 *Martin makes odds:* Duke Zeibert

173 *Williams drinks night before:* Betty Killay

173 *Williams's oral arguments:* oral argument, *U.S.* v. *Silverman,* argued December 5, 1960, National Archives recordings, Washington, D.C.

173 *"Hey, Bob, maybe we weren't guilty":* Duke Zeibert

174   *"ice cracking around* Olmstead*":* Yale Kamisar

174   *court's decision in* Silverman*: U.S.* v. *Silverman,* 365 US 505 (1961)

175   *Williams asks Joe DiMaggio to check for Chinese laundries:* Earl Dudley, Joe DiMaggio

175   *oral arguments:* oral argument, *Wong Sun* v. *U.S.,* argued October 8, 1962, National Archives recordings, Washington, D.C.

175   *court's decision: Wong Sun* v. *U.S.,* 371 U.S. 471 (1963)

175   *"one of the two or three best advocates":* William Brennan

175   *"This isn't a murder case": Washington Star,* April 28, 1964

176   *"Ed, I'm pleased":* Arthur Goldberg to EBW, October 8, 1962, WP

176   *Kronheim's described:* William Brennan

176   *EBW late to Supreme Court: Washington Post,* February 8, 1955; Harold Willey to EBW, February 7, 1955, WP

176   *Williams's friendship with Earl Warren:* John Charles Daley; Agnes Williams

177   *"fell in love":* Katharine Graham

177   *"insider-outsider bond":* Bill Graham

178   *Philip Graham's sickness:* Chalmers Roberts, *The Washington Post: The First 100 Years* (Boston: Houghton Mifflin, 1977), pp. 331–32, 360–63; Halberstam, *The Powers That Be,* pp. 376–83

179   *Graham's will:* Records of Estate of Philip L. Graham, Administration No. 109.223, U.S. District of Columbia (1963); Pack, p. 61

179   *Graham's collapse:* Katharine Graham; Benjamin Bradlee

180   *Stassen's photo on wall:* Nick Chase

180   *"the John Birchers":* Pack, p. 24

180   *EBW and Maryland politics:* Ellen Berlow

181   *"hate being a freshman":* Joseph Tydings

181   *"Democrats were incumbents!":* Peter Taft

181   *"an urban figure":* George Will

181   *cheering Al Smith:* EBW interview with Michael Scully, WP

182   *Baker described: Time,* March 6, 1969

183   *"Only you can save Bobby":* Michael Tigar

183   *"biggest congressional investigation": New York Herald Tribune,* February 26, 1964

183   *"Mongoloid idiot":* Bobby Baker, *Wheeling and Dealing* (New York: Norton, 1978), p. 187

183   *congressional questioning: New York Herald Tribune,* February 26, 1964

184   *"took Five and I'm still alive": Newsweek,* March 2, 1964

184   *Gridiron Dinner: Washington Post,* April 26, 1964

184   *Capitol Vending suit settled: Newsweek,* November 16, 1964

CHAPTER 15

185   *EBW and Burt Lancaster, Robert Stroud:* Pack, p. 139

185   *"It's criminal":* Washington Post, August 11, 1963

185   *EBW meets Helen O'Connell:* Jewel Baxter

186   *"crush"; "infatuated":* Helen O'Connell

186   *EBW at Liston-Patterson fight:* William Fugazy; Irving Kupcinet; Helen O'Donnell

186   *Mailer denies fight:* Norman Mailer to author May 10, 1990. Mailer says EBW and he had "a drunken conversation" about whether the fight was "fixed" (Williams arguing that it was) and "took leave of each other on mild terms of disagreement." But "Williams never laid a hand on me. We may have been holding each other's elbows in drunken solemnity."

186   *Fugazy bails out Williams:* William Fugazy

186   *"a popular recording lark":* Walter Winchell, *Variety,* December 26, 1962

186   *Costello freed; "It's a square bunch":* New York Herald Tribune, February 18, 1964; *U.S.* v. *Costello,* 376 U.S. 120 (1964)

187   *"feel naked":* Time, February 28, 1964

187   *only EBW and Wolf at funeral:* Ellen Williams

187   *EBW represents Genovese:* Washington Star, October 21, 1963; Robert Weinberg

187   *"Free Vito":* Vincent Fuller

187   *"Bad defendants":* Andrew Maloney

187   *Thurgood Marshall confides to EBW:* Robert Weinberg

188   *EBW arm's length from mob:* Peter Taft; Judith Richards Hope

188   *"stop lying":* Judith Richards Hope

188   *Alderisio described:* Peter Taft

188   *Alderisio acquitted: Miami Herald,* October 30 and November 1, 1964

189   *"Wait till the jury finds out":* Peter Taft

189   *EBW and Billy Conn:* Thomas Wadden

189   *"You can't pimp for me":* Morris Siegel

189   *"Representing that slime":* Andrew Maloney

190   *"sniff test":* Michael Tigar

190   *"eminent brain surgeon": Newsday,* April 3, 1964

190   *"better to give than receive":* Robert Weinberg

190   *"take off your pants":* Andrew Maloney

191   *Williams and Sinatra:* Andrew Maloney and Robert Morgenthau

CHAPTER 16

193   *EBW and Herbert Miller:* Thomas Wadden

193   *"toss around the football":* Ibid.

193   *"Where is Mr. Williams?":* William Hundley

194   *"hit like a mule"*: Thomas Wadden

194   *"dead fuck"*: Peter Taft

195   *Del Monico freed:* Nicholas Katzenbach; *Evansville Press*, February 1, 1965

195   *"It stinks"*: *Newsweek*, February 22, 1965

195   *Giancana described:* William Brashler, *The Don: The Life and Death of Sam Giancana* (New York: Harper & Row, 1977), passim; *Time*, June 30, 1975

195   *"never threatened"*: William Hundley

196   *Giancana case tainted by illegal bugs:* Ibid.

196n   *EBW turns down Katz case:* Robert Weinberg

197   *Hanrahan immunizes Giancana:* Edward Hanrahan; Nicholas Katzenbach; see William Roemer, *Man Against the Mob* (Chicago: Donald J. Fine, 1989), pp. 291–302

197   *EBW's strategy for Giancana:* Thomas Wadden; Peter Taft

197   *Giancana tells EBW about CIA role, Judith Exner:* Judith Richards Hope

198   *"get Sam off the hook"*: Nicholas Gage, "2 Mafioso Linked to C.I.A. Treated Leniently by U.S.," *New York Times*, April 13, 1976

198   *"What the hell happened?"*: Thomas Wadden

199   *"He knew how to pitch me"*: Nicholas Katzenbach

199   *"dumbest thing I ever did"*: Edward Hanrahan

199   *Judge Campbell, Hanrahan believe fix:* Ibid.; Thomas Campbell (Judge Campbell's son)

199   *Giancana shot:* *Newsweek*, June 30, 1975

199   *"He hated Williams"*: Robert Morgenthau

199   *EBW dislikes Hoover:* Peter Taft; Judith Richards Hope; Vincent Fuller

199   *Turner and Williams:* William Turner to EBW, May 19, 1962, WP

200   *Las Vegas casino and mob:* Fox, *Blood and Power*, pp. 283, 284; confidential interview with author

200   *bugging report leaked:* William Hundley; confidential interview with author

201   *Hundley and EBW in Las Vegas:* William Hundley

201   *"eager source"*: Richard Harwood; Harwood's series ran in the *Washington Post*, June 18, 20, and 21, 1966

201   *"That rat"*: Ibid.

202n   *Kennedy knew about bugging:* William Hundley

202n   *"Oh, my God, not that!"*: C. D. DeLoach to Clyde Tolson, June 22, 1966, courtesy of FBI Files, Washington, D.C.

202n   *"Kennedy will be seriously wounded"*: C. D. DeLoach to Clyde Tolson, June 24, 1966, courtesy of FBI Files, Washington, D.C. For a description of FBI bugging controversy, see Victor Navasky, *Kennedy Justice* (New York: Atheneum, 1971), pp. 66–95

202   *"particularly gleeful"*: J. Edgar Hoover to Clyde Tolson, June 8, 1966, courtesy of FBI Files, Washington, D.C.

202   *Bugging EBW?*: David Webster; Judith Richards Hope; Thomas Wadden; Vincent Fuller

CHAPTER 17

204   *"something out of Tom Wolfe"*: Judith Richards Hope

204   *Taft and the hitman:* Peter Taft

205   *Wadden described:* Peter Taft; Judith Richards Hope

205   *Fuller described:* Ibid.; Corinne Metcalf

205   *hiring practices:* Peter Taft; David Povich; Michael Tigar

206   *"be the best"*: Judith Richards Hope

206   *"do it by the rules"*: Ibid.

206   *"only real ethic was to win"*: Barbara Babcock

206   *"greater glory"*: Corinne Metcalf

206   *"ruthless"*: Judith Richards Hope

207   *"didn't trust women"*: Corinne Metcalf

207   *"didn't believe that women belonged in the courtroom"*: Barbara Babcock

207   *"I hate to lose"*: Judith Richards Hope

207   *Sunshine case described: Kolod* v. *U.S.*, 371 F 2d 983 (1967)

207   *"half convince the jury"*: Confidential interview with author

208   *"Everyone's trying to knock me off"*: Andrew Maloney

208   *EBW's finances:* Austin Doyle

208   *EBW generous:* Thomas Wadden

208   *borrows for bonuses:* Austin Doyle

209   *"never discussed the* law*"*: Andrew Maloney

209n   *Borgese case:* Ibid.; *U.S.* v. *Borgese*, 235 Fed.Supp. 286 (1964); 372 F. 2d 950 (1967); see also *U.S.* v. *Desist*, 384 F. 2d 889, 900 fn. 21

209   *Ormento and Galante:* Thomas Wadden; Vincent Fuller; *U.S.* v. *Bentvena et al*, 193 F. Supp. 485 (1960); 288 F. 2d 442 (1961); *U.S.* v. *Galante*, 298 F. 2d 72 (1962)

210   *firm withdraws from case:* Pat Wall; Vincent Fuller

210   *"face of a gargoyle"*: *Time*, June 30, 1975

210   *"He had a wild look"*: Paul Curran

210   *"vowel practice"*: Earl Dudley

210   *EBW versus Louis Nizer in Paramount case:* Flora Lewis, "Nizer, Williams Vie in Paramount Battle," *Washington Post*, October 9, 1965; *Variety*, December 22, 1965; David Webster

211   *Balaban wet his pants:* David Webster

211   *Connolly and Williams:* David Webster; Mary Connolly

212   *"What will our corporate clients say about Ed?"*: Jeremiah Collins. Barrett Prettyman does not dispute this, but he does not recall it.

212   *"not going to turn this firm over to the Roman Catholics"*: Ibid.

212   *firm becomes Williams & Connolly:* Jeremiah Collins; David Webster
212   *"until I saw Ed's bills":* Jim McCarrick
212   *"Do you want water tomorrow?":* Steven Umin
212   *"mean side to Ed":* Andrew Maloney
213   *Wadden "broken-hearted":* Peter Taft
213   *"wasn't the right place for me":* Thomas Wadden
CHAPTER 18
214   *Baker charged: U.S.* v. *Baker,* 262 F. Supp 657 (1966)
214   *"you've got four thousand of mine":* Michael Tigar
214   *drinking contest:* Bobby Baker
214   *"Bobby is a big bullshitter":* Michael Tigar
215   *"Next time you want to talk to Agnes":* Oliver Gasch
215   *"This man hates my guts":* Bobby Baker
215   *"Midwestern shitkicker":* Ibid.
215   *"kill them all":* Michael Tigar
215   *Bittman and FBI:* William Bittman
215   *"intimidated":* Ibid.
216   *"blarney didn't work":* Austin Mittler
216   *"almost defies belief":* Pack, p. 306
216   *"I went crazy":* William Bittman
216   *"we were objective":* Oliver Gasch
216   *"making the case go away":* Michael Tigar
216   *Murchison role; Fortas role:* Ibid.
217   *"guilt by association":* Ramsey Clark
217   *"the most important case of your life":* Bobby Baker
217   *LBJ and Hoover:* C. D. DeLoach to Clyde Tolson, January 17, 1967,
      courtesy of FBI Files, Washington, D.C.
217   *"bring down the White House":* William Hundley
217   *bribe to LBJ?:* Judith Richards Hope; Boris Kostelanetz; William Bittman;
      Austin Mittler
217   *"official bagman"; Baker describes payoffs:* Baker, *Wheeling and Deal-
      ing,* pp. 51, 192–96, 271–72
218   *"big mouth":* Peter Taft
218   *"got a lot of guts":* Ibid.
218   *"He didn't trust us":* Ramsey Clark
218   *"certain moves were made":* William Bittman
218   *"Baker case would be my downfall":* Nicholas Katzenbach
219   *Baker offered a deal?:* Baker, *Wheeling and Dealing,* pp. 207–208
219   *"in a New York minute":* Michael Tigar
219   *"It's just Ed":* Ibid.
219   *payoff to Kerr?:* Ibid.
220   *"What kind of defense is that?":* Peter Taft

220   *"I felt we had lost":* Austin Mittler

220   *Gasch cuts off EBW's questions on senators: Washington Post,* January 13, 1967; Michael Tigar

220   *"Shut up, Bobby":* Michael Tigar

221   *cleaning up Baker's life-style: Washington Star,* January 23, 1967

221   *Baker testimony: U.S.* v. *Baker,* CR 39-(19)66, U.S. District Court for the District of Columbia trial transcript, pp. 1, 982–2063; see p. 2178 for Baker's arrogant manner.

221   *"you're the worst witness":* Bobby Baker

221   *EBW and Bittman clash: U.S.* v. *Baker,* trial transcript, pp. 2717–19

222   *Bittman's closing argument:* Ibid., pp. 3131–90

222   *"We have all enjoyed what you said":* Ibid., p. 3278; Barbara Babcock

222   *"knew it was all over":* Judith Richards Hope

222   *"Baker had nothing to go on": Washington Star,* January 30, 1967

222   *"lay it off on the dead":* Oliver Gasch

222   *EBW inconsolable:* Baker, *Wheeling and Dealing,* p. 219; Vincent Fuller

223   *EBW phones LBJ:* Horace Busby

223   *EBW casts blame:* Michael Tigar; Peter Taft; Boris Kastelanetz

223   *Baker appeals:* Sarah Duggin; *U.S.* v. *Baker* petition for writ of Error Coram Nobis, November 6, 1985, courtesy of Williams & Connolly

CHAPTER 19

225   *"sick of this shit":* William Hundley

225   *EBW knocked off* Time, Newsweek *covers:* Richard Stout, Jay Iselin

225   *new generation of lawyers: Newsweek,* April 17, 1967

225   *"I wouldn't take the case":* Morris Siegel

226   *running for office:* John Reilly

226   *advice to LBJ about Hoover:* William Hundley

226   *EBW for attorney general:* Jack Valenti

226   *EBW for United Nations: Washington Post,* June 27, 1967

227   *LBJ offers EBW mayoralty of Washington:* William Fugazy; Agnes Williams

227n   *Rowe urges EBW as mayor:* James Rowe to President Johnson, August 17, 1967, courtesy of LBJ Library, Austin, Texas

227n   *Califano urges a black mayor:* Joseph Califano

227   *"the Secret Society": Washington Post,* June 6, 1967

227   *RFK drops grudge:* RFK to EBW, December 13, 1966, courtesy of Kennedy Library, Boston

228   *Brumus:* Schlesinger, *Robert Kennedy and His Times,* p. 810

228   *"most disgusting thing":* confidential interview with author

228   *EBW and Vietnam:* Clark Clifford

229   *EBW and women:* Nancy Dickerson; Sally Quinn; Betty Killay; Barbara Howar; Pamela Harriman

229   *"Ed saved me":* Barbara Howar, *Laughing All the Way* (New York: Stein & Day, 1973), pp. 18–21, 82–93, 134–42, 146–49, 179–84

230   *"a free cry":* Dick and Shirley Clurman

230   *Jeanne Vanderbilt described:* John Corry, *Golden Clan* (Boston: Houghton Mifflin, 1977), pp. 109–17

230   *EBW and Jeanne Vanderbilt:* Jeanne Vanderbilt

231   *disapproves of Jacqueline Onassis marriage:* Ibid.

231   *EBW and Lauren Bacall:* Lauren Bacall

CHAPTER 20

233   *"drawn to him":* Sally Quinn

234   *the "Club" described:* Art Buchwald; Benjamin Bradlee

234   *"no matter how rich":* William Barry Furlong, "What Kind of Man Defends John Connolly?", *New York Magazine,* May 19, 1975

234   *EBW and Yiddish:* Larry Lucchino

234   *"primitive":* Benjamin Bradlee

234   *Duke's described:* Lynn Rosellini, "Macho Washington Dines at Zeibert's," *Washington Star,* June 27, 1976

235   *Sans Souci described: Wall Street Journal,* October 23, 1970

235   *the diet bet:* Art Buchwald, "The $100-a-pound Bet," *Epicure,* Spring 1973

236   *squash with Sullivan:* Brendan Sullivan

236   *joking at lunch:* Benjamin Bradlee; Art Buchwald; confidential interview with author

236n   *letter to Mrs. Graham:* EBW to Katharine Graham, April 2, 1970, WP

237   *Alsop play:* Art Buchwald, "My Broadway Journal," *New York Magazine,* September 21, 1970

237   *"locker room stuff":* Sally Quinn

237   *"Benjy-Artie-Eddie" offputting:* Robert Donovan; Hugh Sidey

238   *family troubles:* confidential interview with author

238   *"no friends!":* Art Buchwald

238   *"that's how I felt":* Benjamin Bradlee

CHAPTER 21

239   *"a healing ground":* Richard Helms

239   *the box described:* Benjamin Bradlee; Art Buchwald; Philip Geyelin

240   *"On what theory?": Washington Post,* January 1, 1970

240   *EBW revives Redskins:* Robert Boyle, "A Legal Eagle and His Boy Scouts," *Sports Illustrated,* July 25, 1966

240   *EBW before United Mine Workers case:* Earl Dudley

241   *Marshall will dispute:* Pack, pp. 76–85; Bernard Nordlinger; J. Paul Marshall; Catherine Marshall; In re Appointment of a Conservator for George Preston Marshall, CA 2979-(19)63; In re Estate of George P. Marshall,

Administrator no. 1741-(19)69, U.S. District Court for the District of Columbia

241 *EBW obsessed with suit:* Judith Richards Hope; David Webster

241 *"really blew":* David Webster

242 *"a conflict":* Paul McArdle

242 *Dr. Jones's role:* Pack, p. 84; Stephen Jones

243 *"She's drunk":* Stephen Jones

243 *"murderer":* Catherine Marshall

243 *works out with Redskins: Washington Post,* July 26, 1965

243 *makes up sports background:* Ibid.; *Washington Star,* September 26, 1971

243 *EBW on sidelines:* Bobby Mitchell

243 *pep talk:* Ibid.; Sonny Jurgensen

244 *hires Otto Graham:* Shirley Povich

244 *"rather lose":* Boyle, "A Legal Eagle and His Boy Scouts"

244 *Joe Don Looney:* John Carmody, "Ed Williams Looks at His Redskins," *Washington Post Magazine,* September 29, 1968

245 *EBW and Jurgensen:* Sonny Jurgensen; Morris Siegel

246 *"good owner":* Brig Owens

246n *Hundley and NFL:* Dan Moldea, *Interference: How Organized Crime Influences Professional Football* (New York: William Morrow, 1989), pp. 170–71; William Hundley; Brian Gettings

246 *"like slaves":* William Hundley

246 *EBW on NFL owners and Rozelle:* Howard Cosell

246 *"to play with themselves":* Art Modell

246 *Graham's demise:* Sonny Jurgensen; *Washington Star,* September 20, 1970

247 *"betrayal of success":* EBW interviewed by David Frost, reprinted in Congressional Record, H 9734, October 7, 1970

247 *Lombardi hired:* Tom Dowling, "Coach," *Washington Star,* September 9, 1970

247 *EBW "shaking with pleasure":* Bobby Mitchell

248 *EBW and Lombardi:* Morris Siegel; Benjamin Bradlee

248 *Shor's decline:* Halberstam, *Summer of '49,* pp. 275–76

249 *Lombardi wake; Shor's outburst:* William Fugazy

249 *"drunk and exhausted":* Jean Barry Pochna

CHAPTER 22

250 *"anathema to the public":* Landon School News, January 28, 1977

251 *"They need a toastmaster!":* Michael Tigar

251 *"bad case of the generation gap":* Ibid.

251 *Tigar described:* Furlong, "What Kind of Man Defends John Connolly?"

251 *Tigar and SDS:* Michael Tigar

251   *"bomber in Maryland"*: Ibid.
251   *D.C. Nine: Washington Star,* February 8, 1970; William McDaniels
252   *"fat and indolent"*: *U.S. News & World Report,* September 21, 1970
252   *"order to have progress"*: *Newsday,* March 17, 1970
252   *"pure hokum"*: *Los Angeles Times,* September 21, 1970
252   *"Don't be so sure"*: Robert Weinberg
252   *On Chicago Seven . . . "sickens me"*: *Washington Post,* February 26, 1970
253   *"I would become a Republican"*: Dean Acheson to EBW, February 28, 1970, WP
253   *"his bottom line"*: Michael Tigar
253   *Rheault case:* Robert and Caroline Rheault; Robert Kaiser
254   *White House about-face:* Stanley Resor
255   *"panic button"*: Robert Rheault
255n   *Koster case: New York Times,* January 30, 1971
255   *Yarrow case: Washington Star,* September 14, 1970
255   *ex parte Curran:* James Rowe, Jr.; Jeremiah Collins
256   *Fletcher case: Washington Post,* December 16, 1971; *U.S.* v. *Fletcher,* trial transcript, pp. 1–135, courtesy of Williams & Connolly
257   *TV set for Indians: San Francisco Examiner,* December 15, 1970
257   *changing Redskins fight song:* Nancy Dickerson; *Washington Post,* March 30, 1972; *Washington Star,* January 27, 1972
257   *EBW during Washington riots:* Leroy Washington
258   *"They all look alike"*: Benjamin Bradlee
258   *EBW defends black militants: People* v. *Hagan,* 289 NY Supp 2d 384
258   *helps Muhammad Ali:* Charles Morgan
259   *helping Jesuits:* Father James Connor
259   Tilton *v.* Richardson: Jeremiah Collins
259   *"including guest lecturer"*: Norman Sheresky manuscript, WP
260   *"their mere* presence": *Fortune,* September 1969
260   *Clifford and the Arabs story:* Jack Tigue
261   *logs of FBI tapes on EBW:* Confidential source
261   *EBW describes Hoover leaks:* EBW memo to file, February 7, 1972, WP
262   *"It is too hard for me"*: EBW to Clark Clifford, February 22, 1972, courtesy of Clark Clifford
262   *"Rest assured"*: Clark Clifford to EBW, February 24, 1972, courtesy of Clark Clifford
262   *gave Humphrey $5,000: Potomac Magazine,* September 29, 1968
262   *dined with presidential hopefuls: Signature,* September 1970
263   *flattering Mondale:* EBW to Walter Mondale, February 24, 1970, WP
263   *"We're going to New Hampshire!"*: Steven Umin
263   *Fortas:* Pack, p. 360

263   *"Joe awed by Ed":* Ben Heineman

264   *Califano joins firm:* Joseph Califano

264   *"State Department":* Washington Post, April 29, 1971; Joseph Califano

264   *Pentagon Papers background:* Halberstam, *The Powers That Be,* pp. 564–78

265   *Bradlee consults EBW:* Benjamin Bradlee

266   *Sonneborn case:* Tom Patton; David Webster; Sheldon Cohen

267   *"band of brothers":* Larry Lucchino

268   *EBW hired by* Washington Post: Katharine Graham

CHAPTER 23

269   *"What if this goes into the White House?":* Joseph Califano

270   *"We don't have to take your shit":* Washington Post, June 27, 1972

270   *Hunt in the bathroom:* Daniel Schorr

270   *"impugn my motives":* Pack, p. 7

270   *deposing CREEP:* Ibid., pp. 8–9

271   *"brown shorts":* Greg Craig

271   *"This is going to be huge!":* Lee Iacocca

271   *"We?":* Joseph Califano

271   *"within an eyelash":* Pack, p. 9

271   *Nixon tapes discussing EBW:* transcript is in WP (Williams kept it on the wall of his office)

273   *Mitchell threatens Post:* Bob Woodward and Carl Bernstein, *All the President's Men* (New York: Simon & Schuster, 1974), pp. 103–105

273   *Nixon considers removing EBW from Redskins:* Pack, p. 15

273   *"go to hell":* Joseph Califano

273   *IRS to "zing" Williams:* Sheldon Cohen

273   *house burglarized:* Agnes Williams

274   *office swept for bugs:* Washington Post, June 25, 1972

274   *Jaworski worried:* Pack, p. 16

274   *"Does it not seem strange?":* Washington Post, June 25, 1972

274   *"Pick a client":* Joseph Califano

274n   *Agnew:* Ibid.

275   *"You all know Deep Throat":* Remnick, "The Ultimate Trial of Edward Bennett Williams"

275   *"I didn't get anything":* Benjamin Bradlee

275   *"you've got them":* Ibid.

275   *"going to blow":* Bob Woodward

275   *"Keep your eye on the money":* Newsweek, July 2, 1973

276   *Vesco's role:* Gregory Craig; Baker, *Wheeling and Dealing,* pp. 249–50; Arthur Herzog, *Vesco* (New York: Doubleday, 1987), pp. 171–72

276   *EBW on reporters, Sullivan case:* Kevin Baine; Benjamin Bradlee; Robert Flanagan

276   *Woodward, Bernstein, and Sirica:* Bob Woodward; Benjamin Bradlee;
      Joseph Califano; Woodward and Bernstein, *All the President's Men,* p.
      210
277   *EBW and Snyder:* Richard Snyder
278   *"weren't so sure about the First Amendment":* Ben Heineman
CHAPTER 24
279   *EBW and mother:* Stephen Jones; Geraldine Ray
280   *"Don't be like your father":* Tom Kelly
280   *EBW as father:* Ned, Ellen, Dana, Tony, Jobie, and Bennett Williams
281   *"As for discipline":* National Observer, December 16, 1972
281   *Jobie's troubles:* Jobie Williams
282   *Agnes Williams described:* Ned and Dana Williams Fulham; Brendan Sul-
      livan; Betty Killay
283   *"She was perfect for him":* Art Buchwald
283   *eating habits:* Tony and Dana Williams Fulham; Benjamin Bradlee
284   *diet "Disaster":* "Georgetown Diet Management Program," July 3–11,
      1979, WP
284   *"Please drink some whiskey!":* David Brinkley
284   *McPherson and EBW:* Morris Siegel
284   *at father's funeral:* Betty Killay
284   *passed out at Christmas:* Jobie Williams
285   *"chewed his ass":* Benjamin Bradlee
285   *stomping on the brakes:* Leroy Washington
285   *strange man in Ellen's bedroom:* Peter Taft
285   *EBW's fender-benders:* "Release" in which Laura Bertram agrees not to
      sue EBW for damages from collision between his Lincoln and her Volks-
      wagen, September 17, 1970; and EBW to James Womeck, September 15,
      1971, enclosing check for $261.98 for damages in collision on River
      Road, WP
285   *EBW's insomnia:* Stephen Jones
286   *EBW on Nantucket:* Brendan Sullivan
286   *EBW in Las Vegas:* Ned and Tony Williams
286   *uncomfortable with "green pants set":* Betty Killay
287   *EBW on Vineyard:* Art Buchwald; John Charles Daley
287   *EBW at home:* Ned and Tony Williams
287   *EBW, the doctor, and the law:* Tony Williams
287   *EBW and sports:* Larry Lucchino
288   *"teensy weensy" racket:* Walter Cronkite to EBW, December 2, 1976,
      WP
288   *EBW and Ned's tennis:* Agnes Williams
288   *Ping-Pong:* Thomas Taylor
288   *squash:* Brendan Sullivan

288   *softball:* Steven Umin; Paul Wolff; Steve Porter
289   *"Panic Button":* John Underwood, "The Ice Cream Man Cometh," *Sports Illustrated,* October 25, 1971
289   *relationship with George Allen:* Ibid.; *Sports Illustrated,:* April 9, 1973
289   *Redskins finances: Los Angeles Times,* April 3, 1973; Joseph Nocera, "The Screwing of the Average Fan," *Washington Monthly,* June 1978
290   *"Old-Time Religion":* Underwood, "The Ice Cream Man Cometh"
290   *the "People's Plane":* Nancy Dickerson; Benjamin Bradlee
290   *EBW at Super Bowl:* Phil Geyelin; Mary Connolly
291   *"fast enough":* William Hundley
CHAPTER 25
292   *burn White House Tapes ("put my nose down"):* Benjamin Bradlee; James Wechsler, "Advice of Counsel," *New York Post,* May 27, 1975
292   *EBW and Vesco:* Tom Patton; Herzog, *Vesco,* p. 222
293   *"just get rid of" the case:* Dwayne Andreas; *Minneapolis Star,* December 31, 1972
293   *"going to be a long day":* Charles Ruff. Judge McManus confirmed this account.
294   *"judicial irresponsibility":* Roger Witten
294   *EBW with McBride and Koeltl:* Thomas McBride; John Koeltl
294   *"never undercut him":* John Vardaman
295   *"stolen it back again":* John Koeltl, "Steinbrenner Offer of Proof," October 16, 1973, Watergate Special Prosecutor's Office (hereafter WSP), National Archives, Washington, D.C.
295   *"paranoid":* John Koeltl, "Conversation with Fuller," November 12, 1973, WSP
295   *government's offer:* John Koeltl, "Prosecutorial Decision re American Ship Building—Discussion with Steinbrenner Attorneys," November 9, 1973, WSP
296   *"We didn't have the resources":* Thomas McBride
296   *go to trial:* John Koeltl, "Renegotiations with Steinbrenner," January 17, 1975, WSP
296   *government backs down:* Thomas McBride to Leon Jaworski, August 8, 1974, WSP; John Koeltl, "Plea Negotiations re Steinbrenner," August 13, 1974, WSP
296   *judge merciful to Steinbrenner: Philadelphia Inquirer,* September 30, 1974
296   *"It's unbelievable": New York Times,* August 31, 1974
296   *"public sentiment": Philadelphia Inquirer,* September 30, 1974
297   *EBW and Kuhn:* Bowie Kuhn, *Hardball: The Education of a Baseball Commissioner* (New York: Random House, 1987), p. 202
297   *"cop a plea":* William Fugazy
297   *Hefner case background:* David Rubin

297   *"best name dropper"*: Ibid.

297   *"my friend Warren Beatty"*: Hugh Hefner

297   *"This is paradise"*: Ibid.

297   *orders Redskinettes to cover navels:* Washington Post, September 20, 1978

298   *"thought it was porn"*: Steven Umin

298   *Hefner described:* Bella Stumbo, "The Playboy With a Cause," *Los Angeles Times,* December 30, 1984

298   *"throne room"*: David Rubin

298   *progress of case:* Ibid.

299   *"Not much"*: Steven Umin

299   *no case:* Samuel Skinner

299   *the bill:* David Rubin

CHAPTER 26

300   *billing practices:* Joseph Califano; David Webster

300   *hiring practices:* Steven Umin; Peter Taft; Joseph Califano; Earl Dudley

301   *hires Porter:* Stephen Porter

302   *"Billy should ride sidecar"*: Katharine Graham

302   *"Liddy" Dole:* Steven Umin

302   *"how would you know?"*: Peter Taft

302   *"treat you as God"*: Sheldon Cohen

302   *resentment against Califano:* Steven Umin; Paul Wolff

303   *Young Turks revolt:* Steven Umin; Paul Wolff; Jack Vardaman; Earl Dudley; William McDaniels; Vincent Fuller; David Webster

304   *"looked pretty skeptical"*: Lloyd Cutler

304   *Wolff partnership:* Steven Umin; Paul Wolff; David Webster; Jack Vardaman

305   *"lot of patsy in Ed"*: Paul Wolff

305   *"wanted to be loved too much"*: Steven Umin

305   *Judith Richards leaves:* Judith Richards Hope

305   *EBW's acolytes:* Steven Umin; Larry Lucchino

306   *EBW and yes-men:* Brendan Sullivan; Earl Dudley

306   *ambivalent about growth:* Jeremiah Collins

306   *"We were hot"*: Joseph Califano

307   *"He's really bitchy"*: Michael Tigar

307   *bait-and-switch:* confidential interview with author

307   *"the Edward Bennett Williams of today"*: Brendan Sullivan

307   *Koster case:* Ibid.

307   *Kerner case:* confidential interviews with author

308   *"Ed wasn't buying that rhetoric"*: Earl Dudley

308 *EBW and Rauh:* Joseph Rauh; Pack, pp. 354–55; Jeremiah Collins

309 *Miller refuses to appear with EBW: Washington Star,* September 18, 1974

309 *gets in press:* John Herling, "The Sensitive Bar," *Washington Daily News,* July 29, 1971; "Cry to the Bank," *Washington Daily News,* June 15, 1972

309 *Collins falls out of favor:* confidential interview with author

310 *EBW's fish tank:* Stephen Jones; Gregory Craig

CHAPTER 27

311 *"didn't pay a . . . lot of attention":* John Connally

312 *"dang thing":* Ibid.

312 *leaks worry Connally:* Al Reinart, "Not Guilty," *Texas Monthly,* June 1975

312 *"poisoned the atmosphere":* Ibid.

312 *Connally hires EBW:* Mickey Gardner

312 *"calm and dispassionate":* John Connally

313 *"by golly, he has now":* Furlong, "What Kind of Man Defends John Connally?"

313 *status of ida:* Mickey Gardner

313 *Simba:* John Connally

313 *watching Nixon resign:* Michael Tigar; Earl Dudley, George Hart to EBW, March 2, 1974, WP

314 *"license to lie":* U.S. v. Connally, discussion in chambers, March 31, 1975, trial transcript pp. 12–13, courtesy of Williams & Connolly

314 *severing charges:* Steven Brill, "Coming on Tough," *New York Times Magazine,* November 18, 1979

315 *preparing Connally:* Michael Tigar

316 *"hang around with sleazebags?":* Richard Keeton

317 *"goddamned $10,000 bribe":* John Connally

317 *sneaking suspicion:* confidential interviews with author

317 *"No Watergate!":* Michael Tigar

317 *old bills/new bills and Rex Cauble:* James Reston, Jr., *The Lone Star: The Life of John Connally* (New York: Harper & Row, 1989), pp. 502–503, 511, 657

318 *"Cauble was potentially dynamite":* Frank Tuerkheimer

318n *"a man . . . who would sacrifice anything":* Reston, *The Lone Star,* p. 571

318n *"Ed sent him to me":* William Hundley

318 *"gone into training":* Time, April 7, 1975

319 *"a little glum":* Larry L. King, "Williams for the Defense," *Atlantic Monthly,* July 1975

319 *"a bunch of black people":* Pack, p. 324

319   *EBW argues no fair trial:* Fred Graham, "The Secret Trial of John Connally," *The New Republic,* June 21, 1975

319   *"a lot of B.S.":* Michael Tigar

319   *"quote the Good Book":* King, "Williams for the Defense"

320   *Safire column: New York Times,* July 7, 1975

320   *"Williams wouldn't take the case":* Newsweek, April 7, 1975

320   *"of the classic mold": New York Times,* April 8, 1975

320   *"the Undertaker":* King, "Williams for the Defense"

320   *"took the sizzle out of the tape":* Frank Tuerkheimer

320   *tape of Connally and Nixon: U.S.* v. *Connally,* trial transcript, pp. 39–40, courtesy of Williams & Connolly

321   *Hart rules inadmissible:* Graham, "The Secret Trial of John Connally"

321   *Jacobsen described: Washington Star,* April 6, 1975; Reinart, "Not Guilty"

322   *"the great face off": Washington Star,* April 8, 1975

322   *"cowering almost":* Reinart, "Not Guilty"

322   *"astonished lizard":* King, "Williams for the Defense"

322   *"Sominex from the spellbinder": Washington Star,* April 8, 1975

322   *"Ed was a bore":* Brendan Sullivan

323   *"Tedium!":* Furlong, "What Kind of Man Defends John Connally?"

323   *road map of trial:* Larry Lucchino

323   *bridling witnesses and Jacobsen cross-examination:* Priscilla Anne Schwab, "Interview with Edward Bennett Williams," *Litigation Magazine,* Winter 1986

324   *"seem like a lowlife":* Dennis O'Toole

324   *"Saturday night":* Richard Keeton

324   *Jake at the urinal:* Ellen Williams

324   *"shipment of silver":* King, "Williams for the Defense"

325   *"reasonable doubts":* Dennis O'Toole

325   *"Why that son of a bitch":* Reston, *The Lone Star,* p. 533

325   *Graham testifies:* Michael Tigar

326   *Tuerkheimer's summation: U.S.* v. *Connally,* trial transcript, p. 1146, courtesy of Williams & Connolly

326   *Williams's summation:* Ibid., pp. 1222–34

326   *"Stand in front of me!":* Michael Tigar

327   *"makes up for the last time":* Ibid.

327   *"Fuck you, Strauss":* Robert Strauss

327   *"Ed, when was the last time":* Michael Tigar

327   *"I can't believe it!":* Ellen Williams

327   *"the greatest criminal lawyer": People,* May 5, 1975

327   *"Pure opera, boy":* Ibid.

327 *"I'm going to take sixty days"*: Furlong, "What Kind of Man Defends John Connally?"

CHAPTER 28

328 *"Slobodkins!"*: Brendan Sullivan

328 *Hammer case:* Louis Nizer; Thomas McBride; *Wall Street Journal,* October 2, 1975; *Washington Star,* December 3, 1975

329 *Hearst case:* Michael Tigar; *Washington Star,* October 13, 1975

329 *EBW contemptuous of Bailey: Time,* February 16, 1976

329 *Mandel case:* William Hundley

329 *EBW presidential ambitions:* Louis Wolfson; John Kennedy; "Williams for President" file, WP

329 *"You never accept defeat"*: Robert Strauss

330 *"What the hell kind of way"*: Steven Porter

330 *run for Senate?:* David Brinkley; Brendan Sullivan; *Baltimore Sun,* March 3, 1975

330 *Strauss and EBW:* Robert Strauss; *Newsweek,* July 19, 1976

331 *"mere lacuna"*: Harry McPherson

331 *Strauss case dropped: Washington Post,* June 14, 1975

331 *EBW dislikes being DNC treasurer:* William Ragan; Pamela Harriman; Robert Strauss

332 *"networks of boring people"*: R. W. Apple

332 *opposes quotas: Washington Post,* December 11, 1974

332 *"he'll come to me"*: Robert Strauss

332 *EBW and Ford:* Gerald Ford

332 *"resented all those jokes"*: Agnes Williams

332 *called "Edward"*: Benjamin Bradlee

333 *"Can you believe it?"*: Dana Williams Fulham

333 *"awed"*: Bennett Williams

333 *collected autographs:* Ralph Newman

333 *Henry Kissinger consults EBW:* Henry Kissinger; Pack, p. 47

334 *President Ford consults EBW:* Gerald Ford

344 *turns down CIA job:* Ibid.; Terry O'Donnell; Agnes Williams; Richard Helms; Mike Miskovsky

335 *EBW on eavesdropping rules and PFIAB:* Edward Levi; Robert Bork; confidential interview with author

336 *"did not make any exception"*: Ivanov v. U.S.; transcript of oral argument in U.S. Supreme Court, October 14, 1968, courtesy of Williams & Connolly

336 *"We defeat our own ends"*: OMF, p. 105

336 *"Ed had a remarkable way"*: Gregory Craig

337 *keeping the courtroom pure:* Michael Tigar

337   *"I was surprised":* Edward Levi

337   *EBW cross at Levi:* Michael Tigar

CHAPTER 29

339   *Helms described:* Thomas Powers, *The Man Who Kept the Secrets* (New York: Knopf, 1979)

339   *Helms retains EBW:* Richard Helms; *Washington Post,* January 12, 1976

340   *"He knew how to play me":* Harold Tyler

340   *"the right to make surreptitious entry":* Washington Post, February 20, 1976

340   *"straighten it out a little":* Gregory Craig

341   *EBW's graymail strategy:* Ibid. Benjamin Civiletti, the assistant attorney general handling the negotiations, says Williams only threatened to reveal CIA activities in Chile, not elsewhere.

341   *1957 case: Stars and Stripes,* June 2, 1957

341   *"like a Shakespeare play":* Bob Woodward

342   *"no more secrets!":* Gregory Craig

342   *"derringer peeping out":* Powers, *The Man Who Kept the Secrets,* p. 299

342   *"Come on, Ed":* Griffin Bell

342   *Bell and EBW meet with Judge Bryant:* Ibid.; Gregory Craig. Judge Bryant refused to comment.

342   *plea negotiations:* Gregory Craig

343   *EBW, Clifford and Helms meet:* Richard Helms; Clark Clifford; Gregory Craig

343   *"Bryant will help us":* Ibid.

344   *"in disgrace and shame":* Time, November 14, 1977

344   *EBW denounces Graham:* Gregory Craig; Richard Helms; Fred Graham

344   *"badge of honor":* Vincent Fuller

344   *"What do I owe you?":* Richard Helms

CHAPTER 30

345   *watching 1976 elections:* George Stevens

346   *"do something":* Washington Post, July 15, 1976

346   *"the big hello":* Art Buchwald

346   *resign as DNC treasurer?:* Robert Strauss

346   *"That'll get Ruff off his ass":* Gerald Ford

346   *PFIAB abolished:* Jimmy Carter to EBW, May 4, 1977, courtesy of Jimmy Carter Library, Atlanta

346   *Califano leaves; salary: Washington Post,* March 2, 1977; *Newsweek,* March 14, 1977

347   *"not sure it was legal":* Michael Tigar

347   *"No telling":* EBW to Joseph Califano, May 31, 1978; WP

347   *hates reporters:* Robert Flanagan

347 *Kaplan article:* EBW memoranda to files, October 4 and 10, 1976; Katharine Graham to Paul Kaplan, October 7, 1976; WP
348 *"very intimidating":* Laughlin Phillips
348 *excises Kissinger reference:* Norman Sheresky manuscript, WP
348 *"leaving the Church":* Leamer, *Playing for Keeps in Washington,* p. 280
348 *"You little shit":* Laurence Leamer
348 *"got to do something!":* John Kuhns
349 *EBW writes* New York Times: EBW to Abe Rosenthal, May 10, 1977, WP
349 *"most difficult period":* EBW to Michael Burke, May 9, 1977, WP
349 *Kearney case dropped: Washington Post,* April 11, 1978
349 *like a pregnant woman:* John Kearney
349 *nervous exhaustion:* Stephen Jones; Remnick, "The Ultimate Trial of Edward Bennett Williams"
349 *"slipped me a mickey":* Joe DiMaggio
349 *cancer diagnosed:* Jim McCarrick
350 *"Ooooh, look at that":* Nancy Dickerson
350 *EBW in hospital:* Ellen Williams
350 *"intestinal disorder": Washington Star,* June 30, 1977
350 *monitors disease:* Stephen Jones
350 *fed up with Allen:* Benjamin Bradlee
351 *prefers Jurgensen: Potomac,* September 21, 1975
351 *Allen described:* Leonard Shapiro and Nancy Scannell, "The Final Plays," *Washington Post Magazine,* January 7, 1978
351 *Redskins money problems: Washington Star,* July 21, 1976
351 *"I just don't understand it":* Leamer, *Playing for Keeps in Washington,* p. 278
351 *Allen badgers EBW:* Bobby Mitchell
352 *EBW saves Allen from owners:* Art Modell
352 *Allen fired:* Shapiro and Scannell, "The Final Plays"; Benjamin Bradlee; Bobby Mitchell
353 *EBW Deep Throat for "Final Plays":* Tom Dowling, "Saint Ed and the Dragon," *Washingtonian,* June 1978
353 *"a fruitcake":* EBW to Joseph Califano, August 22, 1978, WP
354 *"He was kneeling down":* Bobby Mitchell
CHAPTER 31
355 *"no one to talk to":* Joseph Califano
355 *crackdown on white-collar crime:* "White Collar Crime: Lawyer for the Defense," *National Law Journal,* October 16, 1978
355 *Antonelli described:* Gregory Craig; David Kendall. Antonelli refused to comment.
356 *Antonelli case described: Washington Post,* October 2, 1978
356 *"guy's worth $100 million":* Larry Lucchino

356 *real estate tips:* Gregory Craig
356 *theory of Antonelli case:* Ibid.; confidential interview with author
357 *jokes with prosecutors:* Richard Beizer; Henry Schuelke
357 *EBW on Gesell:* Gregory Craig
358 *EBW and Yeldell:* Ibid.
358 *closing arguments: Washington Post,* October 24, 1978
359 *lost touch with black juries:* Gregory Craig
359 *guilty verdict: Washington Post,* October 25, 1978
359 *EBW depressed:* Dana Williams Fulham
359 *"put-up job":* Harry Schuelke
359 *"got to the guy":* Gregory Craig
359 *"Any contest! Any weapons!":* Michael Tigar
359 *"Not in my courtroom":* Richard Beizer; *Washington Star,* November 28, 1978
359 *prosecutors suspicious:* Hank Schuelke
360 *retrial in Philadelphia:* Richard Beizer; Gregory Craig
360 *car celebration:* Brendan Sullivan
360 *"split a double header":* Henry Schuelke
360 *"Hall of Fame":* Peter Fleming
360 *"to whom the great repair": Washington Star,* February 19, 1976
361 *"like a prison":* Michael Tigar
361 *sick of training:* Larry Lucchino
CHAPTER 32
365 *Sporkin described:* Connie Bruck, "Waning Days for the Zealot at the SEC," *American Lawyer,* November 1980
366 *"he'd forgive you":* Donald Oresman
366 *Bluhdorn described:* Paul Gibson, "A $400 Million Credibility Gap," *Forbes,* September 3, 1979
366 *"get the best":* Arthur Liman
366 *EBW meets Bluhdorn:* Donald Oresman
367 *EBW learns securities law:* Jerry Shulman
367 *"tape recorder for a brain":* Lewis Ferguson
367 *delay strategy:* Stanley Sporkin
368 *EBW handles Bluhdorn:* Ibid.
369 *case dropped:* Ibid.
369 *"full of anger":* Donald Oresman
370 *"couldn't live on $60,000 a year":* Brendan Sullivan
CHAPTER 33
371 *Alfalfa Club:* Richard Helms
371 *"the best dinner we have":* EBW to Tony O'Reilly, November 28, 1987, WP
372 *"candy ass":* Father Timothy Healy

372   *advised Jordan about Anderson:* Jack Anderson; Hamilton Jordan; Jerry Rafshoon; *Washington Post,* September 11, 1978
372   *EBW dislikes Carter:* Robert Strauss
372   *advises Ford:* Gerald Ford
373   *EBW spikes* Post *story:* Nicholas Lemann
373   *EBW on Ted Kennedy:* Jack Vardaman
373   *EBW joins open convention movement:* Robert Strauss; Gregory Craig
373   *meets with Ed Muskie:* Edmund Muskie; Berl Bernhard; Leon Billings
374   *EBW at convention:* Tony Williams; Gregory Craig
374   *EBW's speech:* John Nolan; Robert Strauss
374   *stolen speech?:* Pack, p. 43; Gregory Craig
375   *"cost ten grand":* Tony Williams
375   *EBW dines with Jacqueline Onassis: Washington Post,* May 24, 1980
375   *EBW naive about politics:* R. W. Apple; Peter Taft; Art Buchwald
375   *bets on candidates:* Leon Billings to EBW, May 14, 1981, WP
375   *EBW on Committee on the Present Danger:* Paul Nitze
375   *represents Soviet dissidents:* Gregory Craig
376   *agrees with Safire:* EBW to William Safire, June 15, 1978, WP
376   *"all ad hominem":* William Safire
376   *"not policy-oriented":* Victoria Radd
376   *writes on behalf of Bork:* Robert Bork
376   *"meaningless":* Robert Mayer
376   *agrees to counsel Reagan:* Pack, p. 43
376   *"reaching out": Washington Post,* November 19, 1980
377   *The Jefferson redone:* Rose Narva; *New York Times,* March 15, 1981
CHAPTER 34
378   *Davis escapes indictment:* Jack Vardaman; Gregory Craig
378   *Davis described: Wall Street Journal,* February 24, 1981, and June 21, 1989
378   *Davis impressed by EBW; insult each other:* Marvin Davis; Lewis Ferguson
379   *"not Ed's kind of guy":* Benjamin Bradlee
379   *"I love Ed Williams":* Jay Emmett
379   *"I just couldn't say no":* Marvin Davis
379   *"Pretend this is high school":* Ira Harris
379   *"businessman's mind":* Jerry Shulman
380   *meeting with Siegel:* Marvin Davis; Stuart Siegel
380   *buying Fox:* "The Takeover of Fox", *Los Angeles Times,* August 2, 1981; Alex Ben Block, *Outfoxed* (New York: St. Martin's Press, 1990), pp. 14–20
380   *"moy-jahs":* Marvin Davis
380   *EBW-Davis relationship:* Marvin Davis; Jack Vardaman; Dana Williams Fulham

381   *"The one guy I defer to"*: Jack Valenti
381   *"get intelligence"*: Marvin Davis
381   *"I just got a call"*: John Buckley
382   *"He was so wise"*: Benjamin Bradlee
382   *"I'll take care of that"*: Jack Valenti
382   *"Take this case"*: Christopher Mead
382   *negotiates Iacocca's severance:* Lee Iacocca; *New York Magazine,* October 30, 1978
382   *defends Ford: Wall Street Journal,* April 25, 1979
382   *"If you ever leave your wife"*: Jack Valenti
382   *"cold and true"*: Joseph Califano
382   *advice to Graham:* William Graham
382   *advice to John Warner:* confidential interview with author
383   *advice to Marvin Bush:* Marvin Bush
383n *form letter of recommendation:* EBW to Brown University, January 14, 1982; EBW to Lake Forest, January 19, 1982; EBW to Duke, January 24, 1982, WP
383n *code to admissions committee:* Robert Flanagan
383   *"terrible evenness"*: Remnick, "The Ultimate Trial of Edward Bennett Williams"
383   *advises Nitze:* Paul Nitze
383   *advises Apple:* R. W. Apple
383   *advises Harriman:* Pamela Harriman
383   *"It was massacred"*: *Washington Post,* January 27, 1980
383   *"The pearls!"*: confidential interview with author
384   *advises Quinn:* Sally Quinn
384   *advises Kissinger:* Henry Kissinger
384   *advises Ford:* Gerald Ford
384   *advises Dickinson:* Angie Dickinson
384   *advises Howar:* Barbara Howar
384   *helps Dickerson's husband:* Nancy Dickerson
384   *helps Hadden:* Jay Emmett
385   *defends chauffeur's son:* Gregory Craig
385   *represents Hinckley:* Vincent Fuller; Larry Lucchino
386   *"silly respect for the law"*: *Baltimore News American,* April 6, 1981
386   *"show her there's justice"*: Sarah Duggin
386   *Ross case:* Jack and Betty Ross; Steven Urbanczyk
386   *EBW and "little people"*: Larry Lucchino, Robert Flanagan
386   *putting people at ease:* Jerry Shulman; William Fugazy; Betty Schulman; Larry Lucchino
388   *gave away 10 percent:* Robert Flanagan

388n   *congratulations from priests:* John Nicola to EBW, January 21, 1978;
        R. P. Mohan to EBW, January 24, 1978, WP
388n   *move game:* W. Louis Quinn to EBW, September 6, 1979, WP
388   *loved Holy Cross:* Howard Cosell; John Brooks
388   *Goode speech:* Robert Flanagan
389   *defend Georgetown:* Father Tim Healy
389   *"homosexual conduct was a sin":* Robert Flanagan
389   *"wrong side of the law":* Samuel Dash
389   *Snyder case:* Steve Urbanczyk
389   *Knights of Malta:* Robert Flanagan; Paul Dietrich
390   *dresses as a friar:* John Nolan
390   *Sinatra and Knights of Malta:* Jay Emmett; Paul Dietrich
390   *EBW at soup kitchen:* Ellen Williams
390   *inspirational television spot:* Eugene Marino to EBW, April 28, 1978;
        EBW to Eugene Marino, May 24, 1978, WP
391   *pro bono dreaming:* Sarah Duggin; Benjamin Bradlee; Sally Quinn
CHAPTER 35
392   *love of fights:* Larry Lucchino; Jay Emmett; Bennett Williams; Ned
        Williams, and Tony Williams
393   *buys Baker: Washington Post,* January 23, 1976
393   *EBW betting:* Larry Lucchino
393   *given a racehorse:* Ned and Tony Williams
394   *invest with Simon and Cooke, bid on Orioles:* William Simon; Milton
        Gould; Jack Kent Cooke to EBW, August 17, 1978, WP
394   *Simon denounces Hoffberger: Baltimore Sun,* February 6, 1979
395   *EBW and Hoffberger:* Robert Flanagan
395   *buys Orioles:* Ibid.
395   *Baltimore papers question sale: Baltimore News American* and *Baltimore
        Sun,* August 2–9, 1979
395   *EBW press conference:* Larry Lucchino
395   *Orioles move?: Washington Post,* August 8, 1979
395   *"nadir of irresponsible journalism": Baltimore Sun,* January 9, 1979
396   *"did intend to move":* Tony Williams
396   *fans on trial again: Washington Post,* August 6, 1980
396   *promotes Orioles:* James E. Miller, *The Baseball Business* (Chapel Hill:
        University of North Carolina Press, 1990), pp. 268–71, 274–79; Larry
        Lucchino; Jay Emmett
396   *EBW and Cooke:* Larry Lucchino; Benjamin Bradlee; Bobby Beathard
397   *hires Beathard:* Bobby Beathard; Howard Cosell
397   *Cooke fires Pardee: Washington Post,* January 6, 1981
397   *"Go Back Cooke":* Tony Williams

397   *box changes:* Sally Quinn
398   *obsessed with Orioles:* William Ragan; Ned and Tony Williams; Morris Siegel; Jay Emmett
398   *salaries triple: Sports Illustrated,* June 22, 1981
399   *"crazy":* Miller, *The Baseball Business,* p. 254
399   *strike impact on league:* Ibid., p. 252
399   *"like nuclear war": Baltimore Sun,* March 9, 1980
399   *EBW squeezed:* Robert Flanagan
399   *"sell the house":* Bennett Williams
399   *"the last time":* Ibid.
399   *"I'm basically a capitalist": Washington Post,* December 21, 1980
399   *"that's communism!":* Ibid.
400   *"What does he mean":* Morris Siegel
400   *"a little too corporate law":* Larry Lucchino
400   *"the worst year": Baltimore Sun,* June 13, 1981
400   *secret meetings with Moffett:* Larry Lucchino; Ken Moffett
400   *"this way or that": Baltimore Sun,* August 5, 1981
400   *"won't heal easily":* Miller, *The Baseball Business,* p. 262
400   *"do them in": Baltimore Sun,* August 5, 1981
400   *"helping pave the way":* Miller, *The Baseball Business,* p. 262
401   *"Just the Best Run?": Wall Street Journal,* October 5, 1983
401   *"Baltimore is perfect":* Miller, *The Baseball Business,* p. 267
401   *EBW management style:* Larry Lucchino
401   *"the dominant . . . team":* Miller, *The Baseball Business,* p. 267
401   *"Are you crazy?":* Larry King
401   *"We won!":* Dana Williams Fulham
401   *verge of tears:* George Will
402   *"Are you happy now?":* Hank Peters
402   *"I've got a trial":* Larry King
CHAPTER 36
403   *"Trying cases!":* William Murphy and William McDaniel
404   *"model and the seed":* Charles Ruff
404   *"information control":* Mann, *Defending White-Collar Crime,:* pp. 6–8
404   *ethical considerations:* Ibid., pp. 243–50; Geoffrey Hazard, "Quis Custodiet Ipsos Custodes?," *Yale Law Journal* 95 (1986): 1523
404   *"never . . . admit guilt":* Brendan Sullivan
404   *"through World War III":* confidential interview with author
405   *"buy into your feeling":* Michael Tigar
405   *"I've never gotten it":* Joseph Califano
405   *"I returned the money!":* Steven Brill
406   *"probers"* . . . *"nonprobers":* Mann, *Defending White-Collar Crime,* pp. 103–25

406   *"best favor you can perform":* Vincent Fuller
406   *"no venality":* Mark Richard
406   *"gunning for him":* William Hundley
407   *"better to have the camel":* confidential interview with author
408   *"cut and run":* Ibid.
408   *"Thirty-day continuance":* Michael Tigar
408   *"resigned to defeat":* Mark Richard
409   *EBW more subtle:* Sarah Duggin
409   *"horrible to go to court":* Peter Fleming
409   *Velsicol case:* Terry McDonnell
409   *Holtz case:* Abel Holtz; Gregory Craig, Charles Blau; Justin Gillis and Jeff
       Lean, "Dirty Dollars: Laundering Drug Cash," *Miami Herald,* February
       14, 1990
410   *"mousetrapped":* Leon Kellner
410   *EBW and Judge Braman:* Steven Truitt; Judith Richards Hope (EBW told
       Hope, "We don't invoice judges.")
CHAPTER 37
411   *EBW and Judge Barrow:* Jack Tigue; Jack Vardaman
412   *"You're my main man"; photograph:* EBW to Clark Clifford, undated,
       courtesy of Clark Clifford
412   *prosecutorial misconduct: U.S.* v. *Phillips Petroleum Co.,:* 435 F. Supp
       610 (1977). The conspiracy counts were dismissed because the prosecutor
       violated an agreement between Phillips and the Watergate Special Prose-
       cutor's office.
413   *case settled: Tulsa World,* November 23, 1977
413   *Barrow nominates EBW:* Allen Barrow to EBW, March 27, 1978, WP
413   *asks favor:* Ibid., April 27, 1978, WP
413   *"set me up":* Chad Muller
413   *Home State case:* Hugh Culverhouse; Bernard Gilday; James Cissel; con-
       fidential interviews with author; *Cincinnati Enquirer,* August 12, 1985
413   *Marvin Warner described:* Donald Maggin, *Bankers, Builders, Knaves
       and Thieves* (Chicago: Contemporary Books, 1989), pp. 36–58; James
       Cissel; Robert Flanagan. Warner refused to comment.
415   *Marc Rich described:* A. Craig Copetas, *Metal Men: Marc Rich and the
       10-Billion-Dollar Scam* (New York: G.P. Putnam's Sons, 1985), pp. 23,
       85, 103, 134–39, 175–76. Rich refused to comment.
415   *"I can get rid of it":* confidential interview with author
416   *"Let's settle":* Sandy Weinberg
416   *"My clients don't flee":* Ibid.
416   *stonewall strategy:* Peter Fleming; Jack Tigue
416   *courthouse scene:* Copetas, *Metal Men,* p. 190; Sandy Weinberg. After
       the trunks were seized, Williams told Murray Kempton he was quitting the

case (Murray Kempton, "Study in Discretion," *Newsday*, August 17, 1983).

417 *"You spit on the American flag":* Marvin Davis
417 *"don't need this bullshit":* Jack Tigue
418 *"I'm resigning":* Peter Fleming
418 *case settled:* Ibid.; Sandy Weinberg; *New York Times,* September 28 and October 11, 1984
418 *Posner background:* Allen Sloan and Harold Seneker, "How Posner Profited Even Though His Companies Didn't," *Forbes,* April 8, 1985. Posner refused to comment.
419 *"he's going to pay":* Chris Todd
419 *EBW stalls prosecutors:* Ibid.; Gregory Craig
420 *"Whoa!":* William Murphy
420 *Scharrer skeptical:* William Scharrer; Scharrer's affidavit, *U.S.* v. *Posner,* courtesy of Hugh Culverhouse
421 *Culverhouse role:* Hugh Culverhouse; Chris Todd
421 *"ineffective counsel" charge: U.S.* v. *Posner,* hearing transcript, March 11, 1985, courtesy of Hugh Culverhouse
421 *"Williams' Role in Case Questioned":* National Law Journal, November 5, 1984
421 *"we're all grown-ups":* confidential interview with author
422 *EBW vindicated: U.S.* v. *Posner,* Memorandum Opinion and Order Denying Defendant Scharrer's Post-Trial Motion, July 15, 1985
422 *Culverhouse coached:* Hugh Culverhouse; Gregory Craig
422 *"didn't give a shit about me":* William Scharrer
422 *"doesn't come off as well":* Atlee Wampler
CHAPTER 38
423 *"absolute control over the operation":* Schwab, "Interview With Edward Bennett Williams"
423 *"I'm a pervert":* Stephen Jones
423 *medical history:* "Synopsis on E.B.W.," Jerome DeCosse to Emil Frei, February 22, 1985, WP
424 *"heroic things":* Stephen Jones
424 *chances to live:* Jerome DeCosse
424 *EBW recovers:* Ellen Williams; Jay Emmett; Stephen Jones
424 *normal life expectancy:* John Buckley
424 *"minor surgery":* Baltimore Sun, February 27, 1982
424 *eighty-nine times:* travel schedule, December 1982, WP
424 *boasted to Kay Graham:* Katharine Graham
425 *mental attitude:* Ellen Williams; Larry Lucchino
425 *"I'm not going to come back":* Jill Abramson, "Will the Magic Last?," *American Lawyer,* May 1985; Steve Urbanczyk

425   *"You'll do it"*: Peter Fleming
425   *"too painful"*: Bennett Williams
425   *live with cancer:* Ellen, Dana, and Agnes Williams
425   *"that's bunk"*: Barbara Howar
426   *"I got you here"*: Larry Lucchino
426   *"zippers installed"*: John Buckley
426   *marriage:* Betty Killay; Brendan Sullivan
427   *"peek at it"*: EBW to Nancy Dickerson, January 18, 1982, WP
427   *"Get well or move over"*: EBW to Clare Boothe Luce, March 12, 1982, WP
427   *"Lookee here"*: Benjamin Bradlee
427   *slowing down:* Stephen Jones, Tony Williams
427   *"not try to remake them"*: Agnes Williams
428   *"Have a good life for me"*: Jobie Williams
428   *"realist and tolerant"*: Father Tim Healy
428   *as a father:* Ellen, Dana, Tony, Ned, Bennett, and Jobie Williams; Agnes
        Williams; Betty Killay
429   *dislikes inherited wealth:* Sheldon Cohen
429   *"Top This Poor"*: Leamer, *Playing for Keeps in Washington,* p. 245
429   *"Who was that guy?"*: Martin Peretz
429   *EBW dress:* Betty Killay; Tony Williams; Benjamin Bradlee
430   *resists Oriental rugs:* Rose Narva
430   *EBW finances:* Robert Flanagan
431   *office described:* Remnick, "The Ultimate Trial of Edward Bennett
        Williams"; Chris Todd; Robert Flanagan
432   *Julie Allen described:* Benjamin Bradlee, Robert Flanagan
432   *EBW bored and rude:* Brendan Sullivan; confidential interviews with au-
        thor
432   *EBW warm:* Jack Vardaman
433   *EBW punctual:* Bobby Beathard; Larry Lucchino
433   *ordering coffee:* Jay Emmett; Robert Flanagan; Larry Lucchino
433   *EBW attached to phones:* John Brooks
434   *ambivalence about growth:* Victoria Radd
434   *Califano return?:* Joseph Califano; Robert Strauss; Art Buchwald; Vincent
        Fuller
434   *"left me with it!"*: Joseph Califano
434   *"solo practitioner"*: Steven Umin
435   *"bunch of zeros"*: Robert Flanagan
435   *attitude toward associates:* Sarah Duggin; Kevin Baine; confidential in-
        terviews with author
435   *EBW bitter over resignations:* Gregory Craig; William Murphy
435   *EBW's Depression mentality:* Larry Lucchino; Jack Vardaman; George
        Will; Robert Barnett

436   *EBW resists growth:* Lewis Ferguson
436   *turn off the electricity:* Robert Flanagan
436   *billing clients:* Ibid.; Victoria Radd; Paul Wolff
436   *"testing myself":* Remnick, "The Ultimate Trial of Edward Bennett Williams"
437   *"hand in every pie":* Abramson, "Will the Magic Last?"

CHAPTER 39

438   Washington Post *article on Tavoulareas: Washington Post,* November 30, 1979
438   *Tavoulareas consults EBW:* John Parker; Herb Schmertz
438   *"go eight rounds":* Benjamin Bradlee
439   *EBW disgusted with Younger:* Kevin Baine; David Kendall
439   *Graham unhappy:* Katharine Graham; Nicholas Katzenbach
439   *EBW operated on:* Memorial Hospital Record of Operations, September 13, 1985, WP
439   *EBW down after operation:* Tony and Dana Williams Fulham
440   *"iron butt":* Kevin Baine and David Kendall
440   *EBW prepares to argue:* Ibid.
442   *scene outside courtroom:* Benjamin Bradlee; Patrick Tyler; Katharine Graham; John Walsh; David Kendall; Michael Tigar
443   *"fabulous presence":* Kenneth Starr
443–44   *EBW's argument: Washington Post,* October 4, 1985; David Lanter, "On Trial: The Tavoulareas Case," *National Law Journal,* October 21, 1985
444   *"We win!":* Benjamin Bradlee
444   *"really got to me":* Kenneth Starr. The decision is reported at 817 F. 2d 762 (1987)

CHAPTER 40

445   *"not much fun":* George Will
445   *EBW watching games:* Bennett Williams; Jack Valenti; Larry Lucchino
446   *purchases players:* Hank Peters; Larry Lucchino
446   *"I can't let go":* Baltimore Sun, March 3, 1986
446   *"Which one of you bastards?":* Leroy Washington
446   *speech in Boston:* Tony Williams
446   *"Guilty!":* Washington Post, August 14, 1988
446   *"pussy play":* George Will
447   *"Don't think, Joey!":* Ibid.
447   *"You're the rock":* Larry Lucchino
447   *"Sleepy Hollow":* Ibid.
447   *"Williams didn't know":* Hank Peters
447   *"lower metabolism":* George Will

447   *"conservative—are gone":* Washington Post, February 1, 1985
447   *compared to Steinbrenner:* Ibid., September 12, 1986; *Baltimore Sun,*
       September 12, 1986
447   *"teddy bear":* Mark Hyman
448   *spitting at the baseball: Baltimore News American,* February 2, 1984
448   *Cooke and EBW ownership dispute:* Milton Gould; Robert Flanagan; Larry
       Lucchino
449   *"didn't invite me":* Marvin Davis
449   *after the game:* Bobby Beathard
449   *"Your cry":* Jack Kent Cooke to EBW, June 23, 1983, WP
449   *"pick me up":* EBW to Jack Kent Cooke, June 23, 1983, WP
449   *Cooke and Metropolitan Club:* EBW memoranda to files "Jack Kent
       Cooke," June 13 and 27, 1984, WP
449   *Cooke and EBW settle:* Milton Gould; Robert Flanagan
450   *"pillow over Marshall's face":* confidential interview with author
450   *"flush that piece of shit":* Kitty Kelley, "My Life with Jack," *Washing-
       tonian,* August 1988
450   *"don't go there":* Larry King
CHAPTER 41
451   *"fall in love":* Art Buchwald
451   *"to repay you":* EBW to Jerome DeCosse, March 14, 1984, WP
451   *donation to Sloan-Kettering:* Agnes Williams; Nancy Dickerson
451   *EBW at National Cancer Institute:* Robert Flanagan; Jack Valenti; Joseph
       Califano
452   *EBW at Dana Farber:* Larry Horowitz; Joyce McKenna; Emil Frei; Joyce
       McKenna to author, April 4, 1990
452   *EBW with children at Sloan-Kettering:* Jerome DeCosse; Ellen Williams
453   *"tumor is gone":* Dana Williams Fulham
453   *"too old for this":* Confidential interview with author
453   *Posner and girls:* Tony Williams; Hugh Culverhouse; Marvin Davis
453–54   *background of Posner case: Miami Herald,* June 25, 1986; Chris Todd,
       Gregory Craig, opening arguments, *U.S.* v. *Posner,* trial transcript,
       pp. 1–80, courtesy of Chris Todd
454   *preparing Posner:* Hugh Culverhouse; Tony Williams; confidential inter-
       views with author
455   *"Air! Air!":* William Murphy
455   *"something healthy":* Tony Williams
455   *sick in Miami:* Ibid.; Hugh Culverhouse; Chris Todd
456   *"pick the first twelve":* Hugh Culverhouse
456   *"most delightful experience":* Eugene Spellman
456   *jokes with prosecutors:* Chris Todd
457   *EBW in court:* Laurel Leff, "Williams Holds Court," *Miami Review,*

June 27, 1986; Sydney Freedberg, "Life Is Contest for Posner Lawyer,"
Miami Herald, June 30, 1986

458   *"Italian army marches":* Eugene Spellman

458   *EBW v. Todd:* Chris Todd; Hugh Culverhouse

458   *Posner a poor witness:* Laurel Leff, "Posner Paints Different Picture,"
Miami Review,: July 15, 1986; "Attorneys Agree: Posner's Credibility
Key," *Miami Review,* July 22, 1986; *U.S.* v. *Posner,* trial transcript, pp.
2151–2463, courtesy of Chris Todd

459   *EBW pounds chair; despairs:* Chris Todd; Hugh Culverhouse; confidential
interview with author

459   *final arguments: U.S.* v. *Posner,* trial transcripts, pp. 2862–3048, courtesy
of Chris Todd

459   *jury deliberations:* John Dorschner, "An Embarrassment of Riches,"
Tropic Magazine, August 31, 1986

460   *EBW lost his touch:* Hugh Culverhouse

460   *jurors break rules: Wall Street Journal,* July 31, 1986

460   *Spellman orders new trial:* Ibid., September 23, 1986

461   *Posner sentencing:* sentencing hearing excerpted, *Manhattan Lawyer,*
April 5–11, 1988

461   *EBW influence on Spellman:* Leon Kellner; Hugh Culverhouse; Eugene
Spellman

CHAPTER 42

462   *Dreisell case background:* Lewis Cole, "Death, Lies and Basketball,"
Washingtonian, October 1989

462   *EBW and Marshall:* Arthur Marshall

463   *EBW at grand jury:* Lon Babby

463   *"Are you crazy?":* confidential interview with author

463   *worries about image:* Larry Lucchino

463   *"Williams was never out":* Jesse Jackson

464   *EBW and Busch boycott:* confidential interview with author; Frank Watkins

464   *EBW and Jackson:* Jesse Jackson

464–65   *Jackson and PUSH:* Steve Yannick; Diane Weinstein; *Washington
Post,* January 31 and April 10, 1984, October 15, 1988

465   *case settled:* John Showalter; Jesse Jackson

465   *EBW run 1988 campaign?:* Jesse Jackson

465   *"stiff us on the bill":* Robert Flanagan

465   *"lowlife":* Steven Umin

465   *"medicine man":* Ibid.

465   *"charlatan":* Jack Vardaman

465   *EBW on Reagan:* Larry King; Jay Emmett

465   *"I'll tell you, Rick":* Larry Lucchino

465   *"an Alfalfa kind of guy"*: Tony Williams

465   *backs John Glenn:* Agnes Williams

465   *"the liberal party"*: Lars Erik Nelson, "Mouthpiece," *New York Daily News Sunday Magazine,* January 4, 1981

466   *"he knew what was going on"*: Jesse Jackson

466   *on PFIAB: Newsweek,* March 30, 1981

466   *"Go get 'em, boy"*: Bob Woodward, *Veil* (New York: Simon & Schuster, 1987), pp. 54–55

466   *"no doubt in my mind"*: Bob Woodward

467   *beef up counterintelligence:* Leo Cherne

467   *"Only if they're women"*: Bob Woodward

467   *"tough love"*: Martin Anderson, *Revolution* (Orlando, Fla.: Harcourt, Brace, Jovanovich, 1988), p. 362

467   *EBW and Casey:* Eugene Rostow; John McMahon

468   *PFIAB purge:* Anderson, *Revolution,* pp. 353–69

468   *Casey and Safire:* William Safire. According to Stanley Sporkin, the CIA General Counsel, Casey insisted on making Williams the PFIAB counsel.

468   *EBW "off-the-shelf" troubleshooter:* Brendan Sullivan

468   *EBW and Contras?:* Richard Helms; Brendan Sullivan

469   *North comes to Williams:* Brendan Sullivan; Robert Flanagan

469   *EBW and Woodward:* Bob Woodward (Woodward notes read to author)

470   *"representing the* situation": Robert Barnett

471   *EBW advises Post on national security:* Benjamin Bradlee; Bob Woodward; Kevin Baine; Woodward, *Veil,* pp. 446–63

472   *"He wanted the job"*: George Will

472   *Regan approaches EBW:* Donald Regan

472   *"easy out"*: Brendan Sullivan

472   *Smitty dies:* Ned Williams

473   *EBW operated on:* "Discharge summary," Dana Farber Cancer Institute, January 22, 1987, WP

473   *EBW declines CIA job:* EBW to Donald Regan, February 9, 1987, WP

CHAPTER 43

474   *"Beats me"*: Robert Mayer

474   *EBW and Milken:* Richard Sandler

475   *check for $2 million:* Robert Flanagan

475   *"I cautioned him"*: Medical records, Edward Bennett Williams, Dana Farber Cancer Institute, March 4, 1987, WP

476   *"Aggie, are you cold?"*: Betty Killay

476   *outburst in car:* Tony Williams

476   *complains of fatigue, flatulence:* Stephen Jones, Medical records, EBW, Dana Farber Cancer Institute, May 11 and June 15, 1987

476   *"mad at me"*: Emil Frei

476   *"poison you, burn you"*: Robert Flanagan

476   *"didn't hesitate to disagree"*: Robert Mayer

477   *depressed on Vineyard:* Robert Flanagan; Jay Emmett; Katharine Graham; Pamela Harriman

477   *EBW and Sullivan, North:* Brendan Sullivan; Robert Flanagan; Father Tim Healy; Larry King

478   *"helping me die"*: Jay Emmett

478   *"no offense"*: EBW to James Miller, July 22, 1986, WP

478   *"hanking around"*: Richard Justice, "As a Team Owner, Lawyer, Williams Practiced a Relentless Drive to Win," *Washington Post,* August 14, 1988

479   *"even say hello"*: Tom Giordano

479   *EBW and race in Orioles:* Larry Lucchino; Hank Peters

479   *"guilty"* . . . *"village idiots"*: Peter Ueberroth

479   *caustic remarks:* Justice, "As a Team Owner"

479–80   *EBW and Eddie Murray:* Larry Lucchino; Tom Giordano

480   *"poisoned . . . atmosphere"*: Miller, *The Baseball Business,* p. 288

480   *fires Peters:* Hank Peters

480   *"looks very well"*: EBW medical records, September 21, 1987, Dana Farber Cancer Institute, WP

480   *"What do I have to lose?"*: Ann O'Donnell

480   *"I could tell"*: Larry Lucchino

480   *visits DiOrio:* John Brooks

480   *EBW's faith:* Agnes Williams; Walter Burghardt; Father Tim Healy

480   *"Numero Uno"*: EBW to Walter Burghardt, December 3, 1984, WP

481   *"When I was younger"*: Kevin Baine

481   *"gone for the big one"*: Peter Fleming

481   *"monkish life"*: Dana Williams Fulham

481   *"my friend Jackie"*: Jay Emmett

481   *"not happy"*: EBW to Joseph Cooney, March 29, 1984, WP

481   *attitude toward writing a book:* Dana Williams Fulham; Agnes Williams

482   *approaches Woodward:* Bob Woodward

482   *talks with Robert Sam Anson:* Alice Mayhew

482   *lunches with Nixon:* Leonard Garment

482   *"didn't want to talk about it"*: Dana Williams Fulham

482   *"last round"*: Vincent Fuller; Paul Wolff

483   *hospitalized:* Emil Frei to Stanley Order, March 30, 1988, WP

CHAPTER 44

487   *Dana's wedding:* Robert Flanagan; Edmund Muskie; Jack Valenti; Larry King; Sally Quinn; Dana Williams Fulham; Father John Brooks; Father Jim Connor; David Brinkley

488   *at hospital:* Ann O'Donnell

488   *donation to Harvard Medical School:* Emil Frei
488   *"Ed was the Messiah":* Richard Sandler
488   *EBW's attitude changes:* Paul Wolff; Robert Flanagan
489   *EBW at Dingell hearings:* Greg Rushford, "Williams Turns the Tables," *Legal Times,* May 2, 1988
489   *"just call me":* Peter Fleming
490   *EBW and conflicts in Milken case:* Gregory Craig; Vincent Fuller; Steven Umin; Arthur Liman
490   *health deteriorates:* Robert Mayer; Ellen Williams; Robert Flanagan
490   *solace in family:* Ellen Williams
491   *commencement at Spring Hill:* Tony Williams
491   *signs Orioles lease:* Larry Lucchino
491   *"Do you understand me":* Lon Babby
491   *last partner's meeting:* Lewis Ferguson; Paul Wolff
491   *last lunch with Clifford and Strauss:* Clark Clifford to EBW, May 2, 1988, courtesy of Clark Clifford; Robert Strauss
492   *last trip to Holy Cross:* Benjamin Bradlee; Art Buchwald
492   *"so fucking bored":* Marvin Davis
492   *leaves office:* Robert Flanagan
492   *last favors:* Barbara Howar; Father Jim Connor
493   *spars with Cooke:* Milton Gould, Brendan Sullivan
493   *"extortion":* Pamela Brogan, "Cooke's Divorce Lawyer Blasts Williams Role," *Legal Times,* June 8, 1988
493   *"what's coming to you":* Dana Williams Fulham; Larry Lucchino
493   *will:* Robert Flanagan
493   *"power sleeps":* Tony Williams
493   *EBW and the hereafter:* Father Tim Healy; Larry King
493   *"real power":* Tony Williams
494   *EBW collapses:* Agnes Williams
494   *talks with Cuomo, Califano:* Mario Cuomo; Joseph Califano
494   *"smell so good":* Ann O'Donnell
494   *"Can I quit?":* Marc Lippmann
494   *funeral instructions:* Agnes Williams
494   *Last Rites:* Father Thomas Gavigan
494   *dies:* Jobie and Ellen Williams
495   *"It's Ed":* Peter Fleming
495–96   *burial:* Robert Flanagan; Jay Emmett; Larry Lucchino; Benjamin Bradlee; *Washington Post,* August 17, 1988

Acknowledg-
ments

Acknowledgments

THIS BOOK IS based largely on the recollections of the men and women who knew Edward Bennett Williams. It is a very large and varied group. Williams's personal phone book was a Who's Who of the Washington establishment; the legal community; the business, sports, political, and entertainment worlds; and the Catholic church. Much of Williams's work was done on the public record, before a judge and jury, but more was done behind the scenes. While I have taken care to describe Williams's courtroom exploits, the principal focus of my reporting was on the private, off-the-record Williams. I always tried to talk to all sides in any dispute, to prosecutors and clients as well as to Williams's friends and partners.

This is an authorized biography. I had access to Williams's papers and medical records; and his widow, Agnes Williams, opened doors to me that otherwise might have been closed. By contract, I retained complete editorial control over the manuscript, although Mrs. Williams had the right to correct "demonstrable factual errors." The conclusions and judgments are mine, and I solely am responsible for their fairness and accuracy. Mrs. Williams has not always agreed with these conclusions and judgments, but she always treated me in a gracious and straightforward way.

I am grateful to all those who read parts or all of the manuscript and offered comments and corrections: Lauren Bacall, Kevin Baine, Robert Barnett, Ben Bradlee, Art Buchwald, Steve Bundy, Gregory Craig, Maureen Dowd, Jay Emmett, Robert Flanagan, Vincent Fuller, Donald

Graham, Katharine Graham, William Graham, Father Timothy Healy, Sven Holmes, David Kendall, Larry Lucchino, William McDaniels, Sally Quinn, Father William Richardson, Lois Romano, Peter Romatowski, Stephen Smith, Brendan Sullivan, Peter Taft, Michael Tigar, Steve Umin, Jack Vardaman, Agnes Williams, Ellen Williams, Tony Williams, and Paul Wolff.

Geraldine Ray of Hartford, Connecticut, kindly put together a gathering of EBW's childhood friends and cousins for me, and Bill Richardson and Bud Ryan organized a lively dinner of EBW's classmates from Holy Cross. My thanks to them. Robert Pack, an earlier biographer of EBW, generously shared insights and information with me. My thanks, too, to my boss at *Newsweek,* Rick Smith, for giving me a leave to write the book, and especially to Steve Smith, a gifted editor and my friend. Sandra Fine, Gail Tacconelli, and Steve Tuttle rendered invaluable assistance researching the book and organizing its author. I feel lucky to have Amanda Urban as my agent and Alice Mayhew and her assistant George Hodgman as my editors at Simon & Schuster. Alice is to publishing what Ed Williams was to the law: the best.

My daughters, Louisa and Mary, cheerfully distracted me, and my wife, Oscie, was, as always, patient, supportive, and wise. It is to them that I owe the most.

Index

Index

563

Evan Thomas is Assistant Managing Editor and Washington Bureau Chief of *Newsweek*. He is also—with Walter Isaacson—co-author of *The Wise Men*. He lives in Washington, D.C.